P9-DTA-025

Advance Praise for

The Church

"*The Church* is an amazing achievement in one volume; it could be written only by a senior scholar of great breadth and depth. As we've come to expect from McBrien, it is clearly organized and well written, thorough and balanced, faithful and critical as appropriate. It will make an excellent textbook for graduate and undergraduate courses that study ecclesiology. Its clarity and readability also make it ideal for adult education programs and for personal reading by anyone who wants to know 'the whole story' of the Catholic Church."

—**Thomas Groome**, professor of theology and religious education, Boston College, and author of *What Makes Us Catholic*

"As always, McBrien's work is clear, concise, and comprehensive in scope. Undoubtedly this book will become a standard ecclesiological reference point for students and teachers alike."

—**Neil Ormerod**, professor of theology, director of the Institute of Theology, Philosophy and Religious Education, Australian Catholic University

"With characteristic clarity, McBrien artfully tells the story of how Catholic theology developed over two millennia. In tracing the insights, conflicts, and fundamentals of Catholic thought, he has provided a superb resource for readers of all traditions."

—**Mary C. Boys**, S.N.J.M., author of *Has God Only One Blessing? Judaism as a Source of Christian Self-Understanding*

"In the spirit of the great ecclesiologist Yves Congar, McBrien leads us to a deeper appreciation of the mystery of the Church—its complex development over the centuries and the credibility of its message within the postmodern world. This comprehensive yet very accessible study of the Church will prove to be a valuable resource both for Catholics and non-Catholics alike."

—**Keith F. Pecklers**, S.J. professor of Liturgy, Pontifical Gregorian University, professor of Liturgical History, Pontifical Liturgical Institute, Rome

"An extensive survey of theologies of the Catholic Church, an overview of ecclesiologies ranging from biblical texts to contemporary directions, this book is an accessible and rich resource. McBrien offers a great deal of information about the many aspects of the Church as well as giving directions for the Church today, local and global. Highly recommended for teachers and ministers in the Catholic Church, from DRE to bishop."

—**Thomas F. O'Meara**, O.P., Boston College

"Theologian Richard McBrien is one of Catholicism's greatest teachers and this book is a master class in which we can take delight as we deepen our knowledge of the Church. McBrien is the ideal mentor for a generation of theology-hungry Catholics."

—**Eugene Kennedy**, Emeritus Professor of Psychology, Loyola University of Chicago

the CHURCH

Also by Richard P. McBrien

Catholicism

Ministry: A Theological, Pastoral Handbook

The HarperCollins Encyclopedia of Catholicism
(general editor)

Lives of the Popes: The Pontiffs from St. Peter to Benedict XVI

Lives of the Saints: From Mary and St. Francis of Assisi to John XXIII and Mother Teresa

The Pocket Guide to the Popes

The Pocket Guide to the Saints

the CHURCH

The Evolution of Catholicism

RICHARD P. McBRIEN

HarperOne
An Imprint of HarperCollins*Publishers*

In grateful memory of

Yves M.-J. Congar, O.P.
(1904–95),

the greatest ecclesiologist in

the history of the Church

HarperCollins books may be purchased for educational, business, or sales promotional use. For information please write: Special Markets Department, HarperCollins Publishers, 10 East 53rd Street, New York, NY 10022.

HarperCollins Web site: http://www.harpercollins.com

FIRST EDITION

Library of Congress Cataloging-in-Publication Data is available upon request.

ISBN 978–0–06–124521–3

08 09 10 11 12 RRD(H) 10 9 8 7 6 5 4 3 2 1

CONTENTS

PART III

Ecclesiology from the Postbiblical Period to the Mid-Nineteenth Century 61

FOREWORD

Like his monumental volume *Catholicism,* first published in 1980 and still in print more than a quarter century later, Father Richard McBrien's new book on the Church fills an evident and long-standing gap in the field of ecclesiology not only in the English-speaking world, but for other language groups as well. There simply is no other comprehensive, systematic ecclesiology available to general readers or to students and teachers who focus their attention and study on the mystery and mission of the Church.

Not even the late Cardinal Yves Congar, Father McBrien's acknowledged mentor in the field of ecclesiology, whom he praises herein as the greatest ecclesiologist in the entire history of the Church, produced a complete ecclesiology like this one. Père Congar often expressed the hope of writing such a book at some point in his life, but the many demands on his time, especially before, during, and after the Second Vatican Council, and then a lengthy, debilitating illness made that impossible. Fortunately, his devoted disciple has now done that for him and has, in the spirit of filial piety, dedicated the book to his esteemed mentor.

Although written explicitly through the prism of the Catholic theological and ecclesial tradition, this book is also clearly marked by a catholic (lowercase "c") perspective that is at once ecumenical and interfaith in outreach. Readers of any religious tradition will appreciate the book's biblical and historical content. As the years pass all too quickly, many in the younger generations have lost any meaningful connection with the pre–Vatican II Church—a period that encompasses in principle more than nineteen centuries! But Father McBrien includes all the highlights here, trying all the while to help us better understand the reality of the Church, how it came to be what it is today, and what the future might hold for it.

Some readers may disagree with one point or another in this book. Others may wonder why an issue or a topic close to their own hearts is not included or is not given what is in their minds sufficient attention. No project of such broad and ambitious scope could possibly please everyone, not even the author himself. As in the case of his previous books, such as *Catholicism, Lives of the Popes,* and *Lives of the Saints,* and the one-volume *HarperCollins Encyclopedia of Catholicism,* which Father McBrien edited in collaboration with several Notre Dame colleagues, he remains open to suggestions for correction and improvement in subsequent printings and editions.

In the meantime, however, I have no hesitation at all in warmly recommending this book to a wide and religiously diverse audience, whether in universities, colleges, and seminaries, or in parish and diocesan adult education programs, or in more advanced high-school programs and especially high-school teachers of religion. Whether used as a course text or as a personal resource, *The Church* will serve the Christian community well for many years to come.

I salute Father McBrien for his achievement and wish him and the Church a full measure of success in this still young twenty-first century and third Christian millennium. My prayer for the Church and for all who read or consult this book is the same as my own daily invocation, "Come, Holy Spirit."

—Theodore M. Hesburgh, C.S.C.
University of Notre Dame
January 2008

PREFACE

This book presents in a single volume a systematic and relatively comprehensive theology of the Church, that is, of the worldwide Christian community in general and of the Catholic Church, or the Catholic Communion of Churches, in particular. The largest ecclesial component of that communion is the Roman Catholic Church, consisting of over one billion members as of the beginning of the twenty-first century.

As I pointed out in my *Catholicism,*[1] the use of the adjective "Catholic" as a modifier of "Church" became divisive only after the East-West Schism of the eleventh century (culminating in the sack of Constantinople by Latin Crusaders in 1204) and the Protestant Reformation of the sixteenth century. In the former case, the West claimed for itself the title *Catholic* Church, while the East appropriated the name *Holy Orthodox* Church. In the latter case, those in communion with the Bishop of Rome retained the adjective "Catholic," while the churches that broke with the papacy were called *Protestant*. Today, however, many insist that the adjective "Catholic" can also apply to other Christian communities that regard themselves as evangelical, reformed, and Catholic alike.

Indeed, the Second Vatican Council (1962–65) broadened the notion of catholicity to include Churches and other ecclesial communities outside the Catholic Church (Dogmatic Constitution on the Church, n. 8) and spoke of them as possessing varying "degrees" of communion with one another and with the Catholic Church in particular (Decree on Ecumenism, n. 3). The preconciliar language of "membership" was implicitly set aside. It was no longer simply a question of whether one is "inside" or "outside" the Catholic Church. The preconciliar "either/or" dichotomy was supplanted by a "both/and" perspective, represented by the notion of "degrees of communion." These are matters, however, to be explained and elaborated upon within the book itself.

The Scope and Organizational Plan of the Book

Part I begins with an overall description of ecclesiology, defined simply as theological reflection on the nature, mission, ministries, and structures of the Church. This introductory section situates ecclesiology within the larger context of Catholic theology as a whole, while highlighting its ecumenical and interfaith dimensions as well as its abiding pastoral relevance and importance. Part I also identifies and explains the various methods and models operative in ecclesiology and indicates how and why ecclesiology has changed over the centuries and changed so quickly and so dramatically in recent decades, particularly at and since Vatican II.

Parts II and III examine the historical development of ecclesiology—to be sure, in highly schematic and selective fashion—from the New Testament origins of the Church to the threshold of the First Vatican Council (1869–70). At the beginning of Part II, the crucial distinction between the history of ecclesiology and the history of the Church itself is made clear. The history of ecclesiology describes the way in which the Church has grown in its understanding of its own nature, mission, ministries, and structures, while the history of the Church is concerned with the entire life of the Church, not just its theologies, throughout every century of its existence. Part II, however, focuses mainly on the beginnings of the Church and the ecclesiologies of the New Testament.

Part III traces the history of ecclesiology through the early Christian centuries, the Middle Ages, and the centuries immediately following. Specific, but exceedingly abbreviated, attention is accorded in Part III to the East-West Schism and the Gregorian reform (named after Pope Gregory VII, 1073–85) of the eleventh century, the writings and influence of Thomas Aquinas in the thirteenth, the conflicts generated by the Reformation and Counter-Reformation (also known more broadly as the Catholic Reformation) in the sixteenth century, including the Council of Trent, and pertinent post-Tridentine developments up to, but not including, the First Vatican Council.

Many readers (and perhaps some reviewers as well) may find Part III the least satisfying portion of the book, in that it attempts to cover so much historical ground (from the end of the New Testament period to the threshold of Vatican I) and is highly selective in the topics it treats and correspondingly sketchy in its discussion of each topic. Its method, however, is as much provocative as narrative. It is designed to highlight certain peaks, valleys, and paradoxes in the evolution of ecclesiology, while trying all the while to situate these developments within an overarching framework of church history itself. A complete and detailed historical presentation, however, would require a multivolume project that no single historian—much less a theologian—could competently undertake.

Part IV continues the historical/ecclesiological narrative from Vatican I to the beginning of Vatican II, with a particular focus on Vatican I's teachings on papal primacy and papal infallibility. Part IV also takes into account pertinent ecclesiological developments between the two Vatican councils, including Modernism and the anti-Modernist reaction under Pope Pius X (1903–14); the emerging biblical, liturgical, ecumenical, and social apostolate movements; the initial supplanting of neo-Scholastic ecclesiology (a revival of a form of medieval philosophy and theology that emphasized the juridical and nonhistorical aspects of the Church) by Body of Christ ecclesiology; and disputes that erupted in the 1940s and 1950s over membership in, and salvation outside of, the Church, centered in the controversy provoked by Father Leonard Feeney, S.J. (d. 1978), chaplain to Catholic students at Harvard University, a popular writer and a compelling street preacher. Part IV concludes with the election of Pope John XXIII in 1958 (d. 1963) and his call for another ecumenical council.

Part V is devoted entirely to the Second Vatican Council, beginning with an analysis of John XXIII's historic opening address in October 1962, followed by a comparison of and contrast between preconciliar Catholic ecclesiology and the ecclesiology of the council itself, with special attention to elements of continuity and discontinuity with the Tradition of the Church.[2] There is a particular focus on the two most important documents of the council: the Dogmatic Constitution on the Church, known by its Latin title as *Lumen gentium* (Lat., "Light of nations"), and the Pastoral Constitution on the Church in the Modern World, or *Gaudium et spes* ("Joy and hope").

Part V indicates how the ecclesiology of those two documents was applied and reinforced in several other conciliar decrees and declarations, and it works toward a synthesis of the council's ecclesiology. Part V also acknowledges, however, the existence of ongoing debates regarding the proper interpretation of Vatican II in two senses: micro (individual texts and issues) and macro (the significance of the conciliar teachings in relation to the Tradition of the Church). Most commentators, as we shall see, have recognized that the council contained elements of both continuity and discontinuity with the previous history and doctrinal tradition of the Church, while other commentators, including to some extent Pope Benedict XVI himself, insist that the elements of discontinuity are more apparent than real.

Parts VI and VII focus on post–Vatican II developments in ecclesiology. The material is divided into two major segments. Part VI is concerned with issues that pertain to the relationship of the Church to realities beyond itself: the Kingdom, or Reign, of God; the world at large; salvation outside the Church—which includes a discussion of other religions and separated Christian Churches and ecclesial communities; the Church's social teachings; its role in the political order; and liberation theology, especially but not exclusively in Latin America. The relationship between the Church and the Holy Spirit provides a link with the second major segment, in Part VII, on the internal life of the Church: the Church as a communion; authority in the Church; the reception of doctrine and of disciplinary decrees; ministry (ordained and nonordained alike), the sacramental and liturgical life of the Church; the place of Mary in the Church; feminist and nonfeminist ecclesiology by Catholic women; Hispanic and Latino/a ecclesiologies; African and African American ecclesiologies; new movements in the Church; and the emerging world-Church.

Part VIII provides a synthesis of the ecclesiology developed throughout the book, ten pastoral applications, and a reflection on the future of the Church and its ecclesiologies.

A conscious effort has been made to keep the book's scholarly apparatus to a minimum, but many items have nonetheless escaped into the subterranean world of notes out of a sense of academic responsibility to students and practitioners of theology and related sciences.[3] However, intelligent nonspecialists, for whom this book is also written, should be reassured that these notes need not interfere with a continuous, uninterrupted reading of the book, whether from beginning to end or while jumping from part to part. For the convenience of all readers—academic and nonacademic alike—there are also a glossary of terms (which readers should consult if an unfamiliar term is not defined in the text itself), a select bibliography (again, not to impress or overwhelm, but simply to offer guidance to those who may wish to do further study), and indexes of persons and subjects. There is also a detailed table of contents.

The Limits of the Book

On the one hand, this book has been written to fill an evident academic void. There is no comprehensive, up-to-date, one-volume English-language ecclesiology that individuals, teachers, and students can turn to for private study, reference, or formal course work at the graduate and undergraduate levels in colleges, universities, seminaries, and institutes of various kinds or in adult education programs in parochial and diocesan venues. A two- or three-volume work would be much too lengthy to serve such a purpose, and a relatively brief paperback treatment limited to a historical overview, with perhaps particular emphasis on the Second Vatican Council and/or on various current issues, would be insufficiently systematic and comprehensive.

On the other hand, the author is fully aware of the limitations not only of this book but of *any* effort to offer a comprehensive, systematic theology of the Church, whether in a single volume or even in multiple volumes. Such a project is beyond the capacity of any individual theologian, given the global, multicultural, and ecumenical character of what many, following the late Jesuit theologian Karl Rahner (d. 1984), now call the "world-Church."[4] No one ecclesiologist or church historian could possibly grasp the distinctive pastoral characteristics *and histories* of all the churches of Asia, Africa, Oceania, Eastern, Central, and Western Europe, and North, Central, and South America. Indeed, within each continent and region there are vast religious and cultural differences. When one adds to the mix the extraordinary ecumenical diversity of the Church—nationally, regionally, and globally—the task becomes utterly impossible for any one author. For that reason, this book makes no claim to global, multicultural, and ecumenical breadth, much less total comprehensiveness. Not even the greatest ecclesiologist in the history of the Church, the late Dominican theologian and cardinal Yves Congar (d. 1995), would have attempted such a project, much less successfully completed it.

This book's ecclesiology is primarily reflective, first, of the worldwide Catholic tradition (but viewed always ecumenically), and, second, of the North American experience of Church (but acknowledged always as one of many such experiences in the present and past worlds). It is this author's conviction that one cannot do theology, and especially ecclesiology, in a nondenominational way, which is not to say, however, that it cannot be done ecumenically and with sensitivity to the other great religions of the world.

Those who wish to attain a closer, more detailed grasp of one of the various forms of African, Asian, or Latin American ecclesiology should read the works of theologians and pastoral experts from those regions. Some of these books are included in the notes or the bibliography at the end of this book. Better still, those looking for a more detailed examination of the ecclesiologies of other continents and regions should visit one of those areas of the world and spend sufficient time there in order to begin to absorb the distinctive experiences and practices of the local churches. The key words here are "begin to absorb," because even those efforts will be inevitably limited. No one individual or group of individuals can assimilate what only God can know, fully and instantaneously.[5]

The Spirit and Tone of the Book

In the preface to *Catholicism* I insisted that the book was not intended as an exercise in polemical theology. What I presented there on the full range of doctrinal topics was representative of the mainstream of contemporary Catholic theology and biblical scholarship. Unfortunately, a wide gap existed then, as undoubtedly it still does today, between the content of that scholarly mainstream and the understanding of certain Catholics who apparently lack an adequate theological and biblical background and who possess at the same time a narrowly ideological approach to religious issues. Positions that reflected a broad consensus among theologians and biblical scholars were denounced as unorthodox and dangerous to the faith, and no amount of evidence or assurances to the contrary could assuage the critics—very few of whom actually read the book or any significant part of it.

In spite of this almost inevitable resistance, one must continue to pursue a middle course, acknowledging all legitimate sides to a debate while remaining faithful, albeit not uncritically, to the relevant official teachings of the Catholic Church. This spirit and tone are all the more important in a book devoted exclusively to the Church, because ecclesiology, along with sexual ethics, is one of the most controversial areas of Catholic theology. Indeed, ecclesiologists such as Hans Küng, the well-known Swiss theologian, and the Brazilian Leonardo Boff, a former Franciscan, have felt the impact of formal Vatican criticism of their work in relatively recent years, as did Yves Congar before them.[6] Ecclesiology can be controversial because it touches upon potentially divisive matters that deeply impact the lives and thinking of every active member of the Church, for example, the forms of worship (who can preside, in what language, according to what rituals). Ecclesiology focuses at the same time on issues, such as the nature and limits of ecclesiastical authority, that are especially sensitive for those in (or who aspire to be in) positions of pastoral leadership and for their closest allies.

One hopes that the finished product will be read—and used—as a positive and constructive resource for a broad spectrum of Catholics and other Christians and for interested readers outside the worldwide Christian community. As a Catholic work—in both upper- and lowercase senses of the word—its approach throughout is intentionally inclusive rather than exclusive, while always inviting reflection and dialogue rather than confrontation and conflict. In this regard, it follows in the spirit of Pope John XXIII's opening address to the Second Vatican Council in October 1962, in which he insisted that "Divine Providence is leading us to a new order of human relations which . . . are directed toward the fulfillment of God's superior and inscrutable designs. And everything, even human differences, leads to the greater good of the Church."[7]

—Richard P. McBrien
University of Notre Dame
June 2008

ACKNOWLEDGMENTS

This book could not have been written without the fully funded sabbatical leave so generously provided by the University of Notre Dame, or without the encouragement and support of the chair of the Department of Theology, Professor John C. Cavadini, and of the executive associate dean of the College of Arts & Letters, Professor Gregory E. Sterling, who is also a colleague in the Department of Theology.

I am indebted once again to the president emeritus of the University of Notre Dame, Father Theodore M. Hesburgh, C.S.C., for graciously writing the foreword. Father Hesburgh also wrote the forewords to two different editions of my *Catholicism* and to the one-volume *HarperCollins Encyclopedia of Catholicism,* for which I was general editor. Father Hesburgh is truly one of the great figures of modern Catholicism and indeed of the human community itself, and I am proud to call him a mentor and a friend.

I would probably not have undertaken this ambitious project at all if it were not for the constant encouragement—and gentle prodding—of my friend Father Charles E. Curran, Elizabeth Scurlock University Professor of Human Values at Southern Methodist University and, in my judgment, the leading Catholic moral theologian in the United States today.

I am also particularly grateful to several scholars who read portions of the manuscript and offered helpful suggestions, and in the process saved me from several errors: Father Raymond F. Collins, professor emeritus of New Testament and former dean of the School of Religious Studies at The Catholic University of America, for Part II, "Ecclesiology in the New Testament"; my former colleague, Professor Thomas Prügl, a specialist in medieval ecclesiology, for Part III, "Ecclesiology from the Postbiblical Period to the Mid-Nineteenth Century"; Father Hermann J. Pottmeyer, professor emeritus of theology at the University of Bochum in Germany and a specialist on the First Vatican Council, for Part IV, "Ecclesiology from Vatican I to the Threshold of Vatican II"; Brian E. Daley, S.J., a colleague in the Department of Theology and a specialist in Greek patristic thought, for bibliographical assistance with the writings of the early Fathers of the Church; and Professor J. Matthew Ashley, also a colleague in the Department of Theology and a specialist in liberation theology and the writings of Johann Metz, for his assistance with both. But without in any way diminishing my sense of gratitude to these individuals, I am happy to single out my Notre Dame colleague Professor Robert A. Krieg, a specialist in Christology, for his extraordinary generosity in reading the entire manuscript, in offering many helpful suggestions, and, perhaps what is most important, in providing generously encouraging reactions throughout the entire writing process. Anyone who has had the experience of writing a book of some length and substance knows how valuable it is to have a valued colleague like Robert Krieg offering assurances all along the way that you are on the right track and that all the time and effort being invested in the project will prove, in the end, to have been completely worthwhile.

Indeed, I cannot overestimate the extraordinary asset of working on a book project of this sort surrounded by so many colleagues—most of whom are not mentioned here—who collectively create an atmosphere of scholarship, dedication to teaching, and supportive and enriching colleagueship.

I am indebted, as always, to my longtime assistant, Donna Shearer, for her own invaluable role in protecting my time throughout my sabbatical year, organizing all of my other commitments unrelated to the book, and serving on several occasions as a highly efficient research assistant as well. She has seen me through several other book projects over the past two decades and more, and she only gets better with the passage of years.

Keeping abreast of recent books and articles across the whole spectrum of ecclesiology is not an easy task. Rhodora Beaton, my former graduate assistant and student at both the doctoral and master's levels, prepared an extensive bibliography, and both she and another former student and teaching assistant, Stephen Menicucci, offered excellent suggestions about what to include in this book and how to shape some of its key sections. I kept their joint memorandum at hand and consulted it often in formulating the working outline for the book and in the writing of the book itself. Indeed, I am indebted to all of my former students, both academic year and summer, and both doctoral and master's, who have taken my courses in ecclesiology over the past two and a half decades and who helped to refine and sharpen my own thinking about the Church. This word of gratitude also applies to the hundreds of audiences I have addressed around the United States and elsewhere. I have often referred to those events as my "floating laboratory" in ecclesiology because of the questions and comments that regularly surfaced on such occasions.

In various endnotes I have cited the writings of two former professors of mine: Francis A. Sullivan, S.J., and, to a more limited extent, the late Angel Antón, S.J., both of whom were members of the faculty of the Pontifical Gregorian University in Rome where I studied for my doctorate in theology during two of the four years of the Second Vatican Council. Father Antón served as my dissertation director and Father Sullivan was a member of the dissertation committee. Frank Sullivan is currently professor of ecclesiology at Boston College, where I formerly served on its faculty in the late 1960s and throughout the 1970s, and he has been extraordinarily prolific since returning from Rome.

The endnotes also include references to the writings of some of my former students at Notre Dame and who are now serving on various theological faculties throughout the United States. They include Edward P. Hahnenberg, Xavier University in Cincinnati; Richard R. Gaillardetz, the Murray and Bacik Professor of Catholic Studies, the University of Toledo; John J. Markey, O.P., Barry University in Miami;

Natalia Imperatori-Lee, also a former graduate assistant, Manhattan College; Christopher J. Ruddy, another former graduate assistant, the University of St. Thomas, St. Paul, Minnesota; and Elizabeth Groppe, Xavier University in Cincinnati. I should like to add a special word of affection and respect for my late colleague at Notre Dame, Catherine Mowry LaCugna, whose writings are also cited in this book.

Finally, I am grateful to my friend Beverly M. Brazauskas and to my longtime assistant Donna Shearer for their invaluable help once again in preparing the Indices of Persons and Subjects.

There remains only the duty of thanking people at HarperOne who have provided great support, encouragement, and assistance over the years and in the production of this book. They include Mark Tauber, vice president and deputy publisher; Mickey Maudlin, vice president and editorial director; Terri Leonard, executive managing editor; Eric Brandt, senior editor, to whom I am particularly grateful for his careful review of the entire manuscript and for his helpful suggestions; and the many others who assisted directly in the book's production, especially Lisa Zuniga, production editor; Ann Moru, who once again did an excellent job of copyediting the entire manuscript; and Ralph Fowler, who designed the book's interior. I also want to single out Kris Ashley, former assistant editor, who was for several years my most frequent link with the publisher and who always rendered prompt and efficient assistance.

the CHURCH

PART I

Introduction

The Content and Scope of Ecclesiology

What Is Ecclesiology?

Ecclesiology is literally the study of the Church (from Gk. *logos,* "study of," and *ekklesia,* "assembly," or "church"). But this is only a generic, etymological definition. Many other disciplines study the Church, for example, history, anthropology, political science, sociology, and philosophy. What, then, is distinctive about ecclesiology?

Ecclesiology is the *theological* study of the Church, which is to say that it studies the Church as a mystery, or sacrament. The late Pope Paul VI (1963–78), in his address to the opening of the second session of the Second Vatican Council on September 29, 1963, declared: "The Church is a mystery. It is a reality imbued with the hidden presence of God. It lies, therefore, within the very nature of the Church to be always open to new and greater exploration."[1]

To view the Church as a mystery, or sacrament, is to see it not simply as a religious community, institution, or movement (although it is all of these and more), but as the corporate, communal presence of the triune God. The Church is a mystery, or sacrament, because the

Page numbers for references to other Parts of this book can be found listed in the table of contents on page v.

triune God is present and redemptively active in it on humankind's and the world's spiritual and material behalf.

The terms "mystery" and "sacrament," although closely related, are not identical. A sacrament is, in St. Augustine's classic definition, a visible sign of an invisible grace. The word "grace" is from the Greek *charis* (as in "charism"), which means "gift." The "gift" in this instance is God's gift of self. The invisible grace, therefore, is the triune God present and active in the Church. A sacrament is both a sign and an instrument of that grace. The council's Dogmatic Constitution on the Church puts it this way: "The church, in Christ, is a sacrament—a sign and instrument, that is, of communion with God and of the unity of the entire human race— . . . for the benefit of the faithful and of the entire world" (n. 1, para. 1).[2]

Given this understanding of the Church as mystery and sacrament, it follows that only believers can do ecclesiology. When Christians—not just Catholics—recite the Nicene Creed and confess that they "believe in the Church," what they are saying is not that they "believe in" the Church as an institution or that they "believe in" the authority figures and teachings of the Church, but that they "believe in" the presence of the triune God within the Church. Only God is the proper object of faith.[3]

What Is the Church?

TOWARD A DEFINITION

The working definition of ecclesiology as the theological study of the Church, of course, begs a major question: what is the Church? In brief, the Church is the community of those who confess the lordship of Jesus (that he is "the way, the truth, and the life"—John 14:6) and who strive to live their lives in accordance with his example and teachings. The Church is also known as the People of God, the Body of Christ, and the Temple of the Holy Spirit among other names. Those three names, however, accentuate the trinitarian context for an understanding of the Church, a context that is also employed by Vatican II's Dogmatic Constitution on the Church (nn. 2–4).

A more detailed definition, which ecclesiologist Yves Congar (d. 1995) himself adopted,[4] describes the Church as "the whole body, or congregation, of persons who are called by God the Father to acknowledge the Lordship of Jesus, the Son, in word, in sacrament, in witness, and in service, and, through the power of the Holy Spirit, to collaborate with Jesus' historic mission for the sake of the Kingdom of God."[5] Indeed, as Vatican II's Pastoral Constitution on the Church puts it: "The church has but one sole purpose—that the kingdom of God may come and the salvation of the human race may be accomplished" (n. 45).

MISSION

The mission of the Church, which is for the sake of the Kingdom, or Reign, of God, is fourfold: word, sacrament (or worship), witness, and service. The Church is "sent" (the root meaning of the Latin word *missio*) to confess and proclaim that Jesus is "the way, the truth, and the life" (John 14:6; see also the classic missionary text in Matt. 28:19–20). It does this through preaching and teaching in a variety of forms: the official teaching by bishops; the teaching rooted in scholarship by theologians; the formation of adults, children, and converts by religious educators and other pastoral ministers; and the teaching of children by parents and other caregivers.

The Church's mission includes, second, its whole sacramental and devotional life, at the center of which is the Eucharist (Constitution on the Sacred Liturgy, n. 10). Indeed, the Church itself is a sacrament (Dogmatic Constitution on the Church, n. 1). The liturgy, or public worship, of the Church consists of its participation in Christ's eternal worship of his Father (Pope Pius XII, *Mediator Dei*, nn. 3, 20).[6]

Third, the Church has been "sent" to give witness to the validity of Christ's teachings and his own personal and compelling example of how one should live a fully human life. The Church, therefore, has a missionary obligation to practice what it preaches and teaches.

Otherwise, its sacramental character and effectiveness are significantly diminished.[7]

Finally, the Church exists to share its own limited material resources to assist the poor, the sick, the socially marginalized, and others in need of aid (Luke 4:18–21). This encompasses the whole of what was once commonly called the social apostolate of the Church. It includes not only assistance to individuals, but also involvement in institutional change in the causes of social justice, human rights, and peace.[8]

THE CHURCH AND THE KINGDOM, OR REIGN, OF GOD

The Kingdom, or Reign, of God, for which the Church is "sent" and which was at the heart and center of Jesus's preaching and ministry (Mark 1:15; see also Part II.2.4*), is the redemptive presence of God actualized through the power of God's reconciling Spirit. The Holy Spirit is the active, incarnate power of love by which human beings, their communities, and the world at large are healed, renewed, and brought to the fullness of perfection. In brief, wherever the will of God is done, there is the Kingdom of God. God "reigns" wherever and whenever God's will is acknowledged and fulfilled.[9]

Although the Church has never defined the Kingdom, or Reign, of God, the Second Vatican Council's Pastoral Constitution on the Church in the Modern World describes it variously as "the consummation of the earth and of humanity," "a new dwelling place and a new earth where justice will abide, and whose blessedness will answer and surpass all the longings for peace which spring up in the human heart," a "new age," and a reality "of truth and life, of holiness and grace, of justice, love, and peace" (n. 39).

Article 5 of the council's Dogmatic Constitution on the Church was added toward the end of the drafting process to counteract a residual tendency in the direction of triumphalism, that is, the identification of the Church with the Kingdom of God itself. That constitution notes that just as Christ came to proclaim, personify, and begin distributing the benefits of the Kingdom, so the Church exists

* The page numbers for these references to other Parts of the book are listed in the table of contents.

to proclaim, witness to, and serve the Kingdom, which definitively broke into history in the person of Jesus Christ and in the redemptive work he performed on humanity's behalf. Although the Church is not itself the Kingdom, it is on earth "the seed and the beginning" of that Kingdom.

Like Christ himself, the Church exists for the sake of the Kingdom of God, not vice versa. The Kingdom, not the Church, is at the center of the history of salvation and is the ultimate hope and destiny of the whole human race. The Church is its sign and instrument in history (Dogmatic Constitution on the Church, n. 1).[10]

DISTINCTIONS WITHIN THE CHURCH AND BETWEEN THE CHURCHES

This more detailed definition of the Church embraces in principle all Christians: Catholics, Orthodox, Anglicans, Protestants, and non-Orthodox Oriental Christians. In other words, there is "the Church" and there are also "Churches." This is not to say, however, that all Christian communities fully satisfy the criteria implied in the definition. To the extent that they do, they are recognized by the Catholic Church as "Churches." If they do not meet these criteria, officials of the Catholic Church refer to them as "ecclesial communities," a term one finds in Vatican II's Decree on Ecumenism (chap. 3). The ecumenically important notion of "sister churches" will be discussed in VI.3.3.b.

The distinction between the Church and the Churches is not only ecumenical. A distinction is also made between the "Church universal" and the "local church." "Church" refers at once to the whole Body of Christ and the whole People of God as well as to the individual congregations of Christians in a parish or a diocese, for example. In fact, the universal Catholic Church is itself a communion of Churches, the largest of which by far is the Roman Catholic Church. It is, in turn, divided into local, or particular, churches known as dioceses. The universal ecumenical Church is a communion of denominations and they, in turn, consist of a communion of local churches or congregations within each denomination.[11]

THE CATHOLICITY OF THE CHURCH

As made clear in the Preface, this ecclesiological presentation is "primarily reflective" of the Catholic tradition. As such, this book is unapologetically Catholic in its starting point, focus, and overall perspective. But is "Catholic" synonymous with "Roman Catholic"? And is it accurate to refer to the Roman Catholic Church as simply the "Roman Church"? The answer to both questions is no.

The adjective "Roman" applies more properly to the diocese, or see, of Rome than to the worldwide Communion of Churches that is in union with the Bishop of Rome. Indeed, it strikes some Catholics as contradictory to call the Church "Catholic" and "Roman" at one and the same time. Eastern-rite Catholics, of whom there are more than twenty million, also find the adjective "Roman" objectionable. In addition to the Latin, or Roman, tradition, there are seven non-Latin, non-Roman ecclesial traditions: Armenian, Byzantine, Coptic, Ethiopian, East Syrian (Chaldean), West Syrian, and Maronite. Each of the Churches within these non-Latin traditions is as Catholic as the Roman Catholic Church. Thus, not all Catholics are *Roman* Catholic.

To be Catholic—whether Roman or non-Roman—in the ecclesiological sense of the word is to be in full communion with the Bishop of Rome and as such to be an integral part of the Catholic Communion of Churches. To repeat a point made earlier, it is not a matter of either/or—either one is in communion with the Bishop of Rome, or one is not. The council implicitly set aside the category of membership and replaced it with *degrees* of communion. As in a family, there are degrees of relationships: parents, siblings, aunts, uncles, cousins, nephews and nieces, in-laws. In many cultures, the notion of family is broader than blood and legal relationships. In Chinese culture, for example, individuals are designated as aunts and uncles as an expression of respect and affection, even though technically no blood or marital relationships exist. Even in U.S. Caucasian culture, there is increasing acceptance of what sociologists refer to as the "extended family." And more recent disputes about gay and lesbian unions have challenged the traditional concept of family even further.

Where Ecclesiology Fits

Many teachers are tempted to regard their own area of specialization as the most important in an entire curriculum. Theologians are not immune to such temptation. The subject matter of this book, although of great doctrinal and pastoral significance, is not the most fundamental of theological topics. Ecclesiology presupposes other, more basic areas of theology. The faith claim that the Church is the Body of Christ begs the question: who is Jesus Christ? And faith claims about Christ, that he is God incarnate, beg the question: who or what is God? And the God question, in turn, begs the question of the Trinity: who or what is the Holy Spirit? And if God is the ultimate ground and destiny of human existence, the God question begs another, parallel question: what does it mean to be human? Ecclesiology, therefore, presupposes Christology, the mystery of the triune God, and theological anthropology.

Theologian Karl Rahner (d. 1984) describes the place of ecclesiology in similar fashion. "Vatican II says in its Decree on Ecumenism, *Unitatis redintegratio* [Lat., 'The restoration of unity'] (art. 11) that there is an ordered structure or a 'hierarchy of truths' in Catholic doctrine. If we reflect upon this, surely ecclesiology and the ecclesial consciousness even of an orthodox and unambiguously Catholic Christian are not the basis and the foundation of his Christianity." Rahner continues: "Jesus Christ, faith and love, entrusting oneself to the darkness of existence and into the incomprehensibility of God in trust and in the company of Jesus Christ, the crucified and risen one, these are the central realities for a Christian."[12]

Because it is a historical institution and movement with characteristics similar to those of other institutions and movements and with a long history of development besides, ecclesiology also interfaces with the sociology of religion, the philosophy of religion, history, political science, the fine arts, architecture, biblical exegesis, biblical theology, historical theology, and several other cognate disciplines and areas of specialization. Finally, notwithstanding the Rahner quote above, ecclesiology is itself foundational for other areas of theology: social ethics, canon law, liturgical studies, pastoral theology, and the like. Each of these areas of study presupposes some understanding of the Church, its mission, its ministerial life, and its structural operations. Ecclesiology is not the whole of the theological enterprise, but it is central and indispensable to it.

The Ecumenical and Interfaith Dimensions of Ecclesiology

Beginning with the pontificate of Pope John XXIII (1958–63) and the Second Vatican Council (1962–65), and especially its Decree on Ecumenism, ecclesiology—and Catholic theology and pastoral practice in general—took a decisively new turn. The conventional pre–Vatican II claim was that the Catholic Church alone is "the one, true Church of Christ" outside of which there is no salvation. But the council acknowledged the existence of other Churches and ecclesial communities within the worldwide Body of Christ, separated only from "full" communion with the Catholic Church. Indeed, "those who believe in Christ and have been properly baptized are put in some, though imperfect, communion with the Catholic Church." Whatever differences there are in doctrine, discipline, and structures "exist in varying degrees" (Decree on Ecumenism, n. 3).

The new ecumenical spirit that Vatican II generated had a clear impact on postconciliar ecclesiology at academic, pastoral, and official levels alike. Indeed, the council's Decree on Ecumenism insists that theology, especially in seminaries, must always be taught "with due regard for the ecumenical point of view" (n. 10).

In 1973 the original German edition of *The Catholic Catechism: A Book of Christian Faith* appeared, described by its publisher as "the first common catechism or statement of religious belief produced jointly by theologians of the Protestant and Roman Catholic churches since the Reformation of the sixteenth century."[13] The editors made the point that, "in contrast to the time of the sixteenth-century Reformation, the differences between the denominations are sharpest in their ideas about the nature of the Church," and so "it is in this area that the most careful work must be done to clarify the points of dispute."[14] A year later, the late Baptist theologian Langdon Gilkey (d. 2004) delivered a paper at the annual convention of the Catholic Theological Society of America in which he insisted that ecclesiology is "the most vital issue of all—vital because it is at the heart of both the Catholic crisis of the present and the Catholic promise for the future."[15]

There followed several ecumenical statements on the doctrine of the Church, with particular reference to the perennial question of authority. At the risk of interrupting for a moment the flow of our narrative, the list of important statements includes: *Papal Primacy and the Universal Church, Lutherans and Catholics in Dialogue V* (1974); the Anglican-Roman Catholic International Commission's "An Agreed Statement on Authority in the Church" (also known as *The Venice Statement;* 1976); the response to it by the Anglican-Roman Catholic Consultation in the U.S.A., "Authority in the Church: Vital Ecumenical Issue" (1977), which criticized its international counterparts for concentrating too much on papal and episcopal authority and too little on the authority of the whole Church; the U.S.A. Lutheran-Catholic statement on infallibility, "Teaching Authority and Infallibility in the Church" (1978); the statement of the Orthodox-Roman Catholic Consultation in the United States, "Primacy and Conciliarity" (1989); the Anglican-Roman Catholic International Commission's "The Gift of Authority" (1999); and "Anglican-Roman Catholic Consultation [ARC-USA] Proposes Interim Unity Steps" (2003), which included attendance by bishops and other representatives at one another's major church meetings.[16] To be sure, these were not the only official ecumenical statements touching upon the doctrine of the Church. Those that are explicitly referred to here are mentioned by way of example.[17]

However, one also has to take care to recognize the important distinction between "ecumenical" and "interfaith." The former has to do with the movement toward the restoration of unity among Christian Churches and ecclesial communities; the latter concerns the need for dialogue between the Church and the non-Christian religions of the world (see, e.g., Matt. 15:21–28, Mark 7:24–30,

Acts 17:22–31; Heb. 11:4–7). The former challenge is addressed in Vatican II's Decree on Ecumenism; the latter, in the council's Declaration on the Relationship Between the Church and Non-Christian Religions, better known by its Latin title, *Nostra aetate* (Lat., "In our age").

The most important interfaith development after *Nostra aetate* was the issuance of the document *Dominus Iesus: On the Unicity and Salvific Universality of Jesus Christ and the Church* by the Vatican's Congregation for the Doctrine of the Faith on September 5, 2000.[18] Cardinal Joseph Ratzinger, elected to the papacy in 2005 and taking the name Benedict XVI, was at the time the prefect of the CDF. Although the document explicitly reaffirmed the teaching of *Nostra aetate* that "the Catholic Church rejects nothing of what is true and holy in these [other] religions" (n. 2), it tended to ignore some of the major postconciliar developments in interfaith dialogue, including Pope John Paul II's historic interreligious initiative for peace at Assisi in 1986, and looked generally askance at efforts, especially by Asian Catholic theologians and their counterparts elsewhere, to seek paths to a more fruitful dialogue between the Church and the other world religions.

The belief that Christianity (and Catholicism in particular) is the one and only true religion established by God for the salvation of the whole human race may have been easier to hold in the Middle Ages, when the world was thought to be much smaller and, at the same time, overwhelmingly Christian. But through the process of exploration and discovery in subsequent centuries, it became clear to all except those too stubborn to see it that the world was not coextensive with Christendom, that there were many millions of non-Christians living good lives empowered by the Holy Spirit in other parts of the globe, and that most of them had never heard of Jesus Christ. As missionaries attempted to proclaim the gospel in these foreign lands, some of them came gradually to appreciate the cultures and even the religions of these so-called pagan peoples.

In the latter part of the twentieth century a few innovative Catholic theologians attempted an adaptation of Christian doctrine to the cultures and religious practices of many millions of Buddhists and Hindus in Asia and to a lesser extent to Muslims in Asia, the Middle

East, Europe, and the United States. In some few cases they may have taken this approach too far by collapsing any meaningful distinction between Jesus of Nazareth and the Christ of faith. In the process they also relativized the role of the Church in salvation, reducing it from the "ordinary means of salvation" to simply one of many. As a consequence, the Vatican adopted an initially skeptical, then openly censorious, attitude toward the work of most theologians engaged in this quest, even excommunicating an elderly Sri Lankan, Tissa Balasuriya, a longtime member of the Oblates of Mary Immaculate, in January 1997 (only to restore him to full communion the following January) and restricting the teaching and publishing activities of the Jesuit Jacques Dupuis (d. 2006), a former missionary in India and then professor at the Pontifical Gregorian University in Rome.

Dupuis's approach is contained in two of his books: *Toward a Christian Theology of Religious Pluralism* and *Christianity and the Religions: From Confrontation to Dialogue.*[19] In both books he addresses the central question of the Church's necessity for salvation, adopting what he calls a *regnocentric* (Kingdom-centered) rather than an *ecclesiocentric* (Church-centered) perspective on ecclesiology—an approach adopted by this author more than thirty years earlier.[20] Dupuis notes that John Paul II's 1990 encyclical *Redemptoris missio* (Lat., "The mission of the Redeemer"; esp. n. 18, para. 3) is "the first document of the Roman magisterium to distinguish clearly, while keeping them united, between the church and the Reign of God in their pilgrimage through history: the Reign present in the world is a reality which is much broader than the church; it extends beyond its boundaries and includes . . . not only the members of the church but also the 'others.'"[21]

To be sure, where the Reign of God is, there is also the Holy Spirit, and vice versa. The Church is the "privileged locus of the Spirit," and grace (the presence of God) "is destined to find its visible expression" in the Church. There is an "orientation" toward the Church from outside of it "wherever the Spirit is present and working." This orientation "does not imply a universal mediation of the church already operative by way of efficient causality." Rather, the Church is the "sacramental sign of the presence of God's grace among people."[22]

As such, the Church has no monopoly on the Reign of God. Members of other religious traditions "can contribute to the building up of the Reign of God, not only among their followers but in the world. While the church is the 'universal sacrament' of the Reign of God in the world, the other traditions too exercise a certain sacramental mediation of the Reign, different, no doubt, but no less real."[23]

The relationship between Christianity and Judaism is a special component of the interfaith dimension of ecclesiology, because Christians and Jews have a "common spiritual heritage." The beginnings of the Church's faith and election are found in the patriarchs, Moses, and the prophets, so that "all Christ's faithful . . . are daughters and sons of Abraham." Indeed, "the salvation of the church is mystically prefigured in the exodus of God's chosen people from the land of bondage." Moreover, "the Jews remain very dear to God, for the sake of the patriarchs, since God does not take back the gifts he bestowed or the choice he made" (*Nostra aetate,* n. 4).

Ecclesiologically, this special relationship between the Church and the Jews also raises the question of the role of the Church and of other religions, including Judaism, in the salvation of the world. However, the Holocaust, or Shoah, raises yet another question regarding the holiness of the Church. Were all of the atrocities committed against the Jews during World War II the acts of individual Christians alone, or can sinfulness be attributed to the Church itself, notwithstanding its traditional claim to holiness (as well as oneness, apostolicity, and catholicity)?[24] The 1998 Vatican document "We Remember: A Reflection on the 'Shoah'" did not do so. Although it expressed "deep sorrow for the failures of [the Church's] sons and daughters in every age," "We Remember," unlike earlier statements of the French and German bishops, did not accept responsibility for the Church as such.[25]

Nevertheless, there has been an enormous change in Catholic thinking and policy regarding the Jews in the last half century alone, thanks in large part to Pope John XXIII, the Second Vatican Council's *Nostra aetate,* the statements of repentance issued by the Catholic bishops of Germany and France, the overall record of the late Pope John Paul II, and various other statements and initiatives at less elevated levels.[26]

The Pastoral Dimension of Ecclesiology

Ecclesiology is the theological study of the Church and, as such, has a broadly theoretical dimension. But the Church is much more than an idea. It is also inherently pastoral in character. It is a living, tangible reality that functions in many different practical ways—globally, nationally, and locally. It is a place of worship and also a venue for mission and the exercise of a variety of ministries in service to that mission. Differences in ecclesiology also lead to differences in pastoral practice, and differences in pastoral practice are almost always an implicit reflection of ecclesiological differences. This has been particularly the case in the post–Vatican II conflicts within the Catholic Church over liturgical renewal and reform, generating even what some have called "liturgy wars" (for a more extensive discussion of this phenomenon, see Part V.6.2). Innovative pastoral practice can also shape, as well as be shaped by, ecclesiology.

A few years after Vatican II adjourned (in December 1965) the U.S. Catholic bishops commissioned a series of studies on priestly life and ministry: one on the history of the priesthood in the United States, a second on its sociological aspects, and a third on its psychological aspects. The sociological study was conducted under the direction of the well-known sociologist Father Andrew Greeley. The summation of its principal findings was set forth in the form of questions and answers. One in particular had special relevance to ecclesiology:

> Does the dissatisfaction of the young [clergy] with the distribution of [pastoral] power indicate trouble for the Church? *It apparently does precisely because the difference seems to be rooted in quite different values about the nature of the Church and the nature of Christianity. What we are witnessing is not merely a disagreement between those who have power and those who do not, but a disagreement among those with opposing ideologies about the nature of the reality whose power structure is the subject of disagreement. Power conflicts*

that are rooted in ideological differences tend to be much more serious than power conflicts among those who share the same ideologies.[27]

A year later, a canonical colloquium sponsored by the then School of Canon Law at the Catholic University of America in May 1972 issued the following statement:

On the one hand, through Vatican II and the theological developments following it, the whole community is gradually appropriating a new vision of the Church and of its life, including priestly life and ministry. On the other hand, the present legal system of the Western Church dates back more than sixty years and originated in a significantly different understanding of the life of the Christian community. This growing discrepancy between vision and law gives rise to increasing tension. It creates a need for greater flexibility and instruments of harmony, since a community cannot long remain strong with a new understanding of its goals and an old set of norms to realize them.[28]

In 1988 a subcommittee of what was then called the National Conference of Catholic Bishops (now the United States Conference of Catholic Bishops) made essentially the same connection between ecclesiology and pastoral practice:

Polarization and differing ecclesiologies take their toll not only within rectories and presbyterates but also within parish staffs and parish communities. . . . The priest must deal with those who are angry and disillusioned with what they consider the slow pace of renewal; he must also face the unreasoning and often well-organized opposition of the self-styled orthodox and of those who simply do not believe in the decisions and directions of Vatican II. . . . "Caught in the middle" in an apt description.[29]

Many priests, religious, and laypersons who have been active in a parish or diocesan ministry over the past few decades would recognize from unhappy experience the accuracy of the bishops' subcommittee report. This phenomenon has also been acknowledged, along with a constructive effort to address it, in the pastoral letter of Cardinal Roger Mahony, archbishop of Los Angeles, "As I Have Done for You," written in collaboration with ordained and nonordained ministers of the archdiocese.[30] Its important theological content is amply fleshed out with specific and concrete examples derived from actual parish life.

The Controversial Character of Ecclesiology

Ecclesiology is controversial because it touches upon disputed questions that overlap with the daily experience of ordinary members of the Church. Those questions pertain to their attendance at Mass, their contacts with priests, and their awareness of church officials' stands on public issues such as abortion, birth control, embryonic stem-cell research, gay marriage, immigration, social justice, and war and peace. Unlike theological controversies over, let us say, the Trinity or original sin, ecclesiology affects issues that many Christians have hands-on knowledge of and opinions about. What is most controversial about ecclesiology, however, are its reflections on church authority, particularly the selection, quality, and accountability of pastoral leadership. In more recent years, the circle of controversy within ecclesiology has widened to include a Christological dimension, specifically the question of salvation apart from Christ and the Church. The only other area of Catholic theology that vies with ecclesiology for controversial content is sexual ethics, and for essentially the same reason. Sexual ethics touches the lives of ordinary people, who believe—not without reason—that they know more about the subject than those who presume to teach them and attempt to control their behavior.

Many examples from recent church history could be cited to highlight the controversial nature of ecclesiology: the debate about the teaching authority of national episcopal conferences provoked by the U.S. Catholic bishops' pastoral letters on peace (1983) and the economy (1986); questions raised about the proper role of the Church in society by Church-state developments in the 1980s in Eastern Europe (prior to the dissolution of the Soviet Union), the Philippines, and Latin America (particularly with regard to events related to liberation theology); disputes over the involvement of priests and religious in politics in the United States and Central America (particularly Nicaragua); the personal engagement of Pope John Paul II with the Solidarity movement in his native Poland and its impact on the stability of the Warsaw Pact; the divisiveness of the abortion issue in every U.S. presidential election since 1976; the disciplining of various bishops and theologians during the pontificate of John Paul II; and the letter *Dominus Iesus,* on salvation apart from Christ and the Church, issued by the Congregation for the Doctrine of the Faith in 2000. Each of these examples pertains to the exercise of authority in and by the Church.

Models and Methods in Ecclesiology

Ecclesiology, like Church, is a singular word, but it also has a plural form. Just as there are many Churches, or denominations, and local churches, or dioceses, within the one universal and ecumenical Church, so there are many ecclesiologies, or theologies of the Church, beginning with the New Testament period and continuing down to our present day. Because the Church is a mystery, or sacrament, its core reality, namely, the triune God, cannot be directly grasped by human means. Every attempt to understand the ultimate meaning of the Church is just that: an attempt. "No one has ever seen God," the Fourth Gospel reminds us (1:18), and no one, therefore, has ever seen the God who is present and active in the Church, which is the communal and institutional presence of the triune God in the world and its history. For that reason there are many theologies rather than only one, and many ecclesiologies rather than only one.

Because the Church is a mystery, its spiritual essence (as opposed to its external forms) can only be spoken of poetically, that is, through *images,* analogies, similes, metaphors, and symbols, rather than prosaically.[31] The New Testament itself speaks of the Church through the language of imagery. Paul Minear, longtime professor of New Testament at Yale, once calculated that there are more than a hundred images of the Church in the New Testament.[32] The Second Vatican Council's

Dogmatic Constitution on the Church notes that the Bible derives its imagery for the Church "from pastoral life, agriculture, construction work, or from family life and betrothal" (n. 6). The Church is spoken of as a sheepfold, a flock, a farm or field, a vineyard, a vine, a building, a temple, the new Jerusalem, a mother, a body (the Body of Christ), a bride (nn. 6–8), and a people on pilgrimage (chap. 2, nn. 9–17).

Images are comparable to photographs. They provide only snapshots of a reality that is beyond the comprehension of whole galleries of photos. In the religious sphere, images—for example, the cross, St. Peter's dome, or a depiction of a saint—function as symbols, which speak to us existentially, nonconceptually, and even subliminally. In ecclesiology, images and symbols make the Church *become* what they suggest the Church *is*. But they "work" only to the extent that they resonate with the experience of the faithful. Thus, the Church as a pilgrim people works, but a sheepfold does not, especially among well-educated, urbanized people. In a time of rapid change, like ours, some images lose their power, while newer images, drawn, for example, from a new technological age, have not yet emerged.

When an image is employed reflectively, conceptually, and critically to deepen our understanding of the Church, it becomes a *model*. There are two types of models: explanatory and exploratory. Explanatory models synthesize what we already know, for example, that the Church is an institution. Exploratory models lead us to new theological insights, for example, that the Church is a servant or a liberator. Models are verified by experience and by critical theological reflection. They are tested by their pastoral consequences and by their capacity to illuminate and enrich our understanding and living of the gospel. Like images, however, models remain fundamentally inadequate—and for the same reason. The Church is a mystery. Therefore, no one model—not even a combination of all models—can comprehend the inner reality of the Church. Taken alone, one model will inevitably distort the reality it seeks to describe. Consequently, a pluralism of models must always be maintained in some kind of dynamic unity.

In his classic work *Models of the Church*, Avery Dulles lists these six models: institution, mystical communion, sacrament, herald, servant, and community of disciples. He insists that no one model can do justice to the full reality of the Church, although he singles out the institutional model as the only one that "cannot properly be taken as primary."[33]

When a single model does assume dominance in a given historical period and becomes the prism through which the whole reality of the Church, including its many images and models, is interpreted, that overarching model is known as a *paradigm*. "A model rises to the status of a paradigm when it has proved successful in solving a great variety of problems and is expected to be an appropriate tool for unraveling anomalies as yet unsolved."[34] It becomes a kind of umbrella model under which all other models are clustered and integrated.

During much of the Middle Ages the paradigm was the Church as the perfect society—not "perfect" in the sense that it was without fault or deficiency of any kind, but that it possessed every institutional and spiritual component needed to fulfill its mission. During much of the first half of the twentieth century, the Church came to be referred to most often as "Our Holy Mother." In 1943 with his encyclical letter on the Mystical Body, Pope Pius XII gave quasi-canonical status to the image of the Church as the Body of Christ (called "Mystical" to differentiate the Church from the eucharistic body of Christ, his earthly body, his risen body, and his glorified body in heaven), raising it thereby to the level of a paradigm. At Vatican II and in the years immediately following the council, the Mystical Body paradigm ceded its place of honor to the Church as the People of God, to which an entire chapter of the Dogmatic Constitution on the Church is devoted.

Since then, however, some have contested the People of God paradigm because of its democratic and egalitarian overtones and have sought to supplant it with a new paradigm, the Church as a communion. There are two senses in which the notion of communion can be understood: horizontally, emphasizing the communal nature of the Church here on earth, and vertically, emphasizing the Church as an anticipatory participation in the inner communal life of the triune God. Those who prefer communion, or *communio* (Lat.), to People of God tend to favor the latter rather than the former meaning.

Paradigms change, or shift, when, like images and models, they no longer adequately illuminate our experience of the Church and the world or when developments in theological, biblical, and historical scholarship throw their claims to dominance into question. It is only human, of course, to resist a paradigm shift. People feel as if the ground has been cut out from under them. Many laypersons resist such shifts because they are perceived as threatening to their spiritual security. Some theologians resist because the older paradigm provided the context for their answers to problems. And some pastoral leaders resist paradigm shifts because the older paradigm better supported their authority and exercise of power, while the new one is seen as threatening to both. Of course, it can work the other way. Some church members, especially pastoral leaders, may advocate a paradigm shift because the prevailing paradigm (in this case, People of God) is perceived as diluting their authority and reducing their power, while a newer paradigm (the Church as *communio*), at least in their understanding of it, restores a more hierarchical, less democratic concept of the Church. (The notion of Church as a communion will be treated in greater detail in Part VII.1.)

Ecclesiologies are not only differentiated by the images, models, and paradigms they tend to favor, but also by their starting points. Some ecclesiologies begin "from above" and others begin "from below," not dissimilar in their methods from Christologies "from above" and "from below."[35] An ecclesiology "from above" begins with the mystery of the triune God and emphasizes the nature of the Church as a communion in grace that is derived from, reflects, and is drawn into the inner life of the Trinity. As such, the Church is an icon of the eternal communion that exists between the Father, the Son, and the Holy Spirit.[36]

Other theologians begin their exploration of the mystery of the Church "from below," that is, with the Church as an earthly community of human beings who, though transformed by the grace of God and the enduring presence of the Holy Spirit, have a mission in and for the world that includes, in addition to the preaching of the Word and the celebration of the sacraments, activities on behalf of justice, peace, and human rights. As in Christology, one can choose one or the other starting point. But it cannot be an either/or choice. One may begin the story of an airplane flight while it is still in the sky, but eventually it must land at an airport. Or one can begin with the plane taxiing on the runway prior to flight, but eventually the plane must take off. An ecclesiology "from above" that fails to take into account the whole of the Church's social apostolate is a radically deficient ecclesiology, and an ecclesiology "from below" that fails to pay necessary attention to the deeper spiritual, transcendental dimension of the Church is similarly deficient. The proper method is characterized by both/and, not either/or.

Ecclesiological Development

Although we shall outline in some detail the development of ecclesiology from New Testament times to the present in Parts II–VII of this book, it might be helpful here at the outset to explain the extraordinarily rapid development that has occurred in the past half century alone.[37] We have been moving in a relatively brief period of time (but not without resistance) from a highly clericalist, pyramidal, authoritarian, and unecumenical concept of the Church to one that emphasizes the radical equality of all of the baptized, the common ground that the Catholic Church shares with other Christian Churches and ecclesial communities, the world's non-Christian religions, and the human community as a whole, and the opportunities for dialogue that potentially build upon that common ground.[38]

There has been a shift since the middle of the twentieth century from the notion of the Catholic Church as the one, true Church of Christ outside of which there is no salvation to an understanding of the Catholic Church as a portion, albeit the major portion by far, of the whole Body of Christ and as the ordinary, but not the *only,* means of salvation in and for the world. A more modern way of putting it is to describe the Church as "the universal sacrament of salvation" (Decree on the Church's Missionary Activity, n. 1). It is the universal *sign* of what God has done, is doing, and will continue to do redemptively on behalf of the whole human community. But the Church is not the only *means* by which salvation is received as God's gift to humankind. Insofar as the Church is the Body of Christ and Christ is the one and only Mediator of salvation, the Church is the *ordinary* means of salvation. Insofar as God's salvific grace is available to all of humanity, inside and outside the Church, even without explicit reference to Jesus Christ as Savior, the Church is for millions of non-Christians the *extraordinary,* not the ordinary, means of salvation.

But why have such dramatic developments in ecclesiology occurred in so compressed a period of history? There are two principal reasons—not to exclude many others, including various social, cultural, political, economic, and technological changes throughout the twentieth century, many of which Alvin Toffler described in his widely read book *Future Shock*[39] and some of which are enumerated by Vatican II's Pastoral Constitution on the Church in the Modern World (nn. 4–10). The first is the delayed, but profound, impact of recent New Testament scholarship, which has challenged many conventional assumptions in pre–Vatican II ecclesiology about the origins, nature, mission, and structures of the Church.[40] The second is the all-encompassing impact of the Second Vatican Council as both a teaching body (having produced sixteen documents of varying degrees of authority and theological substance) and an event.[41] The impact of New Testament scholarship on ecclesiology will be considered in detail in the next part, the Second Vatican Council in Part V, and the council's impact on ecclesiology in Parts VI and VII.

PART II

Ecclesiology in the New Testament

The preposition in Part II's title is deliberately "in" rather than "of," because there is widespread agreement among Catholic, Protestant, and Orthodox scholars that there is no single New Testament ecclesiology.[1] Throughout the period covered by the New Testament there were both diversity and development in the various local churches, as will become clear in the course of this presentation. On the other hand, one can also find some degree of unity within the various ecclesiologies of the New Testament. One hopes that this will also become clear in the course of this presentation.

The History of Ecclesiology and the History of the Church

What follows in this and the next five parts of this book is an extended, but selective and therefore limited, narrative of the history of ecclesiology from the New Testament through the Second Vatican Council (1962–65) to the present day. It needs to be pointed out again, as we did in the Preface, that the history of *ecclesiology* is not coextensive with the history of *the Church*.[2] We are not proposing here to present a record of the principal events and persons that have shaped the life and history of the Church, for good or for ill, although such is not in principle foreign to the history of ecclesiology. There is much overlapping between the history of ecclesiology and the history of the Church.

On the other hand, ecclesiology, unlike church history, is primarily interested in ideas rather than in persons and events. More accurately perhaps, ecclesiology is interested in persons and events insofar as they illuminate, explain, and embody the ideas of the Church that have influenced and shaped its thinking and actions throughout its history. Thus, the history of ecclesiology is not so much focused on the *content* of the Gregorian reform of the eleventh century as it is on the *idea* of the Church that informed and shaped it. One could substitute any number of topics for the Gregorian reform: multiple conflicts between Church and state over the course of many centuries; the East-West Schism, whose beginning is traditionally set in the eleventh century; the Protestant Reformation and the Catholic Counter-Reformation of the sixteenth century; the founding and growth of the major religious orders from the eleventh century on; the emergence of papal absolutism in the Middle Ages and its reemergence in a different form at the First Vatican Council (1869–70); the anti-Modernist reaction during the pontificate of Pius X (1903–14); and the renewal and reform movements—biblical, liturgical, ecumenical, and social—of the first half of the twentieth century, which together laid the foundations for Vatican II.

The Ecclesiologies of the New Testament

As noted at the end of Part I, the two principal factors that explain the extraordinary leap forward in ecclesiology are the Second Vatican Council's teachings on the Church as well as its *style* of formulating those teachings[3] and the retrieval of New Testament scholarship as it applies to the origins of the Church.[4]

THE NEW TESTAMENT AS A SOURCE FOR ECCLESIOLOGY

As a *source* for ecclesiology today, the New Testament serves both a *descriptive* and a *prescriptive* function. Descriptively, the New Testament provides the best evidence of what the universal Church and the local churches were actually like in this earliest period of their individual and collective histories. Prescriptively, the New Testament provides normative criteria[5] by which to answer the question: how *should* the Church and the churches function today? One must resist the temptation, however, to jump too quickly to the more engaging level of prescription before the hard work of description has been completed.

"THE CANON WITHIN THE CANON"

Both the descriptive and the prescriptive tasks are affected to one degree or another by the matter of the "canon within the canon." The word "canon" is derived from the Greek *kanon* ("rule," or "list"). The canon of Sacred Scripture is the official "list" of books that the Church regards as inspired. However, several biblical scholars, including James D. G. Dunn, refer also to a canon within the canon, that is, an unofficial list of texts and themes that have become normative for some scholars and church traditions in their interpretation of the whole of Scripture, and particularly the whole of the New Testament.

"Whatever the theory of canonicity," Dunn writes, "the reality is that *all Christians have operated with a canon within the canon.* Anyone who uses his NT a great deal will at once acknowledge that some pages are more grubby with finger marks than others. . . . All Christians no doubt operate on the principle of interpreting the unclear passages by means of the clear; but, of course, a passage which gives a clear meaning to one is precisely the unclear passage for another, and vice versa."[6]

Dunn continues:

> *It is not too much of an oversimplification to say that (until recently) the effective NT canon for Roman Catholic ecclesiology has been*

> *Matt. 16.17–19 and the Pastoral Epistles [1 and 2 Timothy and Titus]; the canon for Protestant theology has clearly been the (earlier) letters of Paul (for many Lutherans indeed "justification by faith" is the real canon within the canon); Eastern Orthodoxy and the mystical tradition within Western Christianity draw their principal NT inspiration from the Johannine writings; while Pentecostalism looks for its authentication to Acts. Or again, the canon for nineteenth-century Liberal Protestantism was the (so-called) historical Jesus, whereas after the First World War the focus of authority for many Christian theologians became "the kerygma," while more recently others have sought to orient themselves in relation to "the apostolic witness." Perhaps most arresting of all, we must remind ourselves that since early Catholicism was only one strand within the NT, consequently* orthodoxy itself is based on a canon within the canon. . . . *Like it or not, then, all Christians have operated and continue to operate with a canon within the NT canon. Since the NT in fact enshrines such a diversity of first-century Christianity it cannot be otherwise. It is inevitable that one should find Paul most congenial, while another recoils from Paul and relaxes with John, while yet another turns in puzzlement from both to the simplicities of Acts or the orderliness of the Pastorals. To recognize the reality that each does in fact operate with a canon within the canon should not cause embarrassment or shame; it simply means accepting that Christians are no different in their diversity from their fellow believers of the first century.*[7]

According to Dunn's analysis, every use of the New Testament in support of a particular theological position is inevitably affected by the New Testament books and the texts within those books that the interpreter regards as most important and indeed as the hermeneutical prism through which to read the whole body of biblical data. Dunn's analysis correctly implies that one's ecclesiological perspective has a determinative influence on one's exegesis of texts. To take that analysis a step further, no one comes to the interpretation of texts independently of ecclesiological biases, even if those biases are the product of some nondenominational amalgamation of several different approaches.[8] To be sure, not all ecclesiological perspectives are equally faithful to the New Testament and to the Church's postbiblical Tradition. It is the conviction here that a Catholic ecclesiological perspective offers the least limited and limiting perspective on the reality of the Church. In other words, the approach is Catholic in the fullest sense of the word, both uppercased and lowercased alike.

THE MEANING OF "CHURCH" IN THE NEW TESTAMENT

The Greek word *ekklesia* (Lat. *ecclesia*) originally signified a legislative assembly of those with full civil rights.[9] It had no religious usage. It was adopted, however, by the Septuagint (the Greek version of the Old Testament, or Hebrew Bible) to render the Hebrew word *kahal* (also *qahal*), which, with the Hebrew word *'edah,* signifies the religious assembly of the Israelites, called forth and gathered by God. The word appears about one hundred times in the Septuagint (e.g., Deut. 23:2; Judg. 20:2; Mic. 2:5), often qualified by the phrase "of the Lord" (*kahal yahweh*). The early Jewish Christians applied the term to their own gatherings for prayer, perhaps to distinguish themselves from the Jewish synagogue, but after Gentiles were admitted into the community of disciples, the word *ekklesia* came to be applied to the Christian community itself.

Jesus uses the term three times in the New Testament, once referring to the Church in the larger sense ("You are Peter, and upon this rock I will build my church," Matt. 16:18), and twice to the Jewish-Christian community for which Matthew's Gospel was intended ("If [a sinful brother] refuses to listen . . . , tell the church," 18:17). The word occurs twenty-three times in Acts, often in reference to the church of Jerusalem (5:11; 8:1, 3), but also to the churches in Antioch (13:1), in Asia Minor (14:23), and in Syria and Antioch (15:41). A more generalized usage appears in 9:31: "The church throughout all Judea, Galilee, and Samaria." Although the community also referred to itself as a communion, or *koinonia* (2:42), and as the Way (24:14), eventually the most popular self-designation became *ekklesia,* perhaps because it best reflected the early Christians' sense of continuity with Israel. They did not see themselves as part of a new religion separate from Judaism, but as a renewal movement *within* it. Their hope was that many within Israel would accept the risen Christ, but this was not to be.

The word *ekklesia* appears most frequently in the Pauline material—sixty-five times. In every instance it signifies a local church (1 Cor. 11:18, 20, 33–34; 14:23), but Paul also uses the plural form (e.g., 1 Cor. 11:16; 14:33; 2 Cor. 8:18; 12:13; Gal. 1:2,22; Rom. 16:4,16). The "churches" are gathered in the name of Jesus Christ and regard themselves as churches of Jesus Christ (Rom. 16:16; 1 Thess. 2:14; Gal. 1:22). A half century later, the term comes to refer in Ephesians and Colossians to the whole worldwide assembly of Christians (Eph. 1:22–23; 3:10; 5:22–32; Col. 1:18–20). Sometimes, however, the *ekklesia* is simply a small house community (Rom. 16:5; 1 Cor. 16:5; Col. 4:15; Philem. 2).[10]

The word *ekklesia* is found in the Johannine writings in 3 John 6, 9, and 10, and twenty times in Revelation, always referring to regional or particular churches. In the Fourth Gospel the Christian community is described as a flock gathered into a sheepfold (John 10:1–5) under Jesus, the Good Shepherd. He is also the true vine; his disciples, the branches united to him (15:1–8). In James 2:2 the Church is called a synagogue.

Although most references to the Church in the New Testament are to local congregations, there is no Corinthian division of the Church, but "the church of God that is in Corinth" (1 Cor. 1:2; see also 2 Cor. 1:1) or "the church of the Thessalonians" (1 Thess. 1:1). On the other hand, the Church universal is a living, integrated organism, "the fullness of the one who fills all things in every way" (Eph. 1:23). Thus, Paul speaks also of "the churches of Galatia" (1 Cor. 16:1) and "the churches of Asia" (16:19). The early Christian community understood itself as "Church" in both the universal and particular senses. The relationship is complementary, not competitive. All of the New Testament authors write as members of the one Church of Jesus Christ, and all of the particular, or local, churches are built on the foundation of the Apostles and prophets. Christ is always the capstone (Eph. 2:20).

Ecclesiologically, each local church is the Church in that particular place, while the Church is a communion of all the local churches, which together constitute the one universal Church. The Second

Vatican Council's Dogmatic Constitution on the Church makes this same point: "This church of Christ is really present in all legitimately organized local groups of the faithful which, united with their pastors, are also called churches in the New Testament. For these are in fact, in their own localities, the new people called by God, in the holy Spirit" (n. 26). These local churches are "modelled on the universal church; it is in and from these that the one and unique catholic church exists" (n. 23). (This important topic will be treated again in Part IV, on the First Vatican Council, Part V, on the Second Vatican Council, and as a separate topic in Part VII.1, on the Church as a communion.)

DID JESUS INTEND TO "FOUND" A CHURCH?

The answer to the question of whether Jesus intended to "found" a church is no, if by "found" we mean some direct, explicit, deliberate act by which Jesus established a new religious community and organization. This view is known as *precritical*, or what the late New Testament scholar Raymond E. Brown (d. 1998) called a "blueprint ecclesiology."[11] The answer is yes, if by "found" we mean "lay the foundations for" the Church in various indirect ways, that is, by the gathering of disciples, which set him apart from the rabbis of his day, and by the establishment of a communal meal in direct continuity with the Eucharist, which Vatican II's Constitution on the Sacred Liturgy regards as "the summit toward which the activity of the church is directed [and] the source from which all its power flows" (n. 10). In the latter case, it would be preferable to speak of the Church as having its *origin* in Jesus rather than as having been directly and explicitly founded by him.[12] In contrast, this view is known as *historico-critical.*[13] According to Daniel Harrington in *The Church According to the New Testament:*

> *It has recently become customary in academic circles to refer to the* Jesus movement. *The term refers to the public ministry of Jesus of Nazareth and the impact it had on other people. The term captures the dynamism that Jesus and his first followers displayed as they moved about the land of Israel and proclaimed the kingdom*

> *of God. Conversely, it avoids the static and institutional connotations that are often attached to the word* church. *And it leaves open whether it is proper to speak of "the Church" prior to Jesus' death and resurrection.*[14]

The precritical, or "blueprint," approach to the origins of the Church, whether as the "Jesus movement" or in the more traditional, institutional sense, holds that Jesus founded a new religion distinct from Judaism in his own lifetime. From among his followers he chose twelve Apostles, gave them special training, and established one of them, Peter, as the head of the Church. He also created the structural organization of the Church, complete with offices and ministries with clearly defined authority. Sometime before his death he instituted the sacraments of the Eucharist and Holy Orders and authorized the institution of five other sacraments as well. All of the Apostles saw themselves as priests and bishops of this new religion and were instructed by Jesus that only men could be ordained.

However, there is no evidence in the New Testament for any specific act or acts on Jesus's part by which he founded a Church or gathered together a community of the elect. Had Jesus done so, his initiative would have been viewed as the founding of a separate synagogue and, as such, would have minimized and probably even destroyed the uniqueness of his proclamation of the coming Reign of God. The only explicit reference to the founding of the Church is given in Matthew 16:18, which is generally regarded by biblical scholars as part of a post-Resurrection narrative. Indeed, it was not until after Jesus had risen from the dead that the first Christians even speak of a "Church." A majority of scholars also support the assumption that Jesus expected the end of history to come very soon—first in his own lifetime and then soon after his impending death.[15]

By contrast, the historico-critical approach to the founding of the Church views Jesus as a rabbi, prophet, and itinerant preacher who spoke with unusual authority because of his conviction that he enjoyed an intensely close relationship with God. He was also convinced that God had given him a special mission to proclaim that God's end-time presence (namely, the Reign of God) was coming soon in its final form and was already present through him. By gathering disciples and sending them out "to proclaim the kingdom of God and to heal" (Luke 9:2) and providing for a continued discipleship in the real and symbolic meal that was the Last Supper, Jesus laid the foundations for the Church. However, he foresaw that Jerusalem would reject the call to salvation and that, instead, non-Jews would be invited to the heavenly banquet as a new People of God without regard for ethnic or religious origins (Matt. 8:11–12).

The community of disciples did, in fact, remain together after Jesus was rejected and crucified, faithful to the Lord's charge at the Last Supper to "Do this in remembrance of me" (1 Cor. 11:24; Luke 22:19). Likewise the charge to Simon Peter to "strengthen your brothers" suggests that the disciples understood Jesus as having intended them to stay together (Luke 22:31–34). Indeed, there never was a churchless period in the New Testament following the Resurrection.

On the one hand, Jesus's preaching of the Reign of God as imminent suggests that he did not anticipate a long interval between his own ministry and the final completion of the Kingdom. He noted that some of those standing in his presence "will not taste death before they see that the kingdom of God has come in power" (Mark 9:1; see also Matt. 26:29; Luke 9:27). In the so-called eschatological discourse in Mark's Gospel, he warned that "this generation will not pass away until all these things have taken place" (13:30). On the other hand, he also insisted that the Reign of God was not something to come only later, but was already present in himself. "The kingdom of God," he said, "is among you" (Luke 17:21). In any case, as one theologian puts it, there is "no evidence to support the view that Jesus envisioned a lengthy period with a span of centuries before the complete fulfillment of God's plan. To the contrary, the majority of scholars today support the assumption that Jesus expected the end to come soon."[16]

JESUS AND THE JEWS

There *is* persuasive evidence, however, that the notion of a distinct group known as the Twelve (on the model of the twelve sons of the patriarch Jacob [Gen. 35:23–26] and the twelve tribes of Israel) came from the time of Jesus himself. To be sure, the Gospels attribute the calling of the Twelve to Jesus (Mark 3:13–14; Luke 6:13).

In any case, Jesus saw himself both in continuity with, and discontinuity from, contemporary Judaism, but more the former than the latter.[17] His teaching and ministry were in *continuity* with Jewish beliefs and practices, and his project was not to found a new religion separate from Judaism, but to initiate and inspire a renewal and reform movement within Judaism. He insisted that he had come not to abolish the law and the prophets, but to fulfill them (Matt. 5:17). Indeed, he regarded his mission as directed to the Jews, not to the Gentiles. He had been sent, he pointed out, "only to the lost sheep of the house of Israel" (Matt. 15:24; see also 10:5–6), and there is no evidence in the New Testament that, during his earthly ministry, Jesus provided for a special mission to the Gentiles. On the other hand, there *is* some evidence that Jesus expected that the Gentiles would eventually share in the blessings of the Reign of God, because it was being prepared for all peoples (Matt. 8:11; see also Isa. 56:6–7).

Jesus also saw himself in *discontinuity* from contemporary Judaism in the sense that he consciously proclaimed something new—"new wine . . . into fresh wineskins" and a new patch on a new garment (Mark 2:21–22). However, the temptation to take the next step, from a reform of Judaism to the creation of the Church, is fraught with risk. Frederick Cwiekowski, reflecting the mainstream of recent New Testament scholarship, is master of the understatement: "The relationship between Jesus's ministry and the beginnings of the church is complex and our evidence is not without ambiguity."[18] Which is not to say, however, that the reality of the Church stands or falls solely on what the historical Jesus said and did. The mystery of the Church must be situated within the broader context of the mystery of salvation itself and of the gift of the Holy Spirit, who would guide its life throughout all of its history.

THE PENTECOST EXPERIENCE

Contrary to popular belief, the descent of the Holy Spirit upon the Apostles at Pentecost (Acts 2:1–13) was not the beginning of the

Church, or its "birthday." The Church had already existed by then, although some commentators refer to the pre-Pentecost Christian community as a "Jesus movement" (see Part II.2.4). Immediately following the ascension of Jesus into heaven (1:9), the Apostles gathered in the upper room and "devoted themselves with one accord to prayer, together with some women, and Mary the mother of Jesus, and his brothers" (1:13–14). Indeed, the Church, which in recent years has been referred to frequently as the "community of disciples,"[19] came into existence as soon as Jesus began gathering disciples. Nonetheless, Pentecost is generally regarded as the moment when the Church was specifically endowed with power from on high (Luke 24:49; Acts 1:18). For the early Church, the outpouring of the Holy Spirit upon it was an established fact, and the manifestations of the Spirit's gifts were not in doubt (1 Cor. 12–14).

THE EARLY CHURCH AND CONTEMPORARY JUDAISM

The early Christian community at Jerusalem saw itself as still part of Judaism, not as a religious community completely separate from it. From the 30s to the 60s the disciples of Jesus expected his imminent return and the end of the world as they knew it. In the meantime, they continued their Jewish practices, meeting in homes for prayer, some teaching, and reflection on the sayings of the Lord. What distinguished them from their fellow Jews was their belief that Jesus was the promised Messiah and that in him God's end time had dawned. Because they continued their Jewish practices, they were tolerated by most Jews; others rejected them as a splinter group, referring to them contemptuously as the "sect of the Nazoreans," with Jesus as their "ringleader" (Acts 24:5).

Between the years 46 and 49 Paul, Barnabas, and John Mark made missionary journeys to Cyprus and to the cities of south and central Asia Minor (modern-day Turkey). These journeys are described in Acts 13:4–14:26. It was this mission that brought to the surface the issue of the relationship between gentile and Jewish Christians. Were gentile converts to Christianity to be circumcised and bound to Jewish dietary laws, as some Jewish Christians (known as "Judaizers") insisted, or were they to be admitted into the company of disciples without having to become, in effect, Jews? The conflict reached a head and was addressed at the so-called Council of Jerusalem, described in Acts 15.

There were at the time of that council four basic positions within the early Church (from right to left on the religious spectrum) regarding the Church's relationship with Judaism: (1) Jewish Christians and their gentile converts, known as the "circumcision party" (Acts 11:2) and regarded by Paul as "false brethren" (Gal. 2:4), who insisted on the full observance of Mosaic law, including circumcision; (2) Jewish Christians and their gentile converts who did not insist on circumcision, but who required gentile converts to observe some of the Jewish purity laws (a group that included Peter and James, the brother of the Lord and head of the Jerusalem church); (3) Jewish Christians and their gentile converts who did not insist on circumcision as salvific for gentile converts and who did not require converted Gentiles to observe Jewish dietary laws, but who also did not demand a break with Jewish cultic practices or abandonment of circumcision and the law (Paul); and (4) Jewish Christians and their gentile converts who did not insist on circumcision and Jewish dietary laws and saw no lasting significance in Jewish feasts and worship in the Temple (a group that consisted of the Hellenists, especially Stephen, Philip, and the rest of the Seven, and a position that found expression in the Fourth Gospel and in the Letter to the Hebrews).[20]

The resolution achieved at the Council of Jerusalem was closest to the second position, but with some overlapping with the third. The assembly did not wish to "trouble" the Gentiles who turn to God (Acts 15:19) or to place on them "any burden beyond [certain] necessities," such as abstaining from meat sacrificed to idols . . . and from unlawful marriage (15:28–29). Frederick Cwiekowski delivers himself of yet another understatement: "The story of the evolving relationship between Judaism and emerging Christianity in the first century does not permit easy summarization."[21]

In any case, we should not miss the deeper ecclesiological significance of the Council of Jerusalem. First, it was James, not Peter, who presided, even though Peter was present. James did so as head of the local church of Jerusalem. Second, if Peter had already been acknowledged as pope in the modern sense of the word, he not only would have presided, but he also would not have been attacked, along with Paul and Barnabas, by the Judaizers, also known as the "circumcision party" and the "party of the Pharisees," for receiving Gentiles into the Church without circumcising them and directing them to observe the Mosaic law (15:5). The fact that it was the ultraconservatives in the early Church who were the leading critics of Peter is an ecclesiological irony not to be ignored. One might have expected them to be on the "pope's" side in the dispute. Third, James proposed a pastoral solution that should serve as a model for church leaders of every age. After the issues had been debated (15:7) and then resolved by an apparently overwhelming vote, perhaps even unanimously (15:25), James counseled those present not to flaunt their decision on the central matter of circumcision (namely, that it was not an essential condition for entrance into the Church), but voluntarily to observe various Jewish dietary laws (15:19–20, 28–29). Finally, and most important, the council tacitly accepted Peter's argument that "we are saved through the grace of the Lord Jesus, in the same way as [the Gentiles]" (15:11). Salvation comes *through* the Church, but it does not come only *to* the Church.

THE CHURCH, THE REIGN OF GOD, AND THE EUCHARIST

We have already referred, in a general and highly abbreviated fashion, to the relationship of the Church and the Reign, or Kingdom, of God in Part I.2.3, and also in Part II.2.4.[22] Our interest here is in the New Testament's portrayal of that relationship, and of that relationship, in turn, in connection with the Eucharist.[23]

Jesus's message and ministry were centered on the Reign of God—a reality already present in him (Luke 17:21) and manifested in his healings, exorcisms, and forgiveness of sins, and it is also a reality due to come later in all fullness and perfection (Mark 9:1; 13:30). Although there is clear textual evidence that Jesus expected the Kingdom of

God to come very soon, in his own lifetime (Luke 22:18), he also spoke of it as coming at some indefinite future time (Matt. 24:36; Acts 1:6–7; Mark 13:32). He instructed his disciples to pray for the coming of the Kingdom (Luke 11:2; Matt. 6:9), a reality signified in the many parables attributed to Jesus.

The Church, however, lives "between the times," that is, between the *already* of the decisive inbreaking of the Reign of God in Jesus and the *not yet* of its final manifestation at the end of history. Acts describes the spread of the Church "between the times" as happening in and through the power of the Holy Spirit. Taking their lead from the risen Lord himself (1:3), the Apostles proclaimed the Kingdom of God wherever they went (8:12; 19:8; 20:25; 28:23, 31). This is undoubtedly why Vatican II's Pastoral Constitution on the Church in the Modern World is so emphatic about the matter: "The church has but one sole purpose—that the kingdom of God may come and the salvation of the human race may be accomplished" (n. 45).

Nowhere in the New Testament is the Church identified with that Kingdom. On the other hand, there is a fundamental orientation of the Church toward the Kingdom of God. Vatican II's Dogmatic Constitution on the Church refers to the Church as "the seed and the beginning of that kingdom" on earth (n. 5). That orientation is vividly manifested in the Eucharist, which anticipates the feasting at the Lord's table in the final Kingdom (Luke 22:30) and which, at the same time, is rooted in the very origin of the Church (1 Cor. 11:18–22). The Last Supper itself was celebrated with a view to the coming Kingdom of God, which was the focus of everything that Jesus said and did, not only at this meal but in his whole life and ministry (1 Cor. 11:23–25; Mark 14:22–25; Matt. 26:26–29; Luke 22:15–20). In his account of the Last Supper, Paul notes that he received the tradition from the Lord himself (1 Cor. 11:23).

After the Resurrection the disciples gathered frequently for these shared meals, modeled on the Last Supper, but now with the conviction that the risen Lord was in their midst whenever they came together in his name (Matt. 18:20). The meals were marked by a spirit of joy prompted by their new sense of solidarity and by their experience of the presence of Christ, and also because "every day the Lord added to their number those who were being saved," that is, being brought into the Kingdom (Acts 2:46–47). Patterned after the Church's relationship to the Kingdom of God, the Eucharist has a threefold dimension. It gives thanks for the decisive inbreaking of the Kingdom in Jesus Christ, for the gift of the Kingdom even now through the presence of the Spirit of the risen Christ, and for the promise that the Kingdom will be given in all of its fullness at the end of time. "For as often as you eat this bread and drink the cup," Paul writes, "you proclaim the death of the Lord until he comes" (1 Cor. 11:26).

THE MISSION OF THE CHURCH

It is clear from the New Testament that the then fledgling universal Church did not always understand itself as a missionary community, if by "missionary" we mean a call from God to preach the gospel beyond the Jewish community. The first Christians were missionary in the sense that they reached out to the whole of Israel (Acts 3:11; 4:1; 5:25, 40, 42), even outside of Jerusalem (9:32–43; Gal. 2:8; 1 Cor. 9:5). But it was not until after the Resurrection experience had permeated their collective consciousness and broadened their ecclesiological horizon that they became convinced that they should proclaim the gospel to the Gentiles as well (Matt. 8:11; Luke 13:28).

As pointed out above, during his earthly ministry Jesus had instructed the Twelve not to go among the Gentiles or into Samaritan towns, but rather to the lost sheep of the house of Israel (Matt. 10:5–6). After his death and Resurrection, however, he instructed the Eleven to "Go, therefore, and make disciples of all nations" (28:19–20). He assured his Apostles that they would receive the power of the Holy Spirit to do so, and that they would become his witnesses not only in all Judea and Samaria, but "to the ends of the earth" (Acts 1:8).[24]

To be sure, there was much resistance on the part of the Jewish Christians of Jerusalem, including some of the Apostles. But Luke provided a theological foundation for expanding the mission (Acts 28:25–28), citing an intervention from God and the authority of Peter as key factors in changing the missionary situation (10:1–11:8). However, even as the mission was broadened "to the ends of the earth,"

Jerusalem retained its privileged position, for it was to be from there that the mission to the Gentiles was to begin (1:8; Luke 24:47; Rom. 9–11). In the meantime, Israel was to be given one last opportunity for repentance through the apostolic preaching (Acts 2:38; 3:19; 5:31; Mark 7:27; Rom. 1:16; 2:9).

Paul expected that all of Israel would eventually be saved, in spite of its current "hardening," but only after the conversion of the Gentiles, which he saw as a mystery imbedded in the history of redemption itself (Rom. 11:25). This will be so, Paul insisted, because "the gifts and the call of God are irrevocable" (11:29). The post-Pauline author of Ephesians regarded it as a revelation from the Holy Spirit that the Gentiles are "coheirs of Christ, members of the same body, and copartners in the promise in Christ Jesus through the gospel" (3:5–6). Because of the conversion of the Gentiles through the preaching attributed to Paul, "the manifold wisdom of God might now be made known through the church to the principalities and authorities in the heavens" (3:10).

In the end, it was the Easter event and the faith it generated that empowered the Apostles to preach to the whole world and to baptize. But, alas, none of this happened without much conflict and debate.

STRUCTURES OF THE NEW TESTAMENT CHURCHES

This section could also have been entitled "How the New Testament Churches Organized Themselves for Mission." There are five points to be made about the organizational structures of the Church and the churches of the New Testament, keeping in mind, however, that at no time in the New Testament period or during the subsequent history of the Church did the institutional Church operate in accordance with the highest ecclesial ideals, as if in some post-Easter Garden of Eden.[25]

1. *There is no uniform order or organizational structure to the Church and the churches of the New Testament.* It is not clear, for example, how the Twelve functioned in the Jerusalem church, or why they receded into the background after the call of "the Seven" assistants,

or deacons, in Acts 6:2, or why elders are mentioned with them at the Council of Jerusalem, or what rank and position "the Seven" actually held (6:3–6). Peter's special role in Jerusalem is clear, but not that of James, the "brother of the Lord" and the head of the Jerusalem community (12:17; 15:13–21; Gal. 1:19; 2:9).

We do know that there was a sharing of goods on the part of the Jerusalem community and a rich liturgical and prayer life both in a special meeting place in the Temple and in the houses of members, where they gathered for the breaking of the bread (Acts 2:46; 20:7, 11). The community maintained close ties with its Jewish roots, and so its organizational structure tended to be patterned after that of the Temple and the synagogues. To be sure, there were internal disputes, the most important of which culminated in the Council of Jerusalem, referred to in Part II.2.7.

At Antioch, at the time the third largest city in the Roman Empire, similar disputes broke out between Jewish Christians and their gentile converts. The Antioch community also held regular meetings at which the large congregation was "taught" (Acts 11:26). Prophets and teachers were active here (13:1–3), and the gifts of the Spirit were said to be evident (11:27; 15:32).

The local church of Corinth, a busy port city, was predominantly gentile in origin. Without close ties to Jewish traditions and structures, it tended to be charismatic in character (1 Cor. 1:5–7; 12:8–11). In the absence of clear lines of pastoral authority and ministerial responsibility, there was often confusion in the community. Partisan groups attached to particular missionaries emerged (1:11; 3:4–5, 22). On the other hand, the apostolic preaching and instruction were heard in the assemblies (2 Cor. 3:4–4:6), and worship occupied a central place (1 Cor. 11:17–34). The Corinthian Christians understood themselves as the Church of God (1:2; 10:32; 11:22; 2 Cor. 1:1; 3:17–18; 4:5). It was a church in communion with the church of Jerusalem (for which the great collection was taken up) and with the other churches (1 Cor. 1:2; 7:17; 11:16; 16:1,19; 2 Cor. 1:1; 8:24; 12:13; 13:12).

2. *On the other hand, some degree of order and structure shaped the life and mission of the Church and the churches.* Indeed, the Church and the churches were never without some measure of order and

structure. There was no absolutely egalitarian, structureless "Jesus movement."[26] Thus, although Paul recognized the fundamental equality of all who have been baptized into a newness of life in Christ (Gal. 3:28), he also called upon Christians "to respect those who are laboring among you and who are over you in the Lord and who admonish you" (1 Thess. 5:12). Their offices were derived from the Lord himself (Eph. 4:11). Indeed, the early Church was a community highly differentiated by reason of charisms and ministries (1 Cor. 12:4–11). There is a sacred order of ministers and pastors who are responsible to their heavenly chief shepherd (1 Pet. 5:2–4).

This is not to say that all authority and pastoral responsibility were given only to a hierarchical elite to be exercised on behalf of the many. On the contrary, the whole congregation was involved in important decisions in this earliest of periods (Acts 15; 1 Cor. 5). But there were also some members who served in a leadership capacity of one kind or another. Local churches were guided by presbyters, and others were appointed as overseers (the original meaning of the Greek word for bishop, *episkopos;* see Acts 20:28).[27]

3. *There is no radical opposition between the charismatic and administrative ministries.* All of the gifts and charisms have the Holy Spirit as their common source (1 Cor. 12:11). Some of these gifts are clearly charismatic, for example, the gift of tongues, but others are just as clearly administrative or institutional, for example, teaching and presiding (Rom. 12:7–8; Eph. 4:11–12). Pope Pius XII (1939–58) made the same point in his 1943 encyclical on the Church as the Mystical Body of Christ, *Mystici Corporis:* "One must not think, however, that this ordered or 'organic' structure of the body of the Church contains only hierarchical elements and with them is complete; or, as an opposite opinion holds, that it is composed only of those who enjoy charismatic gifts" (n. 18).[28]

Nevertheless, as is evident in 2 Corinthians, the charismatic church at Corinth did not fully submit to all of Paul's decisions, but what is not clear is which of Paul's decisions they rejected. He had ruled, for example, on the case of the incestuous man (1 Cor. 5:3–5); he provided liturgical directions (11:17, 33); and he admonished the Corinthians and offered concrete prescriptions (7:17; 16:1). However, they implicitly recognized his apostolic authority in referring questions of this sort to him in the first place (1 Cor. 7–10).

4. *Whatever the office or ministry, it is always for the sake of service, never for control or domination.* The model is always Jesus (Mark 10:45). The one who humbles himself will be exalted, and vice versa (Luke 14:11; Matt. 23:12). Paul consistently refers to his own office as that of a servant (1 Cor. 4:1, 9–13; 2 Cor. 4:5, 12, 15; 6:4–10; Phil. 2:17).

5. *The chief ministry of the universal Church is the Petrine ministry.*[29] Peter was the first disciple to be called by Jesus (Matt. 4:18–19); he served as spokesman for the other Apostles (Mark 8:29; Matt. 18:21; Luke 12:41; John 6:67–69); according to the Pauline and Lucan traditions he was the first to whom the risen Lord appeared (1 Cor. 15:5; Luke 24:34); he was the most frequently commissioned of the Apostles following the Resurrection; and he is regularly listed first among the Twelve (Mark 3:16–19; Matt. 10:1–4; Luke 6:12–16). In the Catholic tradition, the biblical basis for associating the primacy with Peter is embodied in three texts: Matthew 16:13–19; Luke 22:31–32; and John 21:15–19. The conferral of the power of the keys to the Kingdom suggests an imposing measure of authority, given the symbolism of the keys.

On the other hand, Peter's authority was neither absolute nor monarchical. It was James, not Peter, who presided over the Council of Jerusalem. Peter also consulted with the other Apostles and was even sent by them (Acts 8:14). He and John are portrayed as acting as a team (3:1–11; 4:1–22; 8:14). Indeed, Peter shared the apostolate with Paul: Peter's to the circumcised, and Paul's to the uncircumcised (Gal. 2:7–8). And Paul confronted Peter for his inconsistency and hypocrisy in drawing back from table fellowship with gentile Christians in Antioch under pressure from some Jewish Christians who arrived later from Jerusalem. Paul "opposed him to his face because he clearly was wrong" (Gal. 2:11; see also vv. 12–14).

Biblical scholars, however, point to a trajectory of images relating to Peter and his ministry as an independent basis for the Church's belief in his primacy: fisherman (Luke 5:10; John 21:1–14, but see also Matt. 4:18–19 and Mark 1:16–20—Mark was written before either Matthew or Luke—where Jesus called others as well as Peter to be "fishers of men"),[30] shepherd (John 21:15–17), martyr (John 13:36; 1 Pet. 5:1), elder (1 Pet. 5:1), proclaimer of faith in Jesus as the Son of God (Matt. 16:16–17), receiver of a special revelation (Mark 9:2–8; 2 Pet. 1:16–18; Acts 1:9–16; 5:1–11; 10:9–16; 12:7–9), guardian of the faith (2 Pet. 1:20–21; 3:15–16), and the rock on which the Church is to be built (Matt. 16:18). It should be clear, therefore, that the notion of the primacy evolved over time. It was not understood in the New Testament as it came eventually to be understood and clearly taught by the First Vatican Council in the nineteenth century and by the Catholic Church today (for much more on the primacy and on the papacy generally, see Part IV).

To be sure, these five points represent a kind of homogenization of texts, leaving aside for the most part the fact of development *within* the texts. There *was* development, however, and the overall ecclesiology and individual ecclesiologies of the New Testament cannot be understood apart from that development, which is the subject of the next, closely connected section.

STRUCTURAL DEVELOPMENT WITHIN THE NEW TESTAMENT

We do not know exactly when the Church was established in Rome, although it was probably in the early 40s.[31] Peter would have still been in Jerusalem and, therefore, not the original missionary to or founder of the local church in Rome. Paul's Letter to the Romans, which is our best evidence, suggests that Peter did not have any significant association with the Roman church before the year 58, and it may be that he did not come to Rome until the early 60s. The principal sources for understanding the development of the Church in the 50s and early 60s are the Pauline Letters.[32] But even they do not yield a full picture of the Church and the churches of this period because they were written, for the most part, in response to specific pastoral needs and situations.

Regarding ministerial structures, Paul never mentions presbyters (elders) in any of his Letters, and he mentions bishops (*episkopoi*) and deacons only in Philippians 1:1. We do know that there were at least three ministerial roles in the churches of the 50s: apostles (that is, missionary leaders, in contrast to local, residential leaders), fellow workers (patrons and protectors, evangelists, and instructors in the faith), and local leaders (some of whom overlapped with "fellow workers"). Women played a prominent role in the churches at Corinth, Philippi, and Rome, performing some of the same functions and displaying some of the same gifts as men.

But even by the 50s the Church still had no cultic leaders who were called "priests," even though the Christian communities gathered regularly for liturgy (1 Cor. 14:26). There were no detailed instructions for the celebration of Baptism, and the central topic of the Eucharist appears only twice in the seven undisputed Letters of Paul, both in 1 Corinthians. Significantly, none of Paul's Letters says anything about who presided at the eucharistic meals. Raymond Brown reminds us that the owners of some of the house churches of this time were women (Chloe in 1 Cor. 1:11; Mary, the mother of John Mark, in Acts 12:12; Aquila and Prisca in 1 Cor. 16:19; and Nympha in Col. 4:15). Although we do not know if there were women presbyters in the New Testament period, Brown acknowledges, the question takes on a special urgency "if there were women householders and if householders had pastoral roles in the churches meeting in their houses."[33]

An important turning point in the Church's structural development occurred during the period from the early 60s to the end of the 70s, also known as the *subapostolic* period. The principal leaders had already died, the Temple and the city of Jerusalem were destroyed, and the Parousia, or Second Coming of the Lord, was obviously delayed. Although there was a serious risk of a leadership gap and a need for stability and guidance, the emergence of the notion of apostolic succession was a far more complex process than traditional, pre–Vatican II Catholic ecclesiology had understood and appreciated.[34]

In both Luke's Gospel and his Acts of the Apostles, the development of the Church was seen as a historical process under the guidance of the Holy Spirit. Thus, by the 80s and 90s, the leadership of the Church passed from Jewish Christians to Gentiles, and from Jerusalem to other important cities in the Roman Empire, especially Antioch, Alexandria, and Rome. There is no evidence, however, that any one individual in the mid-80s functioned in the Petrine role for the universal Church either at Antioch or anywhere else. On the contrary, available evidence suggests that Rome at this time did not have any such leading figure. Indeed, it was not until the middle of the second century that Rome changed from a collegial form of leadership to a monoepiscopal form.[35]

The principal problem facing the churches, which the pastoral Letters tried to address, was the presence of "false teachers" (Titus 1:10–11; 1 Tim. 4:1–2; 2 Tim. 3:6) and the confusion resulting from the spread of their teachings, which may have been an early form of Gnosticism (the belief that salvation comes to those with a special knowledge [Gk. *gnosis*], or private revelation, given only to an elite few). In order to combat this development, greater emphasis was placed on strong pastoral leadership: in particular, supervisors, or overseers (bishops) and elders (presbyters), who were responsible especially for teaching, preaching, governing, and motivating. A special emphasis was placed on protecting and preserving the "deposit" of faith (1 Tim. 6:20; 2 Tim. 1:12, 14). At this time, that is, the last third of the first century, there was still no clear distinction between the *episkopoi* (bishops, overseers) and the *presbyteroi* (elders). This would not emerge for another generation. In the meantime, elders who ruled well were to be given "double honor," consisting perhaps of monetary considerations and added esteem or respect (1 Tim. 5:17).

The model of the church leader was that of the head of the household, known in Latin as the *paterfamilias*, a masculine term. But women also had a role in church leadership as deaconesses (1 Tim. 3:8–13; 5:2) and as widows who had reached the age of sixty and whose ministry consisted of prayer, assistance with the raising of children, hospitality, caring for the sick, and making pastoral visits (1 Tim. 5:3–16). There is also a reference to deaconesses in Romans 16:1, which identifies Phoebe as a deaconess of the church at Cenchreae.[36]

Deacons and presbyters were also part of the structure of the community related to Peter, which viewed itself as a renewed Israel, a chosen race, a royal priesthood, a holy nation, and God's own people (1 Pet. 2:9). However, we do not get a clear picture of the role and function of deacons in the New Testament generally. Biblical scholars today generally reject Acts 6:1–6, where the function of Stephen and the other six is portrayed as relieving the Twelve of such menial duties as serving at table, as the textual foundation for the diaconate. Early postbiblical texts, however, tend to reinforce the New Testament idea that some form of service (the root meaning of the Greek word *diakonos*) was implied, including the preaching of the word and assistance in the liturgy and the sacramental life of the Church.[37] As noted above, the term "presbyter" was used interchangeably with that of "overseer," both of which indicated some form of community leadership. Only at the end of the first century did the presbyter's role become distinct from that of the overseer, or bishop.

By contrast, the Johannine communities showed little or no interest in church structures and offices, not even that of Apostle. They placed great emphasis on discipleship, indeed a discipleship of equals, and continuity with Jesus came not through the Apostles, but through a disciple who was an "eyewitness," whose "testimony is true" (John 19:35; 21:24), and also through the presence of the Advocate, or Spirit (14:16–17, 26; 15:26; 16:7–13).

The post-Pauline Letters to the Ephesians and Colossians also pay little attention to structure, which is not to say none at all. There is a recognition of the diversity of ministries: apostles, prophets, evangelists, pastors, and teachers (Eph. 4:11–12) and the post-Pauline author of Colossians acknowledges the role of his "co-workers for the kingdom of God" (4:11). The ideal Church, however, is the Body of Christ (Eph. 1:15–23; 4:1–16; Col. 1:18) and the spotless bride (Eph. 5:27). The ecclesiological model is organic rather than institutional. But at about the same time the wider Church was moving in the direction of greater institutionalization and a growing emphasis on ecclesial offices.

The final years of the first century and the early years of the second constitute the *postapostolic* period, as reflected in the extrabiblical writings of Clement of Rome and Ignatius of Antioch. By now the church at Rome was exercising a pastoral care that extended beyond its own community, having replaced Jerusalem as the practical center of the growing universal Church. Appeals were made to Peter and Paul, with whom the Roman church was most closely identified.

There was also a tendency to describe church officials in terms of a divinely ordered pattern and as a parallel to Jewish cultic roles as performed in the Temple: apostles (missionaries), presbyter-bishops, and deacons. By the end of the first century, Christians saw themselves as a religious body distinct from Judaism, the Eucharist as the sacramental replacement of the Temple sacrifices, and those who presided at the Eucharist as priests. Regarding church order, Clement appealed to both the order of the universe and the ordered structure of the Roman Empire to justify the growing organizational structuring of the Church (*1 Clement* 20, 37). In fact, he drew exact parallels with the imperial system, insisting that church leaders commanded the same obedience as military and civil authorities.

In tying together the main lines of this structural development, Frederick Cwiekowski, in his *The Beginnings of the Church*, makes an astute observation—again, with some measure of understatement—about its short- and long-term effects: "On the positive side, the Christian church became organizationally a powerful vehicle for evangelization. However, the negative side meant an uncritical acceptance of some organizational structures and styles which at times sadly hindered the witness and mission of the church."[38]

"EARLY CATHOLICISM" IN THE NEW TESTAMENT

"Early Catholicism,"[39] according to Raymond E. Brown, "designates the initial stages of sacramentalism, hierarchy, ordination, dogma—in short, the beginning of the distinctive features of *Catholic* Christianity."[40] Any consideration of structural developments in the Church and churches of the New Testament must take some account of dissenting views of Protestant scholars, like James D. G. Dunn, and of other, unnamed Catholic scholars who might share some of the Protestant reservations about the way the early Church and churches organized themselves for mission and whether any of the New Testament polity is, or might be, normative for the Church today.[41]

Dunn devotes an entire chapter to the topic in his *Unity and Diversity in the New Testament*.[42] He poses the question straightforwardly in the chapter's opening sentence: "To what extent are the features which characterize Catholicism from the (late) second century onwards already present in the NT?" He then unpacks the question's principal elements: "Was Catholicism a post-apostolic development, a falling away from the primeval purity and simplicity of the first century?—as some Protestants have argued. Or was it simply the natural unfolding of what had belonged to the essence of Christianity from the first?—as many Catholics have maintained. Or does the answer lie somewhere in between?"[43]

Discussion among Protestant scholars beginning in the nineteenth century produced various hypotheses: that Early Catholicism arose as a compromise between Jewish and gentile Christianity (Ferdinand C. Baur); that Early Catholicism was inevitable once it came into contact with the gentile world (Adolf Harnack[44]); that Early Catholicism was a consequence of an identification of the invisible dimension of the Church with the visible (Rudolph Sohm); or that Early Catholicism was the institutionalization consequent upon the fading of the Parousia hope (Ernst Käsemann,[45] Martin Werner). The last approach is also Dunn's, arguing on the basis of various New Testament texts.

Dunn offers several overall conclusions to his study of Early Catholicism, marked perhaps (with the possible exception of the first) by his own Protestant background:

1. Early Catholicism can be found already in the New Testament, specifically in the Pastorals and 2 Peter, probably Jude, and possibly Ephesians, but not in the Fourth Gospel or the three Johannine Letters. Luke-Acts, on the other hand, represents a kind of merger between an Early Catholic perspective and the enthusiasm of the first Christians.

2. Early Catholicism, however, was a "late starter" within the New Testament—a reaction perhaps to the disappointments and excesses of such enthusiasm and to the failure of the Pauline vision of the Church as an essentially charismatic community.

3. On the other hand, the organization of the Jerusalem church (still first generation) was in many ways more conducive to Early Catholicism than the Pauline model, largely because of the former's synagogue pattern of government and the Jewish-Christian community's deeply conservative respect for tradition.

4. But Early Catholicism was not the only trajectory or form of Christianity to emerge from the first century. There were also the apocalyptic, the Jewish, the Hellenistic, the Johannine, and the balanced approach of the Acts of the Apostles. However, none of these survived in their original form. Because of the failure of hope in the Parousia, for example, apocalyptic Christianity could not endure beyond a single generation. Early Catholicism, therefore, became increasingly the dominant trajectory in the second and third centuries.

5. In becoming the norm of orthodoxy, Early Catholicism generated in the process several negative effects: the loss of a lively eschatological hope and of a healthy eschatological tension between the present and the future; an overstructuring of the Church; the confinement of the Spirit by office and ritual; and the reduction of faith to formulas and its petrification in set forms. In the end, Early Catholicism, according to Dunn, failed to realize that its "biggest heresy of all" was the insistence that there is only one ecclesiastical orthodoxy.[46]

Raymond E. Brown, on the other hand, argues that the main features of Early Catholicism—sacramentalism, hierarchy, and dogma—were meaningful within the life of the Church of the New Testament and of subsequent centuries and that is why the Church included the later books in the canon of Sacred Scripture. Consequently, "what was truly normative was not a group of writings but the Spirit acting within the living church. It was church usage that led [the Council of] Trent to determine which books should be accepted as canonical; so it also is church usage that determines the degree of normative authority (canonicity) to be attributed to a NT practice or doctrine."[47]

THE CHURCH AS PEOPLE OF GOD, BODY OF CHRIST, AND TEMPLE OF THE HOLY SPIRIT

During the first half of the twentieth century, prior to the theological revival in the aftermath of World War II and the convening of the Second Vatican Council, Catholic ecclesiology did not generally link the mystery of the Church with that of the triune God. At popular levels, the Church was seen through a kind of unitarian prism, that is, as the prolongation of the Incarnation. Slightly more sophisticated binarian renderings emphasized the role of God the Father as the One who called the Church into being to continue the work of the Son. The Holy Spirit, however, was often referred to at this time as "the forgotten Person of the Blessed Trinity," remembered mainly on the feast of Pentecost, at Confirmations, and when young Catholics were taking difficult exams.

It was not until around the time of the Second Vatican Council and during the years immediately following the council that the word "pneumatology" began to work its way into Catholic theology generally and into ecclesiology in particular. Theological works on the Holy Spirit appeared in tandem with newer approaches to the mystery of the Trinity.[48] The Second Vatican Council's Dogmatic Constitution on the Church led the way by explicitly linking the mystery of the Church with that of the triune God (nn. 2–4). The Father gathered together "all the just" in the universal Church, entrusted it to the Son "to restore all things" (see Eph. 1:4–5,10), and then sent the Holy Spirit on Pentecost to sanctify the Church continually "so that believers might have access to the Father through Christ in the one Spirit (see Ephesians 2:18)." That intimate relationship between the Church and the triune God is expressed in three major biblical images, or metaphors: People of God, Body of Christ, and Temple of the Holy Spirit.[49]

People of God

The image of People of God is derived initially from the Hebrew Scriptures, or Old Testament. Israel understood itself as the People of God because of its conviction that God (Yahweh) had called it together as such (Exod. 19:5; 23:22; Deut. 7:6; 14:2; 26:18). "I will take you as my own people, and you shall have me as your God" (Exod. 6:7). That call to peoplehood was linked with the covenant: "I will look with favor upon you. . . . I will set my dwelling among you, and will not disdain you. Ever present in your midst, I will be your God, and you will be my people" (Lev. 26:9–12). A similar connection can be found in the writings of the major prophets (e.g., Jer. 32:38–41).

Toward the end of the first century of the Christian era, the early Church came to appropriate this image for itself: "But you are a chosen race, a royal priesthood, a holy nation, a people of his own, so that you may announce the praises of him who called you out of darkness into his wonderful light. Once you were no people but now you are God's people" (1 Pet. 2:9–10). This passage makes evident allusions to various Old Testament texts, particularly Isaiah 43:20–21 and Exodus 19:6.

The words of Exodus 6:7 ("I will take you as my own people, and you shall have me as your God") are cited several times in the New Testament and applied to the Church. Paul quotes those words in 2 Corinthians 6:16, but taken this time from Ezekiel 37:27 ("I will be their God, and they shall be my people."). Titus 2:14 refers to the same text. In Hebrews 8:10 it occurs in the lengthy quotation from Jeremiah 31:31–34 to show that this prophecy has been fulfilled in the new covenant. The guiding theme of this Letter is that the Church is the new eschatological People of God. And the formula appears finally in Revelation 21:3 in the vision of the future Jerusalem.[50] Although there is no explicit reference to the Church as the *new* People of God, there *are* explicit references to the *new* covenant in Luke 22:20; 1 Corinthians 11:25; 2 Corinthians 3:6; and Hebrews 8:13; 9:15; 12:24, and the Covenant is connected, at least implicitly, to a new community (Heb. 8:8–12, which cites Jer. 31:31–34, where such a link is made). But it is no longer a covenant sealed by bodily circumcision, but by faith in Jesus Christ and "the circumcision of Christ" (Col. 2:11) in Baptism.

Nevertheless, a tension persisted between the old and new People of God, most strongly portrayed in Paul, especially in his Letter to the Romans (9–11). "Israel according to the flesh" sacrifices "to demons, not to God" (1 Cor. 10:18–20), in contrast to "the Israel of God"

(Gal. 6:16). But in the new dispensation, "There is neither Jew nor Greek, there is neither slave nor free person, there is not male and female; for you are all one in Christ Jesus. And if you belong to Christ, then you are Abraham's descendant, heirs according to the promise" (3:28–29).

But affiliation with the new People of God is no guarantee of salvation. There are false prophets in the Church who will be repudiated by the Lord at the end (Matt. 7:22–23) when all evildoers will be cast out (13:41–43). On the other hand, many who did not belong to the Church will be acknowledged by the Son of Man as his brothers and sisters (25:31–46). The final test will be that of a just life. Metaphorically, no one will enter the heavenly marriage feast without a wedding garment (22:11–13).

One thinks of the words of St. Augustine, in his homily on Baptism, taken over and adapted by the theologian Karl Rahner: "Many whom God has, the Church does not have; and many whom the Church has, God does not have."[51] The Church, or new People of God, is not identical with the Reign, or Kingdom, of God. (For the relationship between the Church and the Reign, or Kingdom, of God, see Part I.2.3; Part II.2.4, 2.8.)

Body of Christ

The People of God image underlines the Church's intimate connection with Israel and with God's call to a covenantal relationship. The Body of Christ image, on the other hand, italicizes the Church's intimate connection with Jesus Christ and with God's call to a communal relationship with God (the vertical dimension) and with one another in Christ (the horizontal dimension).

The image of the Body of Christ is distinctively Pauline, although its bears some affinity with the Johannine allegory of the vine and the branches (John 15:1–8). Sometimes it is falsely set in opposition to the Church as People of God. The Church is *both* the People of God *and* the Body of Christ. Both images are rooted in the Old Testament idea of corporate personality.[52]

The Body of Christ image is grounded in the union that exists between the church community and the risen body of Christ. Paul developed the image initially in the face of the deep divisions within the Christian community at Corinth. Factionalism was rampant, as some identified themselves with one or another Christian figure: Paul, Peter, Apollos (a former disciple of John the Baptist), and the Lord himself (1 Cor. 1:12). There were also divisions between the well-to-do and household servants, which spilled over into the celebration of the Eucharist (11:17–22). When the Christian shares in the bread of the Eucharist, Paul insisted, he or she becomes one body with Christ (1 Cor. 10:16–17). Thus, whoever eats or drinks unworthily profanes the body of Christ (11:29). It is in one body that Christ has reconciled us to the Father by his death and resurrection (Eph. 2:16–17; Col. 1:22). The Church has become one body—Christ's own—in which the Holy Spirit dwells (Eph. 4:4). Christians are called one body (Col. 3:15).

It is important to note that there is a development within the Pauline writings. In Romans 12:4–21 and 1 Corinthians 12:4–27, for example, the application of the image of the body of Christ refers more to the union of Christians with one another than with Christ. These texts refer to the diversity of gifts, charisms, ministries, and offices, which, despite their multiplicity, do not compromise the fundamental unity of the Church. The members are one because they are baptized by one Spirit into one body (1 Cor. 12:13). They are called not one body "in" Christ, but one body "of" Christ (12:27). The same identity is presupposed in 1 Corinthians 6:15: "Do you not know that your bodies are members of Christ?" And it is because the Christian is really a member of the Body of Christ that she or he can also be called metaphorically a temple of the Holy Spirit (6:19).

The ideas in these earlier Pauline Letters are presupposed when the Body of Christ image is introduced, with seeming abruptness, in Ephesians 1:23 and Colossians 1:24. These Letters refer not to local churches but to the universal Church. Christ is called the head of his Body, the Church (Eph. 5:23; Col. 1:18; 2:19). As head of the Church, he is the principle of its union and growth (Eph. 4:16; Col. 2:19). The Body of Christ is something that is to be built up (Eph. 4:12, 16), and whatever gifts exist within the Church are for that purpose (1 Cor. 14:12). Paul himself is presented as "filling up what is lacking in the afflictions of Christ on behalf of his body, which is the church" (Col. 1:24), while Christ is said to love the Church as a husband loves his wife (Eph. 5:25).

The Pauline author of Ephesians makes a special appeal to the community "to live in a manner worthy of the call you have received . . . bearing with one another through love, striving to preserve the unity of the spirit through the bond of peace: one body and one Spirit, as you were also called to the one hope of your call; one Lord, one faith, one baptism; one God and Father of all, who is over all and through all and in all" (4:1–6; see also Col. 3:12–15).

It is because the Church is a sacrament that unity is so crucial. Sacraments cause grace (that is, the redemptive presence of God) insofar as they effectively signify it. The Church is called to be a compelling sign of what God is doing and intends to do for the salvation of the whole of humankind.[53]

Temple of the Holy Spirit

The linkage between the Church as Body of Christ and as Temple of the Holy Spirit is highlighted in Ephesians 2:21–22: "Through him the whole structure is held together and grows into a temple sacred in the Lord; in him you also are being built together into a dwelling place of God in the Spirit." Jesus identified himself with the Temple (John 2:19), and the Body of Christ is the new Temple (1 Cor. 3:9, 16–17; 2 Cor. 6:16; Eph. 2:19–22).[54]

Just as catechists in the pre–Vatican II era sometimes erroneously taught that the Holy Spirit comes to young Christians *for the first time* in the sacrament of Confirmation, so many have also thought that the Church first came into existence at Pentecost, popularly regarded as the "birthday" of the Church. However, there has never been a time when the Holy Spirit was absent from the world or the Church. To be sure, there have been special manifestations or outpourings of the Spirit in history. Its sending was first promised after Christ rose from the dead and before he ascended to the Father (Acts 1:8), and then given at Pentecost (Acts 2:3–4, 38; 4:8, 31; 6:8; 9:17; 11:24; 13:52; 19:2) and also at Confirmation. But in none of these instances was it a matter of the *initial* manifestation of the Spirit in the world, in the Church, or in the lives of individuals.

Indeed, the Spirit is manifested in many varied ways, witnessing to and sustaining the presence and activity of God in the Church (Acts 2:3–13; 10:47; 11:17; 15:8). The Spirit teaches the disciples what to say (Luke 12:12), reveals the mysteries of God (1:41,67; Acts 11:28; 13:9), inspires prophecy (2:18), is the source of wisdom (6:3), faith (6:5; 2 Cor. 4:13), encouragement (Acts 9:31), joy (13:52), hope (Rom. 15:13; 1 Cor. 14:14–16; 2:4–5; Gal. 3:5), and love (Rom. 5:5; Col. 1:8; Gal. 5:13–14). The "fruit of the Spirit is love, joy, peace, patience, kindness, generosity, faithfulness, gentleness, self-control" (Gal. 5:22–23).[55]

For Paul, the Church is a community in the Spirit, whose members are united by Baptism into the Spirit, into one Body of Christ (1 Cor. 12:13). The Spirit is the source of the Church's structure—more charismatic than institutional—and ministries (1 Cor. 12). The gifts of the Spirit are for the building up of the Church (1 Cor. 14:12, 26). By their union with the Spirit of the risen Christ, Christians rise in a spiritual body (15:35–50). The present possession of the Spirit is a foretaste (Rom. 8:23) and a pledge (2 Cor. 1:22; 5:5) of the salvation, that is, the final Reign, or Kingdom, of God that is to come.

For Luke, the Spirit is so much the inner force of the Church's life and mission that his Acts of the Apostles has also been known as the Acts of the Holy Spirit. As mentioned above, the risen Lord promised the sending of the Holy Spirit just before he ascended into heaven (Acts 1:8) and then, of course, the promise was fulfilled at Pentecost (2:1–4). The Spirit directs the officers of the Church in important decisions (13:2; 15:28; 20:28) and is conferred upon all members of the Church at Baptism (19:2, 6; 2:38–39; 15:8–9; 8:16–18; 9:17; 10:44; 11:16–17) and at the imposition of hands (8:14–17; 19:6). When James announced the momentous decision made at the Council of Jerusalem, he pointed out that it was "the decision of the holy Spirit and of us not to place any burden beyond these necessities" (15:28), which included abstaining from meat sacrificed to idols, and so forth.

In the Fourth Gospel, Jesus promises to send "another Advocate" who would always be with the Church as "the Spirit of truth" (14:16–17), who would teach everything necessary to the Church's mission and remind it of what it might otherwise forget (4:26). After the Resurrection, Jesus confers the Spirit upon his disciples, urging them to forgive and to retain sins (20:22–23). The Johannine portrayal of the Church anticipated the recent development in ecclesiology in which the Church is seen as a community of disciples, permeated and empowered by the Spirit. According to Raymond E. Brown, the risk in such an emphasis, with a concomitant lack of a clear teaching authority, is a breakdown in ecclesial unity. In fact, the Johannine communities were subsequently torn by schisms.[56] On the other hand, the Johannine writings also provide what Brown calls "an inbuilt conscience against the abuses of authoritarianism."[57]

Summary and Synthesis

Part II has focused on the various ecclesiologies that emerged during the New Testament period, identifying common elements that constitute the overall ecclesiology of the New Testament itself.

1. Part II began with a distinction between the history of ecclesiology and the history of the Church. Ecclesiology is interested in persons and events insofar as they illuminate, explain, and embody the ideas of the Church that have influenced and shaped its thinking and actions throughout its history.

2. The New Testament functions both descriptively and prescriptively. It is our primary source for determining what, in fact, was going on during the formative period of the life of the Church and for identifying the normative criteria by which the Church of subsequent centuries can be measured and critiqued.

3. We must always be mindful, however, that interpreters of the New Testament canon have usually operated with a "canon within the canon"; that is, they read the New Testament through the prism of their own ecclesiological perspective, judging some texts to be more normative than others. For Catholics, for example, Matthew 16:18 ("You are Peter, and upon this rock I will build my church") has always had a more

decisive role in understanding the hierarchical structure of the Church than it has had for Protestants.

4. The word "Church" is derived originally from the Greek *ekklesia,* which referred to an assembly consisting of citizens with full civil rights. It was taken over by the Septuagint to refer to Israel as the *kahal yahweh,* "an assembly called forth by God." The New Testament appropriated the term to describe the Church both in its local and universal manifestations.

5. The question of whether Jesus actually intended to "found" the Church remains centrally important. Although he did not found the Church according to any preconceived structural "blueprint," he did gather disciples and establish a table fellowship with the mandate that the Apostles and other disciples continue to gather for it. The Church today is a self-described "community of disciples," and the Eucharist is at the heart of its life and mission.

6. Jesus, however, never lost his intimate connection with Judaism. He was born a Jew, remained a Jew throughout his life, and died a Jew. At the same time, he did proclaim something new—a fundamental renewal of contemporary Judaism—and for that he was considered a threat who had to be put away.

7. Although the Holy Spirit was present to the world from the beginning and to the Church as soon as Jesus began to gather disciples, the definitive experience by which the Church came into being was that of Pentecost, when the Spirit was given in all its fullness.

8. The relationship between the early Church and contemporary Judaism, however, remained at once ambiguous and ambivalent. For some of the first Christians, one had to become a Jew through circumcision before one could become a disciple of Jesus. These were the so-called Judaizers. At the other end of the spectrum were the Hellenists, for whom Jewish customs

and feasts had to be set aside in favor of the new Way, which Jesus had introduced. And there were various positions in between, as represented by the compromise achieved by the Council of Jerusalem, described in Part II. 2.7. The relationship between Christianity and Judaism has remained difficult John XXIII (1958–63) and the Second Vatican Council's Declaration on the Relationship of the Church to Non-Christian Religions (*Nostra aetate*, Lat., "In our age"). Which is not to say, however, that this conciliar document brought all discussion to an end.

9. Crucial to understanding the nature and mission of the Church is understanding the relationship between the Church and the Reign, or Kingdom, of God and of their link, in turn, with the Eucharist. Nowhere in the New Testament is the Church identified with that Kingdom. On the other hand, there is a fundamental orientation of the Church toward the Kingdom of God. Vatican II's Dogmatic Constitution on the Church refers to the Church as "the seed and the beginning of that kingdom" on earth (n. 5). That orientation is vividly manifested in the Eucharist, which anticipates the feasting at the Lord's table in the final Kingdom (Luke 22:30) and which, at the same time, is rooted in the very origin of the Church (1 Cor. 11:18–22).

10. In the beginning, the mission of the Church, like that of Jesus himself, was directed toward Israel. The original community of disciples was Jewish, and its members considered themselves reformers of contemporary Judaism, not the agents of an entirely new religion. After the death and Resurrection of Jesus and the Pentecost experience, however, the Church's missionary horizon broadened to include the whole world.

11. However, there was no uniform structural organization to carry out this mission. Each local church developed its own style in response to its own particular situation and pastoral

needs. There was no radical opposition between the institutional and charismatic models that one finds in the New Testament, notwithstanding their wide diversity. Any offices that existed were always for the sake of service, never for domination or control. The Petrine ministry was always in the service of the unity of the Church, but it was never monarchical in the modern political sense of the word.

12. This great structural diversity among the local churches developed over several decades. Those communities influenced by Paul at first had minimal structural forms. After the original leaders had died and the city and Temple of Jerusalem were destroyed, there was considerable structural adaptation to newer pastoral challenges—a process believed (especially in Luke-Acts) to be guided by the Holy Spirit. The pastoral Letters, on the other hand, addressed threats to unity from "false teachers" and consequently stressed the need for pastoral authority. By contrast, the Johannine communities showed little interest in church offices,[58] as did the post-Pauline Letters to the Ephesians and the Colossians, where the model was the ideal Church, that is, the Body of Christ and the spotless Bride. The early Church eventually adopted the organizational grid of the Roman Empire, some elements of which hindered rather than facilitated the missionary work of the Church.

13. One of the distinctive characteristics of Catholicism is precisely its hierarchical structure. Is there a basis for this structure in the New Testament? In other words, is there such a reality as Early Catholicism during the Church's formative period? The answer is yes, even according to major Protestant scholars like James D. G. Dunn, although not without some qualification.

14. In the end, the mystery of the Church must always be situated within the context of the mystery of the triune God. As such, the Church is at once the People of God (the Father),

the Body of Christ (the Son), and the Temple of the Holy Spirit (the Third Person of the Blessed Trinity). The first has its roots in the Hebrew Scriptures, and its New Testament emphasis is to be found especially in Paul's Letter to the Romans, where the new People of God are contrasted with Israel, the original People of God; the second has its roots in Paul and to some extent also in John, both of whom stress the intimate relationship between the risen Christ and the Church; and the third has *its* roots in the Acts of the Apostles, also known as the Acts of the Holy Spirit, as well as in Paul, where the connection is drawn, especially in 1 Corinthians, between the Body of Christ and the Holy Spirit.

15. According to the New Testament, the Church is a mystery that shares in and reflects the mystery of Christ himself. The Church is at once universal and local, both of which are permeated by the Holy Spirit. Their mission is for the sake of the Reign, or Kingdom, of God, and that call to mission is ritualized on a regular basis in the celebration of the Eucharist, in which the Church gives thanks for what God has already done, and continues to do, for the salvation of humankind in Christ through the power of the Holy Spirit, and which looks in anticipation to the Second Coming of Christ and to the manifestation of the Reign, or Kingdom, of God in all its fullness at the end of history. How the universal Church and the many local churches organize themselves for mission is largely a matter of adaptation to newly emerging pastoral challenges and needs. There are, however, certain basic structural elements (aspects of "Early Catholicism") that have endured from the time of the New Testament itself.

PART III

Ecclesiology from the Postbiblical Period to the Mid-Nineteenth Century

The Scope of the Problem

The history of ecclesiology covers an enormous amount of biblical, historical, theological, doctrinal, social scientific, and other material. We have already acknowledged, in the Preface, the necessary limits of this book.[1] But how does one construct a history of ecclesiology within such limits? Unfortunately, there are few examples to guide us.[2]

One has to be always mindful that the process is inevitably selective. Which writings, which events, and which issues embodied in those writings and events should be considered, and which are to be left out? Which items are to be accorded greater attention, and which, less? Whose renditions of the various key periods in this history are to be taken as most reliable? Are the data thereby skewed to fit certain preconceived notions, whether tied to a particular denominational tradition or whether self-described as transcending any and all such traditions?[3]

Accordingly, Part III is far more schematic and tentative than any other in the book. It is principally intended to identify historical peaks, valleys, and paradoxes that have had (or should have had) an impact on ecclesiology, and to highlight the theological contributions of some of the major figures within this broad expanse of time.

The History of Postbiblical Ecclesiology: An Overview

Although there were theological interpretations of the nature, mission, ministries, and structural operations of the Church (i.e., ecclesiologies) from the very beginning, including the period covered by the New Testament itself, as we have already seen in Part II, ecclesiologist Yves Congar (d. 1995) reminds us that "up to about the year 1300 . . . there was no treatise expressly dealing with the Church."[4] What follows is a relatively detailed overview—and it is only an overview—of the development of ecclesiology from the beginning of the post–New Testament period to the threshold of the First Vatican Council (1869–70). Readers need to remember that the time frame encompasses more than seventeen centuries and should assess the presentation accordingly. It is not that there are too few historical resources. On the contrary, there is simply far too much data for any one scholar to assimilate and then to incorporate into a single volume or a single portion thereof.

THE EARLY CHURCH

In the early postbiblical period, formerly (and sometimes still) called the patristic period, a composite of church-related issues were addressed as matters of great pastoral, theological, and doctrinal concern: unity; authority; apostolic succession; the role of bishops; the relation between the Church and the Eucharist; the validity of Baptism by heretics, schismatics, and *lapsi* (Lat., "lapsed ones," those who had fallen away from the Church during times of persecution); the Church and the Holy Spirit; the nature of catholicity; the holiness of the Church; the necessity of the Church for salvation; the Petrine primacy and the episcopate generally; discipline for sinners; election and predestination; the connection between the visible and invisible Churches; the Church as the Body of Christ; and the heavenly Church. How were these questions dealt with, and is there an overriding (or underlying) ecclesiological unity in the various approaches?[5]

Although the writings of Clement of Rome (traditionally regarded as pope ca. 91–ca. 101; 88–97 in the Vatican's official list)[6] and Ignatius of Antioch (d. ca. 107)[7] are usually brought forward to support the traditional Catholic understanding of the role of bishops and, in Ignatius's case, of the tripartite system of Holy Orders (bishops, priests/presbyters, deacons), what else was going on among the other local churches? What other contemporary sources were there? Which of them have been lost to posterity (or simply suppressed), and what else might they have disclosed about the ecclesial situation at the time?[8]

Among the known key writers of this period are, in addition to Clement of Rome and Ignatius of Antioch, Irenaeus (d. ca. 200), who emphasized the doctrine of apostolic succession against the Gnostics; Tertullian (d. ca. 225), who, in his Catholic phase, agreed with Irenaeus, but in his Montanist phase became rigoristic and stressed the sinfulness of the Church; Clement of Alexandria (d. ca. 215), who stressed the catholicity of the Church, its connection with the Eucharist, and its heavenly dimension; Origen (d. 254), who insisted on the universality of salvation, a position shared by Gregory of Nyssa (d. ca. 395); Cyprian of Carthage (d. 258), who stressed the unity of the Church, Petrine primacy, and the importance of being in communion with the bishops; Cyril of Jerusalem (d. 386), who wrote compellingly about the catholicity of the Church; Cyril of Alexandria (d. 444), who stressed the oneness of the Church in Christ, as the Body of Christ, through the power of the Holy Spirit and manifested in the Eucharist; Optatus of Milevis (d. ca. 370), who in his conflict with the sectarian Donatists stressed unity and catholicity as marks of the Church over and above holiness, and also that the sacraments derived their validity from God, not from the priest; and especially Augustine (d. 430), who emphasized the presence and role of the Spirit in the

Church, its catholicity and unity, as the Body of Christ, and its distinction from the Reign, or Kingdom, of God.[9] As noted previously, theologian Karl Rahner (d. 1984), paraphrasing Augustine's axiom, has written: "Many whom God has, the Church does not have; and many whom the Church has, God does not have."[10]

The point is that, even though ecclesiology as a separate discipline within Christian theology would not come of age, so to speak, until the twelfth and thirteenth centuries, some of the most important ecclesiological issues were already emerging in the post–New Testament era, and they were being addressed by some of the leading bishops and theologians in the Church. Some of their responses were forged on the anvil of resistance to various dissident views; others, however, were developed for mainly pastoral reasons, that is, in response to liturgical, catechetical, and broadly spiritual needs.

EARLY HERESIES AND SCHISMS

The early Church was frequently engaged in conflicts with individuals and groups deemed unorthodox or at least as imminent threats to the purity of faith and the unity of the Church. Among these heresies were Gnosticism, Montanism, Novatianism, and Donatism. Gnosticism, which is derived from the Greek word gnosis, "knowledge," posited a secret channel of revelation available only to an elite few who were "in the know," so to speak. Over against this view Irenaeus and others insisted on the public nature of revelation, available to all and whose truth is guaranteed by the bishops in a direct line of succession from the Apostles. Montanism, a mid- to late-second-century apocalyptic and charismatic movement, threatened to undermine traditional authorities such as Sacred Scripture and the office of bishop. Novatianism was a rigorist movement that arose in Rome itself, in strong opposition to the restoration of Christians who had apostatized during the Decian persecution (249–51). The Donatists were a North African sect that also held to a rigid standard of holiness and against whom Augustine vehemently contended. The Catholic Church, he pointed out, exists everywhere throughout the known world, whereas the Donatists exist only in a small portion of Africa and not "in all those places in which the writings of the apostles, their discourse, and their actions, have become current."[11] Were these and similar early heretics and schismatics completely wrong? Was orthodoxy completely right? Moreover, was orthodoxy itself obviously "orthodox" at the time?

The heretic sees and "chooses" (the literal meaning of the word "heresy," from the Greek *hairesis*) a portion of truth, but tends to equate that portion with the whole truth. To use a psychological term, heresy is a matter of selective perception. Has the Church always had the capacity to recognize the truth that heretics have claimed to see and then calmly sort out that truth from the heretic's corresponding denials and exaggerations?

PERSECUTIONS

The persecutions of Christians by temporal authorities were local until the middle of the second century, but from then through the end of the third century they occurred throughout the empire as well. Christians were considered traitors to Rome and to Roman society because of their refusal to abide by the official state religion, which consisted of the worship of the Roman gods and even of the emperor himself. These persecutions, however, had both good and bad long-term effects on the life and self-understanding of the Church. They strengthened the faith commitment of the still growing and expanding Christian community, but also generated sectarian tendencies that persist even into the twenty-first century under the umbrella term "countercultural," which perceives the Church as a righteous enclave within secular society, avoiding all contact with the world beyond itself, in the manner of a sect.

To be sure, the Church itself bore some of the marks of a sect in the earliest decades of its existence. Moreover, there is no direct and unbroken line between the sectarianism generated by these early persecutions and modern sectarian movements and ecclesiologies, found mostly within Protestantism but with growing instances within Catholicism as well.[12] But these sectarian tendencies are on the same continuum, at least analogically. There are more similarities than differences.

THE EDICT OF MILAN

Ecclesiology took yet another step forward in reflecting upon the effects of the so-called Edict of Milan (313), also known as the Edict of Constantine and the Peace of Constantine, and the religious and civil impact the edict had on the internal life and structures of the Church and on the relationship between Church and state. After a long period of persecution, the emperor Constantine (d. 337) accorded the Church not only the protection of the state, but favors and privileges as well. The clergy became, in effect, civil servants with all of the advantages, financial and otherwise, attached thereto. The Radical Reformers of the sixteenth century were, and their current descendants have been, caustically critical of what the latter now contemptuously refer to as "Constantinian Catholicism." In their minds, the Constantinian settlement drained the Church of its prophetic, countercultural energy and passion.

Are those criticisms without any foundation? Did the Church, in fact, lose any of its spiritual and missionary integrity by accepting these benefits from the state? Questions such as these compelled contemporary and subsequent theologians to broaden the scope of their reflections on the nature, mission, ministries, and structural operations of the Church, which is exactly what ecclesiology is all about.

It was surely better for the Church *not* to be persecuted, because it was now able to carry out its mission without violent political interference and at the same time to bring some measure of order to its doctrinal and liturgical life. On the other hand, the Church became too closely identified with and dependent upon the political establishment, which did indeed compromise the Church's prophetic calling.

MONASTICISM

In a sense, monasticism represents a form of legitimate sectarianism within the Church. It sets itself apart from the wider Church and offers its adherents a particular way of achieving sanctity. Unlike sectarianism in the classical sense, however, monasticism has never set itself over against the Church, as if monastic communities alone were the true carriers and embodiments of the gospel of Jesus Christ.

What impact did monasticism (which was, in large part, a reaction of protest against the consequences of the Edict of Milan) actually have on the Church generally and on its pastoral leadership in particular? What effect did bishops who had been spiritually formed in monastic communities have on the contemporary life of the Church and on its subsequent history, and specifically on the discipline of obligatory celibacy for diocesan priests and on the more general matters of clerical and lay spirituality? On the one hand, monasticism was a major factor in the preservation and enrichment of culture (literature, music, art), but in its early stages it also represented a withdrawal of the Church from the business and concerns of the wider world. The relationships between Church and culture and between Church and world are among the central questions that ecclesiology has addressed, and continues to address, over the course of many centuries.[13]

ST. AUGUSTINE OF HIPPO

The leading figure by far in this period is St. Augustine of Hippo (354–430), bishop of the diocese of Hippo in North Africa from 395 until his death and one of the four original Doctors of the Church, recognized for their extraordinary learning and sanctity. His range of theological writings, like those of St. Thomas Aquinas in the thirteenth century and Karl Rahner in the twentieth, is virtually boundless. He played a crucial role in three major controversies: Manichaeism (a dualistic movement that viewed reality as consisting of a permanent struggle between Light and Darkness, Good and Evil), Donatism, and Pelagianism (which held that salvation is attained through human effort alone). Only the Donatist controversy was ecclesiological in character.

The Donatists insisted that the sacraments, especially Baptism, Eucharist, and Holy Orders, were valid only if their respective ministers were free of serious sin at the time the sacraments were administered. Over against the Donatists, Augustine argued that the sacraments belong to Christ and the Church, and as such their validity is not dependent upon the holiness of the minister. He also criticized the Donatists for their parochialism, having separated themselves not only from Rome, but from all other patriarchal sees. They were pure sectarians in that they regarded themselves alone as the true communal embodiment of the gospel.

For the sake of economy, we are concentrating here on this and other ecclesiological issues and, even at that, in a highly selective and exceedingly abbreviated fashion. The literature on Augustine is far too vast for our limited purposes. It is sufficient that readers are aware of his major positions on the doctrine of the Church and, of course, are free to pursue any one or group of them in greater depth.

The Church and the Holy Spirit

With great theologians like Augustine, there are always difficulties in the interpretation of their work. We encounter one immediately here. In his *Sermon 268.2* he declares: "Whoever is outside the Church has not the Holy Spirit."[14] This assumes that the Holy Spirit is present only in the Church, a view no longer common within Catholic theology or in mainstream Protestant, Anglican, and Orthodox theology. To be sure, Augustine was addressing the problem of schism, and particularly of that perpetrated by the Donatists (see Part III.2.6.c). The Donatists claimed that the Spirit is present only within a small portion of the Church, namely, their own sect, but Augustine makes clear that the Spirit is present in every part of the Body of Christ and "gives life to all the parts."

The Visible and Invisible Churches

Augustine distinguishes between the Church as an "enclosed garden, my sister and bride, a sealed fountain, a well of living water, an orchard of choice fruit" (Song 4:12–13) and those who "share a common baptism," but not "a common charity." Citing Cyprian of Carthage, "they have renounced the world only in word, not in deed; and yet he admits that they are within the Church" (*On Baptism* 5.38). Augustine compares the Church to a lily that is surrounded by brambles. The Church contains a "fixed number of the saints, foreordained before the creation of the world," while the brambles "surround her on the outside, above that number, whether openly or secretly separated from her." But "in the ineffable foreknowledge of God many who seem to be outside are within: many who seem to be within are outside."

The Catholicity of the Church

In a letter to Vincentius, a bishop who supported a schismatic group similar to the Donatists, Augustine insists that one must be in communion with the worldwide Church. It is not sufficient that one observes all the divine commands and all the sacraments (*Epistle 93.3*). In a separate letter to Honoratus, a Donatist bishop, he asks: "Do you happen to know why it should be that Christ should lose his inheritance, which is spread over the whole world, and should suddenly be found surviving only in the Africans, and not in all of them? The Catholic Church exists indeed in Africa, since God willed and ordained that it should exist throughout the whole world. Whereas your party, which is called the party of Donatus, does not exist in all those places in which the writings of the apostles, their discourse, and their actions have been current" (*Epistle 49.3*). Elsewhere he insists that "there is one Church which alone is called Catholic. It is this Church, not those separated bodies, who in fact gives birth [in Baptism] to these children" (*On Baptism* 1.4).

The Church as the Body of Christ

Augustine points out that in Paul (Eph. 5:32; 1 Cor. 11:3) the Church's relationship to Christ is portrayed as a conjugal one. They are one flesh, which he describes as a "great mystery." When Paul (then Saul) was confronted by a voice from heaven ("Saul, Saul, why are you persecuting *me*?"—Acts 9:4; italics in Augustine's text), he came to see that "the head is joined to the body." The Church is the Body of Christ, and "with its head is one Christ" (*Sermon 341.12*). His notion of the Church as the Body of Christ was also closely tied to his concept of the Church as the whole Christ (Lat. *totus Christus*), Head and members. Indeed, he read and interpreted the psalms as prayers of the "whole body," either of the Head to the Father, or of members to the Head.

The Church and the Eucharist

The Eucharist is a sacrifice offered by Christ, the High Priest, to the Father. But what is offered is the "whole redeemed community, the congregation and fellowship of the saints . . . the Body of so great a Head" (*City of God* 10.5–6). "If you are the body and members of Christ, it is your mystery which is placed on the Lord's table; it is your mystery you receive. It is that to which you answer 'Amen,' and by that response you make your assent. You hear the words 'the body of Christ'; you answer 'Amen.' *Be* a member of Christ, so that the 'Amen' may be true" (*Sermon 272*).

The Church and the Kingdom of God

In one of his most famous and massive works, *The City of God,* Augustine distinguishes the City of God, created and destined to be given in all its fullness at the end of history, from the earthly city, which is made by human hands and is destined to pass away. Many commentators, however, have seen at least a tendency in Augustine to identify the City of God, which is God's heavenly realm, with the Church in history.[15] This would be the equivalent of a wholly realized eschatology in which the final Kingdom of God is given within human history itself. The Kingdom "is not merely immanent; it is here. . . . The *eschaton* [Gk., "the last thing"] has moved from the future to the present, from the sphere of expectation into that of realized experience."[16]

The major focus of *The City of God,* however, is not on the mystery of the Church, but on the unfolding mystery of sin and salvation within human history. The primal sin of pride is reenacted in every individual sin and is most clearly manifested and most fully realized in social structures of domination, such as those of the pagan Roman Empire. These sins, both primal and individual, are overcome by the Incarnation and Redemption. Christ's death on the cross is at once a supreme act of worship and God's supreme act of compassion toward humanity.

The Bishop of Rome

For Augustine, the unity of the Church was guaranteed not only by the presence of the Holy Spirit and by the celebration of the Eucharist, but also by Peter and his successors, the bishops of Rome. He considered Peter an embodiment of the Church, so that it was the whole Church to whom Christ promised the keys to the Kingdom (*Sermons* 149.7, 295.2) and it was the whole Church that confessed that Jesus was the Christ (*Retractions* 1.21.1). At the same time, Augustine also held to a collegial understanding of the episcopate, with the Bishop of Rome at its center and head. All of the bishops are "united with Peter who is one with Christ, and with the bishop of Rome who succeeded Peter" (*Epistle* 53.2).[17]

TRIBAL MIGRATIONS

Have we sufficiently pondered the effects on the Church of the migration of various Teutonic and other tribes (among which are numbered the Visigoths, Vandals, Ostrogoths, Franks, Lombards, Saracens, Scandinavians, and Vikings), also known prejudicially as the "Barbarian invasions," which occurred from the fifth through the tenth centuries? Ecclesiology has been particularly interested in the politicization of church offices and the militarization of church vocabulary, both of which were profoundly affected by these migrations. Not surprisingly, these migrations had both positive and negative impacts on the life and mission of the Church. To be sure, Christianity, like any comparable society, was enriched by its assimilation of a much broader cultural diversity, but the Teutonic influences in particular also introduced elements of militarism and feudalism, reflected in the new regalia worn by bishops (miters, crosiers, rings), in hymns celebrating Christians as "soldiers of Christ," and in the development of a clerical caste system in the Church.

THE GREGORIAN REFORM

The pontificate of Gregory VII (1073–85) and the so-called Gregorian reform, which he promoted so vigorously, have had profound and long-lasting effects on the exercise of papal authority and on the legalization of the papacy itself.[18] When elected, Gregory confronted four interrelated challenges to the integrity of the Church: clerical corruption (including not only violations of celibacy, but also serious failures to attend to one's pastoral responsibilities), simony (the buying and selling of spiritual benefits, including church offices), nepotism (the promotion of one's relatives to high church offices), and lay investiture (the interference of temporal rulers in the internal life of the Church, especially with regard to the appointment and installation of bishops and abbots).

The Gregorian reform strengthened papal authority in its frequent disputes with temporal rulers, particularly Gregory's own bitter conflict with the German emperor Henry IV, and helped to free the Church from political domination. However, the reform also tended to exaggerate the powers and role of the papacy, declaring the pope to be the supreme judge of all, including of bishops and abbots, with unlimited powers of absolution and excommunication and the right to depose emperors. Some of these claims were listed in the papal document *Dictatus Papae* (Lat., "Pronouncements of the Pope"), drafted (but never formally published) in March 1075. To establish a legal basis for such claims, Gregory encouraged the growth of a new "cottage industry," canon law.

In the eleventh century there were concerted efforts to assemble older collections of ecclesiastical laws and regroup them according to the needs of the time. This led eventually to the formation of the new discipline of canon law, with its most famous collection, Gratian's *Concordia Discordantium Canonum* (Lat., "Concordance of Discordant Canons"), also known simply as the *Decretum* ("Decree"), which was completed by the famous Italian jurist around the year 1140. It became the standard textbook in canon law until the new Code of Canon Law appeared in 1917. The *Decretum*'s topics included papal, conciliar, and episcopal authority, various ministries, ordained and nonordained alike, the conditions for church membership, and the sacraments.

Ecclesiology became, to a large extent, a subset of canon law, rather than vice versa. To put it another way, ecclesiology became a kind of ecclesiastical political science. Unfortunately, this concept persisted even into the middle of the twentieth century and was not officially dispelled until the Second Vatican Council (1962–65) with the retrieval of the notion that the Church is first and foremost a mystery, that is, "a reality imbued with the hidden presence of God" (Paul VI). A residue of the older juridical and legalistic approach continues, however, in some quarters of the Catholic Church even to this day.

THE ESTABLISHMENT OF UNIVERSITIES

What is to be said about Catholicism in the light of its promotion of two mutually opposed movements beginning in the twelfth century, the establishment of the Inquisition (or, more accurately, of a network of local inquisitions) and the founding of the world's first universities, including Paris and Bologna? The latter development reinforced the critical and systematic dimension of theology and laid the foundations for a learned clergy and eventually a learned laity as well. On the other hand, the development of institutions of higher learning also tended to make the Church's theology more academic and less pastoral.[19] The establishment of inquisitorial agencies, however, had no known good effects on the life of the Church. Ecclesiologists today (and most other Christians, one assumes) would support unequivocally St. Bernard of Clairvaux's axiom *Fides suadenda, non imponenda* (Lat., "Faith comes by persuasion, not by force").[20] So too did the Second Vatican Council's Declaration on Religious Freedom (*Dignitatis humanae*), which insists on the need for "psychological freedom and immunity from external coercion" in all matters pertaining to religious faith (n. 2, and passim).

PURIST MOVEMENTS

The so-called purist movements, from the mid-twelfth to the fourteenth centuries, included the Albigensians, or Cathari, and the so-called Spiritual Franciscans, also called Zealots (It., *Zelanti*) or simply "Spirituals," who interpreted their founder, St. Francis of Assisi, literally when they advocated that Franciscans should own absolutely no property. They rejected what they regarded as the worldliness of the

Church, but they also introduced elements of fanaticism and pastoral unrealism into the life of the Church, for which they were censured by Popes Nicholas III (1277–80), Clement V (1305–14), and John XXII (1316–34). The Spiritual Franciscans' distinctive ecclesiology shaped their views on the role of religious communities in the Church and on the uncompromising, countercultural example that the Church must offer to the world. Noting the extremes to which these purist movements were inclined to go, however, ecclesiologists began to refine their own understanding of the Church-world relationship and of the role of religious communities within the Church.[21] They viewed the Church increasingly as having a leavening role within society rather than a totally negative, adversarial relationship, and they came to regard religious communities as healthy stimulants to the overall mission of the Church, placing new emphasis on previously neglected apostolates, such as preaching (in the case of the Dominicans, or Order of Preachers) and service to the poor (in the case of the Franciscans, notwithstanding the excesses of the above-mentioned *Zelanti*).

THE EAST-WEST SCHISM

Does the East-West Schism, traditionally associated with the mutual excommunications of pope and patriarch in 1054, mean that Orthodox Christians, who are no longer in full communion with the Bishop of Rome, have no claim to Catholicity? If not, what *are* the ecclesiological consequences of the schism?[22] What is the nature of schism and how does it differ from a break with communion based on fundamental differences in doctrine and pastoral practice? What sort of communion exists now between the Catholic Church and these separated Churches of the East? Even the Congregation for the Doctrine of the Faith, in its widely discussed and controversial document *Dominus Iesus* (2000), refers to these Churches as "true particular churches," which, "while not existing in full communion with the Catholic Church [because of their rejection of papal primacy], remain united to her by means of the closest bonds, that is, by apostolic succession and a valid eucharist" (n. 17).[23] The Congregation grounded its teaching, in large part, on Vatican II's Decree on Ecumenism, nn. 14–15.

Prior to Vatican II, many Catholics regarded the Orthodox Churches of the East, for all practical purposes, as having no greater ecclesiological standing than even Unitarians or Quakers. A particular non-Catholic community was either in full communion with the Catholic Church or not in any form of communion at all. As we have already pointed out (see Part I.2.5), the Second Vatican Council introduced the notion of "degrees" of communion (Decree on Ecumenism, n. 3). One of the most significant developments in recent ecclesiology has been the emergence of the notion of communion as a central theological category.[24] It is closely aligned with the almost simultaneous emergence of the notion of Church as a "community of disciples," which Avery Dulles, in the 1987 expanded edition of his classic, *Models of the Church,* adds as a sixth model.[25]

ST. THOMAS AQUINAS

Alongside Augustine of Hippo, Thomas Aquinas (ca. 1225–74) is one of the most important theologians in the entire history of the Church. Few theologians have shaped so much subsequent theology as Aquinas did. His various writings, including his classic *Summa Theologiae,* covered the whole spectrum of Christian doctrine. He is one of the four original Doctors of the Church and was given the title "the Angelic Doctor."

Significantly, Aquinas wrote no separate treatise on the Church, but that was equally true of St. Bonaventure (ca. 1217–74), Alexander of Hales (ca. 1185–1245), St. Albert the Great (ca. 1200–80), and other Scholastics of that era. As Yves Congar points out, "Before the 'first treatises on the Church,' no other method was known."[26]

For Aquinas, the Church is a body whose soul is quickened by the Holy Spirit. It is a community that is one in faith, hope, and love. The triune God dwells within it. It is holy because it has been washed in the Blood of Christ. The Church is Catholic spatially or geographically, compositionally (it includes all kinds and conditions of persons), and temporally (from Abel to the end of the world and then into heaven).[27] Finally, the Church is apostolic because it has, in addition to Christ himself, the Apostles and their doctrine as its foundation.[28] Congar argues that "the entire *Secunda Pars* [Second Part] of the *Summa Theologica* is ecclesiology."[29] For St. Thomas, the Church is "the whole economy of the return towards God," which is what the *Secunda Pars* is all about.[30] His ecclesiology is above all theocentric and only after that Christocentric.

"The ecclesiological thought of St. Thomas," Congar writes, "is so rich and there are in his work so many ecclesiological elements that, to fulfill our aim of studying his idea of the Church, a whole treatise on the Church would have to be written."[31] But such a treatise would not resemble that of James of Viterbo (ca. 1255–1308) or Cardinal Robert Bellarmine (1542–1621). For Thomas, "the Church is not a separate reality, something outside the Christian-Trinitarian mystery, outside the anthropologic, christologic, sacramental thing which is the subject of theology."[32]

Congar believes that Thomas deliberately refused to write a separate treatise on the Church, because the mystery of the Church pervaded his whole theology. That overarching concept of the Church simply reflected the broad Catholic tradition as carried forward by the Fathers of the Church. "That tradition," Congar concludes, "can be characterized by three marks: the Church is contemplated as a Spirit-moved, Spirit-known and Spirit-defined reality, as the Body whose living Soul is the Spirit of Life. The Church is contemplated in Christ, as Christ is contemplated in the Church. And the inward Church is not separated from the outward Church, which is its sacramental veil and vehicle. I think no one will deny this to be the ecclesiology of the Fathers. And I hope that I may have proved it to be that of St. Thomas Aquinas."[33]

Another great ecclesiologist in his own right, Avery Dulles, has also synthesized the ecclesiology of Thomas Aquinas.[34] He notes that Catholic ecclesiology, from the fifteenth century, developed along lines different from those laid down by Thomas Aquinas. Cardinal Juan de Torquemada (1388–1468), whose *Summa de ecclesia* set the pattern for many centuries afterward, placed the weightier stress on the external, visible features of the Church, as did Cardinal Robert Bellarmine, whose ecclesiology was shaped and fashioned against the Protestants, and Thomas Stapleton (1535–98). All three, while defending the existence of the papal office, were considered moderates on the issue of papal temporal power, for which Bellarmine's canonization was held up until 1930.

The tide began to turn back in Aquinas's direction with the encyclicals of Pope Leo XIII on the Holy Spirit, especially *Divinum munus* (Lat., "This divine function," 1897), and his earlier encyclical *Aeterni Patris* ("Eternal Father," 1879), which called for a restoration of Christian philosophy and particularly that of Thomas Aquinas. The trend continued with Pius XII's *Mystici Corporis Christi* ("On the Mystical Body of Christ," 1943), which emphasized, as Thomas did, the Church as the Body of Christ, and reached its climax at the Second Vatican Council.[35]

But measured against present ecclesiological standards, some elements of Thomas Aquinas's ecclesiology seem worse than quaint, given the sharp contrast between the historical situation of the thirteenth century and that of the twenty-first. Thus, he insisted on subjection to the pope as a prerequisite for salvation. In his *Summa Theologiae* he held that heretics, if pertinacious, are to be excommunicated and turned over to the civil authorities for capital punishment (II-II, q. 11, art. 3, response). On the other hand, he acknowledged that all the baptized, unless they have culpably separated themselves from the Church, are members of the Body of Christ.

Although Thomas revered the Bible as much as the Protestant Reformers did, he did not have access to the biblical and historical scholarship that is commonly available today. He believed, Dulles writes, "that the faith, sacraments, and ministries of the Church had been, in all essentials, established by Christ in the lifetime of the apostles." But had he lived in our own time, Dulles insists, Thomas "would not have failed to utilize new linguistic, philosophical, and sociological methods. . . . For the contemporary ecclesiologist scarcely any ideal could be more challenging than to try to say what Aquinas might have said if he were alive today."[36]

THE GREAT (WESTERN) SCHISM

What have ecclesiology and the wider Church learned about the importance of the papacy in the light of the Great Schism (1378–1417), also known as the Great Western Schism?[37] For some forty years there were at least two claimants to the Chair of Peter, both with considerable support from Catholic rulers of various European countries. In 1409, a council held in Pisa tried to settle the schism by deposing the two claimants and electing in their place Alexander V.[38] But the decisions made at Pisa failed to achieve universal acceptance, and subsequently there were three simultaneous claimants to the papacy. And yet the Church survived over the course of two generations, notwithstanding the fact that thousands of its members were in sharp disagreement over the identity of the legitimate Bishop of Rome.

The principal historical elements of the Great Schism challenge an ecclesiological assumption that was common from Vatican I to Vatican II, namely, that, in the end, the pope alone determines the nature and moral demands of the Catholic faith and that, without a pope, the Church can only drift in a rudderless, circular fashion. The ecclesiological foundation for both assumptions was laid down, in large part, during the pontificate of Gregory VII in the late eleventh century and remained normative for many Catholics throughout the second Christian millennium, reaching its initial apex in the pontificates of Innocent III (1198–1216) and Boniface VIII (1295–1303)[39] and then being reconstituted in a more sophisticated and nonimperial form in the lengthy pontificate of John Paul II (1978–2005).

It was the Council of Constance (1414–18) that finally brought the Great Schism to an end by deposing two of the claimants to the papal throne (regarded by the council's majority as antipopes), securing the voluntary abdication of a third (Gregory XII, whom the Vatican's official list of popes recognizes as the legitimate successor of St. Peter at this time), and electing Martin V (1417–31). It did so in accordance with the decree *Haec Sancta* (Lat., "This holy [synod]"), promulgated by the council in April 1415, which declared that the council was legitimately assembled by the Holy Spirit, with authority directly from Christ and requiring obedience from all Christians, including the pope. It empowered the council to depose popes if they are hindering church unity and paved the way for the depositions that followed soon thereafter. Constance also mandated, in its decree of October 1417, *Frequens* ("The frequent [celebration of general councils]"), that general councils be held in five, seven, and thereafter at least every ten years (a mandate not observed following the prolonged Council of Basel-Ferrara-Florence-Rome, often called simply the Council of Florence, 1431–45).

Did the Council of Constance, in which there were nonepiscopal, even lay, delegates with the right of full participation, including in the election of Martin V, and which mandated that future general councils meet at regular intervals, represent a victory for conciliarism over papal absolutism? If so, why was the victory so short-lived? Why did the ecclesiology of Constance not permeate the Church beyond the body of the council itself? Indeed, why did so many in subsequent centuries raise questions about Constance's legitimacy as an ecumenical council, if not because of their inability or outright refusal to yield their own papal-juridical ecclesiology to that of the council's?[40]

Although some theologians, canonists, and other church and temporal leaders, lay and clerical alike, may have attempted to push conciliarism to an extreme during and after the Council of Constance, to the potential detriment of papal authority, this same dynamic did not occur at the Second Vatican Council almost five and a half centuries later (see Part V, passim). Vatican II's retrieval of the doctrine of collegiality was always balanced against the doctrine of papal primacy, as reaffirmed by Vatican I in the nineteenth century and in Vatican II's Dogmatic Constitution on the Church (chap. 3).

THE PROTESTANT REFORMATION

There is, of course, a vast body of literature on the nature and history of the Protestant Reformation.[41] There is no intention, much less attempt, here to summarize or synthesize that literature. Our interest remains focused, as always throughout Part III, on the ecclesiological assumptions that led to the Reformation, informed it, and then shaped its consequences as well as on the Catholic Church's reactions to it.

The ecclesiological causes of the Reformation included the corruption of the Renaissance papacy, marked by nepotism, simony, military expeditions, financial manipulation, political intrigue, and even murder. One of these popes was the notorious Alexander VI (1492–1503). A second ecclesiologically significant factor was the Great Schism itself, which compromised the papacy's ability to serve as a symbol and instrument of church unity at a time when it was gravely threatened. The rise of national states also served to diminish the influence of the papacy, which had already taken on an imperial cast. The ecclesiology of contemporary popes and leading bishops viewed the Church less as the People of God than as a hierarchical, indeed absolutely monarchical, institution. (One need only compare Boniface VIII's papal bull *Unam Sanctam* [1302], in which the pope claimed sovereignty over both the sacred and temporal realms, with the Second Vatican Council's Dogmatic Constitution on the Church [1964].) Finally, the papal resistance to legitimate calls for reform in the early sixteenth century proved to be one of the most grievous miscalculations on leadership's part in the entire history of the Church. The blatant failures of Lateran Council V (1512–17), on the very eve of the Reformation, represent an enormously tragic case in point.[42]

The Reformers' ecclesiology was really a form of reaction and rejection "of the whole of the Church's mediation: magisterium, priesthood, sacraments, the authority of tradition and the role of the teaching Church in the rule of faith, prelatial authority, the episcopal dignity, the pope's primacy."[43] In their place, the Reformers offered a dualistic approach to the Church: the true, invisible Church of the saints, on the one side, and the visible, institutional organization that was not truly the Church, on the other.

Catholic treatises on the Church were similarly reactive. "This controversial literature," Yves Congar observes, "was to have such a success that, at least in ecclesiological questions, it unhappily came to determine the content of Catholic theology as taught in the schools. Ecclesiologically, this theology was polemical, anti-Gallican and anti-Protestant throughout, even when it was presented eirenically and with quiet scholarship."[44] Because the Reformers emphasized the priority of the invisible Church, Catholic ecclesiologists (more apologists, however, than theologians) claimed that Christ founded the Church as a visible, hierarchical, juridical society. Ecclesiology became, in a word, "hierarchology."[45]

To be sure, the sixteenth-century Reformers were not entirely wrong about their central criticisms of the contemporary Church, nor was the response of the Catholic hierarchy, and in particular of the papacy, completely right. The Reformers did succeed in some significant measure in spite of the resistance of church officials, but the Reformation also brought disunity and division to the universal Church from which it continues to suffer.

There were at least four dimensions to the Reformation, a word that also has a plural form. There were the magisterial Reformations of Martin Luther (Protestant) and John Calvin (Reformed); the Evangelical, or Radical, Reformation (actually a series of reformations, including Anabaptists and others); and the English Reformation, provoked in large part by King Henry VIII. Each had a distinctive ecclesiology.[46]

Luther's Ecclesiology

For Martin Luther (1483–1546), the Church was no longer apostolic, that is, faithful to its New Testament foundations. He proposed seven criteria by which to determine apostolicity: the Word of God proclaimed audibly and visibly (the constitutive element), Baptism, Eucharist, the office of keys (reconciliation), public ministry, worship (public prayer), and the cross and suffering.

For Luther, the Church is an event rather than an institution. It "happens" only when and where the Word is proclaimed. The Church is both a visible fellowship (composed of saints and sinners, *simul iustus et peccator*) and a hidden community of true Christians—a view reminiscent of Augustine's (see Part III.2.6.b). The Church must be the embodiment of the gospel. Consistently with Luther's view, the Augsburg Confession defined the Church as "the congregation of saints wherein the Gospel is purely preached and the sacraments rightly celebrated."[47]

Calvin's Ecclesiology

The ecclesiology of John Calvin (1509–64) needs to be contextualized within his overall theological perspective, in which there are four overarching themes: (1) the sovereignty of God and predestination (Luther, by contrast, was Christocentric); (2) the glorification of God (Luther was more concerned with personal salvation); (3) human instrumentality (Luther insisted on "God alone" working on our behalf); and (4) sanctification, or living out one's call in the world (Luther emphasized justification, although he too placed high importance on the concept of vocation). The principal elements in Calvin's ecclesiology included the following: (1) Scripture is the one and only authority for the Church; (2) the unity of the Church is realized through representative assemblies (individuals cannot be trusted); (3) there is a parity of ministries (the terms "bishop," "presbyter," and "minister" are used interchangeably, without hierarchical rank); (4) the people possess the right to elect their ministers (in Calvin's *Ordinances* there are four orders: pastor, doctor/teacher, elder/presbyter, and deacon; in his *Institutes of the Christian Religion* pastor and doctor are combined); and (5) the Church is supreme over the state.[48]

Evangelical, or Radical, Ecclesiology

The left wing of the Reformation is also known as the Radical Reformation. It consisted of those who wanted to reinstitute, or restore, rather than reform the pre-Constantinian Church (i.e., the Church prior to 313), making it entirely separate from the world in the manner of a sect. George H. Williams, the leading expert on this phenomenon, divides the Radical Reformation into three movements: (1) Spiritualists (led by, e.g., Thomas Münzer, Casper Schwenckfeld), who believed that the Spirit alone constitutes the Church; the community has no need for Scripture, much less structures; (2) Anabaptists (e.g., Menno Simons), who favored rebaptism into a pre-Constantinian community of the elect and the perfect consisting of a voluntary community in which there is no infant baptism, no church organization, and from which sinners are expelled and shunned; the moral perspective is shaped by pacifism and nonviolence generally;

and (3) Evangelical Rationalists (e.g., Michael Servetus, Fausto Sozzini), who were characterized by a form of applied humanism holding that, since the Trinity is not in the New Testament, it has no claim to our belief—an approach that produced Unitarianism.[49]

The Radical Reformers especially attacked (1) control of the Church by the state; (2) infant baptism (automatic membership); and (3) the just-war ethic (justification of violence). For them, the Church is a purely voluntary community brought into being by a confession of faith and Baptism (the Quakers, however, dissent from the practice of baptism). Faithful to the early Luther and to the early Ulrich Zwingli (1484–1531), the Radical Reformers affirmed the autonomy of each local congregation. For them the Church happens through a conversational process among the members. Discipleship is an overriding concept for the Christian life. Ministry is something called out of the congregation. The wider unity of the Christian body exists when others get together for conversation.[50] The influence of the Radical Reformation continues in the emergence of sectarianism mainly in Protestantism, but in some segments of Catholicism as well.[51]

Ecclesiology of the English Reformation

King Henry VIII was excommunicated in 1533 for his marriage to Anne Boleyn. Subsequently all church business and properties were brought officially under the supremacy and control of the crown rather than the papacy (Act of Supremacy, 1534). At first, the break with Rome was schismatic in nature, rather than Protestant. Indeed, Henry refused to allow any doctrinal changes. Only after his death did the Church of England begin to assume a Protestant character (under Edward VI), reflected in the Book of Common Prayer (1550) and the Forty-two Articles (1553). After a Catholic interlude under Queen Mary, the trend toward Protestantism was resumed and consolidated under Elizabeth, with the Thirty-nine Articles (1563).[52]

The ecclesiology of Luther and other Reformers on the Continent influenced English theologians in Cambridge and Oxford. They debated issues related to church authority, specifically the relationship between papal and biblical authority; justification, whether the Church's sacraments are a means to, or the result of, salvation; and priesthood, specifically the relationship between the offering of the eucharistic sacrifice and the finished work of Christ. To be sure, there has been a much closer ecclesiological relationship between Anglicans and Roman Catholics since Vatican II on questions of this sort.[53]

THE CATHOLIC REFORMATION, OR COUNTER-REFORMATION

Historians have debated whether the renewal and reforms within the Catholic Church during the sixteenth and seventeenth centuries were exclusively a reaction against the Reformation (thus, the Counter-Reformation), or whether both the Protestant and Catholic Reformations developed from the same impetus for reform (thus, the Catholic Reformation). The consensus today seems to favor the single-impulse theory. Nevertheless, it is still possible to speak of a Counter-Reformation, in which the reforms initiated by the Catholic Church were in direct reaction to specific challenges posed by the Protestants and were designed to thwart Protestant advances.

By the 1530s all of Scandinavia, the British Isles, and much of Germany, Austria, and France had broken communion with Rome. Even though Luther himself had called for a general council to examine his doctrines, nothing was done until 1545. The failure was partly political and partly ecclesiological. The latter had to do with the perceived threat of conciliarism. There was a general fear in Rome that, if a general council were convened, the authority of the papacy would be seriously threatened.

The belated response of the Catholic Church to the initial successes of the Reformers emanated mainly from the Council of Trent, which met over a long period of time in three separate segments: 1545–47, 1551–52, and 1562–63. Trent and similar initiatives introduced some needed reforms into the Catholic Church, such as the establishment of a seminary system for the theological education and spiritual formation of future priests, the reform of the liturgy, and the revision of the Latin Vulgate version of the Bible. But the council also reinforced the Church's hierarchicalism, its legalism, and its defensive and polemical approach to the doing of theology.[54] It had little to say about the Church itself, except for its sacramental life. It clearly defined the meaning and number of the sacraments, especially the Eucharist and Matrimony.

At the heart of the Catholic Reformation, and largely responsible for whatever success it had, was the newly established Society of Jesus, founded by Ignatius of Loyola (1491–1556). By and large, however, the post-Tridentine Church, following the ecclesiology of the times, continued to emphasize those practices that came under particular attack by the Protestants: veneration of the saints, Marian devotions, and eucharistic adoration.[55] The last of the three tended to diminish the active role of the laity in the celebration of Mass, which remained increasingly the affair of the clergy. The liturgy itself, which is supposed to be the heart of the Church's life, as stipulated by Vatican II's Constitution on the Sacred Liturgy (n. 10), became in this Baroque period a grand spectacle rather than an act of communal worship.[56] The situation did not begin to change until the liturgical renewal of the twentieth century and the renewal of ecclesiology beginning in the nineteenth century and at Vatican II in the mid-twentieth.

THE FRENCH REVOLUTION

The French Revolution of 1789 unwittingly liberated the Church from its feudal and medieval accretions (sometimes called "the grace of destitution"), thereby freeing it to expend more effort on its perennial mission to preach the gospel, but it also destroyed some of the Church's greatest assets (monasteries, churches, art). In crushing Gallicanism (the highly nationalistic and antipapal movement within the French Church), the French Revolution actually made the surviving French clergy more dependent than ever on Rome (thereby feeding the new spirit of Ultramontanism, looking literally "beyond the mountains," the Alps, to Rome) and generated an extreme counterreaction among Catholic laity known as Romanticism and later Integralism (a nineteenth- and early-twentieth-century movement in France that functioned as a self-appointed "watchdog" of Catholic orthodoxy).

The three-pronged agenda of the Revolution—liberty, equality, and fraternity—was later equated with that of Vatican II by Archbishop

Marcel Lefebvre (d. 1991), the founder of the only major schismatic movement after the council (the Priestly Society of St. Pius X). He denounced what he claimed were Vatican II's parallel teachings on religious liberty, ecumenism, and the collegiality of bishops. Overall, the French Revolution had little impact on the history of ecclesiology except in the negative sense that it generated reactions in the forms of Ultramontanism and Gallicanism and, in the twentieth century, Integralism and the Lefebvreites.

Yves Congar cites a historical study of the catechisms and works of pastoral theology in use during the second half of the eighteenth and the first half of the nineteenth century. The authors of these works had the same ecclesiological defects as some of the Counter-Reformation controversialists. These texts said nothing about the Church as mystery, but were concerned only with its organization as a society and the exercise of its hierarchical powers. The Holy Spirit does not animate the whole People of God. Only the hierarchy and priests are important. The laity are passive observers at the liturgy and have no direct role in the life and mission of the Church.

This "narrowing down" of the treatise on the Church solely to its hierarchical powers was "the more regrettable," Congar notes, "in that it happened at a time when in many parts of ancient Christendom human society was being secularised. . . . From the beginning of the fourteenth century society began slowly to assert its independence. . . . The Church in more than one place was finding herself reduced to the state of a priestly system without a Christian people."[57] Thus it was that, although the mainstream Catholic ecclesiological tradition held together the institutional and communal aspects of the Church, the theological treatises of the day "practically ignored that one according to which a role of the laity could be *a priori* conceivable."[58]

MISSIONARY EXPANSION

The missionary expansion of the Church, especially in the nineteenth and early twentieth centuries, brought the gospel to a much wider and more diversified circle of peoples and cultures (the beginnings of what Karl Rahner called the world-Church), but it was also the carrier of colonialism and cultural oppression. Too often the Church found itself so beholden to the secular powers and their economic interests that the spiritual needs of new converts became secondary—and worse. Two diverse ecclesiological approaches to mission have been effectively portrayed in the films *The Mission* (1986), in which the eighteenth-century Spanish Jesuit missionaries in Paraguay followed the principle of inculturation while opposing Portugal's economic oppression of the native people, and *Black Robe* (1991), in which seventeenth-century French Jesuit missionaries looked upon the native people of northern Quebec as simply pagans who needed to be saved from the fires of hell by the waters of Baptism.

DEMOCRATIC MOVEMENTS OF THE NINETEENTH CENTURY

Democratic movements in the nineteenth century, on the Italian peninsula and elsewhere, encouraged rule by the people; freedom of speech, of the press, and of assembly; due process; and various other civil liberties. These movements also brought about the stripping of the remaining Papal States in Italy and the end of the anomalous situation, in force for over ten centuries, in which the Bishop of Rome functioned simultaneously as a spiritual leader and a temporal ruler. The Papal States were regarded as a major obstacle to Italian unification because they stretched across the whole of central Italy, cutting off the south from the north.[59] Needless to say, the movement for Italian unification (known as the *Risorgimento*) provoked a strongly negative reaction on the part of Pope Pius IX (1846–78), expressed particularly in his *Syllabus of Errors* (1864) and in the promulgation of the dogma of papal infallibility (1870). The pope had pressured the First Vatican Council to approve the latter as a way of enhancing the authority and prestige of an otherwise beleaguered papacy.

Each of the events generated by the democratic movements of the time also surfaced a number of fundamental theological questions concerning the proper role of the Church in the world. These questions, in turn, served to underscore the extraordinarily wide scope and inner complexity that have always characterized the history of ecclesiology.

ECCLESIOLOGY ON THE EVE OF VATICAN I

Johann Adam Möhler (d. 1838), the central Catholic figure at the University of Tübingen in the nineteenth century, had a major influence on Vatican II (but not Vatican I) and on the leading ecclesiologist of the twentieth century, Yves Congar. Möhler's major work on the unity of Church, *Die Einheit in der Kirche* (Ger., "The Unity of the Church," 1825), translated into French but not into English, treated the Church as a living tradition and an organic unity, created and sustained by the Holy Spirit. His work anticipated the nonjuridical approach in ecclesiology that emerged just prior to and during the Second Vatican Council.[60] For Möhler, all of the externals of the Church are the product of the Holy Spirit, who is the Church's life-giving principle.

In his later book, *Symbolik* (Ger., "Symbolism," 1836), a comparative study of Catholic and Protestant approaches to Christian doctrine, translated into English in 1906, he distanced himself from his strong emphasis on the Holy Spirit in *Die Einheit,* but anticipated yet another aspect of mid-twentieth-century ecclesiology, namely, its ecumenical dimension. Given the contemporary revival of a brand of postmedieval theology known as neo-Scholasticism, Möhler's writings were for the most part ignored until the twentieth century, when they were retrieved and rehabilitated by Josef R. Geiselmann (d. 1970), theologian of the modern-day Tübingen school, and especially by the aforementioned Yves Congar.

The Five Wounds of the Church, by Antonio Rosmini-Serbati (d. 1855), which was placed on the Index of Forbidden Books in 1849,[61] called attention to the need for the renewal and reform of the Church, specifically the gap between clergy and laity at worship; the deficient education of the clergy; disunity among the bishops because of territorialism, nationalism, and inequities in wealth; the nomination of bishops by civil authorities rather than by election; and restrictions on the Church's use of its own temporal assets and its enslavement to riches.

Matthias Scheeben (d. 1888), described as "one of the more important and creative theologians of the nineteenth century,"[62] viewed the Church within the larger theological context of the mystery of the

Trinity. The Church was for Scheeben a living organism: the Body of Christ and his true bride, both key ecclesial images. For him, the Church is the most intimate communion between God and humankind—a communion that achieves its truest and most perfect expression in the Eucharist. In his *The Mysteries of Christianity* (1860) he treats the Eucharist after the Incarnation and before the Church and the sacraments. His ecclesiological vision, however, is not merely Christological. "In all its members," he writes, "the Church is a temple of the Holy Spirit who dwells in it as the soul in its own body, and manifests His divine and divinizing power in it."[63] Moreover, the Church's jurisdictional structures are essentially maternal, and the laity also share in the Church's motherhood.[64]

Scheeben was a strong supporter of papal infallibility at the time of the First Vatican Council. He retained the Scholastic division between the power of orders and the power of jurisdiction. Teaching was proclaimed by the power of orders and imposed by the power of jurisdiction. But in some sense he may have also anticipated the Second Vatican Council with his notion of the sacramentality of the Church itself.[65]

Cardinal John Henry Newman (d. 1890) was one of the greatest figures in nineteenth-century Catholicism. He declined an invitation from bishops and the pope himself to serve as a theological consultant to the First Vatican Council. He did so because he opposed efforts, led by the pope, to define papal infallibility, even though as a Catholic he believed in it. His *Letter to the Duke of Norfolk* in 1875 later defended the dogma, but pointed out some of its negative ecumenical implications.

Newman had already opened new ecclesiological pathways in his *An Essay on the Development of Christian Doctrine* (1846), which established continuity between the teachings of the early Church and those of the nineteenth century. He converted from Anglicanism to Catholicism while completing this work. In 1858 he published a controversial article in the journal *The Rambler* on consulting the faithful even on matters of doctrine, for which he was attacked and delated (reported) to Rome. His response was the essay *On Consulting the Faithful in Matters of Doctrine* (1859). His opposition to the pope's retention of temporal power was the occasion for a serious falling-out between himself and fellow convert Cardinal Henry Manning (d. 1892), who was one of the strongest supporters of papal infallibility at Vatican I.

Cardinal Newman's last and most complete work of ecclesiology was the 1877 preface to the third edition of *Lectures on the Prophetical Office* (later retitled *The Via Media*), in which he reflected on the Church's three offices and their interrelationships: the prophetic, exercised by theologians; the priestly, by clergy and laity alike; and the kingly, or governing, by the pope and the other bishops. The preface sought to deal frankly but sympathetically with the apparent flaws and failures of the Church, including its authoritarianism, its inadequate emphasis on Sacred Scripture, and its legalistic approach to morality. It has been said that Newman's thought had some influence on the Second Vatican Council, particularly its theology of the laity and its notion of the *sensus fidelium* (Lat., "sense of the faithful"), namely, that the faith of the whole Church is a sure norm of orthodoxy and of the Church as a communion.[66]

But neither Rosmini, Möhler, Scheeben, nor Newman was typical of nineteenth-century ecclesiology, which, for the most part, was neo-Scholastic, legalistic, and hierarchically oriented, in continued reaction against the Protestant Reformation. Meanwhile, the pre–Vatican I pontificates of Gregory XVI (1831–46) and Pius IX (1846–78) set themselves against the winds of liberalism, and nowhere more defiantly than in the latter's *Syllabus of Errors* (1864), which proclaimed that the pope "cannot and should not be reconciled and come to terms with progress, liberalism, and modern civilization" (n. 80). The climax of Pius IX's efforts to restore the authority of the papal office was Vatican I's dogmatic definition of papal infallibility, about which much more is to be said in Part IV.

PART IV

Ecclesiology from Vatican I to the Threshold of Vatican II

The principal, although by no means sole, topic addressed in Part IV is the papacy. This was the major ecclesiological issue debated and voted upon at the First Vatican Council (1869–70), which, in turn, cast a lengthy theological and pastoral shadow over much of twentieth-century Catholicism. Because of the unsettled political circumstances in Rome at the time of Vatican I, however, the council was unable to complete its proposed agenda, specifically issues that concerned the episcopacy as a whole. That unfinished business would be taken up almost a century later by the Second Vatican Council (1962–65) in its teaching on episcopal collegiality.

Part IV consists of five major units: (1) Peter and the Papacy: The Ecclesiological Context for Vatican I, which includes an overview of official Catholic teaching on the papacy, Peter in the New Testament, official Catholic teaching on papal primacy and papal infallibility, Petrine succession, Petrine ministry, and the pope as Vicar of Peter; (2) Vatican I, which covers its purpose, preparations, composition, and teachings on primacy and infallibility; (3) Post–Vatican I Developments, which includes Leo XIII's encyclicals on the Church,

Pius X's anti-Modernist documents, Pius XII's encyclical *Mystici Corporis Christi,* and the dispute involving Father Leonard Feeney and the question of salvation outside the Church; (4) Pre–Vatican II Ecclesiology, including Protestant, Anglican, and progressive Catholic theologians and the ecclesiology of the Latin manuals; and (5) Pope John XXIII, which focuses on his role in the Church's transition from one ecclesiological perspective, reflected in the Latin manuals of theology, to another, reflected in the documents of Vatican II.

Peter and the Papacy: The Ecclesiological Context for Vatican I

The two principal doctrines approved by the First Vatican Council and promulgated by Pope Pius IX (1846–78) were the doctrine of papal primacy and the dogma of papal infallibility.[1] What follows here is a detailed outline of the ecclesiological context for these two doctrines. The context consists of five principal elements: (1.1) The Papacy in Catholic Teaching: An Overview; (1.2) Peter in the New Testament; (1.3) Papal Primacy in Catholic Teaching; (1.4) Papal Infallibility in Catholic Teaching; and (1.5) Petrine Succession, Petrine Ministry, and the Pope as Vicar of Peter.

THE PAPACY IN CATHOLIC TEACHING: AN OVERVIEW

The papacy is the office of, and the jurisdiction exercised by, the Bishop of Rome, known more popularly as the pope.[2] The papacy is also known as the Petrine ministry (see Part IV.1.5.b) because the Catholic Church considers the pope to be the Vicar of Peter (see Part IV.1.5.c), that is, the one who personally succeeds to the distinctive ministry of St. Peter for the sake of the unity of the universal Church (see Part IV.1.5.a).

The title of "pope," which means "father" (It. *papa*), was in earlier centuries of church history applied to every bishop in the West, while in the East it seems to have been used of priests as well and was a special title of the patriarch of Alexandria. In 1073, however, Pope Gregory VII formally prohibited the use of the title for all except the Bishop of Rome.

In addition to the Bishop of Rome, which is his primary title, the pope has several other titles: Vicar of Peter, Vicar of Jesus Christ, Successor of the Chief of the Apostles, Supreme Pontiff of the Universal Church, Primate of Italy, Archbishop and Metropolitan of the Roman Province, Sovereign of Vatican City State, and Servant of the Servants of God. (The title Patriarch of the West was dropped, with the approval of Pope Benedict XVI, in 2006.)

According to traditional Catholic belief, the papacy was established by Jesus Christ himself when he conferred its responsibilities and powers upon the Apostle Peter at Caesarea Philippi: "And so I say to you, you are Peter, and upon this rock I will build my church, and the gates of the netherworld shall not prevail against it. I will give you the keys to the kingdom of heaven. Whatever you bind on earth shall be bound in heaven; and whatever you loose on earth shall be loosed in heaven" (Matt. 16:18–19).[3] It is because of the ancient tradition that the two principal leaders of the apostolic church, Sts. Peter and Paul, were martyred and buried in Rome that the papacy, from its beginnings, has been linked with this former imperial city.

PETER IN THE NEW TESTAMENT

Catholic tradition regards Peter (d. ca. 64) as the first pope, but the first succession lists identified Linus (ca. 66–ca. 78), not Peter, as the first pope.[4] Peter was not regarded as the first Bishop of Rome until the late second or early third century. Peter's original Hebrew name was *šim'ôn,* rendered in Greek as Simon. It is also rendered as Simeon twice in the New Testament (Acts 15:14; 2 Pet. 1:1). Jesus gave him a new name, the Aramaic word for "rock," *kêpā',* later transliterated into Greek as *Kephas*. But the name Kephas appears only nine times in the New Testament, once in John and eight times in the Letters of Paul. The name Peter is a Greek translation of the Aramaic word *kêpā'* and is used more than 150 times in the Gospels and in the Acts of the Apostles. This name conveyed to Greek-speaking Christians far more about Peter's function in the Church than the noncommittal *Kephas.* He had been chosen by Christ to be the "rock," or foundation, of the Church and the leader of the Apostles. Finally, the double name Simon Peter occurs about twenty times in the New Testament, mostly in John.

That Peter was married and remained so even after becoming a disciple of Jesus is clear from the account of Jesus's healing of Peter's mother-in-law (Mark 1:29–31) and from Paul's reference to the fact that Peter and the other Apostles took their wives along on their apostolic journeys (1 Cor. 9:5). The pious belief that the Apostles, including Peter, "put away" their wives once they received the call from Jesus has no historical basis. Rather, it arises from the mistaken, and essentially unchristian, assumption that celibacy is more virtuous than marriage because sexual intimacy somehow compromises one's total commitment to God and the things of the spirit.

Catholic tradition has regarded Peter as the first pope because of the special commission he received from Jesus Christ and because of the unique status he enjoyed and the central role he played within the college of the twelve Apostles. He was the first disciple to be called by Jesus (Matt. 4:18–19). He served as spokesman for the other Apostles (Mark 8:29; Matt. 18:21; Luke 12:41; John 6:67–69). According to the tradition of Paul and Luke (1 Cor. 15:5; Luke 24:34), he was the first to whom the Lord appeared after the Resurrection. (Mary Magdalene is the primary witness to the Resurrection in the tradition of Matthew, John, and the Marcan appendix, but even in Mark the angel at the tomb instructs Mary Magdalene and the other women to "go and tell his disciples and Peter" [16:7].) Peter is, in fact, the most frequently commissioned of the Twelve following the Resurrection.

Peter is also the most frequently mentioned disciple in all four Gospels and is regularly listed first among the Twelve (Mark 3:16–19; Matt. 10:1–4; Luke 6:12–16). This latter point alongside others is of particular significance because, in the ancient world, respect and authority resided in the first of a line, first born or first chosen. He is thus prominent in the original Jerusalem community—described by Paul as one of its "pillars" (Gal. 2:9)—and is well known to many other churches (Acts 1:15–26; 2:14–40; 3:1–26; 4:8; 5:1–11, 29; 8:18–25; 9:32–43; 10:5; 12:17; 1 Pet. 2:11; 5:13). Paul himself had been "entrusted with the gospel to the uncircumcised" (Gal. 2:7), but it was Peter who took the decisive step in ordering the baptism of the Gentile Cornelius without first requiring circumcision (Acts 10). Although Peter's own ministry was largely focused on his fellow Jews (Gal. 2:7), his influence was nevertheless felt in gentile areas as well (1 Cor. 1:12; 1 Pet. 1:1).

His role, however, was not always a singular one. He often shared his position of prominence with James and John, constituting with them a kind of inner elite within the Twelve. All three accompanied Jesus to the raising of Jairus's daughter (Mark 5:37), at the Transfiguration (9:2), at the Mount of Olives for a special farewell discourse (13:3), and to the Garden of Gethsemane (14:33).

Peter's activities are not reported following the Council of Jerusalem, where he exercised an important, though not necessarily "papal," role in opening the mission of the Church to the Gentiles (Acts 15:7–12). Significantly, it was James, not Peter, who presided over the council and ratified its decisions. However, there is increasing agreement among historians and biblical scholars that Peter did go to Rome and was martyred there (by crucifixion, according to the North African theologian Tertullian [d. ca. 225]). The Roman leader Clement (regarded as Peter's third successor, ca. 91–ca. 101) describes Peter's trials in Rome (*1 Clement* 5:4), and Eusebius of Caesarea (d. ca. 339) reports an ancient story about Peter's crucifixion there (*Ecclesiastical History* 2.25.5, 8). St. Irenaeus of Lyons (d. ca. 200) assumes that Peter and Paul jointly founded the church of Rome and inaugurated its succession of bishops (*Against Heresies* 3.1.2; 3.3.3). However, there is no evidence that, before his death, Peter actually served the church of Rome as its first bishop, even though that "fact" is regularly taken for granted by a wide spectrum of Catholics and others.

The ancient text known as *The Shepherd*, attributed to Hermas, a lay member of the Roman community, contains hints of disputes about rank among church leaders (*Visions* 2.2.6; 3.9.7), who are sometimes referred to as "the elders who are in charge of the Church" (2.4.3). Significantly, the references are all in the plural. Where bishops are mentioned (again in the plural), they are usually linked with other bishops, teachers, and deacons (3.5.1), as if the Church were a tower under construction and these leaders were numbered among its stones. By the late second or early third centuries, however, Peter did become identified in tradition as the first Bishop of Rome. But tradition is not a fact factory. It cannot make something into a historical fact when it is not.

Peter is credited with writing two Letters that are part of the New Testament canon: 1 and 2 Peter. Although biblical scholars generally accept his authorship of the first, they regard his authorship of the second as unlikely. Nevertheless, as a compendium of highly flattering traditions about Peter, the second Letter is an important witness to the stature he enjoyed and the respect he was accorded in the early Church. He is said, for example, to have the gift of inspiration (2 Pet. 1:20–21) and to have received revelations about future false prophets (2:1–3) and special traditions about the Parousia, or Second Coming of Christ (3:8), and about the regeneration of the world (3:11–12). A body of apocryphal literature associated with the name of Peter emerged in the second century: the *Apocalypse of St. Peter,* the *Acts of St. Peter,* and the *Gospel of St. Peter.* Even if not authentically Petrine in authorship, these writings attest to Peter's increasing prestige in the early Church.

In the Catholic tradition, the biblical basis for associating the primacy with Peter is embodied in three texts: Matthew 16:13–19; Luke 2:31–32; and John 21:15–19. The fact that Jesus's naming of Peter as the "rock" occurs in three different contexts in these three Gospels raises a question about the original setting of the incident itself. Scholars are not sure if the naming occurred during Jesus's earthly ministry or after the Resurrection with what is called a subsequent "retrojection" into the accounts of Jesus's earthly ministry. The conferral of the power of the keys to the Kingdom surely suggests an imposing measure of authority, given the symbolism of the keys, but there is no explicit indication that the authority conferred was meant to be exercised over others, much less that it was to be absolutely monarchical in kind (as claimed and exercised by later popes, especially in the Middle Ages and even into the late twentieth century). In Acts, in fact, Peter is shown consulting with the other Apostles and even being sent by them (8:4). He and John are portrayed as acting as a team (3:1–11; 4:1–22; 8:14). And Paul confronts Peter for his inconsistency and hypocrisy in drawing back from table fellowship with gentile Christians in Antioch under pressure from some Jewish Christians who arrived later from Jerusalem. Paul "opposed him to his face because he clearly was wrong" (Gal. 2:11; see also 2:12–14).

Scholars, however, point to a significant trajectory of images relating to Peter and his ministry as an independent basis for the primatial claims. He is spoken of as the fisherman (Luke 5:10; John 21:1–14), an occupation that, in fact, he and his brother Andrew had practiced, as the shepherd of Christ's sheep (John 21:15–17), as the Christian martyr (John 13:36; 1 Pet. 5:1), as an elder who addresses other elders (1 Pet. 5:1), as a proclaimer of faith in Jesus as the Son of God (Matt. 16:16–17), as the receiver of a special revelation (Mark 9:2–8; 2 Pet. 1:16–18; Acts 1:9–16; 5:1–11; 10:9–16; 12:7–9), as the guardian of the true faith against false teaching and misunderstanding (2 Pet. 1:20–21; 3:15–16), and, of course, as the rock on which the Church is to be built (Matt. 16:18).

This trajectory of biblical images continued in the life of the early postbiblical Church, and these images were enriched by others: missionary preacher, great visionary, destroyer of heretics, receiver of the new law, gatekeeper of heaven, helmsman of the ship of the Church, co-teacher and co-martyr with Paul. This is not to suggest, of course, that Peter was portrayed always and only in a positive fashion. He is also presented as a weak and sinful man. He is reproached by Paul (Gal. 2:11–14), misunderstands Jesus (Mark 9:5–6; John 13:6–11; 18:10–11), weakens in faith after beginning to walk on water (Matt. 14:30–31), is rebuked by Jesus (Mark 8:33; Matt. 16:23), and, in spite of prior boasts to the contrary (Mark 14:29,31; John 13:37), denies Christ (Mark 14:66–72). But he is always repentant and is eventually rehabilitated. The risen Lord appears to Peter, and he becomes once again a source of strength to the Church (Luke 22:32).

Peter's unique importance as Jesus's first and chief disciple and as the leader of the college of the twelve Apostles is clear enough. No pope in history has achieved his status, and it is no accident that none of the more than 260 individuals whom Catholic tradition regards as his successors have taken the name Peter II, including two whose own baptismal names were Peter (John XIV, elected in 983, and Sergius IV, elected in 1009). What can be said, however, about Peter's enduring significance for the papacy and for the Church itself?

PAPAL PRIMACY IN CATHOLIC TEACHING

We consider here the first of Vatican I's two major doctrines pertaining to the papacy: primacy and infallibility. Recognition of the papacy, or of the Petrine ministry as exercised by the Bishop of Rome, is not characteristic of the Catholic tradition alone.[5] Other Christian traditions acknowledge the Bishop of Rome as the "first [bishop] among equals" (Lat. *primus inter pares*), but only the Catholic Church accepts him as the earthly head of the worldwide Communion of Churches. This is also known as the doctrine of papal primacy, linked, in turn, with the primacy of the Roman see itself.

St. Ignatius of Antioch is traditionally regarded as the first major witness to the primacy of Rome. In his famous letter to the church at Rome not long before he himself was martyred there, he addressed "the church holding chief place in the territories of the district of Rome—worthy of God, worthy of honor, blessing, praise, and success; worthy too in holiness, *foremost in love*" (emphasis added). Remarkably, however, it is the only one of Ignatius's classic letters to the seven churches of the ancient Mediterranean world that makes no mention at all of a local bishop.[6] This lends credence to the supposition of historians and theologians that the monoepiscopal structure of church governance (i.e., a diocese with one bishop as its pastoral head) did not even come to Rome until the middle of the second century, probably with the pontificate of Pius I (ca. 142–ca. 155).

It would have been extraordinary, however, if Rome had *not* been singled out for a special role and position of authority in the early Church. Not only was it the place traditionally regarded as the site of the martyrdoms and burials of both Peter and Paul; it was also the center of the Roman Empire. Gradually Rome did emerge as an ecclesiastical court of last resort, the local church to which other local churches and their bishops would appeal when disputes and conflicts could not be settled between or among themselves. For example, in the controversies with Gnosticism, a particularly virulent early Christian heresy that denied the full humanity of Jesus Christ, defenders of orthodoxy appealed to the faith of episcopal sees founded by the Apostles, and especially to the faith of the Roman church because of its close association with Peter and Paul. Rome subsequently intervened in the life of distant churches, took sides in theological controversies, was consulted by other bishops on doctrinal and moral questions, and sent delegates to distant councils.

The correlation between Peter and the Bishop of Rome, however, did not become fully explicit until the pontificate of Leo I (also known as Leo the Great) in the mid-fifth century (440–61). Leo insisted that Peter continued to speak to the whole Church through the Bishop of Rome. It was Leo who decisively intervened in the great Christological controversies and whose letter, or *Tome,* to Flavian, patriarch of Constantinople, in 449 provided the basis for the definitive formulation of faith two years later at the Council of Chalcedon.

With the beginnings of the East-West Schism in 1054, the shape of the papacy changed even more significantly. Before the split the Bishop of Rome had been viewed primarily as the patriarch of Rome alongside the patriarchs of Constantinople, Antioch, Alexandria, and Jerusalem. After the split, however, the Roman patriarchal office and the papal office merged. The patriarchal office was completely absorbed by the power of the papacy. In the eyes of many Eastern Christians, Western Christianity became thereby a papal church, that is, a church that relates so predominantly to the see of Rome that the pastoral autonomy of the local churches and their bishops is all but lost. The Bishop of Rome came to regard himself, and be regarded as, the universal primate of the universal Church. It was as if he were the bishop of every local church and the local bishops were simply his vicars or delegates.

Following this long and complex history, the Second Ecumenical Council of Lyons in 1274 claimed for the Roman church "the supreme and full primacy and authority over the universal Catholic Church." That formal declaration laid the foundation, in turn, for the dogmatic definition of the First Vatican Council, in 1870, that "in the disposition of God the Roman church holds the preeminence of ordinary power over all the other churches."

This is not to say, however, that the evolution of the doctrine of papal primacy has proceeded in a direct, unbroken line from the time of the New Testament to the present day. On the contrary, there is a major difference in the way the papacy was perceived and exercised by the whole Church—East and West—during the first thousand years of Christian history and the way it has been perceived and exercised—in the West—during the second Christian millennium.

Before the beginning of the second millennium and of the pontificate of Gregory VII in particular (1073–85), popes functioned largely in the role of mediator. They did not claim for themselves the title "Vicar of Christ." They did not appoint bishops. They did not govern the universal Church through the Roman Curia. They did not impose or enforce clerical celibacy. They did not write encyclicals or authorize catechisms for the whole Church. They did not retain for themselves alone the power of canonization. They did not even convene ecumenical councils, as a rule—and certainly not the major doctrinal councils of Nicaea (325), Constantinople (381), Ephesus (431), and Chalcedon (451).

The Second Vatican Council brought the Church's understanding of the papacy, and of papal primacy in particular, more in line once again with that of the first Christian millennium, in contrast with that of the second Christian millennium. The council viewed the papacy in increasingly (but not completely) communal and collegial terms. In other words, the pope is no longer to be conceived of as an absolute monarch—an impression clearly left by the one-sided, because unfinished, teaching of the First Vatican Council. (Vatican I, as we pointed out in the opening paragraph of Part IV, had to suspend operations because of the political turmoil in Italy.)

According to the Second Vatican Council, the pope exercises supreme authority over the whole Church, but the other bishops also share in that authority. To be sure, the supreme authority vested in the college of bishops cannot be exercised without the consent of the pope. "This college, insofar as it is composed of many, expresses the variety and universality of the People of God, but insofar as it is assembled under one head, it expresses the unity of the flock of Christ" (Dogmatic Constitution on the Church, n. 22). Although the pope retains "full, supreme, and universal power over the Church," the other bishops are no longer perceived as simply his stand-ins or delegates. They also receive from Christ "the mission to teach all nations and to preach the gospel to every creature" (n. 24). They govern their own dioceses not as "vicars of the Roman Pontiff, for they exercise an authority which is proper to them" (n. 27). Whatever authority the pope and the other bishops enjoy, it is always to be exercised within a communion of local churches through the faithful preaching of the gospel, the administration of the sacraments, and pastoral service.

The Catholic Church is not an absolute monarchy. Its governmental structure is communal and collegial, even if also hierarchical. Insofar as the universal Church is a *communion* of local churches, the papal office serves the unity of the whole Church as "the perpetual and visible source and foundation of the unity of the bishops and of the multitude of the faithful" (Dogmatic Constitution on the Church, n. 23). Papal primacy, therefore, is a primacy of service—in the service of unity. Insofar as the universal Church is a communion of local *churches,* the papal office must respect the legitimate diversity of these churches and practice a collegial mode of decision making (n. 23). The bishops, therefore, truly collaborate with the pope in the work of the Holy Spirit, which is the work of unity. They do so in their collegial confession of one faith, in their common celebration of divine worship, especially the Eucharist, and in their promotion of the loving harmony of the family of God (Decree on Ecumenism, n. 2).

PAPAL INFALLIBILITY IN CATHOLIC TEACHING

The second major doctrine formulated by the First Vatican Council and defined and promulgated as a dogma of faith was that of papal infallibility.[7] Infallibility means, literally, immunity from error. Theologically it refers to a charism, or gift, of the Holy Spirit by which the Church is protected from fundamental error when it solemnly defines a matter of faith or morals. Catholic theologians are careful to point out, however, that the charism is a negative charism; that is, it only guarantees that a particular teaching is not erroneous. The charism of infallibility does not ensure that a particular teaching is an adequate, appropriate, or opportune expression of faith or morals. Furthermore, *papal* infallibility is a dimension of the *Church's* infallibility, not vice versa. The pope's infallibility is the same infallibility "with which the divine Redeemer willed His Church to be endowed" (Dogmatic Constitution on the Church, n. 25).

Unlike for the doctrine of papal primacy, there is no explicit basis for the doctrine of papal infallibility in the New Testament. It was not until the middle of the third century that special importance began to be accorded the faith of the church of Rome. Some Roman emperors included the faith of the Bishop of Rome in the official norm of orthodoxy, and the biblical image of the Church "without spot or wrinkle" (Eph. 5:27) began to be applied to the church of Rome. Rome became *the* apostolic see. According to the *Formula of Pope Hormisdas,* written in the year 515, "the catholic religion has always been preserved immaculate" in Rome. This conviction was expressed in different ways by different sources well into the Middle Ages.

But there were also challenges to such claims, not only in the East but in the West as well. Eastern Christians regarded Rome as only one of several apostolic sees to which the protection of the faith had been entrusted. And not all of Rome's bishops effectively fulfilled this important ministry. Marcellinus (296–304) complied with imperial orders to hand over copies of Sacred Scripture and to offer incense to the gods, for which he was probably deposed. Liberius (352–66) was a weak pope who at first opposed the excommunication of St. Athanasius (d. 373), the great enemy of Arianism, but then relented under political pressure from the Arian emperor, Constantius, who deposed him from office and sent him into harsh, but temporary, exile in Thrace. Vigilius (537–55) vacillated on the teaching of the Council of Chalcedon (451) and was even excommunicated by a synod of African bishops. Honorius (625–38) became an unwitting adherent of Monothelitism, a heresy that held there is only one (divine) will in Christ, and after his death was formally condemned by the Third Council of Constantinople (680).

Certain Western metropolitans (archbishops with some form of jurisdiction over suffragan dioceses in the same geographical area) even in the early Middle Ages sometimes contradicted papal decisions. Prophetic voices, including those of saints like Bernard of Clairvaux (d. 1153) and Catherine of Siena (d. 1380), were also raised against the style and practice of the papal ministry centuries before the Reformation. Medieval theologians and canonists admitted that individual popes had erred in matters of doctrine and even conceded that a pope could deviate from the faith.

Nevertheless, the formula "Rome has never erred" survived and over the course of time came to be understood as "Rome *cannot* err." The legal maxim "The first see is judged by no one" appeared initially in the sixth century and was later interpreted to mean that the pope's teaching authority is supreme. St. Thomas Aquinas (d. 1274) would later argue that the pope's teachings must always be followed because he represents the universal Church, which "cannot err."

The formal concept of infallibility, however, was not applied to the papacy until the fourteenth century, during a controversy over poverty in the Franciscan order. Advocates of a rigorist position (that Franciscans must divest themselves of all property, regardless of practical need) employed the term "infallibility" to defend the binding authority of statements by earlier popes against the more liberal decisions of their successors.[8] Under the impact of the Reformation, the concept gained wider currency among the Counter-Reformation theologians (Robert Bellarmine [d. 1621] and others). There were also appeals to infallibility in the condemnations of Jansenism and Gallicanism (two largely French dissident movements) in the seventeenth and eighteenth centuries. Under strong personal pressure from a beleaguered Pope Pius IX, the First Vatican Council formally defined the dogma of infallibility in 1870.

The key words of the Vatican I text placed certain restrictions on the exercise of papal infallibility: "When the Roman Pontiff speaks *ex cathedra* [Lat., "from the chair"], that is, when . . . as pastor and teacher of all Christians in virtue of his highest apostolic authority he defines a doctrine of faith and morals that must be held by the Universal Church, he is empowered, through the divine assistance promised him in blessed Peter, with that infallibility with which the Divine Redeemer willed to endow his Church." Thus, (1) he must be speaking formally as earthly head of the Church (*ex cathedra*); (2) he must be speaking on a matter of faith or morals (not governance or discipline); and (3) he must clearly intend to bind the whole Church. Indeed, the revised Code of Canon Law (1983) stipulates that "no doctrine is understood to be infallibly defined unless it is clearly established as such" (can. 749.3).

Infallibility, therefore, is not a personal prerogative of the pope. It would be inaccurate to say, without qualification, that "the pope is infallible." A pope is only infallible, according to Vatican I, when he is in the act of defining a dogma of faith or morals under the conditions specified.

Neither does the dogma of infallibility mean that the pope is somehow above the Church. Vatican I's declaration that the definitions of popes are "irreformable by themselves [*ex sese*] and not by reason of the agreement of the Church [*non autem ex consensu ecclesiae*]" was added to the definition in order to oppose Gallicanism, an attitude prevalent in France that maintained that papal definitions and other decisions did not go into effect unless and until they were subsequently ratified by the Church. On the other hand, the official presenter of the dogma of papal infallibility at Vatican I, Bishop Vincenz Gasser (d. 1879), made it clear during the debate that the consent of the Church can never be lacking to an infallible pronouncement.

Nor did Vatican I intend to say, in using the word "irreformable," that infallible teachings can never change. If that were the case, it would be difficult to see how there could be a development of dogma as well as of noninfallible doctrines. Dogmas, or infallible pronouncements, are formulated in human language and are expressive of human concepts. As such, even dogmas are historically conditioned (*Mysterium Ecclesiae*, Congregation for the Doctrine of the Faith, 1973).[9] This means that, although the truth of infallible teachings cannot change, the way that truth is expressed can change, through an improvement in its wording or an alteration, even a correction, in its conceptual underpinnings.

Like the dogma of papal primacy, defined by the Council of Florence (1431–45), the dogma of papal infallibility, defined by Vatican I, was set in a larger context by the Second Vatican Council. The charism of infallibility, the council insisted, can be exercised by the whole college of bishops, in communion with the pope, either when assembled in an ecumenical council or when scattered throughout the world. In principle, the whole Church, not just the pope and the other bishops, is infallible (Dogmatic Constitution on the Church, n. 25). This follows from the broader principle, enunciated by Vatican II, that the Church is the whole People of God and includes more than the pope and the rest of the hierarchy (Dogmatic Constitution on the Church, n. 30, and chap. 2 generally).

PETRINE SUCCESSION, PETRINE MINISTRY, AND THE POPE AS VICAR OF PETER

Petrine Succession

History provides a long list of popes following Peter, beginning with Linus (ca. 66–ca. 78) and continuing into the twenty-first century and the beginning of the third Christian millennium with such popes as Pius XII (1939–58), John XXIII (1958–63), Paul VI (1963–78), John Paul I (1978), John Paul II (1978–2005), and Benedict XVI (2005–).[10] Catholic tradition regards all of these popes as successors of Peter. In what sense are they his successors, and in what sense are they not?

Regarding at least two of his apostolic roles, Peter could *not* have had successors: first, as the traditional co-founder with Paul of the apostolic see of Rome (although, more precisely, they are the co-founders of the *apostolic authority* of Rome); and, second, as one of the Twelve who were personal witnesses of the Risen Lord.[11] These are unique, nonrepeatable, and nontransmittable aspects of Peter's apostleship. On the other hand, the bishops of Rome do continue Peter's ministry of evangelizing the world and maintaining the unity of the whole Church. They also continue to exercise within the college of bishops the same kind of pastoral authority that Peter exercised within the original company of the Twelve. The word "continue" is important. The popes do not succeed Peter in the sense of *replacing* him, as a newly inaugurated president of the United States, for example, replaces his predecessor. The popes carry on Peter's ministry, but Peter as such is irreplaceable. He (and the Petrine authority that he and his successors exercise) is the "rock" on which the Church is built.

Indeed, for St. Cyprian of Carthage (d. 258) every bishop in his own episcopal see, or diocese, is in some sense a successor of Peter. As successors of the Apostles, all bishops are signs of unity and bearers of the apostolic tradition. St. Hilary of Poitiers (d. 367) too referred to all bishops as "successors of Peter and Paul." St. Augustine of Hippo (d. 430) pointed out that in Peter the whole Church, and not only Peter, received the keys to the Kingdom. Moreover, the Orthodox churches maintain that Rome is not the only see in which Peter exercised his apostolic primacy and in which an episcopal succession occurred. They cite Antioch as one of these other apostolic sees.[12] Nevertheless, it is a matter of Catholic doctrine that Petrine succession, like apostolic succession, is a development guided by the Holy Spirit and, in that sense, is of divine institution.

Petrine Ministry

According to Catholic tradition, the ministry the Bishop of Rome exercises in his capacity as Vicar of Peter (see Part IV.1.5.c) is a continuation of Peter's own ministry on behalf of the universal Church. As such it is called the Petrine ministry, which Jesus is believed to have conferred upon Peter at the Last Supper when he declared, "I have prayed that your own faith may not fail; and once you have turned back, you must strengthen your brothers" (Luke 22:32). The ministry of pastoral leadership exercised by Peter in the first part of Acts is the model and the norm for the Petrine ministry exercised by the pope. It involves witnessing to the faith, overseeing the way in which local churches preserve and transmit this faith, providing assistance and encouragement to fellow bishops in their own local and universal ministry of proclaiming and defending the faith, speaking in the name of the bishops and their local churches when the need arises, and articulating the faith of the Church in the name of the whole communion of local churches, which together constitute the universal Church. In sum, the Petrine ministry is that of a "servant of the servants of God" (Lat. *servus servorum Dei*): a servant of his brother bishops, and a servant of the whole People of God.

The Pope as Vicar of Peter

The most traditional title accorded the pope (from the end of the fourth century) is that of Vicar of Peter.[13] The Bishop of Rome does not take the place of Peter. Unlike Peter, the pope is neither an Apostle nor an eyewitness of the Risen Lord. These are qualities that cannot be transmitted to those who follow. The popes can only continue Peter's ministry by keeping alive the faith that has been handed on to them. The closest English word to "vicar" is "substitute." Like a substitute teacher in a classroom, the pope stands in for Peter, but does not replace him. Although the title Vicar of Christ is practically synonymous today with the person and office of the pope, it does not have the same historical standing in the Catholic tradition as that of Vicar of Peter. Originally, all bishops were considered vicars of Christ. Not until the pontificate of Eugenius III (1145–53) did the title Vicar of Christ become exclusively identified with the Bishop of Rome. Subsequently, Pope Innocent III (1198–1216) appealed to the title as the basis of his universal power, even over temporal authorities. Nevertheless, in 1964 the Second Vatican Council affirmed that "bishops govern the particular churches entrusted to them as the vicars of Christ and his ambassadors" (Dogmatic Constitution on the Church, n. 27). The pope is Vicar of Christ insofar as he is a bishop, not insofar as he is a pope. The title that captures his distinctive Petrine responsibilities is Vicar of Peter.

Vatican I (1869–70)

PURPOSE, PREPARATIONS, AND COMPOSITION

Pope Pius IX intended Vatican I to serve as a counterweight to the pervasive principles and spirit of the previous century's Enlightenment and French Revolution. He was especially concerned with those ideologies and forces that he and many other Catholics perceived as hostile to the Church and its authority: rationalism, materialism, atheism, socialism, Communism, liberalism, democracy, nationalism, and modern theology insofar as it had been "infected" with any of these ideas. From the time of the French Revolution in the late eighteenth century until 1944, the popes held that a Catholic monarchy that gave legal recognition to the Catholic Church alone was the ideal form of government. It was in his Christmas message of 1944, seven months after the city of Rome had been liberated from the German forces, that Pope Pius XII explicitly recognized the positive value of democracy, thereby marking a break from that older tradition.[14]

The council's agenda would closely follow Pius IX's encyclical *Quanta cura* (Lat., "How much care," 1864), to which was attached the more famous *Syllabus of Errors,* which contained eighty condemned propositions, or theses, pertaining to Pantheism and naturalism, the interplay between faith and reason, and Church and state. At a time when the Church's possession of the last remaining Papal States (including the duchy of Rome) and its exercise of temporal authority generally were under attack, the *Syllabus* sought to preserve the autonomy of the papacy and of the Church generally with regard to its right to property, the selection of bishops, the regulation of the life of the faithful, and the communication of its teachings.

It was just two days before the encyclical's publication on December 8, 1864, that Pius IX, in the presence of a few cardinals, announced for the first time that he intended to convene an ecumenical council. The preparatory commissions began their work in 1865. Those commissions were composed largely of supporters of Ultramontanism, a contemporary intellectual and political movement in European countries "beyond the mountains" (the Alps), namely, France, Germany, Spain, and England. Ultramontanists exalted the papacy as the bulwark against political liberalism and modern philosophical and scientific trends. They were committed to the declaration of the dogma of papal infallibility and to a reaffirmation, if not an outright dogmatic pronouncement, of the doctrine of papal primacy.

Beginning in 1867, Bishop Ignatius von Senestréy of Ratisbon (Regensburg), Archbishop Henry Manning (d. 1892) of Westminster, and the editors of the Jesuit journal *Civiltà Cattolica* strongly advocated for the definition of papal infallibility. They were joined by Victor Augustus Deschamps (d. 1883), archbishop of Malines and primate of Belgium, and such prominent laymen as William G. Ward (d. 1882) of England and Louis Veuillot (d. 1883) of France. Lined up on the other side were the former Anglican Father John Henry Newman (d. 1890) and the lay historian Lord John Acton (d. 1902) in England, the church historian Father Johann J. von Döllinger (d. 1890) in Bavaria, the bishop of Orléans Félix A. P. Dupanloup (d. 1878), the French historian Charles Montalembert (d. 1870), and most of the German, Austrian, and American bishops. Many opponents of defining papal infallibility insisted that there was no historical support for it; others argued that such a definition would be inopportune in the current ecumenical situation because of the expected negative reaction of non-Catholic Christians (and thus were called the "inopportunists"). The latter group included Martin Spaulding (d. 1872), archbishop of Baltimore, who unsuccessfully proposed a compromise definition, and fourteen German bishops, who informed Rome in the late summer of 1869 of their lack of support for the definition.

Pius IX convoked the council in 1868 (i.e., officially announced that the council would be held, with formal papal approval) and then convened it the following year, with a solemn opening on December 8, 1869. Of the approximately 1,050 eligible participants, about 750 were actually present. Two-thirds of these were Europeans, almost all of whom were bishops, and one-third of the Europeans were Italian.[15] Most of the missionary bishops were European. There were 48 bishops and 1 abbot from the United States.[16] There were no non-Catholic Christian observers, as there would be at Vatican II almost a hundred years later, but it has been suggested that the invitations to Orthodox, Anglican, and Protestant representatives were merely pro forma in nature or ineptly communicated.[17]

Of the fifty-six schemas, or draft decrees, only six were discussed and only two of those were acted upon—in part. The first was the Dogmatic Constitution on the Catholic Faith (*Dei Filius,* Lat., "Son of God"), promulgated in final form on April 24, 1870, and the second, which is of primary interest here, was the Dogmatic Constitution on the Church of Christ (*Pastor Aeternus,* "Eternal Pastor"). It was decided that two of the issues contained in the latter document would be discussed before other issues treated in the schema. The first discussion, however, concerned the opportuneness of the proposed definition on papal infallibility. That debate lasted from May 13 to June 3 and was suspended by closure (normally a two-thirds vote to end discussion). A debate on papal primacy followed, during which the minority of progressive bishops objected to the schema's description of papal jurisdiction as ordinary, immediate, and truly episcopal, as if the pope were, in principle, bishop of every diocese, pastor of every parish, and spiritual director of every individual member of the Church.

The debate on papal infallibility, which was resumed following the debate on the primacy, ended on July 4. On July 13 the definition of papal infallibility received 533 affirmative votes (Lat. *placet,* "it pleases"), 88 negative votes (*non placet*), and 62 affirmatives with qualifications (*placet iuxta modum*). In a public session on July 18, the entire constitution *Pastor Aeternus,* which included three chapters on papal primacy and one chapter on papal infallibility (the entire text will be described and analyzed in the next two sections, 2.2 and 2.3), was passed with the same 533 affirmative votes, but with only 2 negative votes (including 1 cast by Edward Fitzgerald [d. 1907], the bishop of Little Rock, Arkansas). The remaining 148, who had voted no (*non placet*) or yes with qualifications (*placet iuxta modum*) on the definition of papal infallibility on July 13, either abstained from the vote on the constitution as a whole, held on July 18, or left the council before the final vote was taken. (The 533 affirmative votes represented just over half of the bishops and other prelates who were eligible to participate in the council itself.) Pope Pius IX officially promulgated the definition on the same day. The next day war broke out between France and Prussia, and French troops, which had been protecting the pope, were removed from the city.

The army of Victor Emmanuel II, who had become the first king of a united Italy in 1861, occupied Rome on September 20. In early October a plebiscite approved the incorporation of Rome in the new Italian state. Then, on October 20, 1870, nine months after convening the council, Pius IX adjourned it indefinitely. The council, however, was never to resume. Its work, especially on the relationship between the papacy and the episcopate, would not be completed for another century, at the Second Vatican Council.

VATICAN I ON PAPAL PRIMACY

What follows here is a synthesis of Vatican I's teaching on the juridical (as opposed to honorary) primacy of the pope over the whole Church and over the whole body of his fellow bishops. However, because the council was prevented from completing its intended work on the episcopate, as just noted above, its teaching on papal primacy lacked a broader ecclesiological context, namely, Vatican II's doctrine-to-be on collegiality. Between Vatican I and Vatican II, therefore, a clear impression was abroad in the minds of many Catholics, including many bishops, pastors, theologians, and laypersons, that the Church was structurally an absolute monarchy with the pope at the top of a kind of hierarchical pyramid. It would take many years before that impression was effectively challenged, although it is still not completely displaced even today.

The Dogmatic Constitution on the Church of Christ (*Pastor Aeternus*), which was the first of an intended pair of constitutions on the Church, consists of a prologue and four chapters: the first three are concerned with papal primacy; the fourth, with papal infallibility. The prologue grounds the teaching on primacy and infallibility on the special authority of St. Peter, whom the Lord placed "over the rest of the apostles and instituted in him the permanent principle of both unities [of faith and communion] and their visible foundation."[18]

Chapter 1, "On the Institution of the Apostolic Primacy in Blessed Peter," teaches and declares that New Testament evidence supports the papal claim to "a primacy of jurisdiction over the whole church of God" and that it was "immediately and directly promised to the blessed apostle Peter and conferred on him by Christ the lord." Christ changed his name from Simon Bar-Jona to Peter, or "rock," upon which he would build his Church (Matt. 16:16–19). And it was to Peter alone, not to the whole Church, that Christ "confided the jurisdiction of supreme pastor and ruler of his whole fold" (John 21:15–17).

The chapter concludes with the formula: "Therefore, if anyone says that blessed Peter the apostle was not appointed by Christ the lord as prince of all the apostles and visible head of the whole church militant; or that it was a primacy of honor only and not one of true and proper jurisdiction that he directly and immediately received from our lord Jesus Christ himself: let him be anathema."

It should be noted here that for centuries it was understood that the anathematizing of a doctrinal position (*anathema sit,* Lat., "Let him/her be anathema") was the equivalent of an excommunication of its adherents. The 1983 Revised Code of Canon Law abolished the use of the word, so that it no longer has any official penal application. One should also note in this summary formula the use of other non-biblical, legalistic terms: "prince," "militant," and "jurisdiction."

Chapter 2, "On the Permanence of the Primacy of Blessed Peter in the Roman Pontiffs," teaches that the primacy "will stand firm until the end of time." The Lord conferred the keys to the Kingdom on Peter and his successors, the bishops of the see of Rome, which Peter "founded and consecrated with his blood." (There is no evidence, however, that Peter founded the church at Rome. He is not even mentioned, for example, in Paul's Letter to the Romans.) The chapter concludes with the formula: "Therefore, if anyone says that it is not by the institution of Christ the lord himself (that is to say, by divine law) that blessed Peter should have perpetual successors in the primacy over the whole church; or that the Roman pontiff is not the successor of blessed Peter in this primacy: let him be anathema." Again, one should note the use of the canonical expression *iure divino* (Lat., "by divine law") and the imperial title *Romanum pontificem* ("Roman pontiff").

Chapter 3, "On the Power and Character of the Primacy of the Roman Pontiff," indicates that the council is promulgating "anew" the definition of the Council of Florence that "the apostolic see and the Roman pontiff hold a world-wide primacy, and that the Roman pontiff is the successor of blessed Peter," with "full power . . . to tend, rule and govern the universal church." As such, "by divine ordinance, the Roman church possesses a pre-eminence of ordinary power over every other church" and this "jurisdictional power . . . is both episcopal and immediate," that is, not given to him by any body or person in the Church, other than Christ himself. Consequently, clergy and laity, of whatever rite or rank, both singly and collectively, "are bound to submit to this power by the duty of hierarchical subordination and true obedience, and this not only in matters concerning faith and morals, but also in those which regard the discipline and government of the church throughout the world. . . . This is the teaching of the catholic truth, and no one can deviate from it without endangering his faith and salvation."

Although even casual readers will not miss the juridical and theologically maximalist content and tone of the paragraph, it is followed by yet another paragraph that significantly qualifies it: "[This papal power] by no means detracts from that ordinary and immediate power of episcopal jurisdiction, by which bishops, who have succeeded to the place of the apostles by appointment of the holy Spirit, tend and govern individually the particular flocks which have been assigned to them." Of great ecclesiological importance is the council's acknowledgment that the appointment of bishops is by the Holy Spirit. In other words, the episcopate is divinely established, and its existence is not dependent upon the approval of the pope. The paragraph also quotes Pope Gregory the Great (590–604) to the effect that his "honor" as the Bishop of Rome is the honor of the whole Church and that he receives it only "when it is denied to none of those to whom honor is due."

Nevertheless, the Bishop of Rome is always the court of last resort, since he is "the supreme judge of the faithful" (para. 5). Whatever judgments he renders are "not subject to revision by anyone." Not even an ecumenical council is superior in authority to the pope.

Once again, the concluding formula:

So, then, if anyone says that the Roman pontiff has merely an office of supervision and guidance, and not the full and supreme power of jurisdiction over the whole church, and this not only in matters of faith and morals, but also in those which concern the discipline and government of the church dispersed throughout the whole world; or that he has only the principal part, but not the absolute fullness, of this supreme power; or that this power of his is not ordinary and immediate both over all and each of the churches and over all and each of the pastors and faithful: let him be anathema.

As the French Dominican theologian Jean-M. R. Tillard (d. 2000) has pointed out, the "authentic meaning" of the doctrine of papal primacy "has to be discovered not only in the affirmations of Vatican I but also in the very important clarifications of Vatican II. The ecclesiological language of Vatican I was strongly juridical. This council was the culmination of a long process of development in Western theology that had, since 1054, been isolated from any vital dialogue with the Eastern churches."[19] By contrast, Vatican II constructed its theology of the papacy (as we shall see in Part V) within the broader context of the principle of communion and its structural expressions, namely, the collegiality of the bishops and the synodality of their local churches (see Part IV.1.4).

The Irish Carmelite theologian Christopher O'Donnell has made a similar observation, which is also typical of many commentaries that compare Vatican I and Vatican II. It was evident from the debate on papal primacy that "the council fathers clearly lacked both a sufficient general ecclesiology and a theology of the episcopate within which to place the primacy doctrine."[20]

In early 1875, just over four years after the abrupt termination of the council, the German bishops issued a rejoinder to an earlier statement in 1872 by the German chancellor, Otto von Bismarck (d. 1898). This statement had maintained (as many Catholics following the council also assumed) that the teaching of Vatican I regarding the direct and universal jurisdiction of the pope reduced the bishops to mere executive organs of the pope and degraded them to the status of mere officials. The "Collective Declaration by the German Hierarchy" affirmed that it is "in virtue of the same divine institution upon which the papacy rests that the episcopate also exists" and that the bishops have rights and duties given by divine ordinance that "the Pope has neither the right nor the power" to change. Thus, the German bishops concluded, "It is a complete misunderstanding of the Vatican decrees to believe that because of them 'episcopal jurisdiction has been absorbed into the papal,' that the Pope has 'in principle taken the place of each individual bishop,' that the bishops are now 'no more than tools of the Pope, his officials, without responsibility of their own.'"[21]

Less than a month later, Pope Pius IX, in an apostolic brief dated March 6, 1875, gave his approval to the statement of the German bishops in unusually solemn form: "Your declaration gives the genuine Catholic doctrine, which is also that of the holy Council and of this holy See; it defends it with illuminating and irrefutable reasoning, and sets it out so clearly that it is plain to any honest person that there is no innovation in the definitions attacked."[22]

Commentaries on the First Vatican Council's teaching on papal primacy must take into serious account this exchange between the German bishops and Pope Pius IX as well as the subsequent teaching of the Second Vatican Council on collegiality. *Pastor Aeternus* cannot be read and interpreted in a vacuum.

VATICAN I ON PAPAL INFALLIBILITY

As noted in IV.1.4, the infallibility of the whole Church has been a belief of the Church for centuries. What was at issue at Vatican I was whether the broad concept of infallibility could and should be applied to the pope as an individual pastoral leader of the Church. The bishops at Vatican I were divided into three groups on this question.[23] The smallest group of "infallibilists," under the leadership of Archbishop Manning of England, Bishop Senestréy of Belgium, and others, upheld the infallibility of *all* papal teachings and asserted that papal infallibility is the source of the Church's infallibility, not vice versa. The second group, consisting of the majority of the council, was open to a definition, but mainly to strengthen the authority of the pope in a newly hostile environment. The third group, the minority in opposition to the definition, comprised a fifth of the council fathers and was composed primarily of bishops from Germany, France, and Austria-Hungary. Archbishop Peter Kenrick (d. 1901) of St. Louis belonged to this group, on the grounds that all the bishops share in this gift of the Holy Spirit and not the pope alone. When the definition passed over his objections, however, he accepted it but no longer spoke about the issue for the rest of his life. Others opposed the definition for ecumenical reasons, and still others rejected the ecclesiology of the Ultramontanists because it conflicted with the ecclesial structure and practice of the ancient Church. (The text of the definition follows, below.)

The infallibility party was able to stack the most important delegations with its own members and close allies. They presented Pius IX with a list of four hundred supporters of the definition. In light of this support, the pope decided to expand the schema on the Church to four chapters, including a fourth on infallibility, and then to separate the chapters on papal primacy and papal infallibility, so that they could be acted on separately as the Dogmatic Constitution on the Church of Christ.

In the conciliar debate, the minority hardened its opposition to the definition, insisting that the exercise of infallibility by the pope would always have to be supported by the infallible tradition of the faith of the whole Church and that it could never operate independently from it. This was also the understanding of the majority of the bishops, but they did not want to become bogged down in a discussion of the precise procedures the pope would have to follow. Neither the infallibilists nor the minority in opposition were able to prevail. In protest, sixty-one members of the minority left Rome before the final vote. Most members of the minority gradually accepted the decision on condition of its reception by the Church as a whole and because of the subsequent clarification by the pope in response to the "Collective Declaration of the German Hierarchy." In German-speaking countries, however, protests against the definition led to the formation of the Old Catholic Church. One of the leading opponents of the definition, the eminent church historian Johann von Döllinger (d. 1890), refused to accept it and was excommunicated in 1871 by the archbishop of Munich.

Chapter 4, "On the Infallible Teaching Authority of the Roman Pontiff," begins with a lengthy paragraph that reaffirms the Church's teaching on papal primacy, citing both the Council of Florence and the Second Council of Lyons (1274). The second paragraph continues in that vein, but focuses more on the purity of teaching and the need for it to be "unblemished by any error." Paragraph 3 speaks of the "gift of truth and never-failing faith" conferred on Peter and his successors, so that the "whole flock of Christ might be kept away by them from the poisonous food of error and be nourished with the sustenance of heavenly doctrine."[24]

A brief fourth paragraph is followed by the paragraph containing the substance of the definition on papal infallibility:

> *Therefore, . . . we teach and define as a divinely revealed dogma that when the Roman pontiff speaks* ex cathedra, *that is, when, in the exercise of his office as shepherd and teacher of all Christians, in virtue of his supreme apostolic authority, he defines a doctrine concerning faith or morals to be held by the whole church, he possesses, by the divine assistance promised to him in blessed Peter, that infallibility which the divine Redeemer willed his church to enjoy in defining doctrine concerning faith or morals. Therefore, such definitions are of themselves, and not by the consent of the church, irreformable.*
>
> *So then, should anyone, which God forbid, have the temerity to reject this definition of ours: let him be anathema.*[25]

The definition contains several key elements. (1) There are three conditions according to which the pope can exercise this negative charism ("negative" because it guarantees only immunity from error, not the best or clearest expression of the truth): he must be speaking as shepherd and teacher of all Christians (*ex cathedra*); he must be defining a matter of faith or morals; and he must intend to bind the whole Church to accept the teaching. (2) Papal infallibility is not in a separate category, something exercised by the pope alone. It is the same infallibility "which the divine Redeemer willed his church to enjoy." (3) Papal infallibility is exercised only when the pope is in the act of exercising it. (4) The definitions are "of themselves, and not by the consent of the church, irreformable" (Lat. *ex sese, non autem ex consensu ecclesiae*). That last phrase was added in order to exclude the tendency of some Gallicans and Conciliarists to regard approval by the bishops as necessary to bestow infallibility on any papal definition. Moreover, the word "irreformable" does not mean that the wording or the conceptual underpinnings of infallible pronouncements are immune from change. Such definitions are always historically conditioned and therefore subject to revision, in accordance with the teaching of *Mysterium Ecclesiae* (1973), issued by the Congregation for the Doctrine of the Faith.[26] However, the essential truth of the infallible teaching remains the same.

A SUMMARY ASSESSMENT OF *PASTOR AETERNUS*

The German theologian Hermann Pottmeyer has correctly described the overall content and tone of *Pastor Aeternus* as one-sided. "As the minority [in opposition] anticipated," he writes, "this document has proved harmful to the Church. It was also unnecessary, because the supreme pastoral authority of the papacy was not contested at the time. Nevertheless, the minority did prevent the acceptance of the extreme definition of papal infallibility, and eventually the views of the minority were confirmed by Vatican II (1962–65)."[27]

On the other hand, the notion of a monarchical papacy was strengthened by the council's teaching on papal primacy, and a "creeping infallibility" developed under pressure from those who became impatient with a defined charism that was, for all practical purposes, unusable because of the careful restrictions placed upon it. Many Catholics, especially during the first half of the twentieth century and even into the long pontificate of John Paul II, assumed that every papal pronouncement was to be regarded "as if" it were infallible—a position that was unwittingly close to that of the extreme infallibilists at Vatican I.

Post–Vatican I Developments

LEO XIII'S *SATIS COGNITUM* AND *APOSTOLICAE CURAE* (1896)

More than twenty-five years after the suspension of the First Vatican Council (1870), Pope Pius IX's successor, Leo XIII (1878–1903), issued two documents—one an encyclical and the other a papal bull (so called because it is stamped with a lead seal [Lat. *bulla*])—that were indicative of his full agreement with the teaching of the council on the matter of papal primacy. In the encyclical, *Satis cognitum* ("Known enough"; in this case the English title is meaningless, but it follows the pattern of all ecclesiastical documents, whose Latin title is taken from the first two or three words of the official Latin text), Leo XIII defended the Counter-Reformation ecclesiology, which had stressed the concept of the Church as "a perfect society" (one that is self-sufficient because it possesses all of the institutional wherewithal to fulfill its essential purposes, or mission). This ecclesiology was represented especially by Robert Bellarmine (see Part III.2.15). It had also informed the thinking of Pius IX and the majority of the bishops at Vatican I. The encyclical insisted that Jesus founded one Church, namely, the Catholic Church. Those who depart from it "have left the path of salvation and are heading for destruction."[28]

Jesus instituted in this Church "a living, authentic and never-failing teaching authority" that he "endowed with His own power, and with the Spirit of Truth." The encyclical continues: "Since the divine founder of the Church decreed that it was to be one in faith, in government, and in social organization, He chose Peter and his successors to be the source and centre of this unity. . . . The episcopal order is considered to be in proper union with Peter, as Christ commanded, if it is subordinate to Peter and obeys him."[29]

Three months later, Leo XIII issued a papal bull on Anglican orders entitled *Apostolicae curae* (Lat., "Of apostolic concern"), which condemned them as "absolutely null and utterly void" on the grounds (no longer upheld by Roman Catholic theologians and ecumenists) that there was a defect in the form of the ordination ritual used by the Anglicans, because it allegedly failed to include the power to offer the eucharistic sacrifice, and also a defect in the intention of the consecrators of Matthew Parker as archbishop of Canterbury in 1559 "to do what the Church does."[30]

PIUS X'S ANTI-MODERNIST DOCUMENTS (1907, 1910)

Counter-Reformation ecclesiology continued to inform official church teachings in the anti-Modernist campaign of the early twentieth century. "Modernism" is an umbrella term, coined and applied by Pope Pius X (1903–14) and those within his curial circle, that covered a variety of theological positions alleged to have been advocated at this time. It existed as a coherent system, however, only in Pius X's 1907 encyclical letter *Pascendi Dominici gregis* (Lat., "Feeding the Lord's flock"), which called it a "synthesis of all the heresies."[31] To the extent that it was a usable term, Modernism was, instead, a general intellectual orientation on the part of those Catholics who were wrestling with new questions posed by contemporary scholarship in various fields. It is clear in hindsight that the condemnations of this so-called Modernism by both the pope and what was then known as the Holy Office (the forerunner of the Congregation for the Doctrine of the Faith) actually would have applied only to a relatively tiny group within the Church led by the English theologian George Tyrell (d. 1909). Tyrell argued that the Church, as an evolving historical community sustained by the religious experiences of its members, should be guided by free discussion among its members rather than by an ecclesiastical magisterium.

The 1907 decree of the Holy Office *Lamentabili sane exitu* (Lat., "A lamentable departure indeed") condemned sixty-five propositions associated with the pope's understanding of Modernism, some of which pertained directly to the Church. Among the condemned ecclesiological views were the following: the learning Church (*Ecclesia discens*) and the teaching Church (*Ecclesia docens*) work together in defining truths of faith, and the only function of the teaching Church, or magisterium, is to ratify generally held opinions of the learning Church (n. 6); the Church cannot demand internal consent from its members regarding the condemnation of errors (n. 7); Christ did not intend to establish the Church as a society that would last for centuries (n. 52); the organic constitution of the Church is not unchangeable, but is subject to perpetual evolution, just as human society is (n. 53); dogmas, sacraments, and hierarchy are nothing but evolutions and interpretations of Christian thought (n. 54); Peter never even suspected that Christ entrusted the primacy to him (n. 55); and the Roman church became the head of all other churches because of political conditions, not because of divine providence (n. 56).

The Oath Against Modernism, which was contained in the pontifical letter *Sacrorum antistitum* (Lat., "Presiding priest," a Ciceronian expression) in 1910, was imposed on all those about to be ordained, on clergy, new pastors and new bishops, and on theologians teaching in seminaries and other ecclesiastical institutions. The oath was suppressed by Paul VI in 1967 and replaced by a much shorter text. The original oath required the firm acceptance of each and every defined teaching of the Church and the belief that the Church was personally and directly instituted by Jesus during his lifetime on earth, that it is built upon Peter and his successors through the ages, that dogmas do not evolve, that the Church's teachings and condemnations are true and binding, and that the bishops are in a direct line of succession from the Apostles.[32]

In early 1989 and in light of canon 833 of the Revised Code of Canon Law (1983), the Congregation for the Doctrine of the Faith published an updated "Profession of Faith" (with three additional paragraphs) and an "Oath of Fidelity on Assuming an Office to Be Exercised in the Name of the Church."[33] Among the categories of persons covered are newly appointed seminary rectors, seminary professors of theology and philosophy, rectors of ecclesiastical or Catholic universities, and university teachers of disciplines dealing with faith or morals. Bishops and cardinals had already been required to take an oath of fidelity. In 1998 Pope John Paul II issued an apostolic letter, *Ad tuendam fidem* (Lat., "To defend the faith"), which added a paragraph to canon 750 of the Revised Code of Canon Law and made amendments as well to Code of Canons of the Eastern Churches "to protect the Catholic faith against errors," particularly those committed by professors of theology. The apostolic letter underlines the assent required when dealing with church teaching proposed "definitively" and provides for "just penalties" imposed on those who deny these teachings.[34] (Reference is also made to the definitiveness of church teaching in Part VII.2.5.c, Örsy on papal teaching.)

PIUS XII'S *MYSTICI CORPORIS CHRISTI* (1943)

Pope Pius XII's encyclical *Mystici Corporis Christi* (Lat., "The Mystical Body of Christ") was the most important ecclesiological document to appear in the period between the anti-Modernist campaign of

Pius X in the early twentieth century and the beginning of the Second Vatican Council in 1962. The encyclical represented the first significant shift in ecclesiology since the Counter-Reformation of the late sixteenth and early seventeenth centuries. For the first time in the modern history of the Church, a pope was rooting his teaching on the Church in Scripture, especially in the writings of St. Paul on the Church as the Body of Christ. As noted below, the encyclical qualified the Pauline image with the adjective "mystical" to distinguish it from the Eucharist and the earthly, risen, and glorified bodies of the Lord. Although a residue of a juridical understanding of the Church permeates the encyclical, it nonetheless marked a point of transition and prepared the way to some extent for the Second Vatican Council, which would take several significant leaps beyond the encyclical.

The first section focuses on the heart of the encyclical's ecclesiology, namely, its understanding of the Church as the Body of Christ. Other important ecclesiological components include its understanding of the Church as both hierarchical and charismatic and its relationship to the Holy Spirit.

The Church as Body of Christ

A revival of the theology of the Church as the Mystical Body of Christ had begun already in the 1930s with the writings of the Belgian theologian Émile Mersch (d. 1940), who retrieved the Eastern patristic tradition, especially of Cyril of Alexandria (ca. 375–444). Cyril had stressed the physical and organic union between Christ, the Head of the Church, and the members of the Church.[35] Sebastian Tromp, a Jesuit professor of ecclesiology at the Pontifical Gregorian University in Rome, also did important research on the notion of the Mystical Body in the fathers of the Church, but, as ecclesiologist Avery Dulles writes, his tendency was "to harmonize ancient Mystical Body ecclesiology with the more juridical approach current in Western Catholicism since Robert Bellarmine."[36] Bellarmine was a Counter-Reformation theologian, as previously noted in Part IV.3.1, whose influence perdured until the onset of Vatican II.

Although Pope Pius XII has remained a controversial figure because of his allegedly passive response to the Holocaust, perpetrated against six million Jews during Nazi Germany's Third Reich (1933–45) and World War II (1941–45), the pope prepared the way—wittingly or not—for the Second Vatican Council. He opened Catholic theology to the fruits of modern biblical scholarship in his 1943 encyclical *Divino afflante Spiritu* (Lat., "Inspired by the Holy Spirit"), which Catholic biblical scholars quickly dubbed the Magna Carta of Catholic biblical scholarship. He provided a major boost to the Catholic liturgical renewal with his 1947 encyclical *Mediator Dei* ("Mediator of God") and his 1956 restoration of the ancient liturgies of Holy Week. And in his 1943 encyclical *Mystici Corporis Christi,* he brought about a discernible turn away from the neo-Scholastic ecclesiology of the Counter-Reformation era[37] in favor of an ecclesiology centered on the Pauline portrayal of the Church as the Body of Christ, although not without some measure of ambivalence.[38] It is also a matter of some interest that, like *Divino afflante Spiritu, Mystici Corporis Christi* was written in the teeth of World War II and includes several oblique references to that most brutal of conflicts (see, e.g., n. 108).

The encyclical insists, citing Leo XIII's *Satis cognitum,* that the Church is a visible reality because it is a body. It is an error, Pius XII pointed out, to imagine the Church to be "invisible, intangible, a something merely 'pneumatological'" (n. 14).[39] The Mystical Body, which the encyclical distinguishes from Jesus's earthly body, his risen and glorified body, and his eucharistic body (n. 60), is analogous to a human body, where all the parts work together as one for the good of the whole. But it is more than a body. It is the Body of Jesus Christ, who is "the Founder, the Head, the Support and the Savior of this Mystical Body" (nn. 25, 69). It is a Body in which the union of all the faithful with Christ is paramount (nn. 71–83), and their union is supremely manifested and realized in the Eucharist (nn. 82–83), which is "a striking and wonderful figure of the unity of the Church" (n. 83).

The Church as Hierarchical and Charismatic

It is of great significance that the encyclical rejects both ecclesiological extremes: "One must not think, however, that this ordered or 'organic' structure of the Body of the Church contains only hierarchical elements and with them is complete; or, as an opposite opinion holds, that it is composed only of those who enjoy charismatic gifts" (n. 17). Indeed, Pius XII deplores and condemns "the pernicious error of those who dream of an imaginary Church, a kind of society that finds its origin and growth in charity, to which, somewhat contemptuously, they oppose another, which they call juridical" (n. 65). He continues in the same paragraph: "There can, then, be no real opposition or conflict between the invisible mission of the Holy Spirit and the juridical commission of Ruler and Teacher received from Christ, since they mutually complement and perfect each other—as do the body and soul in man—and proceed from our one Redeemer."

While emphasizing that "those who exercise sacred power in this Body are its chief members," the encyclical points out that the Church also includes everyone else, namely, those who exercise a variety of ministries, hold a diversity of offices, and have a number of different responsibilities, both within and outside religious communities. Parents too "occupy an honorable, if often a lowly place in the Christian community." Moreover, they can "reach the heights of supreme holiness," which "will never be wanting to the Church" (n. 17).

The Church and the Holy Spirit

Such holiness rests upon the foundation of Christ (n. 98), who is the Head of the Church (nn. 19, 25, 30, 31, 34, and passim), and upon the sacramental life he bequeathed to it (nn. 18–19). He "shares His most personal prerogatives with the Church in such a way that she may portray in her whole life, both external and interior, a most faithful image of Christ.... It is He Who through the Church baptizes, teaches, rules, looses, binds, offers, sacrifices" (n. 54). We have here a tentative anticipation of the sacramentality of the Church itself, a notion that surfaced just prior to the Second Vatican Council in the works of Otto Semmelroth (d. 1979), Karl Rahner (d. 1984), and Edward Schillebeeckx, culminating in the council's Dogmatic Constitution on the Church: "The church, in Christ, is a sacrament—a sign and instrument, that is, of communion with God and of the unity of the entire human race" (n. 1).

"If we examine closely this divine principle of life and power given by Christ," the encyclical declares, "in so far as it constitutes the very source of every gift and created grace, we easily see that it is nothing else than the Holy Spirit" (n. 56). Pius XII continues: "To this Spirit of Christ, also, as to an invisible principle is to be ascribed the fact that all the parts of the Body are joined one with the other and with their exalted Head, entire in the Body and entire in each of the members" (n. 57).[40] This is one of the most significant and far-sighted statements in the entire encyclical, running directly contrary to the common view at the time that the Spirit is present only in the hierarchy and that the hierarchy alone is guided by it. Later in the passage, Pius XII quotes his predecessor Leo XIII, who in his 1897 encyclical letter *Divinum illud munus* (Lat., "This divine function") referred to Christ as the Head of the Church and to the Holy Spirit as its soul (n. 57). It is both Christ and the Spirit who are the sources of holiness in the Church. And the Church itself is composed of all the baptized: "He has purchased with His Blood His members, *who constitute the Church*" (n. 59, italics mine).

The Pope and the Other Bishops

Although Peter and his successors in the primacy are Vicars of Christ, the Church has only one Head, namely, Christ. After his glorious Ascension into heaven, however, "this Church rested not on Him alone, but on Peter too, its visible foundation stone. That Christ and His Vicar constitute only one Head is the solemn teaching of Our predecessor of immortal memory Boniface VIII [1295–1303] in the Apostolic Letter *Unam Sanctam;* and his successors have never ceased to repeat the same" (n. 40). They "walk in the path of dangerous error" who claim to accept Christ as the Head of the Church while rejecting his Vicar on earth (n. 41).

Bishops, in turn, "must be considered as the more illustrious members of the Universal Church," and each one is "a true Shepherd [who] feeds the flock entrusted to him and rules it in the name of Christ" (n. 42). Such shepherds, however, are "not altogether independent, but are subordinate to the lawful authority of the Roman Pontiff, although enjoying the ordinary power of jurisdiction which they receive directly from the same Supreme Pontiff" (n. 42). These words, of course, were written some two decades before Vatican II's

Dogmatic Constitution on the Church and its teaching on episcopal collegiality (see Part V).

"The One, True Church"

The encyclical makes clear that the contours of this Mystical Body encompass only Catholics: "Only those are to be included as members of the Church who have been baptized and profess the true faith and who have not been so unfortunate as to separate themselves from the unity of the Body or been excluded by legitimate authority for grave faults committed" (n. 22). As we shall see in due course, when this position was taken to its logical extreme, "Outside the Church, no salvation," by Father Leonard Feeney, S.J. (d. 1978), the Vatican was compelled to make a distinction between actual membership (Lat. *in re,* or *reapse*) and membership by desire (*inscio quodam desiderio ac voto*), which served to broaden the scope and salvific outreach of the Church. Even the encyclical seems to have partially anticipated this move in acknowledging that individuals can have "a certain relationship with the Mystical Body of the Redeemer" by "an unconscious desire and longing" (n. 103). Vatican II would later set aside the category of membership entirely in favor of "degrees of communion" (see Part I.2.5).

The encyclical also anticipated the teaching of the council's Declaration on Religious Freedom, insisting that if "anyone is compelled to embrace the Catholic faith against his will, Our sense of duty demands that We condemn the act. For men [and women] must be effectively drawn to the truth by the Father of light through the spirit of His beloved Son" (n. 104). Nevertheless, a spirit of triumphalism permeates the encyclical's final "Exhortation to Love the Church" (nn. 91–100). Nothing, Pius XII writes, is "more glorious, nothing nobler, nothing surely more honorable can be imagined than to belong to the One, Holy Catholic, Apostolic, and *Roman* Church" (n. 91, italics mine).[41]

But, again, whatever the encyclical's deficiencies by present-day standards, it did mark the tentative beginning of the transition from the prevailing neo-Scholastic, Counter-Reformation ecclesiology to one more biblically based and more open to the role of the Holy

Spirit in its life and mission. This transition would become more fully developed at the Second Vatican Council, and it continues even to this day.

THE HOLY OFFICE AND THE FATHER FEENEY CASE (1949)

Father Leonard Feeney, S.J, chaplain to Catholic students at Harvard University and based at St. Benedict's Center in Cambridge, Massachusetts, took the medieval axiom formulated by Pope Boniface VIII, "Outside the Church, no salvation" (Lat. *Extra Ecclesiam nulla salus*), to an extreme, arguing that only Catholics can be saved and, in effect, placing all non-Catholic Christians in the same moral category as non-Christians and nonbelievers. Since the controversy had erupted in the archdiocese of Boston and since Father Feeney's followers, who called themselves the Slaves of the Immaculate Heart of Mary, were applying pressure directly upon Archbishop Richard J. Cushing (d. 1970), the archbishop appealed to Rome for assistance. The assistance came in the form of a letter from the Holy Office to the archbishop of Boston, dated August 8, 1949.

While emphasizing the ancient doctrine that the Church is necessary for salvation, it clarified the meaning of this doctrine for each and every individual. To be sure, if one is to be saved, one must be related in some way to the Church. Actual membership, however, is not absolutely required. One can be related to the Church by desire, which may be explicit in the case of catechumens or implicit in the case of the great majority of humankind who are outside the Church, but who are nonetheless persons of goodwill. If they knew of God's intentions for their salvation within the context of the Church, they would join the Church. But they are ignorant of its role in salvation.

Their ignorance can be, in turn, invincible or vincible. If invincible, that is, beyond their ability to dispel it, the ignorance of the true Church is not culpable. If vincible, that is, if the ignorance could be overcome with some reasonable effort, the ignorance is culpable. Those in the latter category of vincible ignorance suspect that God's will for them is to enter the Church, but like ill people who resist going to the doctor for fear of what they might learn about the true state of their health and what would be required to improve it, they remain in deliberate ignorance. However, the Holy Office letter insists that "no one who knows that the Church has been divinely established by Christ and, nevertheless, refuses to be a subject of the Church or refuses to obey the Roman Pontiff, the vicar of Christ on earth, will be saved."[42]

The Holy Office letter reaffirms the traditional teaching of the Church on the necessity of the Church for salvation, but insists that "this dogma is to be understood as the Church itself understands it." The letter teaches that it is possible for someone who is not an actual member of the Church to be saved if the helps provided by God "are used only in desire and longing." Thus, "To gain eternal salvation it is not always required that a person be incorporated in reality [*reapse*] as a member of the Church, but it is required that one belong to it at least in desire and longing [*voto et desiderio*]. It is not always necessary," the Holy Office letter continues, "that this desire be explicit, as it is with catechumens. When one is invincibly ignorant, God also accepts an implicit desire, so called because it is contained in the good disposition of soul by which a person wants his or her will to be conformed to God's will." The letter cites Pius XII's *Mystici Corporis Christi* in support of its teaching. (Pertinent passages from the encyclical have been cited above.)

According to the letter, "With these prudent words the Pope censures those who exclude from eternal salvation all those who adhere to the Church only with an implicit desire, and he also censures those who falsely maintain that people can be saved equally well in any religion." The latter position is known as religious indifferentism. The implicit desire, however, must always be "informed with perfect charity" and faith. That faith too can be implicit.

Father Feeney was dismissed from the Society of Jesus and excommunicated from the Church in 1953 for refusing, in effect, to recant his strict interpretation of the medieval axiom. Pope Paul VI lifted the excommunication prior to Feeney's death in 1978, at the urging of the cardinal-archbishop of Boston, Humberto Medeiros (d. 1983). Some commentators said at the time that Cardinal Medeiros was himself sympathetic to Leonard Feeney's ecclesiology, which may be why he readmitted Father Feeney to the Church without requiring him to make a public retraction of his beliefs or teachings. Medeiros's predecessor, Cardinal Cushing, had taken tongue-in-cheek pride in the fact that he would always be a footnote in Catholic theology because of the letter of the Holy Office to the archbishop of Boston, which also came to be known simply as the Cushing Letter.

PIUS XII'S *HUMANI GENERIS* (1950)

Apart from the reaffirmation of the teaching in *Mystici Corporis Christi* that "the Mystical Body of Christ and the Roman [*sic*] Catholic Church are one and the same thing" (n. 27), the ecclesiological content of the encyclical *Humani generis* (Lat., "Of the human race") was mainly limited to the role theologians are expected to play in the life of the Church. The encyclical as a whole was designed to address the problem of the so-called *nouvelle théologie* (Fr., "new theology") in post–World War II France, particularly with regard to original sin (some theologians allegedly denied that it was a sin inherited from a historical person, namely, Adam) and the supernatural order (some theologians were accused of erasing the distinction between it and the natural order). Among the implied targets of the encyclical were two French theologians who later took a decisive turn in a conservative direction and were created cardinals: Henri de Lubac, S.J. (d. 1991) and Jean Daniélou (d. 1974).

When the popes "carefully pronounce on some subject which has hitherto been controverted," the encyclical declared, "it is obvious that that matter, according to the mind and will of the Pontiffs, cannot be any longer considered a question open to discussion among theologians" (n. 20).[43] By clear implication, this meant that every papal pronouncement, particularly through the vehicle of an encyclical letter, is to be regarded as definitive, a term that is equivalent in many minds to "infallible."

"It is also true that theologians must always return to the sources of divine revelation: for it belongs to them to point out how the doctrine of the living Teaching Authority is to be found either explicitly or implicitly in the Scriptures and in Tradition" (n. 21). Again, there is a clear implication that the role of a Catholic theologian is mainly to find support for official teachings that have already been formulated and proclaimed. There is little room for a critical function generally, much less for public disagreement with a papal pronouncement of any kind. More than a decade before the opening of Vatican II and long before disagreement with the hierarchical magisterium became at least an occasional occurrence, theologians expressed considerable concern regarding the content, tone, and implications of this encyclical.[44]

Pre–Vatican II Ecclesiology

Catholic and non-Catholic theology moved along parallel paths in the decades prior to the Second Vatican Council. Catholics, on the one hand, and Protestants, Anglicans, Orthodox, and other separated Eastern Christians, on the other, generally did not read one another's writings. Catholic students of theology (mostly in seminaries) were warned against reading works by non-Catholic authors. In ecumenically advanced courses, where the books and articles of non-Catholic authors were included in the bibliographies, non-Catholic works would be marked by an asterisk, which served the purpose of a "Proceed with Caution" sign. It was not until the council was already under way that the practice of reading one another's theology became more common.

What follows is a survey of that pre–Vatican II ecclesiological landscape, given in three parts: first, Protestant and Anglican ecclesiologies that anticipated, at least indirectly, the advances made by the council as well as related developments in Catholic theology; second, Catholic ecclesiologies that prepared the way for Vatican II and were eventually embraced as the operative ecclesiology of the council; and, third, traditional, neo-Scholastic Catholic ecclesiologies that were encased in the manuals of theology (Latin textbooks in wide use at the time in Catholic seminaries and pontifical universities) and in various monographs written largely in English, French, and German rather than in Latin. Progressive pre–Vatican II ecclesiologists, like Yves Congar, viewed the Church as a historical, dynamic community, while the Latin manuals, as we shall see below, understood the Church as a static, juridical institution.

PROTESTANT AND ANGLICAN ECCLESIOLOGIES

Dietrich Bonhoeffer

The world had "come of age," Dietrich Bonhoeffer (d. 1945) wrote in his celebrated *Letters and Papers from Prison,* published after his execution at the hands of the Nazis just before the end of World War II.[45] In his key letter of April 30, 1944, he posed two questions: "How can Christ become the Lord even of those with no religion?" and "What is the significance of a Church . . . in a religionless world; . . . in what way are we the *Ekklesia,* 'those who are called forth,' not conceiving of ourselves religiously as specially favored, but as wholly belonging to the world?"

"God," he wrote, "is the 'beyond' in the midst of our life. The Church stands not where human powers give out, on the borders, but in the center of the village." And in "An Outline for a Book," published as an appendix to the *Letters and Papers* and delineating a book he never lived to write, he insisted that the "Church is her true self only when she exists for humanity." Just as Christ was "the man for others," so the Church "must tell men [and women], whatever their calling, what it means to live in Christ, to exist for others." The Church must be, like Christ himself, a servant, and a suffering servant at that.

It is not surprising that Bonhoeffer, though a Lutheran, had enormous appeal, posthumously, to Catholics—an appeal that grew when his more spiritually oriented writings were published.[46] Bonhoeffer's approach was at once sacramental and mediatory. God is present in the neighbor in need, and the Church is called to a life of service on behalf of that neighbor.

John A. T. Robinson

Bonhoeffer's insights were taken up in the early and mid-1960s by the Anglican theologian John A. T. Robinson (d. 1983), bishop of the suffragan see of Woolwich in South London. His ideas were initially expressed in his extraordinarily popular little book *Honest to God,*[47] but he developed and modified the ecclesiological portion of that book in a sequel, *The New Reformation?* The role of the Church, he wrote, is to strip Christ of his incognitos and allow him to be known again in the gracious neighbor and in the gracious community, in release for prisoners and recovery of sight for the blind (Luke 4:18), even if they never say, "Lord, Lord."[48]

The key ecclesiological premise in Robinson's writings is that the Church must always be seen in the context of its subordinate relationship to the Kingdom of God. "The Church," he writes, "stands between the Kingdom accomplished and the Kingdom acknowledged."[49] Thus, Robinson's ecclesiological formula: Have as high a doctrine of ministry as you like, so long as your doctrine of the Church is higher; and have as high a doctrine of the Church as you like, so long as your doctrine of the Kingdom is higher.[50] "We shall not get our theology of the Church and the Ministry right until we get our eschatology right."[51] At this time, however, Catholic ecclesiology did not have a similarly broad eschatological outlook. On the contrary, Catholic theologians and preachers generally regarded the Kingdom of God as an image or even a synonym for the Church, which Vatican II would later criticize as a form of triumphalism and then correct in article 5 of its Dogmatic Constitution on the Church (see Part V).

But Robinson always retained a high doctrine of the Church. It was not only a servant community in subordination to the Kingdom of God; it was also "the carrier now of the Divine glory (*endoxon*)." "Nothing," therefore, "could be more exalted than the doctrine of the Church which the New Testament presents—indeed it is impossible to be a biblical theologian without being a high Churchman."[52] Robinson, himself a New Testament scholar, laid the foundations for this high-church position in his widely respected book *The Body: A Study in Pauline Theology,*[53] in which he rejected a metaphorical interpretation of Paul's identification of the Church with the body of Christ. On the contrary, he argued, "It is almost impossible to exaggerate the materialism and crudity of Paul's doctrine of the Church as literally now the resurrection *body* of Christ."[54] And what stamps the

Church as an eschatological community is "its common possession of the Spirit . . . that enables those who are in the Body of Christ to participate already, in this age, in the resurrection mode of existence."[55]

Harvey Cox

For the American Baptist Harvey Cox, a longtime member of the faculty at the Harvard Divinity School, the Church is an agent of God's revolutionary activity in the world with a threefold missionary function. The Church must be *kerygmatic* (the revolution—the coming of the Kingdom of God—is already under way; the pivotal battle has been fought and won by Jesus Christ; the Church must seize the centers of communication and broadcast the overthrow of the old regime and the establishment of the new); *diakonic* (the Church must begin distributing the benefits of God's revolution in the manner of the good Samaritan); and *koinoniac* (the Church must be a kind of "model city"—a popular political term in the United States in the mid-1960s—to serve as a demonstration community, or what Catholics would call a sacrament of Christ's presence and redemptive activity).[56]

Like Bishop Robinson, Cox situated the Church within a broader eschatological context. The doctrine of the Church is "a secondary and derivative aspect" of the need to bring about the Kingdom of God. Adapting the thought of a contemporary writer, Archie Hargraves, Cox compared the Kingdom to a "floating crap game" and the Church to a "compulsive gambler" who needs to be "where the action is."[57]

"Death of God" Theologians

An even more radical approach to the Church—and to the God question that lay at its foundation—developed in the early 1960s among a small group of younger American Protestant theologians. They were influenced in one way or another by a variety of sources, including one of the twentieth century's most influential Protestant theologians, Karl Barth (d. 1968), the playwright Samuel Beckett (d. 1989), author of *Waiting for Godot,* the celebrated German philosopher Georg W. F. Hegel (d. 1831), and the contemporary English poet

William Blake (d. 1827). The group, consisting for the most part of only three scholars, Thomas J. J. Altizer, William Hamilton, and Paul Van Buren, who came to be labeled "death of God" theologians, even though the terms were contradictory, given the fact that theology is by definition the study of God. The fledgling movement at first attracted wide media attention, but then almost as quickly faded from sight, giving way to the theology of hope, embodied in a major work of the same title by the German theologian Jürgen Moltmann.[58] The widely respected Protestant ecumenist Robert McAfee Brown (d. 2001) had provided a prescient review, an excerpt of which was reproduced on the cover of the "death of God" trio's signature book, Thomas J. J. Altizer's *The Gospel of Christian Atheism*. "It is not a gospel; . . . it is not Christian; . . . and it is not atheism," Brown wrote. "In an attempt to celebrate 'the death of God,' this book succeeds only in demonstrating the death of the 'death-of-God-theology.'"

These "death of God" theologians, especially Altizer and Hamilton, thought Dietrich Bonhoeffer too moderate in his views. "The call for a 'religionless Christianity,'" Altizer wrote in his *The Gospel of Christian Atheism*, "can mean nothing less than this, nor can it have any real meaning apart from a resolution to abandon the whole religious body of Christianity, even if that body should prove to comprehend very nearly everything which Christianity once knew as faith."[59] His antipathy to the specifically Catholic understanding of Christianity was more evident in his earlier work, *Oriental Mysticism and Biblical Eschatology*, in which he asserted that "the transition from primitive Jewish Christianity to the Hellenistic Catholic Church marks the abandonment of the church's charismatic quality as well as of its eschatological message."[60] Hamilton had made a similar observation in *Radical Theology and the Death of God,* coauthored by Altizer: "I do not see how preaching, worship, prayer, ordination, the sacraments can be taken seriously by the radical theologian."[61]

Paul Van Buren, the theological moderate of the original trio of "death of God" theologians, saw a place for the Church, but not as the Body of Christ in the sense that John A. T. Robinson understood St. Paul's portrayal of it. For Van Buren, "body of Christ" is "obviously not a description. It is a reference to the historical perspective which the members presumably have in common, and it suggests the harmony that would exist between people who shared this perspective."[62] The mission of the individual Christian—and, by extension, the Church—is to be at the side of Jesus in the service of the neighbor, not to make the neighbor Christian but to serve the neighbor. "His mission is simply to be a man, as this is defined by Jesus of Nazareth."[63] The emphasis here was clearly on the social mission of the Church.

PROGRESSIVE CATHOLIC ECCLESIOLOGIES

Karl Rahner

Although the principal theological contributions of Karl Rahner (d. 1984) were not in the area of ecclesiology, he too prepared the way for the Second Vatican Council. Among his key ecclesiological insights was the idea of the Church as a diaspora community. The Church exists in the world as a "scattered" community and everywhere as a minority (with some exceptions, such as the Iberian peninsula: Spain and Portugal). As previously noted, Rahner adapted a saying of St. Augustine, found in his homily on Baptism: "Many whom God has, the Church does not have; and many whom the Church has, God does not have" (see Part III.2.6.b).[64] In other words, there are many in the Kingdom (doing the will of God, knowingly or not) who are not in the Church, and many in the Church (confessing the Lordship of Jesus) who are not in the Kingdom. Where is it said, Rahner asks, that the Church must have the whole 100 percent? God must have all.

He noted that some events in the history of salvation "ought not" to be, but are and "must" be so (e.g., the crucifixion of Jesus). The minority, diaspora condition of the Church is one of those "musts" of salvation history. It is a situation not only permitted by God, but positively willed by God for reasons beyond our understanding. But we must draw our conclusions from this. It means that the Church is no longer "in possession" and cannot act as if it were. The age of Christendom is over. The Church must attract people to itself on the basis of free choice rather than social and cultural convention or in response to political pressure. Those who belong to the Church must do so as a matter of personal conviction, not simply of habit.

But is the Church's minority status not a countersign of God's will on behalf of the Church? Rahner reminds us that beginnings are often disappointingly meager, a point that Yves Congar also made (see Part IV.4.2.f). St. Benedict of Nursia (d. ca. 550) did not know that he was founding a new Western civilization when he went out with a few monks to reestablish monasticism on Monte Cassino. In the diaspora situation, Rahner argued, the initiative can still be the Church's, if Christians are Christian by faith and conviction rather than by cultural or political attachments.[65]

Another of Rahner's pre–Vatican II ecclesiological insights, contained in his exceedingly important book *The Church and the Sacraments,* is that the Church itself is a sacrament—the *fundamental* sacrament of Christ, who is, in turn, the *primordial* sacrament of God's saving presence and redemptive activity on our behalf: "Viewed in relation to Christ, the Church is the abiding promulgation of his grace-giving presence in the world. Viewed in relation to the sacraments, the Church is the primal and fundamental sacrament."[66]

Edward Schillebeeckx

Edward Schillebeeckx, a Belgian Dominican theologian who spent most of his academic career in the Netherlands at the University of Nijmegen, first became known internationally because of his major pre–Vatican II work *Christ, the Sacrament of the Encounter with God,* first published in Dutch in 1960.[67] Schillebeeckx argued that apart from the sacramental principle, there is no basis for contact (encounter) between God and humanity. God is totally spiritual, and we are bodily creatures. Thus, it is only insofar as God adapts to our material condition that God can encounter us and we can encounter God. The embodiment of the spiritual in the material and the communication of the spiritual through the material is, in essence, the sacramental principle. Christ is the great sacrament of God, because God addresses us through the humanity of Christ and we respond through the same humanity of Christ. The influential Latin father of the Church Tertullian referred to the humanity of Christ as the *cardo salutis* (Lat., "the hinge of salvation").[68]

The Church, in turn, is the sacrament of Christ, who otherwise would be removed from our range of daily, bodily existence. The seven sacraments are, finally, the principal ways by which the Church communicates the reality of Christ and of God and by which we respond to Christ and to God in discipleship and worship. The essence of the Church, therefore, "consists in this, that the final goal of grace achieved by Christ becomes visibly present in the *whole* Church as a visible society."[69] The Church is not only a means of salvation; it is the principal sign, or sacrament, of salvation. It is not only an institution, but also and foremost a community. Better still, it is an institutionalized community. The important missionary implication is not whether the whole world eventually enters the Church, but whether the Church itself gives credible and compelling witness to the presence and redemptive activity of Christ and of the triune God within the human community.[70]

Henri de Lubac

A similarly sacramental perspective was advanced, although in less substantive fashion, by the French Jesuit Henri de Lubac (d. 1991) in his *Catholicism: A Study of Dogma in Relation to the Corporate Destiny of Mankind.* "Humanity is one, organically one by its divine structure," he writes. "It is the Church's mission to reveal to [humankind] that pristine unity that they have lost, to restore and complete it." The Church is "not merely that strongly hierarchical and disciplined society whose divine origin has to be maintained. . . . If Christ is the sacrament of God, the Church is for us the sacrament of Christ." Indeed, "it is through [his or her] union with the community that the Christian is united to Christ."[71]

Hans Küng

The Swiss theologian Hans Küng, who has spent almost all of his academic career in Germany at the University of Tübingen, was only thirty-three years old when he published his *The Council and Reunion.* It was perhaps the single most influential book in Vatican II's preparatory phase, because it alerted so many in the Catholic world to the possibilities for renewal and reform through the medium of the forthcoming council. For Küng, quoting the German theologian Michael Schmaus (d. 1993), the Church is "the People of God of the New Testament, founded by Jesus Christ, hierarchically organized, serving to advance the reign of God and the salvation of men [*sic*]; and which exists as the mystical body of Christ." "Renewal and reform of the Church," Küng continued, "are permanently necessary because the Church consists, first, of human beings, and, secondly, of sinful human beings."[72]

Although Küng's book is remarkably comprehensive in its proposed conciliar agenda, its basic ecclesiological point is that "the chief difficulty in the way of reunion lies in the two different concepts of the Church, and especially of the concrete organizational structure of the Church."[73] Non-Catholic Christians tend to look askance at a highly centralized authority that leaves too little room for diversity and freedom of conscience. Catholics, on the other hand, have tended to be more comfortable with the functioning of a hierarchy that bears much of the pastoral weight in the governance of the Church. For Küng, the difference between these two concepts is most sharply focused in the matter of ecclesiastical offices: their origins, powers, scope of authority, and forms. The central question concerns the papacy: "Do we need a pope?" Küng noted that Pope John XXIII, then still in office, was creating for the papacy a whole new style and perhaps in the process eliminating or diminishing many of the historic objections to the office from the Protestant side. Almost all of the reforms Küng advocated were eventually adopted, for example, the establishment of national episcopal conferences, the abolition of the Index of Forbidden Books, and the simplification of the liturgy.

John Courtney Murray

John Courtney Murray, S.J. (d. 1967), was perhaps the most respected theologian in the United States in the mid-twentieth century. A longtime professor at the Jesuit theologate in Woodstock, Maryland, he was a *peritus* (Lat., "expert") at the Second Vatican Council and is generally regarded as the chief architect of its Declaration on Religious Freedom (*Dignitatis humanae*). Although he was not a specialist in ecclesiology, his best-known writings touched on the relationship between Church and state and the correlative question of religious liberty.[74] Not invited to the first session of the council because of his controversial views on both subjects, Murray was brought to the second session as a personal *peritus* to Cardinal Francis Spellman (d. 1967), archbishop of New York.

Murray's preconciliar contributions to the discussion of the Church-and-state relationship and religious freedom were done through scholarly articles in the Jesuit quarterly *Theological Studies*, in which he subjected certain traditional teachings, especially those of Pope Leo XIII, to careful historical and theological reinterpretation.[75] He argued not that the Leonine doctrine was false, but that it was archaic because it was based on a paternalistic rather than a constitutional concept of political authority. Leo's teachings were also formulated in the context of the Continental laicist state, and Leo confused society with the state just as they were confused in the philosophies of so-called pagan antiquity. Murray argued that, given developments in Catholic social philosophy and in the political character of much of the modern world, the Leonine teachings can no longer hold. (For further elaboration of Pope Leo XIII's teaching on Church and state, see Part VI.5.2.)

The fruits of Murray's efforts were realized in the council's Declaration on Religious Freedom, which ended the so-called double standard by which the Catholic Church demanded freedom for itself when in a minority position, but refused to acknowledge the same right for other Christian denominations or non-Christian religions when the Catholic Church is in a politically dominant situation. The conciliar decree declared as a matter of principle that the dignity of the human person and the freedom of the act of faith demand that everyone should be immune from coercion of every kind, private or public, in matters pertaining to the profession of a particular religious faith (n. 2). No one can be compelled to accept the Christian faith, nor can anyone be penalized in any way for not being a Christian or even a religious person (n. 9).

In his commentary on the conciliar documents he placed particular emphasis on article 76 of the Pastoral Constitution on the

Church in the Modern World, to which we shall return in Part V. The council's teaching had been anticipated and then formulated by Murray himself, including its insistence that the Church cannot be "identified with any political community nor . . . tied to any political system" (para. 2). Indeed, Church and state are "autonomous and independent of each other in their own fields" (para. 3). The Church has a role to play in society and in the political order when issues touch upon fundamental human rights or the salvation of souls, but it should never expect or accept privileges accorded to it by civil society, lest they compromise the credibility of its witness (para. 5).[76]

Yves Congar

French Dominican theologian Yves Congar (d. 1995), created a cardinal by Pope John Paul II in 1994, a year before his death, was the most important ecclesiologist in the twentieth century and probably in the entire history of the Church. No theologian contributed more to the success of the Second Vatican Council than Congar. Indeed, the council's major ecclesiological themes were already anticipated in various of his writings.

There were at least six major components of his ecclesiological approach: (1) The Church is the People of God. The laity as well as the clergy and religious are called to full participation in the Church's life, mission, and ministries (see his *Lay People in the Church*). (2) The hierarchy exists to serve the Church, not to dominate it (see his *Power and Poverty in the Church*). (3) The Church is a minority in the service of the majority. It exists in itself, but not for itself. It prepares the way, like the French underground of the 1940s, for the coming of the Kingdom of God (see his *The Wide World, My Parish*). (4) The Church must always be engaged in institutional and communal renewal and reform, in both head and members (see his *Vraie et Fausse Réforme dans l'Église*). (5) The Church is a communion in which structures are only a means to enable the Church to fulfill its mission (see his *The Mystery of the Temple*). (6) The Church is ecumenical in nature and scope (see his *Divided Christendom*).[77]

Avery Dulles, a thoroughly sympathetic commentator on Congar's writings, has nevertheless acknowledged that, without prejudice to

Congar's later works, "one must say that these early works embody his major insights. . . . Committed to the movement of *ressourcement* [Fr., "return to the sources"], Congar sought to reclaim for ecclesiology the experience of the first millennium, when the Church did not as yet dominate by its massive power."[78] During this early period, Congar argued, the Church practiced a more intense spirituality and was more open to conversion and reform. Congar looked upon institutional structures and offices as mere means to facilitate the actions of the Holy Spirit and the dimensions of interiority, and this eventually gave rise to an ecclesiology of communion a few decades later. In the end, Congar preferred to define the Church, as the Fathers did, as a community in the Spirit, a *congregatio fidelium* (Lat., "congregation of the faithful"). Indeed, his last major work, in three volumes, was *I Believe in the Holy Spirit.*[79]

One cannot conclude this summary analysis of Congar's pre–Vatican II ecclesiology without making some reference to the painful experiences he suffered in his dealings with the Vatican, and specifically the Holy Office (the forerunner of the Congregation for the Doctrine of the Faith) under the direction of its prefect, Cardinal Alfredo Ottaviani (d. 1979). These are detailed in his diary for the years 1946–56, published posthumously and as yet untranslated.[80] A much shorter version of this diary serves as the preface to his book *Dialogue Between Christians: Catholic Contributions to Ecumenism.*[81] His works were withdrawn from circulation (*Vraie et Fausse Réforme dans l'Église*); he was prohibited from revising previously published books (*Chrétiens désunis*) and then was denied the right to continue teaching and lecturing, especially on ecumenical topics, and attending ecumenical conferences. He was exiled from the Dominican theologate, Le Saulchoir, to England and then to the Holy Land, where, at the Dominican *École Biblique,* he wrote his *Mystery of the Temple.* The death of Pope Pius XII in 1958 and the subsequent election of John XXIII brought this period of persecution to an end, and Congar became a major force at the Second Vatican Council; then, as noted above, was created a cardinal by John Paul II in 1994. By this time, however, he was too ill to travel to Rome for the consistory and was given his red hat in the chapel of Les Invalides (hospital) in Paris, where he was confined until his death the following year.

THE ECCLESIOLOGY OF THE MANUALS

First, a pedagogical point. This section has been deliberately placed at the end of the survey of pre–Vatican II ecclesiologies in order to highlight the contrast between the prevailing, quasi-official ecclesiology of the Latin manuals in use in seminaries and pontifical universities at the time and the ecclesiological achievements of the Second Vatican Council itself. To be sure, the preceding section on progressive Catholic ecclesiologies could just as appropriately been placed at the end of this survey in order to make the point that the council was the culmination of ecclesiological trends already evident in the decades immediately preceding Vatican II. It is simply a judgment call to have organized the material as we have done here. As noted above, whereas progressive Catholic ecclesiology just prior to the council presented the Church as a historical, dynamic community, the Latin manuals presented it as a static, juridical institution. Vatican II clearly reflected the former approach.

The Spanish Summa: *Joachim Salaverri*

Nowhere is the traditional pre–Vatican II ecclesiology more clearly set forth than in Joachim Salaverri's "*De Ecclesia Christi*" (Lat., "On the Church of Christ") in the first volume of the "Spanish *Summa,*" so called because the four-volume work was produced by the Jesuit theological faculty at the University of Salamanca in Spain.[82] The tract's central ecclesiological assumptions are evident in the way in which the material is organized. Indeed, organization is the first and fundamental act of interpretation. An ecclesiology textbook that begins with papal infallibility, for example, reflects one basic understanding of the Church; a work that begins, as Vatican II's Dogmatic Constitution on the Church does, with the Church as mystery, signals a very different approach.

It is of much significance, therefore, that the Salaverri tract on the Church, which is divided into three main parts, or books, begins with the Church's social constitution. Its content immediately becomes clear. Chapter 1 of book I is "On the Institution of a Hierarchical Church," which includes thesis 3: "Christ conferred on the Apostles the power of ruling, teaching, and sanctifying, to which he obliged everyone to submit themselves: consequently, he is the author of a hierarchical society, which he called the Church."[83] It is of some significance that the "ruling" power comes first here, whereas the more common listing places "teaching" first.

According to chapter 2 of book I of the Spanish *Summa,* this hierarchical society is also monarchical. The chapter focuses on the primacy promised and conferred on Simon Peter, who is the Vicar of Christ and to whom all of the other Apostles are subject (arts. 1–3). Chapter 3 is on the permanence of the Church, specifically its hierarchy and papal primacy (art. 1). The bishops are the successors of the Apostles (art. 2), and the Roman Pontiffs [*sic*] succeed St. Peter in the primacy. Thesis 10, article 4, is especially revealing of the manual's prevailing ecclesiology: "The primatial power of the Supreme Pontiff is universal, ordinary, immediate, truly episcopal, supreme and full, and no other power on earth is superior to its judgment." The conclusion of book I baldly asserts: "The Roman Catholic Church alone is the true Church of Christ." We have already referred to the encyclicals of Pius XII, *Mystici Corporis Christi* and *Humani generis* (in Part IV.3.3 and 3.5), which, in effect, dechurchified millions of non-Roman, non-Latin-rite Catholics all around the Catholic world.

Book II is "On the Magisterium of the Church and Its Sources." Chapter 1 is devoted to the "divine institution" of the magisterium. Chapter 2 addresses the matter of the magisterium's infallibility, focusing in sequence on the infallibility of the bishops, whether teaching within or outside of an ecumenical council and always under the Roman Pontiff (art. 1), on the infallibility of the pope, or Supreme Pontiff (art. 2), and on the "merely authentic," that is, official, teachings of the Holy See, to which every Catholic is bound to give "internal and religious assent" (art. 3).

Chapter 3 of book II is on the "object" of the infallible magisterium. The primary object are truths that are per se revealed (art. 1); the secondary object are truths that are necessarily connected with truths that are per se revealed (art. 2). Chapter 4 is on the sources of the magisterium, which include the deposit of faith and revelation given through Scripture and Tradition (arts. 1–2). Chapter 5 is on the criteria of "divine Tradition." These include the consensus of the Fathers (art. 1) and, significantly, the consensus of theologians (art. 2). There are various appendices or corollaries, known as "scholia," one of which concerns the relative authority of various types of church teachings.

Finally, in book III, "On the Supernatural Nature and Properties of the Church," the tract touches upon the noninstitutional, nonorganizational aspects of the Church. Chapter 1 refers to the supernaturality and "eminence" of the Church. Thesis 22 points out that the purpose of the Church is the supernatural sanctification or salvation of humankind. Thesis 23, however, is utterly characteristic of the neo-Scholastic ecclesiology of the period: "The Church is a perfect and absolutely independent society, with full legislative, judicial, and coercive [*sic*] power." Chapter 2 is on the Church as the Mystical Body of Christ, whose "quasi-soul" is the Holy Spirit (art. 1). One becomes a member of the Church through valid Baptism (art. 2) and forfeits that membership by heresy, apostasy, schism, or excommunication (art. 3). However, sanctity and predestination to glory do not in themselves constitute one as a member of the Church (art. 4). The Church is necessary for the salvation of all, even by a "necessity of means" (art. 5).

It should be noted here that a distinction was drawn in the older theology between "necessity of means" and "necessity of precept." The latter refers to a condition that "ought" to be fulfilled because the Lord asked us to do so, but it remains possible to reach a particular end without fulfilling the condition. The former, "necessity of means," refers to a condition that not only "ought" to, but "must" be fulfilled if the end is to be attained.

Chapter 3 of book III focuses on the properties and notes of the Church: one, holy, catholic, and apostolic. Article 1 is on the unity and visibility of the Church. The orientation, however, is apologetical. The four notes, or marks, of the Church function to help us discern the one, true Church from all the "false" churches (thesis 29; art. 3, thesis 31). Article 2 is devoted specifically to these four notes. Chapter 4 offers a recapitulation of the entire tract on the Church, summing everything up in thesis 32: "Christ the Lord established as the primary law for his whole Church the threefold power which he conferred on the Apostles and their successors, namely, of ruling, teaching and sanctifying" (again, "ruling" is placed first, ahead of "teaching"; the "sanctifying" power remains last in both instances).

To repeat the point made at the beginning of this summary of the Salaverri tract on the Church: the key to understanding its ecclesiological perspective is to be attentive to its structure, that is, how the author organizes the material, what topics he treats first, how much attention he accords to other topics, what he chooses to highlight in dealing with these other topics, what issues he fails to address, and so forth. All of the pre–Vatican II Latin manuals need to be interpreted in the same way, that is, structurally and organizationally. Joachim Salaverri's "*De Ecclesia Christi*" happens to be the best of them.

Fundamentals of Catholic Dogma: *Ludwig Ott*

A once widely used textbook by the German theologian Ludwig Ott, *Fundamentals of Catholic Dogma*,[84] follows basically the same approach adopted by Joachim Salaverri. The section on the Church is part 2 of book IV, "The Doctrine of God the Sanctifier." Chapter 1 is "The Divine Origin of the Church." Chapter 2 is "The Constitution of the Church," with almost exclusive reference to the primacy and infallibility of the pope and only one relatively small section on bishops, in which it is pointed out that the bishops receive their pastoral authority directly from the pope. Chapter 3, "The Internal Constitution of the Church," focuses on the relationships of Christ (as the Founder and Head) and the Holy Spirit (as the soul) to the Church. Chapter 4, "The Properties of Essential Attributes of the Church," treats the indefectibility, infallibility, and visibility of the Church and then in sequence its unity, sanctity, catholicity, and apostolicity—all considered within an apologetical perspective. Chapter 5 is "The Necessity of the Church," and chapter 6 is "The Communion of Saints," with the traditional divisions among the Church on earth (militant), the Church in heaven (triumphant), and the Church in purgatory (suffering).

Ott's ecclesiology reflects the highly juridical, hierarchical perspective that tended to be dominant, especially in seminary education, in the decades prior to the Second Vatican Council. There was no emphasis on the Church as the People of God, no mention of collegiality, no room for the Church's social apostolate, and no ecumenical dimension at all.

Other Ecclesiologies in the Manual Tradition: Timoteo Zapelena

One could add various other examples of Latin manuals from the first half of the twentieth century that embodied these same ecclesiological characteristics. These textbooks were used almost exclusively in seminary education, because theology at this time was very much of interest and concern only to future priests and the professors who taught them. Graduate-level theology for the laity did not begin to become commonplace until after Vatican II had adjourned in December 1965. Even a flagship Catholic institution like the University of Notre Dame did not initiate graduate programs in theology until 1966, beginning with summer courses in liturgical studies. Since many of the seminarians from around the world who studied in Rome at this time were destined for higher pastoral office in the Church, we should not neglect the manuals they would have been given in the principal Roman universities: the Pontifical Gregorian University, the Angelicum (the University of St. Thomas in the City), and the Lateran University. The manual authored by Timoteo (Timothy) Zapelena, S.J., of the Gregorian University, is simply one example among many others.

As Avery Dulles points out, prior to Vatican II "the neo-scholastic manuals of ecclesiology . . . remained in full vigor."[85] And he cites in particular the ecclesiology taught by Father Zapelena in Rome, as contained in his *De ecclesia Christi: Pars apologetica* (Lat., "On the Church of Christ: Apologetical Part").[86] This particular manual exhibits the characteristic strengths and weaknesses of the genre. It emphasizes the societal and institutional aspects of the Church, refers to it as the Kingdom of God in its present form on earth, insists that the hierarchical structure given to it by Christ is incompatible with democratic and charismatic elements, and portrays in largely juridical terms the papal primacy handed down to all the popes from Peter, who are, "by divine right," Peter's successors. The four notes of the Church—one, holy, catholic, and apostolic—converge to demonstrate beyond doubt that the Roman Catholic Church is the true and legitimate Church of Jesus Christ.[87]

"Generally speaking," Dulles points out, "these Latin manuals showed a predilection for juridical categories. Christ was seen as the founder of the Church; the Church was presented as a 'perfect society' in which the officeholders had jurisdiction over the members; the pope, as vicar of Christ, was depicted as ruler of the entire society. The bishops were seen as deriving their jurisdiction from the pope. The functions of the Church were studied primarily under the rubric of power," that of order and jurisdiction. "Many of the theses in these manuals," Dulles observes, "were polemically directed against Protestantism, and particularly against Liberal Protestants who looked upon the Church as essentially invisible or charismatic"[88]

The contrast with Vatican II's Dogmatic Constitution on the Church—not to mention the Pastoral Constitution on the Church in the Modern World, the Decree on Ecumenism, the Declaration on Religious Freedom, and other conciliar documents—is stark, as we shall see in our analysis of the council's ecclesiology in Part V.

Charles Journet

Charles Journet (d. 1975) was a Swiss theologian who was later created a cardinal by Pope Paul VI. His singular contribution to pre–Vatican II ecclesiology was his three-volume work *L'Église du Verbe incarné* (Fr., *The Church of the Word Incarnate*), only one volume of which has been translated into English.[89] In contrast to the manualists', Journet's approach was more deeply rooted in the older Scholastic tradition (rather than neo-Scholastic), including the work of Thomas Aquinas. Like the manualists, however, Journet identified the Church with the Kingdom of God. In the end, it was an ecclesiology constructed "from above," that is, based more on dogma than on history, and deductive rather than inductive in method. For Journet the Church was "an organism of love, having charity as its 'created soul'. It was totally sinless."[90]

Pope John XXIII

With the death of Pope Pius XII at Castel Gandolfo on October 9, 1958, the Catholic Church came to the end of an era. The Church and the world at large had no idea, however, of the significance of the transition from the papacy of Pius XII to that of John XXIII. Fifty-one cardinals gathered for the conclave, of whom eighteen were Italian. Age did not disqualify Angelo Giuseppe Roncalli, patriarch of Venice, from the ranks of viable and oft-mentioned candidates, because twenty-four of the cardinal-electors were actually older than he was. In spite of his humble origins (his large family consisted mostly of peasant farmers), Cardinal Roncalli had wide diplomatic experience, was highly cultured, and was proficient in French, Bulgarian, Russian, Turkish, and modern Greek. Once again the cardinals were looking for someone different in style from the previous pope, whom they had found aloof and autocratic. The conclave went to eleven ballots before Roncalli was finally elected by his fellow cardinals.

At his coronation Mass at St. Peter's Basilica on November 4 the new pope broke with tradition and preached the homily himself. He insisted that he wanted to be, above all else, a good shepherd. Later, on November 23, when he took possession of his cathedral church, the Basilica of St. John Lateran, he reminded the congregation that he was not a prince surrounded by the signs of outward power, but "a priest, a father, a shepherd." Only two months later, on January 25, 1959, he announced the calling of an ecumenical council, reducing some eighteen cardinals in attendance at the Basilica of St. Paul Outside the Walls to stunned silence. The new pope attributed the idea to a sudden inspiration of the Holy Spirit and referred to the coming council as a "new Pentecost." By the time of his death on June 3, 1963, John XXIII had become the most beloved pope in history.[91]

But the transition did not only involve the replacement of one style of papal presence and the exercise of papal authority with another. It also marked the end of the quasi-official status of the ecclesiology of the manuals and of neo-Scholasticism and the Counter-Reformation.

That would become clear from the very beginning of the council, with John XXIII's opening address on October 11, 1962, and with the rejection by a majority of the bishops soon thereafter of the Theological Commission's proposed schema on the Church. The first rays of sunlight were illuminating the dawn of a new day.

PART V

The Ecclesiology of the Second Vatican Council

Introduction and Overview

Along with the delayed impact of recent Catholic biblical scholarship,[1] the Second Vatican Council[2] proved to be one of the two most significant factors in the renewal of Catholic ecclesiology and in its "great leap forward" beyond the prevailing neo-Scholastic,[3] Counter-Reformation[4] ecclesiology of the Latin manuals and of official church teachings and decrees. That older, preconciliar ecclesiology was embodied in the council's preliminary schema on the Church drafted by the Theological Commission (also known as the Doctrinal Commission) under the leadership of Cardinal Alfredo Ottaviani (d. 1979), prefect of the Roman Curia's then "supreme" congregation, the Holy Office (now the Congregation for the Doctrine of the Faith). Part V intends to show that the Second Vatican Council (1962–65) is both an extension and a transcending of the First Vatican Council (1869–70).

We have already reviewed in Part II the ecclesiologically pertinent material found in the New Testament and in recent biblical scholarship. Part V is devoted entirely to the ecclesiology of Vatican II, and Parts VI and VII will attempt to show how that conciliar ecclesiology continued to shape the development of Catholic ecclesiology in subsequent decades up to the present. It is important to emphasize here, at the outset of Part V, that the author makes no claim to completeness in the examination of the various conciliar documents (or, for that matter, in the recognition of the major contributions of individual prelates, such as Maximos IV Sayegh [d. 1967], the Melkite Catholic patriarch, who was the leading spokesman for the non-Latin, Eastern Churches). Rather, attention is focused on the council's two principal documents: the Dogmatic Constitution on the Church (*Lumen gentium,* Lat., "Light of nations") and the Pastoral Constitution on the Church in the Modern World (*Gaudium et spes,* "Joy and hope"). Nevertheless, key ecclesiological teachings contained in the other conciliar documents are considered herein and also treated in various other parts of this book. That is the case, for example, with the council's highly significant and groundbreaking Declaration on the Relation of the Church to Non-Christian Religions (*Nostra aetate,* "In our age"), to which reference is made in Parts I and VI.

Neither Pope John XXIII (1958–63) nor his brother bishops knew how long this council would last or how many and which documents it would eventually approve. We have the advantage of historical hindsight. There were four sessions in all, meeting in the fall months of 1962, 1963, 1964, and 1965, respectively. As important as each of these sessions was, the nine months or so between each of them, when bishops and theologians worked together on the various documents, were almost as determinative of the council's letter and spirit as were the actual debates in St. Peter's Basilica. The most dramatic and most important of the four sessions was the first, which included John XXIII's historic opening address and, as we shall see, the refusal of the bishops to accept the Curia's organization of the conciliar commissions, the initial debate over the document on the liturgy, the debate over the document on revelation, and the rejection of the Curia's draft document on the Church. Together these developments signaled a new mood and direction for the Catholic Church.

Pope John died the following June 3 and was succeeded by Cardinal Giovanni Battista Montini, then archbishop of Milan, who took the name Paul VI and served as pope until his own death on August 6, 1978. One of his first acts was to announce that the council would continue under his leadership. In his opening address on September 29, 1963, he listed four aims of the council: the development of a clear idea of the Church, its renewal, the unity of all Christians, and dialogue between the Church and the world.

The most contentious issue of the second session had to do with the doctrine of collegiality (specifically, the pastoral and magisterial relationships of all the world's bishops among themselves and with the Bishop of Rome), but the most dramatic moment came on November 8, when Cardinal Josef Frings (d. 1978), archbishop of Cologne, openly criticized the Holy Office (now the Congregation for the Doctrine of the Faith) for its dealings with theologians and called for a reform of the Curia. Cardinal Alfredo Ottaviani, the prefect of the Holy Office, immediately took the floor to denounce Cardinal Frings's attack on his congregation as an attack on the pope himself, but Paul VI telephoned Frings later that afternoon to express approval of what he had said.

At the end of the second session, the first two (of sixteen) documents were formally approved: the Constitution on the Sacred Liturgy (*Sacrosanctum concilium,* Lat., "The sacred council") and the Decree on the Instruments of Social Communication (*Inter mirifica,* "Among marvelous [technological inventions]"), both on December 4, 1963. The former laid the groundwork for a thoroughgoing renewal and reform of the Eucharist and the other sacraments, including the full and active participation of the laity in the Eucharist, and the celebration of the Mass and the other sacraments in the vernacular rather than in Latin. The latter offered guidance on how the Church might constructively employ such new technological inventions as television and other media. The Internet had not yet been developed at this time.

The pace quickened in the third session, with discussion on a wide variety of complex topics: religious liberty, the Jews, the laity, the Church in the modern world, marriage, culture, the missions, and the formation of priests. After a "Preliminary Explanatory Note" (Lat. *nota explicativa praevia*), discussed in Part V.7.1, was added to the document on the Church, reaffirming the authority of the pope, conservative opposition to the document disappeared and the Dogmatic Constitution on the Church (*Lumen gentium*) was approved on November 21, with only ten negative votes. By the end of the session, the progressive majority had become discouraged by the sidetracking of the document on religious freedom, last-minute changes ordered by the pope in the Decree on Ecumenism (*Unitatis redintegratio,* "The restoration of unity"; passed also on November 21) to satisfy the conservative minority, and the postponing of a vote on the document on non-Christian religions. The mood was somber at the closing ceremonies of the third session, and when Paul VI was carried into St. Peter's Basilica, there was no applause.

The fourth and final session began on September 14, 1965, with an announcement by Paul VI that he would establish the long-awaited Synod of Bishops, which he did the next day. (The synod continues to function to the present time.) Thanks to an intervention by Cardinal Francis Spellman (d. 1967), archbishop of New York, the document on religious freedom was put back on the conciliar agenda and debated. Discussions also resumed on the documents on the missions, religious life, priestly formation, priestly life and ministry, and non-Christian religions. The bulk of this fourth session, however, was devoted to a careful, section-by-section discussion of the Pastoral Constitution on the Church in the Modern World. That document, *Gaudium et spes,* was approved overwhelmingly on December 6, and on the same day a reform of the Roman Curia was announced, with an expression of hope that it would become more international in membership and would represent thereby the multicultural and multiethnic character of the universal Church. *Gaudium et spes* received a second vote of approval at the final plenary meeting of the fourth session on December 7. The pope also removed the excommunication of 1054 against the patriarch of Constantinople, a highly significant gesture, given the millennium-long estrangement between the two Churches. The next day, the feast of the Immaculate Conception, there was a closing ceremony in St. Peter's Square.

Among the other documents approved during the fourth session were the Decree on the Bishops' Pastoral Office in the Church (*Christus Dominus,* Lat., "Christ, the Lord"), the Decree on Priestly Formation (*Optatum totius,* "The wish of the whole [Church]"), the Decree on the Renewal of the Religious Life (*Perfectae caritatis,* "Of perfect charity"), the Declaration on the Relationship of the Church to Non-Christian Religions (*Nostra aetate*), and the Declaration on Christian Education (*Gravissimum educationis,* "The most serious [importance] of education")—all on October 28; the Dogmatic Constitution on Divine Revelation (*Dei Verbum,* "Word of God") and the Decree on the Apostolate of the Laity (*Apostolicam actuositatem,* "The apostolic activity"), on November 18; the Decree on Eastern Catholic Churches (*Orientalium Ecclesiarum,* "of the Eastern churches"), on November 21; and the Decree on the Ministry and Life of Priests (*Presbyterorum ordinis,* "The order of priests"), the Decree on the Church's Missionary Activity (*Ad gentes divinitus,* "divinely [sent] to the nations"), and the Declaration on Religious Freedom (*Dignitatis humanae,* "Of the dignity of the human [person]")—all on December 7.

It should be noted here that constitutions touch substantively upon doctrinal and universal pastoral matters that pertain to the very essence, or "constitution," of the Church. Decrees and declarations are directed at practical questions or specific pastoral concerns. As such, these latter documents presuppose the doctrine, theology, and pastoral directives of the four constitutions (on the Church, on the Church in the modern world, on the liturgy, and on revelation). However, the various decrees and declarations have not had the same lasting impact. Some, like the Decree on the Instruments of Social Communications, have been consigned to the dustbin of history, while others, such as the Decree on Ecumenism, the Declaration on Religious Freedom, and the Declaration on the Relationship of the Church to Non-Christian Religions have been of enduring importance in the life of the Church and in Catholic ecclesiology.

Part V has twelve sections, a listing of which provides an outline of the coverage and analysis of Vatican II: (1) Introduction and Overview; (2) The Announcement of and Preparations for the Council; (3) Pope John XXIII's Opening Address; (4) The First Days of the

Council; (5) Vatican II in Historical and Theological Perspective; (6) The Ecclesiology of Vatican II: Six Basic Themes (the Church as mystery, or sacrament, as People of God, as servant, as a communion, as an ecumenical community, and as an eschatological community); (7) The "Twin Pillars" of Vatican II's Ecclesiology: *Lumen gentium* and *Gaudium et spes;* (8) Vatican II: Continuity or Discontinuity? (9) The Style of Vatican II; (10) Approaches to the Interpretation of Conciliar Texts; (11) Pope Paul VI's *Ecclesiam Suam* (1964); and (12) Concluding Reflections.

The Announcement of and Preparations for the Council

It was on January 25, 1959, the feast of the Conversion of St. Paul, that Pope John XXIII announced at the Basilica of St. Paul Outside the Walls, during a brief address to a small group of cardinals marking the end of the Week of Prayer for Christian Unity, that he intended to convene a diocesan synod for Rome and an ecumenical council. With regard to the latter, he said that he was motivated "solely by a concern for the 'good of souls' and in order that the new pontificate may come to grips, in a clear and well-defined way, with the spiritual needs of the present time."[5] (Two years later, the pope noted that the cardinals had received his announcement in "impressive, devout silence."[6]) He had invited the assembled cardinals to submit confidential opinions and suggestions about his idea for a council, but few did so, and those who did expressed their views "in cold and formal language."[7] The cardinals who had just elected him three months earlier had expected John XXIII to be a transitional pope, not a groundbreaker. His announcement of the council was all the more disconcerting to the cardinals because the pope made it clear that his decision was final. He said that he was "humbly resolute" in it, and that it was "a decisive resolution."[8]

John XXIII indicated that the council would be a key element in the renewal of the Church, with the hope that it would become easier for the Church to discern between what is a matter of sacred principle and the gospel, on the one hand, and what belongs to the changing times, on the other. This distinction would occupy an important place in his historic opening address to the council on October 11, 1962, to which we shall return in due course.

The reaction to the pope's announcement covered the spectrum from dismissiveness, even within the Vatican, to excitement and anticipation within various quarters of the Catholic Church and among non-Catholic Christian bodies, such as the World Council of Churches. A few months after the announcement some, inside and outside the Catholic Church, were beginning to wonder whether the idea for a council had begun to subside within Vatican quarters. Nothing much seemed to be happening. And then, on May 17, 1959, the decision to form a preparatory commission was made public, catching many people by surprise. Plans for the council had not been abandoned after all. Indeed, as the Church approached the feast of Pentecost that year, John XXIII began referring to the council as a "new Pentecost," a new outpouring of the Holy Spirit upon the Church.[9] On July 14, the pope wrote to Cardinal Domenico Tardini, his Secretary of State, making it clear that the council would not simply be the completion of the First Vatican Council. It would be a new and distinct council, to be known as Vatican II. But here again, it is not a matter of either/or, but of both/and. Vatican II was indeed a new and distinct council, but one in continuity with Vatican I.

The preparations for this Second Vatican Council were the most extensive in the history of the Church.[10] Ideas for the council's agenda were solicited from every bishop in the Catholic world, from the heads of clerical religious orders (but not orders of religious women), and from Catholic universities and theological faculties as well as members of the Roman Curia. Over 9,300 proposals were submitted.[11] The material was indexed and distributed to eleven preparatory commissions appointed by the pope in June 1960 to formulate draft documents for discussion. These commissions met between November 1960 and June 1962 and produced over seventy documents, or schemata. These documents, in turn, were reduced to twenty separate texts, each of which was reviewed and revised by the Central Preparatory Commission before being submitted to the pope for his approval.

In July 1962 seven of these documents were circulated among the bishops of the universal Catholic Church in preparation for the planned opening of the council in October. The documents were concerned with the sources of revelation, the moral order, the deposit of faith, the family and chastity, liturgy, media, and church unity. By contrast with the final documents approved by the council itself and promulgated by Pope Paul VI, these schemata, with the exception of the schema on the liturgy, were generally neo-Scholastic in orientation. Fearful of the council's possible impact on its traditional ways of conducting the business of the universal Church, the Roman Curia evidently saw to it that only the safest, mostly Rome-based theologians were appointed to serve on the preparatory commissions. Cardinal Leo Josef Suenens (d. 1996) of Belgium and Cardinal Paul-Émile Léger (d. 1991) of Canada met with the pope to express their concerns about this development.

John XXIII had officially convoked the council on Christmas Day 1961 in an apostolic constitution, *Humanae salutis* (Lat., "Of human salvation"). The council itself was formally convened on October 11, 1962.[12] Its first order of business was a formal address by John XXIII, to which we now turn our attention.

Pope John XXIII's Opening Address

The pope expressed the hope in his historic address on the first day of the council that Vatican II would bless the Church with greater spiritual riches and new energies, so that the Church might "look to the future without fear."[13] Then he launched into his oft-quoted criticism of unnamed curial officials who are burdened, he said, with a negative, pessimistic view of the world and of the future of the Church:

> *In the daily exercise of our pastoral office, we sometimes have to listen, much to our regret, to voices of persons who, though burning with zeal, are not endowed with too much sense of discretion or measure. In these modern times they can see nothing but prevarication and ruin. They say that our era, in comparison with past eras, is getting*

> *worse and they behave as though they have learned nothing from history, which is, nonetheless, the teacher of life. They behave as though at the time of former councils everything was a full triumph for the Christian idea and life and for proper religious liberty.*

The pope referred to these critics as "prophets of gloom, who are always forecasting disaster, as though the end of the world was at hand." Over against their pessimism, the pope insisted: "In the present order of things, Divine Providence is leading us to a new order of human relations which . . . are directed toward the fulfillment of God's superior and inscrutable designs. And everything, even human differences, leads to the greater good of the Church."

Although the "greatest concern" of the council must be that "the sacred deposit of Christian doctrine should be guarded and taught more efficaciously," the "salient point" of Vatican II is not a discussion of one or another article of faith or doctrine of the Church. "For this," the pope observed, "a council was not necessary. . . . The substance of the ancient doctrine of the Deposit of Faith is one thing, and the way it is presented is another." It is the latter, he insisted, that needs to be taken into great consideration by a magisterium that must always be "predominantly pastoral in character."

Errors come and go, "like fog before the sun." The Church has always opposed errors regarding the faith and, in the past, did so "with the greatest severity. Nowadays, however, the spouse of Christ prefers to make use of the medicine of mercy rather than of severity. She considers that she meets the needs of the present day by demonstrating the validity of her teaching rather than by condemnations." At this council, the pope continued, the Catholic Church "desires to show herself to be the loving mother of all, benign, patient, full of mercy and goodness toward children separated from her" and "she spreads everywhere the fullness of Christian charity, than which nothing is more effective in eradicating the seeds of discord, nothing more efficacious in promoting concord, just peace and the brotherly unity of all." He concluded: "This council now beginning rises in the Church like daybreak, a forerunner of most splendid light. It is now only dawn."

It was only in the light of subsequent developments during the council itself and then immediately after it that the significance of John XXIII's opening address became unmistakably clear. Nowadays, it is practically impossible to understand the work of the council, both as an event and as the producer of sixteen documents, except through the prism of this speech.

The pope and his council had broken with the habits and customary approaches of the post-Tridentine, Counter-Reformation Catholic Church—approaches that had held sway since the middle of the sixteenth century.[14] The spirit of the conciliar Church was to be characterized by a hope that would banish fear and pessimism. But it would not be a superficial hope, equivalent to false optimism. This hope is a theological virtue (along with faith and love) and is rooted in the workings of the Holy Spirit and Divine Providence.

The Church's stance in the face of error and dissent was to be no longer one of condemnations and punitive actions, but one of patience and mercy. The most effective way to deal with error, the pope had said, is through a positive and compelling presentation of the truth. And even there, the Church must always be mindful of the crucially important distinction between the substance of faith and the way in which it is presented. In all things, charity. Finally, John XXIII made it clear that Vatican II was only the beginning of a new day, not its climax, much less its fulfillment. "It is now only dawn."

The First Days of the Council

Indications that the council would indeed inaugurate a whole new day for the Church were swift in coming. The pope made a special effort to meet with the diplomatic corps, the press, and the non-Catholic observers in several gatherings held in the Sistine Chapel and the Hall of the Consistory. Perhaps the most impressive of the meetings was with the ecumenical observers, who represented all of the important non-Roman communions except for the Greek Orthodox, the World Baptist Alliance, and certain fundamentalist bodies. After receiving them in the Hall of the Consistory, the pope sat with them in a square—not on his throne but on the same kind of chair as the observers had. Charity, he said, was the key to ecumenical progress.

Each day's plenary meeting (more precisely, Congregation) opened in St. Peter's Basilica with the enthronement of the Book of Scriptures and the celebration of the Eucharist—not only in Latin but in at least twenty-six different rites, celebrated on different days, over the entire course of the council. This underscored the ecclesiologically important point that the Catholic Church embraces more than the "Roman," or Latin-rite, Catholic Church, as we have already pointed out in Part I.2.5.

The first plenary meeting (First General Congregation) was held on Saturday, October 13. The agenda called for the election of members of the ten conciliar commissions, which were the successors to the Preparatory Commissions. Sixteen members were to be elected to each commission by the council fathers,[15] and eight were to be appointed by the pope. As soon as the Secretary General announced that the council would proceed to the election, Cardinal Achille Liénart (d. 1973), archbishop of Lille, who was concerned about the composition of the Curia's list of nominees for the various commissions, rose and read a prepared statement that voting should be delayed until the bishops could meet in national or regional caucuses in order to get to know one another better and to agree on their own slate of candidates. Cardinal Josef Frings, archbishop of Cologne, immediately seconded the proposal, indicating that he was doing so in the name of the other German-speaking cardinals. His intervention was greeted with vigorous applause. The will of the council was clear. No formal vote was taken on the motion and the meeting ended after just fifteen minutes.

This procedural development was of enormous ecclesiological importance. The great majority of the council fathers were sending a message to all concerned parties that this was to be their council, not the Curia's alone. It was the bishops, abbots, and other prelates who would decide on the council's leadership and agenda. When the results were announced a few days later, there was a general feeling that both the elected and appointed members of the various commissions "turned out to be fairly representative of the Church, both as to schools of thought and nationalities."[16]

Vatican II in Historical and Theological Perspective

No theological essay published in the aftermath of the Second Vatican Council was more influential in identifying the historical and theological significance of the council than Karl Rahner's "Basic Theological Interpretation of the Second Vatican Council."[17] He suggested that the council marked "the beginning of a tentative approach by the Church to the discovery and official realization of itself as *world-Church*."[18] Although it is true that there were episcopal representatives of churches in Asia and Africa at the First Vatican Council in the nineteenth century, they were, in almost every case, missionary bishops of European or American origin. There were relatively few native hierarchies throughout the Catholic world—until the decades leading up to Vatican II and thanks in large part to the farsighted teachings of Pope Benedict XV (1914–22) on the missions. In his 1919 encyclical *Maximum illud* (Lat., "This greatest") he urged that missionary bishops, most of whom were from Europe, form a native clergy as quickly as possible and never place the interests of their European countries of origin ahead of the pastoral needs of the people they serve. Under Benedict's successor, Pius XI (1922–39), the total number of native priests in mission lands rose from almost three thousand to over seven thousand. At the beginning of Pius XI's pontificate there were no mission dioceses under the direction of a native bishop. Upon the pope's death in 1939, there were forty such dioceses. "Vatican II," Rahner wrote, "was really a first assembly of the world-episcopate such as had not hitherto existed."[19]

Rahner also challenged the traditional division of Western church history into antiquity, the Middle Ages, and modern times. He divided that history, instead, into three great epochs: first, a short period of Judeo-Christianity (from the Resurrection of Christ to the so-called Council of Jerusalem [ca. 49/50], when the early Church became for the first time a Church of the Gentiles); second, the period (ca. 50–1962) in which the Church became incarnated in a particular cultural group, that of Hellenistic and then European culture and civilization; and, third, the period (1962 into the indefinite future) in which the Church's living space is from the very outset the whole world (or, more accurately, when the Church *began to become* a true world-Church at Vatican II).[20] Dividing one epoch from another are caesurae, breaks created by highly significant, nonrepeatable happenings or events, namely, the Council of Jerusalem and Vatican II. Rahner's thesis is that "today we are for the first time living again in a period of caesura like that involved in the transition [inaugurated by Paul and ratified by the Council of Jerusalem] from Judaeo-Christianity to Gentile Christianity . . . when the Church ceased to be the Church of the Jews and became the Church of the Gentiles."[21]

Rahner argues that the Church nowadays needs to look at itself objectively, as an essentially Western export that has made little or no impact on the ancient civilizations of the East or on the world of Islam. This is so, Rahner believes, because Western Christianity has refused to take the risk of "a really new beginning." But "*either* the Church sees and recognizes these essential differences of the other cultures, into which it has to enter as world-Church, and accepts with a Pauline boldness the necessary consequences of this recognition *or* it remains a western Church and thus in the last resort betrays the meaning of Vatican II."[22]

The Ecclesiology of Vatican II: Six Basic Themes

Is there an overarching ecclesiology of the council or is it more akin to the New Testament, in which there are several different ecclesiologies that invite a synthesis not found as such in the biblical texts themselves (see the opening paragraph in Part II)? Joseph Komonchak, a theologian at The Catholic University of America, refers to various unnamed authors who claim that there is, in fact, no single ecclesiology in the council, but only a variety of images or models of the Church. Komonchak makes the counterargument that the reason for this variety is to be found in the council's choice of a more biblical, patristic, and liturgical language. "The council," he writes, "sought to set out the elements of the Church's life but it left it to theologians to construct a synthesis of them. These elements are many, but the council's ecclesiology includes them all and is, therefore, single in intention."[23] Thus, according to Komonchak, even if there is no single synthesis within the documents themselves, there is a singleness of intention from which a synthesis can be constructed.

The two major sources of the conciliar ecclesiology are the Dogmatic Constitution on the Church (*Lumen gentium*), approved on November 21, 1964, and the Pastoral Constitution on the Church in the Modern World (*Gaudium et spes*), approved on December 7, 1965, both of which can be described as the twin pillars on which the entire conciliar ecclesiology rests. The former is concerned primarily with the internal life of the Church (*Ecclesia ad intra,* Lat., "the Church within") and the latter, with the relationship of the Church to the religious and secular worlds beyond it (*Ecclesia ad extra,* "the Church beyond"). In the beginning, both documents were intended to be part of a single document, *De Ecclesia*. The two documents will be analyzed more fully in Part V.7.1 and 7.2.

There are at least six basic ecclesiological themes that together, but never singly, constitute the overarching ecclesiology of Vatican II and from which some form of synthesis can be developed: the Church as mystery, or sacrament, as People of God, as servant, as a communion, as an ecumenical community, and as an eschatological community

THE CHURCH AS MYSTERY, OR SACRAMENT

The council defined the Church at the outset of its Dogmatic Constitution on the Church (*Lumen gentium*) as a mystery, or sacrament. The distinction between the two theological categories is, for all practical purposes, without any real difference. "Mystery," Pope Paul VI indicated in his opening address to the second session of the council, is "a reality imbued with the hidden presence of God. It lies, therefore, within the very nature of the Church to be always open to new and greater exploration."[24] The first chapter of *Lumen gentium* is entitled "The Mystery of the Church," and article 1 declares that the Church is, in Christ, as "a sacrament—a sign and instrument, that is, of communion with God and of the unity of the entire human race." A "sacrament" is, in the Augustinian sense of the word, "a visible sign of invisible grace" (Lat. *invisibilis gratiae visibilis forma*).[25] Grace is, in turn, a gift—in this case, God's gift of self. Grace, therefore, is the presence of God, which means that a sacrament is a visible sign of the invisible presence of God.

The council's understanding of the Church as mystery, or sacrament, represents a transcending of the preconciliar concept of the Church as primarily an institution or organization. In the latter instance, one "belongs" to the Church; in the former, one participates in the life of the Church and, with all its other members, constitutes the very reality of the Church. The main difference between the ecclesiology of Vatican II and preconciliar ecclesiology becomes clearly evident when comparing and contrasting the first chapter of *Lumen gentium* and Joachim Salaverri's tract on the Church in the Spanish *Summa* (see Part IV.4.3.a). Chapter 1 of *Lumen gentium* is concerned with the Church as mystery, sacrament, and community, while the Latin manuals of the preconciliar period were concerned primarily with the Church's institutional and structural aspects.

It should also be noted that the sacramentality of the Church has to be understood eschatologically as well as incarnationally. Although the Church already embodies the presence of the triune God, it does not yet possess it in its fullness. A purely incarnational understanding of sacramentality can lead to a triumphalistic ecclesiology, as if the Church were already, in its present earthly form, the corporate presence of God and, therefore, beyond fundamental criticism and the need for renewal and reform. Protestant theologians like Jürgen Moltmann and George Lindbeck have called attention to this important distinction between the incarnational and eschatological notions of sacramentality as it applies to the Church.[26]

The call of the whole Church to holiness (chap. 5 of *Lumen gentium*) is a direct consequence of the sacramentality of the Church. If the Church is, in fact, the corporate presence of the triune God, who is holiness itself,[27] then it must look and act like a community transformed by that divine presence. It must be a Church that is "at once holy and always in need of purification," which means that it is called "constantly" to follow "the path of penance and renewal" (n. 8). Indeed, this is the primary pastoral consequence of the sacramentality of the Church. It is a community that must practice what it preaches and teaches to others.

THE CHURCH AS PEOPLE OF GOD

The second chapter of *Lumen gentium* is entitled "The People of God." In teaching (in chap. 1) that the Church is a mystery, or sacrament, the council underscored the point that the Church, like a sacrament, has a visible and an invisible side. The invisible side is the presence of the triune God. The visible side is primarily the baptized persons who constitute the Church. (The adverb "primarily" is used here because there are structural and other institutional elements that are also part of the Church's visibility in the world, but none is as significant as the people who *are* the Church.) The Church is not something apart from the baptized to which they "belong" as recipients and beneficiaries of its principal spiritual assets, namely, the sacraments. The People of God *are* the Church. Whatever structures and other institutional elements exist within the Church are to assist the People of God to fulfill their mission and ministries. These elements, therefore, exist to serve the whole People of God, not the other way around. Indeed, according to the fourth chapter, on the laity in the Church, the laity share in the threefold office of Christ: of teaching, ruling, and sanctifying (n. 30). The lay apostolate is no longer conceived as a delegated participation in the ministry of the hierarchy (as it was understood by the Catholic Action movement of the 1930s, 1940s, and 1950s), but as a direct sharing in the mission of the Church through Baptism and Confirmation and then "communicated and nourished" by the Eucharist (n. 33).

The notion of the Church as People of God is in stark contrast to the preconciliar tendency to identify the Church with the hierarchy, thereby reducing ecclesiology to a kind of hierarchology. Even today, many years after Vatican II, there are Catholics for whom the Church is still equivalent to the hierarchy, while the laity are only, in effect, their spiritual clients. According to this mentality, the laity's eligibility for receiving spiritual benefits from the hierarchy, usually through the sacramental ministrations of the lower clergy, is dependent upon the laity's faithful observance of the teachings and regulations laid down by the hierarchy, and by the pope in particular, whose subordinates the bishops are.[28]

Nowhere is this contrast more evident than in the debate among the council fathers regarding the placement of chapters 2 and 3 of *Lumen gentium*. In previous drafts the chapter on the hierarchy preceded the chapter on the People of God. Those who preferred the status quo did so on the grounds that the laity (which they equated with the People of God, excluding from it the hierarchy, the clergy, and the religiously professed) are subject to the authority of the hierarchy. Those who argued for the reversal of the order of the two chapters did so on the grounds that the Church is the whole People of God—laity, religious, and clergy alike—and that the hierarchical structure of the Church exists to serve the whole People of God, not to dominate or control it. The latter argument prevailed and the chapters were reversed, winning subsequent praise from Cardinal Karol Wojtyla (later Pope John Paul II, 1978–2005) in his book *Sources of Renewal: The Implementation of Vatican II*.[29]

The pastoral implications of this conciliar emphasis on the Church as People of God have been officially realized already, albeit in often tentative forms of uneven quality, in the development of parish and diocesan councils. For the most part, however, lay groups, such as Call to Action and Voice of the Faithful in the United States, have been formed independently of the hierarchy and usually without its subsequent approval and support.

Nowhere, however, have the implications of the council's People of God ecclesiology been more evident, and as a result more controversial, than in the reform of the liturgy mandated by the Constitution on the Sacred Liturgy (*Sacrosanctum concilium*), approved on December 4, 1963. In the Latin Tridentine Mass, authorized by the Council of Trent and promulgated by Pope Pius V (1566–72), the main human focus of the celebration was on the priest. He alone had the sacramental power to "confect" the Eucharist, that is, to change the bread and wine into the body and blood of Christ. The role of the laity was to be present for it and to attune their minds and hearts to the sacred action being performed by the priest at the altar, with his back to the congregation. The modern liturgical movement, with its beginnings in the late nineteenth century, gradually restored the focus to its original meaning in the New Testament and the early Church. The Eucharist is an action of the whole congregation, laity as well as clergy, because the Church itself is more than the clergy; it includes all of the baptized, whether ordained or religiously professed or neither (n. 7, paras. 3–4; nn. 10–11; and esp. nn. 14, 27–30).

Many of the so-called liturgy wars that erupted after Vatican II focused on changes in the language of the Mass (from Latin to the vernacular) as well as on various other ritual aspects (e.g., the handshake in place of the kiss of peace, the reception of Holy Communion in the hand and while standing, the laity's singing and audible responses to the prayers of the priest-celebrant, and the functioning of laypersons as lectors and eucharistic ministers). But what has been underneath these several discrete conflicts is a fundamental conflict of ecclesiologies.

Those who have accepted to one degree or another the liturgical changes have also accepted, at least implicitly, the council's renewed emphasis on the Church as the People of God. Those who have opposed to one degree or another these same liturgical reforms have remained attached—again, at least implicitly—to the neo-Scholastic ecclesiology of the preconciliar period, which tended to identify the Church with the hierarchy and to regard the laity as essentially passive beneficiaries of the clergy's sacramental ministrations and teachings. According to this preconciliar ecclesiology, there was a clear line of distinction between the teaching Church (Lat. *Ecclesia docens*) and the learning Church (*Ecclesia discens*) as well as a clear line of distinction, represented by the Communion rail, separating the laity from the sanctuary and hence from the clergy.

Accordingly, the council's insistence to the contrary that the Church consists of the whole People of God has had its most immediate and practical impact on the Church's liturgical and ministerial life, and that is the main reason why the Mass has become the flash point of so much conflict within the Roman Catholic Church. The "liturgy wars" are at root "ecclesiology wars."

THE CHURCH AS SERVANT

Referring to the Church as a servant does not mean that it has merely a subordinate, if not also passive, relationship to the world around it. Its service to others often requires it to exercise courage and take serious risks on behalf of the poor and the oppressed and as an advocate and agent of justice, human rights, and peace.

The mission of the Church, to be sure, includes essentially, but not exclusively, the preaching of the gospel and the celebration of the sacraments. Until Vatican II, however, the so-called social apostolate (which encompassed all of the Church's pastoral activities in service to individuals in their physical and economic needs, but which also included the reform of unjust political and economic structures, demanded by the virtue of social justice) was generally subsumed under the heading of "pre-evangelization," that is, ecclesial activities that were considered a necessary precondition for the effective implementation of its essential missionary responsibilities of word and sacrament, but not an integral part of that mission. Thus, the term "*pre*-evangelization." In the same period, the social teachings of the Church, stretching back to the landmark encyclical of Pope Leo XIII *Rerum novarum* (Lat., "Of new things"), published in 1891, were treated only in moral theology under the virtue of justice and, more specifically, *social* justice.

With the promulgation of Vatican II's Pastoral Constitution on the Church in the Modern World (*Gaudium et spes*) in 1965, formal consideration of the Church's social teachings was also included within ecclesiology. Indeed, *Gaudium et spes* provided those teachings with an ecclesiological foundation.[30] As the pastoral constitution points out in its preface, "The Church is not motivated by earthly ambition but is interested in one thing only—to carry on the work of Christ under the guidance of the Holy Spirit, who came into the world to bear witness to the truth, to save and not to judge, to serve and not to be served" (n. 3). The "single intention" of the Church is "that God's kingdom may come" (n. 45), a kingdom of "justice, love, and peace" (n. 39).

Two major concerns pervade this pastoral constitution: first, to reaffirm the traditional distinction between the sacred and the temporal orders as well as the transcendence of the Church over the temporal order; and, second, to insist upon the active role of the Church in the world, so that "the earthly and heavenly city penetrate each other" (n. 40).[31] Regarding the first concern, the pastoral constitution insists that the Church has "no proper mission in the political, economic, or social order. The purpose which [Christ] set before it is a religious one. . . . Moreover, in virtue of its mission and nature, it is bound to no particular form of human culture, nor to any political, economic, or social system." The Church asks only that, "in pursuit of the welfare of all, it may be able to develop itself freely under any kind of government which grants recognition to the basic rights of person and family and to the demands of the common good" (n. 42).

Regarding the second concern, the pastoral constitution restates the traditional paradox of a Church existing for a spiritual purpose and yet situated in, and committed to serve, a temporal world. The pastoral constitution points to a resolution of the paradox in its notion of the Church as "a leaven and as a kind of soul for human society as it is to be renewed in Christ and transformed into God's family." The relationship between the two realms is captured in the word "compenetration" (Lat. *compenetratio*), but it is a reality that is "accessible to faith alone" (n. 40). The Church not only "communicates divine life" to women, men, and children alike, but also contributes toward making the human family and its history more human "by its healing and elevating impact on the dignity of the person, [and] by the way in which it strengthens the seams of human society and imbues the everyday activity of people with a deeper meaning and importance" (n. 40).

If one were looking for a single formulation by which to resolve the problem addressed in *Gaudium et spes*, namely, the relationship of Church and world, that formulation might be found in article 76: "For [the Church] is at once a sign and a safeguard of the transcendence of the human person." According to the Jesuit theologian John Courtney Murray (d. 1967), the text suggests that "the Church may neither be enclosed within the political order nor be denied its own mode of spiritual entrance into the political order. It indirectly asserts the rightful secularity of the secular order, at the same time that it asserts the necessary openness of the secular order to the transcendent values whose pursuit is proper to the human person."[32]

Indeed, the cooperation of Church and state in the service of the human person is stated in the document as a principle: "In their proper spheres, the political community and the Church are mutually independent and self-governing. Yet, by a different title, each serves the personal and social vocation of the same human beings. This service can be more effectively rendered for the good of all, if each works better for wholesome mutual cooperation, depending on the circumstances of time and place" (n. 76).

To fulfill its role in society, the Church asks only the freedom to preach and to teach and to pass moral judgment even on matters that belong to the political order "whenever basic personal rights or the salvation of souls make such judgments necessary." On the other hand, the Church "does not lodge its hope in privileges conferred by civil authority" and is even ready to renounce those that have been granted already if they raise any doubts about the sincerity or credibility of the Church's witness (n. 76).

As noted above, with this document Catholic social teachings take a decisive ecclesiological turn. That turn also involves a renewed openness to ecumenicity. The Decree on Ecumenism notes that "cooperation [among Christians] in social matters . . . vividly expresses that bond which already unites them, and it sets in clearer relief the features of Christ the Servant. . . . Through such cooperation, all believers in Christ are able to learn easily how they can understand each other better and esteem each other more, and how the road to the unity of Christians may be made smooth" (n. 12).

The council's stress on the servanthood of the Church has had explicit consequences in the Church's intensified engagement in the temporal sphere on behalf of justice, peace, and human rights in the postconciliar encyclicals and apostolic letters of Paul VI

(*Populorum progressio,* Lat., "On the progress of peoples,"1967; and *Evangelii nuntiandi,* "Of proclaiming the gospel," 1975) and those of John Paul II (*Laborem exercens,* "On doing work," 1981; *Sollicitudo rei socialis,* "Solicitude for social concerns," 1988; and *Centesimus annus,* "The hundredth year," 1991); in the 1971 World Synod of Bishops' *Iustitia in mundo* ("Justice in the World"); in the U.S. Catholic bishops' pastoral letters "The Challenge of Peace" (1983) and "Economic Justice for All: Catholic Social Teaching and the U.S. Economy" (1986); in various pastoral letters of the Latin American Bishops' Conference (CELAM) as outgrowths of their meetings in Medellín, Columbia (1968), and Puebla, Mexico (1979)—the Medellín documents reaffirmed and reinforced the teachings of *Gaudium et spes;* in the development of Latin American liberation theology, inspired by the writings of the Peruvian theologian Gustavo Gutiérrez, especially his *A Theology of Liberation* (1971); and in the growing interplay between ecclesiology and social ethics.

THE CHURCH AS A COMMUNION

Although the council's teaching on the Church as a communion is one key to understanding its overall ecclesiology, it is not the *only* key or even the principal one, as some theologians, pastoral leaders, and others of a similarly conservative bent have suggested or assumed. They like to place the concept of communion in opposition to that of People of God, as if the two cannot coexist with one another as basic elements of the council's ecclesiology. Communion for them highlights the transcendental, otherworldly nature of the Church, while People of God seems to them to stress too much its human dimension and even implies an egalitarian or democratic aspect to the Church.[33]

Rather than set the concept of Church as a communion over against the Church as People of God, the Church as a communion should be more properly set over against the preconciliar notion of the Church as an absolute monarchy with the pope at the top of the structural pyramid. Rather than a single Church with the pope as its earthly head, the Church universal is a communion of local churches (regional, national, diocesan, and parochial), each of which is the

Body of Christ in that place (*Lumen gentium,* n. 26; chap. 3 generally). The structural equivalent of communion is collegiality. The college of local churches is represented by the college of diocesan bishops. Their local churches are not merely administrative divisions and subdivisions of the one, universal Church. Together, in communion with one another and with the Bishop of Rome, these local churches constitute the Church universal, and the collegial unity of their bishops is an expression of the communal nature of the whole Church (*Lumen gentium,* e.g., nn. 24–25). When gathered in ecumenical council, under the presidency of the chief bishop, the Bishop of Rome, they manifest in the most visible fashion the communal and collegial nature of the Church (see also *Lumen gentium,* nn. 8, 13, 18).

As important as the notion of communion surely is, the Second Vatican Council did not make it the centerpiece of its ecclesiology. The explicit references to the Church as a communion are remarkably few in number. The internal bond among the members of the Church is described as a communion in *Lumen gentium* (n. 13, para. 2: "All the faithful scattered throughout the world are in communion with each other in the Holy Spirit"), in the Dogmatic Constitution on Divine Revelation (n. 10, which refers to "the communion of life"), and in the Decree on Ecumenism (n. 2: "It is the Holy Spirit . . . who brings about that wonderful communion of the faithful"). It is in that last document, the Decree on Ecumenism, that the concept of the Church as a communion has its most practical force. As pointed out earlier in the book (I.2.5, and passim), the category of communion—more specifically, *degrees* of communion—replaced that of membership in describing the ecclesial relationship between the Catholic Church (including the whole Catholic Communion of Churches, East and West alike) and other Churches and ecclesial communities in the Body of Christ. This is especially clear in the Decree on Ecumenism (nn. 3, 4, 14, 18, 19, 22) and also in *Lumen gentium* (n. 15). Irish Carmelite theologian Christopher O'Donnell observes that "communion is so much at the heart of the Church that it signifies the desired aim of ecumenism [the movement designed to restore unity to the worldwide Church]. It is a dynamic unifying principle of the Church."[34]

It is also important to note that there are vertical and horizontal dimensions to the communal nature of the Church. The faithful are united with God (the vertical dimension) and also with one another and the entire human race (the horizontal dimension). The Church is a sign and instrument of "communion with God and of the unity of the entire human race" (*Lumen gentium,* n. 1).

The postconciliar implementation of the communal/collegial nature of the Church consisted of various initiatives. The first initiative was the establishment of world synods of bishops as mandated by the council's Decree on the Bishops' Pastoral Office in the Church (n. 5), approved on October 28, 1965. However, the Apostolic Synod had already been formally instituted by Pope Paul VI in September 1965 in the document *Apostolica sollicitudo* (Lat., "Apostolic solicitude"). These synods have been held at regular intervals since 1967. The second initiative was the development of national episcopal conferences, which were recommended for the entire Church by *Lumen gentium* (n. 22) and the Decree on the Bishops' Pastoral Office in the Church (nn. 37–38) and formally established by Paul VI in 1966.

The third initiative was the growing practical importance of the principle of subsidiarity, by which nothing is to be done at a higher level of the Church that can be done as well, if not better, at a lower level. The corollary is that decisions ought always to be made at the level closest to their immediate impact and with the participation, direct or indirect, of those whom the decision is most likely to affect. The principle of subsidiarity is violated when, for example, the Vatican overrides, as it did in 2006, the pastoral authority of episcopal conferences to determine how liturgical texts are most appropriately translated into their own vernacular language or when, in 1980, Pope John Paul II convened a national synod for the Dutch Church in Rome rather than in Holland and allowed members of the Roman Curia to cast votes on an equal basis with the attending Dutch bishops. Indeed, an excessive centralization of authority is the ecclesiological antithesis of this principle of subsidiarity and of the larger principles on which it is based, namely, those of collegiality and communion.

THE CHURCH AS ECUMENICAL COMMUNITY

In the years and decades, indeed in the centuries, preceding Vatican II, the common assumption of Catholics and the official teaching of the Catholic Church was that the Catholic Church is "the one, true Church of Christ." All other Churches and ecclesial communities (they were never referred to as "Churches" during this period) were regarded as "false churches," completely outside the Body of Christ and, therefore, beyond the pale of salvation. Only gradually did the Catholic Church of modern times come to officially recognize the possibility of salvation for non-Catholic Christians and then for non-Christians and even agnostics and atheists.[35]

Vatican II decisively changed that earlier mentality and doctrine in its Decree on Ecumenism. First, it defined the goal of the ecumenical movement as the "restoration" of Christian unity, not the "return" of the separated brethren to the preexisting unity of the Catholic Church (n. 1). The separation that began at the time of the East-West Schism in the eleventh century and the Protestant Reformation of the sixteenth seriously disrupted communion between the various Churches and ecclesial communities within the Body of Christ, but it did not destroy that communion completely. Consequently, the council viewed the goal of the ecumenical movement as the restoration of "*full* communion with the Catholic Church" (n. 3, my italics).[36]

The council also acknowledged that "people on both sides were to blame" for the historic breach of Christian unity, but it exempted those living today from direct responsibility. Indeed, "those [today] who believe in Christ and have been properly baptized are put in some, though imperfect, communion with the Catholic Church."[37] The differences between separated Christians "exist in varying degrees," and in spite of those differences "it remains true that all who have been justified by faith in baptism are incorporated into Christ" and therefore "have a right to be called Christians, and with good reason are accepted as sisters and brothers in the Lord by the children of the Catholic Church."

Indeed, some, "even very many," of the most significant ecclesial elements can exist outside the visible boundaries of the Catholic

Church: "the written Word of God; the life of grace; faith, hope and charity, with the other interior gifts of the holy Spirit, as well as visible elements." The separated brothers and sisters also carry out many authentically Christian liturgical actions that can "engender a life of grace, and . . . are capable of giving access to that communion in which is salvation." These separated Churches and communities are "by no means deprived of significance and importance in the mystery of salvation. For the Spirit of Christ has not refrained from using them as means of salvation which derive their efficacy from the very fullness of grace and truth entrusted to the Catholic Church." The document nonetheless holds to the traditional teaching that it is "through Christ's Catholic Church alone . . . that the fullness of the means of salvation can be obtained." The key word here is "fullness." The council did not say that the "means of salvation" do not exist at all outside the Catholic Church, much less that Catholics alone can be saved. There are "degrees" of participation in the Church and in the means of salvation that are available within it.

The ecclesiological consequences of the council's teaching on the ecumenicity of the Church have been formal dialogues (also known as "consultations" and "bilaterals") between the Catholic Church and other Christian Churches and ecclesial communities at local, national, and international levels; a common pursuit of renewal and reform (indeed, the Decree on Ecumenism, n. 4, called this the "primary duty" of the Catholic Church); cooperation in the social apostolate; joint theological study in seminaries, colleges, and universities; common prayer, especially on special national holidays and during the Week of Prayer for Christian Unity (January 18–25); and initiatives taken toward the eventual mutual recognition of the ordained ministries of separated Churches and ecclesial communities.

The council also called for a legitimate pluralism in the life, mission, ministries, and structural operations of the Church. "While preserving unity in essentials," there must also be "a proper freedom in the various forms of spiritual life and discipline, in the variety of liturgical rites, and even in the theological elaborating of revealed truth. In all things let charity prevail" (n. 4).

One of the most controverted texts in the entire corpus of conciliar documents is that of article 8 of the Dogmatic Constitution on the Church, with a parallel reference in the Decree on Ecumenism (n. 4, para. 3). The Church, "constituted and organized as a society in the present world, subsists in the Catholic Church, which is governed by the successor of Peter and by the bishops in communion with him" (*Lumen gentium*, n. 8). The original text used the copulative verb "is," thereby perpetuating the common notion that the Body of Christ and the Catholic Church are one and the same reality, as Pope Pius XII insisted in *Humani generis* (Lat., "Of the human race," 1950, n. 44) and before that in *Mystici Corporis Christi* ("Of the Mystical Body of Christ," 1943). A majority of the council fathers objected, and the verb was changed to "subsists in." A few attempts to water down the change were rejected by the Theological Commission: *subsistit integro modo* ("subsists in an integral manner"), which was proposed by nineteen bishops; and *iure divino subsistit* ("subsists by divine law"), which was proposed by twenty-five bishops. The change to *subsistit* brought out the point that the Catholic Church is wholly within the Body of Christ and its life is sustained and enriched by that union, but that there is room for other Christian Churches and ecclesial communities within the same Body of Christ, even if their union with it is not of the same order as the Catholic Church's. Here again we have the principle of "degrees of communion." The council is no longer teaching within the preconciliar category of membership, where one is either inside or completely outside the one, true Church of Christ according to the specific criteria of membership, namely, faith, Baptism, and communion with the Bishop of Rome.[38]

Other changes in this text worth noting include the dropping of the adjective *Romana* in *in Ecclesia Romana catholica* and the replacement, at the insistence of the Eastern-rite bishops, of *a Romana Pontifice* (Lat., "by the Roman Pontiff") with *successore Petri* ("by the successor of Peter").

The controversy over the correct interpretation of article 8 of *Lumen gentium* achieved renewed intensity in July 2007 with the publication of the document *Responses to Some Questions Regarding*

Certain Aspects of the Doctrine on the Church by the Vatican's Congregation for the Doctrine of the Faith (CDF) with the explicit approval of Pope Benedict XVI.[39] The document raised and answered five questions that, in the CDF's judgment, had become the source of confusion and even error in recent theological discussions regarding the Church. Questions 2 and 3 focused on the change from "is" to "subsists in" in article 8 of *Lumen gentium:* "What is the meaning of the affirmation that the church of Christ subsists in the Catholic Church?" and "Why was the expression *subsists in* adopted instead of the simple word *is*?"

The CDF document takes issue with the common interpretation given by theologians and council fathers alike, namely, that the council changed the verb from "is" to "subsists in" in order to make clear that the Catholic Church is not to be simply equated with the Body of Christ. There is room, in other words, for other Churches and ecclesial communities in the Body of Christ, even though there are "varying degrees" of communion between them and the Catholic Church.

The CDF declares, in its response to Question 2, that the "*subsistence* means this perduring historical continuity and the permanence of all the elements instituted by Christ in the Catholic Church, in which the church of Christ is concretely found on this earth." The word "subsists," the document continues, "can only be attributed to the Catholic Church alone precisely because it refers to the mark of unity that we profess in the symbols of the faith (I believe . . . in the 'one' church); and this 'one' church subsists in the Catholic Church."

In its response to Question 3, the CDF insists on "the full identity of the church of Christ with the Catholic Church," even though, in the words of the council itself (as translated in the CDF document), "numerous elements of sanctification and of truth" are to be found outside the structure of the Catholic Church, "but as gifts properly belonging to the church of Christ" and which "impel toward Catholic unity" (*Lumen gentium,* n. 8, para. 2). The CDF also acknowledges, with the council, that although these separated Churches and ecclesial communities suffer from "defects," they are "deprived neither of significance nor importance in the mystery of salvation." In fact, the

Spirit of Christ uses them as "instruments of salvation, whose value derives from that fullness of grace and of truth that has been entrusted to the Catholic Church" (Decree on Ecumenism, n.3, para. 4).

The CDF makes its point with even greater force in its accompanying commentary. What the council intended by the change of verbs from "is" to "subsists in," the commentary insists, was "simply . . . to recognize the presence of ecclesial elements proper to the church of Christ in the non-Catholic Christian communities. It does not follow that the identification of the church of Christ with the Catholic Church no longer holds nor that outside the Catholic Church there is a complete absence of ecclesial elements, a 'churchless void.'" Indeed, "the change from *est* to *subsistit in* takes on no particular theological significance of discontinuity with previously held Catholic doctrine." This change "does not signify that the Catholic Church has ceased to regard herself as the one true church of Christ. Rather it simply signifies a greater openness to the ecumenical desire to recognize the truly ecclesial characteristics and dimensions in the Christian communities not in full communion with the Catholic Church."[40]

Catholic readers in particular will certainly want to take into serious and respectful account the interpretation of article 8 given in this CDF document. On the other hand, the weight of interpretation continues to favor the great majority of theologians and bishops who have directly commented on this issue. Francis Sullivan, S.J., for many years professor of ecclesiology at the Pontifical Gregorian University in Rome and subsequently an adjunct professor at Boston College, has pointed out that the words *subsistit in* are often mistranslated. The verb means literally "to continue to exist." Thus, the church of Christ "continues to exist fully only in the Catholic Church." The key word here again is "fully."

"This implies the recognition that the church of Christ continues to exist, but not fully so, in other churches. This interpretation," Sullivan continues, "is consistent with" *Dominus Iesus* (n. 17), namely, that "the separated Eastern churches [are] 'true particular churches.' Vatican II teaches that the universal church of Christ exists 'in and out of' the particular churches. I do not know," Father Sullivan concludes, "how we could recognize the Orthodox as 'true particular churches' if we did not also recognize that the universal church of Christ is wider and more inclusive than the Roman Catholic Church."[41]

THE CHURCH AS ESCHATOLOGICAL COMMUNITY

The council taught, finally, that the Church cannot be understood except in relationship to the Kingdom, or Reign, of God. The Church is not an end in itself, but a means to and a manifestation and anticipation of a higher end, namely, the final Kingdom, or Reign, of God. The Pastoral Constitution on the Church in the Modern World puts it succinctly: "The Church has but one sole purpose—that the Kingdom of God may come and the salvation of the human race may be accomplished" (n. 45). Everything that the Church is and does is always subordinate to and in service of the coming Kingdom of God.

This teaching is in contrast to the common preconciliar assumption that the Church is the Kingdom of God on earth. Thus, parables of the Kingdom were regularly interpreted by preachers, catechists, and theologians alike as parables of the Church. The tendency to equate the Church with the Kingdom of God was denounced as a form of "triumphalism" in a famous intervention at Vatican II by Bishop Emile Jozef De Smedt (d. 1995) of Bruges, Belgium.[42] Indeed, article 5 of the Dogmatic Constitution on the Church was added to the document in its final drafting stage to counteract the residual traces of triumphalism in the document as a whole. Just as Jesus came to announce, personify, and bring about the Kingdom of God, so too the Church exists to proclaim, witness to, and help establish the Kingdom on earth and to facilitate its fulfillment at the end of history. But unlike Jesus, the Church cannot claim to be itself the Kingdom of God. It is at most "the seed and the beginning of that Kingdom. While it slowly grows to maturity, the Church longs for the completed Kingdom and, with all its strength, hopes and desires to be united in glory with its king."

The whole of chapter 7 of the Dogmatic Constitution on the Church is devoted to the eschatological nature of the Church under the title "The Pilgrim Church." The Church is "the universal sacrament of salvation," existing in "the final age of the world," whose renewal is "irrevocably under way." The Church is already enlivened by the Holy Spirit and in communion with the Lord, but it still belongs to the present age and "carries the mark of this world which will pass" (n. 48). Nevertheless, some of its members have gone ahead and already enjoy the fullness of eternal glory in heaven. These constitute the Church triumphant in the vast communion of saints. They become for the Church on earth (also known in the post-Reformation tradition as the Church militant) exemplars and models of Christian discipleship and holiness and as such are signs of the Kingdom itself and a "cloud of witnesses" to it (n. 50).

The implications of the eschatological nature of the Church have been realized already in the postconciliar Church in the form of increased self-criticism leading to the ongoing renewal and reform of the Church. This is clear in the readiness of church members to disagree publicly with their pastoral leaders, in their public exposure of various church faults, as tragically manifested, for example, in the sexual-abuse scandal in the priesthood in the early years of the twenty-first century, and in the various efforts to bring about structural change in the way in which bishops are selected and in the standards of eligibility for ordination to the priesthood.

SUMMARY CHART

Pre–Vatican II Ecclesiology	**Vatican II Ecclesiology**
Church as institution	Church as mystery, or sacrament
Church as hierarchy	Church as People of God
Mission: word and sacrament	Mission: word, sacrament, servant
Church as absolute monarchy	Church as a communion
One, true Church	Church as ecumenical community
Triumphalism (Church = Kingdom)	Church as eschatological community

The "Twin Pillars" of Vatican II's Ecclesiology: *Lumen gentium* and *Gaudium et spes*

Toward the end of the first session of Vatican II (December 4, 1962), in one of the most important speeches of the entire council, Cardinal Leo Jozef Suenens, then archbishop of Malines-Brussels in Belgium, formally introduced the now famous distinction between the Church *ad intra* and the Church *ad extra* in describing the council's overall agenda.[43] The conciliar documents, he said, must attend both to the inner life of the Church (*ad intra*) and to its relationship with the world beyond the Church (*ad extra*). As things developed over the next three years (the council adjourned on December 8, 1965), the two most important conciliar documents embodied fairly closely the distinction that Cardinal Suenens had pointed out that day. The Dogmatic Constitution on the Church (*Lumen gentium*) focuses largely, although not exclusively, on the internal life of the Church, while the Pastoral Constitution on the Church in the Modern World (*Gaudium et spes*) focuses almost entirely on the relationship of the Church to the world outside of it. It was said that Suenens's address was "received with great applause."[44]

It must be emphasized here that there is no adequate substitute for reading these two constitutions (and all of the other fourteen conciliar documents) in full, with a theologically and historically critical commentary at the ready.[45]

THE DOGMATIC CONSTITUTION ON THE CHURCH (*LUMEN GENTIUM*)

The first draft of *Lumen gentium* (then still known as *De Ecclesia*, Lat., "On the Church") was prepared by the council's Theological Commission (*De doctrina fidei et morum;* Lat., "On the Doctrine of Faith and Morals"), headed by Cardinal Alfredo Ottaviani, prefect of the Holy Office (now the Congregation for the Doctrine of the

Faith).[46] The Commission's secretary was Father Sebastian Tromp, S.J. (d. 1975), formerly professor of ecclesiology at the Pontifical Gregorian University in Rome and considered to have been the principal author of Pope Pius XII's encyclical *Mystici Corporis Christi* (1943), on the Church as the Mystical Body of Christ.

The first draft of *De Ecclesia* (which was to become *Lumen gentium*) consisted of eleven chapters and an appendix:

1. The nature of the Church militant.
2. The members of the Church and the necessity of the Church for salvation.
3. The episcopate as the highest grade of the sacrament of orders; the priesthood.
4. Residential bishops.
5. The state of evangelical perfection.
6. The laity.
7. The teaching office of the Church.
8. Authority and obedience in the Church.
9. Relationships between Church and state and religious tolerance.
10. The necessity of proclaiming the gospel to all peoples and in the whole world.
11. Ecumenism.
12. Appendix: Virgin Mary, Mother of God and Mother of Men [*sic*].

This initial draft was discussed in six separate plenary meetings (or Congregations) during the final week of the council's first session (December 1–7, 1962). Although there was some praise for the Theological Commission's work, the most significant comments called attention to the deficiencies of the first draft. Several bishops found the draft "too juridical" in tone and too little concerned with the Church as mystery, faulted its lack of structural coherence (a point raised explicitly by Milan's cardinal-archbishop Giovanni Battista Montini [later Pope Paul VI]), complained that the draft portrayed the laity as mere appendages of the hierarchy, expressed concern that the document was insufficiently sensitive to the legitimate role of the state alongside that of the Church, deplored the absence of any genuine ecumenical dimension, and criticized its lack of attention to the works of the Eastern fathers of the Church and to various biblical images of the Church, especially that of People of God. It was Bishop De Smedt of Belgium who synthesized these criticisms in a ringing, three-pronged attack on the first draft. He challenged its "triumphalism," "clericalism," and "juridicism."

Subsequent to Cardinal Suenens's intervention regarding the Church *ad intra* and the Church *ad extra,* a portion of the *De Ecclesia* draft dealing with the relationship of the Church to the wider world was separated off from the rest of the document and became known for a while as "Schema 17" (because it was the last of seventeen schemata), and then "Schema 13" (still last, but in a reduced list of schemata). The document eventually developed into *Gaudium et spes.* It was Cardinal Suenens who also suggested the title *Lumen gentium* ("Light of nations") for the Dogmatic Constitution on the Church, insisting, however, that Christ alone is the "light of nations."

A Central Commission was appointed to direct and coordinate the work of the various conciliar commissions, including the Theological Commission, during the nine-month recess between the first and second sessions. One of the six norms laid down to guide the work of the Central Commission, based on the various criticisms of the first draft of *De Ecclesia* and the opening address of Pope John XXIII, was that the pastoral nature of the council was always to have priority over the doctrinal or the juridical.

The Theological Commission, which was no longer under Cardinal Ottaviani's dominance, prepared a second draft of the *De Ecclesia* document and presented it to the council at the beginning of the second session in September 1963. It contained only four chapters:

1. The Mystery of the Church.
2. The hierarchical constitution of the Church and the episcopate in particular.
3. The People of God and the laity in particular.
4. The call to holiness in the Church.

The revised draft elicited a more positive reception than the first draft had received.[47] The first chapter no longer spoke of the Church as the Church militant. The Church is primarily a mystery and a community still on pilgrimage through history. It is not yet finished or perfected. Cardinal Raul Silva Henriquez (d. 1999), of Santiago, Chile, had proposed that an additional chapter be included on the People of God.

Chapter 2, on the hierarchical constitution of the Church, evoked the greatest controversy because of the issue of collegiality, that is, the collaboration of the worldwide episcopate with the Bishop of Rome in the governance of the universal Church. Various Italian and Spanish bishops expressed serious reservations about the concept. They preferred a more juridical understanding of the episcopate in which each individual bishop is related vertically and subordinately to the pope, without horizontal relationships with the other bishops. Opposition to collegiality was rooted in a concern that it might compromise the primacy of the pope and perhaps also the sovereignty of the bishop in his own diocese. However, the great majority of the council fathers, including Pope Paul VI himself, did not regard these as serious dangers, and it was clear that collegiality would remain in the text.

As the discussion moved to the third chapter of the second draft, it was evident that the council fathers wanted the chapter divided and the material on the People of God moved to a position between chapter 1, on the mystery of the Church, and chapter 3, on the Church's hierarchical structure. The bishops were also in favor of a portrayal of the laity as full partners with the hierarchy in the life and mission of the Church. It was determined, however, that most of the pastoral applications would be reserved for a separate document, which would become the Pastoral Constitution on the Church in the Modern World (*Gaudium et spes*).

The discussion of the second draft focused finally on the role of Mary in the history of salvation. A separate schema had already been prepared and entitled "The Blessed Virgin, Mother of the Church." The debate was among the sharpest in all of the council's four sessions. One side strongly favored having a separate schema on Mary, while the other wanted to incorporate it into the constitution itself. On October 25, 1963, the council moderators asked the bishops to come to a decision. A debate was arranged.

Cardinal Franz König (d. 2004), of Vienna, spoke on behalf of incorporation, and Cardinal Rufino Santos (d. 1973), of Manila, spoke on behalf of a separate schema. Cardinal Santos argued that Mary's role in salvation history transcended her place and function in the Church, but Cardinal König's arguments—that Mary is a type of the Church and its preeminent member and that she should not be isolated from the unity of the economy of salvation or from the central ecclesiological focus of the council—prevailed, but by the slimmest of margins: 1,114 to 1,074. The final text avoided the Scylla and Charybdis of Marian maximalism and Marian minimalism.[48] It situated Mary in the context of the mystery of the Church itself, leaving her with an exceedingly important place in the Christian life and in Catholic devotional life particularly, but without supplanting Jesus Christ at the center.

In a meeting at the North American College in Rome just prior to the vote, the Passionist biblical scholar Barnabas Mary Ahern (d. 1995) was invited to speak to the American bishops on the issues involved in the debate. Ahern, in full religious habit, was a compelling speaker, exuding a special kind of asceticism that almost always persuaded his more conservative audiences to embrace the findings of modern biblical scholarship. He reassured his audiences that they could embrace a more biblically based understanding of the role of Mary in our salvation that preserved the unique and indispensable role of Christ without abandoning their own traditional devotional attachments to the Blessed Mother. His approach was equally successful with the U.S. bishops. Given the fact that the winning margin was only forty votes, Ahern's intervention may indeed have made the difference in the final vote. It is a matter of some interest, however, that the practically definitive *History of Vatican II,* edited by Giuseppe Alberigo, makes no mention of this event.

Between the second and third sessions of the council the Theological Commission tried to bring the text into line with various criticisms and suggestions. Pope Paul VI also worked hard to win the widest possible support for the emerging document. In his opening address to the third session (September 14, 1964), the pope linked the work of Vatican II with that of Vatican I. As mentioned in IV.1.1, the earlier council had defined papal infallibility and reaffirmed the dogma of papal primacy, but was unable to complete its intended work on the episcopacy. Paul VI said that the role of the college of bishops in the governance of the Church was "the weightiest and most delicate" subject still facing Vatican II. If the current council did not address this issue, the false impression would persist that Vatican I had limited the authority of the bishops and had rendered superfluous any future ecumenical councils.[49]

The four chapters of the second draft were expanded to six, and two new chapters were added—one on the eschatological nature of the Church and the other on Mary—to bring the total to eight. A new article was added to chapter 1 to counteract what Bishop De Smedt had called the residue of triumphalism in the document. Article 5 underscored the common ground between the Church and the Kingdom of God, while making it clear that the two are not identical. The relationship of the Catholic Church to the Body of Christ was carefully nuanced in article 8 to leave room in the Body of Christ for non-Catholic Christian Churches and ecclesial communities. A separate chapter was added on the People of God to bring out the historical nature of the Church and the fundamental equality of all the baptized (chap. 2). Another chapter was added on the laity to emphasize their participation in the prophetic, priestly, and kingly ministries of Jesus (chap. 4). A separate chapter on members of religious communities was approved (chap. 6) and, as mentioned above, there were two new chapters, on the eschatological nature of the Church (chap. 7) and on Mary (chap. 8).

The major debate over this penultimate draft, however, had to do with the doctrine of the episcopate in chapter 3. The drafters were caught between two forces: the one jealous of papal prerogatives and fearful of any undermining of papal primacy; the other, suspicious of papal absolutism and supportive of collegiality. The text bent over backward to reassure the former group. To the extent that it may have satisfied more conservative bishops in the West, it weakened the text in the eyes of the Eastern bishops and patriarchs. On the final vote at this stage, more than two-thirds approved, although about five hundred voted *placet iuxta modum* (which means, loosely translated, "Yes, but with reservations").

Because of the significant critical mass of outright opponents and other concerned bishops, a *nota explicativa praevia* (Lat., "preliminary explanatory note"), also known simply as a *nota praevia* ("preceding note") and as a *nota explicativa* ("explanatory note,")[50] was appended on November 16, 1964, to the final text of the constitution, at the request and with the approval of Paul VI. The *nota* insisted that the word "college" was not to be taken in a juridical sense, that the college does not even exist without its head, whose "*function as Vicar of Christ and pastor of the universal Church*" is left "*intact,*" and that the pope, "as supreme pastor of the Church, may exercise his power at any time, as he sees fit, by reason of the demands of his office."[51] The majority of the bishops were deeply unhappy that the pope forced the *nota* on the council, while the minority, who were strongly opposed to collegiality, regarded it as a "modest gift."[52] Although the third session of the council ended in an atmosphere of considerable tension, the entire Dogmatic Constitution on the Church was approved with near unanimity in a first reading on November 19, 1964, followed by a final solemn vote on November 21. To the thunderous applause of the assembled bishops and non-Catholic observers, Pope Paul VI immediately promulgated the document for the universal Church.

The final version of *Lumen gentium* thus has eight chapters, the titles and principal topics of which are:

1. *The Mystery of the Church:* the Church as sacrament; the trinitarian framework for the mystery of the Church; various

biblical images of the Church, especially that of Body of Christ; the relationship of the Body of Christ to the Catholic Church and other Churches and ecclesial communities; the ongoing need for the renewal and reform of the Church.

2. *The People of God:* the Church on pilgrimage through history; the Church and Christ's threefold mission as prophet, priest, and king; the Church and the sacraments; the Church and non-Catholic Christians and non-Christians.
3. *The Hierarchical Structure of the Church, with Special Reference to the Episcopate:* the New Testament basis for the episcopate; the relationship between the episcopate and the papacy; collegiality; the local church; bishops, priests, and deacons.
4. *The Laity:* the fundamental equality of the laity with clergy and religious; the place of the laity in both the Church and the temporal world.
5. *The Call of the Whole Church to Holiness:* the holiness of groupings within the Church—bishops, clergy, religious, laity; the holiness of the Church itself.
6. *Religious:* the nature and importance of consecration and religious profession and of the observance of the evangelical counsels.
7. *The Eschatological Nature of the Pilgrim Church and Its Union with the Heavenly Church:* the Church and the Kingdom of God; death and the resurrection of the body; the communion of saints; the role of saints as models of Christian discipleship.
8. *The Blessed Virgin Mary, Mother of God, in the Mystery of Christ and the Church:* the role of the Blessed Virgin in the economy of salvation; the Blessed Virgin and the Church; devotion to the Blessed Virgin in the Church; Mary as a sign of sure hope and of solace for God's people on pilgrimage.

Preliminary Explanatory Note: a "theological qualification" of the doctrine of collegiality adopted as an appendix to the constitution, with special reference to chapter 3, in order to safeguard the primacy and pastoral independence of the pope.[53]

Among the most important ecclesiological teachings in *Lumen gentium* are:

1. The Church itself is a sacrament and does not simply administer the seven sacraments (n. 1). It is "the universal sacrament of salvation" (n. 48).
2. The Church exists for the sake of the Kingdom of God, but is not identical with it (n. 5).
3. The Body of Christ is larger than the Catholic Church (n. 8).
4. The Church is at once holy and always in need of renewal and reform (n. 8).
5. The Church is the whole People of God, not simply the hierarchy, the clergy, and religious (chap. 2).
6. All of the baptized participate in the one priesthood of Christ, even though the priesthood of the ordained differs "essentially" from that of the nonordained and not only "in degree" (n. 10).
7. There are degrees of incorporation into or communion with the Church (n. 14).
8. Non-Christians and nonbelievers can also be saved (n. 16).
9. The bishops, together with the Bishop of Rome, are the subject of supreme and full authority over the universal Church. They exercise that supreme authority in the most solemn way in an ecumenical council (n. 22).
10. The Bishop of Rome is "the perpetual and visible source and foundation of the unity of the bishops and of the multitude of the faithful," but the individual bishops exercise this same

authority and pastoral responsibility in their own dioceses (n. 23).

11. The universal Church consists of the communion of each of the local churches with one another (n. 23).
12. Infallibility is a gift to the whole Church, but it is officially exercised by the Bishop of Rome under certain limited conditions and by the whole body of his brother bishops (n. 25).
13. The local churches are each the Body of Christ in their own places; they are not simply administrative subdivisions of the one, universal Church (n. 26). And bishops are not mere "vicars" of the Bishop of Rome; they exercise an authority that is proper to them and not simply delegated by the pope (n. 27).
14. Priests and bishops constitute one priesthood, although there are different functions within that priesthood (n. 28).
15. Everything that has been said concerning the People of God in chapter 2 applies equally to the laity, religious, and clergy. The laity are not confined to the temporal sphere, but also have an important role to play in the Church (n. 30).
16. The laity participate directly in the mission of the Church by reason of their Baptism. They do not simply participate in the work of the hierarchy, by delegation of the hierarchy (n. 33). There is a legitimate and necessary public opinion in the Church and the freedom to express it (n. 37).
17. The pursuit of sanctity is not simply for priests and religious; all the baptized are called to holiness (chap. 5).
18. The saints are primarily models or exemplars of Christian discipleship rather than intercessors or miracle workers (n. 50).
19. Although Mary's greatest title is Mother of God, she is also a type of the Church and her dignity and role in the economy

of salvation cannot be understood apart from the mystery of the Church (nn. 60–65).

THE PASTORAL CONSTITUTION ON THE CHURCH IN THE MODERN WORLD (*GAUDIUM ET SPES*)

The story of the evolution of the second major document of Vatican II, *Gaudium et spes,* is long and complex. One of the key experts (Lat. *periti*) at the council, Canon Charles Moeller, at the time a member of the faculty at Louvain University in Belgium, has written perhaps the definitive—and certainly the most detailed—history of the Pastoral Constitution in the five-volume *Commentary on the Documents of Vatican II,* edited by the German theologian Herbert Vorgrimler.[54] A simpler, more condensed version, prepared by one of the most important contributors to the Pastoral Constitution, Archbishop Marcos McGrath (d. 2000), C.S.C., of Panama, is available in *Vatican II: An Interfaith Appraisal.*[55]

As Archbishop McGrath pointed out in his presentation at the University of Notre Dame's international conference on the council in March 1966, just over three months after the council's final adjournment, *Gaudium et spes* is the longest document ever produced by any of the twenty-one general, or ecumenical, councils recognized by the Catholic Church. He also underscored what is evident to anyone who has studied the history of the pastoral constitution, namely, that its length is of "dubious merit, especially for those [including himself] who over the course of three years had to rework the entire document of this Council, not merely by quantitative criterion [*sic*], but because it is the first time a Council has so directly and assiduously addressed itself to the whole broad question of the Church and the temporal order."[56]

Indeed, there was no other document even resembling the final version of *Gaudium et spes* when the council convened in October 1962. It was the product of a collaborative process within the council itself. One of the council fathers referred to it as "the prolongation of the Constitution on the Church." As already noted above, it was Cardinal Suenens, following the lead of Pope John XXIII himself, who emphasized the council's need to address both the internal life of the Church (Lat. *ad intra*) and its relationships with the rest of the world (*ad extra*). This is why the original document on the Church (*De Ecclesia*) had to be broken into two parts, with the pastoral constitution serving as the second.

First Stage: Emergence of the Idea

It was John XXIII's inaugural address to the council that opened the way forward to the preparation of a separate document on the Church's outreach to the modern world (for a review of this address, see section 3 above).[57] A delay of three days followed the opening assembly so that each national hierarchy could propose candidates to ensure that the commissions responsible for this document and others would be broadly representative of the worldwide Church. The council fathers then offered a message to the entire world as they were about to begin their first debates. They insisted that they were "not estranged from earthly concerns and toils," but were focused on the needs of the poor and those who suffer hunger, misery, and ignorance and that they were committed to the causes of peace and social justice.[58] Various developments that served collectively to broaden the council's vision of its agenda[59] were brought to clear expression by the influential speeches of Cardinal Suenens of Maline-Brussels, Cardinal Giacomo Lercaro (d. 1976) of Bologna, and Cardinal Montini of Milan (the future Pope Paul VI), in the closing days of the council's first session, insisting that the council should center its attention on the double theme encapsulated in the Latin phrases *ad intra* and *ad extra*.

Second Stage: Preparation of a Schema for Conciliar Debate

Pope John XXIII established a Coordinating Commission, which, soon after the close of the first session, reduced the number of preconciliar schemata from more than seventy to seventeen, the first of which was *De Ecclesia* and the last, *De praesentia activa Ecclesiae in mundo* (Lat., "On the active presence of the Church in the world"). This latter document was referred to then and for a time afterward as Schema 17, because it occupied the last place on the list. Schema 17 was to be drafted by a mixed commission consisting of the Theological Commission (also known as the Doctrinal Commission) and the Commission on the Lay Apostolate. Cardinal Suenens, as one of the seven cardinal-members of the Coordinating Commission, was named the *relator* (or chief presenter and floor manager) of the schema by his commission colleagues. Drawing upon some of the preconciliar schemata wherever possible, the commission prepared a new schema consisting of six chapters: the first on vocation in its full human and Christian meaning, and the other five on persons and personal rights, marriage and the family, culture and its spread, the socioeconomic order, and the community of nations and peace.

The work, however, proceeded slowly, given the need to consider other documents, especially the one on revelation, the first draft of which had been withdrawn the previous November by order of the pope himself (because so many of the council fathers had objected to its neo-Scholastic framework), and also the original document on the Church. At the end of May 1963, when the various subcommittees of the mixed commission began submitting their new drafts, John XXIII entered his final death agony. He died on June 3. Everything was left up in the air until a new pope could be elected and his desires for the council made known.

In his inaugural address at the opening of the council's second session in late September 1963, Pope Paul VI made no mention of Schema 17, although he included it by implication in citing the four ends of the council: meditation on the Church, renewal of the Church, the ecumenical effort, and the building of a bridge from the Church to the world. Most of the discussions during the second session were focused on the constitution on the Church. Little was said about Schema 17. In late November a meeting of a new body known as the Council of Presidents (including the twelve presidents, the four moderators, and members of the secretariat of the council) decided that the schema that had been completed in May was not yet mature enough for formal discussion on the council floor.

A debate ensued between those who insisted that the council's approach to social questions must be theological and doctrinal and those who argued that a document designed to speak to the modern world must begin with a consideration of the world's problems and communicate with people in language that is readily understandable and persuasive. (Jesuit church historian John W. O'Malley refers to this as a clash of cultures, what he calls Culture Two and Culture Three.[60]) A smaller steering committee (called a central mixed commission) was formed to try to resolve the differences and develop a text that would be acceptable to both sides. The committee proposed that the first, "doctrinal" chapter be developed at greater length, but that several other chapters be treated as appendices and neither debated nor voted upon. According to Archbishop McGrath, "the well-intentioned proposal reflected the lingering unwillingness of the commission members to plunge the Council into the debate of many temporal issues that seemed too passing, too contingent to become the object of a Conciliar document meant to stand for the ages."[61] Others were concerned about the lack of time.

The steering committee met before the end of the second session and decided that yet another draft should be attempted. The draft was completed by the end of January 1964 and was sent to the members of the mixed commission. After another meeting in March, further revisions of the draft were undertaken and were resubmitted to the mixed commission in early June. The revised schema was sent to the Coordinating Commission of the council, which approved it for distribution to the council fathers and for discussion on the council floor at the third session. By now it was called Schema 13, after the list of schemata was once again reduced. Many continued to regard the document as lightweight, stronger on sociology than on theological and doctrinal substance. It would take the pressure of debate at the third session plus the mounting interest of the press and others in various countries of the world to change that perception.

Third Stage: Council Debate and Revision

The new text contained a brief prologue identifying the Church with the "joys and sorrows" of the world and underscoring the council's desire to speak to the faithful and to anyone else who would listen regarding the "signs of the times" and what the Church should do in response to them. "No council, certainly not Trent," John O'Malley writes, "ever spoke like this about joys and sorrows."[62] There was continued concern and discussion about certain biblical, doctrinal, and theological elements and an added concern that the document was too European and Western in orientation. As a result, more bishops were added to the steering committee from Africa, Asia, and Latin America and from nations under Communist domination.

The most serious criticisms of the text were directed at its apparent dualism, setting the Church off from the world as if the two were completely separate entities, rather than seeing the Church as part of the world. By the end of January 1965, a new team of writers produced another draft that was carefully scrutinized and revised yet again by a large and diverse group of *periti,* including about twenty laymen and laywomen auditors, meeting at Aricca, near Rome. The plenary mixed commission worked assiduously from March 29 to April 6, 1965, approved more changes, and then left to the team of writers the task of incorporating all the revisions in a final text. On May 11 the schema was approved by the council's Coordinating Commission and sent to the council fathers for discussion, even though many recognized that it was still not in final form.

The discussion of Schema 13 within the council itself began on September 24 and proceeded for two weeks. As further revisions were suggested, they were incorporated into the text by the various subcommittees. The document returned to the council floor in early November and was voted upon, part by part. There were over twenty thousand *modi,* or proposed amendments, to consider. The modified texts were read and approved by the entire mixed commission, again part by part. The entire text was finally approved in early December, a feat that Archbishop McGrath described as "somewhat of a miracle."[63] Although, in the end, the Pastoral Constitution had a strong doctrinal content, its overall purpose remained essentially pastoral, directed toward motivating Christians to act together and singly in service to the whole world, through dialogue and cooperation with all persons of goodwill.

Among the most important ecclesiological teachings in *Gaudium et spes* are:

1. The Church cannot address only its own members when presuming to teach about matters of faith and morals; it also has a responsibility to address the whole of humanity on issues that are of concern to all (n. 1).

2. The Church is a servant Church, not motivated by earthly ambition but interested only in bearing witness to the truth under the guidance of the Holy Spirit; its mission is to save and not to judge, to serve and not to be served (n. 3). It has but a single intention: that God's Kingdom may come and the salvation of the human race may be accomplished (nn. 45, 72).

3. In every age the Church has the responsibilities of reading the "signs of the times" and of interpreting them in the light of the gospel (nn. 4, 44).

4. The Church must counter what it regards as error, including atheism, by presenting a positive version of the truth and by lending intrinsic credibility to that teaching by the quality of its own life (n. 21).

5. The Church must recognize that the growth of the Kingdom of God is moving toward the consummation of the earth and of humanity itself. Indeed, earthly progress is "of vital concern" to the coming Kingdom of God, which is a Kingdom not only of truth and of life, but also of justice, love, and peace (n. 39). The Church, therefore, must act as a leaven in society, challenging the false dichotomy between religious life and the demands of justice and peace (nn. 40, 43).

6. Although Christ did not bequeath to the Church a mission in the political, economic, or social order (n. 42), it is concerned with issues in these spheres whenever fundamental human rights or the salvation of souls require it (n. 76). At the same time, the Church must recognize that the political community as well as the Church are autonomous and independent of each other in their own fields (nn. 76, 89).

7. The Church may never employ methods of preaching, teaching, or missionary activity that are at odds with the gospel or the welfare of humanity (n. 76).

8. The Church can never tie itself to any one culture or to any political, economic, or social system (nn. 42, 76).

9. The laity, whose ministerial role is largely in the world beyond the Church, are also called to participate actively in the entire life of the Church (n. 43). They should be accorded a legitimate freedom of inquiry, thought, and expression consistent with the level of theological and professional competence they have achieved (n. 62).

10. The Church is itself a sacrament or sign of the human solidarity that makes possible sincere dialogue and strengthens it. But it can fulfill this role only to the degree that there is mutual esteem and harmony within the Church itself, an acknowledgment of all legitimate diversity within the Church, and fruitful dialogue among its own members, leaders and rank-and-file alike (n. 92).

Vatican II: Continuity or Discontinuity?

In his survey of fifty years of ecclesiology, Avery Dulles (later Cardinal Dulles) suggests that there is a division in the hermeneutics, or interpretations, of Vatican II between those who argue that the council's reaffirmations of previous official teachings of the Church were more central than its innovations and those who argue the reverse. Benedict XVI, in his Christmas address to members of the Roman Curia in 2005 and before that as Cardinal Joseph Ratzinger, has taken a position similar to Dulles's. The conflict, both agree, is between a hermeneutics of continuity (what Ratzinger called "reform") and a hermeneutics of discontinuity (what Ratzinger called "rupture"), and both express a preference for the former.[64]

However, when Cardinal Ratzinger and Avery Dulles were expressing their initial reservations about certain interpretations of the council in 1985 and 1989, respectively, the massive five-volume *History of Vatican II,* undertaken by the so-called Bologna school[65] and edited by Giuseppe Alberigo, had not yet begun to appear. The publication of that history provoked a delayed—and strongly negative—reaction from Archbishop Agostino Marchetto, a church historian, Secretary for the Pontifical Council for Migrants and Itinerant People, and formerly apostolic nuncio to the United Nations Food and Agriculture Organization.[66] He is sharply critical of the Bologna school's interpretation, which he accuses of being "ideological" and "unbalanced" in favoring a hermeneutic of discontinuity over a hermeneutic of continuity.[67]

Unfortunately, proponents of the so-called revisionist, or "contrapuntal," interpretation of the council have tended to pose the issue in an either/or fashion, when, in fact, the two hermeneutics, of continuity and of discontinuity, are complementary rather than contradictory—both/and, not either/or. Examples of this more balanced approach are provided by such theologians as Hermann Pottmeyer, emeritus professor at Bochum University in Germany, and Gustave Thils (d. 2000), longtime professor at the Catholic University of Louvain, in Belgium.[68] Pottmeyer and Thils have acknowledged that the so-called progressive interpretations associated with the hermeneutics of discontinuity "have occasionally forgotten that the Council retracted nothing in the dogmas of Trent and Vatican I," while the so-called conservative interpretations associated with the hermeneutics of continuity "have occasionally forgotten that despite their will to continuity the council fathers attached differing values to the theses in question. The theses defended by the minority do not represent the will of the Council in the same degree as the theses that passed by an overwhelming majority."[69]

Since Avery Dulles has linked this author with advocates of a hermeneutic of discontinuity, albeit in the enviable company of Edward Schillebeeckx,[70] I shall enumerate, contrary to Dulles's categorization, some examples of conciliar teachings that represent *reaffirmations* of the Catholic ecclesiological tradition *and* some that represent *innovations* in the sense of fresher, less rigid interpretations and/or retrievals of elements of that tradition. The reaffirmations:

1. The Church is the Body of Christ (*Lumen gentium,* n. 7).
2. The Church is at once divine and human, an invisible communion in grace and a visible, structured community. Together the two form one interlocking reality, not two separate realities (*Lumen gentium,* n. 8).
3. It is through the sacraments (and the exercise of the virtues) that the sacred nature and organic structure of the Church are brought into operation (*Lumen gentium,* n. 11).
4. The Eucharist is the center and source of this sacramental life (*Lumen gentium,* n. 11) and is the sign and instrument of the unity of the Church (Decree on Ecumenism, n. 2).
5. The Catholic Church is the fullness of the Body of Christ (*Lumen gentium,* n. 14).
6. The Petrine office, or papacy, is essential to the Church (*Lumen gentium,* n. 18).
7. The episcopate is essential to the Church (*Lumen gentium,* n. 20).
8. The Church is called to proclaim the gospel to all people (Decree on the Church's Missionary Activity, n. 1).
9. The Church is the universal sign and instrument of salvation for all humankind (Decree on Ecumenism, n. 3; Decree on the Church's Missionary Activity, n. 3).
10. The Church, like Jesus, is a servant community (*Gaudium et spes,* n. 3).

The innovations:

1. The Church is itself a sacrament (*Lumen gentium,* n. 1).

2. The Church is not itself the Kingdom of God on earth, but its "initial budding forth" (*Lumen gentium,* n. 5).

3. The Church of Christ "subsists in" in the Catholic Church and is, therefore, not simply identical with it (*Lumen gentium,* n. 8; see also #10 below).

4. The Church is itself both holy and sinful and, therefore, always in need of being purified and incessantly pursues the path of penance and renewal (*Lumen gentium,* n. 8).

5. Salvation is available outside as well as inside the Catholic Church (*Lumen gentium,* n. 16; see also #11 below).

6. Bishops are not vicars of the pope (*Lumen gentium,* n. 27). They are constituted as members of the college of bishops not by the conferral of jurisdiction by the pope, but by sacramental consecration (*Lumen gentium,* n. 22).

7. The governance of the Church devolves upon the whole college of bishops, upon the pope as earthly head of the Church, upon bishops meeting in regional, international, and ecumenical councils, and upon the individual bishop in his own diocese (*Lumen gentium,* nn. 22–23).

8. The laity participate directly in the mission of the Church by reason of Baptism and Confirmation and not by episcopal delegation (*Lumen gentium,* n. 33).

9. The whole People of God—laity, clergy, and religious—participate in the threefold mission of Jesus as prophet, priest, and king or shepherd (*Lumen gentium,* n. 30).

10. The Body of Christ is composed of more than Catholics (Decree on Ecumenism, n. 3).

11. Non-Christian religions may also function as instruments of salvation for their own adherents (Declaration on the Relationship of the Church to Non-Christian Religions, n. 2).

12. Religious freedom is required for all, including non-Catholics, because of their human dignity and the freedom of the act of faith (Declaration on Religious Freedom, nn. 2–4).

In the current controversy regarding continuity versus discontinuity, Avery Dulles and others have voiced some of the concerns of Vatican II's minority, namely, that Vatican II was being portrayed by many in the majority as discontinuous from Vatican I. But there is more to the interpretation of a council than a careful analysis of its documents. There is also such a thing as its "style."

The Style of Vatican II

By way of a codicil to the preceding section, we turn here to the recent work of a distinguished Jesuit church historian and specialist on the Second Vatican Council, John W. O'Malley, for many years professor at the Weston Jesuit School of Theology in Cambridge, Massachusetts, and subsequently as chaired professor at Georgetown University. O'Malley has offered a distinctive prism for interpreting the conciliar teachings and the council as an event, namely, its style of teaching and of functioning as a council, with the consequences that it brought about—or hoped to effect—in the way the Church "does business."[71]

"Vatican II," O'Malley points out, "for all its continuity with previous councils, was unique in many ways but nowhere more than in its call for an across-the-board change in church procedures or, better, in church *style*."[72] His own interpretation of the council differs from two others: a minority view that sees Vatican II as an aberration from which nothing is to be learned or applied to the life of the Church and a second, quasi-official view that insists that the council did not introduce anything at all that was truly new or different. On the contrary, O'Malley holds that the council represented, in fact, "a significant break with the past"—but not one in which the Church became something other than itself, anymore than France became something other than France after the French Revolution.

One cannot ignore the reality that the great majority of the council fathers, as they came to the end of their deliberations, were indeed convinced that something of deep significance had happened. And that was borne out in changes that actually occurred immediately following the council, such as the phenomenon of Catholics praying with their Protestant neighbors, particularly at weddings and funerals, where such participation had been strictly forbidden prior to the council. Moreover, the "battles in the council over the decrees on ecumenism and religious freedom were fought not only with great passion but, especially by those opposed to them, almost as life-and-death issues. That minority, which was small but intelligent and fiercely loyal to the church, was utterly convinced that these decrees were changes so large that they could not be tolerated." In seeing them as changes of such great magnitude, O'Malley notes, they were "absolutely correct," even though the actual wording of the documents gave little hint that the council had decided to move the Church along "a remarkably new path."

These and other specific changes the council made are important, O'Malley insists. But they do not tell us *what* the Church is, but *how* it is. "'*How* is the church?' That is where Vatican II becomes radical . . . that is, what kind of procedures does it use; what kind of relationships does it foster among its members; what is its *style* as an institution?" (italics in the original). What made Michelangelo a great painter, O'Malley observes, was not *what* he painted but *how* he painted, his *style.*

For the same reason, it is the style, or spirit and form, of the council's documents that makes them unique in the history of councils. "In dramatic fashion," O'Malley writes, "the council abandoned for the most part the terse, technical, juridical and other punitive language of previous councils." There were no ultimata, no threats of punishment. Rather, the council's style was "invitational." The Scholastic mode of discourse during the medieval period was essentially dialectical, involving debates against the adversary, but the council's style was based for the most part, as was the approach of the early fathers of the Church, "on rhetoric, the art of persuasion, the art of finding common ground. . . . It looked to winning assent to its teachings rather than imposing it." Thus, words like "dialogue," "collaboration," "cooperation," and "collegiality" often recur in the documents.

In the nineteenth century and first half of the twentieth, the style of leadership, especially at the papal and curial levels, was often intransigent and highly autocratic. That mode of leadership prevailed until the election of Pope John XXIII in 1958 and the convening of the Second Vatican Council in 1962. That earlier mode of leadership had "ignored or badly minimized the horizontal traditions of Catholicism." Although the council did not wish to change the Church into a democracy, "it did want to redefine how that authority (and all authority in the church) was to function, for instance, with a respect for conscience that transformed the members of the church from 'subjects' into participants." The Church would not abdicate its role as teacher of the gospel, but "like all good teachers, needed to learn as it taught."

O'Malley summarizes the content of this new style of being Church in five points. First, the Church changed from an exclusively top-down form of behavior to one of cooperation, collaboration, and collegiality. The Church would now act like the People of God. Second, the Church would be more servant than controller. To serve effectively requires that one be in touch with the needs of those being served, rather than supplying them with "prefabricated solutions." Third, the council used words like "development," "progress," and even "evolution." This represented a break from "the static framework of understanding doctrine [and] discipline." Fourth, the council replaced the vocabulary of exclusion with that of inclusion. Instead of anathemas and excommunications, the documents are filled with references to "sisters and brothers" and "men and women of goodwill." Fifth, the council moved from a vocabulary suggesting passive acceptance of church teachings to one of active participation and engagement. Nowhere was this more evident than in the liturgical reforms, which stressed the active participation of the congregation in the celebration of the Mass and the sacraments. "If the way we pray," Father O'Malley concludes, "is a norm for the way we believe, may it not also be a norm for the way we behave? That is, may it be constitutive of our style as church?"

Approaches to the Interpretation of Conciliar Texts

By way of example only, there are at least three complementary and often overlapping approaches to the interpretation of conciliar texts in addition to John W. O'Malley's interpretation of their style (above): those of the Australian theologian Ormond Rush, those of the Final Report of the Extraordinary Synod of 1985, and those of the author of this book.

ORMOND RUSH

Ormond Rush is past president of St. Paul's Theological College in Banyo, Queensland, Australia. He is not an ecclesiologist by specialization, but rather has lectured in foundational theology, theological hermeneutics (which was the subject of his doctoral dissertation),[73] Christology, and the theology of creation. His book *Still Interpreting Vatican II: Some Hermeneutical Principles,*[74] offers some practical, if also somewhat repetitive, rules for interpreting the various conciliar documents.

The first of three sets of rules, in the form of a series of questions, is called *diachronic,* referring generally to the historical development of the documents from the preconciliar period through the four sessions and three intersessions of the council itself, and which Rush calls a "hermeneutics of the authors":[75]

1. How does the history of a text affect our understanding of it?
2. How did the text change, if at all, during the course of the council?
3. Did the council anticipate and provide for development of the topic following the council?
4. How did the council critically "receive" and incorporate earlier theological positions?

5. Did the council deliberately leave some questions open?
6. What significance is there in the council's decision to avoid certain theological formulations?

The second set of rules in the form of questions is called *synchronic*, which Rush calls a "hermeneutics of the text," referring to the need to read each text in relation to comparable conciliar texts:[76]

1. How should a particular text be read in the context of the whole corpus of conciliar documents?
2. Are there some texts that provide a hermeneutical key for interpreting other texts?
3. What weight should be accorded to one conciliar text over another?

The third set of rules, in the form of questions, Rush calls "a hermeneutics of the receivers." It interprets the texts in the light of their subsequent *reception* in the life of the Church (also a topic of Rush's dissertation):

1. What themes have been emphasized or neglected in the postconciliar life and teaching of the Church?
2. What themes have been emphasized or neglected in post-conciliar theological literature?
3. What conciliar teachings have or have not had an impact on church law, structures, and pastoral practice?

THE EXTRAORDINARY SYNOD OF 1985

Pope John Paul II convened the Extraordinary Synod to celebrate the twentieth anniversary of Vatican II's final adjournment on December 8, 1965.[77] Although many Catholics at the time were concerned that the synod would somehow revoke the reforms of the council, it did not do so. On the contrary, in its Final Report it unanimously affirmed the council "as a grace of God and a gift of the Holy Spirit, from which have come forth many spiritual fruits for the universal church and the particular churches, as well as for the men [*sic*] of our time" (I.2).

The Extraordinary Synod also pointed to various "deficiencies and difficulties in the acceptance of the council, . . . in part due to an incomplete understanding and application of the council, in part to other causes" (I.3). Included among these causes are "a partial and selective reading of the council, as well as a superficial interpretation of its doctrine in one sense or another" (I.4). There followed a paragraph in I.5, "A Deeper Reception of the Council," in which the following principles of interpretation are found, as paraphrased by Avery Dulles:

1. Each passage and document of the council must be interpreted in the context of all the others, so that the integral teaching of the council can be rightly grasped.

2. The four constitutions of the council (liturgy, Church, revelation, and Church in the modern world) are the hermeneutical key to the other documents, namely, the council's nine decrees and three declarations.

3. The pastoral import of the documents ought not to be separated from, or set in opposition to, their doctrinal content.

4. No opposition may be made between the spirit of the council and the letter of the council.

5. The council must be interpreted in continuity with the great tradition of the Church, including other councils.

6. Vatican II should be accepted as illuminating the problems of our day.

Like his fellow Jesuit Avery Dulles, John W. O'Malley believes these rules to be fundamentally sound and "could hardly be improved upon."[78] However, O'Malley, unlike Dulles, argues that the Extraordinary Synod's list of norms needs to be complemented by a seventh that would take into account the element of discontinuity. "As a historian,"

O'Malley writes, "I believe that we must balance the picture by paying due attention to the discontinuities. When we do so, one thing at least becomes clear: the council *wanted* something to happen."[79] The council was not simply to be a reiteration of previous councils, but was to embark on a different course in response to new and unprecedented pastoral challenges.

TEN PRACTICAL NORMS

The following principles of interpretation do not neglect any of the criteria given above, although they would seem to be more complete than those of the Extraordinary Synod and less repetitious and complex than those of Ormond Rush:

1. What does the text actually say (in the original Latin and in translation)?

2. What does a specific passage mean, given its immediate context within the document itself?

3. How was the text formulated? What is its developmental history?

4. What is the *wider* context of the text, that is, in relation to other pertinent conciliar documents and developments within the Body of Christ? Does it appear in one of the four constitutions or in a decree or declaration? Is the text reaffirmed in other conciliar texts as well?

5. What is the *widest* context of the text, that is, in relation to developments—religious, social, political, cultural—in the world beyond the Body of Christ?

6. Do the arguments and assumptions embodied in the text hold together? Are they *internally* coherent?

7. Can the arguments and assumptions be validated? In other words, are they also *externally* coherent? Is the text consistent,

therefore, with biblical, historical, theological, and doctrinal sources?

8. Is the text consistent with the current theological discussion of the issue(s) at hand and with the experience and convictions of qualified and interested parties?

9. How has the text been received? Has it actually influenced the self-understanding and pastoral practice of the Church? To what extent?

10. What did the council leave out of given texts and the various documents? How does this absence, intended or not, affect the interpretation of the texts that remain?

This discussion regarding the controversy over Vatican II's continuity with or discontinuity from Vatican I might give rise to confusion in the minds of some readers regarding Paul VI's actual attitude toward the Second Vatican Council. Indeed, the critics of the Alberigo school of interpretation have charged this school of thought with harboring a negative view of the pope who presided over three of the council's four sessions. Such an impression would be misleading and even erroneous. For that reason, Part V ends with an essentially positive consideration of Paul VI's role in the council, and specifically his first encyclical, *Ecclesiam Suam,* which appeared just prior to the council's third session.

Pope Paul VI's *Ecclesiam Suam* (1964)

Pope Paul VI's first encyclical, *Ecclesiam Suam* (Lat., "His Church"), was published on August 6, 1964, during the break between the council's second and third sessions. It was at the third session that the council debated the issues of papal primacy and collegiality, so the encyclical was read with an eye toward discerning how the pope himself might come down on these issues. Paul VI made it clear early in this lengthy and what he called "conversational" document that he did not intend to intrude upon the "full liberty of investigation and discussion" of the council fathers (n. 33).[80]

However, concerns were expressed at the time that the encyclical's ecclesiology reflected too much the preconciliar approaches of theologians such as Charles (later Cardinal) Journet, the Swiss theologian whose work fell somewhere between the rigidly juridical ecclesiology of the Latin manuals and the more advanced and openly ecumenical approach of ecclesiologist Yves Congar and the Mystical Body theology of Pope Pius XII. It seemed to some of the bishops and other commentators that the encyclical had been written to mollify the minority who were anxious about the possible dilution of papal authority. There was, for example, only one mention of the People of God in the document, and then only in the citation from 1 Peter 2:9 on the royal priesthood. On the other hand, one of the contributors to Giuseppe Alberigo's *History of Vatican II,* which has been typecast by conservative interpreters of the council as a one-sided advocate of the hermeneutics of discontinuity, argued the contrary position, namely, that both the history of the encyclical and also the spirit that animated it "established a close link between it and the ecclesiology of Vatican II."[81]

In any event, the encyclical made only limited impact on the council itself. It was rarely cited in conciliar documents, but it did lend papal support to the orientation that was evident in the drafting of the Pastoral Constitution on the Church in the Modern World (*Gaudium et spes*). Indeed, the distinguished moral theologian Bernard Häring (d. 1998), who was one of the drafters of *Gaudium et spes,* insisted that the encyclical had made a "decisive contribution" to the document because of its emphasis on the need for dialogue between the Church and the world.[82] In the case of the Decree on Ecumenism, on the other hand, the lack of reference to the encyclical was a function of timing. The decree had already been approved by the pope the previous April and was finally promulgated, after minor editing, on November 21, 1964.

The encyclical itself is organized in three major sections: the first calls the Church to a deeper self-knowledge (nn. 9–40); the second, to renewal and reform (nn. 41–57);[83] and the third, to dialogue on multiple levels (nn. 96–end). Although the encyclical covers a broad range of issues that were before the council, the longest and perhaps most enduringly relevant part concerns the matter of dialogue. "The Church," Paul VI writes, "can regard no one as excluded from its motherly embrace, no one as outside the scope of its motherly care. It has no enemies except those who wish to make themselves such. Its catholicity is no idle boast. It was not for nothing that it received its mission to foster love, unity and peace among men [*sic*]" (n. 94).

Dialogue must occur at four different levels, which the pope describes as concentric circles (nn. 96–end): the first and widest comprises all the people of the earth, with whom dialogue must be initiated and sustained on each of the great problems of the world; the second circle includes all religious people apart from Christianity; the third, all non-Catholic Christians; and the fourth, all Catholics. Although the spirit of the encyclical's approach to dialogue is consistently positive, the words have an occasionally defensive, even slightly authoritarian, tone. Thus, for example, it speaks of the need for all Catholics to be "obedient" to the Church's "canonical regulations" and to their "lawful superiors" (n. 115).

Nevertheless, the encyclical ends on a hopeful note: "We rejoice and find great consolation in the fact that this dialogue, both inside and outside the Church, has already begun. The Church today is more alive than ever before" (n. 117). One might say, thanks in large measure to John XXIII, Paul VI himself, and especially the Second Vatican Council.

Concluding Reflections

The Second Vatican Council was surely the most important religious event of the twentieth century, notwithstanding some recent efforts to downgrade its significance and to impede its long-term impact on the life of the Church (see section 8 above). The critics are careful, however, not to attack the council directly. That would fly in the face of countless positive statements about the council by Pope John

Paul II, such as his insistence that "the best preparation for the new millennium, therefore, can only be expressed in a renewed commitment to apply, as faithfully as possible, the teachings of Vatican II to the life of every individual and to the whole Church."[84] An attack on Vatican II itself would also contradict the central conclusion of the Extraordinary Synod, which the same pope convened in 1985 to celebrate the twentieth anniversary of the council's adjournment. The synod, in its Final Report, unanimously declared, as previously noted, that the council was "a grace of God and a gift of the Holy Spirit, from which have come forth many spiritual fruits for the universal church and the particular churches, as well as for the men [*sic*] of our time" (I.2). Indeed, on the day of the council's final adjournment, December 8, 1965, Pope Paul VI issued an apostolic brief, or letter, in which he noted that the council had been "without doubt among the greatest events of the Church," "the richest because of the questions which for four sessions [were] discussed carefully and profoundly," and "the most opportune" because it had addressed "the necessities of the day, . . . sought to meet pastoral needs," and "made a great effort to reach not only Christians still separated from communion with the Holy See, but also the whole human family."[85]

The tactic that some of the council's critics have employed, beginning soon after the council adjourned, has been much more prudent and pragmatic than a direct, frontal attack would have been. Their approach, instead, has been to insist that the council changed nothing at all. And if it changed nothing, it requires no change in the Church, in any of its members, or in any of its pastoral leaders.

While doing research for this part of the book, I came across a column I had written at Christmas 1966, one year after Vatican II had closed. The column is entitled "Did the Council Change Anything?" It begins with the words: "The strongest and, in the long run, the most effective opposition to the Second Vatican Council comes not from the vocal detractors of the Council's spirit and orientation, but rather from those who insist that the Council really changed nothing at all."

It continues: "When opponents of Vatican II insist that the Council really changed nothing at all, they are right if they mean that it brought to a fuller flowering the authentic tradition of the Church. But one may seriously question if this is what they mean. For the Council does, in fact, pose a challenge to change. It has changed much that was once considered a part of the authentic tradition of the Church: some of the theology of our catechisms and seminary manuals and pulpit oratory" characteristic of the first half of the twentieth century. What the Second Vatican Council demonstrated was that this theology, which was for so long assumed to be "traditional," was not traditional at all.[86]

Nevertheless, the revisionist reaction is understandable, even if not wholly justifiable, because the council did challenge many conventional assumptions about the nature and mission of the Church: that the Church is equivalent to the hierarchy, that the laity have no active role to play in it, that the pope alone is in charge of the universal Church, that the mission of the Church is limited to the preaching of the word and the celebration of the sacraments, that only Catholics are in the Body of Christ, that all Catholics are "Roman" Catholics, and that any form of worship with non-Catholic Christians is always forbidden. Adjusting to, much less embracing and implementing, such changes as these and others like them has been exceedingly difficult for many Catholics, although by no means for the great majority.

As the eminent nineteenth-century theologian Cardinal John Henry Newman once said, "To live is to change, and to be perfect is to have changed often." Indeed, the only evidence we have of life, he pointed out, is growth. Accordingly, those who resist growth unwittingly suppress the capacity for life, and in the process they also close off our God-given quest for perfection.

More than three years before the opening of Vatican II, in October 1962, Pope John XXIII began referring to the coming council as "a new Pentecost," that is, a new outpouring of the Holy Spirit upon the Church.[87] More than a decade later, Cardinal Leo Josef Suenens, primate of Belgium and one of the leading figures at the council, tried to keep alive John XXIII's dream in his own book *A New Pentecost?* whose epilogue begins with these words: "The Spirit remains at the heart of the Church, directing us toward the future. We should like to have a glimpse of that future, so as to read better the signs of the time. But that is not essential: our hope for the future is not based on statistics and charts. It derives entirely from faith in the Spirit, who is with the Church as it moves into the future."[88]

The first Pentecost has sometimes been referred to as the "birthday of the Church." In reigniting the fires of the original Pentecost, the Second Vatican Council also brought about a rebirth of the Church itself.

PART VI

Post–Vatican II Ecclesiology

The Church ad Extra

As Parts III and IV suggest, the Catholic Church adopted an increasingly defensive stance toward the world beginning especially in the sixteenth century, during its Counter-Reformation phase, and continuing to the very threshold of the Second Vatican Council in the second half of the twentieth century. Internally, Catholicism also began to stress even more the juridical and institutional aspects of the Church.

However, as Part V discloses, the Second Vatican Council (1962–65) retrieved much of the ancient Church's more dialogical stance toward the world and the Church's emphasis on its communal, participatory life (see Part II.2, on the New Testament period, and Part III.2.1–6, on the postbiblical Church). Parts VI and VII will show how and to what extent post–Vatican II theology and official teachings have carried forward and developed further the Church's newly retrieved dialogical stance toward the world and its renewed emphasis on the communal nature of its ecclesial life.[1]

Parts VI and VII adopt, for organizational purposes, the twofold division proposed at the Second Vatican Council by Belgium's Cardinal

Leo Jozef Suenens and embraced by Popes John XXIII (1958–63) and Paul VI (1963–78) and by the great majority of council fathers, namely, between the Church *ad extra* and the Church *ad intra* (see Part V.7). The former is considered here in Part VI; the latter, in Part VII.

The Church *ad extra* is concerned with the relationship of the Church, and specifically the Catholic Communion of Churches, to realities external to it, without prejudice to the inevitable overlapping of the two spheres *ad extra* and *ad intra*. The Church *ad intra* is concerned with the internal life of the Church, but again without prejudice to the inevitable overlapping of the two spheres. Issues pertaining to the Church *ad extra* were most directly addressed in the council's Pastoral Constitution on the Church in the Modern World (*Gaudium et spes,* Lat., "Joy and hope"). Issues pertaining to the Church *ad intra* were most directly addressed in the council's Dogmatic Constitution on the Church (*Lumen gentium,* "Light of nations"). Both together—not separately, much less in opposition to each other—represent the ecclesiological mind of Vatican II.

Part VI is concerned with (1) the relationship of the Church to the Kingdom, or Reign, of God;[2] (2) the relationship of the Church to the world at large;[3] (3) salvation outside the Church—for non-Catholic Christians, non-Christians, and nonbelievers alike;[4] (4) Catholic social teaching as it impacts the world outside (but also inside) the Church;[5] (5) the role of the Church in the political order;[6] (6) liberation theology, a form of political theology that focuses on the role of the Church in specific settings, especially but not exclusively in Latin America; and (7) the relationship of the Church and the Holy Spirit.[7] This last topic provides a bridge to Part VII, which is concerned with the internal life of the Church.

Issues pertaining to the life of the Church *ad intra* in Part VII include (1) the Church as a communion;[8] (2) authority in the Church;[9] (3) the reception of doctrine and disciplinary decrees;[10] (4) ministry, both ordained and nonordained;[11] (5) an excursus on the Church's liturgical and sacramental life; (6) the role of Mary in the Church;[12] (7) feminist and nonfeminist ecclesiology by Catholic women; (8) Hispanic and Latino/a ecclesiologies; (9) African and African American ecclesiologies; (10) new movements in the Church, including basic ecclesial communities; and (11) the emerging world-Church,[13] which provides a link back to the various issues treated in Part VI under the general heading of the Church *ad extra*.

It is important to note that references, by way of thumbnail sketches, to various theologians in Parts VI and VII are generally limited to major figures like Yves Congar and Karl Rahner, from whose writings others have derived some of their own key ideas about the Church. Therefore, the bibliographical references throughout Parts VI and VII and in the Select Bibliography at the end of this book are not to be regarded as complete. Far from it. Readers, including teachers and students of ecclesiology, are encouraged to develop their own, more detailed bibliographies drawn from recent and current theological monographs and from articles in various theological and popular journals.

It is also important to note that the topics and issues considered in Parts VI and VII are too numerous and too broad in scope for anything approaching adequate treatment. Readers will be introduced to each issue, with some few bibliographical references by way of illustration only. Undoubtedly some readers, especially those who teach ecclesiology or who are involved in graduate-level study of the subject, will wonder why this or that issue was not included. Perhaps one or more of these missing topics can be considered for incorporation in a future edition. The author, however, is confident that most, if not all, of the principal topics and issues found in post–Vatican II ecclesiology are considered herein.

Part VIII, finally, summarizes and synthesizes the material presented throughout the book, draws some overarching conclusions about the present state of ecclesiology, and then offers a few tentative reflections on the future of the Church and ecclesiology.

The Church and the Kingdom, or Reign, of God

Much has been written since Vatican II concerning the central connection between the Church and the Kingdom, or Reign, of God.[14]

The summaries included herein are intentionally brief, designed only to provide a general sense of the ecclesiological work being done on this important topic since the council. There is no substitute, of course, for actually reading these and other authors' writings on this and other subjects treated in this part.

What is of general significance, however, is that, following the council, ecclesiology took a major turn in an eschatological direction. The Kingdom, or Reign, of God was no longer seen as an image of, much less a synonym for, the Church, particularly in Roman Catholic theology. The Kingdom became for ecclesiology—Catholic, Protestant, and Anglican alike—the central point of reference, second only to Jesus Christ himself. Post–Vatican II ecclesiology has also taken a pneumatological turn consistent with the emphasis in Orthodox ecclesiology, as will become clear in our subsequent discussions of the relationship of the Church and the Holy Spirit (page 270) and the Church as a communion (see Part VII.1).

KARL RAHNER

Jesuit theologian Karl Rahner (d. 1984) insists that there is an intimate relationship between human effort and divine initiative in the coming of the Kingdom of God[15] and also an intimate connection between the Church, the world, and the Kingdom.[16] (The Church-world relationship in Rahner's thought will be addressed in the next section.) The Church, he writes, is not identical with the Kingdom of God; it is the sacrament of the Kingdom. That is, the Church is "the eschatological and efficacious manifestation (sign) in redemptive history that in the unity, activity, fraternity, etc., of the *world,* the kingdom of God is at hand."[17] "As long as history lasts," Rahner argues, "the Church will not be identical with the kingdom of God, for the latter is only definitively present when history ends with the coming of Christ and the last judgment."[18] And yet the Kingdom is not due simply to come about later. It begins even now in history wherever the will of God is done, inside or outside the Church, and not only inwardly but also socially and politically.[19]

EDWARD SCHILLEBEECKX

Dominican theologian Edward Schillebeeckx also moved in the very early postconciliar years to a more eschatologically oriented understanding of the Church. In his *God, the Future of Man* he describes Christian hope as centered on the Kingdom of God, specifically "this radically new and final Kingdom [that] stimulates [us] never to rest satisfied with what has already been achieved in this world. Historically we can never say *this* is the promised future."[20] For Schillebeeckx, therefore, the proper approach for the Church is one of "permanent criticism of the actual situation: secular institutions, social structures and their dominant mentality," bringing with it "the firm conviction that this building up of a more human world is genuinely possible."[21]

The Church's abiding responsibility for the Kingdom is toward a reality brought about by human beings in cooperation with God, expressed in their caring for one another, especially the dispossessed and the outcasts.[22] Jesus is himself the supreme exemplar of this behavior and therefore of the Kingdom itself. "He becomes the servant of all, even to the point of death on the cross."[23] It was Jesus's conviction that "there is an essential link between the coming of the kingdom of God which he proclaimed and his praxis of the kingdom of God." His followers, then and now, must continue that same mission until the end of time. "It is as simple as that."[24]

HANS KÜNG

The Church, by Swiss theologian Hans Küng, was the first major post–Vatican II book on ecclesiology and the first, before or after the council, to situate the mystery of the Church in the context of the Kingdom, or Reign, of God.[25] Indeed, he devotes some fifty pages at the beginning of the book to the connection between the Church and the Kingdom, highlighting their similarities and differences. However, because of his tendency to rely more on Lutheran than Catholic New Testament exegesis,[26] he is also prone to emphasize, as Martin Luther did, the divine initiative in the coming of the Kingdom and correspondingly to deemphasize the need for human (and specifically the Church's) collaboration and cooperation with God.

Küng implicitly embraces Luther's two-kingdoms understanding: the transcendental Kingdom, which is produced by God alone, and the earthly kingdom, which is produced by human effort and is destined to pass away at the end of history. "God alone," Küng writes, "can bring his reign; the Church is devoted entirely to its service."[27] For Luther, the Church's abiding mission is of one of preaching the gospel and celebrating the sacraments until God's Kingdom comes in all its fullness, through God's efforts alone and in God's own good time. Indeed, Küng had consigned his discussion of the Church's social mission to a brief epilogue. He subsequently attempted to meet criticism of this limited approach in his later book *On Being a Christian,* but his emphasis there is still largely on church reform rather than the Church's social mission.[28]

AVERY DULLES

In his widely celebrated *Models of the Church,* Avery Dulles (later Cardinal Dulles) acknowledges the close and essential connection between the Church and the Kingdom of God.[29] He views the Church as "an anticipation of the final Kingdom," "a sign or representative of the salvation to which we look forward," and as "the proclaimer of the coming Kingdom in Christ" with "the task of introducing the values of the Kingdom into the whole of human society, and thus of preparing the world . . . for the final transformation when God will establish the new heavens and the new earth."[30] That final Kingdom, however, will be "the work of God, dependent on his initiative," but not without antecedent human effort of a collaborative kind in response to the gift of divine grace. "The coming of the Kingdom will not be the destruction but the fulfillment of the Church," Dulles insists, and it will also disclose "the future of the world, insofar as God's gracious power is at work far beyond the horizons of the institutional Church."[31]

It is a matter of some interest that Dulles, especially in his later writings, differs from other theologians who emphasize the subordination of the Church to the Kingdom of God. He resists the idea that the Kingdom, not the Church, is at the center of the history of salvation, which this author once referred to as a "Copernican revolution" in ecclesiology.[32] He even goes so far as to suggest, contrary to the consensus of modern biblical scholarship and of conciliar interpreters, that Vatican II actually identified the Church and the Kingdom, just as had been done in Catholic theology for many years before the council. "To say that the goal of the church is the kingdom of God," Dulles concludes, "is not to deny that the church is, in a certain sense, an end in itself."[33]

PROTESTANT AND ANGLICAN THEOLOGIANS

It is now a matter of general agreement among Catholic theologians, with some measure of nuanced dissent on the part of Avery Dulles and those who agree with his thinking, that the Kingdom of God is not identical with the Church, as was formerly and widely assumed, and that it is at the heart and center of the Church's mission, just as it was of Jesus's preaching and ministry. Protestant and Anglican theologians too have recognized the importance of this relationship, although they were not as inclined before Vatican II to identify the Kingdom with the Church.[34] For instance, the Lutheran theologian Wolfhart Pannenberg views the Kingdom, not the Church, as final. The Church has a preliminary role in history, critiquing everything, including the Church, in the light of the coming Kingdom of God.[35] George Lindbeck, also Lutheran, argues that the Second Vatican Council adopted a new vision of the world and of the Kingdom of God as the transformation of the world, both of which are correlated with a new vision of the Church as the messianic People of God and as a sacramental sign, or witness, of the Kingdom begun and to be completed in Christ.[36]

Finally, for the Reformed Protestant Jürgen Moltmann the Church lives within the horizon of the expectation of the Kingdom of God. The Church is "the community of those who on the ground of the resurrection of Christ wait for the kingdom of God and whose life is determined by this expectation."[37] The Church's "existence is completely bound to the fulfilling of its service. For this reason it is nothing in itself, but all that it is, it is in existing for others,"[38] a position that differs sharply from Avery Dulles's. The Church, Moltmann concludes, "is not in itself the salvation of the world, so that the 'churchifying' of the world would mean the latter's salvation, but it serves the coming salvation of the world and is like an arrow sent out into the world to point to the future."[39]

The Church and the World

From the time of the Reformation, the Counter-Reformation, and the Catholic Reformation of the sixteenth century until the threshold of the Second Vatican Council in the mid-twentieth century, the hierarchy of the Catholic Church and many Christian theologians tended to view the world in negative terms, as a place of testing and probation, of no lasting value in itself. The purpose of the Church is to guide people into heaven. The world is simply the place where the quest for salvation occurs. It is as if, in ecclesiologist Yves Congar's words, "We are aboard a vessel whose destiny is to go to the bottom; man will be saved by journeying in another ship built wholly by God."[40] Congar characterizes this as the dualistic-eschatological view, which is by no means limited to Catholics. He points out that it was a view strongly held by Martin Luther and his twentieth-century Calvinist counterpart Karl Barth (d. 1968).

On the other hand, some Catholic theologians, like Congar himself and the famous Jesuit scientist Teilhard de Chardin (d. 1955), adhered to an incarnationalist view, which affirms the intrinsic value of the world because it has been transformed and redeemed by Jesus Christ, permeated now by the Holy Spirit, and destined for eternal glory in accordance with the Creator's designs. Such theologians were not creating something brand-new, but were retrieving a perspective and a set of insights that were more consistent with those of the early Church than with the neo-Scholastic theology of the Counter-Reformation. The retrieval process, known as *ressourcement* (also rendered *resourcement,* Fr., "a return to the sources," i.e., Scripture and the writings of the Fathers of the Church), was especially prominent in Europe, particularly France, in the years immediately after World War II.

The incarnationalists anticipated Vatican II's Pastoral Constitution on the Church in the Modern World (n. 39) when they insisted that our human efforts on behalf of justice and peace, and indeed all of our good works, would somehow be incorporated into the final Kingdom of God.[41] At the popular level, however, the former view continued to be more widespread in preaching, catechesis, and other forms of communication within the Church. The council was a major factor—perhaps *the* major factor—in replacing this negative, dualistic view with a world-affirming, incarnationalist view. Post–Vatican II ecclesiology has clearly followed the latter path.

KARL RAHNER

"The relation between Church and world has a history," Karl Rahner writes, albeit somewhat opaquely. "The relation is not and must not always be the same. It is historically changing because the world as an individual and collective history of freedom and also the Church in its official ministry and above all in its members is subject to faults and even succumbs to guilt."[42] The Church, Rahner notes, "only slowly" came to acknowledge the legitimate autonomy of the world, including its sciences and its social, political, and economic organizations. "Changes in the Church and in the world mutually interact. . . . The Church comes to know itself more and more as 'not of this world' and at the same time as the sacrament of the absolute future of the world," which is the final Kingdom of God.[43]

Rahner identifies two fundamental ways of misconceiving the relation between Church and world. The one he calls Integrism (a term already in circulation in early-twentieth-century France) and the other, Esotericism. "Integrism," he points out, "regards the world as mere material for the action and self-manifestation of the Church, and wants to integrate the world into the Church." Esotericism, on the other hand, is also a "false attitude towards the world . . . in which what is secular is regarded as a matter of indifference for Christianity, for a life directed towards salvation and therefore towards God's absolute future."[44]

Both Integrism and Esotericism reject from opposite extremes the intrinsic value of the world. For the former, the world cannot be sanctified unless and until it has been brought under the domain of the Church. For the latter, the world is so evil that mere contact with it is corrupting and must always be avoided. In Protestant theologian H. Richard Niebuhr's terminology, the integrist approach is equivalent to his model of "the Christ of culture"; the esotericist approach, to Niebuhr's model of "Christ against culture."[45] For Rahner, the "true relation of the Christian and the Church to the world lies in the mean between these two extremes."[46]

EDWARD SCHILLEBEECKX

For Edward Schillebeeckx the Church is the sacrament of the world (Lat. *sacramentum mundi*). The world in this context "means the confraternity, or other orientated existence, of men [*sic*] in the world—man's [*sic*] mode of existence in dialogue with his fellow-men [*sic*]. The Church must, according to the council, really be the sacrament of this brotherhood [*sic*]."[47] But the Church's sacramental role also has a prophetic and action-oriented dimension. "The Church's critical function is not that of an outsider, pursuing a parallel path, but rather that of one who is critically involved in the building of the world and the progress of nations."[48]

HANS KÜNG

Only in his epilogue to *The Church* does Hans Küng point out, albeit in highly general terms:

> *The world is always involved in what [the Church] does or does not do in the middle of a secular world. Sometimes the world will listen, sometimes it will ignore; sometimes it will be silent and sometimes it will speak; sometimes it will protest and sometimes it will be grateful.*

> *The Church can exist in no other way but in giving witness to the world. . . . The Church is a minority serving a majority . . . a sign among the nations. . . . It is a living invitation to the world to unite itself with the Church and join in testifying to the great things the Lord has done, not only for the Church but for the whole world.*[49]

The Church "does not merely interpret but transforms the broken world in virtue of its unshakable hope in the coming kingdom of complete justice, of eternal life, of true freedom, of unlimited love, and of future peace: hope therefore of the removal of all estrangement and the final reconciliation of mankind with God."[50] These ideas, however, do not permeate the bulk of his book, or most of his other writings for that matter. Avery Dulles, therefore, points out, not without reason: "The idea of the Church as transformer of the world, so prominent in the secular theologies of the 1960s, is almost totally absent" in Küng.[51]

JOHANN METZ

Johann Baptist Metz is perhaps the theologian in the post–Vatican II period who has written the most about the Church-world relationship. His key essay, "The Church and the World," represents the clearest synthesis of his approach to the topic.[52] He refers to modernity's understanding of the world as "fundamentally oriented toward the future,"[53] as a reality that is not imposed upon us but is open to development through human effort. The world is history, and the relationship of the Church to the world as history is characterized by the virtue of hope. Indeed, it is only "in the eschatological horizon of hope [that] the world appear[s] as history [and] . . . as an *arising* reality, whose development or process is committed to the free action of man [*sic*]."[54]

The Church must renounce the world, but not flee from it. It is not called to "flight *out* of the world, but a flight *with* the world 'forward' [which] is the fundamental dynamism of the Christian hope in its renunciation of the world. . . . The Christian is moved to flee and to renounce the world not because he despises the world but because he hopes in the future of the world as proclaimed in God's promises."[55] Such a faith, guided by hope, is "primarily not a doctrine, but an initiative for the passionate innovating and changing of the world toward the Kingdom of God."[56]

It is only within this perspective that the Church's relationship with the world can be properly understood. It should be clear that the Church is not the nonworld, but is itself a part of the world—the part that "attempts to live from the promised future of God, and to call *that world* in question which understands itself only in terms of itself and its possibilities. The decisive relationship between the Church and the world is not spatial but temporal."[57] For Metz, the Church's mission toward the world is shaped by a "creative and militant eschatology." "The eschatological City of God is *now* coming into existence, for our hopeful approach *builds* this city. We are workers building this future, and not just interpreters of this future."[58] In this view, the world is not just a "waiting-room . . . until God opens the door to his office and allows the Christian to enter."[59] The Church has responsibilities toward the world of our brothers and sisters, "since this hope fulfills itself in love for the other, for the least of our brothers [and sisters]."[60]

PROTESTANT THEOLOGIANS

One finds comparable views within mainline Protestant theology in the work of Wolfhart Pannenberg,[61] George Lindbeck,[62] and Jürgen Moltmann,[63] by way of example only. Each of them acknowledges an active role for the Church in the world generally, and in the political order particularly, in spite of Martin Luther's own caution about collapsing the distinction between the two realms. It is "God alone," after all, who brings about the Kingdom. It should also be noted that Moltmann established a close, collaborative relationship with Metz, giving him full credit for coining the term "political theology." None of these theologians was as specific about the secular role of the Church as was Metz.

To be sure, there is also an element of sectarianism in portions of contemporary Protestantism, represented in the writings of such prominent theologians as Stanley Hauerwas.[64] George Lindbeck in his later years moved noticeably in that direction as well.[65]

Apart from this sectarian thrust that one finds in certain segments of the Protestant theological community, but including also a significant number of younger Catholics in the field of moral theology,[66] the theologians represented above reflect the core of Catholic and mainline Protestant thinking on the Church-world relationship. It is an approach that is entirely congruent with the Second Vatican Council's Pastoral Constitution on the Church in the Modern World, as described already in Part V.7.2, and with the approach presented throughout this book.

The Church and Salvation

Salvation is the achievement of full, holistic "health" (the literal translation of the Latin word *salus*) for both the individual and the human community at large. To be saved is to attain the fullness of our humanity, in both its spiritual and physical dimensions, through complete and final communion with God and with one another in the communion of saints. Christians believe that salvation was definitively won for us through the redemptive work of Jesus Christ—his earthly ministry, his death on the cross, his Resurrection, and his ascension into heaven and exaltation at the right hand of the Father. In a sense, all creation is called to, and destined for, salvation (Rom. 8: 19–23).

The title for this section, "The Church and Salvation," may be misleading for some readers, who will expect to find here a full and detailed synthesis of the discussion regarding salvation itself since Vatican II. However, salvation, like faith, cannot be studied apart from its connections to specific religious traditions. And so the discussion of the Church and salvation is presented here always in relationship to specific religious traditions: first non-Christians, then Jews, and then other Christian Churches and ecclesial communities. The last category is, in turn, subdivided into specific issues that have been at the heart of the ecumenical discussion of the nature, mission, ministries, and structural operations of the Church: dialogues and consultations, "sister churches," particular Churches and ecclesial communities, intercommunion or eucharistic sharing, and the mutual recognition of ordained ministries.

THE CHURCH AND NON-CHRISTIANS

For much of the history of the Church, it was simply taken for granted that salvation was available only to Christians (and perhaps only to Catholics) who had shown themselves worthy of it during their lifetimes. A traditional Catholic way of putting it was "dying in the state of grace." From the earliest centuries until the threshold of the Second Vatican Council, the Catholic Church's theological understanding and official teaching on the matter was embodied in the medieval axiom "Outside the Church, no salvation" (Lat. *Extra Ecclesiam nulla salus*). The concept was given definitive status by the Council of Florence (1431–45), which proclaimed that everyone outside the Church—not only pagans, but also Jews, heretics, and schismatics—"will *go into the everlasting fire which was prepared for the devil and his angels* [Matt. 25:41], unless they are joined to the catholic church [*sic*] before the end of their lives."[67]

This most severe interpretation of the axiom "Outside the Church, no salvation" was rejected even by Pope Pius IX (1846–78) in 1854 and 1863 as invalid for those "invincibly ignorant of the true religion."[68] It was rejected in 1943 by Pope Pius XII (1939–58) in his *Mystici Corporis Christi* (Lat., "On the Mystical Body of Christ"), wherein he allowed for the possibility of non-Catholics being "ordained to the Mystical Body by some kind of unconscious desire or longing" (n. 117); and again in 1949 by the Holy Office in its letter to Archbishop Richard Cushing of Boston regarding the case of Father Leonard Feeney, S.J., who had retrieved and aggressively promoted the most narrow interpretation of the medieval axiom on salvation outside the Church (see Part IV.3.4). Finally it was denied by Vatican II's Dogmatic Constitution on the Church, which declares: "Those who, through no fault of their own, do not know the Gospel of Christ or his church, but who nevertheless seek God with a sincere heart, and, moved by grace, try in their actions to do his will as they know it through the dictates of their conscience—these too may attain eternal salvation" (n. 16). Few theologians after Vatican II have examined this history as closely as Francis A. Sullivan in his *Salvation Outside the Church? Tracing the History of the Catholic Response.*[69]

This doctrinal trajectory, beginning in the nineteenth century and continuing through the Second Vatican Council in the twentieth, encouraged theologians after Vatican II to stress not only the universal salvific will of Christ mediated through the Church, but also to grant a fresh and sympathetic look at the intrinsic salvific value of the various non-Christian religions. This latter trend was aided in large part by the growing awareness, through enhanced communications and mobility,[70] of the vast numbers of non-Christians around the world.

Post–Vatican II mainline Christian, and especially mainline Catholic, theologians fall into one of three groups, albeit of unequal size.[71] In the first are those few who hold to the traditional view that there is but one true religion, while appreciating the authentic values and even saving grace in others. These are, in effect, "anonymously Christian" communities—a position identified especially with Karl Rahner. A second view acknowledges the salvific value in each of the non-Christian religions and underscores, as the first view does, the universality of revelation and grace. However, adherents of the second view do not speak of the other religions as "anonymously Christian," but instead implicitly regard them as lesser, relative, and extraordinary means of salvation. This position was articulated by Vatican II itself and is held today by a declining number of theologians. These first two approaches are also known as inclusivist, because they "include" non-Christian religions in the fulfillment of the divine plan of salvation that God established in Christ and through the Church.

Without prejudice to the uniqueness and truth of Christian faith, a third view affirms the intrinsic value of the other great religions of the world and, going beyond the second view, insists on the necessity and worthwhileness of dialogue with them. These other religions are not only to be respected; they are to be recognized as having something positive to teach Christians not only about themselves and their own non-Christian beliefs, but also about God, life, and even Christ and the Church's own doctrines. In this third view, these other religions are not regarded, however benignly, as merely deficient expressions of Christianity or as secondary instruments of salvation in Christ.

This third view was at least implicit in the Second Vatican Council's call for dialogue with non-Christian religions (e.g., in the Decree on the Church's Missionary Activity, n. 34, and the Declaration on Christian Education, n. 11) and in the establishment by Pope Paul VI in 1964 of the Secretariat for Non-Christians, which was renamed, with a modified function, by Pope John Paul II (1978-2005) in 1988 as the Pontifical Council for Interreligious Dialogue. That same year the pope organized his historic—and controversial—meeting of the world's religious leaders at Assisi in order to pray together for peace, thereby recognizing, at least implicitly, the spiritual unity that exists at some level between Christianity and the other world religions. Catholic theologians who have been identified with this third view include Hans Küng, Jacques Dupuis (for a fuller summary of Dupuis's approach, see Part I.4), Heinz Robert Schlette, Raimundo Pannikar, and others.[72]

Each of these three views, their sometimes considerable differences notwithstanding, respects the uniqueness and truth of Christianity and, in varying degrees, the intrinsic spiritual and salvific value of non-Christian religions. A fourth view, considerably to the left of the third, has been advanced by John Hick and Paul Knitter.[73] Some commentators assume that the Congregation for the Doctrine of the Faith's *Dominus Iesus* had such theologians as these in mind when it severely criticized the view that, in the CDF's mind, places all religions on an equal footing.[74]

It is in this broader ecclesiological context that the widely discussed and controverted document *Dominus Iesus,* formulated by the Congregation for the Doctrine of the Faith (CDF), appeared in September 2000, while Cardinal Joseph Ratzinger (later Pope Benedict XVI) served as the congregation's prefect. Consideration has already been given to this document in Part I.4 of this book. The declaration, which is as much Christological as ecclesiological in content and concern, is most critical of the fourth view just mentioned above, but without identifying any of its proponents. It criticizes the tendency to argue that "all religions may be equally valid ways of salvation," labeling it "relativistic." The Church, it insists, is still necessary for the salvation of all humanity, but that does not lessen the sincere respect the Church has for the religions of the world.

For the most part the declaration of the CDF simply reiterates traditional Catholic teaching on Christ, salvation, and the Church. Indeed, if the document had been released on the day after the Second Vatican Council adjourned in December 1965, it would probably not have incurred any serious criticism, except perhaps for its redundancy in relation to the conciliar teachings. The declaration did make clear, contrary to Avery Dulles (see Part VI.1.4), that "the kingdom of God . . . is not identified with the Church in her visible and social reality" and that Christ and the Holy Spirit also act "outside the Church's visible boundaries" (n. 19).

What seemed to have bothered most critics of the declaration who were otherwise in general agreement with its basic reaffirmation of Catholic doctrine was its overall tone. Not only was the declaration polemical; it was also authoritarian. Its arguments were based, according to some, on a proof-text approach to Sacred Scripture, the documents of Vatican II, and the pronouncements of Pope John Paul II. Its appeal was almost always to authority, and its demand was almost always for obedience.

As for the declaration's understanding of the relationship between the Church and non-Christian religions, perhaps Jesuit theologian Francis X. Clooney, then of Boston College and subsequently an endowed professor at Harvard University, put his finger on the essential value of dialogue with other religions: "Learning from other religions does not change the timeless truths of our faith, but it certainly does enrich and deepen our way of following Jesus, driving out not only relativism and indifferentism, but also arrogance and ignorance."[75]

THE CHURCH AND JEWS

The relationship of the Church to Jews[76] is one important area where practice has led the way toward and reinforced new ecclesiological understandings. Most of the developments regarding this relationship, since the council's historic Declaration on the Relation of the Church to Non-Christian Religions (*Nostra aetate*, Lat., "In our age"), have occurred in various interfaith contacts, largely at official levels, and in various official documents, papal and episcopal alike. Although much was made—and legitimately so—of Pope John XXIII's dropping of the adjective "perfidious" before the word "Jews" in the Good Friday liturgy and also of his stopping his car at Rome's chief synagogue to bless the congregation gathered outside that place of worship, nothing in recent papal history has matched in sheerly dramatic effect the visit of Pope John Paul II to the Western Wall and to Yad Vashem, the Holocaust memorial in Jerusalem, in March 2000.

A Reuters photo on the front page of many of the world's leading newspapers showed the diminutive pope, bent with age and bowed in prayer, standing before the massive wall, his white cassock in sharp contrast to the ancient stones, darkened over many centuries. Another photo, taken closer in, depicted the pope placing a customary note to God in a crevice of the wall. The note contained the same message that he had proclaimed at the Mass of Reconciliation in St. Peter's Basilica a week earlier. It asked forgiveness for the sins perpetrated against the Jews, and it committed the Church to "genuine brotherhood with the people of the covenant." Jerome Murphy-O'Connor, prominent Dominican biblical scholar and longtime member of the faculty of the École Biblique in Jerusalem, commented at the time: "By standing there [at the Western Wall], this symbolized the humility of the Church which for Jews has been viewed as arrogant. By standing there he transformed the relationship of Christianity toward Judaism. It is a complete reversal of history."[77]

Pope John Paul II's dramatic words at Yad Vashem were overshadowed only by his physical presence there and his gesture of leaving his chair to shuffle across the darkened hall, leaning on his cane, to greet six Holocaust survivors. "As Bishop of Rome and successor of the Apostle Peter, I assure the Jewish people," he said on that occasion, "that the Catholic Church, motivated by the Gospel law of truth and love and by no political considerations, is deeply saddened by the hatred, acts of persecution, and displays of anti-Semitism directed against the Jews by Christians at any time and in any place." He prayed for "a new relationship between Christians and Jews" marked by a "mutual respect required of those who adore the one Creator and Lord and look to Abraham as our common father in faith."[78]

These historic words and gestures in Jerusalem, during the pope's Jubilee Year visit there, were anticipated by other similarly dramatic developments at high official levels. On January 25, 1995, the German Catholic bishops' conference issued a statement commemorating the fiftieth anniversary of the liberation of the Auschwitz concentration camp in Poland. The German bishops condemned the silence and behavior of Christians in the face of the Holocaust, noting that the "failure and guilt of that time have also a church dimension," a Church that "looked too fixedly at the threat to [its] own institutions and who remained silent about the crimes committed against the Jews and Judaism." The only way to test the "practical sincerity of our will of renewal," the German bishops' statement continued, is through "the confession of this guilt and the willingness to painfully learn from this history of guilt of our country *and of our church as well.*"[79]

Two and a half years later the French bishops issued a similar statement to commemorate the fifty-seventh anniversary of the enactment of the first of more than 160 anti-Semitic laws and decrees under the wartime Vichy government, which had collaborated with Nazi occupation forces in France. Church leaders, the French bishops wrote, "failed to realize that the Church, called at that moment to play the role of defender within a social body that was falling apart, did in fact have considerable power and influence, and that in the face of the silence of other institutions, its voice could have echoed loudly by taking a definitive stand against the irreparable."[80] The Church's "anti-Jewish tradition," the bishops continued, "stamped its mark in differing ways on Christian doctrine and teaching, in theology, apologetics, preaching and in the liturgy. It was on such ground that the venomous plant of hatred for the Jews was able to flourish."[81] The French bishops' statement ended on a ringing note: "In the face of so great and utter a tragedy, too many of the Church's pastors committed an offense, by their silence against the Church itself and its mission.... *This failing of the Church of France* and of her responsibility toward the Jewish people are part of our history. We confess this sin. We beg God's pardon, and we call upon the Jewish people to hear our words of repentance."[82]

In 1998 the Vatican's Commission for Religious Relations with the Jews, under the leadership of Cardinal Edward Cassidy, an Australian, issued a highly publicized document on the Holocaust entitled "We Remember: A Reflection on the Shoah." Many Jewish leaders were disappointed in the statement because the earlier statements of the German and French hierarchies had actually gone much further in acknowledging that the Church itself, and not just some individual members, bears responsibility for the moral climate that allowed Nazism to flourish in Christian Europe. Nevertheless, at the end of the "We Remember" statement, the commission did testify to its "deep sorrow for the failure of [the Church's] sons and daughters in every age" and to its desire to make an act of repentance since, as members of the Church, "we are linked to the sins as well as the merits of all her children." The statement also expressed the Church's "firm resolve to build a new future in which there will be no more anti-Judaism among Christians or anti-Christian sentiment among Jews, but rather a mutual respect."[83]

THE CATHOLIC CHURCH AND OTHER CHRISTIANS

Dialogues and Consultations

The Second Vatican Council's Decree on Ecumenism (*Unitatis redintegratio,* Lat., "The restoration of unity") presupposes and reinforces the council's Dogmatic Constitution on the Church (*Lumen gentium*). Both address the relationship of the Body of Christ to the Catholic Church (*Lumen gentium* 8; *Unitatis redintegratio* 4); both refer to the degrees of communion that exist within the Body of Christ (14; 3, 14, 22); both acknowledge that "many elements of sanctification and of truth" exist outside the structure of the Catholic Church (8; 3); and both apply the terms "churches" and "ecclesial communities" to Christian bodies that are not in full communion with the Catholic Church (15; 19).

Not everything found in the Dogmatic Constitution on the Church, however, is also to be found in the Decree on Ecumenism. The following enduringly relevant principles contained only in the Decree on Ecumenism are listed by way of example:

1. The unity of the Church does not exist already in the Catholic Church. Ecumenism, therefore, is not a matter of non-Catholics' returning to a preexisting Catholic unity. Ecumenism's goal is the restoring of the unity that has been lost and that does not now exist (n. 1).

2. The disunity among Christians is not something that we should simply learn to live with. On the contrary, it "openly contradicts the will of Christ, provides a stumbling block to the world, and inflicts damage on the most holy cause of proclaiming the good news to every creature" (n. 1).

3. It is wrong to attribute blame for the disunity to one side or the other. The divisions between East and West and then, within the West, between Catholics, on the one hand, and Protestants and Anglicans, on the other, were created by "developments for which, at times, people of both sides were to blame" (n. 3).

4. The differences that separate Eastern from Western Christians, and Catholics from Protestants and Anglicans, are not always differences in kind, but more likely differences in degree (n. 3). For that reason we can no longer speak of the Catholic Church as if it and the Body of Christ were "one and the same," as Pope Pius XII once taught in his encyclical *Humani generis* (1950). Other Churches and ecclesial communities are also part of the Body of Christ.

5. What unites the Christian Churches and ecclesial communities, even in their state of ecclesiastical separation, is more important than what continues to divide them. All Christians are justified by faith in Christ and are incorporated into him through the same Baptism, which is the "fundamental

sacramental bond of unity" (n. 22); they accept the same Scriptures as the Word of God and are animated by the same life of grace and by the same virtues of faith, hope, and love along with the gifts of the Holy Spirit (n. 3).

6. All of the Christian Churches and ecclesial communities, each in its own way, have "significance and importance in the mystery of salvation." Indeed, the Holy Spirit uses them as "means of salvation" (n. 3).

7. Nevertheless, it is also the teaching of the council that the Catholic Church is "the all-embracing means of salvation" and that it is through the Catholic Church that "the fullness of the means of salvation can be obtained" (n. 3).

8. The principal human means of collaborating with God in the quest for Christian unity are the elimination of words, judgments, and actions that falsely or unfairly characterize other Christians; opening and sustaining dialogue with other Churches and ecclesial communities; cooperating with other Churches and ecclesial communities in the pursuit of the common good under the light of the gospel (see esp. n. 12); common prayer; and simultaneous efforts toward the renewal and reform of the separated Churches and ecclesial communities, so that the whole Body of Christ can be renewed and reformed in accordance with the Lord's will (n. 4).

9. "While preserving unity in essentials," we must "preserve a proper freedom in the various forms of spiritual life and discipline, in the variety of liturgical rites, and even in the theological elaborations of revealed truth" (n. 4; also nn. 16–17). In any case, charity must always prevail (n. 4).

10. Catholics have much to learn from and be edified by the faith and virtues of non-Catholic Christians (n. 4).

11. "Every renewal of the Church essentially consists in an increase of fidelity to its own calling." Renewal and reform must touch upon areas of ecclesiastical conduct, church

discipline, and even the process by which doctrines are formulated (n. 6).

12. Normally common worship (intercommunion, or eucharistic sharing) is forbidden because of the lack of unity the Eucharist is meant to signify. On the other hand, the Eucharist is also a means of achieving that unity. Both truths have to be honored, not just the first (n. 8).

13. Not all elements of Christian faith or of Catholic doctrine are of equal weight. There is a "hierarchy of truths," based on their relative distance from the "foundation" of the Christian faith (n. 11).

Relations between the Catholic Church and the World Council of Churches grew closer after the council, but they stopped short of membership. In 1968, however, the Catholic Church became a full member of the WCC's Faith and Order Commission. The Secretariat for Promoting Christian Unity (now the Pontifical Council for Promoting Christian Unity) issued two directories, in 1967 and 1970, to guide those involved in ecumenical activities, and in 1993 *The Directory for the Application of Principles and Norms on Ecumenism*[84] brought together "existing norms and legislation, rather than breaking much significant new ground."[85]

Since Vatican II international bilateral dialogues have occurred between the Catholic Church and over ten denominational bodies, including the Orthodox Churches, the Anglican Communion (which has produced the Anglican–Roman Catholic International Commission, better known as ARCIC), the Lutheran World Federation, the World Methodist Council, the Baptist World Alliance, the World Alliance of Reformed Churches, the Disciples of Christ, and various evangelical and Pentecostal groups. Similar dialogues have occurred at national and local levels as well.[86]

As ecumenical contacts developed throughout the twentieth century and were given new impetus by Pope John XXIII and the Second Vatican Council, it became increasingly clear that the preconciliar axiom "Doctrine divides; action unites" needed some serious revision.

The many bilateral and multilateral consultations, at both national and international levels, disclosed an extraordinary measure of common ground on matters of doctrine, but also revealed many other areas of division on practical, action-oriented matters of personal and social ethics, for example, abortion, euthanasia, divorce, same-sex unions and marriages, homosexuality, the rights and roles of women in society and in the Church as well as issues related to peace, human rights, and the economy.

The Week of Prayer for Christian Unity, established as the "Church Unity Octave" in 1908, is observed each year between January 18, formerly the feast of the Chair of St. Peter (now celebrated on February 22), and January 25, the feast of the Conversion of St. Paul, as a reminder that there is an equal need for a spiritual ecumenism such as was envisioned by the council's Decree on Ecumenism (n. 7). Ecumenical ecclesiology is not only advanced by formal dialogues, theological writings, and joint discussions, but also by joint prayer that invokes the Holy Spirit to assist in the Church's abiding quest for reconciliation and the healing of long-standing divisions.

"Sister Churches"

One of the most important ecumenical developments since Vatican II is the growing, albeit controversial, recognition on the part of the Catholic Church of the existence of various non-Catholic Churches as "sister Churches." This recently retrieved ecclesiological concept makes it possible for the Catholic Church and these other "sister Churches" (mainly the Churches of the Anglican Communion and the various Eastern Churches not in full, canonical communion with Rome) to acknowledge and enter into communion with one another, but without the non-Catholic ecclesial partner's being asked or required to renounce its own ecclesial identity and traditions. It is a way through the long-standing either/or dilemma that made any type of formal ecclesial communion between the Catholic Church and other Churches in the Body of Christ practically impossible.

The first explicit use of the expression "sister Churches" following Vatican II was in a papal brief, *Anno ineunte* (Lat., "At the beginning of the year"), sent by Pope Paul VI to Ecumenical Patriarch

Athenagoras I in July 1967.[87] The word "sister" is also found, with an ecclesial meaning, in Vatican II's Decree on Ecumenism: "Hence, it has been, and still is, a matter of primary concern and care among the Orientals to preserve in a communion of faith and charity those family ties which ought to exist between local churches, as between sisters" (n. 14). The use of the word "sister" by Paul VI has had significant ecclesiological implications,[88] given the pope's allusion to the contemplative Mary, the sister of Martha, as a symbol of the contemplative East, along with his citation of Acts 15:28, in which the recently concluded Council of Jerusalem had insisted that the Church was "not to place on [the Gentiles] any burden beyond what is indispensable." Reference to this New Testament text is also made elsewhere in the Decree on Ecumenism in support of the Church's effort "to restore communion and unity or preserve them" (n. 18). The clear implication of *Anno ineunte* is that there existed here "a new moment in the relation between the two Churches and new opportunities to be seized."[89] Paul VI had also used the term in reference to the Anglican Communion in connection with his canonization of a group of English martyrs in 1970.[90]

However, in June 2000 the Congregation for the Doctrine of the Faith issued "Note on the Expression 'Sister Churches,'" which seemed to downplay, if not dismiss, the notion.[91] In an accompanying letter addressed to the presidents of episcopal conferences around the world, Cardinal Joseph Ratzinger, then prefect of the CDF (later Pope Benedict XVI), pointed out that the meaning of the expression "sister Churches" had in recent years been distorted "in certain publications and in the writings of some theologians involved in ecumenical dialogue . . . leading people to think that in fact the one church of Christ does not exist but may be re-established through the reconciliation of the two sister churches,"[92] namely, the Catholic Church and the Orthodox Churches.

"In addition," Cardinal Ratzinger continued, "the same expression has been applied improperly by some to the relationship between the Catholic Church on the one hand, and the Anglican Communion and non-catholic ecclesial communities on the other."[93] The cardinal indicated further that the "theology of sister churches" or an "ecclesiology of sister churches" is "characterized by ambiguity and discontinuity with respect to the correct original meaning of the expression as found in the documents of the magisterium." It was in order to "overcome these equivocations and ambiguities in the use and application of the expression *sister churches*" that the congregation judged it necessary to prepare its "Note on the Expression 'Sister Churches.'"[94]

The CDF "Note" suggests that the expression began to be used in the East from the fifth century, when the idea of the pentarchy, or five patriarchates, gained ground. The note also points out that the Bishop of Rome never recognized an "equalization of the sees or accepted that only a primacy of honor be accorded to the See of Rome" (n. 2). The expression "sister Churches" appeared again in two letters of the metropolitan Nicetas of Nicodemia (1136) and the patriarch John X Camaterus (1198–1206), protesting Rome's presenting itself as "mother and teacher" rather than as simply "first among sisters of equal dignity" (n. 3). More recently, the Orthodox patriarch of Constantinople, Athenagoras I, revived the expression in an exchange of letters with Pope John XXIII, with the hope that unity between the sister Churches (Catholic and Orthodox) might be reestablished in the near future (n. 5).

The note does acknowledge that the Second Vatican Council adopted the expression "sister churches" in its Decree on Ecumenism (n. 14) to describe the relationship between and among particular churches, that is, local churches and the patriarchates of the East. Then, as mentioned above, the first papal document following Vatican II in which the word "sister" is applied ecclesiastically is Paul VI's apostolic brief *Anno ineunte.* The brief's relevant text, as cited in the note, follows: "Since this mystery of divine love is at work in every local church, is not this the reason for the traditional expression *sister churches,* which the churches of various places used for one another? For centuries our churches lived in this way like sisters, celebrating together the ecumenical councils which defended the deposit of faith against all corruption. Now, after a long period of division and mutual misunderstanding, the Lord, in spite of the obstacles which arose between us in the past, gives us the possibility of rediscovering ourselves as sister churches."[95]

The note, however, does not mention that Paul VI also referred to the Anglican Communion as an "ever-beloved sister" in 1970 on the occasion of his canonizing the English martyrs, whose feast day is October 25. It does acknowledge, however, that John Paul II also used the expression "in numerous addresses and documents," including his encyclicals *Slavorum Apostoli* (Lat., "Apostles to the Slavs") in 1985 and *Ut unum sint* ("That they may be one") in 1995, as well as in a letter to the bishops of Europe in 1991 ("Note," n. 8). At the same time, the note insists that the local church of Rome is a "sister church" only to those particular churches within the Catholic Communion of Churches, but that the universal Catholic Church is the *mother* of all others (n. 10).[96] Moreover, the term "sister Church," according to the note, can only be applied to those churches "that have preserved a valid Episcopate and Eucharist" (n. 10), thereby excluding (from the CDF's point of view) the Churches of the Anglican Communion. There is at least an apparent discrepancy between the ecclesiology of the CDF's note and the aforementioned teachings and references employed in the council's Decree on Ecumenism and by both Paul VI and John Paul II.

The note is correct, however, in insisting that the Body of Christ as a whole is not a sister Church to any other Church. But neither is the Body of Christ as a whole simply identical with the Catholic Church (as the note's interpretation of *Lumen gentium*, n. 8, implies). The expression "sister Church" applies to the relationships between and among individual churches—whether they be called particular or local—within the one Body of Christ. That this would include the Churches of the Anglican Communion seems to be warranted not only by Paul VI's remarks at the canonization of the English martyrs in 1970, but also in the remarkable and highly symbolic gesture of John Paul II when, in 1996 on the occasion of the fourteen hundredth anniversary of Gregory the Great's dispatching of Augustine of Canterbury and forty other monks to re-Christianize Britain, the pope invited the then archbishop of Canterbury, George L. Carey, to join him at a Vesper service in the church of St. Gregory the Great in Rome and to walk in procession together in episcopal regalia. On the same occasion, John Paul II gifted Archbishop Carey with a gold pectoral cross. According to the pre–Vatican II manuals of theology, such a gesture would have been considered an act of aiding and abetting the simulation of a sacrament, since Anglican orders had been declared in the bull of Pope Leo XIII (1878–1903) *Apostolicae curae* (Lat., "Of apostolic concern"), exactly a hundred years earlier, to be "absolutely null and utterly void."[97]

Particular Churches and Ecclesial Communities

The CDF's "Note on the Expression 'Sister Churches'" was released just prior to the publication of its better-known and more widely discussed declaration *Dominus Iesus: On the Unicity and Salvific Universality of Jesus Christ and the Church* (see Part I.4 of this book).[98] Both documents distinguish between particular churches and ecclesial communities (*Dominus Iesus,* nn. 16–17). True particular churches, *Dominus Iesus* says, "while not existing in perfect communion with the Catholic Church, remain united to her by means of the closest bonds, that is, by apostolic succession and a valid Eucharist." All of the churches of the Anglican Communion and all of the Protestant Churches have been, in effect, dechurchified in one fell swoop. On the other hand, the declaration reaffirms, with Vatican II, that the individual members of these non-Church, ecclesial communities "are by baptism incorporated in Christ and thus are in a certain communion, albeit imperfect, with the [Catholic] Church" (n. 17).

Dominus Iesus does not cite a specific conciliar text in support of its own understanding and portrayal of the distinction between true particular churches and ecclesial communities because no such text exists. Indeed, the position taken by *Dominus Iesus,* namely, that the Church of Christ is present only in so-called true particular churches, is at apparent odds with John Paul II's encyclical *Ut unum sint,* which states: "To the extent that these elements [of sanctification and truth] are found in other Christian communities, the one church of Christ is effectively present in them" (n. 11, para. 3). One might argue that the CDF's position is also at odds with that of the council itself, if one were to adopt the ecclesiological interpretation given by the council's Doctrinal Commission, namely, that these various non-Catholic Christian communities possess "ecclesiastical elements which they have preserved from our common patrimony, and which confer on them a truly ecclesial character. In these communities the one sole Church of Christ is present, albeit imperfectly."[99]

The late Father John Hotchkin (d. 2001), formerly executive director of the U.S. Catholic Bishops' Committee on Ecumenical and Interreligious Affairs, pointed out in an address to the Canon Law Society of America in October 2000 that the term "ecclesial communities" is "something of a neologism," coined to cover a span of meanings. Thus, there is no Anglican Church as such, but a communion of churches (e.g., the Churches of England, Canada, and Ireland, and The Episcopal Church in the United States), which together constitute the Anglican Communion. The same holds true for Lutheranism and the Lutheran World Federation, for Methodism and the World Methodist Council, for the Alliance of Reformed Churches, and so forth.

Indeed, if the council wanted to dechurchify all except the Orthodox and Old Catholics, for example, why did it not refer to the others as simply "Christian" communities rather than "ecclesial" communities? Father Hotchkin cited one of Cardinal Ratzinger's predecessors as head of the CDF, Jerome Hamer (d. 1996), O.P., who pointed out that there were three variants of the church/community terminology in successive schemata or drafts of the conciliar texts: "separated churches and communities" (employed in the Decree on Ecumenism, n. 3); "Christian communities" (used in an earlier draft of the subtitle of the third chapter of the Decree on Ecumenism and subsequently changed to "churches and ecclesial communities"); and "ecclesial communities separated from the Catholic Church" (used in the same decree, n. 22). Cardinal Hamer insisted that the council used this diverse terminology "because it did not wish to prejudge or definitively pronounce on the [validity of the] ordained ministries of those Protestant communities in which it perceived this possible deficiency or defect by stating that they were nonetheless *churches* in the full theological sense of the word. The council did not wish to preempt this question, but to leave it open."[100] Because Vatican II did decide to leave open the question of the validity of Protestant orders, Hotchkin concluded that we can "draw no hard and fast distinction between churches [particular or otherwise] and ecclesial communities as we know them at this time."[101]

Intercommunion, or Eucharistic Sharing

The term "intercommunion" (known prior to Vatican II as *communicatio in sacris,* Lat., "communication in sacred realities," namely, the Eucharist and the other sacraments) refers to full eucharistic sharing (also known in some ecumenical circles as "eucharistic hospitality") between separated Christians.[102] It describes the reception of Holy Communion by a single separated Christian in a Church other than her or his own, or it refers to the future possibility of full Church to Church, or Christian community to Christian community, reciprocity in the celebration and reception of the Eucharist.[103] Prior to the Second Vatican Council any type of intercommunion between Catholics and other Christians was expressly forbidden by the Catholic Church.

The principle of intercommunion, or eucharistic sharing, however, was endorsed by Vatican II's Decree on Ecumenism: "As for common worship [*communicatio in sacris*], however, it may not be regarded as a means to be used indiscriminately [*indiscretim*] for the restoration of unity among Christians. Such worship depends chiefly on two principles: it should signify the unity of the Church; it should provide a sharing in the means of grace. The fact that it should signify unity generally rules out common worship. Yet the gaining of a needed grace sometimes commends it" (n. 8).

Implementation of this principle was left to the Secretariat for Promoting Christian Unity (now the Pontifical Council for Promoting Christian Unity). This Vatican agency issued an *Ecumenical Directory* in 1967 and released a special instruction on intercommunion in 1972. The conditions under which intercommunion is allowed are these: (1) Admission to the Eucharist is confined to particular cases of those Christians who have a faith in the sacrament in conformity with that of the Catholic Church. (2) Such Christians must experience a serious spiritual need for the eucharistic sustenance. (3) They must be unable for a prolonged period to have recourse to a minister of their own community. (4) They must ask for the sacrament of their own accord. (5) They must have proper dispositions and lead lives worthy of a Christian. These principles were derived from Vatican II's Decree on Eastern Catholic Churches (*Orientalium Ecclesiarum*, n. 27) and were confirmed by the 1983 revised Code of Canon Law (can. 844.2–4).

Even if these conditions are fulfilled, however, "it will be a pastoral responsibility to see that the admission of these other Christians to communion does not endanger or disturb the faith of Catholics." According to the 1972 special instruction on intercommunion, these rules do not apply to Orthodox Christians, who, "though separated from us, have true sacraments, above all, because of apostolic succession, the priesthood and the eucharist, which unite them to us by close ties, so that the risk of obscuring the relation between eucharistic communion and ecclesial communion is somewhat reduced." The 1993 *Directory for Ecumenism* added a word of caution about intercommunion between Catholics and Orthodox Christians: "Eastern churches, on the basis of their own ecclesiological understanding, may have more restrictive disciplines in this matter, which others should respect. . . . A Catholic who legitimately wishes to communicate with Eastern Christians must respect the Eastern discipline as much as possible, and refrain from communicating if that Church restricts sacramental communion to its own members to the exclusion of others" (nn. 122, 124).[104]

The revised Code of Canon Law, cited above, stipulates: "Whenever necessity requires or genuine spiritual advantage suggests and provided that the danger of error or indifferentism is avoided, it is lawful for the faithful for whom it is physically or morally impossible to approach a Catholic minister, to receive the sacraments of penance, Eucharist, and anointing of the sick from non-Catholic ministers in whose churches these sacraments are valid" (can. 844.2). However, concelebration with ministers of other Churches is forbidden (can. 908), and non-Catholic ministers are also forbidden to preach at a Catholic Eucharist (can. 767).

The overriding and still unresolved ecclesiological question is whether complete agreement on every doctrinal issue is required for institutional unity and, therefore, for regular eucharistic sharing. As Christopher O'Donnell and many other theologians and pastoral ministers have pointed out over the years, "People, with very erroneous positions on matters of faith, do in fact receive the Eucharist in the Catholic Church."[105] The conciliar teaching on the "hierarchy of truths" is particularly relevant here: "When comparing doctrines with one another, [Catholic theologians] should remember that in Catholic doctrine there exists an order or 'hierarchy' of truths, since they vary in their relation to the foundation of the Christian faith" (Decree on Ecumenism, n. 11). That "foundation" is Jesus Christ and the Redemption that he wrought on behalf of all humankind and the whole created order (Rom. 8:19–25). It is an important topic to which we shall return in Part VII.2.4.c, when discussing the process of interpreting doctrinal statements.

The Mutual Recognition of Ordained Ministries

Prior to the Second Vatican Council, the Catholic Church did not recognize the validity of ordained ministries beyond its own boundaries, with the exception of those of the Orthodox Churches. Even so, preconciliar regulations did not allow for intercommunion, or eucharistic sharing, between the Catholic Church and the Orthodox Churches except in cases of emergency or necessity (as listed already in the previous section). The Orthodox remained in an ecclesiologically anomalous situation because the preconciliar Catholic Church regarded itself as the "one, true Church of Christ." Those who were not members of the Catholic Church were outside the Body of Christ entirely. With the Second Vatican Council and concurrent and subsequent developments in Catholic ecclesiology, the notion of "degrees of communion" emerged to replace, or at least substantially modify, the previous either/or approach (see also Part I.2.5 and Part V.6.4). That new approach, in turn, reshaped the question of the validity of the ordained ministries of other Churches and ecclesial communities. If there could be degrees of communion between the Catholic Church and various other non-Catholic Churches and ecclesial communities, there could also be degrees of validity in the ordained ministries of these various Churches and ecclesial communities.

There are many ecumenical statements—international, national, and denominational—too numerous here to mention, much less comment upon.[106] The ecclesiological sticking point from the Catholic point of view is apostolic succession. The Catholic belief is that an ordained ministry, especially that of the episcopate and presbyterate, can be regarded as valid only if the sacramental orders can be traced back in an unbroken historical line to the Apostles themselves. This view is shared, in full or in large part, by the Orthodox Churches, the Anglican Communion, other Eastern Churches not in full communion with the Catholic Church, and the Old Catholics, which consist of three schismatic groups of Dutch, German and Austrian, and Polish Catholics, who separated themselves from the Catholic Church in the nineteenth century, mainly, but not exclusively, because of Vatican I's definition of papal infallibility. But this approach to apostolic succession is almost mechanistic in character. It depends in the final analysis upon a firm, but historically unverifiable, conviction that there has, in fact, never been a break of any kind in the transmission of apostolic authority through episcopal ordination over the course of some twenty centuries. An alternate approach views the reality of apostolic succession as fulfilled, to one degree or another, if the Church or ecclesial community in question continues to be faithful to the apostolic word, witness, and service.[107] To the degree that it does so, its ordained ministries are valid.

It is clear, however, that the official teaching of the Catholic Church and of the Second Vatican Council's Dogmatic Constitution on the Church (n. 20), namely, that the episcopacy is of divine institution (Lat. *ex divina institutione*), is closer to the former understanding of apostolic succession than to the latter.[108] Nevertheless, there has been a growing recognition on the part of the Catholic Church and Catholic theologians of the apostolic character of the faith and ordained ministries of Protestant Churches and ecclesial communities. At the same time, there has also been a growing appreciation on the part of Protestants that episcopal ordination is a necessary sign of the apostolicity of ministry.[109] But the issue is far from resolved in the early years of the twenty-first century.

A word ought to be added here regarding the Pastoral Provision, also known as the Anglican Use, a canonical arrangement approved in 1980 by the Congregation for the Doctrine of the Faith, whereby Anglican priests who enter into full communion with the Catholic Church and who are eligible for ordination to the Catholic priesthood may be dispensed from the discipline of clerical celibacy. In 2007 the CDF tightened the regulations for former Protestant ministers, requiring at least a three-year period of theological, biblical, liturgical, and sacramental formation before ordination. However, the process for former Anglican priests remains in effect.[110]

Catholic Social Teaching

Since this is a section of Part VI that focuses on post–Vatican II developments in ecclesiology as they apply to the Church *ad extra,* the emphasis here will be on official documents and theological commentaries that appeared after 1965.[111] We have already made the point (in Part V.6.3) that Catholic social teachings became a matter of direct concern for ecclesiology, and not only for moral theology, with Vatican II's Pastoral Constitution on the Church in the Modern World (*Gaudium et spes*). In other words, these teachings are concerned not only with Christian moral behavior in the social, political, and economic orders, but also with the mission of the Church itself.

The list of ecclesiologically relevant post–Vatican II documents includes Pope Paul VI's *Populorum progressio* (Lat., "The progress of peoples," 1967), *Octogesima adveniens* ("In the eightieth year," 1971),[112] and *Evangelii nuntiandi* ("Proclaiming the gospel," 1975); Pope John Paul II's *Redemptor hominis* ("Redeemer of humankind," 1979), *Laborem exercens* ("On human work," 1981), *Sollicitudo rei socialis* ("Solicitude for social concerns," 1987), and *Centesimus annus* ("On the hundredth year," 1991); the Synod of Bishops' *Iustitia in mundo* ("Justice in the world," 1971) and the Final Report of the Extraordinary Synod (1985); the U. S. Catholic Bishops' "The Challenge of Peace" (1983), "Economic Justice for All: Catholic Social Teaching and the U. S. Economy" (1986), and "A Century of Social Teaching: A Common Heritage, a Continuing Challenge" (1990); and the Medellín (Colombia) documents of the Second General Conference of Latin American Bishops (1968) and the Puebla (Mexico) documents of the Third General Conference of Latin American Bishops (1979). Each and every one of these documents (and similar documents issued by other episcopal conferences in Asia, Africa, and Oceania) merits our careful attention, but the limited space of this book precludes our providing detailed summaries of, much less commentaries on, this corpus of texts.[113]

A sustained study of these documents and those antedating them, beginning with Pope Leo XIII's *Rerum novarum* (Lat., "Of new things," 1891), discloses that no consistent and coherent ecclesiology has shaped this more than century-long evolution of Catholic social teachings. To be sure, it would be surprising if it were otherwise, given the extraordinary changes in theology and the life of the Church since the late nineteenth century and especially those brought about by the Second Vatican Council. The various ecclesiological elements of these documents are listed and explained below.

MISSION

For Vatican II's *Gaudium et spes* and John Paul II's *Sollicitudo rei socialis,* the Church is a servant Church with "a single intention: that God's kingdom may come" (*Gaudium et spes,* n. 45). It is a kingdom not only of "truth and life, of holiness and grace, [but also] of justice, love, and peace" (n. 39). Both *Gaudium et spes* and the Final Report of the 1985 Extraordinary Synod of Bishops insist that there is no opposition between the spiritual mission of the Church and the Church's concern for justice and peace. There is a distinction between the two, but no separation, much less opposition. On the contrary, as the document *Iustitia in mundo* of the Third World Synod of Bishops declares, the Church's "action on behalf of justice and participation in the transformation of the world . . . [are] a constitutive dimension . . . of the Church's mission for the redemption of the human race and its liberation from every oppressive situation" (para. 6).

MINISTRY

Until the pontificate of John XXIII (1958–63), the ministry of the Church was generally defined in a narrowly clerical manner. Only the ordained were regarded as ministers in any formal sense of the word. On the other hand, the laity have been acknowledged from the time of Leo XIII to have an important role to play in the implementation of Catholic social teachings. That role, however, tended to be interpreted, until Vatican II, according to the model of Catholic Action, which was traditionally defined as the participation of the laity in the work of the hierarchy. Pope Pius XI (1922–39) had, in fact, referred to the laity in *Quadragesimo anno* (Lat., "After forty years," 1931) as "auxiliary soldiers of the Church," and "Church" in that context clearly meant the hierarchy (n. 141).

John XXIII's *Mater et magistra* (Lat., "Mother and teacher," 1961) and *Pacem in terris* ("Peace on earth," 1963) placed strong emphasis on lay social ministry, but it was Paul VI who took the next step and insisted that the laity may often have to take the initiative in the social apostolate, "without waiting passively for orders and directives" from the hierarchy (*Populorum progressio,* n. 81). Moreover, the laity should be given some meaningful share in the responsibility for making decisions in this area (*Octogesima adveniens,* n. 47).

As much as Paul VI and the Third World Synod of Bishops (*Iustitia in mundo,* paras. 3–8) advanced the role of the laity in the world, it was the council, especially in *Lumen gentium,* that laid the ecclesiological foundations for it. The Dogmatic Constitution on the Church declared that everything it had said about the People of God's sharing in the prophetic, priestly, and kingly functions of Christ was to be explicitly applied "equally to the laity, religious, and clergy" (n. 30). In direct contradiction to the preconciliar idea behind Catholic Action, it described the lay apostolate as "a participation in the saving mission of the Church itself" (n. 33). This participation was not something granted juridically, that is, by hierarchical delegation, but sacramentally, that is, by Baptism, Confirmation, and the Eucharist.

STRUCTURE

With regard to structure too the Second Vatican Council provided the turning point in the development of recent ecclesiology. Before the council, it was generally taken for granted within the Catholic community that "the Church" meant the hierarchy and that the pope was at once a part of the hierarchy and above it. The council set Catholic ecclesiology on a different course with its doctrine of collegiality (*Lumen gentium,* chap. 3). However, some subsequent papal statements have continued to warn against an exaggerated emphasis on the role of the local church and have, at the same time, underscored the importance of the universal Church and of the papal office, which is responsible for maintaining its unity (Paul VI, *Evangelii nuntiandi,* nn. 67–68).

THE CHURCH'S RIGHT AND DUTY TO TEACH

No assertion appears more frequently or more forcefully in Catholic social teachings—from Leo XIII to the present—than the insistence that the Church has the right and duty to teach officially on matters pertaining to social justice and peace. In essence, the argument has been that the issues, although also economic and political in content, are laden with moral concerns. Indeed, so central are these concerns to the gospel and to Christian faith generally that the Church's social teachings can be regarded as a constitutive part of its evangelizing mission (the Third World Synod's *Iustitia in mundo,* intro., para. 6; John Paul II's *Redemptor hominis,* n. 10, paras. 1–2; his *Sollicitudo rei socialis,* nn. 41, 47; and his *Centesimus annus,* nn. 5, 54).

According to Paul VI, the Church's teaching responsibility is a double one: "first, to enlighten minds in order to assist them to discover the truth; . . . and, secondly, to take part in action and to spread, with a real care for service and effectiveness, the energies of the Gospel" (*Octogesima adveniens,* n. 48). It is "a double task of inspiring and of innovating, in order to make structures evolve, so as to adapt them to the needs of today" (n. 50). In other words, the Church is not limited to enunciating principles; it also has the right and duty to suggest moral courses of action and to pass moral judgment on practical solutions proposed by others.

MODE OF TEACHING

With methodology the dividing line comes slightly earlier than the council. With John XXIII Catholic social teaching became more tentative, more sensitive to the complexities of social problems, more modest in suggesting concrete solutions, and more ecumenical and open to dialogue with others, in contrast to the Church's official teachings on human sexuality and reproduction.[114] The Church's official teachers had come to see their task as one of providing a moral framework and proclaiming a moral vision within which particular problems can be analyzed and addressed (*Octogesima adveniens,* n. 42). In matters of social justice and peace, prudential judgments are engaged. People of goodwill can, with a clear and informed conscience, find themselves at times in disagreement with the Church's official teachers not over the basic moral principles, but over their application to concrete circumstances (the U.S. Catholic Bishops' "The Challenge of Peace," n. 10). Hereafter, the official teachers have to take care to distinguish among various levels of authority that their teachings are intended to have (n. 9). Not everything in a papal, episcopal, synodal, or even conciliar document is of equal doctrinal weight.

Moreover, the teaching Church (*Ecclesia docens*) must be a learning Church as well (*Ecclesia discens*). It must be able to read the "signs of the times" and interpret them in the light of the gospel (*Gaudium et spes,* n. 4). It must first listen to those whom it would presume to teach, just as the U.S. bishops did in the preparation and formulation of their two major pastoral letters of 1983 and 1986. Following the example of John XXIII in his 1963 encyclical *Pacem in terris,* official teachers must be aware of the wider and more diverse audience they are addressing on matters of social justice and peace—not only fellow Catholics or even other Christians, but the whole civic community, including non-Christians and nonbelievers ("The Challenge of Peace," nn. 16–17). And that wider, more diverse community is now a global, multicultural one as well (*Populorum progressio,* n. 3; *Sollicitudo rei socialis,* n. 42; *Centesimus annus,* passim).

Finally, the Church's social teaching must demonstrate a preferential option for the poor. This was evident already in the Medellín and Puebla documents of the Conference of Latin American Bishops, in Paul VI's *Evangelii nuntiandi* (n. 29), and in the Final Report of the 1985 Extraordinary Synod of Bishops (see Part V.10.2), but also in John Paul II's *Sollicitudo rei socialis* (n. 42) and *Centesimus annus* (nn. 11, 57).

CHURCH AND STATE

One of the most significant ecclesiological elements in the corpus of Catholic social teachings has been their consistent affirmation of the autonomy of the Church and the state in their respective spheres of responsibility. Before Leo XIII, however, this was not the case. Official Catholic teaching, especially from the Middle Ages to the latter part of the nineteenth century, insisted that the temporal sphere was always subject to the Church. The Church alone could claim to be a "perfect society," that is, one that possesses all that it requires to fulfill its essential functions (see Part I.7).

Catholic social teachings, as expressed in the council's *Gaudium et spes* (esp. n. 76), in Paul VI's *Evangelii nuntiandi* (n. 32), and in the synodal document *Iustitia in mundo* (Part II, para. 9), call upon the Church to free itself from entangling political alliances in order to provide even more effective and credible moral witness on the great social issues of the day. It involves a dual process, which theologian J. Bryan Hehir has referred to as depoliticization and resocialization.[115] The Church is more active than ever in the social order, but more independent of partisan political movements, parties and officials.[116]

The relationship between Church and state, therefore, is neither one of union nor of separation. It is a relationship of cooperation. Members of the Church are also citizens of the state. And all human beings, Catholic or not, are created by God and called by God to their one common destiny in the Kingdom of God. However, upon entering the public forum, the Church can no longer demand or expect any special considerations, much less privileges. The Church must make its case not on the basis of its spiritual authority alone, but on the basis of arguments that are accessible and compelling to all people of goodwill (*Gaudium et spes,* n. 76).

THE WITNESS OF THE CHURCH

There are only two places in the entire corpus of Catholic social teachings where the teachings on social justice and human rights are explicitly applied to the Church itself: *Iustitia in mundo* (chap. 3) and the U.S. Catholic Bishops' pastoral letter "Economic Justice for All" (n. 347). Neither document, however, properly grounds its argument in the principle of sacramentality. It is because the Church itself is a sacrament, a visible sign of the invisible presence of the triune God, that it has a missionary obligation to practice what it preaches and teaches (see *Lumen gentium,* n. 1). There are, to be sure, other documents in which some connection is made, at least indirectly, between the social teachings of the Church and the life and example of the Church itself: Paul VI's *Evangelii nuntiandi* (nn. 15, 23, 30, 41) and John Paul II's *Sollicitudo rei socialis* (nn. 31, 40). Elsewhere, when the sacramentality of the Church is explicitly referred to, no practical application is made to the inner life and structures of the Church (e.g., *Lumen gentium,* n. 1; *Gaudium et spes,* n. 92).

THE PRINCIPLE OF SUBSIDIARITY

The principle of subsidiarity (namely, that nothing should be done or imposed at a higher level that can be done or fulfilled as well or even more effectively at a lower level, that is, at the point closest to where it will have its immediate and greatest impact) was first enunciated in Pius XI's *Quadragesimo anno* (n. 79),[117] then reaffirmed by John XXIII in both *Mater et magistra* (n. 53) and *Pacem in terris* (n. 140) and by John Paul II in *Centesimus annus* (n. 48). The reference in *Pacem in terris* is particularly significant because, although John XXIII did not apply the principle directly to the Church, he did indicate that "within each political community the relations between individuals, families, *intermediate associations* and public authority are governed by the principle of subsidiarity" (my emphasis). Since the Church is one of those "intermediate associations," it would seem that the principle does, or at least should, apply to it as well as to the state and to economic institutions.

Pope Pius XII had made that very leap in an address in 1946 when, in repeating his predecessor's definition of subsidiarity, he continued: "Such words are indeed enlightening; they apply not only to society but also to the life of the Church within its hierarchical structure."[118] The preface to the Latin edition of the Revised Code of Canon Law (1983) makes the same connection: "Careful attention is to be given to the greater application of the so-called principle of subsidiarity within the Church. It is a principle which is rooted in a higher one because the office of bishops with its attached powers is a reality of divine law" (n. 5).[119]

THE UNFINISHED AGENDA

As Catholic social teaching continues to develop during this new century, it will have to be shaped even more directly by the ecclesiology of the Second Vatican Council. This will require underscoring, even more than it has, the reality of the Church as the whole People of God and not simply its equation with the hierarchy. The social apostolate itself will have to become increasing less clerical in character, and the laity should be encouraged not to wait passively for guidance and directions from the hierarchy to take action in the social order, as Paul VI himself urged in his *Octogesima adveniens* (n. 48).

Second, Catholic social teachings will have to recognize and respect the legitimate diversity and pluralism that characterize the universal Church and especially the autonomy of the local churches. Very few of the most difficult social problems yield to universal solutions based on universal principles. The social teaching of national episcopal conferences will have to assume an increasingly significant role.

Third, other episcopal conferences will have to follow the lead of the U.S. bishops in the formulation of their pastoral letters in the 1980s. The U.S. bishops gave the Church a compelling example of a new mode of teaching marked by openness to all relevant views, dialogue, tentativeness, and competence. That model could also be adopted more broadly to include the Church's official teachings on sexual ethics as well.[120]

Fourth, the Church's social teachings have yet to apply directly the principle of subsidiarity to the inner life and structures of the Church. Initiatives undertaken by the Church's central administration in the Vatican should be in the category of "last resort," as in the criteria for a just war. The principle of subsidiarity is also linked closely with the doctrine of collegiality. Just as the doctrine of collegiality requires the Church to acknowledge and respect the pastoral autonomy of each local church, without prejudice to its abiding bond of communion with all of the other local churches in the Body of Christ and particularly with the church of Rome and its bishop (the pope), so the principle of subsidiarity requires the Church to respect the particular pastoral experiences, sights, and judgments of the local churches as they strive to fulfill their missionary responsibilities in the world.

Finally, and most important, the Church must emphasize more than it has heretofore that these social teachings apply not only to the world beyond the Church, but to the Church itself, and that the latter application is grounded in the principle of sacramentality. Simply put, the Church has an abiding missionary obligation to practice what it preaches and teaches, especially on matters of social justice and human rights. Thus far, only two documents in over one hundred years of Catholic social teachings have made this point, albeit without explicit reference to the principle of sacramentality.

The Church and Politics

THE MEANING OF "POLITICS"

When people say, "The Church should stay out of politics" or "Religion and politics don't mix," it is not always clear what they mean.[121] Do they mean only that clergy and religious should stay out of elective politics, or that religious leaders—the bishops in particular—ought never to address public policy issues having to do with war and peace, social justice, human rights or governmental responsibility to the poor, the sick, and children? The late Jesuit Robert F. Drinan (d. 2007) was directly involved in politics as an elected member of the U.S. House of Representatives from 1971 to 1981, and the late Pope John Paul II was also involved in politics, albeit in a nonelective fashion, in bringing the considerable powers of the papacy to bear on the then Communist government of his native Poland and on the Sandinista government of Nicaragua.

Although no member of the U.S. hierarchy has ever run for political office (although it would be his constitutional right to do so, however imprudent it might also be), the United States Conference of Catholic Bishops has issued pastoral letters on the nuclear arms race in 1983 and on the U.S. economy in 1987. Were these letters concerning foreign policy and the economy political? What about episcopal interventions on behalf of governmental aid to private and parochial schools or initiatives on abortion or civil unions and marriages for gays and lesbians?

The word "politics" is derived from the Greek word *polis*, or "city." From the tenth century BCE, the word denoted the Greek city-state, which was small enough to permit face-to-face discussions among all of its citizens. The word "politics," therefore, pertains fundamentally to the affairs of the city, that is, with the public forum and the process of decision making that occurs there. Running for public office is only one aspect of politics.

The essence of the politics of Jesus is usually reduced to a kind of aphorism: "Repay to Caesar what belongs to Caesar, and to God what belongs to God" (Mark 12:17; Matt. 22:21; Luke 20:25). Indeed, the central theme of his whole ministry was to "seek first [God's] kingdom" (Matt. 6:33; also Mark 1:15). That tradition was carried forward by Paul: "Let every person be subordinate to the higher authorities, for there is no authority except from God, and those that exist have been established by God" (Rom. 13:1).[122]

CHURCH AND STATE

The Church's relationship to the political order, J. Bryan Hehir observes, is addressed primarily in its teaching on Church and state, which is only marginally included in the social encyclical tradition.[123] Pope Leo XIII played a pivotal role in the development of the Church's teaching on Church and state, but different from the role he played in the social-encyclical tradition. Although he initiated the social-encyclical tradition with his classic *Rerum novarum* in 1891, his views on Church and state were largely inherited from Popes Gregory XVI (1831–46) and Pius IX (1846–78). Both popes had denied any legitimacy to the democratic revolutions of the eighteenth century, including the American Revolution, opposed religious freedom, and affirmed the "Catholic state" as normative.[124]

Although Leo XIII did not change any of these conclusions, his contribution, as Jesuit theologian John Courtney Murray has demonstrated, "lay in recasting the church-state question so that both institutions and their relationship were to be seen and judged in light of the welfare of the citizen."[125] Leo prepared for change in the Church's understanding and articulation of the relationship, but he did not bring it about himself. Pius XII did so in his Christmas message of 1944.[126] He reversed the first of the nineteenth-century conclusions (which denied the legitimacy of the eighteenth-century democratic revolutions), while affirming the value and dignity of democratic governance.

John XXIII built on Pius's foundation in his own *Pacem in terris* (1963) by reaffirming the new relationship of official Catholic teaching and the democratic state and affirming "cryptically" (Hehir's word) "the right to honor God according to the dictates of an upright conscience, and therefore the right to worship God privately and publicly" (n. 14). This was a major step forward beyond both Leo XIII's and the medieval Church's teaching, which generally failed to defend the rights of individual conscience and the right to worship God in other than Catholic ways, whether privately or publicly. Such teachings were on a continuum with the later view of Cardinal Alfredo Ottaviani, the leader of the minority at Vatican II, that "error has no rights."

The full expression of this new turn is to be found in Vatican II's Declaration on Religious Freedom (*Dignitatis humanae,* Lat., "Of the dignity of the human [person]"), which Cardinal Ottaviani and his allies strongly opposed, and chapter 4, "The Political Community" (nn. 73–76), in the Pastoral Constitution on the Church in the Modern World (*Gaudium et spes*). Father Hehir summarizes this new dimension of the Church's social role as follows: (1) The Church now affirmed the right of religious liberty for each person based on his or her human dignity; (2) it accepted a "positive but limited" definition of the role of the state in society (what Murray termed the "constitutional state");[127] and (3) it reduced the previously normative status of the "Catholic state" to a contingent application of more general principles.[128] John Paul II, Hehir points out, added his own teaching to this conciliar consensus.[129]

In light of this recent development, the following principles should govern the relationship between Church and State:[130]

1. The Church cannot use the state to further its own spiritual purposes; that is, the state cannot act as a Church. It would do so, for example, if it attempts to write and/or mandate prayer in the public schools. There is a rightful secularity and autonomy to the temporal order, and the Church must remain transcendent to every political system (*Gaudium et spes*, n. 40).

2. The state cannot use the Church for its own purely political purposes. This would violate the principle of the freedom of the Church (*Dignitatis humanae*, n. 4).

3. On the other hand, the Church must have an active role in society. It must have the freedom "to preach and to teach, and to pass moral judgment even on matters that belong to the political order, when human rights or the salvation of souls are at stake" (*Gaudium et spes*, n. 76). But the Church, Pope Paul VI insisted, does not offer a set of ready-made practical solutions to such issues of public policy. It offers only a framework of values or a moral vision through which political leaders might more easily arrive at specific, practical solutions (*Octogesima adveniens*, n. 42).

4. The Church seeks no special status and should be accorded none (*Gaudium et spes*, n. 76). The Church always owes the

public a careful accounting of how it came to its moral conclusions regarding matters of public policy. The Church must also translate its teachings into language and arguments that a religiously and politically pluralistic society can understand and agree upon as the moral foundation of these policy positions. Finally, the Church must address issues in a way that underscores their moral interrelatedness, reminiscent of the late Cardinal Joseph Bernardin's (d. 1996) consistent-ethic-of-life, or "seamless garment," approach.[131]

5. The relationship between the Church and the state must be one of neither union nor absolute separation, but one of cooperation, for the sake of the common good. "In their proper spheres, the political community and the Church are mutually independent and self-governing. Yet, by a different title, each serves the personal and social vocation of the same human beings" (*Gaudium et spes,* n. 76).

BISHOPS IN POLITICS

It is always hazardous to write about time-bound topics, especially with regard to such an ephemeral sector of life as politics, because circumstances can change so rapidly. What would have been pertinent in one period of time may seem irrelevant and outdated only a few years later. It is with that limitation in mind that we make some references here to the activity of bishops in politics, especially Catholic bishops of the United States. (Readers in other countries can make the appropriate applications to their own ecclesiastical and political situations.)

The Administrative Committee of the United States Conference of Catholic Bishops (USCCB) has issued quadrennial statements to help prepare Catholic citizens to vote responsibly in the various presidential elections, beginning in 1975. In 2007 the quadrennial statement, "Forming Consciences for Faithful Citizenship: A Call to Political Responsibility from the Catholic Bishops of the United States," was approved for the first time by the whole body of bishops rather than by the Administrative Committee. The key paragraph in the 2003 statement "Faithful Citizenship: A Catholic Call to Political Responsibility" is: "As bishops, we seek to form the consciences of our people. We do not wish to instruct persons on how they should vote by endorsing or opposing candidates. We hope that voters will examine the position of candidates on the full range of issues as well as on their personal integrity, philosophy and performance. We are convinced that a consistent ethic of life should be the moral framework from which to address issues in the political arena."[132] The words "or opposing" in the second sentence cited are of great significance. They were first added in 1987 after the dubious behavior of some prominent bishops, including Cardinals John O'Connor (d. 2000) of New York and Bernard Law of Boston, in the 1984 campaign, when their attacks upon the Democratic candidates, and particularly the nominee for vice president, Congresswoman Geraldine Ferraro, led many to believe these high-ranking bishops were opposed to the election of the (Walter) Mondale–Ferraro ticket, even if they were not explicitly endorsing the reelection of President Ronald Reagan.[133] The words "or opposing" remain in the bishops' quadrennial statements to this day.

In the 2004 presidential campaign between President George W. Bush and Senator John Kerry of Massachusetts, several bishops more than implied that a vote for Senator Kerry would be tantamount to a vote in favor of abortion and, therefore, seriously sinful. Indeed, a handful of bishops announced that Senator Kerry would be refused Holy Communion in their dioceses, even though his own bishop in Boston made no such statement. One archbishop defended his own involvement by insisting that people of faith have a right to speak out on issues of importance to them. To be sure, that is the case. However, a problem arises when the speaking out crosses the line into overt criticism of a particular candidate or granting a politically beneficial photo-op with the favored candidate. Both practices have been explicitly rejected by the USCCB as a matter of conference policy.[134] "As an institution," the bishops' 2003 statement declares, "we are called to be *political but not partisan*. The Church cannot be chaplain for any one party or cheerleader for any candidate. Our cause is the protection of the weak and vulnerable and defense of human life and dignity, not a particular party or candidate."[135]

During the 2004 election campaign itself, the bishops' conference as a whole issued a statement, "Catholics in Political Life," in which the bishops repeated the central principles about nonpartisanship that had been reaffirmed in the 2003 statement of the Administrative Committee. In addition to encouraging communication between the bishops and Catholic politicians, the bishops' statement rejected the misuse of the Eucharist for political ends, even as it respected the right of individual bishops to make different judgments for their own dioceses. Two years later the Task Force on Catholic Bishops and Catholic Politicians, chaired by Cardinal Theodore McCarrick, then archbishop of Washington, D.C., issued its final report. It was similar in its conclusions to the earlier statement, "Catholics in Political Life," but also included a concluding plea for nonpartisanship and tolerance: "However, there should be no place in the body of Christ for the brutality of partisan politics, the impugning of motives or turning differences in pastoral judgment into fundamental disagreements on principle."[136]

CLERGY AND RELIGIOUS IN POLITICS

The word "clergy" usually applies to the ordained: bishops, priests, and deacons. The term is used here in a wider sense to include anyone whose actions in the public forum could reasonably be construed as somehow representative of the Churches and ecclesial communities to which they belong. In the Catholic Church, this includes religious women and nonordained religious men (brothers).

There are at least eight levels of political involvement on the part of clergy and religious:[137]

1. Participation in public debate on public policy issues. The pastoral letters of an episcopal conference would be one example of this first level.

2. Personal association with officeholders with the intention of influencing their political behavior, directly or indirectly. The role of the Reverend Billy Graham during several recent U.S. presidencies would be a case in point.

3. Public action designed to call attention to deficiencies in the political system. The participation of the Reverend Martin Luther King Jr. (d. 1968) in marches, demonstrations, and sit-ins on behalf of civil rights, in which he was joined by many priests, ministers, rabbis, and nuns, and the activities of the Berrigan brothers, Philip (d. 2002) and Daniel, in the anti–Vietnam War movements are clear examples of this third level of clergy and religious involvement in the political order.

4. Leadership of organized religio-political movements with a broadly based agenda of social and political issues. Father Charles Coughlin (d. 1979) was founder of the National Union of Social Justice in 1934, which formed a third party in opposition to President Franklin D. Roosevelt in 1936, and the Reverend Jerry Falwell (d. 2007) founded the Moral Majority in 1979 for similar purposes.

5. Active support of, or opposition to, candidates for public office by means of voter registration drives, fund-raising, direct mailings and communications via the Internet, endorsements from the pulpit, and the like. These practices have been more common among U.S. Protestant churches, both liberal and conservative, Caucasian and African American.

6. Indirect support of, or opposition to, candidates for public office by means of public appearances and public statements of various kinds. Various bishops have engaged in this sixth level of political involvement, as noted above, in the U.S. presidential campaigns of 1972, 1984, 1988, and 2004.

7. The acceptance and exercise of appointive public office, such as a Cabinet post. Sister Alice Mary Mansour, a Sister

of Mercy in Detroit, was forced out of her religious community in 1983 because she refused to resign her post as head of Michigan's Department of Social Services. No U.S. clergyman, however, has served in more high-level positions in the federal government than Theodore M. Hesburgh, C.S.C., president emeritus of the University of Notre Dame, for example, as chair of the U.S. Commission on Civil Rights. Perhaps the most controversial cases outside of the United States have occurred in Central America and specifically in Nicaragua, where priests served in the Sandinista government as foreign minister and as minister of culture. The latter, Father Ernesto Cardenal, was given a tongue-lashing by Pope John Paul II during a papal visit in 1983. The photo of Father Cardenal on one knee before the pope, with his beret in hand, was sent all over the world and confirmed the pope's reputation as an unyielding, tough-minded leader.

8. Active candidacy for, and service in, elective public office. Scores of Protestant clergy have served in the U.S. House of Representatives and Senate. For example, John Danforth of Missouri, an Episcopal priest, was a member of the U.S. Senate from 1977 to 1995. The most celebrated case involving a Catholic priest was that of Father Robert F. Drinan, S.J., to whom we referred to on page 257. He was elected to the House of Representatives in 1970, but was prevented by the Vatican from seeking reelection to a sixth term in 1980. At least three Protestant clergymen in recent years have been candidates for the presidency: Jesse Jackson, Pat Robertson, and Al Sharpton. In 1984 two Rhode Island nuns resigned from their religious communities rather than abandon their political careers, as Father Drinan had reluctantly done: Elizabeth Morancy, a state representative, and Arlene Violet, who was later elected attorney general of Rhode Island.

The Catholic Church's Code of Canon Law does not forbid involvement at all eight levels. Canon 285 stipulates only that clerics cannot hold public office, elective or appointive, "without the permission of their ordinary," that is, their bishop. Nor are they to have an active role in political parties. The rest is governed by prudence rather than by canon law.[138]

THE POLITICAL THEOLOGY OF JOHANN METZ

No theologian—Catholic, Protestant, Anglican, or Orthodox—has written more on political theology than Johann Baptist Metz; he has achieved thereby the status of preeminent commentator on the topic (see Part VI.2.4). Our interest in him, however, is not in his understanding and elaboration of political theology across the whole spectrum of its theological components, but in its ecclesiological dimensions only.[139] And Metz has written much on the connection between political theology and the Church, including his key paper at a post–Vatican II conference at St. Xavier College in Chicago, "The Church and the World," and pertinent portions of his monographs *Theology of the World, Faith in History and Society: Toward a Practical Fundamental Theology,* and *The Emergent Church: The Future of Christianity in a Postbourgeois World.*[140]

We have already provided a general definition of "politics" VI.5.1. According to Metz, political *theology* reflects on the presence and activity of God in "the city" (Gk. *polis*), which is the temporal order, or the realm of society. Political theology is the study of God as political Actor and of other theological components, including the Church, insofar as they are related to, or expressive of, God's activities in the many "cities" of the world. It is "a positive attempt to formulate the eschatological message under the conditions of our present society."[141] Political theology measures all reality in the light of the promised Kingdom, or Reign, of God. And because the Kingdom has not yet come in all its fullness and perfection, there is nothing, including the Church, that escapes the attention and critical gaze of political theology.[142] The Church itself, therefore, is not exempt from criticism, because the Church is also part of the world.[143] "For it is *that world* which attempts to live from the promised future of God, and to call *that world* in question which understands itself only in terms of itself and its possibilities. . . . The Church is the eschatological community and the exodus community. . . . The Church is not the goal of her own strivings; this goal is the Kingdom of God."[144] The Church has a hope and witnesses to a hope, but its hope is not in itself. The hope is in the Kingdom as the world's future. The Church is the universal sacrament of hope for the salvation of the whole world. It is precisely because of this that the Church must be "the liberating and critical force of this one society."[145] Hope, according to Metz, is living for the other.[146]

That hope, he writes, should be "creative and militant." This means that we human beings—and the Church—cannot simply wait in expectation for the Kingdom to come as "ready-made." "We are workers building this city," which is the eschatological city of God and which is even now coming into existence with our collaboration. For Metz "a theology of the emerging political and social order . . . must be a *political theology*."[147]

Although for most of his theological career he was indebted to his "father in the faith," Karl Rahner, in developing a fundamental theology, Metz moved beyond Rahner in his later years through his contacts with the Church in Latin America and his increasingly close identification with liberation theology and the plight of the poor and the powerless of the world.[148] The Church became a matter of concern, even emphasis, in his later work, in which he insisted that the "church's crisis is due to a deficit of discipleship and to difficulties in adapting to Jesus." It must make the transition from being a traditional "church for the people" to a "living 'church of the people.'"[149] Such a Church of discipleship must also be a "*church of poverty*."[150] At an eschatological level, this transition is from "a church of evolutionistically softened eschatology to a church of the imminent expectation; or the church in the field of tension between apocalyptic and politics. . . . Discipleship and imminent expectation belong inseparably together." He asks if Christians who speak of hope actually hope for anything anymore. "Do they still expect an end at all—not only for themselves but for the world and its time? Is the church still apocalyptic in this sense?"[151] Although the Church has no divinely sanctioned plan for history, for Metz it exists to prevent any inner-historical force or ideology from being absolutized, from becoming an end in itself.[152]

The Church and Liberation

This section on liberation theology also properly belongs in Part VII, on the internal life of the Church. Like feminist ecclesiology, it is an integral part of the life of the Church itself. The fact that the topic is treated here as well as in Part VII (with sections on Hispanic and Latino/a, and African and African American ecclesiologies) only highlights the porous character of some of the distinctions that are prominent throughout this book. Categorization is always a judgment call, with valid arguments on either side.

Liberation theology is a form of political theology that takes as its central theme the freeing of the poor and the powerless from economic, social, and political exploitation and oppression. It initially emerged in Latin America, thereby leading many to believe, erroneously, that liberation theology and Latin American liberation theology are one and the same. In fact, there are diverse forms of liberation theology in Africa[153] and Asia[154] and within specific segments of the human community at large, namely, people of color (black theology)[155] and women (feminist theology).[156] Ecclesiologically, liberation theology views the Church as a potentially liberating community and institution, investing its vast moral, spiritual, and even financial and political resources in the causes of social justice, human rights, and peace.[157] It also critiques and judges the Church by how well it fulfills its liberating responsibilities.

The "father" of Latin American liberation theology is Gustavo Gutiérrez,[158] a Peruvian diocesan priest who entered the Dominican order soon after Juan Luis Cipriani Thorne, a member of Opus Dei, became archbishop (later cardinal) of Lima in 1999. It was Gutiérrez who provided the methodological framework for doing theology in a liberationist fashion, and it was also he, almost alone among liberation theologians, who incorporated the principle of sacramentality into its ecclesiological perspective. "As a sacramental community," he writes, "the Church should signify in its own internal structure the salvation whose fulfillment it announces. . . . As a sign of the liberation of man [*sic*] and history, the Church itself in its concrete existence ought to be a place of liberation. . . . If we conceive of the Church as a sacrament of the salvation of the world, then it has all the more obligation to manifest in its visible structures the message that it bears."[159]

Moreover, the Church is not an end in itself. Rather, "it finds its meaning in its capacity to signify the reality in function of which it exists." That reality, he insists, is the Kingdom of God, "which has already begun in history. The break with an unjust social order *and* the search for new ecclesial structures . . . have their basis in this ecclesiological perspective."[160]

Otherwise there is relatively little ecclesiological content to Gutiérrez's presentation of liberation theology, except that he writes from the perspective of an active and committed member of the Church and through the prism of its faith in Jesus Christ as mediated through the Scriptures and the preaching of the Church. For Gutiérrez, the Church is "born from the blood of martyrs." Its members must always be, "like the God in whom we believe," in solidarity with the poor, the powerless, and the oppressed and showing themselves thereby "capable of stubbornly sustaining the hope of the dispossessed."[161]

The "heart of the message" is to be "faithful to the God of Jesus Christ" through "acts of love towards our neighbor, and especially the weakest among them." It is this message and our commitment to it "that brings us together as a community, as a Church, within which we try to think through our faith. Theology is done in a Church which must provide in human history the testimony to a life victorious over death. To be a witness to the resurrection means choosing life, personal and social life, life in all its forms, since nothing escapes the universality of the Kingdom of God."[162] He continues:

> *This life we celebrate in the Eucharist, the first duty of the ecclesial community. In sharing bread, we remember the love and trust of Jesus who was taken to His death, and the confirmation of His mission towards the poor through the resurrection. The breaking of bread*

is both the point of departure and destination of the Christian community. This act represents the profound communion with human suffering caused in many cases by the lack of bread, and it is the recognition, in joy, of the Resurrected Jesus who gives life and lifts the hopes of the people brought together by his acts and his word.[163]

Perhaps the most ecclesiologically explicit of liberation theologians is Leonardo Boff, a former Franciscan who ran afoul of the Congregation for the Doctrine of the Faith because of his criticisms of the Church as a dysfunctional family, notwithstanding strong support from two fellow Brazilian Franciscans, Cardinals Paulo Evaristo Arns, former archbishop of São Paulo, and Aloisio Lorscheider (d. 2007), former archbishop of Fortaleza.[164] Boff's major ecclesiological work is *Church: Charism and Power: Liberation Theology and the Institutional Church.*[165] He is also the author of *Ecclesiogenesis: The Base Communities Reinvent the Church.*[166]

He argues in the former book that traditional incarnational ecclesiology (the Church as the communal continuation of Christ in history) is too narrow, because it fails to take into account the decisive event of the Resurrection. Through the Resurrection, Jesus entered an entirely new Spirit-filled existence, giving him a "global relationship to all reality." Boff's ecclesiology, therefore, is rooted in pneumatology. "The Church must be thought of not so much as beginning with the risen Christ, now in the form of the Spirit, but rather as beginning with the Holy Spirit, as the force and means by which the Lord remains present in history and so continues his work of inaugurating a new world."[167]

Consequently, the Church is the body not only of Christ, but of the Holy Spirit. Like the risen Christ, its boundaries are the whole cosmos. Its life and structures are essentially charismatic, not institutional, and charisms are available to everyone.[168] Everything in the Church—dogmas, rituals, liturgy, canon law, hierarchical structures—must be measured against the standard of the Holy Spirit. Nothing can be allowed to inhibit the work of Christ acting through the Holy Spirit. In the communion of Persons in the Trinity, there is no subordination or hierarchy. If modeled on the Trinity, hierarchy and authority can only be allowed provided they are for the service of the whole.[169]

The Church and the Holy Spirit

PNEUMATOLOGY YESTERDAY AND TODAY

The Holy Spirit has been central to this entire presentation on the mystery of the Church. There are numerous references to the Spirit in each of the parts (see, e.g., Part II.2.13.c, on the Church as the Temple of the Holy Spirit), and there is neither need nor intention to recapitulate all of that material here. Moreover, the purpose of this section of Part VI is not to lay out a complete theology of the Holy Spirit, also known as pneumatology. Rather, it is to provide a link between our consideration of the Church's relationships with realities beyond itself (Lat. *Ecclesia ad extra*), and outside the Catholic Church in particular, and our subsequent consideration in Part VII of issues that pertain to the internal life of the Church (*Ecclesia ad intra*).

The Holy Spirit empowers the Church to reach out to individuals, groups, communities, and institutions of every kind and is, at the same time, the Church's ultimate life force that makes it possible for the Church to become what it is called to be, namely, a community of grace that is bound together by faith in Jesus Christ, by hope in the promise of eternal life, and by its commitment to the practice of brotherly and sisterly love toward one another and thence to the whole of the human community. To the extent that the Church is faithful to this call to embody and live out the theological virtues of faith, hope, and love, it is a credible sign, lifted up among the nations, of God's universal love for all of humankind and of our common destiny for eternal happiness in the Kingdom, or Reign, of God.

Christopher O'Donnell cites a Vatican II "vignette," attributed to Yves Congar, that has since become "classic." "During the discussion of the schema *De Ecclesia* at the second session of the council," Congar writes, "we were speaking one day with two friends who were Orthodox observers, Fr. [Nikos] Nissiotis and Fr. Alexander Schmemann [d. 1983]. They said to us: 'If we had to write a *De ecclesia* we would write one chapter on the Holy Spirit and one chapter on Christian man [*sic*]. Then we would stop. We would have said what was essential.'"[170] Even though, O'Donnell points out, such an ecclesiology would have been one-sided, the remarks of these two distinguished Orthodox theologians highlighted a major weakness in pre–Vatican II Catholic ecclesiology, which lacked any substantial pneumatological dimension. Indeed, many catechists and their young students in those years used to refer to the Holy Spirit as "the forgotten Person of the Blessed Trinity," liturgically rescued from obscurity on only two occasions: the feast of Pentecost and the celebration of the sacrament of Confirmation.

As O'Donnell and other commentators have shown, supported by numerous bibliographical examples, there has been an outpouring of writings on the Holy Spirit since Vatican II (not to mention the cognate developments in Catholic spirituality).[171] In spite of the great importance of the Holy Spirit in the Bible, in Christian theology generally, and in creeds and doctrinal formulations over the course of many centuries, pneumatology did not begin to inform ecclesiology until the time of Johann Adam Möhler, in the third and fourth decades of the nineteenth century, and then in Leo XIII's encyclical *Divinum illud munus* (Lat., "This divine function" [1897]), a document that relied heavily on the writings of Augustine and Thomas Aquinas. That encyclical anticipated Pius XII's 1943 encyclical *Mystici Corporis Christi* in identifying the Holy Spirit as the soul of the whole Church, hierarchy and laity alike, as the source of its truth and sacramental life and of the holiness of its individual members (for a more detailed description and analysis of the encyclical, see Part IV.3.3). Apart from *Mystici Corporis,* however, the Holy Spirit did not have any significant place in Pius XII's extensive teachings on the Church.

There are only thirteen references to the Holy Spirit in Vatican II's Dogmatic Constitution on the Church (*Lumen gentium*), but they are ecclesiologically important.[172] The constitution begins with a trinitarian exposition of the mystery of the Church. The Church is called by God the Father to carry forward the work of God the Son, in and through the power of the Holy Spirit (nn. 2–4). The council's central pneumatological insight is that "the Holy Spirit was sent to sanctify the Church continually and so that believers would have through Christ access to the Father in one Spirit (see Ephesians 2:18)" (n. 4). Similarly, the Decree on the Church's Missionary Activity (*Ad gentes divinitus,* Lat., "divinely [sent] to the nations") teaches that the Holy Spirit vivifies the whole Church in everything that it does (n. 4).

That conciliar pneumatology was carried forward, but without an equivalently sharp ecclesiological focus, in John Paul II's 1986 encyclical *Dominum et vivificantem* (Lat., "And the life-giving Lord"). That encyclical reaffirms the relatively recent official teaching that the Holy Spirit is the soul of the Church and that the grace of Pentecost is perpetuated in the Church through the sacraments, especially Holy Orders and Confirmation.[173]

THE PNEUMATOLOGY OF YVES CONGAR

To be sure, the doctrine of the Holy Spirit has always been a matter of singular emphasis in the writings of the Eastern Fathers of the Church from the earliest centuries and of Orthodox theologians in our own day, as the "vignette" above makes clear. On the other hand, there has also been a resurgence of interest in the Holy Spirit among Roman Catholic theologians, none of whom has been more deeply immersed in Eastern thought than Yves Congar. Indeed, his last major work was a three-volume study of the Holy Spirit in the life of the Church, *I Believe in the Holy Spirit.*[174]

In the first volume, Congar acknowledges that Pius XII's *Mystici Corporis Christi* "contains a profound theology of the Holy Spirit," but he pays relatively little attention to the encyclical because, in his judgment, it "never reaches the point where it becomes a full pneumatology," so "restricted" is it "by its concentration on the institution."[175] Although Pius XII reinforced the teaching of Leo XIII that the Holy Spirit is the soul of the Church, Congar himself went considerably beyond both popes in identifying the Holy Spirit as the Church's co-institutor, along with Jesus himself. Jesus laid the foundations for the Church during his earthly life and ministry, and the Spirit has guided the Church throughout its subsequent history and will do so until the end of time. The Spirit does so by guaranteeing the efficacy of the sacraments, forming and reforming the members into a coherent, unified community, and providing wisdom and courage for the fulfillment of the Church's mission and ministries.

In one of the most insightful observations in this first volume, Congar points out that certain pre–Vatican II styles of Marian devotion served to displace what should have been a liturgical and theological focus on the Holy Spirit. He concedes the legitimacy of certain Protestant criticisms that Catholics have attributed to Mary what really belongs to the Holy Spirit, for example, the titles and functions of comforter, advocate, and "soul of the Church."[176] Similarly Mary's maternity is such that we are not left as orphans. She reveals Jesus to us, who in turn reveals the Father. And she also forms Jesus in us. But, again, those are roles proper to the Holy Spirit alone, Congar insists.

He cites six elements of Vatican II's otherwise underdeveloped pneumatology that have continued to shape the postconciliar theology of the Holy Spirit: (1) its Christological basis, underscoring the essential point that the Holy Spirit is the Spirit of Christ (*Lumen gentium,* nn. 7, 8, 14); (2) the essential role of the Holy Spirit in the life of the Church (n. 8); (3) the triune context for ecclesiology; (4) the Holy Spirit as the source of the Church's charismatic nature, such that the Spirit is "co-constitutive" of the Church;[177] (5) the Church as a whole is a communion of Churches and the Holy Spirit is the principle of that communion;[178] and (6) the Spirit is already active in history, and was so even before the Incarnation (*Presbyterorum ordinis,* n. 22; *Gaudium et spes,* nn. 11, 26).

The second volume of *I Believe in the Holy Spirit* reflects on the presence and activity of the Holy Spirit in the Church as co-institutor and as the source of its unity, catholicity, and holiness (Part One), in individual members of the Church (Part Two), and in the charismatic renewal (Part Three). Congar insists that the Church is the product of a twofold mission: that of the Son and that of the Holy Spirit. He rejects the false opposition between what is derived from the Spirit (charisms) and what is of the Son (institutional elements). If such a false opposition were accepted, "the unity of the Church as the Body of Christ is destroyed and the claim is made that everything can be regulated and conducted, on the one hand, without spirituality and exclusively in the name of power and, on the other, anarchically, in the name of the Spirit."[179] Congar rejects both extremes: the tendency to subordinate the charismatic to the institutional and the opposite, the tendency to subordinate the institutional to the charismatic. The Holy Spirit is the source of the Church's unity, catholicity, apostolicity, and holiness.[180]

Volume 3 offers a lengthy and detailed comparative analysis of Western and Eastern approaches to the study of the Trinity, with particular reference to the Third Person, the Holy Spirit. Congar shows that our access to knowledge of the Holy Spirit comes through our experience of the effects of the Spirit's action in the world, that is, in the economy (Gk., "household") of salvation. Much of Western theology, at least until the middle of the twentieth century, seems to have been predicated on the assumption that we can achieve direct insight into the inner workings of the Godhead itself.

Congar notes that the Church "as a whole is sacramental in its nature," with a threefold temporal dimension: past, present, and future. The unity of all three is ensured by the Holy Spirit, and not by an "earthly means" or by the institution of the Church. Indeed, the entire "life and activity" of the Church on this earth and in human history "can be seen totally as an epiclesis," that is, a constant "calling down" of the Holy Spirit upon the Church and upon the world the Church serves.[181]

The Spirit's role in Confirmation is obvious.[182] For Congar, the Eucharist "follows the structure of the economy of salvation." The Holy Spirit had to sanctify, anoint, and guide Jesus, the Word made flesh. "It was necessary for the Holy Spirit to 'pneumatize' him.... The Christ whom we receive in sacramental communion is the Christ of Easter who has been 'pneumatized' or penetrated by the Spirit."[183] But the Holy Spirit is involved in all seven sacraments and to various other nonsacramental rituals within the Church, such as religious profession, the reading of Scripture, and preaching.[184]

In the end, there are six principal elements to Congar's own pneumatology as it informs his theology of the Church:[185]

1. The Holy Spirit is not simply the animator of the Church; the Spirit is co-institutor of the Church with Jesus Christ. This insight is congruent with Congar's view of the historic *Filioque* controversy,[186] namely, whether the Holy Spirit proceeds from the Father *through* the Son (Lat. *per Filium*), which is the Eastern understanding, rather than from the Father *and* the Son (*Filioque*), in subordinate fashion, as if from two coequal principles, which has been the typical, though not exclusive, Western understanding as enshrined in the Nicene Creed since the ninth century.

2. The Holy Spirit is co-institutor of the Church. As such, the Spirit ensures the efficacy of the sacraments, especially the Eucharist, forms and reforms the members of the Church into a community, confers charisms upon the institutional Church and its individual members, and inspires and guides the Church's mission and ministries. There is no opposition, therefore, between the institutional and charismatic dimensions of the Church, that is, between Christ as the institutor of the structures of the Church and the Holy Spirit as the source of its charisms.

3. The entire life of the Church is "one long epiclesis," that is, of the Church's calling down of the Holy Spirit upon itself and upon the world it has been sent to serve. The epicletic character of the Church is evident in many aspects of the Church's activities, but especially its sacramental life.

4. The Holy Spirit is with the Church now, but also ahead of it, drawing it forward in history toward the fulfillment of the Reign of God, which is the final destiny of the Church and of the whole world, of which the Church is a part.

5. The universal Church is a communion of local churches, and the Holy Spirit is the source and ground of that communion as well as of its holiness, catholicity, and apostolicity.

6. The Church is the Body of Christ, and the Holy Spirit is the Spirit of the Risen and exalted Lord. The primary basis of pneumatology, therefore, is Christology.

Alas, it is not what Yves Congar wrote about the Holy Spirit that will endure for decades, even centuries, but what he wrote about the Church. But here again, it is not a matter of either/or but of both/and. His pneumatology is, in the end, a function of his ecclesiology.

Brief Summation

As pointed out at the beginning of Part VI, the Catholic Church had adopted an increasingly defensive stance toward the world in the sixteenth century and maintained it to the very threshold of the Second Vatican Council in the second half of the twentieth century. At the same time, Catholicism also began to stress even more than it had in previous centuries the juridical and institutional aspects of the Church, especially during its own Counter-Reformation.

The Second Vatican Council retrieved much of the ancient Church's more dialogical stance toward the world and its emphasis on its communal, participatory life. Part VI has attempted to show how and to what extent post–Vatican II ecclesiology and official teachings carried forward and developed further the Church's newly retrieved dialogical stance toward the world (the Church *ad extra*). Part VII will focus on the Church's renewed emphasis on the communal nature of its ecclesial life (the Church *ad intra*).

PART VII

Post–Vatican II Ecclesiology

The Church ad Intra

Part VII is the second half of a detailed synthesis of post–Vatican II ecclesiology, and of Catholic ecclesiology in particular, organized in accordance with the division proposed at the Second Vatican Council (1962–65) by Belgium's Cardinal Leo Jozef Suenens, namely, between the Church *ad extra* (the Church's relationship to realities beyond itself) and the Church *ad intra* (the internal life of the Church). Beginning with Vatican II, the Church has been moving away from the juridical, legalistic understanding of the Church, common since the High Middle Ages (thirteenth–fifteenth centuries) and the Counter-Reformation (sixteenth century), to a more communal notion of the Church that is at once less legalistic, less authoritarian, and less clerical and more encouraging of broad participation on the part of the laity in its mission, ministries, and sacramental life. This also has involved a reconsideration of the role of the papacy in the authority structure of the Church and a renewed appreciation for other centers of authority within the Church.

In this part, the following topics will be considered: (1) the Church as a communion; (2) authority in the Church; (3) the reception of doctrine and disciplinary decrees; (4) ministry, both ordained and nonordained; (5) a brief excursus on sacraments and liturgy; (6) Mary and the Church; (7) feminist and nonfeminist ecclesiology by Catholic women; (8) Hispanic and Latino/a ecclesiologies; (9) African and African American ecclesiologies; (10) new movements in the Church; and (11) the emerging world-Church. (For references to previous considerations of most of these topics throughout this book, see the opening paragraphs of Part VI. On the liturgical controversies, see Part V.6.2.)

The Church as a Communion

THE GENERAL CONCEPT

For most Catholics and other Christians, the first meaning of the word "communion" is eucharistic. Communion is something one receives at Mass or upon a sickbed, and the word is usually modified by the uppercase adjective "Holy." According to official Catholic teaching, pronounced definitively at the Council of Trent in the sixteenth century, *Holy* Communion is the eucharistic body and blood of Jesus Christ under the appearances of bread and wine.

In more recent years, the word "communion" has taken on a broader ecclesiological meaning, especially in Catholic theology. It refers not only to the sacrament of Holy Communion, but also to the reality of the Church itself. Indeed, the Final Report of the Extraordinary Synod of Bishops in 1985 concludes that the "ecclesiology of communion is the central and fundamental idea of the [Second Vatican] council's documents."[1]

But all this might seem highly abstract to many readers. Words like "ecclesiology" and expressions like "ecclesiology of communion" (also known as "communion ecclesiology") have an academic ring to them. If ecclesiology is simply the theological study of the Church (see Part I.1), what does "ecclesiology of communion" mean, and what practical difference does it make for an understanding of the nature and mission of the Church?

To speak of the Church as a communion means, among other things, that the Church is a community of baptized persons who are interiorly united with God in Christ through the reconciling presence and power of the Holy Spirit. This communion is visibly expressed and realized especially in the sacraments.[2] It is the Holy Spirit who unites us one with another into a single, although divided, community, which is the Body of Christ. The Greek word that the New Testament employs for this reality is *koinonia,* which is difficult to render precisely in English. It is usually translated as "fellowship," "participation," "solidarity," or simply "communion."

COMMUNION AND VATICAN II

Although the word, but especially the concept of *koinonia,* continued to be used in the postbiblical history of the Church, it tended to fade from the scene in Roman Catholic ecclesiology, but not in Anglicanism or Eastern Orthodoxy. There was a retrieval of interest in the notion of communion within Roman Catholicism around the time of the Second Vatican Council.[3] As stated above, the Final Report of the Extraordinary Synod of Bishops pointed out in 1985 that "communion" became a "central and fundamental idea" within the council's own ecclesiology.

The internal bond among the faithful is described as a communion in the council's Dogmatic Constitution on the Church (*Lumen gentium,* Lat., "Light of nations," n. 13) and the Decree on Ecumenism (*Unitatis redintegratio,* "The restoration of unity," n. 2). This communion, according to the council, is brought about by the Holy Spirit (*Lumen gentium,* n. 4; *Unitatis redintegratio,* n. 2; Pastoral Constitution on the Church in the Modern World [*Gaudium et spes,* "Joy and hope"], n. 32). For Vatican II, the visible, structural expression of this communion is the collegiality of bishops, each of whom represents and embodies his own local church or diocese. The bishops' collegiality with one another is a representative expression of the communal nature of the universal Church. Their union is the corporate expression of the union of each of their local churches with one another and with the local church of Rome, whose bishop is their visible center of unity (*Lumen gentium,* nn. 22–23). The archbishop of Canterbury and the various patriarchs of the Eastern Orthodox Churches serve a similar function within their own communion of churches, but with important canonical differences, to be sure.

Communion is a key notion in the council's Decree on Ecumenism. Separated Churches and ecclesial communities are regarded as not in full communion with the Catholic Church (*Unitatis redintegratio,* n. 3; for the distinction between Churches and ecclesial communities, see Part I.2.4; Part V.6.4 of this book),[4] but those who believe in Christ and are baptized are said to be in some real, though imperfect, communion with the Catholic Church (*Unitatis redintegratio,* n. 3; *Lumen gentium,* n. 15). The notion that there are *degrees* of communion (not to be confused with references to "impaired communion," employed within Anglicanism because of the controversy precipitated by the ordination of V. Gene Robinson, an openly partnered gay priest, as bishop of New Hampshire in 2003) has been a major ecumenical step forward beyond the pre–Vatican II concept of membership in the Church (for "degrees of communion," see Part V.6.4–5). In pre–Vatican II Catholic ecclesiology, either one was a member of the one, true Church of Christ or not. It was a matter of all or nothing. According to that approach, Anglicans would have been no more a part of the Body of Christ than, let us say, Muslims.

This either/or mentality came to the fore in the late 1940s during the controversy within Catholicism over Father Leonard Feeney's insistence, based on his interpretation of the medieval axiom "Outside the Church, no salvation," that only Catholics can be saved (previously discussed in Part IV.3.3.e, 3.4). Vatican II sidestepped the controversy over membership entirely—whether non-Catholics could be members of the Church or not, given their lack of communion with the Bishop of Rome—and allowed for degrees of affiliation, or communion, within the Body of Christ. Even those who are not Christian, the council pointed out, are related to the Church in one way or another (*Lumen gentium,* n. 16).

COMMUNION AND EUCHARIST

However, it is in the celebration of the Eucharist and in the reception of Holy Communion within the Eucharist that the Church becomes more fully what it is already: a communion of grace, that is, a community created and sustained by the sanctifying presence of the triune God.[5] The eucharistic celebration, or Mass, expresses both the vertical and horizontal dimensions of the Church as a communion.

Vertically, the Eucharist is an anticipation of the heavenly banquet. Those who participate in the Eucharist are drawn up into intimate communion with the triune God and the communion of saints (for a brief excursus on this topic, see Part VII.1.5).[6] But horizontally, the Eucharist is also a communal act of thanksgiving and celebration. The Church is most visibly itself when it is gathered for the Eucharist.[7] The communion that is experienced in and through the Church is not only with Christ and ultimately with the triune God; it is also a communion with one another in Christ, actualized by the power of the Holy Spirit. By reason of a shared faith, the sacrament of Baptism, and the gift of grace, the members of the Church become one family, one body, one community.

There are, of course, ecumenical dimensions to the matter of eucharistic communion. The Church is not to be equated with the Catholic Church (or the Catholic Communion of Churches). The Body of Christ is larger than any one ecclesial entity within it, including the Catholic Church. When Christian individuals and communities that are not in full communion with one another participate in the Eucharist together, it is called "*inter*communion." It is an ecclesiologically ambivalent experience because, as Vatican II's Decree on Ecumenism insists, intercommunion, or eucharistic sharing, "is not to be considered as a means to be used indiscriminately for the restoration of unity among Christians." On the other hand, the Eucharist is not only a sign of unity, but also a means to achieve it (n. 8). (We have already discussed the issue of intercommunion, or eucharistic sharing, in Part VI.3.3.d.)

STRUCTURAL ASPECTS OF COMMUNION

This "ecclesiology of communion" applies also to the structures of the Church, to the ways in which the Church organizes itself for mission at the local, regional, and international levels. (This is why the current topic regarding the Church as a communion overlaps at some point with the next topic in Part VII, authority in the Church.) The global, or universal, Church is composed of many local churches, and each local church is the Body of Christ in a particular place.[8]

The Second Vatican Council's Dogmatic Constitution on the Church makes this very point: "This church of Christ is really present in all legitimately organized local groups of the faithful which, united with their pastors, are also called churches in the New Testament. For these are in fact, in their own localities, the new people called by God, in the Holy Spirit and with full conviction (see 1 Thess. 1:5). In them the faithful are gathered together by the preaching of the Gospel of Christ, and the mystery of the Lord's supper is celebrated" (n. 26).

The term "local church" may apply to a parish, a diocese, a regional cluster of churches (such as a province), a national body of churches (such as The Episcopal Church), or a patriarchate. For Catholicism, the communal nature of the Church is expressed not only sacramentally, but also collegially, or structurally—in ecumenical, or general, councils (with the Bishop of Rome as their head), in synods of various kinds, in regional councils, and in national episcopal conferences. But it is not only the Catholic Communion of Churches, of which the Roman Catholic Church is by far the largest part, that has these structured instruments of unity. In the Anglican Communion, for example, there are four such instruments of unity: the archbishop of Canterbury, the Lambeth Conference, the Anglican Consultative Council, and the Primates' Meeting. And all of these are in addition to various local and national expressions of collegiality in diocesan conventions, the General Convention, and in the House of Bishops and the House of Deputies—structures that are characteristic of The Episcopal Church.

"Because the Church is a communion," the Extraordinary Synod's Final Report of 1985 declares, "there must be participation and coresponsibility at all of [the Church's] levels."[9] Some Catholics, however, have tended to interpret the ecclesiology of communion more narrowly. For them, communion has only a vertical dimension. It refers exclusively to the Church's union in grace with the triune God and to the union of the local churches and their bishops with the Holy See. Such an ecclesiology views the Church primarily in otherworldly and hierarchical categories. Those of this particular school of thought founded an international journal of theology soon after the council adjourned in December 1965 to compete with another such journal, which had called itself *Concilium*. *Concilium*'s editorial board included many of the council's leading theological experts, or *periti*. Significantly, the theologians who felt a closer affinity with Vatican II's defeated minority called their journal *Communio,* thereby co-opting the term and making it seem as if communion was the ecclesiological alternative to People of God.[10]

Indeed, the founders of *Communio* tended to be unsympathetic with Vatican II's teaching that the Church is the People of God because, for them, such an emphasis ran the risk of making the Church too human and especially too democratic. Such Catholics tend to downplay the horizontal dimension of communion, that is, the solidarity and coresponsibility of all believers as well as the collegiality of local churches, expressed in councils, synods, and episcopal conferences. According to such an ecclesiological perspective, everything in the Church comes from the top down, or from the center out—from God ultimately, but more immediately from the pope and the Roman Curia. This reflects an incomplete and one-sided understanding of communion and particularly a lack of recognition of the pastoral autonomy of the local churches and their bishops.

If Catholicism before the council and then again during the lengthy pontificate of John Paul II (1978–2005) was prone to exaggerate the central authority structures of the Church—the papacy and the Curia—the problem within Anglicanism has been just the opposite. One finds in Anglicanism a strong emphasis on local autonomy, with a proportionately weaker central authority. Unlike the Bishop of Rome, the archbishop of Canterbury is a *primus inter pares* (Lat., "first among equals"), with some measure of spiritual and moral authority, but little canonical authority. The challenge for both the Catholic and Anglican traditions is to strike somehow a happy balance between the requirements of authority at the center, for the sake of preserving the unity of the universal Church, and the requirements of authority at the local level, to preserve the nature of the Church as a true communion of churches, each of which is the Body of Christ in its own particular place, as *Lumen gentium* insists (n. 26).

In this regard, both sides would do well to examine the Anglican Communion's Windsor Report,[11] a document produced in 2004 by the Lambeth Commission on Communion, under the leadership of Archbishop Robin Eames, of Armagh, and occasioned by the controversial ordination of Gene Robinson as the Episcopal bishop of New Hampshire. According to the Windsor Report, "the very nature of autonomy obliges each church to have regard to the common good of the global Anglican community and the Church universal" (n. 80). "Communion," it insists, "obliges each church to foster, respect and maintain all those marks of common identity, and all those instruments of unity and communion, which it shares with fellow churches, seeking a common mind in essential matters of common concern: in short, to act interdependently, not independently" (n. 51).

Although the Windsor Report acknowledges that there is an important structural difference between the Anglican Communion and the Roman Catholic Church, centered principally in the papacy, the potential for reaching common ground has been enhanced by Catholicism's renewed understanding of the Church as a communion. From that is derived Vatican II's doctrine of the collegiality of the bishops working as true collaborators with the Bishop of Rome and not simply as his vicars (*Lumen gentium*, n. 27).

THE COMMUNION OF SAINTS

The article on the "communion of saints" was first found in the Apostles' Creed at the end of the fifth century and was used much earlier in the East, though not as part of the creed.[12] The doctrine was understood in the first instance as a communion of grace among all Christians who participate in the blessings of salvation and in the communion of God's holy people. The formal term "communion of saints" gradually came to apply principally to the communion between the heavenly Church and the earthly Church. More recently, it has come to apply as well to the exchange of graces and spiritual benefits between individuals on earth (the Church militant) and the saints in heaven (the Church triumphant) and the souls in purgatory (the Church suffering). The doctrine of the communion of saints was affirmed in the Second Vatican Council's Dogmatic Constitution on the Church, nn. 49–51 (see Part V.6.6).

Authority in the Church

By far, the greatest attention in this part of the book is devoted to the question of authority in the Church. It has always been the most neuralgic issue in Catholic ecclesiology, not only because of its inherently controversial character, but also because its various elements, especially the papacy, are so distinctive to the nature, mission, ministries, and structures of the Catholic Church.

AN OVERVIEW

The word "authority" is derived from the Latin *auctor* ("author"), from *augere* ("to cause to grow, to increase, to enlarge").[13] When properly exercised by a healthy "author," authority stimulates growth in freedom, responsibility, and maturity. Its opposite, authoritarianism, stunts that growth by stifling rather than stimulating the creative, life-giving energies of those who are under authority. Ultimately, all authority comes from God, who is the "Author" of all that is: "Let every person be subordinate to the higher authorities, for there is no authority except from God, and those that exist have been established by God" (Rom. 13:1).

Human authority may be *de iure* (Lat., "by right" or "by law," and usually attached to an office) or *de facto* ("in fact," or the way it really is). The ideal is that those holding *de iure* authority also possess *de facto* authority. In other words, they are obeyed not simply because they have the power to command obedience and punish disobedience, but because of the "power" of their humanity, values, and integrity, manifested in their personal example. Many who do not hold *de iure* authority exercise *de facto* authority—often even greater authority than those holding official, or *de iure,* authority. By reason of her personal example in ministering to the poorest and most desperate of God's people, Mother Teresa (d. 1997) possessed far more *de facto* authority throughout the Church and humankind generally than the majority of the Church's bishops. Of course, she also possessed *de iure* authority within the religious community she had founded and led, the Missionaries of Charity.

THE AUTHORITY OF JESUS AND THE APOSTLES

Authority (Gk. *exousia*) and the power (*dunamis*) to exercise it are ascribed to Jesus (John 17:2; 5:27; Rev. 12:10).[14] He preaches with authority (Mark 1:22, and parallels) and has the power to forgive sins (Matt. 9:6–8; Mark 2:5–10) and to heal and cast out demons (Mark 1:27; Matt. 12:27–28; Luke 11:19–20). He interprets the law (Matt. 7:28–29) and teaches in his own name (Matt. 5:21–48). In fact, his manner was so authoritative that he was specifically challenged with the question, "By what authority are you doing these things? Or who gave you this authority to do them?" (Mark 11:28). After his death and Resurrection he was given "all power in heaven and on earth" (Matt. 28:18). All creation is subject to him (Phil. 2:10), and he will judge the living and the dead (Acts 10:42).

However, Jesus always exercises his authority in the manner of a servant (Mark 10:45; Luke 22:27). It is precisely because he did not cling to divinity that he became Lord of all (Phil. 2:5–11). And so he charged his disciples to follow his example: "The kings of the Gentiles lord it over them, . . . but among you it shall not be so. Rather, let the greatest among you be as the youngest, and the leader as the servant

[Gk. *diakonos*]" (Luke 22:25–26; John 13:14–15). His disciples are not to be engaged in any struggles for power or preferment among themselves (Matt. 20:20–28; Mark 10:35–45).

The absolute authority that Jesus claims and exercises (Matt. 28:18) is not transferred to his disciples, not even to Peter. On the contrary, in Acts 1–12, where Peter's leadership is most clearly portrayed, decisions are made by "the Twelve" or "the apostles" or "the church," and not by Peter. His seemingly devious behavior in Antioch even elicits an open rebuke from Paul (Gal. 2:11–14). Nor are "the Twelve" the sole participants in Jesus's authority. There are also prophets, teachers, evangelists, presbyters, and others (1 Cor. 12:28; Eph. 4:11). When Paul was harshly rebuked by some of the Corinthians, he did not claim that he was above criticism because of his status.[15]

The Holy Spirit is given to the whole Church and not only to its pastoral leaders (1 Cor. 12:1–28; Rom. 12:3–8). Because all such authority comes from God, and from the Holy Spirit in particular, church authority is of a unique kind (see Part II.2.10–11).[16]

APOSTOLIC SUCCESSION

Francis A. Sullivan, S.J., longtime professor of ecclesiology at the Pontifical Gregorian University in Rome, defines apostolic succession[17] as "the perpetuation, in the college of bishops, of the pastoral charge given by Christ to the college of the apostles."[18] However, like most other Catholic theologians writing after Vatican II, Sullivan rejects a simplistic, mechanistic notion of apostolic succession, what some refer to derisively as the passing-the-baton theory. This understanding of apostolic succession, which retains widespread support among many Catholics today, even in the hierarchy, assumes that each validly ordained Catholic bishop can trace his episcopal ordination in an unbroken line back to one of the original twelve Apostles.

Sullivan offers two reasons for opposing such a view: first, the Apostles were not bishops in the present-day meaning of the word; today a bishop is a residential pastor of a diocese. They were instead missionaries and founders of local churches. There is no evidence, nor is there likely ever to be any evidence, that any of them ever took up permanent residence in a particular church as its bishop. Second, although some local churches had leaders who were called "bishops" (Gk. *episkopoi;* see Acts 20:17–35), it remains unclear whether these "bishops" were actually appointed or ordained by the Apostle Paul or by any other Apostle. "The New Testament," Sullivan writes, "offers no support for a theory of apostolic succession that supposes the apostles appointed or ordained a bishop for each of the churches they founded."[19]

Nor is there support for such a theory in the early Christian writings, during the early postbiblical period. The *Didache* (Gk., "The Teaching"), an ancient book of basic instructions for Christians, testifies to the existence of communities led by prophets. If such communities were to lack a prophet-leader, they were to choose worthy men as bishops and deacons. But the *Didache* "contains no suggestion that such pastoral officers would derive their authority in any way from a founding apostle."[20] Clement's letter to the Corinthians, known as *1 Clement,* provides good evidence that thirty years after Paul's death the church of Corinth was being led by a group of presbyters, with no indication of a bishop. The letter does affirm that the founding apostles had appointed the first generation of local leaders with instructions to have them replaced after death, but "gives no support to the idea that the apostles had appointed a bishop for each church they founded."[21] The exceptions at this time were the churches of Antioch and several churches of western Asia Minor in the vicinity of Ephesus. Sullivan insists that "nothing in the letter of Ignatius [of Antioch] suggests that he saw his episcopal authority as derived from the mandate Christ gave to the apostles. . . . He never invoked the principle of apostolic succession to explain or justify" the role and authority of bishops."[22]

"One conclusion seems obvious," Sullivan writes. "Neither the New Testament nor early Christian history offers support for a notion of apostolic succession as 'an unbroken line of episcopal ordination from Christ through the apostles down through the centuries to the bishops of today.'"[23] Which is not to say that the doctrine of apostolic succession is without any theological or historical basis. It is just that this particular explanation of it is not valid. The Catholic Church's official teaching on the matter is encapsulated in Vatican II's Dogmatic Constitution on the Church, n. 20.

However, Catholic theologians today also insist that the council's declaration that apostolic succession is "by divine institution" should not be taken to mean that Christ explicitly determined the episcopal structures of the local churches. To return to Father Raymond Brown's "blueprint" metaphor, Jesus did not leave a precise organizational plan to guide the Church (see Part II.2.4).

Francis Sullivan frames the doctrine in positive terms:

> *What is certain is that within a century after the death of the apostles, each church was led by a single bishop, and that these bishops were recognized by all the orthodox Christian churches as the legitimate successors of the apostles and, thus, as guarantors of the authentic apostolic tradition. The argument for divine institution is based on the belief that their development was guided by the Holy Spirit, as part of God's design for the Church. A sound reason for this belief is the fact that from the second century on, Christians everywhere accepted the teaching of their bishops as normative for their faith. It is a basic article of Christian belief that the Holy Spirit maintains the Church in the true faith.*[24]

There is, however, a broad diversity of views on this matter within the worldwide Body of Christ. Although all Christians would agree that apostolicity involves a succession in the faith of the Apostles and a sharing in their mission to proclaim the gospel to the ends of the earth, many Protestant Churches and communities have been content with the aphorism of Martin Luther: "The true apostolic succession is the gospel. Whoever preaches the pure gospel stands in apostolic succession."[25] The great twentieth-century Protestant theologian Karl Barth rejected any view of apostolicity based on historical or juridical grounds or one based on episcopal ordination, because this would presume to control the workings of the Holy Spirit, whereby the Spirit is transferred from person to person. For Barth, there is a legitimate apostolic succession only when there is a following of the Apostles in discipleship, hearing, respect, and obedience, all according to Scripture.[26]

The Anglican Communion, the Orthodox Churches, the separated, non-Orthodox Churches of the East, and the Old Catholics, however, would agree with the Catholic Church, and against Barth, that duly ordained bishops are an essential component of the doctrine. For the Orthodox there is, as Irish Carmelite theologian Christopher O'Donnell points out, a strong accent of the "now" of apostolicity, especially in the Eucharist.[27]

Francis Sullivan notes, however, that a number of ecumenical dialogues have made considerable progress on lessening the gap between Catholic and non-Catholic understandings of apostolic succession. He cites in particular the widely discussed "Lima report," whose formal title is *Baptism, Eucharist and Ministry,* produced in 1982 by the Faith and Order Commission of the World Council of Churches.[28] Section IV of that document, "Succession in the Apostolic Tradition," indicates the degree of agreement that has been reached and the important difference that remains. There is agreement, even among the denominations that do not have an episcopate, that "episcopal succession [is] a sign of the apostolicity of the life of the whole Church" (para. 38). At the same time, the document acknowledges that "a continuity in apostolic faith, worship and mission has been preserved in churches which have not retained the form of historic succession" and that "the reality and function of the episcopal ministry have been preserved in many of these churches, with or without the title 'bishop'" (para. 37).

According to Sullivan, the "remaining difference is also evident, in that Protestants cannot recognize episcopal succession as a necessary element of the apostolicity of the Church, as this could suggest that the ministry in their churches would be invalid until it entered into the historic episcopal succession."[29] He concludes that, "despite the progress that has been made, apostolic succession in the episcopate remains a church-dividing issue."[30]

MAGISTERIUM

The Meaning and Levels of Teaching Authority

The magisterium of the Church is one of the most controversial issues in Catholic theology and in the pastoral life of the Church.[31] The word "magisterium" is derived from the Latin word *magister* ("master" or "teacher"). Magisterium applies ordinarily to the body of the Church's "master-teachers," or simply official teachers, as well as to the teaching authority they exercise in the name of the Church. The magisterium functions at four different levels, three of which are official, that is, linked with an office, and one of which is not.

At its narrowest official level, the magisterium is the teaching authority inherent in and exercised by the Bishop of Rome, the pope. As such, it is known as the *papal* magisterium and is rooted in the pope's episcopal ordination and his subsequent election as Bishop of Rome. The pope, however, never teaches definitively, that is, infallibly, except in communion with the whole college of bishops, of which he is the head. But it is a rare occurrence for a pope to teach infallibly, or dogmatically (see the discussion of papal infallibility in Part IV.1.4, 2.3). For all practical purposes, his teachings, even those directed to the whole Church, are not protected by the charism of infallibility and are communicated through encyclicals, apostolic exhortations, and formal decrees of Vatican congregations that are explicitly approved by the pope.

At a broader official level, this teaching authority is inherent in and exercised by the college of bishops (and by exception by nonbishops, as listed, e.g., in can. 223 of the 1917 Code of Canon Law). This magisterium is known as the *hierarchical* magisterium and is rooted in episcopal ordination and communion with the whole college of bishops. Individual bishops exercise this magisterium for the worldwide Church and for their own dioceses. Groups of bishops exercise teaching authority in national episcopal conferences, in regional councils or synods of bishops, and in world synods of bishops. All the bishops together exercise this teaching authority in ecumenical councils or in a more ambiguous form known as the ordinary universal magisterium, that is, when there is judged to exist a virtual unanimity among the bishops regarding a matter of faith or morals.[32]

The teachings that emanate from the hierarchical magisterium are referred to as "authentic." This does not mean "genuine," but "authoritative." An "authentic" teaching is one that is given by a bishop or body of bishops who teach in the name of the Church by reason of their episcopal office. The bishops are not above the Word of God. They must listen to it, guard it, and explain it faithfully, with the help of the Holy Spirit (Dogmatic Constitution on Divine Revelation, n. 1). Even noninfallible teachings, however, are said to require religious *obsequium,* which is a Latin term that has been translated both as "submission" and as "respect."[33]

At a broader official level still, the magisterium is the teaching authority inherent in and exercised by the hierarchy and theologians alike. It is known by some as the *double* magisterium and is rooted in both episcopal ordination (thus, the pastoral magisterium of the cathedral chair) and theological competence (the magisterium of the professorial chair). Ecclesiologist Avery Dulles bases this distinction on that of St. Thomas Aquinas, namely, between the *magisterium cathedrae pastoralis* and the *magisterium cathedrae magistralis.*[34]

At its broadest, nonofficial level, the magisterium is the teaching authority inherent in and exercised by every member of the Church. It is known simply as the magisterium of the whole Church, the *Ecclesia docens* (Lat., "the teaching Church"), and is rooted in Baptism. In the past, the term *Ecclesia docens* was limited to the hierarchy, while the rest of the faithful were considered the *Ecclesia discens* ("the learning Church"). With Vatican II, that distinction disappeared.

Directed Toward Whom?

Until recent decades the intended audience for teachings of the hierarchical magisterium, and particularly the papal magisterium, has been members of the Catholic Church. There may have been an implicit desire to reach non-Catholics with, but perhaps not bind them to, such teachings, but it was never made explicit. Even as recently as 1961, Pope John XXIII (1958–63) addressed his social encyclical *Mater et magistra* (Lat., "Mother and teacher"), "To Our Venerable Brothers, the Patriarchs, Primates, Archbishops, Bishops and Other Local Ordinaries *in Peace and Communion with the Holy See,* and to All the Clergy and Faithful *of the Catholic World*" (my emphasis). Two years later, however, the same pope directed his final encyclical, *Pacem in terris* ("Peace on earth"), to the same hierarchical companies, but also to the "Faithful of the Whole World and to All Men [*sic*] of Good Will."

By 1983, this new style had been adopted by the United States Conference of Catholic Bishops in its pastoral letter "The Challenge of Peace." The bishops' teaching on matters of war and peace was addressed to

> *two distinct but overlapping audiences. The first is the Catholic faithful, formed by the premises of the gospel and the principles of Catholic moral teaching. The second is the wider civil community, a more pluralistic audience, in which our brothers and sisters with whom we share the name Christian, Jews, Moslems, other religious communities, and all people of good will also make up our polity. Since Catholic teaching has traditionally sought to address both audiences [a dubious claim], we intend to speak to both in this letter, recognizing that Catholics are also members of the wider political community.* (n. 16)

The letter continues: "The conviction, rooted in Catholic ecclesiology, that both the community of the faithful and the civil community should be addressed on peace and war has produced two complementary but distinct styles of teaching" (n. 17). Catholics are formed by the teachings of the Church, and so one magisterial style explicitly draws upon previous official teachings and commends them to Catholics as they form their consciences about these public policy issues. The other magisterial style draws upon the principles of natural law, making the case for its official teachings by appealing to the second audience's reasonableness (nn. 18–19).

Complexity of the Process

The process is magisterial. The subject of the process is the hierarchy (we are speaking here of the hierarchical magisterium). Its intended audience, if the issue is broad enough, is both the Catholic faithful and all people of goodwill, including, of course, brother and sister Christians and their Churches and ecclesial communities. The product of the magisterial process consists of doctrines. In other words, official teachers produce official teachings, which are called doctrines.

First, the debate about doctrines is never only a debate about their truth, but also about law and order, including the demands of obedience and loyalty to the Church and to its pastoral leaders and the possibilities of penalties for noncompliance. Thus, rarely did the debate over the 1968 birth-control encyclical, *Humanae vitae* (Lat., "Of human life"), of Pope Paul VI (1963–78) focus on its moral arguments or its understanding of natural law. It was almost always a debate about loyalty to the pope, the possibility of dissent from official teachings of the Church, and the difference between faithful and unfaithful Catholics.

Second, since every doctrine is, in turn, a theological statement, it must be recalled that theological and doctrinal language never adequately corresponds to the reality to which it refers (ultimately God). God talk at its best is poetic and analogical rather than prosaic and univocal. No one on this earth has ever seen God, except Jesus Christ (John 1:18).

Third, doctrinal statements are always made in a given cultural context, as the Vatican document *Mysterium Ecclesiae* (Lat., "The Mystery of the Church"), formulated in criticism of Hans Küng's book on infallibility, made clear.[35] Küng had denied the validity of papal infallibility because, according to his argument, Pope Paul VI's teaching on birth control in *Humanae vitae* was in error and yet was given as an infallible pronouncement. However, not even Catholic theologians who had been generally sympathetic with Küng's views agreed with his reasoning on this matter. Paul VI did not, in fact, claim infallibility for *Humanae vitae,* and no one of any theological or pastoral stature other than Küng had made such an argument.

But *Mysterium Ecclesiae* was not only concerned with Küng's views on papal infallibility. The document's enduring theological importance consists of its teaching on the historical conditioning of all doctrinal pronouncements of the Church, including even dogmatic ones.

(Dogmas are doctrines that are taught infallibly.) Official teachings of the Church, at whatever level of authority, "depend partly upon the expressive power of the language used at a certain point in time and in particular circumstances," *Mysterium Ecclesiae* points out. Moreover, sometimes even dogmatic statements are expressed incompletely (although not falsely) and need to be improved upon at some later date. Interpreters must also be mindful of the specific questions or errors that a particular pronouncement was originally intended to address. The pronouncement itself cannot be assumed to apply to questions or errors of a different time and set of circumstances. Finally, the truths of faith, enunciated even in dogmatic formulas, always bear the marks of "the changeable conceptions of a given epoch." Those contemporary conceptions also need to be taken seriously into account when attempting to interpret the official teachings themselves.[36]

Fourth, not all doctrinal statements are of equal value. There is a "hierarchy of truths," depending upon their relationship to the core of faith (Decree on Ecumenism, n. 11), as previously noted in Part VI.3.3.d. There was an important ecumenical reason for the council's introduction of this concept. When engaged in formal dialogue with non-Catholic Christians, the Catholic participants—whether they are theologians or bishops—must not demand of the non-Catholics more than what the gospel itself demands.

Catholic dialogue partners cannot insist, for example, that non-Catholics must accept the Catholic belief that Mary is the mediatrix of all graces, namely, that all of the graces of redemption, which come ultimately from Christ, must somehow pass through Mary before reaching any of the redeemed. This is by no means an agreed-upon, foundational truth. There are many other, lower-level examples of nonfoundational truths: belief in guardian angels, the practice of adoration of the Blessed Sacrament (as distinct from belief in the Real Presence of Christ in the sacrament, which is part of the essence of Catholic faith), and obligatory celibacy for priests of the Roman rite. There are, of course, differences of opinion about whether one or another teaching is foundational. The best example is that of the Church's prohibition of the ordination of women. Some theologians and bishops hold that it is a matter of unchangeable faith; most theologians, however, regard it as a matter of discipline rather than dogma and, therefore, subject to change.

Some examples of foundational truths of faith that rest at or near the top of the "hierarchy of truths" are the existence of a loving, triune God who created us, sustains and guides us, and destines us for eternal life; the divinity of Jesus Christ and the redemptive significance of this life, death, and Resurrection; our transformation into new creatures in Christ by the power of the Holy Spirit; the Church as mystery, or sacrament, that is, "a reality imbued with the hidden presence of God" (Pope Paul VI); the forgiveness of sins; the mandate to love one another; the communion of saints; and our hope in eternal life. In other words, the foundational truths that are at the core of Christian faith are those included in the historic creeds, such as the Apostles' Creed and the Nicene Creed.

The "hierarchy of truths" is not meant to provide an escape hatch for Catholics who prefer not to accept certain official teachings. Rather, it serves as a defense against the abiding tendency of some Catholics (and other Christians) to confuse secondary and tertiary teachings with essential truths, thereby diluting and devaluing what truly pertains to the "foundations of the Christian faith."

Fifth, and last, different churches and ecclesial communities may not express themselves about one or another mystery of faith, including the mystery of the Church, in the same way that the Catholic Church does or has done. We cannot assume, therefore, that different modes of expression necessarily indicate a fundamental difference in the understanding Christian faith itself. That is why ecumenical dialogue is so important. It is only in talking with one another that it is possible for us to grow in respect for each other's integrity of faith and to come to a greater understanding of how we each understand the gospel and its implications.[37]

Criteria for Evaluating Magisterial Pronouncements

Certain questions are to be put to a magisterial document itself. Other questions are raised about the antecedent and subsequent processes by which such a document came into being and was later interpreted and applied.

The intrinsic criteria, in the form of questions, include the following: (1) Does the argument advanced in the document hold together? Is it coherent and compelling in its logic? (2) Does the language employed in the document reflect the current state of the discussion and debate, or does it indicate a lack of sufficient awareness of the issues involved and the various positions taken on them? (3) Are the conclusions proposed consistent with the experience and competence of qualified and interested parties? (4) Are they also consistent with the classical sources: Scripture, the early Christian writers, the teachings of ecumenical councils, and the great theologians of the Church, past and present? (5) To what levels of authority does the teaching appeal?

The U.S. Catholic bishops' pastoral letter "The Challenge of Peace" (1983), for example, provides pertinent criteria for interpreting the relative authority of teachings within a given document: Are the principles universally binding? Do they involve statements of recent popes and of Vatican II? Does the document simply apply principles to specific cases? If they do apply to specific cases, the bishops acknowledge that "prudential judgments are involved based on specific circumstances which can change or which can be interpreted differently by people of good will. . . . However, the moral judgments that [the bishops] make in specific cases, while not binding in conscience, are to be given serious attention and consideration by Catholics as they determine whether their moral judgments are consistent with the Gospel" (nn. 9–10).

The extrinsic criteria are also in the form of questions: (1) Were all views represented in the process of formulation? Indeed, was there an open process at all? (2) How has the teaching been received by competent scholars, pastoral leaders, affected constituencies, and the ecclesial and civil communities at large? Has it changed their thinking and practice? (For further consideration of the reception of doctrine and disciplinary decrees, see the next section, 3.)

There is a medieval axiom, *Bonum ex integra causa, malum ex quocumque defectu* (Lat., "[Something can be regarded as] good [if it seems truly so] in every respect, [but] bad [if there is] any defect at all"), which may apply to these criteria. If all of the criteria are positive, the teaching can be accepted. If only a single criterion is doubtful, acceptance can temporarily be withheld until further examination. If the doubt cannot be resolved, then acceptance of the pronouncement can legitimately be withheld.[38] Another name for this is "dissent," which labors, however, under many misunderstandings and pejorative overtones. It is a juridical term that some insist should not be used in theological discourse.

PAPAL AUTHORITY

This section does not intend to reproduce the extensive material on the papacy found already in Part IV, especially regarding the teaching of the First Vatican Council (1869–70) on papal primacy and papal infallibility. The concern in this section is more limited, focusing instead on the post–Vatican II discussions about the role of the pope in a communal, collegial Church. Much of the discussion has been prompted by the governing style of the lengthy pontificate of John Paul II and whether he had initiated, and then accelerated, a process of recentralizing ecclesiastical authority in the papacy to the detriment of the pastoral authority of the other bishops and their local churches. Toward the end of John Paul II's pontificate, a number of high-ranking pastoral leaders and respected Catholic theologians began to raise this very question openly.[39] But first we shall consider what was perhaps the most ecclesiologically significant document issued by John Paul II during his lengthy pontificate, namely, his encyclical on ecumenism, *Ut unum sint* (Lat., "That they may be one").

John Paul II's Ut unum sint *(1995)*

Although the encyclical *Ut unum sint,* issued on May 25, 1995, was devoted entirely to ecumenism and its various ecclesiological dimensions, the brief portion that evoked the greatest attention throughout the worldwide Church was the section devoted to the papacy (nn. 88–99), and particularly John Paul II's remarkably personal reflections on the exercise of the primacy (nn. 95–96).

These are the key sentences: "I am convinced that I have a particular responsibility . . . above all in acknowledging the ecumenical aspirations of the majority of the Christian Communities and in heeding the request made of me to find a way of exercising the primacy which, while in no way renouncing what is essential to its mission, is nonetheless open to a new situation" (n. 95). The exercise of the primacy "is an immense task, which we cannot refuse and which I cannot carry out by myself. Could not the real but imperfect communion existing between us persuade Church leaders and their theologians to engage with me in a patient and fraternal dialogue on this subject, a dialogue in which, leaving useless controversies behind, we could listen to one another, keeping before us only the will of Christ for his Church and allowing ourselves to be deeply moved by his plea 'that they may all be one'?" (n. 96).

Herein, John Paul II makes a key distinction between the papacy as an essential, even nonnegotiable, structural element in the life of the Church, on the one hand, and the manner in which the papal primacy is exercised—something that is entirely negotiable—on the other hand. Indeed, he explicitly invited pastoral leaders and theologians to enter into dialogue with him.[40] As we shall see below, it was this invitation to engage in dialogue with the pope on this sensitive matter of the exercise of the primacy that prompted the retired archbishop of San Francisco, John R. Quinn, to write his book *The Reform of the Papacy*.[41]

Hierarchical Commentators

By way of example only, three bishops, two of whom are or were cardinals, are listed here as having publicly raised questions about the post–Vatican II recentralization of authority in the papal office and in its organizational extension, the Roman Curia. The most extensive commentary was offered by Archbishop Quinn. Others were provided by Cardinal Godfried Danneels of Belgium and the late Cardinal Franz König of Austria. Avery Dulles, although a cardinal, is not included in this section because he has been known throughout his life, and included throughout this book, as a theologian rather than as a member of the hierarchy. In any case, his contributions to the post–Vatican II discussions about the papacy are included in VII.2.5.c.

Archbishop John R. Quinn. Archbishop Quinn's book *The Reform of the Papacy*, published in 1999, was developed from a lecture, "The

Exercise of the Primacy," delivered on the occasion of the centenary of Campion Hall, Oxford University, on June 29, 1996. It was published in *Commonweal* less than a month later.[42]

The first chapter focuses on John Paul II's encyclical *Ut unum sint,* which had appeared a year earlier and which the archbishop characterizes as a "clearly precedent breaking and, in many respects, revolutionary" document.[43] He lists a series of papal responsibilities as an exercise of primatial vigilance and in service of the unity of the Church and notes that the pope himself insisted that these responsibilities are to be fulfilled in communion with the whole college of bishops. "The force of this declaration," Quinn writes, "would seem to be that the normal mode of the exercise of papal authority will be collaborative and consultative, one that respects legitimate church structures such as the patriarchates and episcopal conferences, and one that is dedicated to preserving diversity within the framework of unity."[44]

Subsequent chapters address the issues of reform and criticism in the Church, the papacy and collegiality, the appointment of bishops, the reform of the papacy and the College of Cardinals, and, finally, the reform of the Roman Curia. Taken all together, these chapters argue for the decentralization of authority in the universal Catholic Church in keeping with the understanding of the Church as a communion and of collegiality as the structural expression of communion.

"All that I have been able to deal with here," Archbishop Quinn writes in the conclusion to his book, "leads me to believe that in the exercise of the papacy two things, more than others, are the greatest problem for the Church and for Christian unity. The first is centralization; the other, the need for reform of the Roman Curia. . . . Once the decision is made to move toward decentralization," following the lead of large international corporations, "the substantial reform of the Roman Curia will be inevitable."[45]

No serious observer is suggesting, much less advocating, that the papacy itself be abolished as a condition for ecclesial unity. The archbishop cites the Second Vatican Council as a major example of the importance of the primacy (but exercised always "in communion" with the whole college of bishops). The reforms initiated by the council "did not come about because of a great groundswell among the people, priests, or bishops of the world. It was the result of a papal initiative." However, he concludes, "Without the council it is likely that there would never have been an encyclical like *Ut unum sint*. The combination of this growing openness and the Pope's prophetic call to probe the primacy is one of those unique moments in history. If there is too much delay, too much diffidence, the time will pass. It is imperative not to lose this moment of grace."[46]

Cardinal Godfried Danneels. In an interview in 1997 with *Il Regno,* an Italian magazine, at a time when there were increasing public discussions about the health of Pope John Paul II, his capacity to carry on his responsibilities, and the legacy he would leave following his death or resignation, Cardinal Godfried Danneels, primate of Belgium, made the same point that Archbishop Quinn had made a year earlier in his lecture at Oxford, namely, that the Church "should now begin a broad process of decentralization."[47] The cardinal pointed out what others have also noted, including this author:[48] that the exercise of the papacy in the first Christian millennium was markedly different from its development in the second, when the authority of the universal Church became more centralized in Rome and in the papal office to the detriment of the authority of the other bishops and their local churches.

The cardinal insisted that the Roman Curia should be "an instrument of the pope and nothing more." At the present time, Danneels suggested, the Roman Curia produces too many documents, making it difficult for smaller episcopal conferences, as in Belgium, to answer each one. Moreover, it acts too often as "a command organization that assumes part of the authority of the pontiff." He was hesitant, however, to increase the role and authority of national episcopal conferences. Although they are valuable for communication and forming consensus within a given body of bishops, there is always the risk of reducing the universal Church to a collection of national Churches and of compromising the pastoral autonomy of the local churches or dioceses. "It is necessary to reaffirm that the fixed points are the universal church and the local church. The intermediary bodies are instruments of assistance. The Roman Curia, bishops' conferences, the committees of bishops' conferences and the other similar bodies that exist in the world are only tools and are to be judged by their usefulness, and this usefulness can change."[49]

Cardinal Franz König. One of the most influential figures at Vatican II, Cardinal Franz König (d. 2004), then archbishop of Vienna, continued into his nineties writing articles on the state of the Church in English-language publications such as *The Tablet* (London). He too expressed concern about the recentralization of authority in the Church, especially during the long pontificate of John Paul II: "A gradual decentralisation is needed, so as to strengthen the concern and responsibility of the college of bishops for the whole Church, under and with the Petrine office.... Within the Catholic Church itself, no one has difficulties about the existence of the Petrine office.... What is often felt to be defective is the present style of leadership practised by the authorities in the Roman Curia in dealing with the diverse and multiple dioceses throughout the world."

The cardinal reminded his readers that Pope Paul VI, in his 1969 *motu proprio* (Lat., "On his own initiative") *Sollicitudo omnium ecclesiarum* ("The care of all the churches"), "took pains to remodel the advisory and controlling functions of the curial authorities, in order to bring them into line with the council's intentions. In the post-conciliar period, however, as bishops have not infrequently pointed out, the Vatican authorities have striven to take back autonomy and central leadership for themselves. The intentions of *Sollicitudo omnium ecclesiarum* have not been realised." Although the Church is no longer Eurocentric, the Roman Curia "remains a powerful force tending in the opposite direction, toward centralism." It has "appropriated the tasks of the episcopal college. It is they who now carry out almost all of them." The cardinal expressed special praise for John Paul II's earlier encyclical *Ut unum sint* for moving the discussion in a more communal, collegial direction.

For Cardinal König, the principle of subsidiarity is key. That principle, first articulated in Pope Pius XI's 1931 encyclical *Quadragesimo anno* (Lat., "After forty years"), declares that nothing should be done at a higher level that can be done better or equally well at a lower level. It was also incorporated into the preface to the 1983 Revised Code of

Canon Law. The cardinal also cited Pius XII's Christmas address of 1946 in which the pope pointed out, as we did earlier in Part VI, that the principle applies not only to society but to the Church as well. The bishops, the cardinal insisted, do not exist simply to carry out orders from the pope. As the Dogmatic Constitution on the Church declares, they exercise pastoral authority in their own right, for the sake of their own local churches (n. 27). "Today, however, we have an inflated centralism," according to König.

It is not a question, therefore, of eliminating the papacy. We would not have had Vatican II without John XXIII. It is a matter, rather, of balance. "We have to return to the decentralised form of the Church's command structure as practised in earlier centuries. That, for the world Church, is the dictate of today."[50]

Theologians

Hermann J. Pottmeyer. Emeritus professor of theology at the University of Bochum, Germany, and a priest of the diocese of Münster, Hermann Pottmeyer has been one of the leading figures in the post–Vatican II ecclesiological discussion of the papacy. His major work on the subject is his book *Towards a Papacy in Communion,* but he has summarized his approach in abbreviated form in a subsequent article in *America* magazine, "Primacy in Communion."[51] Unlike his book, which appeared too soon in 1998, the *America* article takes into account a document on the primacy issued by the Congregation for the Doctrine of the Faith in December of that same year, "Reflections on the Primacy of Peter" (see Part VII.2.5.d).[52]

He refers to it as a "remarkable," even "revolutionary," document because it situates the papacy in a communal and collegial context. Instead of speaking of the pope as *the* Vicar of Christ, it cites John Paul II's 1995 encyclical *Ut unum sint,* which, in turn, had cited the council's Dogmatic Constitution on the Church that "all bishops are also 'vicars and ambassadors of Christ'" (n. 27). When referring to the canonical principle that "the First Chair is not subjected to the judgment of another authority," the CDF document insists that "this does not mean, however, that the pope has absolute power. Listening to what the churches are saying is, in fact, an earmark of the ministry of unity, a consequence also of the unity of the episcopal body and of the *sensus fidei* [Lat., "sense of the faith"] of the entire people of God." Then Pottmeyer asks, rhetorically, "Is it possible to level a stronger criticism against the Vatican's centralism and top-down decision-making?"[53]

Pottmeyer also notes approvingly that the CDF document on the primacy acknowledges the historically conditioned and changeable manner in which the primacy has been exercised in response to changing pastoral circumstances. This view, he observes, has never been endorsed by the Roman Curia, which "has always insisted that the present scope of Roman jurisdiction is divinely willed. If what 'Reflections' says is taken seriously," Pottmeyer continues, "then a revision of canon law is overdue, and the Vatican's administrative and doctrinal centralism must end."[54]

According to Pottmeyer, a centralist papacy can only become a papacy in communion (the title of his book) if it normally makes no decrees or decisions affecting the universal Church without formally inviting the input of the local churches and their bishops. At the same time, the local churches and their respective episcopal conferences should determine any regulations that do not, however, threaten the unity of the whole Church. This means also that the Roman Curia should never put itself above the worldwide episcopate. "When the Curia makes decisions that supersede the bishops, it violates the authority and responsibility of the individual bishop for his particular church and of the college of bishops for the universal church."[55]

The same principle, Pottmeyer writes, should be applied to the teaching mission of the Church. The bishops themselves are "official witnesses to the faith of their local churches and of the church at large."[56] Therefore, they should have direct input in every magisterial initiative, from solemn dogmatic pronouncements to matters of lesser importance, but with applicability to the worldwide Church. There should also be greater reliance on the Synod of Bishops and national episcopal conferences without their being subject to subsequent approval, much less correction, by the Curia. Representatives of the local, national, and regional churches should also have a say in the appointment of bishops. In the end, the current two-tiered, or diadic, structure of the Church, in which Rome deals directly with each individual local church and vice versa, must give way to the more traditional three-tiered, or triadic, structure consisting of the local church, or diocese, and its bishop, the regional church and its primate (or episcopal conference), and the universal Church centered in the local church of Rome and its bishop, the pope. In this way, the Church could once again truly be a communion of communities.

"Communion is the church's essential form," Pottmeyer writes,

> *because only when the church is a solidarity in faith, hope and love does it become a sign and instrument of God's reign. . . . The realization of a primacy in communion requires an ecclesiology that understands communion in relation to Jesus' message of God's reign and the church as the sacrament of this kingdom. In other words, the Petrine ministry must flow out of the church as mystery and sacrament. The strongest argument against a centralistic, authoritarian papacy appeals not to democracy, human rights or liberal claims, but to Jesus' promise of God's new creation.*[57]

John W. O'Malley. John W. O'Malley, S.J., the distinguished church historian whose work has already been cited frequently in Part V on the Second Vatican Council and particularly with regard to the council's "style," in section 9, coined the word "papalization" to describe "the most important change" that has occurred in the life and practices of the Catholic Church in contrast to "those of earlier times." Indeed, he refers to the papalization of Catholicism as "the change of the millennium."[58]

O'Malley writes:

> *At the beginning of the last millennium—indeed, as late as Luther's posting of the Ninety-Five Theses [in 1517]—relatively few Christians knew that the papacy existed, and surely only a minuscule percentage believed it had anything to do with the way they lived their lives. . . . Even for bishops and princes it was at best a remote institution, a possible court of appeal if things got rough at home. At worst it was a political rival and an expropriator of financial resources. For the vast, vast majority of Christians, however, the papacy, if they ever heard it*

mentioned, meant about as much to them as names like Scotus and Ockham mean to Catholics today. . . . This was especially true in the countryside, which is where most people lived.[59]

For Catholics today, the pope is the one who "runs the Church." Agreement with and obedience to all of his teachings and practical decrees are readily taken as the measure of one's fidelity to the Church, if not also the integrity of one's faith. "For many Catholics to say that 'the church forbids this or that' is the equivalent of saying that the pope forbids it."[60] It is the pope who makes all the appointments to the hierarchy, and the bishops, in turn, serve as his personal representatives in their respective dioceses. It is a rare Catholic rectory, chancery office, or bishop's residence that does not have a framed portrait of the current pope hanging prominently in the building.

O'Malley asks how "such a profound revolution in consciousness and practice" came about. How did the papacy move "from the outskirts of awareness, at best, to the defining center? How did Mt. 16:16—'Thou art Peter'—become the canon within the canon for Roman Catholics and become emblematic of their very identity?"[61]

John O'Malley points out that we tend to interpret the past in light of our own present-day experience. Because the papacy, especially during the long reign of John Paul II, looms so important today, it is assumed that it was always so. He also cites the invention of printing in the fifteenth century and the subsequent development of electronic communications, including the telephone, as making it easier to disseminate and keep track of information—about the papacy and a myriad of other realities. O'Malley's third and final reason for the papalization of Catholicism is that the papacy itself has changed over the millennia.

During the first Christian millennium, popes were essentially local figures, intent on local issues.[62] The decisive turn occurred during the Gregorian reform (named after Pope Gregory VII) in the eleventh century, when the papacy made new claims entailing much broader authority over others in both the Church and the temporal realm. The next great change occurred during the Reformation of the sixteenth century, when the papacy was under direct attack and

Catholics came to identify themselves as its loyal supporters. In Reformation England, for example, it was both a mark of distinctiveness and of honor to be known as "papists." Nevertheless, the papacy remained too controversial an issue for the Council of Trent to address. O'Malley notes the twofold irony that the Reformation, by attacking the papacy, actually strengthened it, and the Council of Trent, by not saying anything about it, did the same. The same was true of the so-called *Risorgimento* in Italy during the nineteenth century. Pope Pius IX (1846–78) began to see himself as "the prisoner of the Vatican" and became thereby a figure meriting great sympathy from Catholics around the world.

"The cult of a papal personality began to take shape for the first time," O'Malley writes.[63] Pius IX drew more attention to himself with the definition of the dogma of the Immaculate Conception in 1854 and later with the dogma of papal infallibility in 1870. Around this time, the papal encyclical became even more common as a vehicle for communicating with the universal Church. And during the same century, the papal appointment of bishops rather than their canonical election became standard. In 1929 the Lateran Treaty opened the doors of the so-called Vatican prison. Movie cameras were admitted into St. Peter's and even into the Apostolic Palace. For the first time in history, millions of people throughout the Church and the entire world could actually see Pius XI (1922–39), Pius XII (1939–58), and John XXIII bestow their blessings. The invention of television made such contact even more accessible, especially during the pontificate of John Paul II. Popes, beginning with Paul VI, also began to travel by jet, and they moved about on the ground in the popemobile. "What most fascinates me," O'Malley concludes his article, "is not how much the papacy changed in the course of the past millennium but how much its changes have changed us. The papacy isn't what it used to be. But, largely for that reason, neither are we."[64]

Avery Dulles. Like his fellow Jesuit John O'Malley, Avery Dulles, one of the Church's leading ecclesiologists of the twentieth and early twenty-first centuries, who was created a cardinal by Pope John Paul II in 2001, had previously been introduced to the readers of this book in Part I.7, later here in Part V, then again in Part VI.1.4, and, finally, on page 291 on the magisterium. However, his later views on the papacy,[65] especially during the pontificate of John Paul II, diverge significantly from those of John O'Malley and other fellow Jesuits, including Ladislas Örsy, to whom we shall turn in the next section.

In an article for the Jesuit weekly *America* that appeared only three months after O'Malley's,[66] Dulles celebrates what O'Malley refers to critically as the "papalization" of Catholicism, particularly under John Paul II. Dulles argues that the "globalization" of the papacy in the past two centuries has been a positive development for the Catholic Church, especially for its unity. What others see as deficiencies in John Paul II's papal style Dulles views as assets. Where others reinforce the principle of subsidiarity in opposition to the recentralization of authority in the Vatican, Dulles argues that "local questions often have ramifications for the universal church, and therefore require the involvement of higher authority." Against those who have advocated a return to synodal models of church governance, Dulles notes that the patriarchates often quarreled among themselves and the Orthodox Church today is "plagued by rivalries among the autocephalous national churches of Eastern Europe."[67] Over against the stated importance of national episcopal conferences, he reminds us of the dangers of nationalism and how the resurgence of Roman authority in the nineteenth century was a "signal benefit" in this regard.

Dulles insists, at the same time, that he is not arguing for a return to pre–Vatican II structural arrangements and procedures. Decentralization and centralization, he points out, have their own strengths and weaknesses. It is the responsibility of what he calls the "Roman center" to hold everything in balance. He is generally satisfied with the current method of appointing bishops, fearing that a return to a more broadly participatory approach would compromise confidentiality. This might be the case, for example, if a popular candidate were deemed unsuitable by the Vatican to be a bishop because of some serious, but hidden, moral defect. Dulles also opposes granting more powers to the Synod of Bishops, because in his mind it is not supposed to be a legislative body, but simply "a forum for the bishops to express their views on the theme of the meeting and ascertain the degree of consensus among them."[68] For Dulles, it is apparently only for the pope and the Roman Curia to decide what to do or not to do. Consequently, he opposes efforts to strengthen the role of national episcopal conferences and to reform of the Roman Curia in order to weaken its centralized power over the local bishops.

On the specific issue of papal teaching authority, Dulles dissents from fellow theologians and other pastoral leaders, such as those mentioned in Part VII.2.5.b, who have expressed concerns about what they see as an excessive centralization of doctrinal authority in the papacy. Unfortunately, he seems to caricature some of those positions, as if doctrinal issues are to be resolved by the conducting of a poll or a call for a vote prior to any papal initiative. According to Dulles, "the voice of the pope together with a solid majority of bishops over a long period of time obviates the need for a head count."[69] He also characterizes those who advocate the decentralization of authority as restorationists in their own right, advocating the reinstatement of conditions of patristic Christianity, and as tending to be "nostalgic and anachronistic." Given the global character of the Catholic Church today and the rapidity of modern communications, he concludes, the Church needs a stronger, not a weaker, papacy.

Ladislas Örsy. A few months after Avery Dulles's article on the globalization of the papacy appeared, there was a rebuttal in the same journal by another fellow Jesuit, Ladislas Örsy, formerly a professor of canon law at the Gregorian University in Rome, who also served on the faculties of Fordham University, The Catholic University of America, and Georgetown University. Örsy's article was entitled "The Papacy for an Ecumenical Age: A Response to Avery Dulles."[70]

After praising John Paul II for his 1995 encyclical *Ut unum sint* (see Part VII.2.5.a), Örsy chastises Avery Dulles for presenting "partial" information, reporting "the activities of the center faithfully," but failing to speak of the "weaknesses in the provinces," and then, "on the basis of incomplete data, he reaches the conclusion that no significant change is needed."[71] In other words, Örsy observes, for Dulles, in contrast with *Ut unum sint,* "the contemporary way of exercising the papacy is not open to a new situation." Örsy's central thesis is that the Petrine office needs to begin changing its manner of exercising papal authority "*by strengthening the Roman Catholic communion in all its parts*."[72] He then lists eight specific areas that require immediate attention: the universal Church and the particular churches, subsidiarity, collegiality, the appointment of bishops, episcopal conferences, the Synod of Bishops, papal teaching, and the Roman Curia.

Regarding *the universal Church and the particular churches,* Avery Dulles, he suggests, incorrectly assumes that Vatican II gave priority to the universal Church over the particular, or local, churches. Örsy attributes this assumption to a mistranslation on Dulles's part of *Lumen gentium,* n. 27. The universal Church is not "antecedent" to the particular churches, as Dulles holds (even though the conciliar text never uses the word "antecedent"). Rather, the universal Church exists "in and from" (Lat. *in quibus et ex quibus*) the particular churches. In other words, "there is no universal church (not even conceptually) apart from the particular churches. . . . In the post-apostolic Catholic tradition, there has never been, and there could not be, a universal church without particular churches. Such an 'abstract' church could not even have a head, since Peter's successor is the bishop of Rome!"[73]

On *subsidiarity,* "once the 'antecedency' principle is discarded," Örsy continues, "the principle of subsidiarity appears in a new light. . . . It is the intrinsic law of any organic body"—including the Church.[74]

It would have made no sense for Vatican II to have affirmed *collegiality,* nor would there have been any fierce debate over it at the council, if all it meant, as Avery Dulles seems to assume, is "mere consultation." On the contrary, Ladislas Örsy insists, "collegiality means participation in the act of a decision, as it happens precisely at an ecumenical council."[75]

Örsy insists that there is no secular model for the election of bishops, because the *appointment of bishops* is "a unique ecclesial act." But he believes that Dulles is wrong in "insinuating that the only alternative to the present system is the system presently in place. Our tradition is much richer than that."[76]

Episcopal conferences, Örsy points out, emerged in modern times from an "old tradition" of various assemblies and synods. However, their capacity to make a decisive impact on the life of their local churches today has been unduly constrained by Vatican regulations. "In the practical order, episcopal conferences exist and operate at the good pleasure of the Holy See."[77]

If Paul VI instituted the *Synod of Bishops* to build a closer link with the worldwide episcopate and to develop an effective practice of collegiality, Örsy observes, his hopes have not been fulfilled. The synod remains a consultative body. Its members do not control their own agenda. And any documents ensuing from it are edited and put in final form by curial officials. If allowed to function as Paul VI intended, however, Synods of Bishops could be of great benefit to the universal Church.

Regarding *papal teaching*, Örsy believes that the concept of "definitive" teaching was rendered ambiguous during the pontificate of John Paul II. In the past, the term was deliberately reserved for infallible statements, but in the John Paul II years it seemed to be employed in a more elastic fashion. Ever since the widespread public dissent registered by bishops, theologians, and married Catholics alike against Paul VI's birth-control encyclical, *Humanae vitae*, in 1968,[78] the Vatican has been searching for ways and means to enforce its doctrinal declarations. These ways and means were introduced incrementally since 1989. First, there was the publication of an "extended" profession of faith required from all candidates for ordination or for an ecclesiastical office. This was followed by a new Oath of Fidelity to be taken by the same persons. Obedience to "definitive" declarations is clearly included (see Part IV.3.2). In 1998 a new canonical penalty was inserted into the Code of Canon Law applicable to dissenters from "definitive" doctrine. Catholic scholars, Örsy writes, are asking, "*What is 'definitive' doctrine?*"[79] (For more on *Humanae vitae*, see page 322.)

It should be noted here that Pope John Paul II's 1998 apostolic letter *Ad tuendam fidem* (Lat., "To defend the faith"), added a paragraph to canon 750 of the Revised Code of Canon Law and made amendments as well to the Code of Canons of the Eastern Churches "to protect the Catholic faith against errors," particularly those committed by professors of theology. The apostolic letter underlined the assent required when dealing with church teaching proposed "definitively" and provided for "just penalties" imposed on those who deny these teachings.

The letter was published with a commentary that was signed by then Cardinal Joseph Ratzinger and Archbishop (later Cardinal Secretary of State) Tarcisio Bertone, the two top officials of the Congregation for the Doctrine of the Faith. The commentary supplied examples of "definitive" teachings that had been taught by the ordinary and universal magisterium, namely, the ordination of women, the invalidity of Anglican orders, and the moral teaching on euthanasia, prostitution, and fornication.[80]

On the *Roman Curia,* Ladislas Örsy recalls the famous intervention at Vatican II by Cardinal Joseph Frings of Cologne in which he sharply criticized the procedures of what was then called the Holy Office (now the Congregation for the Doctrine of the Faith). Örsy points out that, although the cardinal and others have made good suggestions for improvement, "implementation is the real problem."[81]

Having covered the main points in Avery Dulles's article, Örsy concludes that the methodology employed in the article is neither that of scholastic "disputation" in the style of Aquinas, nor "theological investigation" in the style of Karl Rahner, nor an inquiry according to the "transcendental precepts" of Bernard Lonergan (from research, to understanding, to judgment), nor an aesthetic contemplation of the mystery of the Church in the spirit of Hans Urs von Balthasar. "It is none of these," he writes. "It is advocacy. It is driven by the art and craft of rhetoric. It uses or omits information to support a 'thesis,' which is that the development of the exercise of the papal office has reached a point where no significant changes are needed. There is an irony in what Father Dulles is doing. He wants to support the pope but he does not enter into the dynamics of John Paul's request."[82]

The Congregation for the Doctrine of the Faith

The Congregation for the Doctrine of the Faith (CDF) issued a set of reflections on papal primacy that was published on October 30, 1998. The document, "Reflections on the Primacy of Peter," appeared the following January in *Origins.*[83] We have already devoted some attention to the document in Part VII.2.5.c in our discussion of the writings of Hermann Pottmeyer. "Reflections" was an appendix to the published set of papers from a 1996 symposium, sponsored by the CDF, called "The Primacy of the Successor of Peter in the Mystery of the Church."[84] The 1996 symposium was itself a response to John Paul II's invitation in his 1995 encyclical *Ut unum sint* to reflect with him on the exercise of the papal primacy and to suggest improvements in the manner of that exercise.

"Reflections" asserts that Peter was "expressly assigned by Christ to the first place among the Twelve and was called to exercise a distinctive, specific task in the church. . . . From the beginning . . . the church has understood that . . . the ministry of unity entrusted to Peter belongs to the permanent structure of Christ's church and that this succession is established in the see of his martyrdom" (n. 3). As a result, "the Catholic Church teaches as a doctrine of faith that the bishop of Rome is the successor of Peter in his primatial service in the universal church" (n. 4). This is in keeping with the teachings of both the First and Second Vatican Councils. The document also emphasizes that the Petrine office is not separate from that of the other bishops. "The bishop of Rome is a member of the 'college,' and the bishops are his brothers in the ministry." Nor does episcopal collegiality stand in opposition to the personal exercise of the primacy (n. 5). There is a "mutual interiority" between the universal Church and each and all of the particular churches (n. 6).

The Petrine ministry is "not an office of coordination or management, nor can it be reduced to a primacy of honor or be conceived as a political monarchy." The pope does not make arbitrary decisions, but is always subject to the Word of God and to the Catholic faith (n. 7). The primacy of the pope is always in service of the unity of the bishops and of all the faithful (n. 8). The communion of the bishops with the bishop of Rome is a necessary condition for their own teaching mission (n. 9). Although the power of the primacy is supreme, "this does not mean, however, that the pope has absolute power. Listening to what the churches are saying is, in fact, an earmark of the ministry of unity. It is a consequence also of the unity of the episcopal body and of the *sensus fidei* of the entire people of God. . . . The ultimate and absolute responsibility of the pope is best guaranteed, on the one hand, by its relationship to tradition and fraternal communion and, on the other, by trust in the assistance of the Holy Spirit, who governs the church" (n. 10).

The unity of the Church reaches its "highest expression" in the Eucharist, "which is the center and root of ecclesial communion," which is also based on the unity of the episcopate (n. 11). Moreover, "the fact that a particular task has been carried out by the primacy in a certain era does not mean by itself that this task should necessarily be reserved always to the Roman pontiff; and vice versa" (n. 12). Discerning the appropriate ways to exercise the primacy requires the assistance of the Holy Spirit and fraternal dialogue between the bishop of Rome and the other bishops." However, the pope has "the last word on the ways to exercise his pastoral ministry in the universal church" (n. 13). "Reflections" notes that the reaffirmation of these basic doctrinal points is "useful for avoiding the continual possibility of relapsing into biased and one-sided positions already rejected by the church in the past" (n. 14). The document cites four examples: three on the left (Febronianism, Gallicanism, and Conciliarism) and only one on the right (Ultramontanism). Human error and human frailty have characterized the papacy from the time of Peter himself to the present. We must trust in the Holy Spirit to guide the Church and the papacy along the right paths (n. 15). These responses to *Ut unum sint* show the Church struggling today to strike the right balance between papal authority and the authority rightly exercised by other teachers and teaching bodies in the Church.

COLLEGIALITY

Collegiality is the structured expression of the communal nature of the Church. It applies immediately to the unity that exists among all the local, or particular, churches in the universal Church and to their unity with the local church of Rome and its bishop, the pope. Collegiality also applies to the pastoral collaboration that marks (or should mark) their common work on behalf of the mission of the Church. The collegiality of the bishops of these local churches is, in turn, the structured, representational expression of the collegiality that exists among all of the local churches with each other and in communion with the local church of Rome and its bishop.

We have already discussed this topic several times in this book (see Part IV.2.2; Part V.6.4, 7.1 and elsewhere; and Part VII.1.4). The topic is also inherent in our previous discussion (above) of papal primacy in post–Vatican II ecclesiology.

OTHER STRUCTURES OF AUTHORITY

Other, more specific structures by and through which the authority of the Church is exercised include synods and conferences.

The World Synod of Bishops

Established by Pope Paul VI in 1965 in the document *Apostolica sollicitudo* (Lat., "Apostolic solicitude") and subsequently mandated by Vatican II's Decree on the Bishops' Pastoral Office in the Church (n. 5), the World Synod of Bishops meets every few years at the call of the pope, who is its president. Nevertheless, it is a permanent body, with a permanent general secretariat presided over by a general secretary appointed by the pope. The Code of Canon Law treats of the synod's structure, its responsibilities, and its powers in canons 342–48. The first synod met in 1967.

Other Synods

Synods also exist at the regional and diocesan levels. Regional synods, also known as Special Assemblies of the Synod of Bishops, have been meeting since 1991 as representative of the Church in various parts of the world, such as Europe, Africa, the Americas, Asia, and Oceania. Diocesan synods involve certain clerical, religious, and lay leaders and representatives within the local church whose task is advising the bishop on the various pastoral challenges and opportunities that confront the diocese. The Code of Canon Law does not require the holding of diocesan synods, but allows for their existence "when circumstances warrant it in the judgment of the diocesan bishop, after he has consulted the presbyteral council" (can. 461.1; see also cans. 460–68).

National Episcopal Conferences

National conferences of bishops existed prior to the Second Vatican Council. In the United States, for example, it was called the National Catholic Welfare Conference (and before that, a "Council"), established in 1919. National episcopal conferences were explicitly recommended for the entire Church by the Dogmatic Constitution on the Church (n. 22) and the Decree on the Bishops' Pastoral Office in the Church (nn. 37–38) and were formally established by Paul VI in 1966. According to the 1983 Code of Canon Law (cans. 447–59), an episcopal conference is an association of the bishops of a nation or definite region. A permanent board and a general secretariat are authorized to handle the conference's ongoing work. The conference elects its own officers and committee chairmen.

The pastoral letters of some conferences of bishops have attracted worldwide attention. By way of example only, the two pastoral letters issued by the United States Conference of Catholic Bishops (then called the National Conference of Catholic Bishops) that fall readily into this category are "The Challenge of Peace" (1983) and "Economic Justice for All: Catholic Social Teaching and the U.S. Economy" (1986). There have been continuing controversies, however, on the teaching authority (Lat. *mandatum docendi*) of episcopal conferences. The best statement of the issue is provided by Avery Dulles in his *The Reshaping of Catholicism.*[85] Dulles argues that the influence and impact of these episcopal documents do not depend so much on their canonical or doctrinal authority as on their "intrinsic qualities" and "on the reception accorded to them by discerning critics and by the general public."[86] Although then Cardinal Joseph Ratzinger (later Pope Benedict XVI) came later to reject the notion that episcopal conferences have a teaching mandate,[87] in the first issue of the international theological journal *Concilium,* then Professor Ratzinger wrote: "One not infrequently hears the opinion that the bishops' conferences lack all theological basis and could therefore not act in a way that would be binding on an individual bishop. Here again we have a case where a one-sided and unhistorical systematization breaks down."[88]

ECUMENICAL STATEMENTS

There is a long list of documents, books, and articles that highlight the ecumenical dimensions of ecclesiology.[89] What follows is only a sample of major ecumenical statements that have touched upon the issue of authority in the Church. They are *Baptism, Eucharist and Ministry*, a Faith and Order Paper, also known as the "Lima text" (because of its origin in Lima, Peru) or the *BEM* document, issued by the World Council of Churches in 1982;[90] "The Gift of Authority," issued by the second Anglican–Roman Catholic International Commission (ARCIC II) in 1999;[91] and *The Nature and Mission of the Church*, also a Faith and Order Paper, issued by the WCC in 2005.[92]

Baptism, Eucharist and Ministry *(WCC, 1982)*

Although concern with authority runs throughout the so-called *BEM* document, especially in the third major section on ministry, there is explicit reference to the topic in II.B of the document. It states therein that the authority of the Church—and of the ordained ministry in particular—is rooted in Jesus Christ, who received it, in turn, from God the Father through the Holy Spirit, who is conferred through the act of ordination. This authority, however, "is not to be understood as the possession of the ordained person but as a gift for the continuing edification of the body in and for which the minister has been ordained," to be "exercised with the cooperation of the whole community" (II.B.15). This also means that its exercise must always be marked by a sense of "inter-dependence and reciprocity" rather than "isolation and domination" (II.B.16), that is, in the manner of Jesus himself (Matt. 7:29; 9:36). "Authority in the Church can only be authentic as it seeks to conform to this model."

"The Gift of Authority" (ARCIC II, 1999)

The ultimate root of true authority, "The Gift of Authority" declares, is the triune God (II.7). Jesus exercised this authority in the manner of a servant (Mark 10:45; II.9). "The revealed word, to which the apostolic community originally bore witness, is received and communicated through the life of the whole Christian community" (II.14). This dynamic process of "handing on" (Tradition) is the work of the Holy Spirit, "especially through the ministry of word and sacrament and in the common life of the people of God." Scripture, on the other hand, occupies "a unique and normative place" within Tradition (II.19). The formation of the canon of Sacred Scripture was itself an act of authority, under the guidance of the Holy Spirit, and an integral part of the process of Tradition (II.22). Scripture, in turn, can only be read and interpreted within the context of the Church (II.24). This process is known as reception (see page 322). Sometimes the Church recognizes that some of the formulations of Tradition are "inadequate or even misleading in a new context. This whole process may be termed *rereception*" (II.25).

The process of reception or of "rereception" yields a variety of interpretations and formulations. But such diversity is not a weakness. On the contrary, it is "the practical manifestation of catholicity and confirms rather than contradicts the vigor of Tradition." It is not a matter of uniformity, but of "catholic diversity within the unity of communion" (II.27). Again, it is the "people of God as a whole" who are "the bearer of the living Tradition. . . . The discernment, actualization and communication of the word of God is the responsibility of the whole people of God. The Holy Spirit works through all members of the community. . . . In each community there is an exchange, a mutual give and take, in which bishops, clergy and lay people receive from as well as give to others within the whole body" (II.28). Every individual Christian possesses a *sensus fidei* (Lat., "sense of the faith"), which is "an active capacity for spiritual discernment, an intuition that is formed by worshiping and living in communion as a faithful member of the church." When exercised collectively by the faith, it is called the *sensus fidelium* ("sense of the faithful"). The latter contributes to the former. "By the *sensus fidelium*, the whole body contributes to, receives from and treasures the ministry of those within the community who exercise *episcope* [Gk., "oversight"], watching over the living memory of the Church" (II.29).

"The Gift of Authority" insists, however, that "those who exercise *episcope* in the body of Christ must not be separated from the 'symphony' of the whole people of God in which they have their part to play. They need to be alert to the *sensus fidelium,* in which they share, if they are to be made aware when something is needed for the well-being and mission of the community or when some element of the Tradition needs to be received in a fresh way" (II.30). The document does not ignore the specifically ecumenical dimension of this reality: "When Christian communities are in real but imperfect communion, they are called to recognize in each other elements of the apostolic Tradition which they may have rejected, forgotten or not yet fully understood. Consequently, they have to receive or reappropriate the ways in which they have separately interpreted the Scriptures" (II.31).

The authority Jesus bestowed on his disciples "was, above all, the authority for mission, to preach and to heal (cf. Lk. 9:1–2, 10:1). . . . This authority enables the whole church to embody the Gospel and become the missionary and prophetic servant of the Lord" (III.32). To the extent, however, that the Church is divided, it cannot adequately or credibly preach the gospel of reconciliation. Therefore, "the challenge and responsibility for those with the authority within the church is so to exercise their ministry that they promote the unity of the whole church in faith and life in a way that enriches rather than diminishes the legitimate diversity of local churches" (III.33), the mutual interdependence of which is "integral to the reality of the church as God wills it to be." No local church is self-sufficient. Forms of synodality are needed "to manifest the communion of the local churches and to sustain each of them in fidelity to the Gospel." The ministry of each bishop is crucial to the success of synodality (manifested in synods or councils, whether local, provincial, worldwide, or ecumenical). The communion of the bishops with each other "is expressed through the incorporation of each bishop into a college of bishops" (III.37).

An essential aspect of the episcopal ministry involves consulting the faithful. Each bishop must seek to discern and articulate the *sensus fidelium* in his own local church and in the wider communion of churches. "Roman Catholics and Anglicans share this understanding of synodality," the document notes, "but express it in different ways" (III.38).

"The Gift of Authority" turns next to the exercise of teaching authority, distinguishing between indefectibility, which is the Church's perseverance in the truth, and infallibility, which concerns the preservation of the truth without error, under the guidance of the Holy Spirit and in service to the Church's indefectibility (III.41–42). "When the people of God respond by faith and say amen to authoritative teaching, it is because they recognize that this teaching expresses the apostolic faith and operates within the authority and truth of Christ, the head of the church. . . . The authenticity of the teaching of individual bishops is evident when this teaching is in solidarity with that of the whole episcopal college" (III.43–44).

This brings us to the especially sensitive topic of the primacy, which exists in churches other than the Catholic, but in different forms. Quoting St. Augustine, the document points out that the Lord did not give the keys only to one man, but to "the church in its unity." Peter's preeminence was rooted in his representing and sustaining the Church's universality and unity. It is the whole Church, Augustine insisted, "which has received the keys of the kingdom in heaven." When Christ spoke directly to Peter, Peter "at that time stood for the universal church" (III.46, quoting from Augustine's *Sermon 295*, on the feast of the martyrdom of the Apostles Peter and Paul). The ARCIC II document acknowledges that the primacy exercised by the bishop of Rome is "a specific ministry concerning the discernment of truth," but exercised always within, not outside or over against, the college of bishops. "When the faith is articulated in this way, the bishop of Rome proclaims the faith of the local churches. It is thus the wholly reliable teaching of the whole church that is operative in the judgment of the universal primate" (III.47).

To be sure, human weakness and sin affect individual ministers, at any level of authority, and can distort the very structures of authority. "Therefore, loyal criticism and reforms are sometimes needed" (III.48). Moreover, the exercise of authority "must always respect conscience, because the divine work of salvation affirms human freedom" (III.49).

"We envisage a primacy," the document concludes, "that will even now help to uphold the legitimate diversity of traditions, strengthening and safeguarding them in fidelity to the Gospel. . . . This sort of primacy will already assist the church on earth to be the authentic catholic *koinonia* [Gk., "communion"] in which unity does not curtail diversity, and diversity does not endanger but enhances unity" (III.60).

The Nature and Mission of the Church *(WCC, 2005)*

The Nature and Mission of the Church overlaps in many respects with "The Gift of Authority." It treats of the nature of the Church as People of God and as a communion (I.A.II.a, d), of the relationship between communion and diversity (II.C), of the universal Church as a communion of local churches (II.D), and of the ministry of all the faithful, of the ordained, of bishops, and of the primacy in the context of conciliarity (III.D–G). Its explicit discussion of authority, however, is relatively brief (III.H.105–8).

It notes that Jesus's own ministry was characterized by authority and healing in the service of others. His authority was self-emptying, manifested in the washing of his disciples' feet (John 13:1–17), and its "vindication" is eschatological (1 Cor. 15:28; III.H.105). All authority in the Church is patterned after that of Jesus himself and as such is "relational and interdependent." It is to be exercised as an act of witnessing to him, in and through the power of the Holy Spirit, "to the end of the world" (Acts 1:7–8; III.H.106).

"All authority in the church," the document insists, "comes from God and is marked by God's holiness." Such authority, however, is "effective when holiness shines from the lives of Christians and the ordered Christian community, faithful to the divine teachings." All the sources of authority that are recognized "in varying degrees" by all the churches, such as Scripture, tradition, worship, and synods, "also reflect the holiness of the Triune God" (III.H.107). "One example of the communal aspect of authority in the church," this section of the WCC document concludes, "is the act of ordination. In ordination both the action of the ordaining minister and the assent of the faithful are necessary elements" (III.H.108).

These ecumenical statements are compelling indicators that Catholicism is not alone in reconsidering the role of authority in the Church.

Reception

Reception is a process by which the body of the faithful, or a significant portion thereof, accepts and abides by an official teaching or disciplinary decree of the hierarchical Church (see also Part VII.2.8.b). There are two criteria by which to determine whether a teaching or decree has been accepted: first, there is some evidence of a change in or reaffirmation of the thinking of the Church as a whole or that portion of the Church to which the teaching or decree is directed; and second, there is also some evidence of a change in or reconfirmation of individual and institutional patterns of behavior. Ladislas Örsy writes: "A correct act of promulgation can impose a legally binding norm; yet, its effective reception alone can make it into a vital force, leading to a pleasing sacrifice to God."[93] It is important to note here that such reception can be whole or only partial. Examples of the latter would be the responses to the so-called Lima document (referred to in Part VII.2.8.a) and to ARCIC II's "The Gift of Authority" (referred to in Part VII.2.8.b). Tradition, which is a concept closely related to reception, is a continuous process of the rereception of truths throughout the history of the Church.[94]

In the New Testament, reception concerns the acceptance of the word of God (Mark 4:20), the message of Jesus (Rev. 2:41), and the gospel (1 Cor. 15:1).[95] It also involves the acceptance of Jesus himself and of those whom he sent (Matt. 10:40; John 13:20) and whom he himself had first accepted (Rom. 15:7). This process of acceptance is always under the guidance of the Holy Spirit (1 Cor. 2:10–16).

In the early Church, confessions of faith, liturgies, various conciliar decrees, and the finalization of the biblical canon acquired recognition and authority by means of their reception by the various local churches. Such reception was understood as a reliable indication of their fidelity to the apostolic tradition. Over time, however, the role of the local churches in this process diminished, giving way to that of the central authority in Rome. This occurred particularly in the second Christian millennium and then from the nineteenth century on, when papal authority became even more centralized. Reception also became increasingly tantamount to obedience.

Properly understood, the reception of doctrine does not confer authenticity (i.e., official status) upon the doctrine; it simply recognizes and accepts what was already there. Nonreception of a doctrine does not necessarily mean that the doctrine is in error, but nonreception does require the formulator(s) of the doctrine to reexamine the teaching to see if the nonreception is indicative of a flaw in the doctrinal formulation itself. In the rare case of an infallible teaching, there may be criticism of the form in which the teaching has been framed, but there cannot be rejection of the core of the teaching. As the Dogmatic Constitution on the Church points out: "The assent of the Church can never be lacking to such definitions on account of the same Holy Spirit's influence, through which Christ's whole flock is maintained in the unity of the faith and makes progress in it" (n. 25).

A recent major example of reception is the acceptance and incorporation by Vatican II of the aims of the biblical, liturgical, and ecumenical movements that predated the council. Acceptance of all of the teachings of the council itself has had a more mixed record (as we noted in Part V.8, 10). A major example of nonreception is the negative reaction on the part of the great majority of Catholic married couples of childbearing age to the teaching of Pope Paul VI's 1968 birth-control encyclical, *Humanae vitae.*[96] The reason for the resistance is, very simply, that the teaching is not consistent with the experience of most Catholic married couples of childbearing age. It is not that they have misunderstood the teaching or have found it too difficult to obey. They believe the teaching to be wrong. Moreover, they do not believe themselves to be committing serious sin when they act in accordance with a judgment of conscience that is contrary to the encyclical's central teaching, namely, that every act of marital intimacy must be open to the transmission of human life (n. 14). Rightly or wrongly, the great majority of Catholic married couples doubt the capacity of celibate males to understand their sexual experience within marriage or the physical and economic pressures that constrain them and their families today.

Reception is also a major factor in the acceptance and implementation by affected Churches and ecclesial communities of various ecumenical agreements, such as those produced by the Anglican–Roman Catholic International Commissions (ARCIC I and II) on authority in the Church (see Part VII.2.8.b).

The theology of reception, never lost by the Eastern Churches and the Anglican Communion, experienced a renewal within Catholic ecclesiology in the years immediately after Vatican II, and largely because of the council. In retrieving the doctrine of communion and its structured expression, collegiality, and by once again viewing the Church as the whole People of God, permeated with the Holy Spirit in head and members alike, the council's Dogmatic Constitution on the Church laid the foundation for a recovery of the ancient notion of reception.

Ecclesiologist Yves Congar was a key figure in the renewed attention to the doctrine of reception, which he defined as "the process by means of which a church (body) truly takes over as its own a resolution that it did not originate in regard to its self [*sic*], and acknowledges the measure it promulgates as a rule applicable to its own life."[97] It is more than an act of obedience. That latter assumption is based, he writes, on a pyramidal notion of the Church in which there is "hardly any mention of the Holy Spirit."[98]

Reception, Congar insists, does not confer subsequent validity on a teaching or decree; it declares only that it had been valid from the beginning. On the other hand, nonreception does not retract validity; it indicates that previous teachings or decisions had been invalid from the beginning. However, subsequent assent, or reception, gives a valid teaching or decree "increased effectiveness."[99]

Other post–Vatican II theologians who have helped to retrieve the doctrine of reception have included the Greek Orthodox (now Bishop) John Zizioulas and the Roman Catholic Jean-Marie R. Tillard (d. 2000), both of whom contributed to the documents of the World Council of Churches that touched upon the subject of reception and both of whom also emphasized the eucharistic context for the process of reception.[100] The liturgy itself is a norm of faith: *lex orandi, lex credendi* (Lat., "The law, or rule, of praying is the law, or rule, of believing"). How the Church prays is a sure indication of what the Church believes. Since the Eucharist is the highest form of prayer, how the Church celebrates the Eucharist (the words it uses and the rituals it performs) is the surest liturgical indication of what the Church believes, or, in other words, of the faith that the Church has *received* over the centuries and that it continues to *receive* today in each celebration of the Eucharist.

As Christopher O'Donnell points out, "There has been a very substantial literature on reception in recent decades."[101] The reality, however, is very ancient, even though the process has never been entirely clear. The reception of the first seven ecumenical councils by East and West alike was "not a matter merely of subsequent papal approval; more profoundly operative was the sense of the faith whereby the bishops of the local Churches and their people welcomed them into their liturgy and life. . . . Reception in this classical sense is communitarian; it is a work of the Spirit in the communion within and among the local Churches; it recognizes a special role for the bishop as a witness to tradition and judge of the authenticity of faith. But it also involves the laity, who accept and find life-giving what their pastors acknowledge as authentic."[102] Because it is a work of the Holy Spirit in the whole community of faith, it is not the product of a vote or a modern poll.

COROLLARY ON DISSENT IN THE CHURCH

Dissent is the public or private nonreception of a doctrine or disciplinary decree that has been handed down by some individual official or agency of the Church's teaching and pastoral authority. Only public dissent is at issue here. The term "dissent" is usually applied to the negatively critical reactions of theologians to a particular doctrinal or disciplinary pronouncement, in whole or in part. However, because dissent is also a juridical concept, many prefer not to use the word when referring to the nonreception of doctrinal pronouncements and disciplinary decrees, particularly those emanating from the Vatican. Perhaps the best and clearest explanation of the meaning of and criteria for dissent, or nonreception, is Richard A. McCormick's

"The Church and Dissent: How Vatican II Ushered in a New Way of Thinking."[103]

Therein he lists twelve factors that have encouraged a new critical awareness in the Church and have helped to explain the emergence of dissent, or nonreception, in the post–Vatican II Church. Each factor, he argues, is positively affirmed in Vatican II's Pastoral Constitution on the Church in the Modern World (references are to that document, unless otherwise noted): (1) changing times (n. 4); (2) newness of problems (n. 62); (3) variety of competence in the Church (nn. 43–44); (4) openness to the sciences (n. 62); (5) freedom of theological inquiry and speech (n. 62); (6) the Church's modesty about its own competence (n. 33); (7) the independence of the sciences (n. 36); (8) the fact of doctrinal development (the Dogmatic Constitution on Divine Revelation, n. 8); (9) adaptation to practices (Decree on Eastern Catholic Churches, n. 26); (10) acknowledgment of legitimate pluralism (n. 43); (11) conciliar admission of errors and deficiencies (Decree on Ecumenism, n. 6); and (12) the new task of theology, moving, McCormick says, "from a mere repetition of past formulas to a search for fresh and more appropriate ones, to much more innovation than was envisaged in the past."[104]

He concludes his detailed examination of dissent in the Church with a quotation from Pope John Paul II's book *The Acting Person*, written prior to his election as pope in 1978: "The structure of a human community is correct only if it admits not just the presence of a justified opposition, but also that effectiveness of opposition which is required by the common good and the right of participation."[105] These words, McCormick writes, "are no less true of the church than of any community."[106]

Ministry

Here again, the post–Vatican II literature on ministry, ordained and nonordained alike, is too vast to comprehend within a single section of this book. Nor is it necessary to do so. The purpose of summarizing and synthesizing the ecclesiological content of the various topics in Parts VI and VII is simply to provide an overview of each and, with the help of some bibliographical guidance, to encourage readers to pursue a more extensive and intensive inquiry as interest and need dictate.[107]

Etymologically, ministry (Gk. *diakonia*) is a service. It is a service rendered to another or others who are in need of the service. There are four types of ministry: first, a general, nonreligious ministry that is rooted in our common humanity and that every human being is called to render to others in need; second, a specific, but still nonreligious, ministry that is rooted in some form of licensing or certification; it is the type of service rendered by physicians to patients or plumbers to homeowners; third, Christian ministry, rooted in Baptism and rendered in principle by every member of the Church, whether explicitly or implicitly because of their faith in Christ, to everyone in need, both inside and outside the Church; and fourth, ecclesial ministry, which is rendered to others, inside and outside the Church, in the name of the Church; it is rooted in some form of designation by the Church, whether by ordination or some other form of recognition, and whether conferred by a parish, a diocese, the universal Church, or other ecclesial entities in between.

From the time of the Council of Trent in the sixteenth century and largely in reaction to Protestantism's stress on the "priesthood of all believers," the Catholic Church tended to restrict the notion of ministry to the ordained (bishops, presbyters/priests, and deacons) and to those steps taken in preparation for ordination (the minor orders of lector, acolyte, and exorcist). Today, however, ministry has taken on a much broader meaning, as indicated in the previous paragraph. The history of Christian ministries yields a broad diversity of ministries as well as a wide variety in the ways in which each has been structured and exercised.[108]

The post–Vatican II development of a theology and practice of ministries of various kinds has been impacted largely by the council's emphasis on the Church as the whole People of God (therefore, ministries can be, and are, exercised by laity as well as clergy) and on the participation of all the baptized in the priesthood of Christ. Which is not to say that the council's teaching on ministry is without ambiguity. It insists that the faithful participate in the priesthood of Christ, but it also points out that the difference between the ordained and the nonordained is not only one of degree, but of essence (Dogmatic Constitution on the Church, n. 10).

In the final accounting, however, the council recovered the notion of ministry as a service rather than as an ecclesiastical status. Whatever "sacred power" the ordained possess and exercise is always for the sake of the life, mission, and ministries of the whole People of God. The ordained ministries are not to dominate these other ministries, but to integrate and coordinate them (Dogmatic Constitution on the Church, n. 30). In 1972 Pope Paul VI's apostolic letter *Ministeria quaedam* (Lat., "Certain ministries") set aside the notion, from the time of the Council of Trent, that all ministries below the priesthood are simply steps toward the priesthood. He restored lay ministries, to be conferred by some form of installation other than ordination. The document established two such lay ministries, those of lector and acolyte, and left open the possibility of the creation of others.

Although the resource document on lay ministry "Co-Workers in the Vineyard of the Lord,"[109] approved by the U.S. Catholic bishops in November 2005, received much favorable attention at the time, perhaps the best episcopal statement on ministry, in the form of a pastoral letter, was issued by Cardinal Roger Mahony, archbishop of Los Angeles, more than five years earlier. The letter was entitled "As I Have Done for You," was jointly produced by the cardinal, his priests, and the laity of the archdiocese, and was released on Holy Thursday 2000.[110] The document acknowledges that, given the grave pastoral circumstances the Church faces in the early twenty-first century, "mere adjustments and small shifts in practice will not suffice. What is called for is a major reorientation in our thinking about ministry as well as in our ministerial practice."[111]

The letter insists that lay ministry is rooted in the priesthood of the baptized. As such, it is not a "stopgap measure." Even if there were again an abundance of vocations to the ordained priesthood and the religious life,[112] "there would still remain the need for cultivating, developing and sustaining the full flourishing of ministries that we have witnessed in the church since the Second Vatican Council." At the same time, "there is a pressing need for greater collaboration and inclusivity in ministry in the church of the new millennium," not only the traditional collaboration between priests and bishop, but also between the ministries of the ordained and of the nonordained.[113]

Unfortunately, it has taken the grave shortage of priestly and religious vocations to awaken the Church to an appreciation of the great variety and value of its lay ministries. This has gone hand in hand with a recovery of the theology of Baptism. All ministries, whether ordained or nonordained, are rooted first and foremost in the sacrament of Baptism. "Both ordained and baptismal priesthoods share in this one priesthood [of Christ]. The laity as well as the ordained participate in the threefold office of Christ the prophet, priest and king. What emerges from the Second Vatican Council is a clear theology of the laity rooted in an understanding of the church as the people of God, in the universal call to holiness and in an appreciation of the diversity of the nature of the church both hierarchical and charismatic."[114]

The pastoral letter notes that lay ecclesial ministry "refers to professionally trained or otherwise properly prepared women and men, including vowed religious, who are in positions of service and leadership in the church."[115] Such ministry emerges from a personal call, requires appropriate formation, and is undertaken with the support and authorization of competent church authority. Examples include pastoral associate, business manager, director of religious education (DRE), catechist, director of the RCIA program (Rite of Christian Initiation of Adults), youth/young adult minister, and coordinator of liturgy.

Deacons, on the other hand, serve the Church by assisting bishops and pastors. They "express in a most visible way the character of the church as servant. *Diakonia* is so central to the life of the Church that it is singled out and sacramentalized in diaconal ordination." The priest-pastor, however, is the head of a local parish community. He "addresses challenging prophetic words" to it, exercises a pastoral ministry of oversight and direction of its charisms, and "presides sacramentally as the instrument of Christ's action in the sacraments." But he exercises this headship over the parish community within it, not over it or apart from it. Indeed, it is the "whole church [that] celebrates the sacraments—head and members." "If we are to continue . . . to develop a more collaborative and inclusive approach to ministry," the letter concludes, "then one of the challenges that awaits us now is to gather together priests, deacons, religious and lay leaders to explore how we all might more effectively exercise our ministry as servants of Christ and his church."[116]

An Excursus on Sacraments and Liturgy

The literal meaning of the Latin word *excursus* is a "running forth." It also has a military meaning: an attack. In common English usage, however, it means a digression, or something akin to an appendix. Part VII is already lengthy. Adding a separate section on the sacraments and the liturgy (the distinction between the two is never clear) would inflate the size of this book far too greatly. We dare not even add limited bibliographical notes, as was done above in the section on ministry. There are extensive bibliographies on the sacraments in general, on each of the seven sacraments, especially the Eucharist, and on the Church's liturgical life. (For the benefit of non-Catholic readers, the seven sacraments of the Catholic Church are Baptism; Confirmation; Eucharist; Reconciliation, also known as Penance and, more popularly, as Confession; the Anointing of the Sick, formerly Extreme Unction; Marriage, also known as Matrimony; and Holy Orders, which consists of three levels of ordained ministry—bishops, priests, and deacons.) These topics together or separately would merit a thick volume or several individual volumes in their own right.

It is important, however, to note at some point here in Part VII on the post–Vatican II internal life of the Church, that ongoing post-conciliar discussions of the Church's sacramental and liturgical life have had, and continue to have, significant ecclesiological ramifications. The so-called liturgy wars, referred to earlier in Part V.6.2, are at root conflicts over ecclesiology. They tend to be waged between those who have fully embraced the content and pastoral implications of the council's teaching on the Church as the whole People of God—laity, clergy, and religious alike—and those who continue to view the Church as largely identical with the hierarchy and its clerical adjuncts. For the former, the liturgy and the Church's sacramental life generally invite the active participation of all the baptized; for the latter, these ritual activities are essentially the responsibility of the ordained, who alone are sacramentally empowered to produce and administer them. In this latter view, with few exceptions the laity's role is to "attend" these rituals and dutifully "receive" their spiritual benefits. The laity's role, therefore, is essentially passive rather than active.

Because of the Second Vatican Council and the theology developed under its impact, the sacraments are viewed more clearly now as acts of the Church. To be sure, they are also Christological in nature (acts of Christ), but they are more immediately ecclesiological. This point was being made already just before the council by such major Catholic theologians as Karl Rahner and Edward Schillebeeckx (see Part IV.4.2.a–b).

Those who receive the sacraments or actively participate in the Church's liturgical life are not only related to the triune God and to Jesus Christ in particular; they are also immediately related to the Church. For example, the sacrament of Reconciliation has as its immediate purpose and effect not the restoration of friendship with God, but reconciliation with the Church. The penitent who has committed a serious sin but who has made an act of perfect contrition (which restores union with God) is still required to seek forgiveness in the sacrament. Serious sin compromises the mission of the Church to be, and also to appear to be, a holy people, a sacrament of Christ and of the Reign of God. It is not God alone who is "offended" by the sin. The Church too has been violated. Its sacramentality has been tarnished and diminished. The sinner also has to "make up" with the Church.

The same line of reasoning applies to each of the sacraments and to the Church's liturgical life generally. It is not only because the faithful "belong" to the Church and derive spiritual benefits from it; they *are* the Church, and everything they do sacramentally and liturgically engages the reality of the Church and thereby imposes a great spiritual responsibility upon each and every baptized member.[117]

In the end, liturgy and sacraments are ritualized expressions of ecclesiology. It is impossible to have an authentic renewal and reform of either without careful attention to their ecclesiological dimensions and implications. Moreover, a close analysis of the way the Church worships and celebrates the sacraments will yield the underlying ecclesiology that shapes and animates both actions.

Mary and the Church

The Second Vatican Council marked a significant change in the Church's thinking about both Mary and itself.[118] Specifically, it moved away from idealized, perfectionist notions of both toward a more realistic understanding of their humanity and its corresponding limitations. Mary is now increasingly portrayed and viewed in a larger ecclesiological context. As pointed out already in Part V.7.1, there was a major debate at the council over whether Mary should be treated in a separate document or as an integral part of the Dogmatic Constitution on the Church. Cardinal Rufino Santos (d. 1973) of the Philippines had argued, on behalf of a large number of his fellow bishops, that Mary's role in salvation history transcended her place and function in the Church, but Austrian Cardinal Franz König's arguments—that Mary is a type of the Church and its preeminent member, and that she should not be isolated from the unity of the economy of salvation or from the central ecclesiological focus of the council—prevailed, even if by the slimmest of margins: 1,114 to 1,074.

Mariological expert Stephano De Fiores notes that the early postconciliar years have been referred to as "the decade without Mary."[119] Indeed, another major Mariologist, René Laurentin, concluded as of 1972 that "the marian movement is finished."[120] But Heribert Mühlen (d. 2006), one of the twentieth century's most important ecclesiologists, whose writings have been generally unknown in the English-speaking world because they have not been translated, made a more insightful observation, similar to Yves Congar's, namely, that the crisis in Mariology is at root a pneumatological crisis. People's attention has been redirected from Mary to the Holy Spirit, where it belonged in the first place.[121]

Pope Paul VI in *Marialis cultus* (Lat., "Marian devotion," 1974) noted also the cultural factors involved (n. 34). Women in greater numbers are now working outside the home, often pursuing professional careers in the public and corporate sectors of society. Within the family, roles formerly reserved to wives and mothers are now equally shared with husbands and fathers. Many pre–Vatican II Marian devotions, Paul VI acknowledged, are simply inconsistent with these new cultural realities.

De Fiores, however, faults many postconciliar Mariologists for not integrating the theology of Mary with the whole corpus of theology, including ecclesiology, as Karl Rahner had done in his *Foundations of Christian Faith.*[122] On the other hand, he also faults various postconciliar ecclesiological treatises and dictionary entries on the Church for not making any reference to the patristic teaching on Mary as a type, or symbol, of the Church. But there have been exceptions to that deficiency in the writings, for example, of Otto Semmelroth (d. 1979),[123] Hans Urs von Balthasar (see Part VII.6.1), Louis Bouyer,[124] and Charles (later Cardinal) Journet (d. 1975; his classic three-volume work on the Church is *L'Église du Verbe incarné,* Fr., "The Church of the Word Incarnate," almost all of which, however, had been written before the end of the council). Of all these theologians, however, Balthasar offers by far the most significant application of Mariology to ecclesiology.

HANS URS VON BALTHASAR

According to more critical interpretations than De Fiores's, however, Hans Urs von Balthasar's (d. 1988) understanding of Mary's womanhood and its impact on ecclesiology is dubious, particularly his claim that her femininity is a symbol of the Church as it stands before God:

obedient, receptive, and open. Thus, Mary, as the perfect woman and perfect example of faith, is obedient to God's will, receptive to God's initiative, and open to God's plan for her life.[125]

His emphasis on the Church as mystery stresses its invisible, unknowable dimension at the apparent expense of the visible and knowable. Ecclesial reflection, he writes, should not focus on the outward form of the Church, its presence on earth, or its structure and mission, but rather on "the inmost essence of the Church."[126] When the Church is "stripped of this all-embracing [maternal/feminine] sphere," it is "in danger of being reduced to a purely sociological entity or, at best, is far more vulnerable to sociological criticism than a Church conceived in terms of the ancient *mysterium* vision."[127] He believes that the medieval Church understood this, as reflected in its art.

Balthasar is less enthusiastic about the council's emphasis on the Church as the People of God, which he considers only a "socio-psychological reality"[128] or something more suited to the people of Israel in the pre-Christian era. "It is the mystical, marial element in the Church," he writes, "which distinguishes it from the People the God in the Old Testament."[129] He harks back even further, to "the patristic 'hypostasis' of the pure Church" and its emphasis on the Church as the spotless bride in Ephesians 5.[130]

There are other writers, as pointed out above, who have stressed the archetypical function of Mary for the Church, but Balthasar alone grounds her qualities of receptivity and obedience in her gender. For him, it is determinative of her place in salvation history—which is also why he was not completely satisfied with Vatican II's approach. He faults the council for failing to give any attention to the "man-woman aspect."[131] The relationship between Mary and the Church hinges on his understanding of the relationship between the sexes. For him, woman is man's "vessel of fulfillment specially designed for him."[132] The relationship is one of subordination of the woman to the man.

He describes the Church in terms of a masculine-feminine polarity embodied in the persons of Peter and Mary, with John as a mediating principle within the polarity. He refers to these three as a constellation representing three different spheres in the Church, although he also includes John the Baptist and Paul as members of the theologically significant community that surrounded Jesus.[133] Mary represents the Church of love; Peter, the Church of office. At the foot of the cross, John is given the role of a mediating figure between the feminine Church and the official masculine Church.[134]

But Mary always remains for Balthasar the central focus (after Christ himself) of his ecclesiology. She is the *Realsymbol* of the Church, imparting to it all the qualities of womanliness: openness, receptivity, and responsiveness. Her *Fiat* (Lat., "Let it be done [to me]"), which was a perfect response to God's initiative, is the pinnacle and cornerstone of her femininity and her discipleship. It is "the all-inclusive, protective, and directive form of all ecclesial life. It is the interior form of *communio,* insofar as this is an unlimited mutual acceptance."[135] For Balthasar, the whole Church, male and female alike, is feminine because it is essentially receptive to God's masculine activity. In consenting to the angel, Mary not only participates in the birth of Christ, but also indirectly in the birth of the Church, and her virginal motherhood mirrors and prefigures that of the Church, which gives birth to believers in faith.[136]

Karl Rahner puts his finger on the challenge that male theologians like Hans Urs von Balthasar have in writing about Mary and the Church in the context of femininity. Rahner notes that Mariology needs to incorporate the voices and experiences of women. Such a theology "can perhaps be produced authentically today only by women, by women theologians."[137] One might add that the voices and experiences of women are needed in every area of theology, including ecclesiology.[138]

PAUL VI'S *MARIALIS CULTUS* (1974)

Pope Paul VI's apostolic exhortation *Marialis cultus,* also known by its English title, "For the Right Ordering and Development of Devotion to the Blessed Virgin Mary," points out in its introduction that

Mary remains "a most excellent exemplar of the Church in the order of faith, charity and perfect union with Christ." However, the world and the Church have changed dramatically since many traditional Marian devotions were first developed, rendering some of them "inadequate or unsuitable because they are linked with social and cultural patterns of the past."[139]

Paul VI offers four guidelines for the reordering of Marian devotions, namely, that they should have a biblical imprint, always harmonize with the liturgy and not be mixed in some hybrid form, be ecumenically sensitive (e.g., not giving the impression that Mary is somehow coequal with Christ, our one Mediator and Redeemer), and pay close attention to certain findings of the human sciences. The last has a decidedly different approach to womanhood than Balthasar, stressing women's equality and coresponsibility with men within the family, the legal system, the world of politics, the professions, and the social, scientific, intellectual and cultural sectors generally (*Marialis cultus*, n. 34). Mary herself was "far from being a timidly submissive woman or one whose piety was repellent to others." On the contrary, "she was a woman who did not hesitate to proclaim that God vindicates the humble and the oppressed, and removes the powerful people of this world from their privileged positions (cf. Luke 1:51–53)" (n. 37).

JOHN PAUL II'S *REDEMPTORIS MATER* (1987)

John Paul II's 1987 Marian encyclical *Redemptoris Mater* (Lat., "Mother of the Redeemer"), written to herald the opening of a Marian year in 1987–88, is more devotional in tone than *Marialis cultus*, but it also underscores the ecumenical dimensions of a true understanding of Mary as one "obedient of faith" and applauds the great progress that had been made by various ecumenical dialogues regarding Christian beliefs relating to Mary.[140] His reference to Mary's Magnificat incorporates the Church's "preference for the poor" (n. 37), and his reflection on her discipleship stresses the Church's call to the service of others.

Feminist and Nonfeminist Ecclesiology by Catholic Women

I noted in the preface to the 1994 edition of my *Catholicism* that one of the major changes that had occurred in the Church and in theology since the publication of the first edition in 1980 was "the emergence of women in positions of pastoral and intellectual leadership. Nowhere has this development been more pronounced than in the fields of theology and biblical studies."[141] One looks almost completely in vain for books and articles in theology, and in ecclesiology particularly, that were written by Catholic women prior to 1980. Rosemary Radford Ruether is one of the most visible exceptions.[142] Women theologians did not generally begin to come into their own, so to speak, until the decade of the 1980s, ironically just at the time that the relatively new pontificate of John Paul II was beginning to "crack down" on traditional male theologians like Hans Küng, Charles Curran, and Leonardo Boff.

It would be impossible to do justice in this section, given the spatial limits of this volume, to the post-1980 work of women theologians in general, and even of the far smaller contingent of Catholic women in ecclesiology. The list of books and articles has been growing apace each year since then. We can mention only some of them here.

FEMINIST ECCLESIOLOGIES

Among the leading representatives of feminist ecclesiology are New Testament scholar Elisabeth Schüssler Fiorenza and theologians Elizabeth Johnson, Anne Carr (d. 2008), Rosemary Radford Ruether, and Mary E. Hines.[143] It is important to note Mary Hines's observation that "ecclesiology is perhaps the most difficult area of systematic theology to treat from a feminist perspective within the Roman Catholic tradition." This is so because of, as she puts it, the Catholic Church's "intractably patriarchal and hierarchical" traditions and structures, which cause many "discouraged and alienated" women to move or to work outside that Church.[144]

Elisabeth Schüssler Fiorenza

In her groundbreaking book *In Memory of Her: A Feminist Theological Reconstruction of Christian Origins,* Elisabeth Schüssler Fiorenza presents the Church as a "discipleship of equals" and its women members as "paradigms of true discipleship."[145] In her later collection of essays *Discipleship of Equals: A Critical Feminist Ekklesia-logy of Liberation,* she proposes what she calls an *ekklesia* of women. In the three essays in which the proposal occurs, previously published in 1982, 1991, and 1992, respectively,[146] there is a progression in her thought from a generally exclusive focus on women in the Church, who are sent forth to liberate other women from oppressive structures and ideologies, especially patriarchalism, to a more inclusive understanding of Church. Patriarchy, Schüssler Fiorenza acknowledges in the last of the three essays, is not only a problem of gender, but also of class and race. She recognizes that power differentials exist among women as well.[147] White, educated, economically advantaged First World women are in a far different situation from poorer, socially, politically, and culturally oppressed women in the Third World. These latter women not only exist in the same world as privileged First World (mostly white) women; they exist also in the same Church.[148]

Elizabeth A. Johnson

Elizabeth A. Johnson has focused her research and publications primarily in the areas of Christology, Mariology, and the theology of God and the saints,[149] but her emphasis on the communion of saints in two of her four major books has a clearly ecclesiological dimension. Mary, of course, has long been regarded as a type of the Church and the saints are an embodiment of one of the four essential marks of the Church, namely, holiness. In her *Friends of God and Prophets,* Johnson describes "the whole church" as "a communion of saints," understanding "saints" in the Pauline sense as referring to the whole Christian community (Rom. 1:7; Phil. 1:1; 1 Cor. 1:12; 2 Cor. 1:1). For her, the communion of saints is a synonym for the Church, but interpreted always within the context of what she calls "women's interpreted experience."[150] Indeed, she writes of transforming the Church "into a community of mutuality among equal persons,"[151] that is, in a nonhierarchical, gender-inclusive community empowered always by the Holy Spirit, and therefore all sharing equally in the holiness of God.[152] The lifeblood of this communion is the "vibrant, life-giving Spirit" of Christ,[153] who inspires not only mutuality and compassion, but also action for justice. The action of the Holy Spirit is, in turn, "an integral part of contemporary women's spiritual journey and a liberating paradigm for the ekklesia as a whole."[154]

According to one scholar, Natalia Imperatori-Lee, in Johnson's view Mary becomes "a paradigmatic figure in the best sense, an example of the companionship model of sainthood" as explained in her *Friends of God and Prophets*. Mary highlights "the holiness of lives lived in obscurity, the holiness of the church."[155] "Rather than being paradigmatic in a symbolic or metaphysical sense Mary is exemplary in her compassion and solidarity. And rather than being a 'vessel' of the Holy Spirit, Johnson's Mary is thoroughly permeated by the Spirit, her actions guided by the Spirit, her life lived in response to the Spirit, as all in the church are called to do."[156]

Anne Carr

Anne Carr too rejects a patriarchal model of the Church that focuses on authority and obedience in favor of an egalitarian model similar to that of Elisabeth Schüssler Fiorenza and Elizabeth Johnson.[157] Carr uses the women's ordination issue to make her point about the contrasting ecclesiologies in the Church today. Those who oppose women's ordination to the priesthood "hold a 'high church,' hierarchical, sacramental view in which ... the priesthood of the laity is sharply distinct from the ordained priesthood." The latter represents God or Christ "as masculine and active in relation to the community as feminine or receptive." Those in favor of women's ordination "stress the more biblical, community aspect of the church, and the one priesthood of all believers through baptism. For them, ministry represents the entire community before God and thus symbolically includes both men and women."[158] Carr places herself clearly with the proponents of women's ordination, and for the ecclesiological reasons given.

Rosemary Radford Ruether

Rosemary Radford Ruether's *Women-Church*[159] also follows an approach similar to Schüssler Fiorenza's, which underscores the latter's considerable impact on Catholic theology after 1983. For Ruether, Women-Church is a feminist countercultural movement and an exodus community that is called to abandon the established social order. It is not enough, she insists, to press for change in the Church. "One needs communities of nurture to guide one through death to the old symbolic order of patriarchy to rebirth into a new community of being and living. . . . One also needs deep symbols and symbolic actions to guide and interpret the actual experience of the journey from sexism to liberated humanity."[160] Women-Church, she writes, "means neither leaving the church as a sectarian group, nor continuing to fit into it on its terms. It means establishing bases for a feminist critical culture and celebrational community that have some autonomy from the established institutions."[161]

Mary Hines

Notwithstanding her strong criticisms of Roman Catholicism's "overly institutional ecclesiology," especially prior to Vatican II, Mary Hines celebrates the council's emphasis on the Church as a *communio,* its retrieval of the biblical image of the People of God, and its more open, dialogical approach to the world.[162] "A critical feminist theology of the church," she writes, "can find a more serviceable ecclesial starting point in Vatican II's contextualization of the church's institutional dimensions within its primary understanding of the church as the community of God's people journeying in history toward ultimate fulfillment in the realm of God."[163] Mary Hines is especially supportive of the work of Rosemary Ruether on the notion of Women-Church, but also of Karl Rahner, particularly with regard to his openness toward a wider spectrum of ecclesial images, his emphasis on the local church, and his conceptualization of the Church as a world-Church. But here again, the influence and impact of the writings of Elisabeth Schüssler Fiorenza manifest themselves, particularly in Hines's embrace of her understanding of the Church as a "community of equal disciples."[164] A feminist ecclesiology, Hines concludes, incorporates the "experience of women so that the church may truly become a community of liberation for all humanity."[165]

NONFEMINIST ECCLESIOLOGIES

Here again we can only offer a sample, not a comprehensive list, of women theologians who have specialized in ecclesiology. In this section, however, there are two representatives, Susan K. Wood and Sara Butler, who tend to approach ecclesiological questions from different perspectives. What they have in common is that each approaches ecclesiological questions without a traditionally feminist perspective. Sara Butler, however, claims to be working out of a "new feminist" perspective advocated and approved by Pope John Paul II.

Susan K. Wood

Susan Wood did her doctoral dissertation at Marquette University in 1986 on the ecclesiology of Henri de Lubac (d. 1991), a version of which was subsequently published as *Spiritual Exegesis and the Church in the Theology of Henri de Lubac.*[166] She has also written and edited books on the priesthood, both lay and ordained.[167] In her articles she has tended to focus also on the Church as a communion.[168] Her views on the basic elements of an ecclesiology of communion are fairly standard—particularly with regard to the relationship between the universal Church and the local churches, the nature of collegiality, and the eucharistic dimension of communion. She is included here in our survey because her views on the Church as a communion do not in any apparent way reflect distinctively feminist concerns (for our previous discussion of the Church as a communion in this part, see page 278). With regard to the debate between then Cardinal Ratzinger (and others) and Cardinal Kasper (and others) on the precise relationship between the universal and local churches, Wood argues for "the need to maintain a balance between the two. . . . Ultimately, it is not a question of one over and against the other, for the universal Church is the communion of particular churches. The tension remains."[169]

Sara Butler

In her contribution to the collection *The Gift of the Church*, entitled "Women and the Church,"[170] Sister Sara Butler, a member of the Missionary Servants of the Most Blessed Trinity, provides an overview of various types of feminism and indicates the Church's official critical assessment of each: the "first wave" of modern feminism (socialist, liberal, and cultural); the "second wave" (incorporating the "revival" of the three forms of modern feminism, plus "radical feminism" in which she seems to include such authors as Anne Carr and Elisabeth Schüssler Fiorenza); and finally the "new feminism" proposed by Pope John Paul II in his 1995 encyclical *Evangelium vitae* (Lat., "The gospel of life"), n. 99, and in the same year his "Letter to Women."[171] The "new feminism" advocates economic, political, and social equality for women, but at the same time defends life at every stage of development, acknowledges that women, by the will of Christ, cannot aspire to be ordained to the priesthood, and embraces the values of premarital chastity, motherhood, unpaid work in the home, volunteerism, and solidarity with the poor.[172]

Hispanic and Latino/a Ecclesiologies

Even though serious questions have been raised concerning the historicity of the Guadalupe event and of Juan Diego, the now canonized chief witness to it, the cult of Our Lady of Guadalupe[173] has had some important ecclesiological implications.[174] Key interpreters have referred to it as a "Church-founding event."[175] The many devotional consequences are expressive of the Church's self-understanding as People of God.[176] Theologian Virgilio Elizondo makes the point that, although the story of Guadalupe is typically associated with the conversion of the Indians, the real converts of the narrative are the skeptical bishop and his household:

"theologians, catechists, liturgists, canonists and others."[177] For Elizondo, "The beginning of this great miracle was that the bishop finally came to listen to the voice and call of the poor, ridiculed, crushed, and often ignored."[178] Guadalupe's message converts the Church to the service of the poor, the colonized, and the ostracized. And then, just as Juan Diego is said to have been sent by the Virgin, the entire Church is sent out to the margins of society. The apostolic thrust of the Guadalupan story calls to mind the apostolic character of the Church itself.

For all Hispanics, but especially for Mexicans, "no other popular religious devotion is as closely linked to a people's self-identity, or socio-historical context," theologian Roberto Goizueta points out, "as is the Mexican devotion to Our Lady of Guadalupe."[179] His understanding of the authentic community as being both constitutive of identity and the nexus of true freedom describes what the Church as People of God could truly be.[180]

Ada María Isasi-Díaz echoes some of the same themes in her writings.[181] She sees her own work as an integral part of Latin American liberation theology (see Part VI.6), but one that addresses the plight of women. A *mujerista* (Sp., "feminist") approach to theology, liturgy, and the life of the Church generally must ground its reflections in the experience of working-class Hispanic women, whom she argues experience the Church as more Marian than Christological.[182] Her emphasis on liturgy brings out the active role that women assume in planning and executing ritual. The communal exercise of the liturgy enables women to establish themselves as subjects, as agents in control of their destiny, in the midst of a culture that seeks to make them invisible, on the margins of society. *Mujerista* liturgy relocates the sacred to the world of the margins "instead of the institutional Churches that often do little or nothing to be in solidarity with Hispanic women's struggle for liberation."[183] It takes the power of the Church from the center of society to the margins. In so doing, this liturgy subverts patriarchy's hold on society. The relocating of sacred space reinforces the notion of solidarity with the marginalized that is a central part of the mission of the Church.[184]

Natalia Imperatori-Lee summarizes the Hispanic-Latino/a ecclesiological perspective well: "Because Guadalupe is in solidarity with those who suffer, she points the way for the rest of the Church: where the poor are the Church should be too. Mexican-Americans celebrate the accompaniment and permanence of Guadalupe's presence with their community. In the same way, the Church [is] called to be, and remain, in solidarity with those on the margins."[185]

African and African American Ecclesiologies

African and African American theologies are often identified simply as black theology. Since it is statistically the case that most African Americans are Protestant, it is not surprising that there is a relative dearth of Catholic writings on ecclesiology within the African American community. Indeed, Christopher O'Donnell observed in the mid-1990s that "black theology is only slowly being accepted within Catholicism," even though Pope Paul VI had said to the African Catholic community in 1969, "You must now give your gifts of Blackness to the whole Church."[186] Two religious women are among the most productive: Diana L. Hayes and Jamie T. Phelps.[187] Edward K. Braxton authored two books on the Church, one in 1980 and another in 1990, but he was later appointed a bishop in 1995 and was unable to continue his scholarly publications.[188] Notwithstanding the limited number of samples of African American ecclesiologies, it is important to include them in this broader survey in order to remind readers that the global, multicultural Church is also multiracial.

As already suggested in Part VI.6, black theology has a liberationist emphasis for obvious historical, social, economic, and political reasons. "In the formative experience of slavery, blacks found the white Churches to be the institutions of the slavemasters, whereas their God was found in story, song, and prayer."[189] The key figure in the American civil rights movement was Martin Luther King Jr. (d. 1968), who held a doctorate in theology from Boston University. Although he functioned mainly as a pastor and a civil rights activist, Dr. King's ecclesiology could be reduced to the metaphor "a drum major for justice," which he had applied to himself in a sermon delivered in Detroit.[190] The first major African American theologian after Vatican II was James H. Cone, like Dr. King a Protestant, who authored such liberation-oriented books as *A Black Theology of Liberation, God of the Oppressed,* and *Risks of Faith: The Emergence of a Black Theology of Liberation.*[191] A less controversial theologian, but no less prolific, is J. Deotis Roberts, also a Protestant.[192]

Black theology soon took root in Africa itself, where the ecclesiological emphasis was on the Church as family, but not without a liberationist perspective, especially in South Africa.[193] Black ecclesiology overall is taken into account in a broadly ecumenical survey by Veli-Matti Käikkäinen, *An Introduction to Ecclesiology: Ecumenical, Historical and Global Perspectives.*[194]

New Movements in the Church

While religious communities of men and women alike have been undergoing a process of recovery of their respective missions, there have emerged, in one of the most remarkable developments in the post–Vatican II Catholic Church, various new, largely lay movements. Most of them tend to be conservative or traditional in their theology, spirituality, and pastoral practices. They have been referred to by sympathetic observers as agents of the so-called new evangelization in the Church.[195] They include Opus Dei, the Legion (or Legionaries) of Christ, Communion and Liberation (its Italian name is *Comunione e Liberazione*), the Neo-Catechumenate (also known as the Neocatechumenal Way), the Focolare movement, and the Community of Sant'Egidio, which is the exception to the rule of conservatism.

Opus Dei (Lat., "The Work of God") was founded in Spain in 1928 by Father Josemaría Escrivá de Balaguer (d. 1975) to promote sanctity among lay members through their daily work. In 1982 it was made a personal prelature, that is, an ecclesiastically erected society governed by its own statutes and presided over by a prelate, usually a bishop, as its own proper Ordinary, with the right to establish seminaries, incardinate the seminarians in the society, and promote them to Holy Orders. The society enjoyed special favor during the pontificate of

John Paul II, who beatified Escrivá in 1992 and then canonized him ten years later. The organization, which has upwards of a hundred thousand members worldwide, has been controversial because of its allegedly aggressive activities within the Church, pushing conservative religious and political causes, and for its alleged penchant for secrecy and cultlike practices.[196]

The Legion of Christ, also known as the Legionaries of Christ, was founded in Mexico in 1941 by Father Marcial Maciel Degollado (d. 2008). The organization consists of priests and seminarians who describe themselves as committed to experiencing and knowing Christ in the gospel, the Eucharist, and the cross. Laypersons (as well as other priests and religious) may join its closely allied organization, Regnum Christi (Lat., "Reign of Christ"), also founded by Father Maciel. The Legion suffers from complaints similar to those leveled against Opus Dei. In May 2006 Father Maciel was formally prohibited by the Congregation for the Doctrine of the Faith, with the approval of Pope Benedict XVI, from exercising a public ministry in the Church because of credible allegations of sexual abuse committed against several individuals in earlier years.[197]

Communion and Liberation (It., *Comunione et Liberazione*) was founded in Italy in 1954 by Father Luigi Giussani (d. 2005), who left his position as a seminary professor in Milan to work with young people as a high-school teacher. In its early Italian phase, the movement was identified with conservative politics and anti-Communism and provoked distrust and criticism from some of Italy's bishops. As it became more international in scope, however, it also shifted its focus to charitable and educational work. It is predominantly lay in membership, but includes priests and religious. Like Opus Dei and the Legion of Christ, it flourished during the pontificate of John Paul II.

The Neo-Catechumenate (or Neocatechumenal Way) was founded in 1967 by Kiki Arguello and Carmen Hernandez, Spanish laypersons, ostensibly to promote the renewal initiated by Vatican II. However, the organization moved in a more conservative and independent direction and in the process ran afoul of many bishops. Although the movement enjoyed general support during John Paul II's pontificate, the Vatican withheld formal approbation of its statutes because of their ambiguity regarding the status of its priest-members and of the relations between the organization and local bishops. Tensions have arisen in some dioceses over its catechetical methods and its sometimes disruptive and divisive impact on parish communities. As in the case of the previously mentioned movements, the Neo-Catechumenate has also sometimes been accused of mind control in the formation and retention of its members.

Focolare (It., "fireplace") was founded in 1943 by Chiara Lubich (d. 2008) in Trent, Italy, and won formal Vatican approval in 1962. Focolare has a number of branches throughout the world, which include celibates, lay and clerical, and married persons. Its general purpose is to change the world through the observance of gospel principles and to work toward the world's unity. It has a strong, pre–Vatican II Marian spirituality.[198]

The Community of Sant'Egidio was founded in Rome in 1968 by a group of high-school students led by Andrea Riccardi. They took the name of Sant'Egidio parish (Eng. "St. Giles") in the Trastevere section of the city, where they had their first meeting place. The group is devoted to common prayer, which is inspired by the Bible, and work on behalf of the needy, especially the poor, the elderly, the homeless, and those with AIDS. It is also committed to ecumenical and interfaith reconciliation and is particularly involved in efforts to bring peace to troubled parts of the world, for which the group has received various international awards and been nominated by the Italian Parliament for a Nobel Peace Prize. Although not a political movement, the community is more liberal than the aforementioned groups in its approach to public-policy issues, such as capital punishment.[199]

Of course, other movements have existed in the Church before and after Vatican II, but they have not pursued a conservative religious or political course and, therefore, have not enjoyed the special approbation and support—in varying degrees, to be sure—that the first five above experienced during the pontificate of John Paul II. By way of example only: the Cursillo (Sp., "Little course") movement, founded in Spain around 1949, which sponsors seminars designed to recommit participants to Christian ideals; L'Arche (Fr., "Ark") communities for the handicapped, founded by Jean Vanier in 1964; the Legion of Mary, founded by Frank Duff (d. 1980) in Dublin, Ireland, to reclaim lapsed Catholics and to provide a lay spirituality for its members; Marriage Encounter, founded by Father Gabriel Calvo in Spain in the early 1960s and moving soon after to the United States; and the Christian Family Movement (CFM), a lay couples' social action movement, founded by Patrick (d. 1974) and Patricia (d. 2005) Crowley, that uses Belgian cardinal Joseph Cardijn's (d. 1967) "observe-judge-act" method of Catholic Action, which he incorporated into the Young Christian Workers organization, which he himself had founded in 1925.

This second group of "movements" are to be distinguished from organizations that have a similar preponderance of lay members, such as Call to Action or Voice of the Faithful, based mainly in the United States and Canada, which sponsor conventions, conferences, and individual lectures at the national, regional, and diocesan levels. They neither require nor have sought official ecclesiastical approval. On the contrary, they have been prohibited in some dioceses from using church facilities for their meetings.

Call to Action promotes the ongoing renewal and reforms initiated by Vatican II and was inspired originally by the conference of the same name that was conducted in 1976 under the auspices of the National Conference of Catholic Bishops (now the United States Conference of Catholic Bishops) in Detroit, Michigan. Voice of the Faithful represented at first an ad hoc response to the sexual-abuse scandal in the priesthood that erupted with singular force in January 2002, but has continued as a formal organization to support victims of sexual abuse by priests, to support priests of integrity, and to shape structural change within the Church, including financial management. The organization has been controversial because some bishops see its third purpose as tantamount to challenging the very structures of the Church that, in their minds, have been personally determined by the Lord himself (see Part II of this book, regarding the beginnings of the Church in the New Testament period).

Christopher O'Donnell's concluding observation about these various movements is judiciously balanced: "Given the diversity of movements, it is not possible to make a specific evaluation. In general one must acknowledge that they are a powerful work of the Spirit in this age; each one has one or several notable charisms. But being human, they can have distortions or deviations." Consequently, they need careful supervision "to ensure that they remain within the wider communion of the Church and its mission, and that they remain healthy from both a psychological and spiritual point of view."[200]

There is at least one other form of ecclesial community that deserves mention here, namely, base (or basic) Christian communities, perhaps better known by their original Spanish name, *communidades ecclesiales de base.*[201] In the United States the comparable term is "small Christian communities."[202] Although the term "base Christian communities" can be applied to many kinds of Christian-based groups among the poor, the term conventionally describes the small, Scripture-centered reflection-and-action groups among the poor in Latin America. Unlike the first five movements listed above (Opus Dei, the Legion of Christ, Communion and Liberation, the Neo-Catechumenate, and Focolare), these base communities are not conservative in their religious or political orientation. On the contrary, they represent efforts to put liberation theology (see Part VI.6) into practice, especially in its outreach to the poor and the powerless. There are said to be some eighty thousand such communities operating in Brazil, the world's most populous Catholic nation.[203]

Ecclesiologically, base communities are eucharistic communities within the Church, not simply discussion or political action groups. Their members pray together, minister to one another inside and outside their small communities, and collaborate in works of justice and charity. The Second Conference of Latin American Bishops (CELAM) at Medellín, Colombia, spoke positively of them as "the first and fundamental ecclesiastical nucleus," which "becomes then the initial cell of the ecclesiastical structures and the focus of evangelization."[204] The Extraordinary Synod of Bishops in 1985 did likewise in its Final Report: "Because the church is communion, the new 'basic communities,' if they truly live in unity with the church, are a true expression of communion and a means for the construction of a more profound communion. They are thus cause for great hope for the life of the church."[205]

The Emerging World-Church

Although others have referred to and written about the emergence of a world-Church around the time of the Second Vatican Council in the early 1960s, no theologian has been more explicitly identified with the concept than Karl Rahner, perhaps the greatest Catholic theologian of the twentieth century. As suggested earlier, in Part V.5, no theological essay published in the aftermath of Vatican II was more influential in identifying the historical and theological significance of that council than Karl Rahner's "Basic Theological Interpretation of the Second Vatican Council."[206] He suggests therein that the council marked "the beginning of a tentative approach by the Church to the discovery and official realization of itself as *world-Church*."[207] He points out that, although there were episcopal representatives of churches in Asia and Africa at the First Vatican Council in the nineteenth century (see Part V.5), these bishops were, in almost every case, missionary bishops of European or American origin. There were relatively few native hierarchies throughout the Catholic world during the decades leading up to Vatican II. At the beginning of Pius XI's pontificate (1922), for example, there were no mission dioceses under the direction of a native bishop. Upon the pope's death in 1939, there were forty such dioceses. "Vatican II," Rahner writes, "was really a first assembly of the world-episcopate such as had not hitherto existed."[208]

Rahner also challenges the traditional division of Western church history into antiquity, the Middle Ages, and modern times, as noted previously in Part V. He divides church history instead into three great epochs: first, a short period of Judaeo-Christianity, ending with the so-called Council of Jerusalem (ca. 49/50), described in Acts 15, when the early Church became for the first time a Church of the Gentiles; second, the period (ca. 50–1962) in which the Church adapted itself to Hellenistic and then European culture and civilization; and, third, the period (from 1962) in which the Church is no longer confined by traditional Church-world boundaries. As indicated before, in this third epoch the Church *began to become* a true world-Church.[209] Dividing one epoch from another are, Rahner suggests, caesurae, breaks created by highly significant, nonrepeatable happenings or events, namely, the Council of Jerusalem and Vatican II. To repeat his crucially important point: Rahner's original and highly influential thesis is that "today we are for the first time living again in a period of caesura like that involved in the transition from Judaeo-Christianity to Gentile Christianity . . . when the Church ceased to be the Church of the Jews and became the Church of the Gentiles."[210]

Consequently, if Western Christianity refuses to take the risk of "a really new beginning," it will remain an exclusively Western Church "and thus in the last resort [will] betray the meaning of Vatican II."[211]

The main consequence of Rahner's insight has been that the Church now more fully recognizes itself as a global, multicultural community, and that its theology, particularly its ecclesiology, is being reshaped accordingly (see Part I.4, on the interfaith dimensions of the Church; Part VI.2, on the Church-world relationship; and Part VI.3.1, on the Church and non-Christians). No ecclesiological work underscores that point more emphatically than Roger Haight's three-volume opus *Christian Community in History*.[212] To be sure, the world travels of Pope Paul VI and especially of Pope John Paul II also contributed significantly to this new global consciousness.

Brief Summation

Part VII has looked closely at the internal life of the Church (*Ecclesia ad intra*) to examine its nature as a community; the way in which authority is exercised at various levels in that community; the process by which official teachings and decrees are received and implemented—or not; the means by which the church community fulfills its mission through its many and varied ministries, ordained and nonordained alike; an excursus on the sacramental and liturgical life of the community; the role of Mary and Marian devotions in the Church, with special emphasis on the connection between Mariology and ecclesiology; and the experiences and perceptions of women in the Church, as reflected especially, but not at all exclusively, in feminist and nonfeminist ecclesiology by Catholic women; Hispanic and Latino/a ecclesiologies; African and African American ecclesiologies; the function and impact of "new movements" in the Church, often self-described as expressions and instruments of the "new evangelization"; and the emerging world-Church, a term coined by Karl Rahner, which underscores the fundamental shift, especially since just before Vatican II, from a largely Eurocentric Church to one that is self-consciously global, multiethnic, multiracial, and multicultural.

Part VIII offers a synthesis of the ecclesiology developed throughout this book and proposes pastoral criteria, drawn from that ecclesiology, that might guide and shape the future of the Church and its ecclesiologies throughout this twenty-first century and the beginnings of the third Christian millennium.

PART VIII

The Future of the Church and Its Ecclesiologies

This final part of the book consists of three sections. The first synthesizes the book's main ecclesiological elements. The second offers a set of ten pastoral applications that can be drawn from this synthesis and from other points made throughout the book. And the third provides a brief reflection on the future of the Church and its ecclesiologies.[1]

Synthesis of the Book

BASIC CONCEPTS

Ecclesiology Defined

"Ecclesiology" (derived from two Greek words, *ekklesia* and *logos*) is literally the study of the Church. To be sure, many other disciplines study the Church, for example, history, anthropology, political science, sociology, and philosophy. Ecclesiology is the *theological* study of the Church, which is to say that it studies the Church as a mystery, or sacrament.

The late Pope Paul VI (1963–78), in his address to the opening of the second session of the Second Vatican Council (1962–63) on September 29, 1963, declared: "The Church is a mystery. It is a reality imbued with the hidden presence of God. It lies, therefore, within the very nature of the Church to be always open to new and greater exploration."

To view the Church as a mystery, or sacrament, is to see it not simply as a religious community, institution, or movement (although it is all of these and more), but as the corporate, communal presence of the triune God in the world. The Church is a mystery, or sacrament, because the triune God is present and redemptively active in it on humankind's and the world's spiritual and material behalf.

The Church Defined

The Church, which is the object of ecclesiology's study, is the community of those who confess the lordship of Jesus (that he is "the way, the truth, and the life"—John 14:6) and who strive to live their lives in accordance with his example and teachings. The Church is also known as the People of God, the Body of Christ, and the Temple of the Holy Spirit as well as by other names. The first three titles, however, accentuate the trinitarian context for an understanding of the Church, a context that is also employed by Vatican II's Dogmatic Constitution on the Church (nn. 2–4).

A more detailed definition of the Church, embraced by the Church's greatest ecclesiologist, Yves Congar, himself, describes the Church as "the whole body, or congregation, of persons who are called by God the Father to acknowledge the Lordship of Jesus, the Son, in word, in sacrament, in witness, and in service, and, through the power of the Holy Spirit, to collaborate with Jesus' historic mission for the sake of the Kingdom of God."[2] Indeed, as Vatican II's Pastoral Constitution on the Church expresses it: "The church has but one sole purpose—that the kingdom of God may come and the salvation of the human race may be accomplished" (n. 45).

Of course, the question whether Jesus actually intended to "found" the Church remains centrally important. Although he did not found the Church according to any preconceived organizational "blueprint," he did gather disciples and establish a table fellowship with the mandate that the Apostles and other disciples continue to gather for it. The Church today is a self-described "community of disciples," and the Eucharist is at the heart of its life and mission.

The above definition of the Church embraces in principle all Christians: Catholics, Orthodox, Anglicans, Protestants, and non-Orthodox Eastern Christians alike. In other words, there is "the Church" and there are also "Churches." This is not to say, however, that all Christian faith communities fully satisfy the criteria implied in the definition. To the extent that they do, they are recognized by the Catholic Church as "Churches." If they do not meet all of these criteria, official documents of the Catholic Church refer to them as "ecclesial communities," a term one finds in the title of and throughout chapter 3 of Vatican II's Decree on Ecumenism (nn. 19–24).

Indeed, the Congregation for the Doctrine of the Faith in July 2007 restricted the use of the term "Church" to the Catholic Church and what it referred to as "the Oriental churches separated from full communion with the Catholic Church." The ecclesiological criteria that the CDF used were the possession of "true sacraments and above all—because of apostolic succession—the priesthood and the Eucharist."[3] According to this line of thinking, the Anglican Communion and all Protestant denominations fail to qualify, in spite of the fact that Pope Paul VI referred to Anglicans as a "sister Church."[4] Indeed, the CDF document explicitly excluded from the designation of "Churches" all of the Christian communities "born out of the Reformation of the 16th century" because they "do not enjoy apostolic succession in the sacrament of orders and are therefore deprived of a constitutive element of the church." The document continues: "These ecclesial communities that, specifically because of the absence if the sacramental priesthood, have not preserved the genuine and integral substance of the eucharistic mystery cannot, according to Catholic doctrine, be called *churches* in the proper sense."[5] As should be evident from the pertinent discussions throughout this book, the CDF's restrictive understanding of the scope of the Church is not shared by many Catholic theologians and bishops, nor was it the clear and unambiguous teaching of the Second Vatican Council itself.

To be Catholic—whether Roman (Latin-rite) or non-Roman (non-Latin-rite)—is to be in full communion with the Bishop of Rome and as such an integral part of the Catholic Communion of Churches. But it is not a matter of either/or—either one is in communion with the Bishop of Rome or one is not. The council implicitly set aside the univocal category of *membership* and replaced it with the notion of *degrees of communion*. As in a family, there are degrees of relationships: parents, siblings, aunts, uncles, cousins, nephews, nieces, in-laws. In many cultures, the notion of family is much broader than blood and/or legal relationships. In Chinese culture, for example, individuals are designated as aunts and uncles as an expression of respect and affection, even though technically no blood or marital relationships exist. Even in U.S. Caucasian culture, there is increasing acceptance of what sociologists refer to as the "extended family" or alternate family structures. This broader sociological understanding of the nature of a family also analogously applies to our understanding of the dimensions of the Church.

The distinction between the Church and the Churches (or ecclesial communities), however, is not only ecumenical. There is also a distinction between the "universal Church" and the "local church." The noun "Church" refers at once to the whole Body of Christ and to the whole People of God as well as to the individual congregation of Christians in a parish or a diocese, for example. The universal Catholic Church is itself a communion of local churches, known as dioceses and patriarchates, and of Roman and non-Roman Churches. The universal ecumenical Church is a communion of Churches and ecclesial communities (also known as denominations), and they, in turn, consist of a communion of local churches or congregations within each Church or ecclesial community.

The Content and Scope of the Church's Mission

The mission of the Church, at every level of its existence, is for the sake of the Kingdom, or Reign, of God. That mission of evangelization is fourfold: word, sacrament (or worship), witness, and service.[6]

The Church is "sent" (the root meaning of the Latin word *missio*) to confess and proclaim that Jesus is "the way, the truth, and the life"

(John 14:6). It does this through preaching and teaching in a variety of forms, whether through the official teaching by bishops, the teaching rooted in scholarship by theologians, the formation of adults, children, and converts by religious educators (catechists) and other pastoral ministers, or the teaching of children carried out by parents and other caregivers.

Second, the Church's mission includes its whole sacramental and devotional life, at the center of which is the Eucharist, the "summit" and the "source" of the Church's life (Constitution on the Sacred Liturgy, n. 10). Indeed, the Church itself is a sacrament (Dogmatic Constitution on the Church, n. 1).

Third, the Church has been "sent" to give witness to the validity of Christ's teachings and his own personal example of how one should live a fully human life generally and of Christian discipleship particularly. The Church, therefore, has a missionary obligation to practice what it preaches and teaches, in fulfillment of the principle of sacramentality.

Finally, the Church exists to share its own limited material resources to assist the poor, the sick, the socially marginalized, and others in need of aid of any kind (Luke 4:18–21). This activity encompasses the whole of what was once commonly called the "social apostolate" of the Church. It includes not only direct assistance to individuals, but also involvement in institutional and systemic change for the sake of social justice, human rights, and peace.

The Kingdom, or Reign, of God Defined

The Kingdom, or Reign, of God, for which the Church is "sent" and which was at the heart and center of Jesus's preaching and ministry (Mark 1:15), is the redemptive presence of God actualized through the power of God's reconciling Spirit. The Holy Spirit is the active, incarnate power of love by which human beings, their communities, and the world at large are healed, renewed, and brought to the fullness of perfection. In brief, God "reigns" wherever and whenever God's will is acknowledged and fulfilled.

Like Christ himself, the Church exists for the sake of the Kingdom of God, not vice versa. The Kingdom, not the Church, is at the center of the history of salvation and is the ultimate hope and destiny of the whole human race. The Church is not itself the Kingdom of God on earth, but is "the seed and the beginning" of it in history (Dogmatic Constitution on the Church, n. 5). The Church is its "sign and instrument" in the world, that is, "of communion with God and of the unity of the entire human race" (n. 1).

Basic Structures in Service of Mission

In the earliest years of its existence, the Church had no uniform structural organization to carry out its mission for the sake of the Kingdom of God. Each local church developed its own organizational accommodations to its pastoral situation and needs. There was no radical opposition between the institutional and charismatic models that one finds in the New Testament, notwithstanding their wide diversity. Whatever offices existed were always for the sake of service, never for domination or control. Although the Petrine ministry was in the service of the unity of the whole Church, it was never a monarchical office in the modern political sense of the word.

The great structural diversity that one finds among the local churches of the New Testament period developed over the course of several decades. The communities influenced by Paul at first had minimal structural forms. After the Church's original leaders had died and the city of Jerusalem and the Temple had been destroyed, there was considerable structural adaptation to the newer pastoral challenges—a process believed (especially in Luke-Acts) to have been guided always by the Holy Spirit. The pastoral Letters, 1–2 Timothy and Titus, on the other hand, were addressed to threats to unity from "false teachers" and consequently stressed the need for pastoral authority. By contrast, the Johannine communities showed little interest in church offices, as did the communities of the post-Pauline Letters to the Ephesians and the Colossians, where the model is the "ideal Church," that is, the Body of Christ and the spotless Bride. The early Church eventually adopted, for the most part, the organizational grid of the Roman Empire, some elements of which hindered rather than facilitated the missionary work of the Church.

In the second and third Christian millennia, there was a divergence of structural forms in the Catholic Church. The Church in the West became increasingly a papal Church, with monarchical overtones, in the Middle Ages and especially after the First Vatican Council (1869–70), while the Church in the East—Catholic and Orthodox alike—retained more deliberately the patriarchal, synodal, and conciliar structures of church governance and pastoral practice.

THE HISTORY OF ECCLESIOLOGY AND THE HISTORY OF THE CHURCH

It is important to note that the history of *ecclesiology* is not coextensive with the history of *the Church,* even though there is much overlapping between the two. Both, to be sure, cover an enormous amount of biblical, historical, theological, doctrinal, social scientific, and other material. The process of incorporation of such data is inevitably selective.

Although there have been many different ecclesiological interpretations of the nature, mission, ministries, and structural operations of the Church from the very beginning of its existence, Yves Congar reminds us that "up to about the year 1300 . . . there was no treatise expressly dealing with the Church."[7] However, once ecclesiology developed as a separate area of specialization within the theological enterprise, it has been primarily interested in ideas about the Church. But, like church history, ecclesiology is also concerned about persons and events insofar as they illuminate, explain, and embody the ideas of the Church that have influenced and shaped its thinking and actions throughout its entire existence.

Thus, the history of ecclesiology is not so much focused on the *content* of the Gregorian reform of the eleventh century as it is on the *idea* of the Church that informed and shaped it. One could substitute any number of topics for the Gregorian reform: multiple conflicts between Church and state over the course of many centuries, the East-West Schism beginning in the eleventh century, the Protestant Reformation and the Catholic Counter-Reformation of the sixteenth century, the founding and growth of the major religious orders from the eleventh century on, the emergence of papal absolutism in the Middle Ages and its reemergence at the First Vatican Council, the anti-Modernist reaction during the pontificate of Pius X (1903–14), and the renewal and reform movements—biblical, liturgical, ecumenical, and social—of the first half of the twentieth century, which together laid the foundations for Vatican II (see Parts III and IV).

MODERN ECCLESIOLOGY

The Catholic Church had adopted an increasingly defensive stance toward the world beginning especially in the sixteenth century. Its hierarchy reacted in large part to the various challenges posed by the Reformation, but to other social, economic, political, and cultural developments as well. Catholicism began to stress even more the juridical and institutional aspects of the Church, especially during its own Counter-Reformation. With the First Vatican Council in the nineteenth century and its teaching on papal primacy and papal infallibility, emphasis on the office and person of the pope became more and more pronounced, reaching its highest point in modern history in the pontificate of Pius XII (1939–58).

There are two main reasons why this neo-Scholastic, pyramidal ecclesiology, with the pope at the top, the laity at the bottom, and bishops, priests, and religious in between, has been giving way in recent decades, albeit not without resistance (as pointed out in I.8 and several other locations throughout the book), to a communal, broadly participatory notion of the Church, marked by an openness to dialogue with various constituencies. The two factors that best explain this development are, first, the retrieval and progressive absorption, beginning in the 1940s with the encouragement of Pius XII's 1943 encyclical *Divino afflante Spiritu* (Lat., "Inspired by the divine Spirit"), of historico-critical New Testament studies, especially as they apply to the beginnings of the Church; and, second, the major impact and lasting influence of the Second Vatican Council.

Modern New Testament studies challenged one of the principal ecclesiological assumptions of the first half of the twentieth century, namely, that Jesus left a detailed blueprint according to which the Church was to organize itself, both internally and for its mission to the world. Those studies, in turn, made a significant impact on Vatican II itself. The Church, which was the council's central topic, began to be viewed now in the light of the Bible, and especially the New Testament, rather than the abstract categories of neo-Scholasticism: as the People of God, the Body of Christ, and the Temple of the Holy Spirit among other biblical images. The Church was also seen as a mystery or sacrament and as a servant—an agent of justice and peace in the world and of aid to, and advocacy for, the poor and the powerless.

Parts VI and VII have shown in some detail how and to what extent post–Vatican II theology and the official teachings of the Church have carried forward and developed further the Church's newly retrieved dialogical stance toward the world and its renewed emphasis on the communal and participatory nature of its ecclesial life.

THE CHURCH *AD EXTRA* AND THE CHURCH *AD INTRA*

Toward the end of the first session of Vatican II, in one of the most important speeches of the entire council, Cardinal Leo Jozef Suenens, then archbishop of Malines-Brussels in Belgium, formally introduced, with the approval of Pope John XXIII (1958–63), the now famous distinction between the Church *ad extra* and the Church *ad intra* in describing the council's overall agenda. The Church *ad extra* is concerned with the relationship of the Church, and specifically the Catholic Communion of Churches, to realities external to it, without prejudice to the inevitable overlapping of the two spheres, *ad extra* and *ad intra*. The Church *ad intra* is concerned with the internal life of the Church, but again without prejudice to the inevitable overlapping of the two spheres.

Vatican II's Pastoral Constitution on the Church in the Modern World is the cornerstone for the council's reflections on various issues pertaining to the Church *ad extra*. Vatican II's Dogmatic Constitution on the Church anchors the council's considerations of various issues pertaining to the Church *ad intra*. Both documents together—not separately, much less in opposition to one another—represent the ecclesiological mind of the Second Vatican Council. They have also generated most of the major topics in post–Vatican II ecclesiology, and they frame the discussions of each, as we have seen in Parts VI and VII.

Ten Pastoral Applications

1. The Church should never regard itself—at the parish, diocesan, national, regional, patriarchal, or international levels—as an end in itself (Dogmatic Constitution on the Church, n. 5). It exists not for its own sake, but in service of the Kingdom, or Reign, of God, and in fulfillment of its fourfold mission in relation to the Kingdom:

First, to preach and teach the gospel of Jesus Christ, which requires the best-qualified preachers and teachers as to theological education, spiritual formation, and personal health, not only physical but also psychological.

Second, to celebrate the sacraments, especially the Eucharist, in an intelligible, engaging, and spiritually fruitful manner, encouraging the full and active participation of everyone present at these rituals. The Eucharist in particular is the key manifestation of what the Church is and how and for whom it organizes itself for mission.[8] Alas, it also bears the marks and tensions of the divisions that have fractured the unity of the worldwide Church since the East-West Schism, beginning in the eleventh century, and the Reformation of the sixteenth. Thus, the call to "full and active participation" in the Eucharist is directed first to Catholics; but, given a broader, ecumenical understanding of the Church, eucharistic sharing, or intercommunion, needs also to be seriously considered (see Part VI.3.3.d).

Third, to commit itself without compromise to ongoing renewal and reform, again at every level, so that the Church will appear to others to be what it is in the eyes of faith, namely, the People of God, the Body of Christ, and the Temple of the Holy Spirit—in sum, a mystery and a sacrament of the triune God.

Fourth, to employ whatever limited resources it has, at whatever level and in as effective and generous a fashion as possible, for the sake of those in need of any kind.

2. The Church is not a sect, closed in on itself as a righteous minority, bearing the promise of salvation for those willing to subject themselves to it. It is part of a larger Christian community of communities—Anglican, Orthodox, Protestant, and separated non-Orthodox Eastern Christians alike. Just as the Catholic Church in particular must reach out to other Churches and ecclesial communities (and they, to one another) in the Body of Christ, so the Church must be open to dialogue and collaboration with other religions, especially but not exclusively Judaism, and with the worldwide human community as well.

Although Jesus Christ is the way, the truth, and the life for all, God wills the salvation of all without requiring that everyone confess Jesus as Lord and Savior and accept sacramental Baptism and formal membership in the Church. "Not everyone who says to me, 'Lord, Lord,' will enter the kingdom of heaven, but only the one who does the will of my Father in heaven" (Matt. 7:21). Sectarianism, of both Protestant and Catholic kinds, remains one of the most serious threats to the integrity of the Church and to its call to be truly *catholic* in the fullest sense of the word.

3. The content of Catholic social teaching is an integral part of the Church's mission. Indeed, as Pope John Paul II (1978-2005) insisted in his 1991 encyclical *Centesimus annus* (Lat., "The hundredth year"), that teaching, stretching back to the pontificate of Leo XIII (1878–1903), "pertains to the church's evangelizing mission and is an essential part of the Christian message" (n. 5). Social justice, peace, the defense of human rights, advocacy and support of the poor, the powerless, and victims of discrimination of every kind—all these and more are essential responsibilities of the Church and its ministers at every level. This is the constant and the consistent teaching of the Church since Leo XIII's groundbreaking 1891 encyclical *Rerum novarum* ("Of new things"). Before all else, the Church must practice in its own household what it presumes to demand of others in government, in the corporate world, in the professions, and in the academy.

Because the Church is itself a sacrament, it teaches most effectively by example. As Pope Paul VI wrote in his 1974 apostolic exhortation *Evangelii nuntiandi* ("Of proclaiming the gospel"), "It is therefore primarily by her conduct and by her life that the Church will evangelize the world" (n. 41).

4. The Church must take an active interest in the realm of politics, but church leaders should never give even the appearance of partisan support of, or opposition to, specific candidates and political parties. The Church's only interest is in support for social justice, peace, human rights, the poor and the powerless, and the sick and the voiceless. The closer the Church and its leaders are to the poor and the powerless, the more likely they will understand and sympathize with their plight, and the less likely they will be to identify too closely with the wealthy and the powerful, which is always the stronger temptation.

5. Members of the Church cannot become finally discouraged and demoralized by temporary setbacks in the work of the Church or in the quality and performance of its leadership at various levels. However pietistic it may sound, one can never forget that it is the Holy Spirit who guides and leads the Church. It is a matter of faith and of hope that no human force and no ecclesiastical mistakes of any magnitude can permanently derail the Church from its course in history, and that the promise of Christ to be with the Church "always, until the end of the age" (Matt. 28:20) will be fulfilled.

6. There is no false dichotomy between the Church as People of God and the Church as a communion. As in every other major area of ecclesiology, our instincts should be inclusive rather than exclusive, catholic rather than sectarian, both/and rather than either/or. The Church is *both* the People of God, a this-worldly reality built from the ground up ("ecclesiology from below"), *and* a communion, that is, a community expressive of, and modeled after, the inner communal life of the triune God ("ecclesiology from above"). The two are not mutually opposed; they are complementary. Thus, the Church must encourage a kind of participatory democracy for its own members, while never forgetting that the Church is greater than the members

who constitute it. The Church is a mystery, "a reality imbued with the hidden presence of God" (Pope Paul VI).

7. Authority is absolutely essential in the Church, as it is in every other community, organization, and institution. But authority in the Church is of a unique kind. It is bestowed by the Holy Spirit and is to be exercised always in service of the Church and its mission on behalf of the whole world. The expression coined by Pope Gregory the Great (590–604) that the Bishop of Rome is "the servant of the servants of God" has endured to this day. It sets the bar, as it were, for everyone who is given authority in the Church at any level—from pope and other bishops to parish priests and directors of religious education. All authority is for service, never for domination or control.

8. The process of formulating doctrinal pronouncements and disciplinary decrees should involve, in some representational way, those who will be expected to embrace and to abide by those doctrines and decrees. Such pronouncements and decrees do not acquire their authority only from the official who promulgates them; there is also a process whereby those directly affected by the doctrines and decrees willingly accept and faithfully live by them. This process is known as reception, and it is guided from beginning to end by the Holy Spirit. Reception is an essential component in the teaching and governing mission of the Church. Teaching and disciplinary decrees that lack confirmation by reception lack sufficient authority to command assent and practical implementation.

9. Ministry, like the Church itself, is never an end in itself. One does not become a priest or a bishop, for example, in order simply to attain the status of priest or bishop. One becomes a particular minister in order to *do* the ministry that is conferred. Ministry may be conferred by ordination or by some other nonsacramental designation. Almost all ministries, in fact, are conferred by means other than ordination. The great majority of nonordained ministers are women. The Church, therefore, cannot function on a day-to-day basis without the ministries and dedicated service of nonordained women. To speak, therefore, about the "role" of women in the Church, as if it were a question that needs to be answered or a concern that needs to be

addressed, is tantamount to speaking about the "role" of politicians in government or the "role" of doctors in the medical profession. The Church could not function ministerially without women, nor should it. The major ministerial question facing the Church today is whether all ministries, ordained as well as nonordained, should be as open to qualified women as they are to qualified men.

10. There should be the greatest measure of freedom in the Church to develop new apostolates and new forms of religious communities. But these new communities and movements should never regard themselves, or be allowed to regard themselves, as churches within, and even over against, the Church. Sectarianism, as pointed out previously, remains one of the greatest threats to the unity of the Church and to the integrity of its mission. From the earliest centuries, groups have in effect proclaimed themselves the only "true" Christians, setting themselves above and apart from the worldwide Church. St. Augustine reproached the Donatists by asking how it could be that the Catholic Church "should suddenly be found surviving only in the Africans, and not in all of them" (*Letter 49.3*).

These so-called new movements should take their cue from the Church's great religious orders, which were originally formed to address some particular missionary need and which later broadened their communal purposes and scope of activities within the universal Church. But never have the Jesuits, Benedictines, Franciscans, or Dominicans, for example, set themselves apart as a church (or "personal prelature") within and over against the Church as a righteous remnant of authentic Christianity.

The Future of the Church and Its Ecclesiologies

Article 45 of the Second Vatican Council's Pastoral Constitution on the Church in the Modern World reminds us that the Church has but a single intention: that God's Kingdom, or final Reign, might come. The Kingdom has already come in the past, uniquely and definitively in Jesus Christ. It will come again in all its fullness at the end of history, as the final destiny of the world and of all creation. And the Kingdom is in our midst even now wherever there is renewal and reconciliation, that is, wherever and whenever the will of God is done. As such, the Kingdom, or Reign, of God is at once past, present, and future.

Like the Kingdom of God, the future of the Church—and by extension the future of its ecclesiologies—is also multidimensional. We can distinguish between the *ultimate* future of the Church, the *remote* future of the Church, and the *proximate* and *immediate* futures of the Church.

The *ultimate* future of the Church is the final and absolute realization of the Kingdom of God, a kingdom, as the Pastoral Constitution on the Church in the Modern World points out (art. 39), of justice and peace as well as of holiness and grace. The *remote* future of the Church is relative. "Remote" could mean one hundred years from now or even centuries from the present day. Theoretically, the *remote* future could refer to the day before the final coming of the Kingdom of God—infinity minus one. In the meantime, however, one can only speculate on what the Church will look like in the year 2100, or 3000, or 30,000, even if we had the requisite eschatological imagination to think that far ahead. To be sure, those who presume to make predictions about the *remote* future of the Church will not be around to have those predictions measured against the actual outcomes.

Conventionally, however, when we speak of the future of the Church, it is usually within our own lifetimes or the lifetimes of our children and grandchildren. That is the *proximate,* or even the *immediate,* future of the Church. The *proximate* future of the Church is, like the *remote* future, a relative concept. Is it five years, ten years, twenty-five years, or fifty years from today? And is the *immediate* future also five or ten years from now, or is it something even closer at hand? Obviously, there is some overlapping in these last two categories.

We are speaking here in section 3 about the *proximate* (not the *immediate*) future of the Church and of its ecclesiologies, that is, the Church and the ecclesiologies of the twenty-first century. We are confident in faith and in hope that we know the *ultimate* future of the Church, which is one of glory and fulfillment. We are left to speculate only about the *remote* and *proximate* futures, and we do so by extrapolating from trends that are already known and were given their impetus by Vatican II.

What follows here, therefore, are only a few brief and highly tentative thoughts about the continued evolution and development of the Church and its ecclesiologies over the next several decades. What will the Church and its ecclesiologies of today look like tomorrow? What new pastoral challenges and opportunities will present themselves as the Church moves forward in the twenty-first century and in this still new third Christian millennium?

We suggest here only five trends. The list is by no means exhaustive. First, in the light of the growing interdependence of the world's national and ethnically diverse communities, brought about mainly by the twentieth century's revolutionary advances in communications and transportation, the Church of the twenty-first century is likely to be more self-consciously catholic and less rigidly denominational, more self-consciously multicultural and less culturally monolithic. *Globalization* (in its broadest meaning, not limited to economics) is changing the face and direction of the Church as surely as it is changing the face and direction of the world, which is now more akin to a global village. This is a development that Pope John XXIII acknowledged as early as 1963 in his encyclical *Pacem in terris* (Lat., "Peace on earth," nn. 40–45, 145).

Ecclesiology has already begun to respond to this new situation. There is a greater effort now to relate Christianity to the other great religions of the world and to develop new understandings of the availability of salvation, not only outside the Catholic Church, but outside the Body of Christ as a whole. Ecclesiology has begun to assume an interfaith as well as an ecumenical character. The development, of course, has not been without controversy thus far, as the many debates about *Dominus Iesus,* the document issued by the Congregation for the Doctrine of the Faith in September 2000, dramatically illustrate. But this is the way the world and the Church are moving—in a global and multicultural direction—and so inevitably are the Church's ecclesiologies.

Second, in the light of the growing *ecumenicity* of the Church, so many past differences between Churches and ecclesial communities are viewed today as relatively minor and secondary—more cultural than theological, more political than doctrinal. The Church of the twenty-first century will increasingly recognize the degrees of communion that already exist within it, and it will express and celebrate that fundamental unity in the Eucharist primarily, via some forms of eucharistic sharing, and more generally in common prayer and collaboration in social ministry.

So too there is likely to be a mutual recognition of one another's ordained ministries, as recommended by several of the ecumenical dialogues at both the national and international levels. And the papacy, while remaining the most important single ministry in the worldwide Church, will be more responsive to the input of all of the other bishops of the Catholic Church and that of the pastoral leaders of the other Churches and ecclesial communities within the Body of Christ. The papacy will also be less monarchical in style than that of most modern pontificates since Pius IX in the nineteenth century, with the major exception of John XXIII and, to a lesser extent, of Paul VI. Indeed, one of the most important encyclicals of the second lengthiest pontificate in history, John Paul II's *Ut unum sint* (Lat., "That they may be one"), insists that the exercise of the papal office can be improved upon and even reformed in accordance with the gospel itself (see Part VII.2.5.a).

Ecclesiologically, this will involve a broadening and a deepening of research into the nature and especially the pastoral implications of the notion of communion and into the nature and exercise of authority, particularly of the papacy and of collegiality, in an increasingly ecumenical Church. This development will also require, and is likely to promote, similar probings into the notion of ministry of every kind and at every level of church life.

Third, in the light of the growing emphasis, especially in the Catholic and other high-Church traditions, on the principle of *sacramentality,* the Church will be increasingly challenged to practice what it preaches and teaches and to apply the main elements of its social teachings to itself. It will be increasingly challenged to be more than a Church that preaches against discrimination beyond its own borders; it will hold itself to the same high standard of behavior and oppose discrimination within itself based on gender, race, ethnicity, sexual orientation, and economic status. Women in particular will be more fully incorporated into the ministerial life of the Catholic Church, eventually with no ordained ministry closed to them. This may occur only as a matter of practical necessity, as the Church confronts nearly catastrophic shortages of priests, rather than in fidelity to the principle of equality before God. In this regard, the practice of the Churches of the Anglican Communion and of various mainline Protestant Churches and ecclesial communities will continue to put indirect pressure for change on the Catholic Church as well.

Consequently, ecclesiologists will increasingly recognize the inextricable link between the Church's social teachings and the life and practices of the Church itself. They will see that many of the issues once reserved exclusively to moral theologians and Christian ethicists have an important ecclesiological dimension as well, and must also be of direct concern to ecclesiology, as they have been in this book.

Fourth, in the light of the growing gap between rich and poor and the powerful and powerless of the world, the Church of the twenty-first century will also be challenged to become even more firmly committed to the quest for social justice, human rights, and peace. Even so conservative a pope as the late John Paul II had significantly advanced and enriched the substance of Catholic social teachings in his three major social encyclicals: *Laborem exercens* (Lat., "On doing work") in 1981, *Sollicitudo rei socialis* ("Solicitude for social concerns") in 1987, and *Centesimus annus* (referred to in Part VIII.2.3). There is no reason to doubt seriously that this agenda will be carried forward by the current and subsequent popes, by the bishops of the world, and by an increasing number of socially committed and active Christians all over the globe.

Ecclesiology will necessarily be supportive of this concern by underscoring and developing the link between itself and especially the related discipline of Christian social ethics, as already mentioned above. Practitioners of both areas of the theological enterprise will have to become more conversant with each other's respective methodologies and issues. It is, and will continue to be, impossible to do social ethics without an ecclesiological context.

Fifth, and finally, the Church of the twenty-first century, no matter how many changes occur in its everyday life and structure, will remain a *eucharistic faith community*, gathered around the Lord's table, hearing and proclaiming the word of God, reaching out beyond itself to those in need, witnessing in all that it says and does to the coming of the final Reign of God—a reign of justice and peace as well as of holiness and grace (Pastoral Constitution on the Church in the Modern World, n. 39).[9] In the light of its own history and of Pope John XXIII's historic opening address at Vatican II (see Part V.2), the Church must see itself not as a community apart from, or above, all others in the manner of a sect, but as a community in close relationship with all others in the human community and its family of religions, in the manner of a truly *catholic* Church.

Ecclesiology, therefore, will always have an essentially liturgical dimension. The Church is defined by its sacramental life, at the center of which is the Eucharist. It is the Eucharist—the way in which it is celebrated and the way its several ministries are assigned and exercised—that, more than any other ecclesiastical action, is expressive of the nature, mission, ministerial life, and structural operations of the Church (see the second pastoral application on page 362). That is why the point was made so emphatically earlier in this book that the so-called liturgy wars of the post–Vatican II period are at root conflicts over ecclesiology (see Part V.6.2; Part VII.5).

The future of the Church—whether ultimate, remote, proximate, or immediate—is always in process. Like the Reign of God, it is "already," but "not yet." The Church of today is an important and indispensable part of the "already." Its hope is to see and experience what is "not yet." That hope, in turn, is rooted in a firm and unshakeable faith in Christ, who is "the same yesterday, today, and forever" (Heb. 13:8), and in an equally unshakable confidence in the Holy Spirit, who makes "all things new" (Rev. 21:5). Reflecting on what that means and what its practical implications are for those who count themselves as disciples of Christ and as members of the "community of disciples" is what ecclesiology is all about.

NOTES

Preface

1. *Catholicism,* rev. ed. (San Francisco: HarperSanFrancisco, 1994), p. 4.

2. Uppercased "Tradition" refers to the essential and abiding elements of the Christian faith generally and of Catholicism in particular—those doctrinal elements that are explicitly mentioned in, e.g., the historic creeds of the Church. Lowercased "tradition" refers to elements of Christian (and particularly Catholic Christian) belief and practice that are not part of the core of Christian (or Catholic Christian) faith and thus can, with good reason, be modified or eliminated from the belief and practice of the Church. The classic work on the subject is Yves Congar's *Tradition and Traditions: An Historical and a Theological Essay* (New York: Macmillan, 1966; French ed., 2 vols., Paris: Librairie Arthème Fayard, 1960, 1963).

3. An attempt has been made to strike a happy medium in these notes. On the one hand, there are ample notes to guide both specialists and nonspecialists to the most accessible sources of direct quotations and other pertinent references found in this book. On the other hand, references are not included to sources to which nonspecialists would not have access, much less be likely to consult. And if truth be told, not even specialists would do so as a matter of course. Thus, note references to official church documents, such as encyclicals, are made to commonly available texts—in print or on the Internet—rather than to their location in the *Acta Apostolicae Sedis* (Lat., "Acts of the Apostolic See"; abbreviated *AAS*), which contains the laws, pronouncements, and addresses of the popes and the principal documents issued by the various dicasteries, or departments, of the Vatican (Roman Curia). The same is true of references to the early Christian writers. Most of their works are collected in either the *Patrologia Latina* (*PL*) or the *Patrologia Graeca* (*PG*), edited by Jacques Paul Migne (d. 1875). The former consists of 221 volumes, originally published 1844–64, and the latter, 162 volumes, published 1857–66. Preference here, however, is given to collections

that contain pertinent excerpts of these early Christian writings. For a listing of the principal collections, see Part III, n. 5. There are also no references to the collections of church documents contained in the series known as the *Enchiridion Symbolorum* (Lat., "Handbook of Symbols"), initiated in 1854 by Heinrich Joseph Denzinger (d. 1883) and subsequently issued in over thirty editions and in various translations. The edition most frequently used here is Jacques Dupuis, ed., *The Christian Faith in the Doctrinal Documents of the Catholic Church,* 6th rev. ed. (New York: Alba House, 1996). The collection was originally coedited by Joseph Neuner.

4. See Karl Rahner, *Concern for the Church: Theological Investigations XX,* trans. Edward Quinn (New York: Crossroad, 1981), "Basic Theological Interpretation of the Second Vatican Council" and "The Abiding Significance of the Second Vatican Council," pp. 77–102. The first of the two chapters was delivered originally as an address on April 8, 1979, at an academic convocation at the Weston Jesuit School of Theology in Cambridge, Massachusetts, and published initially under the title, "Towards a Fundamental Theological Interpretation of Vatican II," trans. Leo J. O'Donovan, *Theological Studies* 4/1 (December 1979): 716–27.

5. See my contributions to the "Review Symposium" on the first two volumes of Roger Haight's *Christian Community in History* (New York: Continuum, 2004, 2005). Vol. 1 is subtitled *Historical Ecclesiology;* vol. 2, *Comparative Ecclesiology;* and vol. 3, published in 2008, is subtitled *Ecclesial Existence.* The symposium was published in *Horizons* 32/2 (Fall 2005): 374–97. For my comments, see pp. 384–86. For Roger Haight's response to my criticisms, see pp. 396–97. Haight insists in the preface to his third volume that his "transdenominational" approach is complementary rather than in opposition to other approaches that treat the mystery of the Church through the methodological prism of a particular denominational tradition, which this book does explicitly in the case of the Catholic tradition. It should also be noted here that the ecumenical breadth of my own book makes no claim to comprehensiveness. Although there are literally millions of evangelical, fundamentalist, and Pentecostal Protestants in the world, there is no fully developed ecclesiology in any of these traditions apart from Miroslav Volf's *After Our Likeness: The Church as the Image of the Trinity* (Grand Rapids, MI: Eerdmans, 1998). For Haight's own discussion of the ecclesiology of Pentecostalism, see vol. 2, pp. 452–77. He summarizes its view of the Church as "the place where one encounters Jesus Christ in the Spirit and thus finds salvation. It is also the agency through which the message and the encounter is spread abroad through missionaries" (pp. 463–64).

6. Against Küng, see the *Declaration in Defense of the Catholic Doctrine on the Church Against Certain Errors of the Present Day (Mysterium Ecclesiae),* Congregation for the Doctrine of the Faith (CDF), June 24, 1973 (full text in *Origins* 31/7 [July 19, 1973]: 97, 99–100). On December 18, 1979, the CDF, with the approval of Pope John Paul II, issued a declaration withdrawing his canonical mission to teach Catholic theology. Against Boff, the same congregation issued a critical "Notification on the Book 'Church: Charism and Power' by Father Leonardo Boff, O.F.M." (full text in *Origins* 14/42 [April 4, 1985]: 683, 685–87). Boff was subsequently suspended from teaching and writing for one year. He later resigned

from the Franciscans (the Order of Friars Minor) and from the priesthood. Congar, who was named a cardinal in 1994 by Pope John Paul II, had also been forbidden by the Holy Office (the forerunner of the CDF) to write or to teach, and he served a period of exile in Cambridge, England, and Jerusalem. These and other experiences are detailed in Congar's diary, *Journal d'un théologien 1946–1956* (Paris: Les Éditions du Cerf, 2001).

7. Walter M. Abbott, ed., *The Documents of Vatican II,* trans. Joseph Gallagher (New York: Guild Press, America Press, and Association Press, 1966), pp. 712–13. For a complete list of sources for this important address, see Part V, n. 13.

Part I: Introduction

1. See Walter M. Abbott, ed., *The Documents of Vatican II,* trans. Joseph Gallagher (New York: Guild Press, America Press, and Association Press, 1966), p. 14, n. 1.

2. Unless otherwise noted, English translations of Vatican II documents are taken from Austin Flannery, ed., *Vatican Council II: The Basic Sixteen Documents: Constitutions Decrees Declarations: A Completely Revised Translation in Inclusive Language* (Northport, NY: Costello, 1996). The style throughout this book, except when drawing quotations directly from other sources, is to uppercase "Church" when it refers to a particular denomination or to the universal Church and to lowercase the word when used as an adjective or in referring to a parish or diocese as a local church.

3. The description and definition of ecclesiology reflect, of course, the broadly Catholic theological tradition. By contrast, *The Oxford Dictionary of the Christian Church,* a widely used and highly respected reference work, defines ecclesiology as the "science of the building and decoration of churches." The short entry does acknowledge, however, that "nowadays the term more commonly refers to the theology of the Church" (p. 526). This is from the third edition, edited by E. A. Livingstone and published in 1997 (London: Oxford University Press). The original volume was edited by the late F. L. Cross and published in 1957. A second edition, edited by both Cross and Livingstone, appeared in 1974. It is a matter of some interest that the final sentence of the entry in the second edition was noticeably more tentative than that in the third: "The term is also sometimes used of the theology of the Church" (p. 441).

4. See Yves Congar, "Church: Ecclesiology," trans. Matthew J. O'Connell, in Mircea Eliade, ed., *The Encyclopedia of Religion* (New York: Macmillan and Free Press, 1987), vol. 3, p. 481 (full article, pp. 480–86).

5. Richard P. McBrien, *Catholicism,* rev. ed. (San Francisco: HarperSanFrancisco, 1994), p. 723. Congar, in "Church: Ecclesiology," cited the original edition of *Catholicism,* published in 1980, p. 726. The word "church" is derived from both Hebrew and Greek (see II.2.3 for the use of the word in both Hebrew and Christian Scriptures). Both languages underscore the nature of the Church as *an assembly called forth* by God, just as the definition embraced by Congar emphasizes.

6. For a fuller explanation of the sacramental, liturgical, and devotional prayer life of the Church, see McBrien, *Catholicism,* chap. 29, "Worship: Liturgy, Prayer, Devotions," pp. 1063–75.

7. See McBrien, *Catholicism,* pp. 727–28.

8. See McBrien, *Catholicism,* pp. 728–29. These issues will be taken up later in Parts V and VI. See also Walter J. Burghardt and William G. Thompson, eds., *Why the Church?* (New York: Paulist Press, 1977).

9. For a fuller explanation of the meaning of the Kingdom, or Reign, of God and its relationship to the Church, see McBrien, *Catholicism,* chap. 31, "The Last Things," pp. 1123–83, and pp. 586–87.

10. Breaking the long-standing tendency in Catholicism to identify the Church and the Kingdom of God while developing an understanding of the Church's mission in relationship always to the Kingdom has been a central priority of my writings on the Church from my earliest years as a theologian. See, e.g., my *Do We Need the Church?* (New York: Harper & Row, 1969), which calls for a "Copernican Revolution" in ecclesiology, displacing the Church from the center of the history of salvation in favor of the Kingdom of God (pp. 14–16, and passim). I first came upon and developed this insight in the course of my doctoral studies at the Pontifical Gregorian University in Rome (1963–65) and more specifically while working on my doctoral dissertation. The dissertation was subsequently published under the title *The Church in the Thought of Bishop John Robinson* (Philadelphia: Westminster, 1966; London: SCM, 1966); see pp. 64–65, and passim. Avery Dulles offers a dissenting view on the Church-Kingdom relationship (see VI.1.4).

11. See McBrien, *Catholicism,* p. 723.

12. Karl Rahner, *Foundations of Christian Faith: An Introduction to the Idea of Christianity,* trans. William V. Dyck (New York: Seabury, 1978), p. 324.

13. Johannes Feiner and Lukas Vischer, eds., *The Catholic Catechism* (New York: Seabury, 1975), p. vii. Some of the finest theologians in Germany contributed to the volume, e.g., Heinrich Fries, Alois Grillmeier, Walter Kasper, Karl Lehmann, Heinrich Ott, Wolfhart Pannenberg, Trutz Rendtorff, and Ulrich Wilckens.

14. Feiner and Vischer, eds., *The Catholic Catechism,* p. 632; for the entire section on the Church, see pp. 632–66.

15. *The Catholic Theological Society of America: Proceedings of the Twenty-Ninth Annual Convention* (Chicago: CTSA, 1974), vol. 29, p. 329.

16. Paul Empie and T. Austin Murphy, eds. *Papal Primacy and the Universal Church, Lutherans and Catholics in Dialogue V* (Minneapolis: Augsburg, 1974); "An Agreed Statement on Authority in the Church" (Washington, DC: United States Catholic Conference, 1977); "Authority in the Church: Vital Ecumenical Issue," *Origins* 7/30 (January 12, 1978): 474–76; "Teaching Authority and Infallibility in the Church," *Theological Studies* 40/1 (March 1979): 113–66; for a summary of its main elements, see my *Catholicism,* pp. 763–64; "Primacy and Conciliarity," *Origins* 19/29 (December 21, 1989): 469, 471–72; "The Gift of Authority," *Origins* 29/2 (May 27, 1999): 17, 19–29; "Anglican-Roman Catholic Consultation Proposes Interim Unity Steps," *Origins* 32/44 (April 17, 2003): 726–28.

17. Other statements inevitably have ecclesiological implications, e.g., the Anglican-Roman Catholic International Commission's "Mary: Grace and Hope in Christ," *Origins* 35/3 (June 2, 2005): 33–50, particularly "Mary in the Life of the Church," pp. 46–48. See also Lydia Veliko and Jeffrey Gros, eds., *Growing*

Consensus II: Church Dialogues in the United States, 1992–2004, vol. 7, Ecumenical Documents (Washington, DC: United States Conference of Catholic Bishops, 2005); Randall Lee and Jeffrey Gros, eds., *The Church as Koinonia of Salvation: Its Structures and Ministries, Lutherans and Catholics in Dialogue X* (Washington, DC: United States Conference of Catholic Bishops, 2005); Heinrich Holze, ed., *The Church as Communion: Lutheran Contributions to Ecclesiology* (Geneva: Lutheran World Federation, 1997); John Borelli and John H. Erickson, eds., *The Quest for Unity: Orthodox and Catholics in Dialogue* (Crestwood, NY: St. Vladimir Press, 1996; Washington, DC: United States Conference of Catholic Bishops, 1996); Walter Kasper, ed., *The Petrine Ministry: Catholics and Orthodox in Dialogue* (New York: Newman, 2006); and Brian Daley, "Catholic-Orthodox Dialogue in America," *Origins* 35/22 (November 10, 2005): 363–70.

18. CDF, *Dominus Iesus: On the Unicity and Salvific Universality of Jesus Christ and the Church,* in *Origins* 30/14 (September 14, 2000): 209, 211–19. The document generated many reactions and commentaries. Seven years later, Cardinal Ratzinger's successor as prefect of the Congregation for the Doctrine of the Faith, Cardinal William Levada, issued a document designed in large part to respond to the criticisms of *Dominus Iesus*. This subsequent CDF document was entitled *Responses to Some Questions Regarding Certain Aspects of the Doctrine on the Church* (full text in *Origins* 37/9 [July 19, 2007]: 134–36, with an official commentary, pp. 136–39). There will be a fuller discussion of this document in V.6.4. My own "*Dominus Iesus:* An Ecclesiological Critique" was originally delivered as a lecture at the Centro Pro Unione in Rome on January 11, 2001, and was subsequently published in the semi-annual *Bulletin/Centro Pro Unione* 59 (Spring 2001): 14–22. See also Stephen J. Pope and Charles Hefling, eds., *Sic et Non: Encountering Dominus Iesus* (Maryknoll, NY: Orbis Books, 2002). An earlier Roman document of pertinent interest is the International Theological Commission's "Christianity and the World Religions," *Origins* 27/10 (August 14, 1997): 149, 151–85.

19. Jacques Dupuis, *Toward a Christian Theology of Religious Pluralism* (Maryknoll, NY: Orbis Books, 1997); *Christianity and the Religions* (Maryknoll, NY: Orbis Books, 2002).

20. See n. 10 above.

21. See Dupuis, *Toward a Christian Theology of Religious Pluralism,* p. 341, and also *Christianity and the Religions,* pp. 199–200. See also Mariasusai Dhavamony, *The Kingdom of God and World Religions: Documenta Missionalia,* vol. 31 (Rome: Editrice Pontificia Università Gregoriana, 2004).

22. Dupuis, *Christianity and the Religions,* p. 213.

23. Dupuis, *Christianity and the Religions,* p. 217. For a sympathetic analysis of Jacques Dupuis's work, see Gerald O'Collins, "Jacques Dupuis's Contributions to Interrreligious Dialogue," *Theological Studies* 64/2 (June 2004): 388–97. In the same issue, see James Fredericks, "The Catholic Church and the Other Religious Paths: Rejecting Nothing That Is True and Holy," pp. 225–54.

24. On the notes, or marks, of the Church, see Francis A. Sullivan, *The Church We Believe In: One, Holy, Catholic and Apostolic* (New York: Paulist Press, 1988). On the specific note of holiness, see Christopher O'Donnell, "Holy," in *Ecclesia: A Theological Encyclopedia of the Church* (Collegeville, MN: Liturgical Press, 1996), pp. 198–202.

25. "We Remember: A Reflection on the 'Shoah,'" *Origins* 27/40 (March 26, 1998): 669, 671–75. For the German bishops' statement marking the fiftieth anniversary of the liberation of the Auschwitz concentration camp in Poland, see "Opportunity to Re-examine Relationships with the Jews," *Origins* 24/35 (February 16, 1995): 585–86. For the statement of the French hierarchy commemorating the fifty-seventh anniversary of the enactment of anti-Semitic laws under the wartime Vichy government, which collaborated with Nazi occupation troops in France, see "Declaration of Repentance," *Origins* 27/18 (October 16, 1997): 301, 303–5.

26. See, e.g., the joint statement issued by the U.S. Catholic Bishops' Committee on Ecumenical and Interrreligious Affairs and the National Council of Synagogues, "Reflections on Covenant and Mission," *Origins* 32/13 (September 5, 2002): 218–24. The Roman Catholic participants acknowledged that "Jews are also called by God to prepare the world for God's kingdom" (p. 221).

27. *Study on Priestly Life and Ministry: Summaries of the Report of the Ad Hoc Bishops' Subcommittees on History, Sociology and Psychology* (Washington, DC: National Conference of Catholic Bishops, 1971), p. 39. Today the situation is reversed. The gap is still there, but it is now the younger clergy who are more likely than middle-aged and senior priests to embody pre–Vatican II views of the Church and its priesthood. For a statistical analysis, see Dean R. Hoge, *The First Five Years of Priesthood: A Study of Newly Ordained Catholic Priests* (Collegeville, MN: Liturgical Press, 2002); and Dean R. Hoge and Jacqueline E. Wenger, *Evolving Visions of the Priesthood: Changes from Vatican II to the Turn of the Century* (Collegeville, MN: Liturgical Press, 2003), esp. pp. 47–78.

28. "Canonical Reflections on Priestly Life and Ministry," *American Ecclesiastical Review* 166 (June 1972): 366; cited in my book *The Remaking of the Church: An Agenda for Reform* (New York: Harper & Row, 1973), p. 71.

29. "Reflections on the Morale of Priests," *Origins* 18/31 (January 12, 1989): 501 (full text, 497, 499–505).

30. "As I Have Done for You," *Origins* 29/46 (May 4, 2000): 741, 743–53.

31. What follows is drawn in large part from Avery Dulles's *Models of the Church* (Garden City, NY: Doubleday, 1974; exp. ed., 1987); see chap. 1, "The Use of Models in Ecclesiology," pp. 15–33 (exp. ed.). There are, of course, other models, beyond biblical and theological types, by which the reality of the Church can be interpreted. See, e.g., Thomas F. O'Meara, "Philosophical Models in Ecclesiology," *Theological Studies* 39/1 (March 1978): 3–21. His five philosophical models include: (1) Neoplatonic, (2) Aristotelian, (3) nominalist, (4) idealist, and (5) phenomenological-historical. Each is explained in the article. O'Meara agrees with Dulles that there is "a variety of philosophical models . . . because the mysterious nature of the Church is more than theology or polity can grasp" (p. 19). Any attempt at "an eternal metaphysics, i.e., a perennial definition" of the Church would undermine its historical and eschatological nature. "It belongs to the Church's essence to change," he concludes. "The forms of cultural history are the lessons of ecclesiology" (p. 21).

32. Paul Minear, *Images of the Church in the New Testament* (Philadelphia: Westminster, 1960; Cambridge: Clark, 2006).

33. See Dulles, *Models of the Church* (1974), p. 187; (1987), pp. 198, 205, although Dulles acknowledges in the later 1987 edition that he "may have been somewhat too severe [on] the institutional model" in the original edition, given the anti-institutional atmosphere of the late 1960s and early 1970s (p. 205). For his overall evaluation of the models, see chap. 12, "The Evaluation of Models," in both editions. Dulles therein lists seven criteria for evaluating models: (1) their basis in Scripture, (2) their basis in Christian tradition, (3) their capacity to give church members a sense of their corporate identity and mission, (4) their tendency to foster Christian virtues and values, (5) their correspondence with the religious experience of people today, (6) their theological fruitfulness, and (7) their ecumenical fruitfulness (taking "ecumenical" in its broadest sense as touching not only other Christian communities, but also other religions and humankind itself).

34. Dulles, *Models of the Church* (1987), p. 29.

35. For a summary of each with examples, see my *Catholicism*, pp. 493–517.

36. See Walter Kasper, *Theology and Church*, trans. Margaret Kohl (New York: Crossroad, 1989), p. 152. For an evangelical Protestant view, see Miroslav Volf, *After Our Likeness: The Church as the Image of the Trinity* (Grand Rapids, MI: Eerdmans, 1998).

37. See Avery Dulles, "A Half Century of Ecclesiology," *Theological Studies* 50/3 (September 1989): 419–42.

38. This was the very framework adopted by Pope Paul VI in his first encyclical, *Ecclesiam Suam* (1964), to which we shall return in V.11.

39. Alvin Toffler, *Future Shock* (New York: Random House, 1970). For a synthesis of these developments, see my *Catholicism*, chap. 3, "The Human Condition Today," pp. 77–97.

40. For an excellent synthesis of these developments in New Testament scholarship, see Frederick J. Cwiekowski, *The Beginnings of the Church* (New York: Paulist Press, 1988).

41. See, e.g., Hermann J. Pottmeyer, "A New Phase in the Reception of Vatican II: Twenty Years of Interpretation of the Council," in Giuseppe Alberigo, Jean-Pierre Jossua, and Joseph A. Komonchak, eds., *The Reception of Vatican II* (Washington DC: Catholic University of America Press, 1987), pp. 17–43. See also John W. O'Malley, "Vatican II: Did Anything Happen?" *Theological Studies* 67/1 (March 2006): 3–33; Stephen Schloesser, "Against Forgetting: Memory, History, Vatican II," *Theological Studies* 67/2 (June 2006): 275–319; and Neil J. Ormerod, "'The Times They Are a-Changin': A Response to O'Malley and Schloesser," *Theological Studies* 67/4 (December 2006): 834–55. For a collection of these and other previously published articles, see David Schultenover, ed., *Vatican II: Did Anything Happen?* (New York: Continuum, 2007). As editor Giuseppe Alberigo points out in the conclusion to the five-volume *History of Vatican II* (Maryknoll, NY: Orbis Books, 2006): "The frequent emphasis here on the importance of Vatican II as a total event and not solely for its formal decisions may have led some readers to suspect the intention of playing down the documents approved by the Council." On the contrary, "the very reconstruction of the course of the Council has clearly shown the importance of the conciliar experience for the

correct and full use of the documents themselves. . . . It is the knowledge of the event in all its aspects that provides satisfactory interpretive criteria for grasping the full meaning of Vatican II and its documents" (vol. 5, p. 643). Alberigo makes the same point even more directly in his *A Brief History of Vatican II*, trans. Matthew Sherry (Maryknoll, NY: Orbis Books, 2006): "Vatican II was thus understood, to a certain extent, in the abstract, as if it were merely an abundant, even excessive, collection of documents—nothing but words. But at a distance of forty years, it figures as an event that—in spite of its limitations and shortcomings—has brought to modern life the hope and optimism of the gospel. . . . This is why priority should be given to the phenomenon of the Council itself as an event that assembled a deliberating body of more than two thousand bishops. The same is true of its decisions, which are to be interpreted not as cold, abstract norms but as an expression and continuation of the event itself" (p. xiii).

Part II: Ecclesiology in the New Testament

1. See Christopher O'Donnell, "New Testament Ecclesiologies," in his *Ecclesia: A Theological Encyclopedia of the Church* (Collegeville, MN: Liturgical Press, 1996), p. 320. The entire entry, with copious notes, is found on pp. 320–26. O'Donnell cites, among several other sources, Raymond E. Brown, *The Churches the Apostles Left Behind* (New York: Paulist Press, 1983); Angel Antón, *La Iglesia de Christo: El Israel de la Vieja y la Nueva Alianza* (Madrid: La Editorial Católica, 1977); Thomas P. Rausch, "Unity and Diversity in New Testament Ecclesiology: Twenty-five Years after Käsemann and Brown," *Irish Theological Quarterly* 54 (1988): 131–39; M. A. Chevallier, "*L'unité plurielle de l'Église d'après le Nouveau Testament,*" *Revue d'histoire et de philosophie religieuse* 66 (1986): 3–20; and V. Kesich, "Unity and Diversity in New Testament Ecclesiology," *St. Vladimir's Theological Quarterly* 19 (1975): 109–27. The last two reflect Protestant and Orthodox scholarship, respectively.

2. Roger Haight makes the same distinction in his *Christian Community in History*, 2 vols. (New York: Continuum, 2004, 2005), vol. 1, pp. 2–4.

3. See John W. O'Malley, "The Style of Vatican II," *America* 188/6 (February 24, 2003): 12–15.

4. Still the best synthesis of this scholarship is Frederick J. Cwiekowski's *The Beginnings of the Church* (New York: Paulist Press, 1988). To be sure, there are other excellent sources for this topic, including, e.g., Raymond E. Brown, *The Churches the Apostles Left Behind* (see n. 1); Raymond E. Brown and John P. Meier, *Antioch and Rome: New Testament Cradles of Catholic Christianity* (New York: Paulist Press, 1983); Raymond F. Collins, *The Many Faces of the Church: A Study in New Testament Ecclesiology* (New York: Crossroad, 2003), and also his "Church, Idea of," in *The New Interpreter's Dictionary of the Bible*, vol. 1 (Nashville, TN: Abingdon, 2006), pp. 643–55; and Daniel J. Harrington, *The Church According to the New Testament: What the Wisdom and Witness of Early Christianity Teach Us Today* (Franklin, WI: Sheed & Ward, 2001). Bernard P. Prusak draws upon these and the work of other New Testament scholars in his *The Church Unfinished: Ecclesiology Through the Centuries* (New York: Paulist Press, 2004), pp. 70–119. O'Donnell, in "New

Testament Ecclesiologies," adopts a chronological approach to the various New Testament writings, pointing out that the "task for ecclesiology is to be as comprehensive as possible in bringing out all the relevant teaching of the NT books and applying it to the contemporary local and universal Church" (p. 324).

5. The New Testament and the Scriptures generally are analogous to the constitution of a given nation. They provide—explicitly or implicitly—the norms by which the present preaching and practices of the Church and the churches can be measured. Because the Bible is believed to have been inspired by God, it has an authority equaled by no other written source. It is theologically the *norma normans non normata* (Lat., freely translated, the norm that is the standard for all other norms, but is not itself subject to a higher norm). See also my *Catholicism,* rev. ed. (San Francisco: HarperSanFrancisco, 1994), pp. 59–63. For a fuller and more diverse discussion of canonicity, see Lee Martin McDonald and James A. Sanders, eds., *The Canon Debate* (Peabody, MA: Hendrickson, 2002).

6. James D. G. Dunn, *Unity and Diversity in the New Testament* (Philadelphia: Westminster, 1977; repr., Philadelphia: Trinity Press International, 1990; London: SCM, 2006), pp. 374–75. For a similar, though not identical, reflection on the "canon within the canon," see Raymond E. Brown, *An Introduction to the New Testament* (New York: Doubleday, 1997), pp. 43–44.

7. Dunn, *Unity and Diversity in the New Testament,* p. 375.

8. This seems to be the methodological approach taken, e.g., by Roger Haight in his three-volume *Christian Community in History* (New York: Continuum, 2004, 2005, 2008).

9. This material was previously developed in my *Catholicism,* pp. 579–82.

10. See Raymond E. Brown, "New Testament Background for the Concept of Local Church," *Proceedings of the Catholic Theological Society of America* 36 (1981): 1–14, especially 4–8.

11. See, e.g., Raymond E. Brown, "Roles of Women in the Fourth Gospel," *Theological Studies* 36/4 (December 1975): 688.

12. For this and for what follows on the question of the founding of the Church, see my *Catholicism,* pp. 577–79. See also Raymond F. Collins, "Did Jesus Found the Church? Which Church?" *Louvain Studies* 21/4 (1996): 356–64; and Harrington, *The Church According to the New Testament,* pp. 20–22.

13. The two approaches are clearly compared and contrasted by Raymond Brown's former student and fellow Sulpician priest Frederick Cwiekowski in his *The Beginnings of the Church* (New York: Paulist Press, 1988), pp. 5–7, 60–61.

14. Harrington, *The Church According to the New Testament,* p. 1. Harrington devotes his first two chapters to the "Jesus movement" (pp. 1–25). Prusak also refers to the early Church as a "Jesus movement" in *The Church Unfinished,* chap. 3, pp. 120–75.

15. For an examination of both sides of the discussion regarding the limits or limitlessness of Jesus's knowledge of the end time and other matters, see my *Catholicism,* pp. 548–57.

16. Cwiekowski, *The Beginnings of the Church,* p. 44.

17. The most thorough study of this connection is John P. Meier, *A Marginal Jew: Rethinking the Historical Jesus,* 3 vols. (New York: Doubleday, 1991–2001).

18. Cwiekowski, *The Beginnings of the Church,* p. 60.

19. See Avery Dulles, *Models of the Church*, exp. ed. (Garden City, NY: Doubleday, 1987), pp. 204–26. Dulles acknowledges that he drew the idea from a "passing remark" in Pope John Paul II's first encyclical, *Redemptor hominis*, n. 21 (Washington, DC: United States Catholic Conference, 1979), p. 90. Although the term does not appear anywhere in the documents of Vatican II, they do refer more than twenty times to church members as disciples. "From this," Dulles writes, "it is but a short step to calling the Church the community of disciples, as John Paul II was soon to do" (p. 207).

20. See Cwiekowski, *The Beginnings of the Church*, pp. 91–92. Cwiekowski, in turn, drew upon the work of his mentor, the late Raymond E. Brown, for this schema. Cwiekowski points out that these were not hard-and-fast positions and that scholars acknowledge a spectrum within each group.

21. Cwiekowski, *The Beginnings of the Church*, p. 205.

22. The term "kingdom" is the more traditional, and it remains in one of the most familiar Christian prayers, the "Our Father" ("Thy kingdom come, thy will be done on earth as it is in heaven"). In recent years, however, many theologians and biblical scholars prefer to translate the Greek *basileia* as "reign" to underscore its dynamic quality and also to avoid the implication of gender exclusivity.

23. See Harrington, *The Church According to the New Testament*, chap. 4, "How Early Christians Worshiped," pp. 43–55.

24. The Greek, however, is in the singular and is a reference to Rome, not to the whole world. See Joseph A. Fitzmyer, "The Acts of the Apostles," in *The Anchor Bible*, vol. 31 (New York: Doubleday, 1998), pp. 206–7.

25. This section of Part II relies on the presentation in my *Catholicism*, pp. 593–97 and 583–85 (see n. 5 above). For a realistic assessment of the less-than-ideal circumstances existing in some of the early Pauline communities, see Jerome Murphy-O'Connor, *Paul: His Story* (New York: Oxford University Press, 2004) and Alain Decaux, *Paul: Least of the Apostles*, Celia Sirois, trans. (Boston: Pauline Books and Media, 2006; original French edition, 2003).

26. See Raymond E. Brown, "Early Church," in *The New Jerome Biblical Commentary* (Englewood Cliffs, NJ: Prentice Hall, 1990), p. 1343.

27. For more on ministry and the ministerial structures of the early Church, see Harrington, *The Church According to the New Testament*, chap. 11, "Ministry," pp. 145–58; chap. 12, "Ministers," pp. 159–72.

28. Pius XII, *Mystici Corporis Christi: Encyclical Letter on the Mystical Body of Christ* (New York: Paulist Press, 1943), p. 6. This distinction between charismatic and administrative ministries would not have reflected Paul's own thinking since, in his mind, both result from the gifts of the Holy Spirit.

29. See also my *Lives of the Popes: The Pontiffs from St. Peter to Benedict XVI* (San Francisco: HarperSanFrancisco, 1997; updated ed., 2006), pp. 28–33.

30. To be sure, Luke limits the call to Peter alone, thereby highlighting Peter's "primacy," but Matthew includes Peter's brother Andrew in the call (4:18–19), and Mark includes, in addition to Peter and Andrew, James, the son of Zebedee, and his brother John (1:16–20).

31. This section relies for the most part on Frederick Cwiekowski's *The Beginnings of the Church*, pp. 97–146, and passim. His book, in turn, is a synthesis of recent and current developments in New Testament scholarship, reflecting especially the work of his own mentor, Raymond E. Brown.

32. For another way into Paul's ecclesiology, see Harrington, *The Church According to the New Testament,* chap. 5, "Paul on the Church," pp. 57–68.

33. Brown, "New Testament Background for the Concept of Local Church," p. 6.

34. See, e.g., O'Donnell's "Apostolic Succession," in his *Ecclesia,* pp. 23–26. He acknowledges that we do not know how this succession came about and that there is "wide diversity" in understanding its meaning (p. 25).

35. See my *Lives of the Popes,* p. 39.

36. To be sure, there is no Greek word for "deaconess" in the New Testament. The masculine *diakonos* is used for Phoebe here. In 1 Timothy 3:11 it says "women" (*gynaikai*), though the preferred exegesis takes that to mean "women deacons." According to Raymond F. Collins, the reference in 1 Timothy 5:2 is not to "deaconesses." The author is using a household code in which "elders" means older men and "younger" means younger women. Neither term, Collins believes, refers to church leaders in 5:2. He also holds, along with the majority of New Testament exegetes, that 1 Timothy 5:3–16 does not imply that the widows mentioned are deacons. See his *I & II Timothy and Titus: A Commentary,* New Testament Library (Louisville, KY: Westminster/John Knox, 2002), pp. 132–34 (for the household code), pp. 134–35 (for widows, though the exegesis of the passage extends to p. 143).

37. See, e.g., *1 Clement* 40:5, 42 and Ignatius of Antioch's *Letter to the Philadelphians* 11:1, as cited by O'Donnell, in "Deacons," in his *Ecclesia,* pp. 121–23, at p. 121.

38. Cwiekowski, *The Beginnings of the Church,* p. 184.

39. According to James D. G. Dunn, the term "Early Catholicism" seems to have been coined in Germany (as *Frühkatholizismus*) around the turn into the twentieth century, although the issues involved in it go back at least to the middle of the nineteenth century and the Tübingen school of F. C. Baur. See Dunn, *Unity and Diversity in the New Testament,* p. 341.

40. Raymond Brown, "Canonicity," in *The New Jerome Biblical Commentary* (Englewood Cliffs, NJ: Prentice Hall, 1990), p. 1053.

41. The unnamed Catholic scholars are alluded to in Brown's "Early Church," p. 1343.

42. Dunn, *Unity and Diversity in the New Testament,* chap. 16, pp. 341–66. By contrast, Haight devotes only four, generally unfocused, pages to the topic in his *Christian Community in History,* vol. 1, pp. 83–86.

43. Dunn, *Unity and Diversity in the New Testament,* p. 341.

44. Harnack maintained that in the New Testament there was no Early Catholicism at all, that it was a second-century development that distorted the pristine evangelical character of Christianity. See his *What Is Christianity?* trans. Thomas Bailey Saunders (New York: Harper, 1957; original ed., 1900), pp. 190–99.

45. The Lutheran scholar Ernst Käsemann, in particular, has championed a negative view of Early Catholicism, conceding, contrary to Harnack, that it can be found in Ephesians, Luke-Acts, the Pastorals, Jude, and 2 Peter, but that they represent a regression in New Testament ecclesiology characterized by a universal, abstract Church that is the object of its own theology. See Paul J. Kobelski, "The Letter to the Ephesians," in *The New Jerome Biblical Commentary*

(Englewood Cliffs, NJ: Prentice Hall, 1990), p. 885. Käsemann's solution was to fall back on the "canon within the canon," the content of which is justification by faith. Whatever does not pertain to that is not part of the essential New Testament, and that would include the writings that support the existence of an Early Catholicism. On this point, see Brown, "Canonicity," p. 1053. A much younger Hans Küng accused Käsemann of judging canonicity on the basis of an a priori Protestant bias. See his *Structures of the Church* (New York: Thomas Nelson, 1964), pp. 151–69.

46. Dunn, *Unity and Diversity in the New Testament,* pp. 362–66. The enumeration is mine, not Dunn's.

47. Brown, "Canonicity," p. 1053.

48. E.g., Yves Congar, *I Believe in the Holy Spirit,* trans. David Smith, 3 vols. (New York: Seabury, 1983; original French ed., Paris: Les Éditions du Cerf, 1979–80); Ghislain Lafont, *Imagining the Catholic Church: Structured Communion in the Spirit* (Collegeville, MN: Liturgical Press, 2000); Catherine Mowry LaCugna, *God for Us: The Trinity and Christian Life* (San Francisco: HarperSanFrancisco, 1991); Karl Rahner, *The Trinity,* trans. Joseph Donceel (New York: Herder & Herder, 1970); and William Hill, *The Three-Personed God: The Trinity as a Mystery of Salvation* (Washington, DC: Catholic University of America Press, 1982).

49. What follows is drawn in large measure from my *Catholicism,* pp. 598–602. For more on the Church as People of God, see Harrington, *The Church According to the New Testament,* chap. 6, "The Church and the People of God," pp. 69–81. On Paul's notion of the Church as Body of Christ, see pp. 64–68 of the same volume. Yves Congar's last major work of ecclesiology was on the Church and the Holy Spirit. See his three-volume work *I Believe in the Holy Spirit.* See also my commentary on that work, "*I Believe in the Holy Spirit:* The Role of Pneumatology in Yves Congar's Theology," in Gabriel Flynn, ed., *Yves Congar: Theologian of the Church* (Louvain: Peeters, 2005; Grand Rapids, MI: Eerdmans, 2005), pp. 303–27.

50. See N. T. Wright, *The New Testament and the People of God* (Minneapolis: Fortress, 1992). Also Gerhard Lohfink, *Does God Need the Church? Toward a Theology of the People of God* (Collegeville, MN: Liturgical Press, 1999).

51. Karl Rahner, "A Theological Interpretation of the Position of Christians in the Modern World," in *Mission and Grace* (London: Sheed & Ward, 1963), p. 51. The original is from Augustine's *De Baptismo* 5.38, cited in Henry Bettenson, ed. and trans., *The Later Christian Fathers* (New York: Oxford University Press, 1972), p. 239.

52. See Harrington, *The Church According to the New Testament,* p. 65.

53. We have already briefly explained the sacramentality of the Church in I.1 and underscored its intimate link with the concept of mystery. These central categories will appear repeatedly throughout the book.

54. See Yves Congar, *The Mystery of the Temple,* trans. Reginald F. Trevett (London: Burns & Oates, 1962), esp. sec. 7, "The Christian and the Church as Spiritual Temples," pp. 151–235.

55. The word "love" has more than one referent. In Romans 5:5, e.g., "love" refers to God's love for us. In Galatians 5:22, however, it refers to Christians' love for one another, which makes it a social virtue like the other virtues in that list.

56. See Raymond E. Brown, *The Community of the Beloved Disciple* (New York: Paulist Press, 1979), pp. 145–64. Although there is a tradition going back to Clement of Alexandria (ca. 150–ca. 215) that identified the Beloved Disciple with John the Evangelist, there is no evidence for that equation in the New Testament itself.

57. Brown, *The Community of the Beloved Disciple,* p. 164. Brown points out that, as important as Peter was to the early Church, Jesus loved "a disciple" more than Peter, which Brown describes as "an eloquent commentary on the relative value of church office." He concludes his book with this sentence: "The greatest dignity to be striven for is neither papal, episcopal, nor priestly; the great dignity is that of belonging to the community of the beloved disciples of Jesus Christ."

58. For more on Johannine ecclesiology, see Harrington, *The Church According to the New Testament,* chap. 9, "The Johannine Communities," pp. 115–28.

Part III: Ecclesiology from the Postbiblical Period to the Mid-Nineteenth Century

1. See especially the paragraph concerning Part III in "The Scope and Organizational Plan of the Book" in the Preface. The Australian Catholic theologian Neil Ormerod has made a similar point in "The Structure of a Systematic Ecclesiology," *Theological Studies* 63/1 (March 2002): 6.

2. The closest that the greatest of ecclesiologists, Yves Congar, came to constructing such a history was in his *L'Église de Saint Augustin à l'époque moderne* (Paris: Les Éditions du Cerf, 1970). It is a fine work, but it begins in the late fourth century, ends with Vatican II, and focuses, for the most part, on the institutional aspects of ecclesiology, particularly the papacy. Fully 60 percent of the book is devoted to just six centuries, the eleventh through the sixteenth. For a much shorter overview of the history of ecclesiology, see Congar's "Church: Ecclesiology," trans. Matthew J. O'Connell, in Mircea Eliade, ed., *The Encyclopedia of Religion* (New York: Macmillan and Free Press, 1987), vol. 3, pp. 480–86. See also Eric G. Jay, *The Church: Its Changing Image Through Twenty Centuries* (Atlanta: John Knox, 1980). More recent efforts include Bernard P. Prusak, *The Church Unfinished: Ecclesiology Through the Centuries* (New York: Paulist Press, 2004); and Roger Haight, *Christian Community in History,* vols. 1–2 (New York: Continuum, 2004, 2005). Prusak, like Congar, develops a historical narrative through the prism of the Catholic tradition; Jay and Haight adopt a nondenominational approach (which Haight prefers to call "transdenominational"), although Haight, unlike Jay, is a Catholic and indeed a Jesuit. See also Gerard Mannion, *Ecclesiology and Postmodernity: Questions for the Church in Our Time* (Collegeville, MN: Liturgical Press, 2007), although it has a strongly philosophical dimension and lacks biblical content and a broad historical narrative. Readers may also consult my *Catholicism,* rev. ed. (San Francisco: HarperSanFrancisco, 1994), chap. 10, "The Church in History," pp. 607–54. For one-volume histories of the Church written mainly for nonspecialists, see, e.g., Hans Küng, *The Catholic Church: A Short History,* trans. John Bowden (New York: Modern Library, 2001);

and Thomas Bokenkotter, *A Concise History of the Catholic Church,* rev. ed. (New York: Doubleday, 2004).

3. This latter approach is the one taken by Roger Haight and of which I have been critical in my brief contribution to the review symposium on his first two volumes in the Fall 2005 issue of *Horizons* (32/2: 374–97). Neil Ormerod makes a similar point: "While I agree with Haight that any particular church cannot automatically claim to be identified with the 'universal Church,' I do not agree with his contention that the proper object of ecclesiology is the 'whole or universal Church.' In fact there is a real danger that such an object becomes an idealization. While the churches may be united eschatologically, in the here and now they are divided on many scores, and it would be methodologically unsound not to recognize this" ("The Structure of a Systematic Ecclesiology," p. 7).

4. Yves Congar, *Lay People in the Church: A Study for a Theology of the Laity,* trans. Donald Attwater (Westminster, MD: Newman, 1957), p. 37. Congar agrees with the suggestion that the first such treatise was James of Viterbo's *De regimine christiano* (1301/02), and almost immediately thereafter Giles of Rome's *De ecclesiastica potestate* and John of Paris's *De potestate regia et papali.* Congar notes that all three works were occasioned by the conflict between the French king, Philip the Fair (d. 1314), and Pope Boniface VIII (1295–1303) and consequently tended to emphasize the authority, rights, and governmental structure of the Church. Avery Dulles observes that, although "treatises on the Church had appeared sporadically since the 14th century, ecclesiology had not yet assumed the central position in Catholic theology that it has enjoyed in [the 20th] century" ("A Half Century of Ecclesiology," *Theological Studies* 50/3 [September, 1989]: 419 [full article, pp. 419–42]). For another overview of the ecclesiology of the New Testament and of the first nineteen centuries of the Church's history, see Michael J. Himes, ed., *The Catholic Church in the 21st Century: Finding Hope for Its Future in the Wisdom of Its Past* (Liguori, MO: Liguori, 2004).

5. Relevant texts are available in a variety of collections. See, e.g., Betty Radice and Andrew Louth, eds., *Early Christian Writings: The Apostolic Fathers,* trans. Maxwell Staniforth (Harmondsworth, U.K./New York: Penguin, 1968; new ed., 1987); Bart D. Ehrman, ed. and trans., *The Apostolic Fathers* (Cambridge, MA: Harvard University Press, 2003); Henry Bettenson, ed. and trans., *The Early Christian Fathers* (Oxford/New York: Oxford University Press, 1956); Cyril C. Richardson, ed. and trans., *Early Christian Fathers* (New York: Macmillan, 1970); S. L. Greenslade, ed., *Early Latin Theology: Selections from Tertullian, Cyprian, Ambrose, and Jerome* (Philadelphia: Westminster, 1956); Henry Bettenson, ed. and trans., *The Later Christian Fathers* (New York: Oxford University Press, 1970); James Stevenson, ed., *A New Eusebius: Documents Illustrating the History of the Church to AD 337,* rev. ed., revision ed. W. H. C. Frend (London: SPCK, 1987); James Stevenson, ed., *Creeds, Councils and Controversies: Documents Illustrative of the History of the Church A.D. 337–461* (London: SPCK, 1966); Edward Giles, ed., *Documents Illustrating Papal Authority, 96–454* (London: SPCK, 1952); and J. N. D. Kelly, *Early Christian Doctrines,* 5th rev. ed (San Francisco: Harper & Row, 1978). Bernard Prusak covers this period well—and in greater detail than we have provided here—in his *The Church Unfinished,* pp. 120–75.

6. For a profile of Clement, see my *Lives of the Popes: The Pontiffs from St. Peter to Benedict XVI* (San Francisco: HarperSanFrancisco, 1997; updated ed.,

2006), pp. 35–36. To be sure, Clement was not a "pope" in the modern sense of the word. As pointed out in that same book (p. 25), a monarchical episcopate did not come to Rome until around the middle of the second century.

7. For a very brief profile, see "Ignatius of Antioch, St." in Richard P. McBrien, ed., *The HarperCollins Encyclopedia of Catholicism* (San Francisco: HarperSanFrancisco, 1995), p. 652. For a more complete profile, see "Ignatius, St.," in F. L. Cross and E. A. Livingstone, eds., *The Oxford Dictionary of the Christian Church*, 3rd ed. (Oxford/New York: Oxford University Press, 1997), pp. 817–18.

8. The suppression theory has been advanced by such scholars as Elaine H. Pagels. See, e.g., her *The Gnostic Gospels* (New York: Random House, 1979) and *Beyond Belief: The Secret Gospel of Thomas* (New York: Random House, 2003). See also Karen L. King, *The Gospel of Mary of Magdala: Jesus and the First Woman Apostle* (Santa Rosa, CA: Polebridge, 2003); and John Dominic Crossan, *Four Other Gospels* (Minneapolis, MN: Winston, 1985). The suspicion was fueled at a more popular level by Dan Brown's best-selling novel *The Da Vinci Code* (New York: Doubleday, 2003) and the discussion surrounding the subsequent release of the film based on the novel in 2006.

9. There are brief entries (in alphabetical order) on each of these early Church figures and on the heresies they opposed in both McBrien, ed., *The HarperCollins Encyclopedia of Catholicism,* and Cross and Livingstone, eds., *The Oxford Dictionary of the Christian Church.* This section, however, does not purport to be a compendium of what was once called patristic theology. In this instance and many others, the acknowledged limitations of Part III are more than evident. Nevertheless, because of Augustine's central importance in this period of history, there is a separate treatment of him in 2.6.

10. Karl Rahner, "A Theological Interpretation of the Position of Christians in the Modern World," in *Mission and Grace* (London: Sheed & Ward, 1963), p. 51. The original is from Augustine's *De Baptismo* 5.38, cited in Bettenson, ed. and trans., *The Later Christian Fathers,* p. 239.

11. Cited in Bettenson, ed., *The Later Christian Fathers,* p. 240.

12. Although it can also be argued that sectarianism as we know it today has its origins in the Middle Ages and in the Reformation period rather than in the earliest centuries of the Church, it is nevertheless a fact that there are strong sectarian tendencies in the Church of the twenty-first century. The most prominent representatives of this approach in Protestant theology are Stanley Hauerwas, of Duke University, and George A. Lindbeck, emeritus professor at Yale University. Hauerwas, although a Christian ethicist, has written a number of books and articles with ecclesiological themes, e.g., *A Community of Character: Toward a Constructive Christian Social Ethic* (Notre Dame, IN: University of Notre Dame Press, 1981); *Christian Existence Today: Essays on Church, World, and Living in Between* (Durham, NC: Labyrinth, 1988); *After Christendom? How the Church Is to Behave if Freedom, Justice, and a Christian Nation Are Bad Ideas* (Nashville, TN: Abingdon, 1991); and *In Good Company: The Church as Polis* (Notre Dame, IN: University of Notre Dame Press, 1995). For Lindbeck, see his *The Nature of Doctrine: Religion and Theology in a Postliberal Age* (Philadelphia: Westminster, 1984) and *The Church in a Postliberal Age,* ed. James J. Buckley (Grand Rapids, MI: Eerdmans, 2003). Both Hauerwas and Lindbeck have been styled as sectarian by various commentators, but none so distinguished as James M. Gustafson,

who referred to Hauerwas's work as "an ideal type of sectarian Christian ethics." See Gustafson's "The Sectarian Temptation: Reflections on Theology, the Church and the University," in *The Catholic Theological Society of America: Proceedings of the Fortieth Annual Convention* (Louisville, KY: Catholic Theological Society of America, 1985), vol. 40, p. 84 (entire paper, pp. 83–94). Hauerwas rejected the sectarian label in "Will the Real Sectarian Stand Up?" *Theology Today* 44/1 (1987): 87–94. He has many Catholic disciples—former students at Duke—now teaching in various Catholic colleges and universities in the United States, none of whom has attained individual prominence but who have collectively had a marked influence on Catholic theological education, particularly in the field of moral theology. Like Hauerwas's, their views on Christian ethics are an expression of an underlying sectarian ecclesiological perspective, especially as it relates to the role of the Church in the world. See, for example, David McCarthy and M. Theresa Lysaught, eds., *Gathered for the Journey: Moral Theology in Catholic Perspective* (Grand Rapids, MI: Eerdmans, 2007). For a recent critique of Hauerwas's approach, see Mannion, *Ecclesiology and Postmodernity,* pp. 201–12.

13. One of the classic works on the subject is H. Richard Niebuhr's *Christ and Culture* (New York: Harper & Row, 1951; Torchbook ed., 1956). See also VI.2 of this book for our own treatment of the Church-world relationship.

14. Quotations from Augustine's works in 2.6.a–e are taken from Bettenson, ed., *The Later Christian Fathers,* pp. 237–44.

15. See Benedict T. Viviano, *The Kingdom of God in History* (Wilmington, DE: Glazier, 1988), pp. 30–31. Regarding Augustine's general understanding of the City of God and the Kingdom of God, I should gladly make as my own the words of James Stevenson, editor of *Creeds, Councils and Controversies:* "While it is impossible in a book such as this to delineate the thought of Augustine on the two cities, it is felt that some mention should be made of his great work, the origin of which was rooted in the disasters of his time" (p. 215).

16. Charles H. Dodd, *The Parables of the Kingdom* (London: Collins/Fontana, 1963; orig. ed., 1935), pp. 40–41. To be sure, Dodd is not himself equating the Kingdom of God and the Church here.

17. Texts cited in Bernard Prusak, *The Church Unfinished,* p. 138. References to Augustine's *Retractions* and *Sermons 149* and *295* are also drawn from Prusak, p. 137. Tarcisius van Bavel provides a useful survey of Augustine's ecclesiology, "Church," in Allen G. Fitzgerald, ed., *Augustine Through the Ages: An Encyclopedia* (Grand Rapids, MI: Eerdmans, 1999), pp. 169–75. See also the first (still untranslated) book by Joseph Ratzinger (later Pope Benedict XVI), *Volk und Haus Gottes in Augustins Lehre von der Kirche* (Ger., "The People and House of God in Augustine's Ecclesiology") (Munich: Zink, 1954).

18. Roger Haight has a particularly lengthy treatment of the ecclesiological aspects of the Gregorian reform and its consequences in vol. 1 of his *Christian Community in History,* chap. 5, "The Gregorian Reform and the New Medieval Church," pp. 267–344. See also the entry on Gregory VII in my *Lives of the Popes,* pp. 185–88. Yves Congar has described the Gregorian reform as the "great turning-point" in the history of the papacy and in the legalization of the Church's life and governance. See his "Church: Ecclesiology," p. 483.

19. See Charles Davis, "Theology in Seminary Confinement," *The Downside Review* 81/265 (October 1963): 307–16. Davis's thesis is that there is an ecology of theology whereby Catholic theology in general has been shaped by the various environments in which it has been primarily done, e.g., bishops' houses, monasteries, universities, and seminaries. What applies to theology in general certainly applies to ecclesiology in particular. For an excellent analysis of Catholic universities today, see Melanie M. Morey and John J. Piderit, *Catholic Higher Education: A Culture in Crisis* (New York: Oxford University Press, 2006).

20. Cited in "Inquisition, the," in Cross and Livingstone, eds., *The Oxford Dictionary of the Christian Church,* p. 836.

21. See, e.g., Haight, *Christian Community in History,* vol. 1, p. 344.

22. See Robert F. Taft, "Eastern Schism," in McBrien, ed., *The HarperCollins Encyclopedia of Catholicism,* pp. 445–46. See also Yves Congar, *After Nine Hundred Years: The Background of the Schism Between the Eastern and Western Churches* (New York: Fordham University Press, 1959). It should be pointed out here that the mutual excommunications of 1054 did not actually start the schism. Rather, it was actually a growing alienation during the eleventh to the early thirteenth centuries that led to the break. There are many documents from the late eleventh and twelfth centuries that disclose no awareness of any division between the Greek and Latin Churches. The final, decisive action that has prevented reconciliation to this very day was the sacking of Constantinople by Latin Crusaders in 1204.

23. *Dominus Iesus: On the Unicity and Salvific Universality of Jesus Christ and the Church,* in *Origins* 30/14 (September 14, 2000): 209, 211–19. We shall return to the question of the Church as a communion in various sections of Part VI and again in VII.1.

24. See, e.g., Dennis M. Doyle, *Communion Ecclesiology: Visions and Versions* (Maryknoll, NY: Orbis Books, 2000). For our own treatment of this topic, see VII.1.

25. Avery Dulles, *Models of the Church,* exp. ed. (Garden City, NY: Doubleday, 1987), pp. 204–26. Dulles credits his own idea of a sixth model to a passing remark of Pope John Paul II in his 1979 encyclical *Redemptor hominis,* n. 21. See Part II, n. 19.

26. Yves Congar, "The Idea of the Church in St. Thomas Aquinas," in *The Mystery of the Church* (London: Chapman; Baltimore: Helicon, 1960), p. 98. See also his *Lay People in the Church,* pp. 36–52. For a more recent study of Aquinas's ecclesiology, see George Sabra, *Thomas Aquinas's Vision of the Church: Fundamentals of an Ecumenical Ecclesiology* (Mainz: Grünewald, 1987).

27. The expression "the Church from Abel," evident in some of the early Christian writers, underscored the belief that the just who preceded Christ were also saved, in anticipation of Christ's merits. St. Augustine may have been the first to use the expression, also to make the point that the just of the Old Testament were in a sense already Christians. The expression became commonplace in the Middle Ages, but then ceded ground to the growing institutional emphasis in ecclesiology. For this reason perhaps, Yves Congar revived the ancient theme of the Church from Abel, and it came to be incorporated in Vatican II's Dogmatic

Constitution on the Church, n. 2, highlighting the traditional belief that at the end of history the Church will consist of all the just, including those who lived before Christ. See "Abel, Church from," in Christopher O'Donnell, *Ecclesia: A Theological Encyclopedia of the Church* (Collegeville, MN: Liturgical Press, 1996), p. 1.

28. From Aquinas's *Expositio in Symbolum,* cited in Congar, *The Mystery of the Church,* pp. 99–100.

29. Congar, *The Mystery of the Church,* p. 102.

30. Congar, *The Mystery of the Church,* p. 103.

31. Congar, *The Mystery of the Church,* pp. 116–17.

32. Congar, *The Mystery of the Church,* p. 117.

33. Congar, *The Mystery of the Church,* p. 117.

34. See Avery Dulles, *A Church to Believe In: Discipleship and the Dynamics of Freedom* (New York: Crossroad, 1982), chap. 10, "The Church According to Thomas Aquinas," pp. 149–69.

35. Dulles lists twenty-four items on which the council and Aquinas were in agreement in their respective ecclesiologies (*A Church to Believe In,* pp. 165–66), but also mentions others on which Aquinas and the council diverged from one another. "In place of St. Thomas' pyramidal ecclesiology, with its strong accent on the pope's *plenitudo potestatis* [Lat., 'fullness of power'], Vatican II introduced the idea that the pope and his brother bishops constitute a 'collegium'" (p. 166). There is no idea of episcopal collegiality in St. Thomas.

36. Dulles, *A Church to Believe In,* p. 169.

37. One of the classic works on the subject is Walter Ullmann, *The Origins of the Great Schism* (Hamden, CT: Archon, 1967). For a thumbnail sketch of the schism, see W. David Myers, "Great Schism," in McBrien, ed., *The HarperCollins Encyclopedia of Catholicism,* pp. 585–86.

38. The Catholic Church came eventually to regard Alexander V as an antipope. An antipope was an individual whose claim to the papacy was either rejected by the Church at the time or later recognized as invalid. Because the rules for papal elections have changed over the course of history, it has not always been easy to distinguish between validly elected popes and those invalidly elected or later recognized as such. There have been thirty-nine antipopes in all: the first was St. Hippolytus (217–35), and the last was Felix V (1439–49). My colleague Thomas Prügl suggests that the popes who emerged from the so-called reform councils proved to be much more effective in reestablishing the unity of the Church and ending the Great Schism than were those in the Roman line.

39. In my book *Lives of the Popes,* I sometimes differ, on theological grounds, with the official Vatican dating of various pontificates. Since the pope is the Bishop of Rome, and since several popes, like Boniface VIII, were not bishops at the time of their election, I have concluded, over against the Vatican's previous system of dating, that a person does not become pope until he has been consecrated as a bishop. Boniface VIII was elected on December 24, 1294, but he was not consecrated a bishop until January 23, 1295. The problem no longer exists because in 1996 Pope John Paul II decreed in *Universi Domini gregis* (Lat., "Of the Lord's whole flock") that, if a person elected is not yet a bishop, he is immediately ordained a bishop by the dean of the College of Cardinals. Canon 332.1

of the Code of Canon Law, as revised in 1983, stipulates: "The Roman Pontiff obtains full and supreme power in the Church by means of legitimate election accepted by him together with episcopal consecration. . . ." By contrast, the 1917 Code of Canon Law stipulated that a person becomes pope "as soon as he accepts election" (can. 219).

40. For an illuminating interpretation of the Council of Constance, see Francis Oakley, *Council Over Pope? Towards a Provisional Ecclesiology* (New York: Herder and Herder, 1969). An English translation of the council's key decree, *Haec Sancta,* is available in Klaus Schatz, *Papal Primacy: From Its Origins to the Present,* trans. John A. Otto and Linda M. Maloney (Collegeville, MN: Liturgical Press, 1996), pp. 186–88. Schatz summarizes the discussion regarding this document on pp. 111–14.

41. See, e.g., Hans J. Hillerbrand, "Reformation," in Mircea Eliade, ed., *The Encyclopedia of Religion* (New York: Macmillan and Free Press, 1987), vol. 12, pp. 244–54.

42. See my *Catholicism,* pp. 632–36.

43. Congar, *Lay People in the Church,* p. 38.

44. Congar, *Lay People in the Church,* p. 38.

45. Congar, *Lay People in the Church,* p. 39.

46. Roger Haight devotes most of the second volume of his *Christian Community in History* to the various ecclesiological traditions associated with the Reformation. See the first four chapters: "Luther's Ecclesiology" (pp. 13–81), "Calvin's Ecclesiology" (pp. 82–147), "The Church of England" (pp. 148–217), and "Anabaptist, Baptist, and Roman Ecclesiology" (pp. 218–88).

47. See Ralph F. Smith, "Luther, Martin" in McBrien, ed., *The HarperCollins Encyclopedia of Catholicism,* pp. 799–801.

48. For brief entries, see R. Emmet McLaughlin, "Calvin, John," and Robert A. Krieg, "Calvinism," in McBrien, ed., *The HarperCollins Encyclopedia of Catholicism,* pp. 211, 211–12. There is, of course, a substantial literature on Calvin and Calvinism, just as there is on Luther and Lutheranism. However, such specialized studies are beyond the scope of this book. I would like to single out, however, the work of my colleague Randall C. Zachman, *John Calvin as Teacher, Pastor, and Theologian: The Shape of His Writings and Thought* (Grand Rapids, MI: Baker Academic, 2006).

49. See George H. Williams, *The Radical Reformation,* 3d ed. (Kirksville, MO: Sixteenth Century Journal Publishers, 1992; orig. ed., Philadelphia: Westminster, 1962).

50. I am indebted for this synthesis to the late John Howard Yoder (d. 1997), a former colleague at the University of Notre Dame and a leading theologian in the Radical Reformation tradition.

51. See n. 12 above.

52. See Doreen Rosman, *From Catholic to Protestant: Religion and the People in Tudor England* (London: University College London Press, 1996); Eamon Duffy, *The Stripping of the Altars: Traditional Religion in England, 1400–1580* (New Haven, CT: Yale University Press, 1992); and Stephen Sykes and John E. Booty, eds., *The Study of Anglicanism* (London: SPCK, 1988).

53. See, e.g., Anglican–Roman Catholic International Commission (ARCIC), "The Gift of Authority," *Origins* 29/2 (May 27, 1999): 17, 19–29; and Anglican–Roman Catholic Consultation in the United States, "Anglican–Roman Catholic Consultation Proposes Interim Unity Steps," *Origins* 32/44 (April 17, 2003): 726–28. ARCIC II had also produced "Salvation and the Church," *Origins* 16/34 (February 15, 1987): 611–16, and "The Church as Communion," *Origins* 20/44 (April 11, 1991): 719–27.

54. See Giuseppe Alberigo, "From the Council of Trent to 'Tridentinism,'" trans. Emily Michelson, in Raymond F. Bulman and Frederick J. Parrella, eds., *From Trent to Vatican II: Historical and Theological Investigations* (New York: Oxford University Press, 2006), pp. 19–37; and also Kenan Osborne, "Priestly Formation," in Bulman and Parrella, eds., *From Trent to Vatican II,* pp. 117–35. For a definitive history of the Council of Trent, see Hubert Jedin, *A History of the Council of Trent,* trans. Ernest Graf, 2 vols. (St. Louis: Herder, 1957; London: Nelson, 1957–61; vol. 1, Freiburg: Herder, 1951). See also John W. O'Malley, *Trent and All That: Renaming Catholicism in the Early Modern Era* (Cambridge, MA: Harvard University Press, 2000), and his "Trent and Vatican II: Two Styles of Church," in Bulman and Parrella, eds., *From Trent to Vatican II,* pp. 301–20. For a critical view of Trent's reforms, see Hans Küng, *Christianity: Essence, History and Future* (New York: Continuum, 1995), esp. p. 483.

55. Yves Congar insists that the hierarchically oriented ecclesiology developed in this period and not in the High Middle Ages, when formal treatises on the Church were just being produced. "Rather it was later, in the writings of the Counter-Reformation and those directed against Gallicanism of the seventeenth and eighteenth centuries, that the problems raised in the fourteenth and fifteenth were treated with a marked insistence on hierarchical powers, most especially papal power" (*Lay People in the Church,* p. 38).

56. See Thomas F. O'Meara, "Leaving the Baroque: The Fallacy of Restoration in the Postconciliar Era," *America* 174/3 (February 3, 1996): 10–12, 14, 25–28. See also Anthony M. Stevens-Arroyo, "A Marriage Made in America: Trent and the Baroque," in Bulman and Parrella, eds., *From Trent to Vatican II,* pp. 39–59.

57. Congar, *Lay People in the Church,* p. 41.

58. Congar, *Lay People in the Church,* p. 41.

59. On May 13, 1871, the Law of Guarantees assured the pope of personal inviolability and left him with the Vatican and other buildings. But Pius IX refused to accept the arrangement and never again set foot outside the Vatican, considering himself a prisoner therein.

60. See Michael J. Himes, *Ongoing Incarnation: Johann Adam Möhler and the Beginnings of Modern Ecclesiology* (New York: Crossroad, 1997). See also Christopher O'Donnell, "Möhler, Johann Adam (1796–1838)," in his *Ecclesia,* pp. 309–11.

61. Rosmini was beatified in 2007 and is, at this writing, a candidate for eventual canonization—a reminder that so many who have been persecuted by church authorities were later rehabilitated in remarkable ways. Several of the leading theologians at Vatican II had been silenced and censured in the years prior to the council. Some were later created cardinals, e.g., Yves Congar, Jean Daniélou, Henri de Lubac. In 1887, thirty-two years after his death, forty propositions drawn from

Rosmini's writings were officially condemned by the Holy Office, the forerunner of the Congregation for the Doctrine of the Faith (CDF). In 2001, however, the CDF issued a decree (or *nota*) declaring that the 1887 condemnation has been "superseded." In other words, Rosmini has been officially rehabilitated.

62. Christopher O'Donnell, "Scheeben, Matthias Joseph (1835–1888)," in his *Ecclesia,* p. 419.

63. Matthias Scheeben, *The Mysteries of Christianity,* trans. Cyril Vollert (St. Louis, MO: Herder, 1946), p. 544.

64. Both the bridal and maternal images of the Church were central to Scheeben's ecclesiology and were carried over into his Mariological writings as well. Indeed, the Church's motherhood is exercised through Mary's. See *The Mysteries of Christianity,* pp. 546–47.

65. Scheeben, *The Mysteries of Christianity,* pp. 558–66, 581.

66. See Christopher O'Donnell, "Newman, John Henry (1801–1890)," in his *Ecclesia,* pp. 326–27. For a brief profile, see Mary Katherine Tillman, "Newman, John Henry," in McBrien, ed., *The HarperCollins Encyclopedia of Catholicism,* pp. 913–15. See also Walter E. Conn, "From Oxford to Rome: Newman's Ecclesial Conversion," *Theological Studies* 68/3 (September 2007): 595–617.

Part IV: Ecclesiology from Vatican I to the Threshold of Vatican II

1. Technically, Vatican I defined only one dogma of faith, namely, papal infallibility. However, it also "promulgate[d] anew the definition of the ecumenical council of Florence" regarding papal primacy. See *Pastor Aeternus,* chap. 3, para. 1, in Norman P. Tanner, ed., *Decrees of the Ecumenical Councils,* vol. 2 (Washington, DC: Georgetown University Press; London: Sheed & Ward, 1990), p. 813. The entire document is given in both the original Latin and English translation, pp. 811–16. Hereafter in Part IV, reference is made to the "doctrine" of papal primacy simply to underscore the point that Vatican I defined only papal infallibility as a dogma, not papal primacy as well. That had been defined, as noted above, by the Council of Florence in the fifteenth century.

2. The material in this section is directly reproduced from my book *Lives of the Popes: The Pontiffs from St. Peter to Benedict XVI* (San Francisco: Harper SanFrancisco, 1997; updated ed., 2006), p. 17. See also Jean-M. R. Tillard, "The Papacy," in Richard P. McBrien, ed., *The HarperCollins Encyclopedia of Catholicism* (San Francisco: HarperSanFrancisco, 1995), pp. 953–55. For more fully developed works, see Jean-M. R. Tillard, *The Bishop of Rome* (Wilmington, DE: Glazier, 1983); Patrick Granfield, *The Limits of the Papacy: Authority and Autonomy in the Church* (New York: Crossroad, 1987); Eamon Duffy, *Saints and Sinners: A History of the Popes,* 2d ed. (New Haven, CT: Yale University Press, 2002); and William J. LaDue, *The Chair of Saint Peter: A History of the Papacy* (Maryknoll, NY: Orbis Books, 1999).

3. See Raymond E. Brown et al., *Peter in the New Testament* (Minneapolis, MN: Augsburg, 1973); and Chrys C. Caragounia, *Peter and the Rock* (New York: De Gruyter, 1990).

4. The material in this section is adapted from my *Lives of the Popes*, pp. 28–33. In supplying the dates of Linus's pontificate, I am following the lead of historians of the papacy. The Vatican's official list sometimes gives slightly different dates. In the case of Linus, they are 67–76.

5. What follows in this section is also directly reproduced, with only slight modifications, from my *Lives of the Popes*, pp. 17–20. See also Jean-M. R. Tillard, "Primacy, Papal," in McBrien, ed., *The HarperCollins Encyclopedia of Catholicism*, pp. 1051–53; and Christopher O'Donnell, "Papal Primacy," in his *Ecclesia: A Theological Encyclopedia of the Church* (Collegeville, MN: Liturgical Press, 1996), pp. 344–49. For a more detailed study, see Klaus Schatz, *Papal Primacy: From Its Origins to the Present*, trans. John A. Otto and Linda M. Maloney (Collegeville, MN: Liturgical Press, 1996). See also Joseph Ratzinger (later Pope Benedict XVI), *Called to Communion: Understanding the Church Today*, trans. Adrian Walker (San Francisco: Ignatius, 1996), pp. 47–74. For a very different approach, see Hans Küng, *The Catholic Church: A Short History*, trans. John Bowden (New York: Modern Library, 2001), pp. 40–44; chap. 4, "The Papal Church," pp. 55–76. For an Orthodox approach, see Olivier Clément, *You Are Peter: An Orthodox Theologian's Reflection on the Exercise of Papal Primacy*, trans. M. S. Laid (New York: New City, 2003). See also Walter Kasper, ed., *The Petrine Ministry: Catholics and Orthodox in Dialogue* (New York: Newman, 2006).

6. See Betty Radice and Andrew Louth, eds., *Early Christian Writings: The Apostolic Fathers*, trans. Maxwell Staniforth (Harmondsworth, U.K./New York: Penguin, 1968; new ed. 1987); and Bart D. Ehrman, ed. and trans., *The Apostolic Fathers* (Cambridge, MA: Harvard University Press, 2003).

7. What follows in this section is also taken directly, with modifications, from my *Lives of the Popes*, pp. 20–23. See also John T. Ford, "Infallibility," in McBrien, ed., *The HarperCollins Encyclopedia of Catholicism*, pp. 664–65; Christopher O'Donnell, "Infallibility," in his *Ecclesia*, pp. 212–16; and Paul T. Empie et al., eds., *Papal Primacy and the Universal Church: Lutherans and Catholics in Dialogue V* (Minneapolis, MN: Augsburg, 1974). See also Klaus Schatz, *Vaticanum I (1869–1870): Unfehlbarkeitsdiskussion und Rezeption, Konziliengeschichte* (Paderborn: Schöningh, 1994), vol. 3.

8. See Brian Tierney, *Origins of Papal Infallibility* (Leiden: Brill, 1972).

9. For an especially insightful commentary on the "irreformability" issue as raised by Vatican I's formula of definition, see Hermann J. Pottmeyer, *Towards a Papacy in Communion: Perspectives from Vatican Councils I and II*, trans. Matthew J. O'Connell (New York: Crossroad, 1998), pp. 94–104, esp. pp. 101–4.

10. Material for 1.5.a–c is taken from my *Lives of the Popes*, pp. 32–33.

11. See Jean-M. R. Tillard, "Petrine Succession," in McBrien, ed., *The HarperCollins Encyclopedia of Catholicism*, pp. 995–96.

12. See Raymond E. Brown and John Meier, *Antioch and Rome: New Testament Cradles of Catholic Christianity* (New York: Paulist Press, 1973).

13. See Jean-M. R. Tillard, "Vicar of Peter" and "Vicar of Christ," in McBrien, ed., *The HarperCollins Encyclopedia of Catholicism*, pp. 1310–11.

14. The address, *Benignitas et Humanitas* (Lat., "Kindness and Humanity"), given on December 24, 1944, was published in *The Tablet* 184 (December 30, 1944): 316–18. See Paul E. Sigmund, "Democracy," in Judith A. Dwyer, ed., *The*

New Dictionary of Catholic Social Thought (Collegeville, MN: Liturgical Press, 1999), pp. 269–75. See also *The Major Addresses of Pope Pius XII*, vol. 2, *The Christmas Messages*, ed. Vincent Yzermans (St. Paul, MN: North Central Publishing, 1961), esp. pp. 51–66, 78–90.

15. Sources differ on this point. Dom Cuthbert Butler's authoritative account, *The Vatican Council 1869–1870* (Westminster, MD: Newman, 1962), based largely on Bishop William Ullathorne's letters written during the council, gives the number of active participants as 750 (p. 229). Hermann Pottmeyer puts the number at 774. See his "Vatican Council I," in McBrien, ed., *The HarperCollins Encyclopedia of Catholicism*, p. 1297. In any case, not all present were bishops. Most sources place that number at just under 700. See, e.g., "Vatican Council, First," in E. A. Livingstone, ed., *The Oxford Dictionary of the Christian Church*, 3d ed. (London: Oxford University Press, 1997), p. 1681.

16. See James J. Hennesey, *The First Council of the Vatican: The American Experience* (New York: Herder and Herder, 1963), p. 17.

17. Pottmeyer, "Vatican Council I," p. 1297.

18. Quotations from *Pastor Aeternus* in this section are taken from Tanner, ed., *Decrees of the Ecumenical Councils*, pp. 811–15.

19. Tillard, "Primacy, Papal," p. 1051.

20. O'Donnell, "Papal Primacy," p. 346. See also Gustave Thils, *Primauté et infallibilité du Pontife Romaine à Vatican I et autres études d'ecclésiologie* (Leuven: Leuven University Press, 1989).

21. Cited in Jacques Dupuis, ed., *The Christian Faith in the Doctrinal Documents of the Catholic Church*, 6th rev. ed. (New York: Alba House, 1996), pp. 298–99.

22. Dupuis, ed., *The Christian Faith in the Doctrinal Documents of the Catholic Church*, p. 298.

23. What follows is adapted from the summary of the debate in Pottmeyer, "Vatican Council I," pp. 1297–98.

24. Tanner, ed., *Decrees of the Ecumenical Councils*, p. 816.

25. Tanner, ed., *Decrees of the Ecumenical Councils*, p. 816.

26. Otherwise known as the "Declaration in Defense of the Catholic Doctrine on the Church Against Certain Errors of the Present Day." The full text is in *Origins* 3/7 (July 19, 1973): 97, 99–100. Pertinent excerpts are provided in the appendices to my *Catholicism*, rev. ed. (San Francisco: HarperSanFrancisco, 1994), pp. 1209–10. See also the reflection on the "irreformability" clause in Pottmeyer, *Towards a Papacy in Communion*, pp. 94–104, esp. pp. 101–4.

27. Pottmeyer, "Vatican Council I," p. 1298. Some may legitimately wonder about Pottmeyer's observation that *Pastor Aeternus* was unnecessary "because the supreme pastoral authority of the papacy was not contested at the time." If that were the case, why was there was such intense discussion at Vatican I regarding "opportuneness"? The reason is that Pope Pius IX was severely beleaguered at the time by the forces of the nationalistic *Risorgimento* (It., "resurgence"), who coveted the remaining Papal States, including Romagna, Umbria, the Marches, and Rome itself, an area that stretched across the whole of central Italy, cutting off the south from the north. As the states were peeled away one by one until Rome alone was left, the pope became convinced of the need for a strong reaffirmation of his supreme

authority in the Church as a counterweight to the setbacks on the temporal side. He pushed hard for the definition of papal infallibility and for the reinforcement of the dogma of papal primacy. The great majority of bishops supported his cause—some under intense papal pressure, others willingly and even enthusiastically. It was Pius IX himself who made "the supreme pastoral authority" an issue, even though it was not subject to challenge at the time within the Church.

28. J. Neuner and Jacques Dupuis, eds., *The Christian Faith in the Doctrinal Documents of the Catholic Church* (Westminster, MD: Christian Classics, 1975), p. 229. Excerpts from the encyclical were not repeated in the 1996 edition of this collection (see n. 21).

29. Neuner and Dupuis, eds., *The Christian Faith in the Doctrinal Documents of the Catholic Church,* pp. 229–30.

30. See Christopher O'Donnell, "Anglican Orders," in his *Ecclesia: A Theological Encyclopedia of the Church* (Collegeville, MN: Liturgical Press, 1996), pp. 10–12; and George H. Tavard, "Anglican ordination," in McBrien, ed., *The HarperCollins Encyclopedia of Catholicism,* pp. 50–51. In 1996, on the fourteen hundredth anniversary of Pope Gregory the Great's sending of missionaries to re-Christianize England and one hundred years after Leo XIII's papal bull on Anglican orders, Pope John Paul II received George L. Carey, then archbishop of Canterbury, as, in effect, a brother bishop and conferred on him a pectoral cross as a personal gift.

31. See C. J. T. Talar, "'The Synthesis of All Heresies'—100 Years On," *Theological Studies* 68/3 (September 2007): 491–514. For commentaries on Modernism in general, see also Gregory Baum, "Modernism," in McBrien, ed., *The HarperCollins Encyclopedia of Catholicism,* pp. 877–78; and Christopher O'Donnell, "Modernism," in his *Ecclesia,* pp. 308–9.

32. Dupuis, ed., *The Christian Faith in the Doctrinal Documents of the Catholic Church,* 6th rev. ed. (1996), pp. 51–54.

33. The full texts of both documents are available in *Origins* 18/40 (March 16, 1989): 661, 663. The three paragraphs in the "Profession of Faith" added to the Nicene Creed require the individual to profess belief in all of the teachings of the Church, whether taught "definitively" or not.

34. The full text of the apostolic letter is available in *Origins* 28/8 (July 16, 1998): 113, 115–16. Following the text is a commentary by then Cardinal Joseph Ratzinger on the concluding paragraphs of the "Profession of Faith" (pp. 116–19). It was in this commentary that Cardinal Ratzinger listed various examples of official teachings that must be embraced, including "truths connected to revelation by historical necessity and which are to be held definitively." One of the examples cited was Leo XIII's declaration of the invalidity of Anglican orders in 1896 (p. 119). This created some measure of controversy at the time, because many regarded it as not only ecumenically insensitive but also theologically dubious to describe this teaching as "definitive." See n. 30.

35. See Émile Mersch, *Le Corps mystique du Christ: Études de théologie historique* (Paris: Desclée De Brouwer, 1933); English ed., *The Whole Christ: The Historical Development of the Doctrine of the Mystical Body in Scripture and Tradition,* trans. John R. Kelly (Milwaukee: Bruce, 1938); and *La théologie du Corps mystique,* 2 vols. (Paris: Desclée De Brouwer, 1944); English ed., *The Theology of*

the Mystical Body, trans. Cyril Vollert (St. Louis: Herder, 1951). The second book was published posthumously. Father Mersch died in a bombing raid in 1940, at the beginning of World War II, while ministering to a group of wounded.

36. Avery Dulles, "A Half Century of Ecclesiology," *Theological Studies* 50/3 (September 1989): 422 (full article, pp. 419–42). See also Sebastian Tromp's textbook on the Church in use for a number of years at the Gregorian University: *Corpus Christi quod est ecclesia*, 4 vols. (Rome: Pontifical Gregorian University, 1937–72).

37. Although the dates of the Counter-Reformation are given as the mid-sixteenth century to the end of the Thirty Years' War in 1648 in E. A. Livingstone, ed., *The Oxford Dictionary of the Christian Church*, 3d ed. (London: Oxford University Press, 1997), p. 423, its impact continued to be felt on Catholic ecclesiology and practice to the very threshold of Vatican II.

38. The encyclical, Avery Dulles remarks, "was by no means a repudiation of previous official teaching, but in many ways it was a welcome advance beyond the more juridical ecclesiologies of the manuals. It capitalized on the rich sources of renewal made possible by recent patristic studies and in turn stimulated further studies of the kind" ("A Half Century of Ecclesiology," p. 422). There is general agreement among theologians, including Dulles, that the principal author behind the encyclical was Sebastian Tromp, S.J., a professor of ecclesiology for many years at the Pontifical Gregorian University in Rome. Tromp was a firm advocate of the view that the Body of Christ and the Catholic Church are one and the same; he later served on the Theological Commission of the Second Vatican Council, under the presidency of Cardinal Alfredo Ottaviani (d. 1979), the prefect of what was then known as the Holy Office and the leader of the minority in opposition to the council's reformist agenda.

39. The English-language edition used here is on the Vatican Web site at www.vatican.va/holy_father/pius_xii/encyclicals/documents/hf_p-xii_enc_29061943_mystici-corporis-christi_en.html.

40. The translation of this sentence is far more pointed and powerful in Dupuis, ed., *The Christian Faith in the Doctrinal Documents of the Catholic Church*, 6th rev. ed., p. 303. The latter part of it reads: ". . . for the whole Spirit is in the Head, the whole Spirit is in the Body, and the whole Spirit is in each of the members."

41. The Catholic Church, also known as the Catholic Communion of Churches, is larger than the Roman, or Latin-rite, Catholic Church. Eastern-rite Churches, which have a collective membership of more than 20 million and which are in communion with the Bishop of Rome, are also Catholic in the fullest sense of the word, but they are not *Roman* Catholic. In a subsequent encyclical in 1950, *Humani generis* (Lat., "Of the human race"), Pius XII compounded the problem by identifying even more bluntly the Body of Christ with the *Roman* Catholic Church: "The Mystical Body of Christ and the Roman Catholic Church are one and the same thing" (*unum idemque esse*, n. 27).

42. Quotations from the Holy Office letter here and following are from Dupuis, ed., *The Christian Faith in the Doctrinal Documents of the Catholic Church*, 6th rev. ed., pp. 305–7.

43. For the complete text see www.vatican.va/holy_father/pius_xii/encyclicals/documents/hf_p-xii_enc_12081950_humani-generis_en.html.

44. See, e.g., Gustave Weigel, "The Historical Background of the Encyclical *Humani Generis,*" *Theological Studies* 12/2 (June 1951): 208–30; and "Current Theology: Gleanings from the Commentaries on *Humani Generis,*" *Theological Studies* 12/4 (December 1951): 520–49.

45. Dietrich Bonhoeffer, *Letters and Papers from Prison* (New York: Macmillan, 1962). The definitive biography of Bonhoeffer was written by his friend Eberhard Bethge, *Dietrich Bonhoeffer: Man of Vision, Man of Courage,* trans. Eric Mosbacher et al. (New York: Harper & Row, 1970). An excellent collection of essays by leading Protestant scholars is Martin E. Marty, ed., *The Place of Bonhoeffer: Problems and Possibilities in His Thought* (New York: Association Press, 1962).

46. E.g., Dietrich Bonhoeffer, *The Cost of Discipleship,* trans. Reginald H. Fuller (New York: Macmillan, 1963); and *Life Together: Prayerbook of the Bible,* Geffrey B. Kelly, ed., trans. Daniel W. Bloesch and James H. Burtness (Minneapolis: Fortress, 1996; first English ed., 1954).

47. John A. T. Robinson, *Honest to God* (New York: Macmillan, 1965). For an overall assessment of Robinson's ecclesiology, see my *The Church in the Thought of Bishop John Robinson* (Philadelphia: Westminster; London: SCM, 1966).

48. See John A. T. Robinson, *The New Reformation?* (Philadelphia: Westminster; London: SCM, 1965), pp. 35–37, 46–50.

49. See John A. T. Robinson, "Kingdom, Church and Ministry," in Kenneth M. Carey, ed., *The Historic Episcopate in the Fullness of the Church,* 2d ed. (London: Dacre, 1960), p. 16. This is one of the most important, but least known, ecclesiological essays written during this period. It was among the first to situate ecclesiology within the larger context of eschatology. In *Honest to God* Robinson wrote that the true radical is the one who subjects the Church to the judgment of the Kingdom (p. 140).

50. Robinson, "Kingdom, Church and Ministry," p. 17.

51. Robinson, "Kingdom, Church and Ministry," p. 17.

52. Robinson, "Kingdom, Church and Ministry," p. 16.

53. John A. T. Robinson, *The Body: A Study in Pauline Theology* (London: SCM, 1952).

54. Robinson, *The Body,* p. 51.

55. Robinson, *The Body,* p. 72.

56. See Harvey Cox, *The Secular City: Secularization and Urbanization in Theological Perspective* (New York: Macmillan, 1965), pp. 127–48.

57. Cox, *The Secular City,* pp. 125–26.

58. Jürgen Moltmann, *Theology of Hope: On the Ground and the Implications of a Christian Eschatology,* trans. James W. Leitch (London: SCM; New York: Harper & Row, 1967; original German ed., 1965).

59. Thomas J. J. Altizer, *The Gospel of Christian Atheism* (Philadelphia: Westminster, 1966), p. 40.

60. Thomas J. J. Altizer, *Oriental Mysticism and Biblical Eschatology* (Philadelphia: Westminster, 1961), pp. 105–6.

61. William Hamilton, *Radical Theology and the Death of God* (Indianapolis, IN: Bobbs-Merrill, 1966), p. 7.

62. Paul Van Buren, *The Secular Meaning of the Gospel* (New York: Macmillan, 1963), p. 184.

63. Van Buren, *The Secular Meaning of the Gospel,* p. 191.

64. Karl Rahner, *Mission and Grace: Essays in Pastoral Theology,* trans. Cecily Hastings, (London: Sheed & Ward, 1963), vol. 1, p. 51. The chapter (pp. 3–55) is entitled "A Theological Interpretation of the Position of Christians in the Modern World." The essay was published originally in 1961, but written earlier than that. For thumbnail sketches of the various Catholic theologians profiled in this section, see my *Catholicism,* pp. 659–64.

65. Rahner, *Mission and Grace,* pp. 51–55.

66. Karl Rahner, *The Church and the Sacraments,* trans. W. J. O'Hara (Freiburg: Herder; Edinburgh-London: Nelson, 1963), p. 19. This is one of the most significant pre–Vatican II books that anticipated and laid the foundation for the council's teaching on the sacramentality of the Church (see the Dogmatic Constitution on the Church, n. 1).

67. Edward Schillebeeckx, *Christ, the Sacrament of the Encounter with God,* trans. Paul Barrett and N. D. Smith (New York and London: Sheed & Ward, 1963). Page references are to the Stagbooks edition, published in London.

68. Tertullian *De Resurrectione carnis* (Lat., "On the resurrection of the flesh") 8. For the translation of the full text, see *Ante-Nicene Fathers,* vol. 3, trans. Peter Holmes (Peabody, MA: Hendrickson, 1994), p. 551.

69. Schillebeeckx, *Christ, the Sacrament of the Encounter with God,* p. 56.

70. See Schillebeeckx, *Christ, the Sacrament of the Encounter with God,* esp. sec. 2, "The Church, Sacrament of the Risen Christ," pp. 55–109.

71. Henri de Lubac, *Catholicism: A Study of Dogma in Relation to the Corporate Destiny of Mankind,* trans. Lancelot C. Sheppard (New York: Sheed & Ward, 1958), pp. 19, 29, 35. The English translation was made from the fourth French edition (Paris, 1947).

72. Hans Küng, *The Council and Reunion,* trans. Cecily Hastings (London: Sheed & Ward, 1961), pp. 15, 17; U.S. ed., *The Council, Reform and Reunion* (New York: Sheed & Ward, 1962); original German ed., *Konzil und Wiedervereinigung* (Freiburg im Breisgau: Herder, 1961).

73. Küng, *The Council and Reunion,* p. 188.

74. See John Courtney Murray, *We Hold These Truths: Catholic Reflections on the American Proposition,* new ed. (Lanham, MD: Rowan & Littlefield, 2005; original ed., New York: Sheed & Ward, 1960).

75. His five major articles in *Theological Studies* in the early 1950s constitute the main body of his pre–Vatican II writings on the subject: "The Problem of State Religion," 12/2 (June 1951): 155–78; "The Church and Totalitarian Democracy," 13/4 (December 1952): 525–63; "Leo XIII: Two Concepts of Government," 14/4 (December 1953): 551–67; "Leo XIII on Church and State: The General Structure of the Controversy," 14/1 (March 1953): 1–30; and "Leo XIII: Two Concepts of Government: II. Government and the Order of Culture," 15/1 (March 1954): 1–33. A sixth article, "Leo XIII and Pius XII: Government in the Order of Religion," already in galley proofs, was to be published the following year in *Theological Studies,* but was withdrawn upon order of the Vatican. It was subsequently published in John Courtney Murray, *Religious Liberty: Catholic Struggles with Pluralism,* ed. J. Leon Hooper (Louisville, KY: Westminster/John Knox, 1993), pp. 49–125.

76. See his commentary "The Declaration on Religious Freedom," delivered at an international theological conference at the University of Notre Dame three months after the adjournment of the council, in John H. Miller, ed., *Vatican II:*

An Interfaith Appraisal (Notre Dame, IN: University of Notre Dame Press; New York: Association Press, 1966), pp. 565–76, followed by a summary of the discussion, pp. 577–85.

77. Yves Congar, *Lay People in the Church: A Study for a Theology of the Laity,* trans. Donald Attwater (Westminster, MD: Newman, 1957); *Power and Poverty in the Church,* trans. Jennifer Nicholson (Baltimore: Helicon, 1964); *The Wide World, My Parish,* trans. Donald Attwater (Baltimore: Helicon, 1961), esp. the first three chapters, pp. 1–26; *Vraie et fausse réforme dans l'Église* (Paris: Les Éditions du Cerf, 1950); *The Mystery of the Temple,* trans. Reginald F. Trevett (London: Burns & Oates, 1962); and *Divided Christendom* (London: Geoffrey Bles, 1939); original French ed., *Chrétiens désunis: principes d'un "oecuménisme" catholique* (Paris: Les Éditions du Cerf, 1937).

78. Dulles, "A Half Century of Ecclesiology," pp. 424–25.

79. Yves Congar, *I Believe in the Holy Spirit,* trans. David Smith, 3 vols. (New York: Seabury, 1983; original French ed., Paris: Les Éditions du Cerf, 1979–80).

80. Yves Congar, *Journal d'un théologien 1946–1956* (Paris: Les Éditions du Cerf, 2001).

81. Yves Congar, "The Call and the Quest 1929–1963," in *Dialogue Between Christians: Catholic Contributions to Ecumenism,* trans. Philip Loretz (Westminster, MD: Newman; London: Chapman, 1966), pp. 1–45, esp. "Difficulties: A Time for Patience," pp. 28–45.

82. *Summa,* 5th ed. (Madrid: Biblioteca de Autores Christianos, 1962). The 1962 edition is a particularly apt exhibit for purposes of comparison and contrast, because it appeared in the same year that the Second Vatican Council opened and was, by general agreement, the finest expression of the so-called manual theology of the preconciliar period.

83. *Summa,* vol. 1, p. xiii. Quotations hereafter in this section on the manuals of theology are to the Spanish *Summa*'s highly detailed Table of Contents (Lat. *Index Generalis*), pp. xii–xvii, which provides the corresponding page numbers for the treatment of each topic within the text itself.

84. Ludwig Ott, *Fundamentals of Catholic Dogma,* trans. Patrick Lynch (Rockford, IL: Tan Books, 1974). The original German edition was published in 1952.

85. Dulles, "A Half Century of Ecclesiology," p. 419.

86. Timoteo Zapelena, *De ecclesia Christi: Pars apologetica,* rev. ed. (Rome: Pontifical Gregorian University, 1950; original ed., 1940). See also his second volume, *Pars altera: Apologetica-dogmatica* (Lat., "Second Part: Apologetical-Dogmatic"), 1940, revised 1950 and 1954. Zapelena was succeeded in the chair of ecclesiology by the American Jesuit theologian Francis A. Sullivan. Dulles notes that Sullivan's approach differed from Zapelena's in that it was "structured more along the lines of the encyclical *Mystici Corporis Christi*" ("A Half Century of Ecclesiology," p. 420).

87. See Dulles, "A Half Century of Ecclesiology," pp. 419–20.

88. Dulles, "A Half Century of Ecclesiology," p. 420.

89. Charles Journet, *The Church of the Word Incarnate,* vol. 1, trans. A. H. C. Downes (New York: Sheed & Ward, 1955); *L'Église du Verbe incarné,* 3 vols. (Bruges: Desclée De Brouwer, 1941, 1951, 1969).

90. Dulles, "A Half Century of Ecclesiology," p. 421.

91. For a brief profile of Pope John XXIII, see my *Lives of the Popes*, pp. 369–75.

Part V: The Ecclesiology of the Second Vatican Council

1. For a detailed synthesis of biblical scholarship as it relates to the origins of the Church, see Frederick Cwiekowski's *The Beginnings of the Church* (New York: Paulist Press, 1988). For similar works, see Part II, n. 4.

2. The literature on the Second Vatican Council is vast, even when limited to English-language books and articles. The major source, however, is Giuseppe Alberigo's five-volume *History of Vatican II,* ed. Joseph A. Komonchak, English ed. (Maryknoll, NY: Orbis Books; Leuven: Peeters, 1995, 1997, 2000, 2003, 2006). Matthew J. O'Connell is listed as the translator of the fifth volume. The volumes appeared simultaneously in Italian, French, German, Spanish, Portuguese, and English. See also Alberigo's *A Brief History of Vatican II,* trans. Matthew Sherry (Maryknoll, NY: Orbis Books, 2006). The most substantive commentary on each of the documents is Herbert Vorgrimler, ed., *Commentary on the Documents of Vatican II,* 5 vols. (New York: Herder and Herder, 1967–69). The individual volumes were translated from the original German by several different individuals. A more recent five-volume commentary, as yet untranslated, is Peter Hünerman and Bernd Jochen Hilberath, eds., *Herders theologischer Kommentar zum zweiten Vatikanischen Konzil* (Freiburg: Herder, 2004–6). There are also highly useful commentaries and discussions by some of the leading experts (Lat. *periti*), a few of the fathers of the council, and several non-Catholic observers, given at an international theological conference held at the University of Notre Dame in March 1966, in John H. Miller, ed., *Vatican II: An Interfaith Appraisal* (Notre Dame, IN: University of Notre Dame Press; New York: Association Press, 1966). The documents themselves are available in the original Latin and in English translation in Norman P. Tanner, ed., *Decrees of the Ecumenical Councils* (Washington, DC: Georgetown University Press; London: Sheed & Ward, 1990), vol. 2, pp. 817–1135. The latest gender-inclusive, English-language edition is Austin Flannery, ed., *Vatican Council II: The Basic Sixteen Documents* (Northport, NY: Costello, 1996). All of the documents are available in several languages on the Vatican's official Web site: www.vatican.va. By far, the best detailed summary of, and theological guide to, all sixteen documents for nonspecialist readers is Edward P. Hahnenberg, *A Concise Guide to the Documents of Vatican II* (Cincinnati, OH: St. Anthony Messenger Press, 2007). For a useful summary of the daily sessions, see *Council Daybook,* 3 vols. (Washington, DC: National Catholic Welfare Conference, 1965, 1966). An excellent insider's journalistic account of each of the four yearly sessions is provided by Xavier Rynne (pseudonym of Redemptorist Francis Xavier Murphy), *Vatican Council II* (Maryknoll, NY: Orbis Books, 1999; orig. ed., 1966). The Church's leading ecclesiologist and a council *peritus,* Yves Congar, has provided the most authoritative daily journal by a single individual in *Mon Journal du Concile,* ed. Éric Mahieu, 2 vols. (Paris: Les Éditions du Cerf, 2002). See also John W. O'Malley's *What Happened at Vatican II* (Cambridge, MA: Harvard University Press, 2008). Jesuit church historian O'Malley is an especially acute

commentator on the council, as subsequent references to him in both the text and notes of Part V will clearly indicate. For quick overviews, see my "Vatican Council II," in Richard P. McBrien, ed., *The HarperCollins Encyclopedia of Catholicism* (San Francisco: HarperSanFrancisco, 1995), pp. 1299–1306; and Christopher O'Donnell's "Vatican II, Council of (1962–1965)," in his *Ecclesia: A Theological Encyclopedia of the Church* (Collegeville, MN: Liturgical Press, 1996), pp. 457–63. There is also a five-cassette video entitled *Faithful Revolution: Vatican II,* exec. prod. Sherry Revord (New York: Lyrick Productions, 1997). Finally, for a brief, but highly substantive, essay of appreciation for the council, for Popes John XXIII and Paul VI, and for Vatican II's ecumenical and interfaith breakthroughs, especially in the relation of the Church to the Jews, see Cardinal Franz König, "It Must Be the Holy Spirit," *The Tablet* 256 (December 21–28, 2002): 4–6.

3. Neo-Scholasticism was a revival of medieval Scholasticism (the philosophy and theology of "the Schools," thus the term "Scholasticism"), with a heavy emphasis on nonhistorical orthodoxy (a propositional and even legalistic approach to Christian faith) that shaped the content and tone of the Latin manuals of Catholic theology from the sixteenth century to Vatican II.

4. The Counter-Reformation was the official Catholic response—papal, conciliar, theological, and pastoral—to the Protestant Reformation of the sixteenth century. At the center of the Counter-Reformation was the Council of Trent and its reform of Catholic doctrine, liturgy, law, and seminary education. For the relation between the Counter-Reformation and the Catholic Reformation, see III.2.15.

5. Cited in Alberigo, *History of Vatican II,* vol. 1, p. 1.

6. Alberigo, *History of Vatican II,* vol. 1, p. 2.

7. Alberigo, *History of Vatican II,* vol. 1, p. 2.

8. Cited in Alberigo, *A Brief History of Vatican II,* p. 1. But even the theologian Yves Congar expressed reservations. He wrote in his diary that in regard to the unity of the Christian Churches, "it seemed that the Council was being held twenty years too soon" (*Mon Journal du Concile,* vol. 1, p. 4).

9. *Acta et Documenta Concilio oecumenico Vatican II apparando* (Typis Polyglottis Vaticanis, 1960–61), vol. 1, pp. 19, 24.

10. What follows in the remainder of this section is drawn directly from my entry "Vatican Council II," in McBrien, ed., *The HarperCollins Encyclopedia of Catholicism,* pp. 1301–2. For a more detailed exposition of this material, see Alberigo's *History of Vatican II,* vol. 1, *Announcing and Preparing Vatican Council II: Toward a New Era in Catholicism.*

11. There was so little understanding of John XXIII's intentions for the council that many of the suggested agenda items were trivial by present-day standards. On a personal note, one of my own seminary professors unblinkingly acknowledged that he had submitted to the cardinal-archbishop of Boston a proposal that the council clarify the Church's teaching on servile work. Many readers nowadays would not even know what servile work is, namely, physical labor forbidden on Sundays and holy days, in presumed conformity with the Third Commandment to "Keep holy the Sabbath."

12. Convocation is the official announcement by the pope that a council will be held. The convening of a council is its official opening by the pope.

13. The English text of the opening address is available on various Web sites; in Walter M. Abbott, ed., *The Documents of Vatican II,* trans. Joseph Gallagher (New York: Guild Press, America Press, and Association Press, 1966), pp. 710–19; and in Floyd Anderson, ed., *Council Daybook: Vatican II, Sessions 1 and 2* (Washington, DC: National Catholic Welfare Conference, 1965), pp. 25–29. The critical text, compiled on the basis of later revisions by the pope, was edited by Giuseppe Alberigo and Alberto Melloni and published as "*L'allocuzione "Gaudet mater Ecclesia" di Giovanni XXIII*" in *Fede Tradizione Profezia: Studi su Giovanni XXIII e sul Vaticano II* ["Faith Tradition Prophecy: Studies on John XXIII and Vatican II"] (Brescia, 1984), pp. 185–283.

14. Xavier Rynne makes the same point in his *Vatican Council II:* "This inaugural address to the Council . . . marked the end of the closed mentality that had characterized not a few Catholic bishops and theologians since the sixteenth century" (p. 48).

15. The term "council fathers" consists of "the bishops and others called to the council." These include all cardinals, patriarchs, archbishops, residential bishops (even if not yet consecrated), auxiliary bishops, heads of independent abbeys and prelatures, abbots primate, abbots who are superiors of monastic congregations, and superiors general of exempt congregations of professed religious. Experts (Lat. *periti*) and non-Catholic observers are not included in this category. See Anderson, ed., *Council Daybook,* vol. 1, p. 32.

16. Anderson, ed., *Council Daybook,* vol. 1, p. 54. For a sustained reflection on the political mechanics of the council, see Philippe Levillain, *La Mécanique Politique de Vatican II: La majorité et l'unanimité dans un Concile* (Paris: Éditions Beauchesne, 1975).

17. Karl Rahner, *Concern for the Church: Theological Investigations XX,* trans. Edward Quinn (New York: Crossroad, 1981), "Basic Theological Interpretation of the Second Vatican Council," pp. 77–89.

18. Rahner, *Concern for the Church,* p. 78.

19. Rahner, *Concern for the Church,* p. 80.

20. Rahner, *Concern for the Church,* pp. 82–83.

21. Rahner, *Concern for the Church,* p. 85.

22. Rahner, *Concern for the Church,* p. 86, my italics.

23. Joseph Komonchak , "The Significance of Vatican II for Ecclesiology," in Peter C. Phan, ed., *The Gift of the Church: A Textbook on Ecclesiology* (Collegeville, MN: Liturgical Press, 2000), p. 76. I would generally agree with Komonchak's conclusion.

24. See Abbott, ed., *The Documents of Vatican II,* p. 14, n. 1.

25. St. Augustine of Hippo, *Letter 105,* 3, 12. See also Johann Auer, *The Church: The Universal Sacrament of Salvation* (Washington, DC: The Catholic University of America, 1993), and Colm O'Doherty, *Church as Sacrament: The Need for Self-Questioning* (Dublin: Columba, 1994).

26. See Jürgen Moltmann, *Theology of Hope: On the Ground and the Implications of a Christian Eschatology,* trans. James W. Leitch (London: SCM; New York: Harper & Row, 1967; original German ed., 1965), pp. 325–26; and George Lindbeck, *The Future of Roman Catholic Theology: Vatican II—Catalyst for*

Change (Philadelphia: Fortress, 1970), p. 47, n. 34. Significantly, Moltmann is in the Reformed tradition of Protestantism, while Lindbeck is from the Lutheran side of the so-called magisterial Reformation.

27. On the holiness of God and its application to the saints and to the Church itself, see my *Lives of the Saints: From Mary and St. Francis of Assisi to John XXIII and Mother Teresa* (San Francisco: HarperSanFrancisco, 2001), pp. 3–4, 10–11. For explicit references to the holiness of the Church in the teachings of Vatican II, see my *Catholicism,* rev. ed. (San Francisco: HarperSanFrancisco, 1994), pp. 1043–44.

28. For our previous discussion of the People of God in the Bible, see II.2.13.a. There are, of course, many references to the Church as People of God throughout this book.

29. Karol Wojtyla, *Sources of Renewal: The Implementation of Vatican II,* trans. P. S. Falla (San Francisco: Harper & Row, 1980; original Polish ed., 1972), pp. 146–47. Cardinal Wojtyla described the change as "significant" because it brought out the "organic link" between the People of God and the hierarchical structure of the Church and also emphasized the truth, rooted in the gospel, that authority is a form of service, which Christ himself taught by word and example. See also Alberigo, *History of Vatican II,* vol. 3, pp. 80–81.

30. See J. Bryan Hehir, "The Social Role of the Church: Leo XIII, Vatican II and John Paul II," in Oliver F. Williams and John W. Houck, eds., *Catholic Social Thought and the New World Order* (Notre Dame, IN: University of Notre Dame Press, 1993), p. 36.

31. The material for this paragraph and several subsequent paragraphs is drawn from my paper "An Ecclesiological Analysis of Catholic Social Teachings," in Williams and Houck, eds., *Catholic Social Thought and the New World Order,* pp. 155–57.

32. John Courtney Murray, "The Issue of Church and State at Vatican II," *Theological Studies* 27/4 (December 1966): 602–3.

33. One of those commentators, Joseph Ratzinger, became Pope Benedict XVI in 2005. In an article published in 1976, "*Taufe, Glaube und Zugehörigkeit zur Kirche*" (Ger., "Baptism, Faith and Membership in the Church"), *Internationale katholische Zeitschrift Communio* 5 (1976): 218–34, and reprinted in *Principles of Catholic Theology: Building Stones for a Fundamental Theology,* trans. Mary Francis McCarthy (San Francisco: Ignatius, 1987), pp. 27–55, then Cardinal Ratzinger set the Church as People of God in opposition to the Church as a sacrament and as a communion (see pp. 45, 53–55). The "deepest meaning" of the Church as "sacrament of unity" is the Church as a communion, i.e., "God's communing with men [*sic*] in Christ and hence the communing of men [*sic*] with one another" (p. 53). The future pope expressed the concern back in 1976 that "the isolated concept of 'people of God' could become a caricature of conciliar ecclesiology" (pp. 54–55). His additional concern was that the notion of the Church as sacrament might eventually be lost entirely in favor of People of God. This concern should be alleviated by the ecclesiological synthesis provided in this book, where the concept of the Church as mystery, or sacrament, is placed first in order, ahead of the Church as People of God, just as it is in the Dogmatic Constitution on the Church itself.

34. Christopher O'Donnell, "Communion–Koinonîa," in his *Ecclesia*, p. 96. See also Michael A. Fahey's succinct entry "communion, Church as," in McBrien, ed., *The HarperCollins Encyclopedia of Catholicism*, p. 337.

35. For a historical survey, see Francis A. Sullivan, *Salvation Outside the Church? Tracing the History of the Catholic Response* (New York: Paulist Press, 1992). The Dogmatic Constitution on the Church speaks of the Church as being "from Abel," indicating, in agreement with some of the early fathers of the Church, that the Church existed before the Incarnation and included all of the just who "will be gathered together with the Father in the universal church" (n. 2). Yves Congar has written the classic work on the subject, "*Ecclesia ab Abel*" in M. Reding, H. Elfers, and F. Hoffmann, eds., *Abhandlungen über Theologie und Kirche: Festschrift für Karl Adam* (Dusseldorf: Patmos, 1952), pp. 79–110.

36. Until otherwise noted, the following quotations are from the same article of the decree.

37. Some may ask what "properly baptized" means. In the Catholic Church and in other mainline Churches and ecclesial communities, Baptism consists of the pouring of water while saying the words: "I baptize you in the name of the Father and of the Son and of the Holy Spirit." The same sacramental result can be achieved, of course, by immersion, although the practice is not common in the Catholic and other mainline Churches and ecclesial communities. The baptismal rite is an expression of the recipient's faith in Jesus Christ as the Son of God and our Redeemer, and it is the intention of the minister to initiate the recipient into the Body of Christ, not necessarily into one particular denomination within it. In other words, for the Catholic Church, as for most others, Baptism can be validly administered outside of one's own ecclesiastical tradition, so long as the matter and the form (the pouring of the water and the recitation of the words) are observed. See, e.g., Kenan B. Osborne, *The Christian Sacraments of Initiation: Baptism, Confirmation, Eucharist* (New York: Paulist Press, 1987). For an abbreviated presentation, see Anthony Sherman, "Baptism," in McBrien, ed., *The HarperCollins Encyclopedia of Catholicism*, pp. 133–38.

38. See Aloys Grillmeier's commentary on article 8 in Vorgrimler, ed., *Commentary on the Documents of Vatican II*, vol. 1, pp. 146–52.

39. *Responses to Some Questions Regarding Certain Aspects of the Doctrine on the Church*, in *Origins* 37/9 (July 19, 2007): 134–36, with the CDF's own commentary on pp. 136–39. This CDF document should be read in close connection with its earlier document *Dominus Iesus*, in *Origins* 30/14 (September 14, 2000): 209, 211–19.

40. *Responses to Some Questions*, commentary, pp. 137–38.

41. Francis Sullivan, "Subsists," *America* 188/9 (March 17, 2003): 15. See also Sullivan's "Quaestio Disputata: A Response to Karl Becker, S.J., on the Meaning of *Subsistit In*," *Theological Studies* 67/2 (June 2006): 395–409, esp. 407–9, and his later "Quaestio Disputata: The Meaning of *Subsistit in* as Explained by the Congregation for the Doctrine of the Faith," *Theological Studies* 69/1 (March 2008): 116–24. For a good summation of the debate, see Richard R. Gaillardetz, "The Church of Christ and the Churches," *America* 197/5 (August 27–September 3, 2007): 17–20.

42. See Alberigo, *A Brief History of Vatican II*, p. 30.

43. See Alberigo, *History of Vatican II,* vol. 2, pp. 343–44.

44. Alberigo, *History of Vatican II,* vol. 2, p. 344.

45. Some of these commentaries are mentioned in n. 2.

46. The material for this section is drawn largely from my previously published commentary on *Lumen gentium,* "The Church (*Lumen Gentium*)" in Adrian Hastings, ed., *Modern Catholicism: Vatican II and After* (New York: Oxford University Press; London: SPCK, 1991), pp. 84–95. Among the best commentaries on the document is the multi-authored "Dogmatic Constitution on the Church," in Herbert Vorgrimler, ed., *Commentary on the Documents of Vatican II,* vol. 1, pp. 105–305. Individual sections include "History of the Constitution," by Gerard Philips, pp. 105–37; "The Mystery of the Church," by Aloys Grillmeier, pp. 138–52; "The People of God," also by Grillmeier, pp. 153–85; "The Hierarchical Structure of the Church, with Special Reference to the Episcopate" (arts. 18–27 by Karl Rahner; art. 28 by Aloys Grillmeier; and art. 29 by Herbert Vorgrimler), pp. 186–230; "The Laity," by Ferdinand Klostermann, pp. 231–52; "The Call of the Whole Church to Holiness," by Friedrich Wulf, pp. 261–72; "Religious," also by Wulf, pp. 273–79; "The Eschatological Nature of the Pilgrim Church and Her Union with the Heavenly Church," by Otto Semmelroth, pp. 280–84; "The Role of the Blessed Virgin Mary, Mother of God, in the Mystery of Christ and the Church," also by Semmelroth, pp. 285–96; and "Announcements and Prefatory Notes of Explanation," by Joseph Ratzinger, pp. 297–305. There is also a comparable commentary in Portuguese and in French, but still untranslated into English. The French edition is Yves Congar, Guilherme Baraúna, et al., eds., *Vatican II: L'Église de Vatican II: la Constitution dogmatique sur l'Église,* 3 vols. (Paris: Les Éditions du Cerf, 1965–66). Meanwhile, more popular commentaries abound. See, e.g., Richard R. Gaillardetz, *The Church in the Making: Lumen Gentium, Christus Dominus, Orientalium Ecclesiarum* (New York: Paulist Press, 2006.)

47. For an analytical narrative of the various debates on the second draft of *De Ecclesia,* see Alberigo, *History of Vatican II,* vol. 3, pp. 40–115.

48. On the distinction, see my *Catholicism,* pp. 1104–5. Marian minimalism tends to withhold any and all veneration of Mary, while Marian maximalism assumes that there are practically no limits to such veneration.

49. This was a relatively common view prior to and at the time of the Second Vatican Council. Many readers who are too young to remember or even to have been alive in the 1950s and 1960s might be surprised to hear this. However, by way of a personal anecdote, my own professor of ecclesiology in seminary urged us to pray that Vatican II would never be held. Paul VI's address is discussed briefly in Alberigo's *History of Vatican II,* vol. 4, pp. 8–10.

50. It may seem incongruous that it is called "a preceding [or preliminary] note" when it appears in the appendix of the document, but the reason is that the note "came before" the Theological Commission's comments on the various last-minute *modi* (Lat., "amendments").

51. Text is available in Flannery, ed., *Vatican II: The Basic Sixteen Documents,* pp. 92–95; quotations from p. 94; italics are in the text itself. The text is also available, in both Latin and English, in Tanner, ed., *Decrees of the Ecumenical Councils,* vol. 2, pp. 898–900.

52. See Alberigo, *History of Vatican II,* vol. 3, p. 445. The entire controversy is described on pp. 432–55 and here and there in chap. 6, "The 'Black Week' of Vatican II (November 14–21 1964)," pp. 387–452.

53. For a fuller analysis, see my "The Church (*Lumen Gentium*)," in Hastings, ed., *Modern Catholicism,* esp. pp. 88–94.

54. Charles Moeller, "Pastoral Constitution on the Church in the Modern World: History of the Constitution," in Vorgrimler, ed., *Commentary on the Documents of Vatican II,* vol. 5, pp. 1–76.

55. Archbishop McGrath's commentary is the one followed here. It appears in Miller, ed., *Vatican II: An Interfaith Appraisal,* pp. 397–412.

56. McGrath, in Miller, ed., *Vatican II: An Interfaith Appraisal,* p. 397.

57. I am employing in the discussion that follows Archbishop McGrath's categories and titles.

58. See Anderson, ed., *Council Daybook,* vol. 1, pp. 45–46.

59. These are listed in Archbishop McGrath's presentation in Miller, ed., *Vatican II: An Interfaith Appraisal,* pp. 398–99.

60. See John W. O'Malley, *Four Cultures of the West* (Cambridge, MA: Harvard University Press, 2004), pp. 176–77, and passim.

61. McGrath, in Miller, ed., *Vatican II: An Interfaith Appraisal,* p. 401.

62. O'Malley, *Four Cultures of the West,* p. 177.

63. McGrath, in Miller, ed., *Vatican II: An Interfaith Appraisal,* p. 410.

64. See Avery Dulles, "A Half Century of Ecclesiology," *Theological Studies* 50/3 (September, 1989): 430–31. Pope Benedict XVI, in his Christmas address of 2005, referred to the latter view as one of "discontinuity and rupture." He advocated instead a "hermeneutics of reform," which focuses more on the final documents of the council than on the council as an ecclesial event. He had also expressed this view as Cardinal Joseph Ratzinger in an interview in Vittorio Messori, *The Ratzinger Report: An Exclusive Interview on the State of the Church* (San Francisco: Ignatius, 1985), p. 35. The full text of the pope's Christmas address is available on the Internet at www.asianews.it/view.php?l=en&art=4944#; see esp. pp. 4–5. Australian theologian Ormond Rush suggests an alternative distinction between "macro-rupture" (which the council never intended) and "micro-rupture," the latter representing a genuine innovation with regard to some aspect of the tradition, but one that can also be interpreted as "rejuvenating that broader tradition." See Rush's *Still Interpreting Vatican II: Some Hermeneutical Principles* (New York: Paulist Press, 2004), p. 7. Rush's book is a highly useful, balanced primer for interpreting the council and has begun to influence younger theologians, like Richard R. Gaillardetz, who embraces Rush's work in his own *The Church in the Making,* pp. xvi–xx. For a more recently expressed view by Avery Dulles, arguing on behalf of the hermeneutic of continuity, see his "Vatican II: The Myth and the Reality," *America* 188/6 (February 24, 2003): 7–11, with strongly critical rejoinders by two fellow Jesuits, John F. Long, a *peritus* at Vatican II, pp. 14–15, and Francis A. Sullivan, longtime professor at the Pontifical Gregorian University in Rome and later at Boston College, p. 15.

65. The "Bologna school" was centered at an institute for research in religious studies in the archdiocese of Bologna, Italy, originally directed by Professor

Giuseppe Dossetti, later ordained a priest and for whom Giuseppe Alberigo had served as an assistant. The institute was closely connected to the local archbishop, Cardinal Giacomo Lercaro (d. 1976), who played an important part in the Second Vatican Council and before that was a leading candidate to succeed Pius XII as pope in 1958.

66. See Agostino Marchetto, *Il Concilio Ecumenico Vaticano II: Contrappunto per la sua storia* [It., "Vatican Council II: A Counterpoint to Its History"] (Vatican City: Libreria Editrice Vaticana, 2005). The book was publicly and formally introduced in July 2005 by Cardinal Camillo Ruini, at the time the pope's vicar for the diocese of Rome and president of the Italian Bishops' Conference (see *Espresso* reporter Sandro Magistro's account of the celebratory event at www.chiesa.espressoline.it/dettaglio.jsp?id=34283&eng=y, July 27, 2005). Ruini explicitly attacked the so-called Bologna school, comparing it, as Archbishop Marchetto himself had done in his book (pp. 378–79), with Paolo Sarpi's history of the Council of Trent (1619), which suggested that the council had been part of a papal conspiracy to prevent the reform of the Church. Sarpi's book was immediately placed on the Index of Forbidden Books.

For a brief commentary on this event, see John W. O'Malley, "Vatican II: Did Anything Happen?" *Theological Studies* 67/1 (March 2006): 3–33, at 3–6. O'Malley specifically challenges the odious comparison with Sarpi. After careful study of all five volumes, O'Malley concludes that they are "a remarkable achievement of historical scholarship . . . [comparable] not to Sarpi but to the authoritative history of Trent published in the last century by Hubert Jedin" (p. 6). See also O'Malley's "Trent and Vatican II: Two Styles of Church," in Raymond F. Bulman and Frederick J. Parrella, eds., *From Trent to Vatican II* (New York: Oxford University Press, 2006), pp. 301–20. Also in Bulman and Parrella, eds., *From Trent to Vatican II,* see Joseph Komonchak, "The Council of Trent at the Second Vatican Council," pp. 61–89, and Giuseppe Alberigo, "From the Council of Trent to 'Tridentinism,'" pp. 19–37.

67. See his interview with Catholic Online, July 14, 2005, at www.yourcatholicvoice.org/print.php?print=news&ID=2357. Archbishop Marchetto mentions other works in line with his own "contrapuntal" interpretation of the council, e.g., Cardinal Leo Scheffczyk, *Aspecte der Kirche in der Krise: Um die Entscheidung für das authentische Konzil* [Ger., "Aspects of the Church in Crisis: Towards an Authentic Interpretation of the Council"] (Siegburg, Germany: F. Schmitt, 1993); and Annibale Zambarbieri, *Il Concilio del Vaticano* (Cinisello Balsamo, Italy: San Paolo, 1995).

68. See Hermann Pottmeyer, "A New Phase in the Reception of Vatican II: Twenty Years of Interpretation of the Council," in Giuseppe Alberigo, Jean-Pierre Jossua, and Joseph A. Komonchak, eds., *The Reception of Vatican II* (Washington, DC: Catholic University of America Press, 1987), pp. 27–43; and Gustave Thils, "*En pleine fidélité au Concile du Vatican II*" (Fr., "In Complete Fidelity to Vatican Council II"), *La foi et le temps* 10 (1980): 278–79, and "*Trois traits charactéristiques de l'Église postconciliaire*" (Fr., "Three Characteristic Traits of the Postconciliar Church"), *Bulletin de théologie africaine* 3 (1981): 233–45 (cited in Pottmeyer, "A New Phase in the Reception of Vatican II," pp. 40–41).

69. Pottmeyer, "A New Phase in the Reception of Vatican II," p. 40. He also quotes Thils to the same effect.

70. See Dulles, "A Half Century of Ecclesiology," pp. 430–31.

71. The clearest, popular explanation of O'Malley's thesis regarding the change in style is contained in his "The Style of Vatican II," *America* 188/6 (February 24, 2003): 12–15. A more academically elaborate presentation is his "Vatican II: Did Anything Happen?" *Theological Studies* 67/1 (March 2006): 3–33. For background to both, see his *Four Cultures of the West* (Cambridge, MA: Harvard University Press, 2004), esp. "Introduction: Athens and Jerusalem," pp. 1–36, and "Culture Three: Poetry, Rhetoric, and the Common Good," pp. 127–77; reflections on the Culture Three style of discourse in the documents of Vatican II are found on pp. 175–77. This section of Part V draws from O'Malley's *America* article, but with the strong recommendation that readers also consult his longer, annotated article in *Theological Studies* as well as his *Four Cultures of the West* book. "To this day," O'Malley insists in the book, "the council has become an object of confusion and controversy, to a large extent because interpreters miss that they are dealing here with literary genres altogether different from those of all preceding councils. This obliviousness is all the more amazing because the first thing that strikes one when reading the documents is that they are written in a style no previous council ever adopted" (p. 176). See also his more recent monograph *What Happened at Vatican II* (Cambridge, MA: Harvard University Press, 2008).

72. O'Malley, "The Style of Vatican II," p. 12, italics in the original. In the remainder of this discussion in section 9, quotations from O'Malley's work are from "The Style of Vatican II" (pp. 12–15).

73. Ormond Rush, *The Reception of Doctrine: An Appropriation of Hans Robert Jauss' Reception Aesthetics and Literary Hermeneutics* (Rome: Pontifical Gregorian University, 1997).

74. Ormond Rush, *Still Interpreting Vatican II: Some Hermeneutical Principles* (New York: Paulist Press, 2004). Richard R. Gaillardetz, currently a chaired professor of Catholic Studies at the University of Toledo, is generous in his praise for Rush's approach, referring to it as "the most balanced hermeneutical framework to date for interpreting council documents, one which avoids a false absolutizing of either continuity or discontinuity" (*The Church in the Making*, p. xvi). Over against Gaillardetz's view, I should argue that the both/and approach is, in fact, the more common one by far. Few mainline theologians and church historians who have addressed this matter have absolutized either side of the hermeneutical dialectic. It is only a minority who have done so, and most of those tend to absolutize the hermeneutics of continuity. Nevertheless, I am indebted to Richard Gaillardetz for his useful summaries of Rush's rules of interpretation, which he provides on pp. xviii–xx of his own *The Church in the Making*, and which I am reproducing here, with some modifications for the sake of clarity and simplification.

75. See Rush, *Still Interpreting Vatican II*, pp. 1–34; and Gaillardetz, *The Church in the Making*, pp. xviii–xix.

76. See Rush, *Still Interpreting Vatican II*, pp. 35–51.

77. The rules of interpretation listed in this section are in John W. O'Malley's "Vatican II: Did Anything Happen?" p. 32, as paraphrased by Avery Dulles in his "Vatican II: The Myth and the Reality," p. 9. For the full text of the Extraordinary Synod's Final Report, see *Origins* 15/27 (December 19, 1985): 444–50; for the synodal norms for interpreting the conciliar texts, see I.5 on pp. 445–46.

78. O'Malley, "Vatican II: Did Anything Happen?" p. 32.

79. O'Malley, "Vatican II: Did Anything Happen?" p. 33.

80. References are to the official Vatican translation of the encyclical, available at www.vatican.va/holy_father/paul_vi/encyclicals/documents/hf_p-vi_enc_06081964_ecclesiam_en.html.

81. Evangelista Vilanova, "The Intersession (1963–1964)," in Alberigo, *History of Vatican II,* vol. 3, p. 454.

82. Vilanova, "The Intersession," p. 457.

83. According to Yves Congar, Paul VI, when still cardinal-archbishop of Milan, had written to ask for a copy of Congar's *Vraie et fausse réforme dans l'Église* (Paris: Les Éditions du Cerf, 1950), a book that had been ordered withdrawn from circulation by the Holy Office. See Vilanova, "The Intersession," p. 452, n. 358.

84. *Tertio millennio adveniente* (Lat., "As the third millennium draws near"), n. 20. Full text in *Origins* 24/24 (November 24, 1994): 401, 403–16, at 407.

85. *In Spiritu Sancto* (Lat., "In the Holy Spirit"), para. 1. For the full text, see www.vatican.net/holy_father/paul_vi/apost_letters/documents/hf_p-vi_apl_19651208_in-spiritu-sancto_en.html.

86. "Essays in Theology" (syndicated column), week of December 23, 1966.

87. See n. 9 above.

88. Leo Josef Suenens, *A New Pentecost?* (New York: Seabury, 1974), p. 229.

Part VI: Post–Vatican II Ecclesiology: The Church ad Extra

1. Post–Vatican II ecclesiology can be characterized in one of three ways: first, as a drawing out of the logical, but sometimes hidden, implications of the council's ecclesiology (in Cardinal Suenens's metaphor, the council documents were like seeds awaiting the sun); second, as a set of new theological developments that are wholly or largely independent of the council; or, third, as an uneven mixture of both. The most plausible characterization of post–Vatican II ecclesiology is the first; the least plausible, the second.

2. The Kingdom, or Reign, of God is central to the doctrine and theology of the Church. It is no surprise, therefore, that it should occupy an exceedingly prominent place throughout this book. For previous treatments of this topic, without which an understanding of the nature and mission of the Church is impossible, see I.2.1–3; II.2.4–5, 8; III.2.6.f; IV.4.1.b–c, 4.2.f; and V.6.6.

3. For previous treatments of the Church-world relationship, see V.5, 6.2, 7.2, particularly with regard to Vatican II's Pastoral Constitution on the Church in the Modern World (*Gaudium et spes*).

4. For previous discussions of this topic, see I.4; I.8; IV.3.4; IV.4.2.a; and V.6.6.

5. See also V.6.3.

6. See also V.6.3.

7. See also II.2.6, 2.13.c; and III.2.6, 12.

8. See also V.6.4.

9. See also I.4; I, passim; and V.9.

10. See also V.10.

11. See also I.5; II.2.10–11; and IV (with special attention to the Petrine ministry).

12. See also V.7.1.

13. See also V.5.

14. Some prefer the term "Reign" because "Kingdom" suggests a masculine bias. Others believe that "Reign" also conveys a more dynamic expression of the Kingdom, i.e., the Kingdom in the process of being realized. The two terms, however, are essentially equivalent. For an overview, see my *Catholicism*, rev. ed. (San Francisco: HarperSanFrancisco, 1994), pp. 692–718, 1141–57. See also John Fuellenbach, *The Kingdom of God: The Message of Jesus Today* (Maryknoll, NY: Orbis Books, 1995). His chapter on the Church and the Kingdom of God is reproduced in almost identical form in *Church: Community for the Kingdom* (Maryknoll, NY: Orbis Books, 2002), chap. 4, pp. 74–90. See also Mariasusai Dhavamony, *The Kingdom of God and World Religions, Documenta Missionalia*, vol. 31 (Rome: Pontifical Gregorian University, 2004).

15. See Karl Rahner's commentary on article 39 of the council's Pastoral Constitution on the Church in the Modern World, "Christianity and the New Earth," *Theology Digest* 15/4 (Winter 1967): 275–82.

16. See Karl Rahner, "Church and World," in Karl Rahner, ed., *Sacramentum Mundi: An Encyclopedia of Theology*, trans. W. J. O'Hara (New York: Herder and Herder, 1968), vol. 1, pp. 346–57.

17. Rahner, "Church and World," p. 348.

18. Rahner, "Church and World," p. 348.

19. Rahner, "Church and World," p. 348.

20. Edward Schillebeeckx, *God, the Future of Man*, trans. N. D. Smith (New York: Sheed & Ward, 1968), p. 157.

21. Schillebeeckx, *God, the Future of Man*, p. 157.

22. See Edward Schillebeeckx, *Jesus: An Experiment in Christology*, trans. Hubert Hoskins (New York: Seabury, 1979), p. 153.

23. See Edward Schillebeeckx, *Christ: The Experience of Jesus as Lord*, trans. John Bowden (New York: Seabury, 1980), p. 835. In his *Interim Report on the Books Jesus and Christ*, trans. John Bowden (New York: Crossroad, 1981), Schillebeeckx points out that the way in which he wrote his two Jesus books shows that he "wanted to help the church to concentrate again on the kingdom of God and the role which Jesus Christ plays in it" (p. 103). It was also to counteract the Church's tendency toward triumphalism, self-righteousness, and severity.

24. See Edward Schillebeeckx, *Church: The Human Story of God*, trans. John Bowden (New York: Crossroad, 1990), p. 155, and passim.

25. Hans Küng, *The Church*, trans. Ray and Rosaleen Ockenden (New York: Sheed & Ward, 1967); see esp. pp. 43–104.

26. This was noted even by Yves Congar in his "Bulletin d'ecclésiologie," *Revue des sciences philosophiques et théologiques* 53 (1969): 693–705, esp. 694. Cited in Avery Dulles, "A Half Century of Ecclesiology," *Theological Studies* 50/3 (September 1989): 433.

27. Küng, *The Church*, p. 96.

28. Hans Küng, *On Being a Christian*, trans. Edward Quinn (Garden City, NY: Doubleday, 1976).

29. Avery Dulles, *Models of the Church*, exp. ed. (Garden City, NY: Doubleday, Image Books, 1987); see chap. 7, "The Church and Eschatology," pp. 103–22.

30. Dulles, *Models of the Church*, p. 121.

31. Dulles, *Models of the Church*, p. 121.

32. See my *Do We Need the Church?* (New York: Harper & Row, 1969), p. 14, and passim.

33. Avery Dulles, *The Reshaping of Catholicism: Current Challenges in the Theology of Church* (San Francisco: Harper & Row, 1988), p. 138; see also pp. 136–38.

34. John A. T. Robinson, an Anglican New Testament scholar and later suffragan bishop of Woolwich in south London, is a good representative of this approach. For his influence on this author, see Part I, n. 10.

35. See Wolfhart Pannenberg, *Theology and the Kingdom of God* (Philadelphia: Westminster, 1969), esp. chap. 2, "The Kingdom of God and the Church," pp. 72–101. See also his *The Church*, trans. Keith Crim (Philadelphia: Westminster, 1983), chap. 4, "The Significance of Eschatology for an Understanding of the Apostolicity and Catholicity of the Church," pp. 44–68.

36. George Lindbeck, *The Future of Roman Catholic Theology: Vatican II—Catalyst for Change* (Philadelphia: Fortress, 1970), pp. 9–10, 27–28. This book is a model of ecumenical theology.

37. Jürgen Moltmann, *Theology of Hope: On the Ground and the Implications of a Christian Eschatology*, trans. James W. Leitch (London: SCM; New York: Harper & Row, 1967; original German ed., 1965), p. 326.

38. Moltmann, *Theology of Hope*, p. 327.

39. Moltmann, *Theology of Hope*, p. 328. For an attempt, albeit unfinished, at a comprehensive ecumenical ecclesiology, see *The Nature and Mission of the Church: A Stage on the Way to a Common Statement*, Faith and Order Paper 198 (Geneva: World Council of Churches, 2005). The document is available on the World Council of Churches Web site at www.oikoumene.org/index.php?id=2617&L=0. This paper could usefully be consulted for each of the topics treated in Part VI of this book. Other important ecumenical statements on the nature and mission of the Church issued by the WCC after Vatican II include *Baptism, Eucharist and Ministry*, Faith and Order Paper 111 (Geneva: World Council of Churches, 1982); *Church and World: The Unity of the Church and the Renewal of the Human Community*, Faith and Order Paper 151, 2d rev. printing (Geneva: World Council of Church, 1990); the statement of the Canberra Assembly of 1991, "The Church as Koinonia: Gift and Calling," in Michael Kinnamon and Brian E. Cope, eds., *The Ecumenical Movement: An Anthology of Key Texts and Voices* (Geneva: World Council of Churches; Grand Rapids, MI: Eerdmans, 1997), pp. 124–25; and *Growing Together in Unity and Mission: Anglican-Roman Catholic International Commission*, *Origins* 37/19 (October 18, 2007): 289,

290–307. Finally, for a helpful overview of ecumenical ecclesiology, see Michael A. Fahey's article of the same name in Phan, Peter, ed., *The Gift of the Church: A Textbook on Ecclesiology in Honor of Patrick Granfield, O.S.B.* (Collegeville, MN: Liturgical Press, 2000), pp. 111–27.

40. See Yves Congar, *Lay People in the Church: A Study for a Theology of the Laity,* trans. Donald Attwater (Westminster, MD: Newman, 1957), p. 78.

41. Congar, *Lay People in the Church,* pp. 80–81.

42. Rahner, "Church and World," p. 348.

43. Rahner, "Church and World," p. 349. See also Thomas F. O'Meara, *God in the World: A Guide to Karl Rahner's Theology* (Collegeville, MN: Liturgical Press, 2007), esp. pp. 94–134.

44. Rahner, "Church and World," p. 350.

45. See H. Richard Niebuhr, *Christ and Culture* (New York: Harper & Row, 1951; Torchbook ed., 1956). For a summary of Niebuhr's various models, see my *Catholicism,* pp. 406–11.

46. Rahner, "Church and World," p. 351.

47. Schillebeeckx, *God, the Future of Man,* p. 123.

48. Schillebeeckx, *God, the Future of Man,* p. 161.

49. Küng, *The Church,* p. 487.

50. Hans Küng, *Signposts for the Future: Contemporary Issues Facing the Church* (Garden City, NY: Doubleday, 1978), p. 36.

51. Dulles, "A Half Century of Ecclesiology," p. 434.

52. The essay was originally delivered as a paper at St. Xavier College, Chicago, in 1966 and published in a collection of symposium papers under the title *The Word in History,* T. Patrick Burke, ed. (New York: Sheed and Ward, 1966), pp. 69–85. It was reprinted in Johann Baptist Metz, *Theology of the World,* trans. William Glen-Doepel (New York: Herder and Herder, 1969), pp. 81–97.

53. Metz, *The Word in History,* p. 71.

54. Metz, *The Word in History,* p. 78 (italics in original).

55. Metz, *The Word in History,* p. 80 (italics in original).

56. Metz, *The Word in History,* p. 81.

57. Metz, *The Word in History,* p. 81 (italics in original).

58. Metz, *The Word in History,* p. 82 (italics in original).

59. Metz, *The Word in History,* p. 83.

60. Metz, *The Word in History,* p. 85.

61. See Pannenberg, *Theology and the Kingdom of God,* p. 84.

62. See Lindbeck, *The Future of Roman Catholic Theology,* chap. 1, "Vision of a World Renewed," pp. 9–25; chap. 2, "The Church's Secular Mission," pp. 27–50. For Lindbeck, the Church's main missionary task in relation to the world is one of witnessing "in all that it is and does, to Christ and to the kingdom" (p. 27). The Church is bound to the world, therefore, sacramentally.

63. See Moltmann, *Theology of Hope,* pp. 327–28.

64. See Part III, n. 12.

65. See Part III, n. 12. By contrast, see *The Nature and Mission of the Church,* Faith and Order Paper 198 (see n. 39).

66. For a collection of essays by some of these younger Catholic moralists, see William C. Mattison, ed., *New Wine, New Wineskins: A Next Generation Reflects*

on Key Issues in Catholic Moral Theology (Lanham, MD: Sheed & Ward, 2005). See also William L. Portier, "In Defense of Mt. Saint Mary's: They Are Evangelical, Not Conservative," *Commonweal* 127/3 (February 11, 2000): 31–33.

67. See Norman P. Tanner, ed., *Decrees of the Ecumenical Councils* (Washington, DC: Georgetown University Press; London: Sheed & Ward, 1990), vol. 1, p. 578. The italicized words are also italicized in the original Latin text.

68. See Francis X. Clooney, "Salvation Outside the Church," in Richard P. McBrien, ed., *The HarperCollins Encyclopedia of Catholicism* (San Francisco: HarperSanFrancisco, 1995), p. 1159.

69. Francis A. Sullivan, *Salvation Outside the Church? Tracing the History of the Catholic Response* (Mahwah, NJ: Paulist Press, 1992). For a comprehensive overview of recent writings on missiology, see Francis Anakwe Oborji, *Concepts of Mission: The Evolution of Contemporary Missiology* (Maryknoll, NY: Orbis Books, 2006).

70. See my *Catholicism*, pp. 82–86.

71. I am drawing here upon my *Catholicism*, chap. 10, "Religion and Its Varieties," esp. pp. 382–85, 389–90. To be sure, there are still many Christians in the fundamentalist, evangelical, and Pentecostalist traditions who hold fast to the older, pre–Vatican II view that only those who explicitly accept Jesus as their Savior can, in fact, be saved. But they are, for practical reasons, beyond the scope of this discussion. The approach taken here includes the crucially important Christological and salvific dimensions of the relationship between the Church and the other religions of the world. For a detailed schema, see J. Peter Schineller, "Christ and Church: A Spectrum of Views," *Theological Studies* 37/4 (December 1976): 545–66.

72. See Hans Küng, *Christianity and the World Religions: Paths of Dialogue with Islam, Hinduism, and Buddhism* (Garden City, NY: Doubleday, 1986); Jacques Dupuis, *Jesus Christ at the Encounter of World Religions* (Maryknoll, NY: Orbis Books, 1991), *Toward a Christian Theology of Religious Pluralism* (Maryknoll, NY: Orbis Books, 1997), and *Christianity and the Religions: From Confrontation to Dialogue* (Maryknoll, NY: Orbis Books, 2002); Heinz Robert Schlette, *Towards a Theology of Religions* (New York: Herder and Herder, 1966); and Raimundo Panikkar, *The Interreligious Dialogue* (New York: Paulist Press, 1999). See also Jeannine Hill Fletcher, *Monopoly on Salvation? A Feminist Approach to Religious Pluralism* (New York: Continuum, 2005). For general texts on world religions, see David S. Noss, *A History of the World's Religions*, 12th ed. (Upper Saddle River, NJ: Pearson–Prentice Hall, 2007); H. Byron Earhart, ed., *Religious Traditions of the World: A Journey Through Africa, Mesoamerica, North America, Judaism, Christianity, Islam, Hinduism, Buddhism, China, and Japan* (San Francisco: HarperSanFrancisco, 1993); Willard G. Oxtoby, ed., *World Religions: Western Traditions* (Toronto: Oxford University Press, 1996); and Willard G. Oxtoby, ed., *World Religions: Eastern Traditions* (Toronto: Oxford University Press, 1996). Jacques Dupuis's last book elicited a formal "Notification" from the Vatican's Congregation for the Doctrine of the Faith. In February 2001 the CDF concluded that the book "contained notable ambiguities and difficulties on important doctrinal points, which could lead the reader to erroneous and harmful opinions." Among such points it mentioned "the value and significance of the

salvific function of other religions." For a defense of Jacques Dupuis, see Francis A. Sullivan, "Ways of Salvation: On the Investigation of Jacques Dupuis," *America* 184/12 (April 9, 2001): 28–30. See also Gerald O'Collins, "Jacques Dupuis's Contributions to Interreligious Dialogue," *Theological Studies* 64/2 (June 2003): 388–97. For another view, closer to Dupuis's than to the Vatican's, see James Fredericks, "The Catholic Church and the Other Religious Paths: Rejecting Nothing That Is True and Holy," *Theological* Studies 64/2 (June 2003): 225–54. Father Dupuis died suddenly of a cerebral hemorrhage on December 28, 2004, at the age of eighty-one.

73. See John Hick and Paul Knitter, eds., *The Myth of Christian Uniqueness: Toward a Pluralistic Theology of Religions* (Maryknoll, NY: Orbis Books, 1987); and Paul F. Knitter, *Introducing Theologies of Religion* (Maryknoll, NY: Orbis Books, 2002).

74. See *Dominus Iesus: On the Unicity and Salvific Universality of Jesus Christ and the Church,* in *Origins* 30/14 (September 14, 2000): 217–18 (sec. 6).

75. Francis X. Clooney, "*Dominus Iesus* and the New Millennium," *America* 183/13 (October 28, 2000): 17 (full article, pp. 16–18). See also his "Learning to Listen: Benedict XVI and Interreligious Dialogue," *Commonweal* 134/1 (January 12, 2007): 11–12, 14–15. He writes: "It is a privilege to speak to people of faith who know their own religion; it is still more fruitful to speak to people who know their own religion and know my religion as well" (p. 15). See also Peter Phan, *Being Religious Interreligiously: Asian Perspectives on Interfaith Dialogue* (Orbis, 2004), and "Speaking in Many Tongues: Why the Church Must Be More Catholic," *Commonweal* 134/1 (January 12, 2007): 16–19. For an important collection of essays on *Dominus Iesus,* see Stephen J. Pope and Charles Hefling, eds., *Sic et Non: Encountering Dominus Iesus* (Maryknoll, NY: Orbis Books, 2002). For my own evaluation, see "*Dominus Iesus:* An Ecclesiological Critique," *Centro Pro Unione Semi-annual Bulletin* 59 (Spring 2001): 14–22.

76. See also I.4 and II.2.5, 2.7. It is important for readers to note that, although this book intends to be comprehensive and systematic in its approach to various church-related topics and issues, its actual scope is necessarily limited for practical reasons, as pointed out in the second section of the Preface. Thus, there is a special section here on the relation of the Church to Jews mainly because the Church grew out of Judaism and has been closely related to it ever since. However, there are no separate treatments of the relation of the Church to Islam or the other non-Christian religions of the world. Suffice it to say that the council's *Nostra aetate* adopts a generally positive and irenic approach to non-Christian religions. See 3.1 above.

77. Cited in my weekly syndicated column, "The Pope in the Holy Land," April 24, 2000 (available at www.richardmcbrien.com).

78. "The Depths of the Holocaust's Horror," *Origins* 29/42 (April 6, 2000): 679.

79. "Opportunity to Re-examine Relationships with the Jews," *Origins* 24/35 (February 16, 1995): 586 (my italics; full text, pp. 585–86).

80. "French Bishops' Declaration of Repentance," *Origins* 27/18 (October 16, 1997): 303 (full statement, pp. 301, 303–5).

81. "French Bishops' Declaration of Repentance," p. 304.

82. "French Bishops' Declaration of Repentance," p. 305 (my italics).

83. "We Remember: A Reflection on the Shoah," *Origins* 27/40 (March 26, 1998): 674 (full text, pp. 669, 671–75). To be sure, there are still bumps in the road toward full reconciliation between Christians (Catholics particularly) and Jews. By way of example, we can point to the beatification in September 2000 of Pope Pius IX, who countenanced the kidnapping of Edgardo Mortara in order to raise him as a Catholic against his parents' wishes, and the refusal to open the Vatican archives to Catholic and Jewish scholars so that an informed judgment could finally be reached about Pope Pius XII's wartime record with regard to the Holocaust. For a critical examination of the former, see David I. Kertzer, *The Kidnapping of Edgardo Mortara* (New York: Knopf, 1997). The book was translated into several languages and has been made into a play, *Edgardo Mine,* by Alfred Uhry, a Pulitzer- and Oscar-winning playwright. See also Walter Kasper, "Christians, Jews and the Thorny Question of Mission," *Origins* 32/28 (December 19, 2002): 457, 459–66; and Richard J. Sklba, "Catholic-Jewish Relations After 40 Years: New Beginnings," *Origins* 35/31 (January 19, 2006): 509–14. As another indication of how much progress has been made by Catholic theologians as well as Catholic bishops, see the joint statement of August 2002, "Reflections on Covenant and Mission," issued by the U.S. Catholic Bishops' Committee on Ecumenical and Interrreligious Affairs and the National Council of Synagogues, in *Origins* 32/13 (September 5, 2002): 219–21.

84. *Acta Apostolicae Sedis* 85 (1993): 1039–1119.

85. Christopher O'Donnell, "Ecumenism and the Roman Catholic Church," in his *Ecclesia: A Theological Encyclopedia of the Church* (Collegeville, MN: Liturgical Press, 1996), p. 149.

86. See, e.g., William G. Rusch and Jeffrey Gros, eds., *Deepening Communion: International Ecumenical Documents with Roman Catholic Participation* (Washington, DC: United States Catholic Conference, 1998); Joseph A. Burgess and Jeffrey Gros, eds., *Building Unity: Ecumenical Dialogues with Roman Catholic Participation in the United States* (New York: Paulist Press, 1989); and Lydia Veliko and Jeffrey Gros, eds., *Growing Consensus II: Church Dialogues in the United States, 1992–2004: Ecumenical Documents,* vol. 7 (Washington, DC: United States Conference of Catholic Bishops, 2005). See also my *Catholicism,* pp. 709–11. For examples of some of these important dialogues, see the Anglican–Roman Catholic International Commission (ARCIC II), "The Gift of Authority," *Origins* 29/2 (May 27, 1999): 17, 19–29; Randall Lee and Jeffrey Gros, eds., *The Church as Koinonia of Salvation: Its Structures and Ministries,* vol. 10, *Lutherans and Catholics in Dialogue* (Washington, DC: United States Conference of Catholic Bishops, 2005); John Borelli and John H. Erikson, eds., *The Quest for Unity: Orthodox and Catholics in Dialogue: Documents of the Joint International Commission and Official Dialogues in the United States, 1965–1995* (Crestwood, NY: St. Valdimir Seminary Press; Washington, DC: United States Catholic Conference, 1996); and Walter Kasper, ed., *The Petrine Ministry: Catholics and Orthodox in Dialogue* (New York: Newman, 2006). For examples of theological work written in the spirit of these national and international bilateral consultations, see Marsha L. Dutton and Patrick Terrell Gray, eds., *One Lord, One Faith, One Baptism: Studies in Christian Ecclesiality and Ecumenism in Honor of J. Robert Wright* (Grand Rapids, MI: Eerdmans, 2006); Walter Kasper, *That They*

May All Be One: The Call to Unity (London: Burns & Oates, 2004); and George H. Tavard, *The Church, Community of Salvation: An Ecumenical Ecclesiology* (Collegeville, MN: Liturgical Press, 1992). For general reference, see Nicholas Lossky et al., eds., *Dictionary of the Ecumenical Movement,* 2d ed. (Geneva: World Council of Churches Publications, 2002). For an overview of the state of ecumenism at the beginning of the twenty-first century, with emphasis on its global and ecclesiological dimensions, see Jeffrey Gros, "Ecumenism 2007: The Challenges," *Origins* 36/34 (February 8, 2007): 541–47. Finally, see also I.4 of this book, which lists some of the most important dialogues and consultations since Vatican II.

87. For the text, see E. J. Stormon, ed., *Towards the Healing of Schism: The Sees of Rome and Constantinople 1958–1984* (Mahwah, NJ: Paulist Press, 1987), pp. 161–63. See also *Acta Apostolicae Sedis* 59 (1970): 753.

88. See John Meyendorff and Emmanuel Lanne, "*Église-soeurs: Implications ecclésiologiques du Tomos Agapis,*" *Istina* 20 (1975): 35–46, 47–74. Unfortunately, the more recent document from the Congregation for the Doctrine of the Faith, *Responses to Some Questions Regarding Certain Aspects of the Doctrine on the Church* (*Origins* 37/9 [July 19, 2007]: 134–36), makes no mention at all of Pope Paul VI's recognition of the Anglican Communion as a "sister Church."

89. Christopher O'Donnell, "Sister Churches," in his *Ecclesia,* p. 425.

90. *Acta Apostolicae Sedis* 62 (1970): 753.

91. "Note on the Expression 'Sister Churches,'" *Origins* 30/14 (September 14, 2000): 222–24.

92. "Note on the Expression 'Sister Churches,'" p. 223.

93. "Note on the Expression 'Sister Churches,'" p. 223.

94. "Note on the Expression 'Sister Churches,'" p. 223. The letter pointed out, however, that the note, although "authoritative and binding," would not be published in official form in the *Acta Apostolicae Sedis* (*AAS*), "given its limited purpose of specifying the correct theological terminology on this subject."

95. The text is cited in n. 7 of the CDF "Note on the Expression 'Sister Churches.'" The official Latin version is found in *Acta Apostolicae Sedis* 59 (1967): 852–53.

96. One theologian who has been directly involved in the Catholic-Orthodox dialogues, Michael Fahey, S.J., whimsically observed that members of various Slavic Churches who were evangelized directly through Constantinople, regarded in the East as the "new Rome," probably look upon the church of the old Rome more as their grandmother rather than their mother. See his "Am I My Sister's Keeper?" *America* 183/13 (October 28, 2000): 13 (full article, pp. 12–15).

97. This issue reemerged in the response in 2001 of the House of Bishops of the Church of England to a 1998 statement of the Roman Catholic Bishops of England and Wales, Ireland, and Scotland entitled "One Bread, One Body." The Anglican response, "The Eucharist: Sacrament of Unity," took particular exception to the assertions of the Roman Catholic bishops that Anglicanism is, like other Protestant churches, "rooted in the Reformation," when, in fact, it "traces its origins back to the beginning of Christianity in England and is continuous with the Church of the Apostles and Fathers." The Anglican bishops also insisted, arguing from the Decree on Ecumenism, n. 8, that full ecclesial communion is the ultimate goal, but it need not already be achieved for there to be any eucharistic

sharing even now. For my comments on this exchange, see my columns, "Essays in Theology," of 11/23/98, 5/7/01, and 5/14/01 at www.richardmcbrien.com. The original documents are available on the Internet at www.catholic-ew.org.uk/resource/obob/index.htm, which is the Web site of the Catholic Church in England and Wales, and www.cofe.anglican.org/ccu/england/, which is the Web site of the Church of England.

98. The material for this section is drawn from my "*Dominus Iesus:* An Ecclesiological Critique," *Centro Pro Unione Semi-Annual Bulletin* 59 (Spring 2001): pp. 19–20.

99. Cited in Francis A. Sullivan, "The Impact of *Dominus Iesus* on Ecumenism," *America* 183/13 (October 28, 2000): 10–11 (full article, pp. 8–11).

100. John Hotchkin, "Canon Law and Ecumenism: Giving Shape to the Future," *Origins* 30/19 (October 19, 2000): 294–95. Hamer's article, "*La terminologie ecclésiologique de Vatican II et les ministères Protestants,*" appeared in *Documentation catholique* 68 (July 4, 1971): 625–28.

101. Hotchkin, "Canon Law and Ecumenism," p. 295.

102. Material for the first part of this section is drawn from my *Catholicism,* pp. 828–29; other material is drawn from Christopher O'Donnell, "Intercommunion," in his *Ecclesia,* pp. 220–22.

103. For a broader ecumenical understanding of the concept, see O'Donnell, "Intercommunion," p. 220.

104. Cited in O'Donnell, "Intercommunion," p. 221.

105. O'Donnell, "Intercommunion," p. 222.

106. One can begin with a search of various Web sites under the heading, "mutual recognition of ordained ministries." See, e.g., the reservations expressed in 1984 regarding the so-called Lima statement "Baptism, Eucharist and Ministry" by the U.S. Bishops' Committee on Ecumenical and Interreligious Affairs (United States Conference of Catholic Bishops Web site, www.usccb.org/seia/lima.shtml).

107. This has been the view also of mainline Protestants like Karl Barth, who insists that there is "legitimate apostolic succession only when there is a following of the apostles in discipleship, hearing, respect and obedience, all according to Scripture." See his *Church Dogmatics* 4:1, trans. G. W. Bromiley (Edinburgh: Clark, 1956), pp. 712–25, cited in O'Donnell, "Intercommunion," p. 25. For a more up-to-date Catholic understanding of apostolic succession, see Francis A. Sullivan, *From Apostles to Bishops: The Development of the Episcopacy in the Early Church* (New York/Mahwah, NJ: Newman, 2001), chap. 1, "Apostolic Succession in the Episcopate: A Church-Dividing Issue," pp. 1–16.

108. See Francis A. Sullivan, "Apostolic Succession," in McBrien, ed., *The HarperCollins Encyclopedia of Catholicism,* pp. 77–79; and Christopher O'Donnell, "Apostolic Succession," in his *Ecclesia,* pp. 23–26.

109. See Francis A. Sullivan, *The Church We Believe In: One, Holy, Catholic and Apostolic* (Mahwah, NJ: Paulist Press, 1988), p. 209. This is also evident in *The Nature and Mission of the Church,* Faith and Order Paper 198, pp. 23–24, no. 89.

110. See "Former Protestant Ministers Who Wish to Become Catholic Priests," *Origins* 37/3 (May 31, 2007): 46–47. Unfortunately, the accompanying letter of

Cardinal William Levada, prefect of the CDF, refers to "former Episcopalian ministers [*sic*]" and "former ministers of *other* Protestant denominations" (my italics), thereby describing Anglicans and their U. S. counterparts as Protestants and their clergy as "ministers" rather than "priests."

111. This section draws mainly upon my "An Ecclesiological Analysis of Catholic Social Teachings," in Oliver F. Williams and John C. Houck, eds., *Catholic Social Thought and the New World Order* (Notre Dame, IN: University of Notre Dame Press, 1993), pp. 147–77, esp. pp. 169–76. Other theologians who have addressed the ecclesiological dimensions of Catholic social teaching include Charles E. Curran, *Catholic Social Teaching 1891–Present: A Historical, Theological, and Ethical Analysis* (Washington, DC: Georgetown University Press, 2002), chap. 3, "Ecclesial Methodology," pp. 101–24; and Richard R. Gaillardetz, "The Ecclesiological Foundations of Modern Catholic Social Teaching," in Kenneth R. Himes, ed., *Modern Catholic Social Teaching: Commentaries and Interpretations* (Washington, DC: Georgetown University Press, 2005), pp. 72–98. For an official collection of documents, see the *Compendium of the Social Doctrine of the Church* (Città del Vaticano: Libreria Editrice Vaticana, 2004), distributed in the United States by the United States Conference of Catholic Bishops.

112. The Latin titles of at least three important papal documents have a chronological reference to the landmark encyclical of Pope Leo XIII *Rerum novarum* in 1891. Thus, Pius XI's encyclical *Quadragesimo anno* appeared forty years after *Rerum novarum;* Paul VI's apostolic exhortation *Octogesima adveniens* appeared eighty years later; and John Paul II's encyclical *Centesimus annus* marked *Rerum novarum*'s one hundredth anniversary.

113. Such summaries and commentaries, through the prism of ecclesiology, are available in my "An Ecclesiological Analysis of Catholic Social Teachings," in Williams and Houck, eds., *Catholic Social Thought and the New World Order*.

114. Charles E. Curran has written the best article on the different methodologies employed by the Church in its social and sexual teachings: "Official Catholic Social and Sexual Teachings: A Methodological Comparison," in his *Tensions in Moral Theology* (Notre Dame, IN: University of Notre Dame Press, 1988), pp. 87–109. No article gives a clearer explanation of why some Catholics have a problem with the Church's teachings on human sexuality and reproduction while embracing without any difficulty its social teachings, and why other Catholics embrace the sexual teachings and remain generally silent about the Church's social teachings. It is one of the most important articles on methodology written since Vatican II, and it has exceedingly important ecclesiological implications.

115. See J. Bryan Hehir, "The Social Role of the Church: Leo XIII, Vatican II and John Paul II," in Williams and Houck, eds., *Catholic Social Thought and the New World Order,* pp. 29–50, esp. pp. 33–40.

116. This does not apply universally, however. There are still instances where church officials, including a handful of bishops, have allowed themselves to cross the line between being official representatives of the Church and being political leaders. See the next section of Part VI on the Church and politics.

117. The text of the encyclical reads: "It is an injustice and at the same time a grave evil and disturbance of right order to assign to a greater and higher association what lesser and subordinate organizations can do. For every social activity

ought of its very nature to furnish help to members of the body social, and never destroy and absorb them."

118. Cited by the late Cardinal Basil Hume (d. 1999), archbishop of Westminster, in an address prepared for the U.S. Catholic bishops and read to them after his death, "A Bishop's Relation to the Universal Church and His Fellow Bishops," *Origins* 29/7 (July 1, 1999): 110.

119. *Code of Canon Law: Latin-English Edition* (Washington, DC: Canon Law Society of America, 1983), p. xxi.

120. See Charles E. Curran, *Catholic Social Teaching 1891–Present*, chap. 3, "Ecclesial Methodology," pp. 101–24, which compares the methods employed by the official Church in its social teachings and its teachings on human sexuality and reproduction.

121. What follows in this section is derived from my *Caesar's Coin: Religion and Politics in America* (New York: Macmillan, 1987), pp. 19–24.

122. For succinct descriptions of the views of Augustine, Thomas Aquinas, John Calvin, Martin Luther, Niccolà Machiavelli, Thomas Hobbes, John Locke, James Madison, and others, see my *Caesar's Coin*, pp. 22–24. For an elaboration of the relationship between religion and politics in a U.S. environment, see *Caesar's Coin*, pp. 35–41.

123. Hehir, "The Social Role of the Church," p. 30. What follows is taken from a brief section of Hehir's article, pp. 30–31.

124. Hehir ("The Social Role of the Church") cites John Courtney Murray, "The Problem of Religious Freedom," *Theological Studies* 25/4 (December 1964): 503–75; see esp. pp. 507–8, 512.

125. Hehir, "The Social Role of the Church," p. 30.

126. *Benignitas et humanitas* (Lat. "Kindness and humanity"), given on December 24, 1944, was published in *The Tablet* 184 (December 30, 1944): 316–18.

127. Murray, "The Problem of Religious Freedom," pp. 545–46.

128. Hehir, "The Social Role of the Church," p. 31.

129. See Hehir's synthesis of John Paul II's contributions, "The Social Role of the Church, pp. 38–40.

130. The principles that follow are derived from my *Caesar's Coin*, p. 131. See also my "Religion and Politics in America: The 1988 Campaign," *America* 158/21 (May 28, 1988): 551–58, esp. p. 556.

131. See Joseph Bernardin, "Consistent Ethic of Life," in Charles E. Curran and Leslie Griffin, eds., *The Catholic Church, Morality and Politics: Readings in Moral Theology No. 12* (New York/Mahwah, NJ: Paulist Press, 2001), pp. 160–69. The entire volume consists of a valuable collection of essays across a broad spectrum of views, including contributions representing a politically and theologically conservative perspective by George Weigel, Richard John Neuhaus, James T. McHugh, Michael Pakaluk, Mary Ann Glendon, Michael Novak, and John M. Finnis. See also Thomas G. Feuchtmann, ed., *Consistent Ethic of Life* (Kansas City, MO: Sheed and Ward, 1988); and Charles Curran, *The Church and Morality: An Ecumenical and Catholic Approach* (Minneapolis: Fortress, 1993).

132. United States Conference of Catholic Bishops (USCCB), "Faithful Citizenship: A Catholic Call to Political Responsibility," *Origins* 33/20 (October 23, 2003): 325 (full text, pp. 321, 323–30). See also their "Forming Consciences for

Faithful Citizenship," *Origins* 37/25 (November 29, 2007): 392, 395 (full text: 389–401).

133. Similar questions had been raised about Cardinal John Krol (d. 1996) of Philadelphia when he stood prominently on center stage between the newly renominated candidates, President Richard Nixon and Vice President Spiro Agnew, at the end of the 1972 Republican National Convention in Miami, and later when Cardinal Krol effusively praised President Reagan during a campaign stop in Doylestown, Pennsylvania, in 1984.

134. USCCB, "Faithful Citizenship," p. 330.

135. USCCB, "Faithful Citizenship," p. 329 (italics in original).

136. Cardinal Theodore McCarrick, "Final Report: Bishops and Catholic Politicians," *Origins* 36/7 (June 29, 2006): 96, 98–100.

137. The principles that follow are derived from my *Caesar's Coin,* pp. 47–49.

138. For a comprehensive and diverse collection of essays on this subject, see Madonna Kolbenschlag, ed., *Between God and Caesar: Priests, Sisters and Political Office in the United States* (New York/Mahwah, NJ: Paulist Press, 1985).

139. A leading interpreter of political theology and of J. B. Metz in particular is my colleague at the University of Notre Dame, J. Matthew Ashley. See his *Interruptions: Mysticism, Theology and Politics in the Work of Johann Baptist Metz* (Notre Dame, IN: University of Notre Dame Press, 1998); his chapter "Johann Baptist Metz," in Peter Scott and William T. Cavanaugh, eds., *The Blackwell Companion to Political Theology* (Oxford: Blackwell, 2004), pp. 241–55; his "Introduction: Reading Metz," in Johann Baptist Metz, *A Passion for God: The Mystical-Political Dimension of Christianity,* trans. J. Matthew Ashley (New York/Mahwah, NJ: Paulist Press, 1998), pp. 7–21; and also his substantial introduction to his retranslation of Metz's *Faith in History and Society: Toward a Practical Fundamental Theology* (New York: Crossroad/Herder, 2007), in which Ashley insists that political theology is "one of the most significant movements in post–World War II European theology," that Metz is "its premier Catholic proponent," and his book *Faith in History and Society* "the most important single text for understanding his approach" (p. 1). Ashley mentions two other well-known founders and practitioners of political theology, both Protestants, Jürgen Moltmann and Dorothee Soelle (d. 2003), who, Ashley points out, later veered off into other themes.

140. Johann Baptist Metz, "The Church and the World," in T. Patrick Burke, ed., *The Word in History* (New York: Sheed and Ward, 1966), pp. 69–85 (also reprinted in Metz, *Theology of the World,* pp. 81–97). Johann Baptist Metz, *Theology of the World,* trans. William Glen-Doepel (New York: Herder and Herder, 1969); *Faith in History and Society: Toward a Practical Fundamental Theology,* trans. David Smith (New York: Seabury/Crossroad, 1980), esp. "Church and People," Part II.8, pp. 136–53; and *The Emergent Church: The Future of Christianity in a Postbourgeois World,* trans. Peter Mann (New York: Crossroad, 1981).

141. Metz, *Theology of the World,* p. 107. See all of chap. 5, "The Church and the World in the Light of a 'Political Theology,'" pp. 107–24.

142. Metz, *Theology of the World,* p. 107.

143. This brief section is derived from my own *Catholicism,* p. 699.

144. Metz, *Theology of the World,* p. 94 (italics in original); see nn. 51, 139.

145. Metz, *Theology of the World,* p. 96.

146. See Metz, "The Church and the World," p. 85.

147. Metz, "The Church and the World," pp. 82–83 (italics in original).

148. See Johann Baptist Metz, "For a Renewed Church Before a New Council: A Concept in Four Theses," in David Tracy, Hans Küng, Johann Metz, eds., *Toward Vatican III: The Work That Needs to Be Done* (New York: Seabury, 1978), pp. 137–45.

149. Metz, "For a Renewed Church Before a New Council," p. 139.

150. Metz, "For a Renewed Church Before a New Council," p. 140 (italics in original).

151. Metz, "For a Renewed Church Before a New Council," p. 143.

152. See Johann Metz, "In Place of a Foreword: On the Biographical Itinerary of My Theology," in his *A Passion for God,* pp. 1–5.

153. African liberation theology emerged, especially in South Africa, in the mid-1970s in response to apartheid and in dialogue with Latin American liberation theologians. See, e.g., Emmanuel Martey, "Liberation Theologies: African," in Virginia Fabella and R. S. Sugirtharajah, eds., *Dictionary of Third World Theologies* (Maryknoll, NY: Orbis Books, 2000), pp. 127–29.

154. See Bastiaan Wielenga, "Liberation theology in Asia," in Christopher Rowland, ed., *The Cambridge Companion to Liberation Theology* (Cambridge: Cambridge University Press, 1999), pp. 39–62. See also a much shorter piece by R. S. Sugirtharajah, "Liberation Theologies: Asian," in Fabella and Sugirtharajah, eds., *Dictionary of Third World Theologies,* pp. 129–31.

155. See Eduardo Antonio, "Black Theology," in Fabella and Sugirtharajah, eds., *Dictionary of Third World Theologies,* pp. 63–88.

156. See Mary Grey, "Feminist Theology: a Critical Theology of Liberation," in Fabella and Sugirtharajah, eds., *Dictionary of Third World Theologies,* pp. 89–106. Of course, the bibliographical resources on this topic are vast. Our interest here is ecclesiological only. Those who wish to explore the phenomena of feminist, black, Asian, and African forms of liberation theology independently of their ecclesiological aspects will need to build their own bibliographies from various standard sources.

157. For a succinct description of its origins, growth, and themes, see Paul J. Wojda, "Liberation Theology," in McBrien, ed., *The HarperCollins Encyclopedia of Catholicism,* pp. 768–69. For an excellent detailed overview, see also Christopher O'Donnell, "Liberation Theologies and Ecclesiology," in his *Ecclesia,* pp. 260–65.

158. See the classic work Gustavo Gutiérrez, *A Theology of Liberation: History, Politics and Salvation,* trans. Caridad Inda and John Eagleson (Maryknoll, NY: Orbis Books, 1973; orig. Spanish ed., 1971). For shorter pieces on Latin American liberation theology by the same author, see "The Task and Content of Liberation Theology," trans. Judith Condor, in Rowland, ed., *The Cambridge Companion to Liberation Theology,* pp. 19–38, and "Liberation Theologies: Latin American," in Fabella and Sugirtharajah, eds., *Dictionary of Third World Theologies,* pp. 131–33. See also Marc H. Ellis and Otto Maduro, eds., *The Future of Liberation Theology: Essays in Honor of Gustavo Gutiérrez* (Maryknoll, NY: Orbis Books, 1989). Many of the essays are pertinent to this section on liberation theology and to other parts of this book, including those on feminist ecclesiologies, African and African American ecclesiologies, Hispanic and Latino/a ecclesiologies, Asian

ecclesiologies, the Church and the Jews, and the Church and non-Christian religions generally.

159. Gutiérrez, *A Theology of Liberation,* p. 261 (or see Gustavo Gutiérrez, *A Theology of Liberation,* 15th anniversary ed. [Maryknoll, NY: Orbis Books, 1988], pp. 147–48). Some few liberationists in the past, in both North and Latin America, tended to discount the importance or even relevance of internal church reform to the overall mission of the Church. In doing so, they overlooked Gutiérrez's insistence herein that the Church must also be a credible sign and practitioner of the message of liberation it proclaims to others.

160. Gutiérrez, *A Theology of Liberation,* p. 261 (my italics).

161. Gutiérrez, "The Task and Content of Liberation Theology," p. 35.

162. Gutiérrez, "The Task and Content of Liberation Theology," p. 37.

163. Gutiérrez, "The Task and Content of Liberation Theology," p. 37.

164. For this and other clashes between the Vatican and practitioners of liberation theology, see Peter Hebblethwaite, "Liberation Theology and the Roman Catholic Church," in Rowland, ed., *The Cambridge Companion to Liberation Theology,* pp. 179–98. For a specific reflection on the Boff case, see Harvey G. Cox, *The Silencing of Leonardo Boff: The Vatican and the Future of World Christianity* (Oak Park, IL: Meyer Stone, 1988).

165. Leonardo Boff, *Church: Charism and Power: Liberation Theology and the Institutional Church,* trans. John W. Diercksmeier (New York: Crossroad, 1985). For the complete text of the Congregation for the Doctrine of the Faith's official "Notification" in criticism of this book, see *Origins* 14/42 (April 4, 1985): 683, 685–87. Boff is also the only theologian mentioned by name in the commentary that accompanied the CDF's later document *Responses to Some Questions Regarding Certain Aspects of the Doctrine on the Church.* See *Origins* 37/9 (July 19, 2007): 137.

166. Leonardo Boff, *Ecclesiogenesis: The Base Communities Reinvent the Church,* trans. Robert R. Barr (Maryknoll, NY: Orbis Books, 1986).

167. Boff, *Church: Charism and Power,* pp. 145, 150.

168. Boff, *Church: Charism and Power,* p. 159.

169. See Leonardo Boff, *Trinity and Society,* trans. Paul Burns (Maryknoll, NY: Orbis Books, 1988).

170. Yves Congar, "The Church: The People of God," *Concilium* 1/1 (January 1975): 13 (full article, pp. 7–19); cited in O'Donnell, "Pneumatology and Ecclesiology," in his *Ecclesia,* p. 367.

171. See my *Catholicism,* chap. 28, pp. 1019–61.

172. There are, however, 258 references to the Holy Spirit in all of the conciliar documents.

173. The preceding material is drawn from O'Donnell, "Pneumatology and Ecclesiology," pp. 369–70.

174. Yves Congar, *I Believe in the Holy Spirit,* trans. David Smith, 3 vols. (New York: Seabury, 1983; orig. French ed., Paris: Les Éditions du Cerf, 1979–80). For Congar's other writings on the Holy Spirit, see n. 1 of my article, "*I Believe in the Holy Spirit:* The Role of Pneumatology in Yves Congar's Theology," in Gabriel Flynn, ed., *Yves Congar: Theologian of the Church* (Louvain: Peeters; Grand Rapids, MI: Eerdmans, 2005), pp. 303–27. What follows here is drawn largely

from that chapter. See also Elizabeth Groppe, *Yves Congar's Theology of the Holy Spirit* (New York: Oxford University Press, 2004).

175. Congar, *I Believe in the Holy Spirit,* vol. 1, p. 157.

176. Congar, *I Believe in the Holy Spirit,* vol. 1, p. 161.

177. Congar, *I Believe in the Holy Spirit,* vol. 1, p. 170.

178. Congar, *I Believe in the Holy Spirit,* vol. 1, p. 171.

179. Congar, *I Believe in the Holy Spirit,* vol. 2, p. 11.

180. Congar, *I Believe in the Holy Spirit,* vol. 2: unity, pp. 15–23; catholicity, pp. 24–38; apostolicity, pp. 39–49; holiness, pp. 52–64.

181. Congar, *I Believe in the Holy Spirit,* vol. 3, p. 271.

182. Congar, *I Believe in the Holy Spirit,* vol. 3, pp. 222, 224.

183. Congar, *I Believe in the Holy Spirit,* vol. 3, p. 264.

184. See my contribution to Flynn, ed., *Yves Congar: Theologian of the Church,* pp. 323–25.

185. For what follows, see my synthesis of Congar's pneumatology in Flynn, ed., *Yves Congar: Theologian of the Church,* pp. 325–27.

186. This question has been a matter of theological disagreement between East and West since the fourth century. In the early ninth century (810), the emperor Charlemagne (d. 814) asked Pope Leo III (795–816) to approve the use of the *Filioque* throughout the Frankish empire. The pope refused, but expressed agreement with its underlying theology. Two centuries later, however, Pope Benedict VIII (1012–24) provided official approval for the practice. Since Vatican II, the Catholic Church has allowed the recitation of the creed without the *Filioque* in ecumenical services with the Orthodox, and indeed Pope Paul VI did so himself. For a fuller summary of the *Filioque* controversy, see Corinne Winter, "Filioque," in McBrien, ed., *The HarperCollins Encyclopedia of Catholicism,* pp. 529–30.

Part VII: Post–Vatican II Ecclesiology: The Church ad Intra

1. "The Final Report of the Extraordinary Synod of Bishops," *Origins* 15/27 (December 19, 1985): 448 (full text, pp. 444–50). Dennis M. Doyle makes a similar claim in his *Communion Ecclesiology: Visions and Versions* (Maryknoll, NY: Orbis Books, 2000), p. 2. On the same page Doyle makes the additional claim, following Joseph Ratzinger, that "communion ecclesiology is the one basic ecclesiology." However, this is by no means a unanimous judgment among Catholic theologians. See, e.g., Neil Ormerod, "The Structure of a Systematic Ecclesiology," *Theological Studies* 63/1 (March 2002): 27–29 (full article, pp. 3–30). Ormerod offers here a theological/sociological critique according to which communion ecclesiology is too idealistic and not sufficiently rooted in the contingencies of history. The unity that it celebrates is not this-worldly in character, but can only be realized at the end of history when the Kingdom, or Reign, of God will be given in all of its fullness. Ormerod argues that "mission," not "communion," is the fundamental category for ecclesiology. Edward Hahnenberg supports Ormerod's view in his "The Mystical Body of Christ and Communion

Ecclesiology: Historical Parallels," *Irish Theological Quarterly* 70/1 (2005): 28–30 (full article, pp. 3–30). For an indication of how an understanding of the Church as a communion impacts the interpretation of *Lumen gentium*, n. 8, on the relationship between the Catholic Church and the Body of Christ as a whole, see Johannes Willibrands, "Vatican II's Ecclesiology of Communion," *Origins* 17/2 (May 28, 1987): 27–33. At a more popular level, Doris Gottemoeller, at the time president of the Sisters of Mercy of the Americas and a past president of the Leadership Conference of Women Religious, points out: "Defining the church as *communio* means that it is neither an otherworldly abstraction nor a purely human organization. It serves as an antidote to ecclesiological reductionism by reminding us that the church is a complex reality involving sacramental, spiritual, juridical and social relationships" (see "A Vision for the Church of 2010," *Origins* 25/9 [July 27, 1995]: 150 [full text, pp. 149–52]).

2. See Walter Kasper, "The Church as Communion: Reflections on the Guiding Ecclesiological Idea of the Second Vatican Council," in his *Theology and Church*, trans. Margaret Kohl (New York: Crossroad, 1989), pp. 148–63 (notes, pp. 220–22). For other major works that present an ecclesiology of communion, see Jean-Marie Roger Tillard, *Église d'Églises* (Paris: Les Éditions du Cerf, 1987; an English translation appeared in 1992, but was withdrawn from circulation because of serious deficiencies); *L'Église locale: Ecclésiologie de communion et catholicité* (Paris: Les Éditions du Cerf, 1995); and *Flesh of the Church, Flesh of Christ: At the Sources of the Ecclesiology of Communion*, trans. Madeleine Beaumont (Collegeville, MN: Liturgical Press, 2001); and John J. Markey, *Creating Communion: The Theology of the Constitutions of the Church* (Hyde Park, NY: New City, 2003). See also Christopher Ruddy, *The Local Church: Tillard and the Future of Catholic Ecclesiology* (New York: Crossroad, 2006).

3. See, e.g., Jérôme Hamer, *The Church Is a Communion*, trans. R. Matthews (Franklin, WI: Sheed & Ward, 1965; orig. ed., 1964); and Yves Congar, *Lay People in the Church: A Study for a Theology of the Laity*, trans. Donald Attwater (Westminster, MD: Newman, 1957), pp. 28–58. Avery Dulles briefly summarizes Hamer's approach in his *Models of the Church* (Garden City, NY: Doubleday, 1974; exp. ed., 1987), pp. 49–50, and develops his own approach in chap. 3, "The Church as Mystical Communion," pp. 47–62. See also Dennis M. Doyle, "Henri de Lubac and the Roots of Communion Ecclesiology," *Theological Studies* 60/2 (June 1992): 209–27; "Journet, Congar and the Roots of Communion Ecclesiology," *Theological Studies* 58/3 (September 1997): 461–79; and *Communion Ecclesiology*, pp. 38–71.

4. For Pope John Paul II's reflections on the ecumenical dimensions of communion, see his 1995 encyclical *Ut unum sint*, nn. 5–14, in which he reaffirms the teaching of Vatican II that there are degrees of communion between the various Churches and ecclesial communities in the one Body of Christ.

5. See Paul McPartlan, "The Eucharist as the Basis for Ecclesiology," *Antiphon* 6/2 (2001): 12–19, and his monograph *Sacrament of Salvation: An Introduction to Eucharistic Ecclesiology* (Edinburgh: Clark, 1995). See also Tillard *Flesh of the Church, Flesh of Christ*, pp. 33–82, 107–31.

6. See Kasper, *Theology and Church*, p. 160. Cardinal Kasper refers to the Church as "an icon of the Trinity." Neil Ormerod acknowledges that "this attempt

to link ecclesiology and trinitarian theology is admirable," but the unity within the triune Godhead, he insists, is "where God is most different from God's creatures, even the creation we call Church. What is first in our knowledge of the triune nature," he continues, "are the divine missions of Word and Spirit, which in turn ground our knowledge of the processions and persons within the Trinity. In this way a *missio* ecclesiology also makes contact with trinitarian theology, not in terms of *communio* and *perichoresis* [Gk., "circulation"], but in terms of *missio* and *processio*. Communion may be our eschatological end in the vision of God, but in the here and now of a pilgrim Church mission captures our ongoing historical responsibility" ("The Structure of a Systematic Ecclesiology," p. 29).

7. See Karl Rahner, *The Church and the Sacraments,* trans. W. J. O'Hara (Edinburgh-London: Nelson, 1963), p. 84: The Church "is most manifest and in the most intensive form" and "attains the highest actuality of [its] own nature, when [it] celebrates the eucharist."

8. The most dramatic debate about the relationship between the universal Church and the individual local churches, within the broader content of an ecclesiology of communion, has been carried out by two major Catholic theologians: Cardinal Walter Kasper and then Cardinal Joseph Ratzinger (later Pope Benedict XVI). The debate has been amply summarized by Kilian McDonnell in "The Ratzinger/Kasper Debate: The Universal Church and Local Churches," *Theological Studies* 60/2 (June 2002): 227–50. Ratzinger's position is that the universal Church is ontologically and temporally prior to the local churches. Kasper argues, over against that view, that if this were the case, the local church could not be fully Church, and the bishops of the local churches could only be delegates of the pope, not vicars of Christ. Kasper underscores the principles of simultaneity and *perichoresis.* The universal Church is present in every local church, and every local church is an embodiment of the universal Church in its own locale. The local church *is* the Church in a given place. Although not simply identifying the universal Church with the local churches, Kasper insists that they cannot be separated because they exist simultaneously and in one another. See also Yves Congar, "De la communion des églises à une ecclésiologie de l'Église universalle," in Yves Congar and B. D. Dupuy, eds.

9. "The Final Report of the Extraordinary Synod of Bishops," p. 449.

10. See, e.g., Joseph Ratzinger, *Principles of Catholic Theology: Building Stones for a Fundamental Theology,* trans. Mary Frances McCarthy (San Francisco: Ignatius, 1987), pp. 53–55.

11. The Windsor Report is available at www.anglicancommunion.org/windsor2004/.

12. What follows here is drawn from my *Lives of the Saints: From Mary and St. Francis of Assisi to John XXIII and Mother Teresa* (San Francisco: HarperSanFrancisco, 2001), pp. 15–16. For an ecclesiology of saint-making, see my article "The Saints: An Ecclesiological Reflection," *Theology Digest* 48/4 (Winter 2001): 303–17. For the "politics of canonization," see my *Lives of the Saints,* pp. 50–54. See also Elizabeth Johnson, *Friends of God and Prophets: A Feminist Theological Reading of the Communion of Saints* (New York: Continuum, 1998). For a succinct summary of the meaning of the doctrine of the communion of saints, see Mary A. Donovan, "Communion of Saints," in Richard P. McBrien, ed., *The*

HarperCollins Encyclopedia of Catholicism (San Francisco: HarperSanFrancisco, 1995), p. 339. See also Christopher O'Donnell, "Communion of Saints," in his *Ecclesia: A Theological Encyclopedia of the Church* (Collegeville, MN: Liturgical Press, 1996), pp. 98–99. On a related matter, see Patricia A. Sullivan, "A Reinterpretation of Invocation and Intercession of the Saints," *Theological Studies* 66/2 (June 2005): 381–400. See also Lawrence S. Cunningham, *A Brief History of Saints* (Oxford: Blackwell, 2005).

13. What follows here in section 2.1 is drawn from my *Catholicism*, rev. ed. (San Francisco: HarperSanFrancisco, 1994), pp. 739–43.

14. Power and authority are closely related, but are not the same thing. Power is attached to *de iure* authority to make it possible to exercise it, but authority exercised only through the use of power, i.e., without *de facto* authority, is authoritarianism. See Eugene C. Kennedy and Sara C. Charles, *Authority: The Most Misunderstood Idea in America* (New York: Free Press, 1997).

15. See Francis A. Sullivan, *From Apostles to Bishops: The Development of the Episcopacy in the Early Church* (New York/Mahwah, NJ: Newman, 2001), esp. chap. 2, "The Apostles," and chap. 3, "Sharers in the Apostles' Ministry," pp. 17–53.

16. For a brief overview of the uses of authority in the Church in the post-biblical period to the present, see my *Catholicism*, pp. 744–50. For a much more comprehensive overview, see Bernard Prusak, *The Church Unfinished: Ecclesiology Through the Centuries* (New York: Paulist Press, 2004), pp. 120–312.

17. This important topic was already touched upon in an ecumenical context in VI.3.3.e.

18. Francis A. Sullivan, "Apostolic Succession," in McBrien, ed., *The HarperCollins Encyclopedia of Catholicism*, p. 77 (full article, pp. 77–79). See also his longer entry, "Apostolic Succession," *New Catholic Encyclopedia*, vol. 1 (Detroit: Thomson/Gale, 2003), 2nd ed., pp. 589–92.

19. Sullivan, *From Apostles to Bishops*, p. 14.

20. Sullivan, *From Apostles to Bishops*, p. 15.

21. Sullivan, *From Apostles to Bishops*, p. 15. See *1 Clement* 44:1–4.

22. Sullivan, *From Apostles to Bishops*, p. 15.

23. Sullivan, *From Apostles to Bishops*, pp. 15–16.

24. Sullivan, "Apostolic Succession," p. 78.

25. Cited by Christopher O'Donnell, in "Apostolic Succession," in his *Ecclesia*, p. 25.

26. Karl Barth, *Church Dogmatics* 4:1, trans. G. W. Bromiley (Edinburgh: Clark, 1956), pp. 712–25. See O'Donnell, "Apostolic Succession," p. 25.

27. O'Donnell, "Apostolic Succession," p. 25. See also John D. Zizioulas, "*La continuité avec les origines apostoliques dans la conscience théologiques des Églises orthodoxes*," *Istina* 19 (1974): 66–94.

28. *Baptism, Eucharist and Ministry*, Faith and Order Paper 111 (Geneva: World Council of Churches, 1982).

29. Sullivan, *From Apostles to Bishops*, p. 9.

30. Sullivan, *From Apostles to Bishops*, p. 9.

31. There is a large body of literature on the general topic of teaching authority in the Church. A few representative examples will have to suffice: Francis A.

Sullivan, *Creative Fidelity: Weighing and Interpreting Documents of the Magisterium* (New York: Paulist Press, 1996), and his earlier work *Magisterium: Teaching Authority in the Catholic Church* (New York: Paulist Press, 1983); Richard R. Gaillardetz, *Teaching with Authority: A Theology of the Magisterium in the Church* (Collegeville, MN: Liturgical Press, 1997); John P. Boyle, *Church Teaching Authority: Historical and Theological Studies* (Notre Dame, IN: University of Notre Dame Press, 1995); David J. Stagaman, *Authority in the Church* (Collegeville, MN: Liturgical Press, 1999); and Bernard Hoose, "Authority in the Church," *Theological Studies* 63/1 (March 2002): 107–22.

32. I refer to this level of official teaching as "ambiguous" because, as Francis Sullivan points out, "at the present time there is no clear consensus among Catholic theologians as to what is included in the secondary object of infallible teaching"—which is what the ordinary universal magisterium would sometimes be concerned with, as opposed to the primary object of infallible teaching, which consists of matters of faith or morals that are explicitly contained in the sources of revelation. See his "Magisterium," in McBrien, ed., *The HarperCollins Encyclopedia of Catholicism,* p. 806 (full entry, pp. 805–7). Richard Gaillardetz, referred to in the previous note, wrote his doctoral dissertation (unpublished) on the topic: "The Development of the Theologies of the Ordinary Universal Magisterium of Bishops from 1840 to 1990" (University of Notre Dame, 1991).

33. Francis Sullivan elaborates on the meaning of religious *obsequium:* "This is best understood as an attitude of willingness to accept the teaching and to do one's best to convince oneself of its truth. It is called 'religious,' since it is based on belief in the divine origin of the teaching authority. However, despite genuine willingness and sustained effort, a person might be unable to give sincere mental assent to some point of nondefinitive teaching. In such a case, an individual's non-assent does not signify a failure to give religious *obsequium* to the authority of the magisterium" ("Magisterium," pp. 806–07). See also Richard A. McCormick, "Magisterium and Morality," in McBrien, ed., *The HarperCollins Encyclopedia of Catholicism,* pp. 807–8.

34. Avery Dulles, *A Church to Believe In: Discipleship and the Dynamics of Freedom* (New York: Crossroad, 1982), p. 109; see also chap. 7, "The Magisterium in History: Theological Considerations," pp. 103–17, and chap. 8, "The Two Magisteria: An Interim Reflection," pp. 118–32. On the use of the term "magisterium" in Aquinas, see p. 189, n. 88. The original citation on the so-called double magisterium is from St. Thomas's *Quodlibetales* (usually rendered *Quodl.*) 3.4.1 ad 3 (Parma ed., 9:490–91).

35. The reference is to Hans Küng's *Infallible? An Inquiry,* trans. Edward Quinn (New York: Doubleday, 1971). For the relevant excerpts from *Mysterium Ecclesiae,* known by its English title as "Declaration in Defense of the Catholic Doctrine on the Church Against Certain Errors of the Present Day," issued by the Congregation for the Doctrine of the Faith on June 24, 1973, see my *Catholicism,* pp. 1209–10. The full text of *Mysterium Ecclesiae* is in *Origins* 3/7 (July 19, 1973): 97, 99–100, 110–12.

36. See my *Catholicism,* p. 1209.

37. For more on the "hierarchy of truths," see Christopher O'Donnell, "Hierarchy of Truths," in his *Ecclesia,* pp. 195–97.

38. For an excellent, well-balanced reflection on the legitimacy of dissent from magisterial teachings and the criteria by which it can be justified, see Richard A. McCormick, "The Church and Dissent: How Vatican II Ushered in a New Way of Thinking," *Commonweal* 125/4 (February 27, 1998): 15–20.

39. See, e.g., John R. Quinn, retired archbishop of San Francisco, *The Reform of the Papacy: The Costly Call to Christian Unity* (New York: Crossroad, 1999). Archbishop Quinn claimed simply to be responding to John Paul II's invitation in his encyclical *Ut unum sint* (1995) to engage in a dialogue with him on how the exercise of the papacy could be improved for the benefit of the Catholic Church and the whole Body of Christ (see p. 9). For other examples, in no particular order of importance or chronology, see Cardinal Godfried Danneels, archbishop of Mechelen-Brussels in Belgium, "On Papal Primacy and Decentralization," *Origins* 27/20 (October 30, 1997): 339–41; Cardinal Franz König (d. 2004), "My Vision for the Church of the Future," *The Tablet* 253 (March 27, 1999): 424–26; Hermann J. Pottmeyer, *Towards a Papacy in Communion: Perspectives from Vatican Councils I and II,* trans. Matthew J. O'Connell (New York: Crossroad, 1998), and "Primacy in Communion," trans. Robert A. Krieg, *America* 182/20 (June 3–10, 2000): 15–18; John W. O'Malley, "The Millennium and the Papalization of Catholicism," *America* 182/12 (April 8, 2000): 8–10, 12, 14–16; Cardinal Avery Dulles, "The Papacy for a Global Church," *America* 183/2 (July 15–22, 2000): 6–11; and Ladislas Örsy, "The Papacy for an Ecumenical Age: A Response to Avery Dulles," *America* 183/12 (October 21, 2000): 9–15. For an important statement on the primacy issued by the Congregation for the Doctrine of the Faith, see "Reflections on the Primacy of Peter," *Origins* 28/32 (January 28, 1999): 560–63.

40. It is not entirely clear, however, whether the invitation was extended to the pastoral leaders and theologians of *all* Churches and ecclesial communities, including the Catholic Church, or whether it was only extended to the pastoral leaders and theologians of the various non-Catholic Christian Churches and ecclesial communities. In any case, Catholic bishops and theologians were not explicitly excluded from the dialogue.

41. See n. 39 above.

42. John R. Quinn, "The Exercise of the Primacy," *Commonweal* 123/13 (July 12, 1996): 11–21.

43. Quinn, *The Reform of the Papacy,* p. 34.

44. Quinn, *The Reform of the Papacy,* p. 29.

45. Quinn, *The Reform of the Papacy,* pp. 178, 180.

46. Quinn, *The Reform of the Papacy,* p. 181.

47. Godfried Danneels, "On Papal Primacy and Decentralization," *Origins* 27/20 (October 30, 1997): 339.

48. See my *Lives of the Popes: The Pontiffs from St. Peter to Benedict XVI* (San Francisco: HarperSanFrancisco, 1997; updated ed., 2006), pp. 395–403.

49. Danneels, "On Papal Primacy and Decentralization," pp. 340–41.

50. All quotations in this section are from Franz König, "My Vision for the Church of the Future," *The Tablet* 253 (March 27, 1999): 424, 426.

51. Hermann Pottmeyer, *Towards A Papacy in Communion: Perspectives from Vatican Councils I and II,* trans. Matthew J. O'Connell (New York: Crossroad,

1998); "Primacy in Communion," trans. Robert A. Krieg, *America* 182/20 (June 3–10, 2000): 15–18.

52. "Reflections on the Primacy of Peter," *Origins* 28/32 (January 28, 1999): 560–63.

53. Pottmeyer, "Primacy in Communion," p. 15.

54. Pottmeyer, "Primacy in Communion," p. 16.

55. Pottmeyer, "Primacy in Communion," p. 16.

56. Pottmeyer, "Primacy in Communion," p. 16.

57. Pottmeyer, "Primacy in Communion," p. 18.

58. John W. O'Malley, "The Millennium and the Papalization of Catholicism," *America* 182/12 (April 8, 2000): 8–16.

59. O'Malley, "The Millennium and the Papalization of Catholicism," p. 9.

60. O'Malley, "The Millennium and the Papalization of Catholicism," p. 10.

61. O'Malley, "The Millennium and the Papalization of Catholicism," p. 10.

62. See my *Lives of the Popes,* pp. 18–20.

63. O'Malley, "The Millennium and the Papalization of Catholicism," p. 16.

64. O'Malley, "The Millennium and the Papalization of Catholicism," p. 16.

65. For some of Avery Dulles's earlier writings on the papacy, see, e.g., *The Survival of Dogma* (Garden City, NY: Doubleday, 1971), p. 165, and *The Reshaping of Catholicism: Current Challenges in the Theology of Church* (San Francisco: Harper & Row, 1988), chap. 6, "Authority and Conscience: Two Needed Voices," pp. 93–109. The most exhaustive study of the change in Avery Dulles's thinking and writing on the general question of the magisterium, both papal and more broadly hierarchical, is an unpublished doctoral dissertation, "The Magisterium and Theologians in the Writings of Avery Robert Dulles," by Dariusz W. Jankiewicz (Andrews University in Berrien Springs, Michigan, 2001).

66. Avery Dulles, "The Papacy for a Global Church," *America* 183/2 (July 15–22, 2000): 6–11. This and a few other articles by Dulles cited herein, especially those on Pope John Paul II, were originally delivered as lectures at Fordham University and were subsequently published in *America* and other journals. For the complete collection, see Avery Cardinal Dulles, *Church and Society: The Laurence J. McGinley Lectures, 1988–2007* (New York: Fordham University Press, 2008).

67. Dulles, "The Papacy for a Global Church," p. 9.

68. Dulles, "The Papacy for a Global Church," p. 10.

69. Dulles, "The Papacy for a Global Church," p. 11.

70. Ladislas Örsy, "The Papacy for an Ecumenical Age: A Response to Avery Dulles," *America* 183/12 (October 21, 2000): 9–15.

71. Örsy, "The Papacy for an Ecumenical Age," p. 9.

72. Örsy, "The Papacy for an Ecumenical Age," p. 11 (italics in original).

73. Örsy, "The Papacy for an Ecumenical Age," p. 11.

74. Örsy, "The Papacy for an Ecumenical Age," p. 11.

75. Örsy, "The Papacy for an Ecumenical Age," p. 11.

76. Örsy, "The Papacy for an Ecumenical Age," p. 11. He offers specific examples on p. 12. See also my *Lives of the Popes,* pp. 406–12.

77. Örsy, "The Papacy for an Ecumenical Age," p. 13.

78. See, e.g., Charles E. Curran, ed., *Contraception: Authority and Dissent* (New York: Herder & Herder, 1969); Anthony Kosnick et al., eds., *Human Sexuality: New Directions in American Catholic Thought: A Study Commissioned*

by the Catholic Theological Society of America (New York: Paulist Press, 1977); and Joseph A. Komonchak, "*Humanae Vitae* and Its Reception: Ecclesiological Reflections," *Theological Studies* 39/2 (June 1978): 221–57. Various bishops' conferences also adopted a mildly critical view, including the bishops of Belgium, Germany, Holland, France, Canada, and Scandinavia. See my *Catholicism*, pp. 990–91.

79. Örsy, "The Papacy for an Ecumenical Age," p. 14 (italics in original).

80. The text of the apostolic letter is available in *Origins* 28/18 (July 16, 1998): 113, 115–16. The text of the commentary is in the same issue on pp. 116–19.

81. Örsy, "The Papacy for an Ecumenical Age," p. 14.

82. Örsy, "The Papacy for an Ecumenical Age," p. 15.

83. "Reflections on the Primacy of Peter," *Origins* 28/32 (January 28, 1999): 560–63. Hereafter, references in the text of this section are to the various articles in the document itself.

84. *Il Primato del Successore di Pietro: Atti del Symposio Teologico* (Vatican City: Libreria Editrice Vaticana, 1998).

85. Dulles, *The Reshaping of Catholicism*, chap. 11, pp. 207–26. See also his "The Teaching Authority of Bishops' Conferences," *America* 148/23 (June 11, 1983): 453–55.

86. Dulles, "The Teaching Authority of Bishops' Conferences," p. 455.

87. Cited in Dulles, "The Teaching Authority of Bishops' Conferences," p. 453.

88. Joseph Ratzinger, "The Pastoral Implications of Episcopal Collegiality," *Concilium* 1/1 (January 1965): 30 (full article, pp. 20–34). For a collection of essays on the subject, see Thomas J. Reese, ed., *Episcopal Conferences: Historical, Canonical, and Theological Studies* (Washington, DC: Georgetown University Press, 1989).

89. Several have been cited in Part VI, n. 86.

90. *Baptism, Eucharist and Ministry*, Faith and Order Paper 111 (Geneva: World Council of Churches, 1982).

91. Anglican–Roman Catholic International Commission (ARCIC II), "The Gift of Authority," *Origins* 29/2 (1999): 17–29. There was a previous, yet tentative, document, "An Agreed Statement on Authority in the Church," also known as "The Venice Statement," published in 1977 (Washington, DC: United States Catholic Conference). In 1981 ARCIC I issued its own document, "The Final Report," which elicited formal responses from Anglicans and Catholics alike. Both sides agreed that the ARCIC I document provided a good foundation for further dialogue on such issues as papal primacy. However, the Anglican–Roman Catholic Consultation in the United States criticized its international counterparts for concentrating too much on the authority of the pope and the other bishops and too little on the authority of the whole Church (see "Authority in the Church: Vital Ecumenical Issue," *Origins* 7/30 [January 12, 1978]: 474–76). The later document from ARCIC II, "The Gift of Authority," represents the joint effort to continue the dialogue and to advance beyond its previous stage.

92. *The Nature and Mission of the Church: A Stage on the Way to a Common Statement*, Faith and Order Paper 198 (Geneva: World Council of Churches, 2005).

93. Ladislas Örsy, "Reception of Law," in McBrien, ed., *The HarperCollins Encyclopedia of Catholicism*, p. 1082. See also James A. Coriden, "The Canonical Doctrine of Reception," *The Jurist* 50/1 (1990): 58–82.

94. See Jean-Marie Tillard, "Reception–Communion," *One in Christ* 28/4 (1992): 312–13 (full article, pp. 307–22).

95. See Hermann J. Pottmeyer, "Reception of Doctrine," in McBrien, ed., *The HarperCollins Encyclopedia of Catholicism,* pp. 1081–82.

96. See Komonchak, "*Humanae Vitae* and Its Reception."

97. Yves Congar, "Reception as an Ecclesiological Reality," in Giuseppe Alberigo and Anton Weiler, eds., *Concilium: Election and Consensus in the Church,* vol. 77 (New York: Herder and Herder, 1972), p. 45 (full article, pp. 43–68). The article is reprinted in Congar's *Église et papauté: Regards historique* (Paris: Les Éditions du Cerf, 1994), pp. 229–66.

98. Congar, "Reception as an Ecclesiological Reality," p. 60; see also p. 62.

99. Congar, "Reception as an Ecclesiological Reality," p. 68; see also pp. 66–68.

100. See, e.g., John Zizioulas, "The Theological Problem of Reception," *One Church* 21 (1985): 187–93; and Jean-Marie Tillard, "The Mission of Councils of Churches," *The Ecumenical Review* 45/3 (July 1993): 271–82. See also Myroslaw Tataryn, "Karl Rahner and the Nature of Reception," *One in Christ* 25/1 (1989): 75–83; and Margaret O'Gara, "Reception as Key: Unlocking ARCIC on Infallibility," *Toronto Journal of Theology* 3/1 (Spring 1987): 41–49.

101. See Christopher O'Donnell, "Reception," in his *Ecclesia,* p. 400 (full article, pp. 400–402). O'Donnell provides useful examples of how reception occurs through various venues, including the liturgy, and instances of nonreception and partial reception. Examples of the pertinent literature on reception include Michael J. Himes, "The Ecclesiological Significance of the Reception of Doctrine," *Heythrop Journal* 33/2 (April 1992): 146–60; Edward J. Kilmartin, "Reception in History: An Ecclesiological Phenomenon and Its Significance," *Journal of Ecumenical Studies* 21/1 (Winter 1984): 34–54; Thomas P. Rausch, "Reception Past and Present," *Theological Studies* 47/3 (September 1986): 497–508; and Richard R. Gaillardetz, "The Reception of Doctrine: New Perspectives," in *Authority in the Roman Catholic Church* (Burlington, VT: Ashgate, 2002), pp. 95–114. Regarding the specific reception of Vatican II, see Joseph Chinnici, "Reception of Vatican II in the United States," *Theological Studies* 64/3 (September 2003): 461–94; Angel Antón, "*La 'receptión' del Concilio Vaticano II y de su eclesiología,*" *Revista espazola de teologia* 48/3 (July–September 1988): 291–319. Regarding the reception of Vatican I, see Klaus Schatz, *Vaticanum I (1869–1870),* vol. 3: *Unfehlbarkeitsdiskussion und Rezeption, Konziliengeschichte* (Paderborn: Schöningh, 1994). Regarding the reception of other councils—Nicaea II, by way of example, see John E. Lynch, "The Reception of an Ecumenical Council: Nicaea II, a Case in Point," *The Jurist* 48/2 (1988): 454–82. Nicaea II (786–87) had been rejected in the West until 1053, when Pope Leo IX explicitly accepted it as one of the seven great councils of the Church. Regarding, finally, the notion of reception in other Christian traditions, see, by way of example only, H. Meyer, "*Les présupposés de la réception ecclésial ou le probleme de la 'recevabilité'—Perspectives luthériennes,*" *Irénikon* 59/1 (1986): 5–19; and Johannes Willebrands, "Ecumenical Dialogue and Its Reception," *Diakonia* 19 (1984–85): 118–28.

102. O'Donnell, "Reception," p. 400.

103. Richard A. McCormick, "The Church and Dissent: How Vatican II Ushered in a New Way of Thinking," *Commonweal* 125/4 (February 27, 1998):

15–20. See also his *The Critical Calling: Reflections on Moral Dilemmas Since Vatican II* (Washington, DC: Georgetown University Press, 1989), chap. 2, "Dissent in the Church: Loyalty or Liability?" pp. 25–46. For a broader sampling of views on the question, see Charles E. Curran and Richard A. McCormick, eds., *Dissent in the Church: Readings in Moral Theology No. 6* (New York: Paulist Press, 1988).

104. McCormick, "The Church and Dissent," p. 18.

105. Cited in McCormick, "The Church and Dissent," p. 20.

106. McCormick, "The Church and Dissent," p. 20.

107. With few exceptions, most of the literature concerns the pastoral implications of the theology of ministry rather than focusing on the theology itself. For a representative mixture of both, see Thomas F. O'Meara, *Theology of Ministry,* rev. ed. (New York/Mahwah, NJ: Paulist Press, 1999); Richard P. McBrien, *Ministry: A Theological, Pastoral Handbook* (San Francisco: Harper & Row, 1987), and "Church and Ministry: The Achievement of Yves Congar," *Theology Digest* 32/3 (Fall 1985): 203–11; Edward P. Hahnenberg, *Ministries: A Relational Approach* (New York: Crossroad, 2003); see also his "Ordained and Lay Ministry: Restarting the Conversation," *Origins* 35/6 (June 23, 2005): 94–99, and "The Vocation to Lay Ecclesial Ministry," *Origins* 37/12 (August 30, 2007): 176, 178–82; Kenan B. Osborne, *Ministry: Lay Ministry in the Roman Catholic Church, Its History and Theology* (New York: Paulist Press, 1993); see also Osborne's *Orders and Ministry: Leadership in the World Church* (Maryknoll, NY: Orbis Books, 2006) and *The Permanent Diaconate: Its History and Place in the Sacrament of Orders* (New York: Paulist Press, 2007); Donald B. Cozzens, *The Changing Face of the Priesthood: A Reflection on the Priest's Crisis of Soul* (Collegeville, MN: Liturgical Press, 2000); Susan K. Wood, ed., *Ordering the Baptismal Priesthood: Theologies of Lay and Ordained Ministry* (Collegeville, MN: Liturgical Press, 2003), esp. Richard R. Gaillardetz, "The Ecclesiological Foundations of Ministry Within an Ordered Communion," pp. 26–51; Walter Kasper, *Leadership in the Church: How Traditional Roles Can Serve the Christian Community Today,* trans. Brian McNeil (New York: Crossroad, 2003), esp. chaps. 1–3, pp. 13–113; Dean R. Hoge and Jacqueline E. Wenger, *Evolving Visions of the Priesthood: Changes from Vatican II to the Turn of the New Century* (Collegeville, MN: Liturgical Press, 2003); Dean R. Hoge, *The First Five Years of the Priesthood: A Study of Newly Ordained Catholic Priests* (Collegeville, MN: Liturgical Press, 2002); Dean R. Hoge and Aniedi Okure, *International Priests in America: Challenges and Opportunities* (Collegeville, MN: Liturgical Press, 2006); Katarina M. Schuth, *Seminaries, Theologates, and the Future of Church Ministry: An Analysis of Trends and Transitions* (Collegeville, MN: Liturgical Press, 1999), and *Priestly Ministry in Multiple Parishes* (Collegeville, MN: Liturgical Press, 2006); Victor J. Klimoski, Kevin J. O'Neil, and Katarina M. Schuth, *Educating Leaders for Ministry: Issues and Responses* (Collegeville, MN: Liturgical Press, 2005); Richard R. Gaillardetz, "Shifting Meanings in the Lay-Clergy Distinction," *Irish Theological Quarterly* 64/2 (Summer 1999): 115–39, and "The Theology Underlying Lay Ecclesial Ministry," *Origins* 36/9 (July 20, 2006): 138–43; Kathleen A. Cahalan, "Toward a Fundamental Theology of Ministry," *Worship* 80/2 (March 2006): 102–20; and Neil Ormerod, "System, History and a Theology of Ministry," *Theological Studies* 61/3 (September 2000): 432–46. For a sample of official statements on various aspects of

ministry, see John Paul II's apostolic exhortation on the laity, *Christi fideles laici* (Lat., "Christ's faithful people"), *Origins* 18/35 (February 9, 1989): 561, 563–95; the 1997 interdicasterial instruction "On Certain Questions Regarding the Collaboration of the Nonordained Faithful in the Sacred Ministry of Priests," *Origins* 27/24 (November 27, 1997): 397, 399–409; United States Conference of Catholic Bishops, "Co-Workers in the Vineyard of the Lord," *Origins* 35/25 (December 1, 2005): 404, 406–27; and Cardinal Roger Mahony's pastoral letter on ministry, "As I Have Done for You," *Origins* 29/46 (May 4, 2000): 741, 743–53.

108. For a brief survey of this history, see my *Catholicism*, pp. 766–71.

109. See n. 107.

110. Roger Mahony, "As I Have Done for You," *Origins* 29/46 (May 4, 2000): 741, 743–53.

111. Mahony, "As I Have Done for You," p. 746.

112. There is no separate section in this book on religious or consecrated life, even though it has, of course, significant ecclesiological dimensions. The author has chosen—not ill-advisedly, one hopes—to leave that discussion to those with actual experience of religious life. One of the best books on the subject is Johannes B. Metz, *Followers of Christ: Perspectives on the Religious Life*, trans. Thomas Linton (New York: Paulist Press, 1978). See also Sandra M. Schneiders, *Finding the Treasure: Locating Catholic Religious Life in a New Ecclesial and Cultural Context*, vol. 1 (New York: Paulist Press, 2000), and *Selling All: Commitment, Consecrated Celibacy, and Community in Catholic Religious Life*, vol. 2 (New York: Paulist Press, 2001); Nadine Foley, ed., *Journey in Faith and Fidelity: Women Shaping Religious Life for a Renewed Church* (New York: Continuum, 1999); Diarmuid O'Murchu, *Consecrated Religious Life: The Changing Patterns* (Maryknoll, NY: Orbis Books, 2005); and Casian J. Yuhaus, ed., *Religious Life: The Challenge for Tomorrow* (New York: Paulist Press, 1994).

113. Mahony, "As I Have Done for You," p. 747.

114. Mahony, "As I Have Done for You," p. 747.

115. Mahony, "As I Have Done for You," p. 748.

116. Mahony, "As I Have Done for You," pp. 749–50, 753.

117. For a fuller treatment of the sacraments and the Church's liturgical life, see my *Catholicism*, chaps. 21–24, pp. 787–880, and chap. 29, pp. 1063–75. For a history of liturgical development from the sixteenth century to today from a Methodist scholar's vantage point, see James F. White, *Roman Catholic Worship: Trent to Today* (Collegeville, MN: Liturgical Press, 2003). For a more recent perspective, see Annibale Bugnini, *The Reform of the Liturgy, 1948–1975*, trans. Matthew J. O'Connell (Collegeville, MN: Liturgical Press, 1990); Piero Marini (Archbishop Marini served for many years as Master of Pontifical Liturgical Celebrations during the pontificates of John Paul II and Benedict XVI), *A Challenging Reform: Realizing the Vision of Liturgical Renewal, 1963–1975*, ed. Mark R. Francis, John R. Page, and Keith F. Pecklers (Collegeville, MN: Liturgical Press, 2007); Bernard Botte, *From Silence to Participation: An Insider's View of Liturgical Renewal*, trans. John Sullivan (Washington, DC: Pastoral Press, 1988); Keith F. Pecklers, *Worship: A Primer in Christian Ritual* (Collegeville, MN: Liturgical Press, 2003), esp. chaps. 4–8, pp. 91–212; Mark R. Francis and Keith F. Pecklers, eds., *Liturgy for the New Millennium: A Commentary on the Revised Sacramentary*

(Collegeville, MN: Liturgical Press, 2000). For a Protestant view on the relation between liturgy and ecclesiology, see Gordon W. Lathrop, *Holy People: A Liturgical Ecclesiology* (Minneapolis: Fortress, 1999). For titles more explicitly concerned with the sacraments in the life of the Church, see the various books by Kenan Osborne, including *Christian Sacraments in a Post-Modern World: A Theology for the Third Millennium* (New York: Paulist Press, 1999), and *Sacramental Theology: A General Introduction* (New York: Paulist Press, 1988).

118. See Anne Carr, "Mary in the Mystery of the Church: Vatican Council II," in Carol Frances Jegen, ed., *Mary According to Women* (Kansas City, MO: Leaven Press, 1985), pp. 5–32, esp. pp. 25–26. For a commentary on chap. 8 of the Dogmatic Constitution on the Church, comparing Mary in the contexts of the mystery of Christ and of the Church, see Stefano De Fiores, *Maria nel Misterio di Christo e della Chiesa: Commento al Capitolo Mariano del Concilio Vaticano,* 3d ed. (Rome: Edizioni Monfortane, 1984). For a highly compressed version, see his "Mary in Postconciliar Theology," in René Latourelle, ed., *Vatican II: Assessment and Perspectives: Twenty-Five Years After (1962–1987)* (New York: Paulist Press, 1988), pp. 470–74 (full article, pp. 469–539).

119. De Fiores, "Mary in Postconciliar Theology," p. 474.

120. De Fiores, "Mary in Postconciliar Theology," p. 475.

121. Heribert Mühlen, *Una Mystica Persona: Die Kirche als das Mysterium der Identität des Heiligen Geistes in Christus und den Christen; eine Person in vielen Personen* (Munich, Paderborn, Vienna: Schöningh, 1967), p. 575. For Congar's comments, see VI.7.2.

122. Karl Rahner, *Foundations of Christian Faith: An Introduction to the Idea of Christianity,* trans. William V. Dych (New York: Seabury, 1978), pp. 387–88.

123. See Otto Semmelroth. "*Quomodo mariologiae cum ecclesiologia coniunctio adiuvet utriusque mysterii interpretationem*" ["How the connection between Mariology and ecclesiology assists both in the interpretation of mystery"], in *Acta Congressus Internationalis de Theologia Concilii Vaticani* (Vatican City, 1968), p. 268.

124. Cited in De Fiores, "Mary in Postconciliar Theology," p. 482, n. 66 (p. 529).

125. See Lucy Gardner, "Balthasar and the Figure of Mary," in Edward T. Oakes and David Moss, eds., *The Cambridge Companion to Hans Urs von Balthasar* (Cambridge: Cambridge University Press, 2004), p. 65. I am indebted in what follows regarding Balthasar's anthropology and ecclesiology to the unpublished doctoral dissertation of my former graduate assistant at Notre Dame, Natalia Imperatori-Lee, "The Use of Marian Imagery in Catholic Ecclesiology Since Vatican II" (2007), chap. 2, pp. 59–92.

126. Hans Urs von Balthasar, *Explorations in Theology II: Spouse of the Word,* trans. A. V. Littledale, with Alexander Dru (San Francisco: Ignatius, 1991), p. 20.

127. Hans Urs von Balthasar, *The Office of Peter and the Structure of the Church,* trans. Andrée Emery (San Francisco: Ignatius, 1986), p. 184.

128. Balthasar, *The Office of Peter and the Structure of the Church,* p. 24.

129. Hans Urs von Balthasar, *Prayer,* trans. Graham Harrison (San Francisco: Ignatius, 1986), p. 72.

130. Balthasar, *The Office of Peter and the Structure of the Church,* p. 195.

131. Hans Urs von Balthasar, *Theo-Drama: Theological Dramatic Theory III: The Dramatis Personae: The Person in Christ,* trans. Graham Harrison (San Francisco: Ignatius, 1992), p. 317.

132. Balthasar, *Theo-Drama,* p. 285.

133. See Balthasar, *The Office of Peter and the Structure of the Church,* pp. 131–82.

134. As Imperatori-Lee points out in her dissertation, "The Use of Marian Imagery in Catholic Ecclesiology Since Vatican II," the fluidity of gender in the symbolism of John is an interesting contrast with the rigid gender roles Balthasar assigns to Mary and Peter (pp. 79–80). Pope John Paul II wrote in support of Balthasar's Mary/Peter distinction in his apostolic letter *Mulieris dignitatem* (Lat., "On the Dignity of Women") in 1995 (n. 27).

135. Balthasar, *The Office of Peter and the Structure of the Church,* p. 208.

136. For a different approach to the motherhood of the Church, see Sally Cunneen, *Mother Church: What the Experience of Women Is Teaching Her* (New York: Paulist Press, 1991). Instead of obedience and receptivity, Cunneen presents the Mother Church as nurturing, enabling, enduring, and sharing.

137. Karl Rahner, "Mary and the Christian Image of Woman," *Theological Investigations,* vol. 19, trans. Edward Quinn (New York: Crossroad, 1983), p. 217 (full article, pp. 211–17).

138. For Imperatori-Lee, "the greatest gift of feminist theology to Mariology and ecclesiology" is its theological anthropology, which undermines the kind of masculine-feminine anthropology advocated by Hans Urs von Balthasar, and with far-reaching implications for one's understanding of the Church ("The Use of Marian Imagery," p. 190).

139. See my *Catholicism,* pp. 1096–97. This brief section on *Marialis cultus* is drawn from my synthesis in *Catholicism,* pp. 1096–98.

140. See William McLoughlin and Jill Pennock, eds., *Mary Is for Everyone: Papers on Mary and Ecumenism Given at International Congresses of the Ecumenical Society of the Blessed Virgin Mary at Winchester (1991), Norwich (1994), and Bristol (1996), and a Conference at Dromatine, Newry (1995)* (Leominster, UK: Gracewing, 1997); Alberic Stacpoole, ed., *Mary and the Churches: Papers of the Chichester Congress, 1986, of the Ecumenical Society of the Blessed Virgin Mary* (Dublin: Columba, 1987); H. George Anderson, J. Francis Stafford, and Joseph A. Burgess, eds., *The One Mediator, the Saints, and Mary: Lutherans and Catholics in Dialogue 8* (Minneapolis: Augsburg, 1992); and Anglican–Roman Catholic International Commission (ARCIC II), *Mary: Grace and Hope in Christ: The Seattle Statement* (2004), available at www.ecumenism.net/archive/arcic/mary_en.htm.

141. McBrien, *Catholicism,* p. xliv.

142. See, e.g., Rosemary Radford Ruether *The Church Against Itself: An Inquiry into the Conditions of Historical Existence for the Eschatological Community* (New York: Herder and Herder, 1967).

143. For a broader perspective, see Natalie K. Watson, *Introducing Feminist Ecclesiology* (Cleveland, OH: Pilgrim, 2002).

144. Mary E. Hines, "Community for Liberation: Church," in Catherine Mowry LaCugna, ed., *Freeing Theology: The Essentials of Theology in Feminist*

Perspective (San Francisco: HarperSanFrancisco, 1993), p. 161 (full article, pp. 161–84). See also her "Ecclesiology for a Public Church: The United States Context," in Michael Downey, ed., *Catholic Theological Society of America: Proceedings of the Fifty-fifth Annual Convention* (Catholic Theological Society of America, 2000), pp. 23–46. As if to reinforce her earlier point—more implied perhaps than explicit—about the difficulty in identifying feminist ecclesiologies or even ecclesiologies written by nonfeminist women, women are cited in only four of the ninety-nine footnotes in her CTSA paper. For another feminist voice, see Mary Grey, "Beyond Exclusion: Towards a Feminist Eucharistic Ecclesiology," in Mary Grey, Andrée Heaton, and Danny Sullivan, eds., *Candles Are Still Burning: Directions in Sacrament and Spirituality* (Collegeville, MN: Liturgical Press, 1995), pp. 3–12.

145. Elisabeth Schüssler Fiorenza, *In Memory of Her: A Feminist Theological Reconstruction of Christian Origins* (New York: Crossroad, 1983); see pp. 140–54, 315–33, respectively.

146. Elisabeth Schüssler Fiorenza, *Discipleship of Equals: A Critical Feminist Ekklesia-logy of Liberation* (New York: Crossroad, 1993), "Gather in My Name: Toward a Christian Feminist Spirituality" (1982), pp. 195–205; "A Democratic Feminist Vision for a Different Society and Church" (1991), pp. 353–72; and "The Ethics and Politics of Liberation: Theorizing the *Ekklēsia* of Women" (1992), pp. 332–52.

147. Schüssler Fiorenza, *Discipleship of Equals,* pp. 341, 346.

148. Latin American liberation theology and feminist theology, of course, share much in common. Both arise out of a situation of relative oppression and marginalization. Women's voices in liberation theology have in more recent years been added to those of its previously dominant male theologians. See, e.g., Ivone Gebara and Maria Clara Bingemer, *Mary: Mother of God, Mother of the Poor* (Maryknoll, NY: Orbis Books, 1989); Ada María Isasi-Díaz *En la Lucha = In the Struggle: A Hispanic Women's Liberation Theology* (Minneapolis: Fortress, 1993). For our earlier discussion of liberation theology, see VI.6.

149. See, e.g., Elizabeth A. Johnson, *She Who Is: The Mystery of God in a Feminist Theological Discourse* (New York: Crossroad, 1992); *Truly Our Sister: A Theology of Mary in the Communion of Saints* (New York: Continuum, 2003); *Friends of God and Prophets: A Feminist Theological Reading of the Communion of Saints* (New York: Continuum, 1998); and *Quest for the Living God: Mapping Frontiers in the Theology of God* (New York: Continuum, 2007).

150. Johnson, *She Who Is,* pp. 60–61.

151. Johnson, *Friends of God and Prophets,* p. 26, also p. 63.

152. Johnson, *Friends of God and Prophets,* p. 221.

153. Johnson, *Friends of God and Prophets,* p. 40.

154. Johnson, *Friends of God and Prophets,* p. 170.

155. Imperatori-Lee, "The Use of Marian Imagery," p. 121 (see n. 125).

156. Imperatori-Lee, "The Use of Marian Imagery," pp. 122–23.

157. See Anne Carr, *Transforming Grace: Christian Tradition and Women's Experience* (San Francisco: HarperSanFrancisco, 1988). See also her "The New Vision of Feminist Theology: Method," in LaCugna, ed., *Freeing Theology,* pp. 5–29.

158. Carr, *Transforming Grace*, p. 53.

159. Rosemary Radford Ruether, *Women-Church: Theology and Practice of Feminist Liturgical Communities* (San Francisco: Harper & Row, 1986). See also her "Women-Church: An American Catholic Feminist Movement," in Mary Jo Weaver, ed., *What's Left? Liberal American Catholics* (Bloomington: Indiana University Press, 1999), pp. 46–64.

160. Ruether, *Women-Church*, p. 3.

161. Ruether, *Women-Church*, p. 62.

162. Mary E. Hines, "Community for Liberation: Church," in Catherine Mowry LaCugna, ed., *Freeing Theology: The Essentials of Theology in Feminist Perspective* (San Francisco: HarperSanFrancisco, 1993), p. 162.

163. Hines, "Community for Liberation," p. 163.

164. Hines, "Community for Liberation," pp. 167–68 (Ruether), 172–73, 176–77 (Rahner), 174–75 (Schüssler Fiorenza).

165. Hines, "Community for Liberation," p. 178. For a broader international view, see Lily Wang, "Ecclesiology and Women: A View from Taiwan," in Virginia Fabella and Sun-Ai-Lee Park, eds., *We Dare to Dream: Doing Theology as Asian Women* (Hong Kong: Asian Women's Resource Center for Theology and Culture, 1989), pp. 24–32.

166. Susan Wood, *Spiritual Exegesis and the Church in the Theology of Henri de Lubac* (Grand Rapids, MI: Eerdmans, 1998).

167. Susan Wood, *Sacramental Orders* (Collegeville, MN: Liturgical Press, 2000); Susan Wood, ed., *Ordering the Baptismal Priesthood: Theologies of Lay and Ordained Ministry* (Collegeville, MN: Liturgical Press, 2003), to which she contributed two articles: one on presbyteral identity within the context of a parish and the other a concluding essay on "convergence points toward a theology of ordered ministries."

168. See esp. Susan Wood, "The Church as Communion," in Peter C. Phan, ed., *The Gift of the Church: A Textbook on Ecclesiology* (Collegeville, MN: Liturgical Press, 2000), pp. 159–76. See also her "Ecclesial *Koinonia* in Ecumenical Dialogues," *One in Christ* 29/2 (1994): 124–45; and "The Sacramentality of Episcopal Consecration," *Theological Studies* 51/3 (September 1990): 479–96.

169. Wood, "The Church as Communion," p. 176.

170. Sara Butler, "Women and the Church," in Phan, ed., *The Gift of the Church*, pp. 415–33. See also her "Women's Ordination and the Development of Doctrine," *The Thomist* 61/4 (October 1997): 501–24. See also her book *The Catholic Priesthood and Women: A Guide to the Teaching of the Church* (Chicago: Hillenbrand, 2006). Butler is one of the few Catholic women theologians actively to oppose the ordination of women to the priesthood.

171. John Paul II, "Letter to Women," *Origins* 25/9 (July 27, 1995): 137, 139–43. The letter was written in anticipation of the United Nations World Conference on Women, to be held in September of that year in Beijing.

172. See Butler, "Women and the Church," p. 432.

173. See Stafford J. Poole, *The Guadalupan Controversies in Mexico* (Stanford, CA: Stanford University Press, 2006); *Our Lady of Guadalupe: The Origins and Sources of a Mexican National Symbol, 1531–1797* (Tucson: University of Arizona

Press, 1995); and D. A. Brading, *Mexican Phoenix: Our Lady of Guadalupe: Image and Tradition Across Five Centuries* (New York: Cambridge University Press, 2001). For a description of Guadalupan devotions and festivals, see Timothy M. Matovina, *Guadalupe and Her Faithful: Latino Catholics in San Antonio from Colonial Origins to the Present* (Baltimore: Johns Hopkins University Press, 2005). See also Orlando Espín, *The Faith of the People: Theological Reflections on Popular Catholicism* (Maryknoll, NY: Orbis Books, 1997); and Jeannette Rodriguez, *Our Lady of Guadalupe: Faith and Empowerment among Mexican-American Women* (Austin: University of Texas Press, 1994).

174. The terms "Hispanic" and "Latino/a" are used interchangeably in this section, as in Roberto Goizueta, *Caminemos con Jesús: Toward a Hispanic/Latino Theology of Accompaniment* (Maryknoll, NY: Orbis Books, 1995), esp. pp. 12–15.

175. E.g., Virgilio Elizondo, "Mary and Evangelization in the Americas," in Doris Donnelly, ed., *Mary, Woman of Nazareth: Biblical and Theological Perspectives* (New York: Paulist Press, 1989), p. 160 (full article, pp. 146–60).

176. See Imperatori-Lee, "The Use of Marian Imagery," pp. 141–42, and passim.

177. Virgilio Elizondo, *Guadalupe, Mother of the New Creation* (Maryknoll, NY: Orbis Books, 1997), p. 95.

178. Elizondo, *Guadalupe*, p. 95.

179. Goizueta, *Caminemos con Jesús*, p. 38.

180. See Imperatori-Lee, "The Use of Marian Imagery," p. 167.

181. See, e.g., Ada María Isasi-Díaz, *En la Lucha = In the Struggle: Elaborating a Mujerista Theology* (Minneapolis: Fortress, 2004).

182. See Ada María Isasi-Díaz, *Hispanic Women: Prophetic Voice in the Church: Toward a Hispanic Women's Liberation Theology* (San Francisco: Harper & Row, 1988), pp. 12–55.

183. Ada María Isasi-Díaz, "*Mujerista* Liturgies and the Struggle for Liberation," in Louis-Marie Chauvet and Francois Kabasele Lumbala, eds., *Liturgy and the Body* (*Concilium* 1995/3) (Maryknoll, NY: Orbis Books, 1995), p. 107 (full article, pp. 104–11).

184. Isasi-Díaz, "*Mujerista* Liturgies and the Struggle for Liberation," p. 108.

185. Imperatori-Lee, "The Use of Marian Imagery," p. 174.

186. Christopher O'Donnell, "Black Theology," in his *Ecclesia*, p. 61 (full article, with ample notes, pp. 61–62). For Paul VI's comment, see "The African Church Today," *The Pope Speaks* 14/3 (Autumn 1969): 219 (full text, pp. 214–20). See also the U.S. black bishops' pastoral letter "What We Have Seen and Heard," *Origins* 14/18 (October 18, 1984): 273–87.

187. See Diana L. Hayes, *And Still We Rise: An Introduction to Black Liberation Theology* (New York: Paulist Press, 1996); Cyprian Davis and Jamie T. Phelps, eds., *"Stamped with the Image of God": African Americans as God's Image in Black* (Maryknoll, NY: Orbis Books, 2003); Jamie T. Phelps, ed., *Black and Catholic: The Challenge and Gift of Black Folk: Contributions of African American Experience and Thought to Catholic Theology* (Milwaukee, WI: Marquette University Press, 1997); and Peter C. Phan and Diana L. Hayes, eds., *Many Faces, One Church: Cultural Diversity and the American Catholic Experience* (Lanham, MD:

Rowan & Littlefield, 2005). See also "The Catholic Reception of Black Theology," *Theological Studies* 61/4 (December 2000): pp. 603–747. See especially Jamie T. Phelps, "Communion Ecclesiology and Black Liberation Theology," pp. 672–99.

188. Edward K. Braxton, *The Wisdom Community* (New York: Paulist Press, 1980), and *The Faith Community: One, Holy, Catholic, and Apostolic* (Notre Dame, IN: Ave Maria, 1990). See also his "Toward a Black Catholic Theology," in G. S. Wilmore and James H. Cone, eds. *Black Theology: A Documentary History 1966–1979* (Maryknoll, NY: Orbis Books, 1979), pp. 325–28.

189. O'Donnell, "Black Theology," p. 61.

190. The "drum major for justice" speech is available on various Web sites. His own theological journey is succinctly presented in Martin Luther King Jr. *Stride Toward Freedom: The Montgomery Story* (New York: Harper & Brothers, 1958; Perennial Library ed., Harper & Row, 1964), pp. 72–88, chap. 6, "Pilgrimage to Non-Violence." His major influences included Reinhold Niebuhr; two of his professors at Boston University, Edgar S. Brightman and L. Harold DeWolf; Mahatma Gandhi; and, of course, Jesus Christ himself.

191. James H. Cone, *A Black Theology of Liberation* (Philadelphia: Lippincott, 1970); *God of the Oppressed* (New York: Seabury, 1975); and *Risks of Faith: The Emergence of a Black Theology of Liberation* (Boston: Beacon, 1999). Diana Hayes has taken account of James Cone's work in "James H. Cone, Black Historical Experience and the Origins of Black Theology," *Louvain Studies* 12/3 (Fall 1987): 245–60.

192. See, e.g., J. Deotis Roberts, *Liberation and Reconciliation: A Black Theology*, 2d ed. (Louisville, KY: Westminster John Knox, 2005).

193. See A. (Agbonkhianmeghe) E. Orobator, *The Church as Family: African Ecclesiology in Its Social Context* (Nairobi, Kenya: Paulines Publications Africa, 2000); Emmanuel Martey, *African Theology: Inculturation and Liberation* (Maryknoll, NY: Orbis Books, 1993); Elochukwu E. Uzukwu, *A Listening Church: Autonomy and Communion in African Churches* (Maryknoll, NY: Orbis Books, 1996); and Oseni Ogunu, ed., *The African Enchiridion: Documents and Texts of the Catholic Church in the African World* (Bologna: Editrice Missionaria Italiana, 2005). For South African ecclesiology, see B. S. Moore, ed., *The Challenge of Black Theology in South Africa* (Atlanta: John Knox, 1974; originally published in Johannesburg, 1972, but subsequently banned).

194. Veli-Matti Käikkäinen, *An Introduction to Ecclesiology: Ecumenical, Historical and Global Perspectives* (Downers Grove, IL: InterVarsity, 2002). For a dissenting voice on the enduring value of black theology, see Alistair Kee, *The Rise and Demise of Black Theology* (Burlington, VT: Asgate, 2006).

195. Pope Paul VI perhaps indirectly promoted the work of these new movements in his 1975 apostolic exhortation *Evangelii nuntiandi* ("Of proclaiming the gospel"). See the United States Catholic Conference edition (Washington, DC: 1976). Some commentators, including this author, regard that document as perhaps Paul VI's finest pronouncement. For another approach, see Joseph Ratzinger, "The Theological Locus of Ecclesial Movements," *Communio* 25 (Fall 1998): 480–500.

196. For a generally sympathetic treatment, however, see John L. Allen, *Opus Dei: An Objective Look Behind the Myths and Reality of the Most Controversial Force in the Catholic Church* (New York: Doubleday, 2005). For a more critical

analysis, see Michael J. Walsh, *The Secret World of Opus Dei: An Investigation into the Secret Society Struggling for Power Within the Roman Catholic Church* (San Francisco: HarperSanFrancisco, 1992; updated ed., 2004).

197. For background, see Jason Berry and Gerald Renner, *Vows of Silence: The Abuse of Power in the Papacy of John Paul II* (New York: Free Press, 2004), esp. parts 2–3, pp. 125–273.

198. For a critical evaluation of this movement and the others already cited, see Gordon Urquhart, *The Pope's Armada: Unlocking the Secrets of Mysterious and Powerful New Sects in the Church* (New York: Bantam, 1995). For self-descriptions, see their respective Web sites. For a more balanced evaluation of these so-called ecclesial movements, see Christopher O'Donnell, "Movements, Ecclesial," in his *Ecclesia,* pp. 313–15. See also John A. Saliba, "Vatican Response to the New Religious Movements," *Theological Studies* 53/1 (March 1992): 3–39.

199. Pope Paul VI made it emphatically clear in his *Evangelii nuntiandi* that evangelization is not complete if it does not take into account the interplay between the gospel and our actual, concrete life in the world. "This is why evangelization involves an explicit message, adapted to the different situations constantly being realized . . . a message especially energetic today about liberation" (n. 29; see also nn. 30–31).

200. O'Donnell, "Movements, Ecclesial," p. 315.

201. For an objective overview of these communities, see Christopher O'Donnell, "Basic Christian Communities," in his *Ecclesia,* pp. 46–47. There are useful bibliographical references in the entry's notes, which need not be reproduced here. See also Margaret Hebblethwaite, *Base Communities: An Introduction* (Mahwah, NJ: Paulist Press, 1994).

202. See, e.g., Thomas A. Kleissler, Margo A. LeBert, and Mary C. McGuinness, *Small Christian Communities: A Vision of Hope for the 21st Century,* rev. and updated ed. (New York: Paulist Press, 1997); Bernard J. Lee, *The Catholic Experience of Small Christian Communities* (New York: Paulist Press, 2000); James O'Halloran, *Small Christian Communities: A Pastoral Companion* (Maryknoll, NY: Orbis Books, 1996); and Robert S. Pelton, *Small Christian Communities: Imagining Future Church* (Notre Dame, IN: University of Notre Dame Press, 1997).

203. Larry Rohter, "As Pope Heads to Brazil, a Rival Theology Persists," *New York Times* 156 (May 7, 2007): A1 (full article, pp. A1, A8).

204. *The Church in the Present-Day Transformation of Latin America in the Light of the Council,* vol. 2: *Conclusions* (Washington, DC: Division for Latin America–United States Catholic Conference, 1968–69), p. 201.

205. "Synod of Bishops: The Final Report," *Origins* 15/27 (December 19, 1985): 449 (full text, pp. 444–50). Pope Paul VI devoted much more space to base communities in his apostolic exhortation *Evangelii nuntiandi,* n. 58, although his comments were tempered with some concerns about their ability to remain within the communion of the Church and in good relations with their bishops.

206. Karl Rahner, in *Concern for the Church: Theological Investigations XX,* trans. Edward Quinn (New York: Crossroad, 1981), "Basic Theological Interpretation of the Second Vatican Council," pp. 77–89.

207. Rahner, *Concern for the Church,* p. 78.

208. Rahner, *Concern for the Church,* p. 80.

209. Rahner, *Concern for the Church,* pp. 82–83.

210. Rahner, *Concern for the Church,* p. 85. The divisions employed in this book, however, follow neither the traditional antiquity–Middle Ages–modern times categories, nor Rahner's, except in Rahner's case to underscore the historic importance of the so-called Council of Jerusalem and the Second Vatican Council. Otherwise, this book adopts a broadly chronological approach, beginning with the New Testament, then carrying the narrative forward to the threshold of Vatican I in the nineteenth century, then taking the narrative from Vatican I to Vatican II (1962–65), followed finally by post–Vatican II developments to the present time.

211. Rahner, *Concern for the Church,* p. 86.

212. Roger Haight, *Christian Community in History,* 3 vols. (New York: Continuum, 2004, 2005, 2008). For books and articles related to the Church in Asia, Africa, and Latin America and Native American Catholics, see also Peter C. Phan, *Christianity with an Asian Face: Asian American Theology in the Making* (Maryknoll, NY: Orbis Books, 2003); Peter C. Phan, ed., *The Asian Synod: Texts and Commentaries* (Maryknoll, NY: Orbis Books, 2002); Thomas Fox, *Pentecost in Asia: A New Way of Being Church* (Maryknoll, NY: Orbis Books, 2002); James H. Kroger and Peter C. Phan, *The Future of Asian Churches: The Asian Synod and Ecclesia in Asia* (Quezon City, Philippines: Claretian, 2002); Edmond Tand and Jean-Paul West, eds., *The Catholic Church in Modern China: Perspectives* (Maryknoll, NY: Orbis Books, 1993); Leonardo Boff, "The Contribution of Brazilian Ecclesiology to the Universal Church," in José Oscar Beozzo and Luiz Carlo Susin, eds., *Brazil: People and Church(es),* trans. Paul Burns (London: SCM, 2002), pp. 78–83; and Carl Starkloff, "Native Americans and the Catholic Church," in Michael Glazier and Thomas J. Shelley, eds., *The Encyclopedia of American Catholic History* (Collegeville, MN: Liturgical Press, 1997), pp. 1009–20.

Part VIII: The Future of the Church and Its Ecclesiologies

1. The noun "ecclesiology" has been rendered here and in the title of Part VIII in the plural. This is a judgment call that could easily have gone either way. The singular form would have underscored the point that there is a basic unity in diversity. The plural form acknowledges the diversity, but without denying the underlying unity. Throughout this part, and especially in section 3, the text moves easily—one hopes, not indiscriminately—from the singular to the plural. There is a similar dialectical tension in the motto of the United States of America, *E pluribus unum* (Lat., "One from many" or, more freely, "Unity in diversity"). It was adopted in 1782 to appear on the nation's Great Seal.

2. See my *Catholicism,* rev. ed. (San Francisco: HarperSanFrancisco, 1994), p. 723. Congar adopts the definition in his entry "Church: Ecclesiology," trans. Matthew J. O'Connell, in Mircea Eliade, ed., *The Encyclopedia of Religion* (New York: Macmillan and Free Press, 1987), vol. 3, p. 481 (full article, pp. 480–86).

3. See CDF, *Responses to Some Questions Regarding Certain Aspects of the Doctrine on the Church,* in *Origins* 37/9 (July 19, 2007): 135 (full text, pp. 134–36).

4. See VI.3.3.b for a full discussion of this important topic, along with pertinent references.

5. CDF, *Responses to Some Questions,* p. 136. The CDF document cites *Dominus Iesus,* n. 22, para. 3. For the complete reference to and discussion of this earlier CDF document, see Part I, n. 18.

6. Indeed, Pope Paul VI insisted throughout his 1975 apostolic exhortation *Evangelii nuntiandi* (Lat., "Proclaiming the gospel") that the whole mission of the Church is one of evangelization.

7. Yves Congar, *Lay People in the Church: A Study for a Theology of the Laity,* trans. Donald Attwater (Westminster, MD: Newman, 1957), p. 37.

8. Karl Rahner compresses the ecclesiological connection between the Church and the Eucharist in less than two pages in *The Church and the Sacraments,* trans. W. J. O'Hara (Freiburg: Herder; Edinburgh-London: Nelson, 1963), pp. 84–85.

9. Whatever hope the Church has a right to embrace, as Sister Doris Gottemoeller points out in a lecture given in England in 1995, "A Vision for the Church of 2010," is an "Easter phenomenon." She cites the post-Resurrection scene on the road to Emmaus, where the forlorn disciples, who know only of the crucifixion, confide in the stranger, "We had hoped . . ." "But Jesus," she continues, "restored their hope in a moment of exquisite *communio,* the breaking and sharing of the bread. We live in the Eastertime, when *communio* with Jesus and with one another is always ours within the church" (*Origins* 25/9 [July 27, 1995]: 152 [full text, pp. 149–52]).

GLOSSARY

The Glossary is only for quick reference. The definitions and descriptions herein are not intended as a substitute for the more detailed explanations provided in the text. The Glossary should always be used, therefore, in conjunction with the indexes of subjects and persons. Readers may also consult *The HarperCollins Encyclopedia of Catholicism,* edited by Richard P. McBrien (San Francisco: HarperSanFrancisco, 1995), for fuller entries and for entries on the many Churches of the Catholic and Orthodox East and the Protestant West.

Acta Apostolicae Sedis (AAS) (Lat., "Acts of the Apostolic See"), the official journal of the Holy See, containing the laws, pronouncements, and addresses of the pope and the principal documents issued by the various departments of the Roman Curia.

Ad gentes divinitus. *See* Decree on the Church's Missionary Activity.

aggiornamento (It., "updating"), a term that became synonymous with Pope John XXIII's program of church renewal and reform leading up to, and including, the Second Vatican Council (1962–65).

anathema (Gk., "accursed," "separated from the fold"), an official condemnation by the Church of a doctrinal or moral position, but without necessarily imposing an excommunication or other grave penalty. References to anathemata do not appear in the 1983 Revised Code of Canon Law.

Anglican Communion, the worldwide network of Churches in communion with the archbishop of Canterbury, who is regarded as *primus inter pares* (Lat., "first among equals" [of Anglican archbishops, or primates]).

Anglican orders, Anglican ordinations to the priesthood declared invalid by Pope Leo XIII in his papal bull of 1896 *Apostolicae curae* (Lat., "Of apostolic concern"). However, the recent practice of the Catholic Church has been to reordain former Anglican priests conditionally rather than absolutely.

Anglo-Catholicism, the name given to the "high church" party within the Anglican Communion ever since the nineteenth-century Oxford movement (q.v.).

Annuario Pontificio (It., "papal yearbook"), official annual publication by the Vatican of a complete list of members of the hierarchy, offices, and officials of the Roman Curia and names of dioceses and religious institutes with pertinent statistics. It also contains a list of the popes with the dates of their pontificates.

antipope, an individual whose claim to the papacy has not been recognized by the Church as valid. There have been thirty-nine antipopes. The first was St. Hippolytus (217–35); the last was Felix V (1439–49).

apostasy (Lat., "defection"), the deliberate, public, and complete abandonment of the Christian faith by a baptized member of the Church.

apostle (lit., "one who is sent"), in the New Testament period, a missionary. Included among the apostles were "the Twelve" (q.v.). In their case, the word "apostle" is appropriately rendered in uppercase.

Apostolicam actuositatem. *See* Decree on the Apostolate of the Laity.

apostolicity, one of the four marks of the Church (along with one, holy, and catholic); it identifies the Church's faith and practice with those of the Apostles.

apostolic succession, in the wider sense, the process by which the whole Church continues, and is faithful to, the word, witness, and the service of the Apostles; in the stricter sense, the legitimization of the office and authority of the bishops because of their linkage with the Apostles (see *Lumen gentium,* n. 20).

ARCIC, Anglican–Roman Catholic International Commission.

Augsburg Confession, the primary confession of faith of the Lutheran Church, written by Philipp Melanchthon (1530), who also wrote the definitive commentary on it.

authenticity of church teachings, a quality of teachings that have authority because they are issued by persons holding a canonically recognized teaching office in the Church.

Baptism, the sacrament required for entrance into the Church. However, baptism of blood (martyrdom) and baptism of desire (explicitly in the case of catechumens, and implicitly in the case of people of goodwill who are not at fault in their ignorance of the gospel) are regarded as analogous to the sacrament of Baptism and as sufficient for salvation.

Baroque Catholicism, a renewal of Roman Catholicism in the seventeenth and eighteenth centuries that emphasized emotion, visual experience, and individual spirituality. The liturgy became more and more elaborate, and devotions, more and more dramatic, even masochistic. It was Baroque Catholicism, more than Counter-Reformation Catholicism, that was directly challenged by Vatican II.

base (or basic) communities, small groups of Christians who gather, under lay leadership, for Bible study and missionary activity.

basilica, a term used originally for certain official buildings in the time of the Roman Empire, later adapted in Christian usage for church buildings. Basilicas are among the principal churches of the Catholic Church. There are four major basilicas in Rome: St. Peter's, St. John Lateran, St. Paul's Outside the Walls, and St. Mary Major.

bishop (Lat. *episcopos,* "overseer"), a priest who has been ordained to the third and highest level of the sacrament of Holy Orders. If he heads a diocese, he is called the Ordinary or local bishop.

Bishops, College of, the worldwide body of Catholic bishops headed by the Bishop of Rome (the pope) who, according to Catholic teaching, succeed to the college of the Apostles in teaching authority and in the pastoral governance of the Church.

Body of Christ, one of the primary biblical and theological images of the Church, sometimes modified by the adjectives "Mystical" and "ecclesial" to distinguish the Church as Body of Christ from the human, earthly body of Christ, his risen and exalted body, and his eucharistic body.

Byzantine rite, sometimes called the "Greek rite," the liturgical system of the Orthodox and Byzantine Catholic Churches, called "Byzantine" because it originated in the Orthodox patriarchate of Constantinople (formerly Byzantium).

Caesaro-papism, a political system in which the temporal ruler claims sovereignty over the Church as well as the state.

Canon Law, Code of, the body of church laws for the Roman Catholic Church that was first promulgated in 1917 and then revised in 1983. The Code of Canons of the Eastern Churches was promulgated in 1990.

"canon within the canon," the interpretation of Scripture through the prism of a single theological point of view.

Cardinals, College of, the body of cardinals under the age of eighty who have been responsible (since 1059) for electing a new pope and for assisting a pope in the governance of the universal Church.

catechumen, an unbaptized person who is undergoing religious instruction in preparation for entrance into the Catholic Church.

Catholic Action, a movement of Catholic laity actively encouraged by Pope Pius XI in his 1931 encyclical *Quadragesimo anno* (Lat., "The fortieth year") involving "the participation of the laity in the apostolate of the hierarchy."

Catholic Church, the Catholic Communion of Churches, both Roman and Eastern, or Oriental, that are in full communion with the Bishop of Rome (the pope).

Catholic Communion of Churches, the union that exists among and between the individual Churches and dioceses of the universal Catholic Church. Its structural expression is the College of Bishops, each of whom represents and embodies his own local church.

Catholic Reformation, or Counter-Reformation, alternate names for the reform movements in response to the Protestant Reformation of the sixteenth century. The former emphasizes the more positive and constructive results of the impetus toward reform; the latter, those aspects that were in reaction and opposition to Protestantism. At the center of both was the Council of Trent (q.v.) and its reform of doctrine, liturgy, and church law. These reform movements also included the founding of new religious orders and the establishment of seminaries.

Catholicism, Early, the initial stages in the New Testament of sacramentalism, hierarchy, ordination, and dogma—in short, the beginning of the distinctive features of Catholic Christianity.

catholicity, one of the four marks of the Church (along with one, holy, and apostolic); it emphasizes its universality, inclusiveness, and openness to all truth and values.

charismatic, pertaining to that fundamental aspect of the mystery of the Church that is directly permeated and inspired by the Holy Spirit. It is complementary to the institutional aspect of the Church. The former is less constrained by structure and authority; the latter, more responsive to the requirements of structure and authority.

Christus Dominus. *See* Decree on the Bishops' Pastoral Office in the Church.

Church, the worldwide body of Christians, known as the Body of Christ, the People of God, the Temple of the Holy Spirit, and the community of disciples.

Church Unity Octave, eight days of prayer for the unity of all Christians, celebrated annually from January 18 (formerly the feast of St. Peter's Chair) to January 25 (the feast of the Conversion of St. Paul).

collegiality, the principle that the universal Catholic Church is a communion of local churches (dioceses), each led by a bishop. The College of Bishops is an extension of the college of local churches, which together constitute the universal Church.

communicatio in sacris (Lat., "communication in sacred things"), full sacramental participation in the liturgy of a Church other than one's own; also known as intercommunion and eucharistic sharing.

Communion, Church as a, a community of baptized persons who are interiorly united with God in Christ, through the reconciling presence and power of the Holy Spirit.

Communion of Churches, the bond of unity, forged by the Holy Spirit, that exists among and between the various Churches and dioceses of the universal Church.

communion of saints, the spiritual union of the whole community of believers in Christ, both living and dead. Those on earth have been called the Church militant; those in heaven, the Church triumphant; and those in purgatory, the Church suffering.

Conciliarism, the medieval movement that viewed an ecumenical, or general, council as superior in authority to the pope.

Concord, Book of, foundational Lutheran confessional statement (1577), formulated to resolve theological differences that surfaced after Martin Luther's death in 1546.

congregation: (1) a department (or dicastery) of the Roman Curia; (2) a religious community (or order) of women or men; (3) an assembly of Christians at worship. *See also* religious congregation.

Congregation, a plenary meeting of an ecumenical council; the term was especially pertinent to Vatican II.

Congregation for the Doctrine of the Faith (CDF), the Roman Curia's most authoritative dicastery, with responsibility for the maintenance of Catholic orthodoxy by bishops and theologians. It was formerly known as the Holy Office and, before that, the Inquisition.

Constantinople, the traditional seat of Eastern Christianity, especially after the emperor Constantine transferred the capital of the Roman Empire from Rome to Constantinople in 330, building the new city on the site of the Greek city of Byzantium. Four ecumenical councils have been held there, in 381, 553, 680–81, and 869–70.

constitution, conciliar, the most solemn and formal type of document issued by an ecumenical council, containing teachings that pertain to the essence of the Church and its faith. At Vatican II there were four such documents: on the Church (*Lumen gentium*), on the Church in the modern world (*Gaudium et spes*), on the liturgy (*Sacrosanctum concilium*), and on divine revelation (*Dei verbum*).

Constitution on the Sacred Liturgy (*Sacrosanctum concilium,* Lat., "The sacred council"), the first major document approved by Vatican II in which the council laid down the principles for liturgical renewal and reform, emphasizing "full and active participation" (n. 14).

council, an official church assembly, which may be ecumenical (general), regional, national, or local (diocesan).

creed, an official profession of faith usually promulgated by a church council and used by the Church in its liturgy. It is also known as a symbol of faith.

Crusades, a series of wars fought under the banner of Christ, with the authority and approval of various popes, for the recovery and/or defense of Christian lands. It was the Fourth Crusade (1202–4) that definitively opened a rift between the Christian East and Christian West, with the sacking of Constantinople in 1204 and the temporary establishment of a Latin empire there.

Declaration on Christian Education (*Gravissimum educationis,* Lat., "The most serious [importance] of education"), a Vatican II document that focuses on the education of the young in the home, the school, and the Church, especially through catechesis and liturgy. Overall emphasis, however, is on formal schooling.

Declaration on the Relation of the Church to Non-Christian Religions (*Nostra aetate,* Lat., "In our age"), a Vatican II document that teaches that everyone comes from the creative hand of God and that non-Christian religions often reflect a "ray of that Truth which enlightens all persons" (n. 2). The declaration encourages dialogue and collaboration with the followers of other religions, but places special emphasis on the Church's relationship with Jews, insisting that all forms of persecution and discrimination against Jews, past and present, are to be condemned (n. 5).

Declaration on Religious Freedom (*Dignitatis humanae,* Lat., "Of the dignity of the human [person]"), a Vatican II document that teaches that no one should be coerced in matters of faith because coercion is incompatible with the freedom of the act of faith and the dignity of the human person. This was by far the most controversial of the council documents because it raised the underlying question of doctrinal development, illustrated by the vast difference between this document and Pope Pius IX's *Syllabus of Errors* (1864).

Decree on the Apostolate of the Laity (*Apostolicam actuositatem,* Lat., "The apostolic activity"), a Vatican II document that insists that the laity are full members of the Church, not merely helpers of the hierarchy, and that their Christian dignity is rooted in their Baptism and Confirmation and in the mandate of the Lord himself (n. 3).

Decree on the Bishops' Pastoral Office in the Church (*Christus Dominus,* Lat., "Christ, the Lord"), a Vatican II document that follows the lead of the Dogmatic Constitution on the Church in insisting that the bishop's pastoral office is rooted in his episcopal ordination and not in the delegation of the pope. A bishop's pastoral responsibilities include the preaching of the Gospel, presiding at worship, and ministering to those in need (n. 16).

Decree on the Church's Missionary Activity (*Ad gentes divinitus,* Lat., "Divinely [sent] to the nations"), a Vatican II document that presupposes both the Dogmatic Constitution on the Church and the Pastoral Constitution on the Church in the Modern World, but differs with them in emphasizing "evangelization and the planting of the Church among those peoples and groups where it has not yet taken root" (n. 6). The distinction is between the "mission of the Church" and "the missions."

Decree on Eastern Catholic Churches (*Orientalium Ecclesiarum,* Lat., "Of the Eastern Churches"), a Vatican II document that proclaims the equality of the Eastern and Western traditions of Christianity (n. 3) as well as the importance of preserving the spiritual heritage of the Eastern Churches (n. 5). It acknowledges that the Eastern Catholic communities are true Churches and not just rites within the Catholic Church (n. 2).

Decree on Ecumenism (*Unitatis redintegratio,* Lat., "The restoration of unity"), a major document of the Second Vatican Council that marked an ecclesiological shift from the idea of the Catholic Church as "the one, true Church of Christ" to that of its being one Church, albeit the central and most important one, within the whole Body of Christ. The decree characterizes the ecumenical movement not as a "return" to preexisting Catholic unity, but as the "restoration" of a unity that has been lost.

Decree on the Instruments of Social Communication (*Inter mirifica,* Lat., "Among marvelous [technological inventions]"), a Vatican II document, promulgated in December 1963, before the council's theology of the Church was fully developed, that insists on the primacy of the moral order in the world of communications and art and on the competence of church authorities to make moral judgments about these realities.

Decree on the Ministry and Life of Priests (*Presbyterorum ordinis,* Lat., "The order of priests"), a Vatican II document that teaches that ordained priests form one presbyterate in a diocese "to whose service they are committed under their own bishop" (n. 8). Whether in parish work, teaching, or some other special activity, priests are "united in a single goal of building up Christ's Body," whether by preaching, presiding at the Eucharist, administering the sacraments, leading a faith-community, or ministering to those in need (nn. 4–6).

Decree on Priestly Formation (*Optatum totius,* Lat., "The wish of the whole [Church]"), a Vatican II document that insists on the close connection between seminary education and pastoral realities (n. 4). It mandates that theological studies in seminary be biblical, ecumenical, historical, and personally formative (nn. 16–17). It also emphasizes the importance of continuing education programs for clergy (n. 22).

Decree on the Renewal of the Religious Life (*Perfectae caritatis,* Lat., "Of perfect charity"), a Vatican II document that bases the renewal of religious life on two principles: a return to the sources of all Christian life and to the original inspiration behind a given community; and a readiness to adapt to the changed conditions of the times (n. 2). Such communities must always see themselves as part of the Church and as active participants in its mission, giving corporate witness to the Gospel by their spirit of poverty and their support for the poor (n. 13).

Dei verbum. *See* Dogmatic Constitution on Divine Revelation.

Denzinger, a collection of excerpts of church documents first published by Heinrich Joseph Denzinger in 1854.

deposit of faith, the content of the essential elements of Christian faith given by Christ and the Apostles and preserved as a treasury by the Church ever since.

dicastery, generic term for a department or agency of church government, especially in the Roman Curia.

Dignitatis humanae. *See* Declaration on Religious Freedom.

diocese, a Christian community, or local church, within given territorial boundaries and presided over by a bishop. It is also known as a see. Larger and more important dioceses are known as archdioceses and are led by an archbishop.

disciple, a follower of Christ. The Church is the community of disciples.

dissent, a judgment of disagreement, in whole or in part, with an official teaching or disciplinary decree of the Church, usually on the part of theologians.

doctrine, an official teaching of the Church.

doctrine, development of, the process by which official teachings are legitimately revised by theologians and the hierarchical magisterium (q.v.) in accordance with changes in historical circumstances and understanding.

dogma, a doctrine promulgated with the highest authority and solemnity. It is presumed to be infallible, and the denial of it is heresy. All dogmas are doctrines; not all doctrines are dogmas.

Dogmatic Constitution on the Church (*Lumen gentium,* Lat., "Light of nations"), one of the two most important Vatican II documents (the other being the Pastoral Constitution on the Church in the Modern World, q.v.). It focuses on the Church *ad intra,* that is, its internal life, emphasizing the reality of the Church as mystery (q.v.) and sacrament (q.v.), and as People of God (q.v.), its collegial structure (q.v., "collegiality"), and the role of the laity (q.v.) in the life of the Church.

Dogmatic Constitution on Divine Revelation (*Dei verbum,* Lat., "Word of God"), one of the four dogmatic constitutions (q.v.) of Vatican II. It emphasizes the mission of the Church to proclaim the Word of God, insisting that the teaching office of the Church interprets the Word of God but is not above it. Sacred Tradition, Sacred Scripture, and the magisterium (q.v.) are "so linked and joined together that one cannot stand without the others" (n. 10).

Donatism, a North African schismatic movement of the fourth and fifth centuries that regarded itself, as most rigoristic movements do, as the doctrinally and spiritually pure remnant of the one, true Church of Christ.

Eastern Churches, those non-Roman-rite Christian Churches whose origins were in the eastern half of the Roman Empire or beyond the empire's eastern frontiers. Some Eastern Churches remain in full communion with the Bishop of Rome; others broke communion with Rome beginning in 1054.

East-West Schism, the disruption of the bonds of communion between Rome and Constantinople beginning with the mutual excommunications by the patriarch of Constantinople and the Bishop of Rome in 1054. The schism was sealed by the Crusades (q.v.) and the sack of Constantinople in 1204.

Ecclesia ad extra (Lat., "the Church beyond"), the mystery and mission of the Church as they relate to realities outside the Church.

Ecclesia ad intra (Lat., "the Church within"), the mystery and mission of the Church as they relate to the Church's internal life.

Ecclesia discens (Lat., "the learning Church"), a term traditionally used by Roman Catholic ecclesiologists for the laity and sometimes the lower clergy. The Second Vatican Council effectively set this notion aside with its teaching that the Church is the whole People of God and that all are learners and teachers alike, albeit in different ways.

Ecclesia docens (Lat., "the teaching Church"), a term traditionally used by Roman Catholic ecclesiologists for the hierarchy and sometimes all the clergy, contrasted with the *Ecclesia discens,* defined above.

ecclesial, pertaining to the Church as a mystery and a community, as opposed to "ecclesiastical," which pertains to the Church as a structured institution.

ecclesial communities, Christian denominations within the Body of Christ that lack one or another institutional element that is deemed essential to the doctrinal, sacramental, and ministerial integrity of a Church. These are referred to in Vatican II's Decree on Ecumenism, chapter 3.

ecclesiology, the theological study of the Church as a mystery, that is, "a reality imbued with the hidden presence of God" (Paul VI). Ecclesiology also reflects on the mission, ministries, and structural operations of the Church.

"ecclesiology from above," a theology of the Church whose starting point is the mystery of the triune God and that emphasizes the nature of the Church as a communion in grace that is derived from, reflects, and is drawn into the inner life of the Trinity. As such, the Church is an icon of the eternal communion that exists between the Father, the Son, and the Holy Spirit.

"ecclesiology from below," a theology of the Church whose starting point is the Church as an earthly community of human beings who, though transformed by the grace of God and the enduring presence of the Holy Spirit, have a mission in and for the world that includes, in addition to the preaching of the Word and the celebration of the sacraments, actions on behalf of justice, peace, and human rights.

ecumenical council, also known as a general council, the assembly of all the world's bishops, under the presidency of the Bishop of Rome (the pope); it is the highest earthly authority in the Church along with, and never without, the pope.

ecumenism, the movement that seeks to restore the unity of the Church that had been lost at the time of the East-West Schism and the Protestant Reformation.

encyclical, a formal letter from the pope to the universal Church and sometimes to the whole human community concerning doctrinal, moral, disciplinary, or pastoral matters. The social encyclicals, the first of which was Leo XIII's *Rerum novarum* in 1891, deal with matters of social justice, human rights, and peace in the context of the mission of the Church.

episcopate/episcopacy, the body of bishops and the office they hold as bishops of individual dioceses.

eschatology (lit., "the study of the last things"), the area of theology that focuses on the Kingdom, or Reign, of God, which is the central purpose of the Church itself.

Eucharist, the most important of the seven sacraments and, according to Vatican II, the summit and the source of the whole Christian life and of the life and mission of the Church itself.

evangelization, the proclamation of the gospel in such a way that the entire mission of the Church is engaged, as pointed out by Pope Paul VI in his 1975 apostolic exhortation *Evangelii nuntiandi* (n. 29).

ex cathedra (Lat., "from the chair"), the highest level of papal teaching, namely, an infallible pronouncement.

excommunication, the penalty in canon law that excludes a member of the Church from full participation in its sacramental and ministerial life.

Extra Ecclesiam nulla salus (Lat., "Outside the Church, no salvation"), the medieval axiom stipulating that unless individuals are somehow related to the Church, they cannot enter into eternal life. The axiom has been superseded by the teachings of Vatican II.

Faith and Order, a study commission of the World Council of Churches that focuses on the ecumenical call to the Churches and other ecclesial communities to engage in common theological investigations regarding matters crucial to the cause of Christian unity.

Febronianism, an eighteenth-century movement in Germany that proposed restricting papal authority to the supervision of church unity and the promulgation of decrees of ecumenical councils (q.v.). It also held that papal teachings would bind the Church only with the consent of the bishops. The movement collapsed after the French Revolution and for lack of support among the German bishops.

Filioque (Lat., "and of the Son"), a word added to the Nicene-Constantinopolitan Creed under the emperor Charlemagne in the early ninth century that contributed to the eventual schism between East and West. The East insisted that the Holy Spirit proceeds within the life of the Trinity from the Father *through* the Son (*per Filium*).

fundamentalism, the literal, unhistorical interpretation of the Bible (Protestant fundamentalism) and/or church doctrine (Catholic fundamentalism).

Gallicanism, a movement that claimed for the Church in France an independence from papal intervention. It declared that papal teachings are not to be considered definitive unless and until they are accepted by a formal vote of the various national Churches.

Gaudium et spes. *See* Pastoral Constitution on the Church in the Modern World.

Gnosticism (from Gk. *gnosis,* "knowledge"), a system of religious belief according to which salvation depends upon a singular knowledge or inner enlightenment about God. In reaction, it generated the doctrine of apostolic succession (q.v.), which declared that revelation is public in character and is proclaimed and preserved by the body of bishops whose episcopal orders are in a direct line back to the Apostles.

Gravissimum educationis. *See* Declaration on Christian Education.

Great (Western) Schism, the period of crisis in the Church (1378–1417) in which two and then three rival popes claimed papal authority. The schism came to an end at the Council of Constance (1414–18), which elected Martin V as pope.

Gregorian reform, the movement of church renewal and reform beginning in the tenth century but reaching its climax under Pope Gregory VII (1073–85). Its principal objects for reform were simony, nepotism, clerical corruption, and lay investiture.

heresy, the formal and deliberate rejection of a defined teaching (or dogma) of the Church.

hierarchy (from Gk., "rule by priests"), the ordered body of clergy (bishops, priests/presbyters, deacons), but, more commonly, bishops alone, including the Bishop of Rome.

hierarchy of truths, a principle that recognizes the relative importance of various Christian doctrines based on their proximity to "the foundation of the Christian faith" (Decree on Ecumenism, n. 11).

Holy Office, the former name (until 1967) for the Congregation for the Doctrine of the Faith.

Holy Orders, the sacrament by which one is received into the ministry of the diaconate, the presbyterate (priesthood), or the episcopate of the Church.

Holy See, the Apostolic See, or diocese, consisting of the pope and those persons and departments of the Roman Curia who assist him in the governance and administration of the universal Church (can. 361). The name also refers to the juridical entity that is the Vatican, which assigns ambassadors (nuncios) and other diplomats to represent it to other countries and juridical entities and to which ambassadors and other diplomats are accredited in their turn.

Holy Spirit, Temple of, the Church as the embodiment of the presence and reconciling activity of the Holy Spirit, who is regarded by Yves Congar as the co-institutor of the Church along with Jesus himself. Pre–Vatican II ecclesiology regarded the Holy Spirit as the soul, or quasi-soul, of the Church.

indefectibility, the promise of Christ that the Church will last until the end of time without fundamental corruption of its faith and teaching, not to be confused with "infallibility" (q.v.).

infallibility (lit., "immunity from error"), a charism, or gift, of the Holy Spirit by which the Church and the pope in particular, when speaking as earthly head of the Church (*ex cathedra*), are preserved from error in their definitive teachings on matters of faith and morals, to be held by the whole Church.

Integrism, also known as **Integralism,** a nineteenth- and early-twentieth-century ultraconservative movement in France that opposed ecumenism, modern biblical studies, and historically based theology. The movement was initially supported by Pope Pius X (1903–14), but brought to an end by Pope Benedict XV in 1914.

Inter mirifica. *See* Decree on the Instruments of Social Communication.

intercommunion. *See communicatio in sacris.*

interfaith, term used of relations between the Church and non-Christian religions. It is to be distinguished from "ecumenical," which is concerned with relations leading toward church unity between Churches and ecclesial communities within the Body of Christ.

irenicism (Gk. *irene,* "peace"), a conciliatory approach to the challenge of church unity that emphasizes points of agreement, with the concurrent risk of watering down existing differences for the sake of achieving that unity, which was called a "false irenicism" by Pius XII in his encyclical *Humani generis* (1950).

Jansenism, a seventeenth-century Catholic reform movement originally in France and the Low Countries. Apart from its many other views on human nature, sin, and grace, it opposed the centralizing tendencies of the Counter-Reformation and set itself against the hierarchy.

Jesuits, popular name for the Society of Jesus, founded in 1540 by St. Ignatius Loyola. The order was a major force in the Catholic Reformation (q.v.) of the sixteenth and seventeenth centuries and remains a major influence within the Catholic Church today.

Josephinism, an eighteenth-century effort on the part of the Austrian emperors to subordinate the Church to national interests, involving an attempt at state control of the Church.

juridical, pertaining to a mentality that views the life and work of the Church primarily in terms of laws, moral obligations, and the duty to obey authority.

Kingdom, or Reign, of God, the reality that comes into being wherever and whenever the will of God is done. It has entered human history definitively in Jesus Christ, will come in all its fullness at the end of history, and in the meantime is present even now to the Church and to all of humanity. It is the Church's central purpose; the Church exists to proclaim it, to celebrate it, and to be a credible and compelling witness of its presence in the world.

laity (from Gk. *laos,* "people"), the Christian faithful who are first initiated into the Church by the sacrament of Baptism.

Latinization, the imposition or imitation of Latin-rite liturgical customs and principles and the resulting erosion or dilution of the Eastern Catholic liturgical traditions.

Latin rite, popular though inaccurate name for the religious usages (liturgical, canonical, monastic) of the Roman Catholic Church.

lay apostolate, the composite of ministries exercised by nonordained members of the Church.

lay investiture, the interference of temporal rulers in the installation of bishops and abbots. The practice was one of the abuses that the Gregorian reform (q.v.) of the eleventh century sought to correct.

liberation theology, a way of doing theology that emphasizes the Church's mission as a liberator of the poor and the powerless and that reflects on their plight while directly sharing their experience. It began in Latin America, but the term applies to any theology with similar emphasis and methods, including feminist theology, black theology, and various theologies of liberation in Africa and Asia.

liturgy, the public worship of the Church, at the center of which is the Eucharist (q.v.). It includes also the six other sacraments and the Liturgy of the Hours.

local church, a diocese, also known as a particular church (q.v.).

Lumen gentium. *See* Dogmatic Constitution on the Church.

magisterium, hierarchical, the body of official teachers in the Church and the teaching authority exercised by them.

marks (or notes) of the Church, one, holy, catholic, and apostolic. The first mark pertains to the unity of the Church and its principal source, which is the Holy Spirit. The unity of the Church is reflected especially in the Eucharist (q.v.). The second mark pertains to the holiness of the Church, indicating that the Church is a communion of saints who are permeated and transformed by the presence of the Holy Spirit. The third mark pertains to the universality of the Church and its openness to all truth and to all people. The fourth mark identifies the faith and practice of the Church with those of the Apostles.

Middle Ages, the historical period that spans the millennium between the collapse of the Roman Empire in 476 and the birth of the modern world at the end of the fifteenth century. Various scholars use other dates. The adjectival form, often used in a pejorative way, is "medieval."

ministry, a service rendered in the name of the Church to those in need, whether inside or outside the Church. Ministries exist at various levels, are of various kinds, and are always for the sake of the Church's mission. Some ministries require ordination (the sacrament of Holy Orders), but most do not. *See also* ordination.

missiology, a special area of study within ecclesiology that focuses on the missionary activity of the Church toward non-Christians.

mission of the Church, that for which the Church has been "sent" by God, namely, to proclaim the gospel of Jesus Christ, to continue Christ's worship of the Father through the sacraments, and especially the Eucharist, to witness to the presence of the triune God by the quality of its own life, and to use its own limited resources to hasten the final coming of the Kingdom, or Reign, of God (q.v.).

models of the Church, conceptual images by which the mystery of the Church can be better understood. As defined and described by Avery Dulles, they are institution, community (or mystical communion), sacrament, herald, servant, and community of disciples.

Modernism, name given to the doctrinal and disciplinary crisis in the Catholic Church in the early years of the twentieth century, particularly during the pontificate of Pius X (1903–14). The negative papal reaction to Modernism had a chilling effect on Catholic scholarship until the Second Vatican Council (1962–65).

Montanism, a mid- to late-second-century apocalyptic and charismatic movement that threatened to undermine traditional authorities such as Sacred Scripture and the office of bishop. In reaction, the Church stressed these traditional sources of authority. Montanism's most famous convert was the prolific early Christian theologian Tertullian (d. ca. 207).

Mother of the Church, a title conferred on the Blessed Virgin Mary by Pope Paul VI in 1964 in response to the concerns of a number of bishops who felt that Vatican II had not sufficiently stressed the significance of Mary in the life of the Church.

mystery, "a reality imbued with the hidden presence of God" (Paul VI), a concept closely related to that of sacrament (q.v.).

neo-Scholasticism, a limited revival of medieval Scholastic theology and philosophy, with emphasis on the Church as a juridical, legalistic, and hierarchical institution, that shaped the content and tone of textbook ecclesiologies from the sixteenth century to the Second Vatican Council.

Nostra aetate. *See* Declaration on the Relation of the Church to Non-Christian Religions.

notes of the Church. *See* marks of the Church.

Novatianism, a third-century movement that arose in Rome in reaction to the Church's liberal policy for the readmission of those who had left the Church during the persecution initiated by the emperor Decius (249–51).

Oath Against Modernism, oath first imposed by Pope Pius X on all those about to be ordained, on clergy, new pastors and new bishops, and on theologians teaching in seminaries and other ecclesiastical institutions. The oath required the firm acceptance of each and every defined teaching of the Church and the belief that the Church was personally and directly instituted by Jesus during his lifetime on earth, that it is built upon Peter and his successors through the ages, that dogmas do not evolve, that the Church's teachings and condemnations are true and binding, and that the bishops are in a direct line of succession from the Apostles. The oath was suppressed by Paul VI in 1967. In 1989 the Congregation for the Doctrine of the Faith produced an updated version of the oath.

Oath of Fidelity, oath imposed in 1989 by the Congregation for the Doctrine of the Faith and known by its full title as the "Oath of Fidelity on Assuming an Office to Be Exercised in the Name of the Church." Among the categories of persons covered are newly appointed seminary rectors, seminary professors of theology and philosophy, rectors of ecclesiastical or Catholic universities, and university teachers of disciplines dealing with faith or morals. Bishops and cardinals had already been required to take an oath of fidelity.

Optatum totius. *See* Decree on Priestly Formation.

Ordinary, the bishop of a diocese. The term also applies to other church office-holders (can. 134).

ordination, the sacramental rite of Holy Orders in which the Holy Spirit is invoked on candidates for the office of bishop, priest, and deacon as they are initiated into these ministries by prayer and the laying on of hands.

Orientalium Ecclesiarum. *See* Decree on Eastern Catholic Churches.

Orthodox Christianity, the original apostolic Churches and the later Churches they founded in the eastern half of the Roman Empire and in other eastern territories beyond the imperial frontiers. The term "orthodox" was applied originally only to those who accepted the teachings of the Council of Chalcedon (451) on the divinity and humanity of Christ. Today the term applies more commonly to Eastern Churches (particularly Russian and Greek Orthodox) that are not in full communion with the Bishop of Rome.

orthodoxy (from Gk., "right praise," "right belief"), a pattern of belief and prayer that is consistent with the basic teachings of the Church. Its opposite is heresy (q.v.).

"Outside the Church, no salvation." *See Extra Ecclesiam nulla salus.*

Oxford movement, the religious reformation begun at Oxford University in 1833 that brought about a spiritual, doctrinal, and liturgical renewal in the Anglican Communion (q.v.) by a return to the church Fathers and the writings of seventeenth-century Anglican theologians.

papacy, the office of the Bishop of Rome, or pope. *See also* Petrine ministry.

particular church, the canonical term especially, but not exclusively, for a local church, or diocese (cans. 368–74). It can also refer to any Church in apostolic succession and with a valid Eucharist.

Pastoral Constitution on the Church in the Modern World (*Gaudium et spes,* Lat., "Joy and hope"), one of the two most important Vatican II documents (the other being the Dogmatic Constitution on the Church, q.v.). It focuses on the Church *ad extra,* that is, its relations with the world beyond the Church. The basic thrust of its teaching is that the Church exists not alongside the world but within the world, and not in domination over the world but as its servant.

patriarch, title for the highest-ranking bishop of an autonomous Church or federation of local churches (dioceses or eparchies). The five major patriarchies have been Rome, Constantinople, Alexandria, Antioch, and Jerusalem. Pope Benedict XVI (2005–) has since abandoned the papal title Patriarch of the West.

patriarchate, an autonomous, self-governing federation of dioceses under the jurisdiction of a chief bishop, called "patriarch," and his synod.

Pentecost (from Gk., "the fiftieth day"), traditionally regarded as the "birthday" of the Church because of the dramatic outpouring of the Holy Spirit, followed by the preaching of St. Peter regarding the heart of the gospel (Acts 2). The Church, however, had first come into existence when Jesus began to gather disciples.

People of God, a common term for the Church, derived from the Bible. By extension it applies to the whole human community. It was the dominant image of the Church at the Second Vatican Council, more prominent even than Body of Christ (see Dogmatic Constitution on the Church, chap. 2).

perfect society, Church as, a common medieval expression for the Church that suggests that the Church possesses whatever institutional elements it needs to fulfill the purposes for which it was founded by Christ. It does not mean that the Church is literally perfect in every way. In the twentieth century the term gave way to the "Mystical Body of Christ" and then to the "People of God."

Perfectae caritatis. *See* Decree on the Renewal of the Religious Life.

Petrine ministry, the pastoral responsibilities exercised by the Bishop of Rome for the sake of the unity of the universal Church and the strengthening of the faith of his brother bishops.

Petrine succession, the process by which the Bishops of Rome follow in the line of St. Peter as his vicars and as earthly heads of the universal Church.

Pontifex Maximus (Lat., "supreme pontiff"), a title of honor accorded to the Bishop of Rome since the late fourth century, but originally a pagan title employed by the emperors of Rome.

pope (from It. *papa,* "father"), the Bishop of Rome. In earlier centuries the title was applied to every bishop in the West, while the East applied it to priests as well. In 1073 Pope Gregory VII limited its application to the Bishop of Rome.

precepts of the Church, requirements enjoined of all Catholics by the Church, of which there are five: (1) to keep holy Sunday and holy days of obligation by participating in the Eucharist and refraining from unnecessary physical work; (2) to keep the days of fast and abstinence that have been determined by the Church; (3) to receive the sacrament of Reconciliation at least once a year; (4) to receive Holy Communion at least once a year during the Easter season; and (5) to contribute to the support of one's pastor.

pre-evangelization, those pastoral activities of the Church that are performed in order to prepare potential converts for the preaching of the gospel and the celebration of the sacraments.

prelate, a priest who has the power of governance in the external (public) forum of the Church, that is, over some canonical portion of the Church. The term is usually limited to bishops.

presbyterate, the union of all priests, diocesan and religious, in a diocese with the diocesan bishop. It can also apply to all of the world's priests or to the ecclesiastical state they entered by ordination (q.v.).

Presbyterorum ordinis. *See* Decree on the Ministry and Life of Priests.

priesthood: (1) the body to which all Christians baptized in Christ belong; in the New Testament, Jesus is the only individual who is called a priest; the whole Church is referred to as a priestly people (1 Pet. 2:5); (2) the most common ordained ministry of the Church.

primacy, papal, the honorary and jurisdictional authority possessed by the Bishop of Rome and exercised over the universal Church. The primacy, however, is always exercised within the College of Bishops, over which the pope presides.

proselytism, the active effort to persuade potential converts, by whatever means, to abandon their present religious community and join another.

Protestant Reformation, the sixteenth-century movement, originating in western Europe, that identified and attacked the abuses found in the Church of the time and that promoted, in effect, the formation of new church communities and often new interpretations of traditional Catholic teachings. The Reformation was multiple in character: Lutheran (Martin Luther), Reformed (Jean Calvin), Radical Reformed (the Anabaptists and others), and English (Henry VIII).

reception, the process by which official teachings and disciplinary decrees of the Church are accepted and applied. The two principal signs of reception within the Church are a change in consciousness (whether accepting a doctrine or decree that was not held prior to the pronouncement or embracing the teaching or decree more firmly than before) and a change in practice—institutional, communal, or individual.

Reformed Churches, in general, all Christian Churches and ecclesial communities whose beliefs and practices have been shaped by the Protestant Reformation, but more particularly by the teachings of John Calvin, especially regarding the Lord's Supper (the common Protestant name for the Eucharist, or Mass). These Churches and ecclesial communities are often known by the name "Presbyterian."

Reign of God. *See* Kingdom, or Reign, of God.

religious congregation, or order, an organized group of Christians who have taken vows to live in community and to observe the evangelical counsels of poverty, chastity, and obedience.

religious life, the type of Christian existence and practice observed by members of religious congregations and orders.

rereception, the process of embracing a doctrine or disciplinary decree that had been forgotten or temporarily rejected.

rite, the form and language of worship employed in a particular Church.

Roman Catholicism, the tradition within the Catholic Communion of Churches that observes the Roman rite. It constitutes by far the largest portion of the Catholic Church, but is not simply coextensive with it.

Roman Curia, the network of secretariats, congregations, tribunals, councils, offices, commissions, committees, and individuals who assist the pope in the governance and administration of the universal Church. It was first organized by Pope Sixtus V in 1588.

Roman Empire, the territory around the Mediterranean and in Europe that was ruled by Rome from the first century before Christ to the end of the fourth century of the Christian era (395), when the empire was divided into East and West. The early Church adopted some of the organizational framework of the Roman Empire for its own structural plan of provinces, metropolitan sees, dioceses, and the like.

Rome, the Italian city that was the seat of the Roman Empire and later of the Catholic Church, especially in the West. It is often used generically for the Vatican.

sacrament, Church as, the reality of the Church as a mystery (q.v.), that is, "a reality imbued with the hidden presence of God" (Paul VI). Sacraments are both signs and causes. The Church, therefore, is a sign of the presence of the triune God in the world and also the instrument by which the triune God acts redemptively on behalf of the unity and salvation of the whole world (Dogmatic Constitution on the Church, n. 1).

sacramentality, principle of, the fundamentally Catholic notion that all reality is potentially and in fact the bearer of God's presence and the instrument of divine action on behalf of all of humanity.

Sacrosanctum concilium. *See* Constitution on the Sacred Liturgy.

saints, those who have been transformed fully by the grace of Christ and are with God in the heavenly kingdom. In the New Testament, the members of the Church were referred to simply as "the saints."

saints, communion of. *See* communion of saints.

St. John Lateran Basilica, one of the four major basilicas in Rome and the cathedral church of the Bishop of Rome, the pope.

St. Paul's Outside the Walls, one of the four major basilicas in Rome, at which Pope John XXIII first announced his intention to convene the Second Vatican Council.

St. Peter's Basilica, one of the four major basilicas in Rome and the Catholic Church's principal church. The other three are St. John Lateran, St. Paul's Outside the Walls, and St. Mary Major.

salvation outside the Church. *See Extra Ecclesiam nulla salus.*

schism, a formal breach of church unity. In Catholic ecclesiology, this occurs when communion with the Bishop of Rome is broken. *See also* East-West Schism.

Scholasticism, a method of intellectual inquiry that was prominent until the sixteenth century in Western medieval thought, especially in universities, in contrast, on the one hand, with the *lectio divina* (Lat., "divine reading"), or meditative reflection on the Bible and other classic sources of theology and spirituality, and, on the other hand, with the more rhetorical type of thought usually found in the monastic schools. Scholasticism is not to be confused with neo-Scholasticism (q.v.).

Scripture, Sacred, the Bible as read and understood as the Word of God rather than simply as literature.

sectarianism, an understanding of the Church as a relatively small, morally pure group of Christians living in a world perceived to be hostile to the gospel and against which the remnant Church must be insulated and protected from contamination.

sensus fidelium (Lat., "sense of the faithful"), the actual belief of Christians held communally down through the ages.

simony, the buying and selling of church offices or spiritual benefits. It was a major problem for the Church in the Middle Ages and was directly addressed during the pontificate of Gregory VII (1073–85). *See also* Gregorian reform.

"sister Churches," a term used by Pope Paul VI to apply to the Anglican Communion and the Orthodox Churches, that is, to Churches that, although not in full communion with the Catholic Church, possess the requisite ecclesiological elements to constitute them as Churches rather than as ecclesial communities (q.v.).

Sistine Chapel, the principal chapel of the Vatican Palace and the place used for papal elections, named for Pope Sixtus IV (1471–84).

sobornost (Russ. *sobŏrnaja,* "catholic"), a Russian theological neologism that defines an ideal of ecclesiology that is conciliar and collegial and based on an interior spiritual communion of freedom and love. It is claimed by some in the East to provide a middle way between the excessive individualism of Protestantism and the legalism and heavy emphasis on hierarchical authority in Roman Catholicism. It is counterclaimed in the West, however, that *sobornost* exists more in theory than in practice in the East.

social doctrine, Catholic, the teachings of popes, councils, and episcopal conferences on matters of social justice, human rights, and peace. The formulation of modern social doctrine was initiated by Pope Leo XIII in his encyclical *Rerum novarum* in 1891.

Spanish *Summa,* the best of the Latin manuals of theology in common use before Vatican II. Its tract on the Church is in striking contrast to the approach taken at the council itself in its Dogmatic Constitution on the Church.

spirituality, Christian, life in the Holy Spirit, who incorporates the Christian into the Church, through which the Christian has access to the triune God in faith, hope, love, and service.

subsidiarity, principle of, the idea that nothing should be done at a higher level that can be done as well, if not better, at a lower level, also that decisions ought always to be taken at a point closest to where they will immediately apply. This principle, first articulated by Pope Pius XI in his 1931 encyclical *Quadragesimo anno,* applies not only to society at large, but to the Church as well.

symbol, a creed or basic belief of the Church. The word is also closely related to "mystery" and "sacrament."

synods, gatherings of church leaders to address matters of concern to the life and mission of the Church. After Vatican II, Pope Paul VI established the World

Synod of Bishops to meet at regular intervals. Synods may also occur at regional, national, or diocesan levels.

Tradition, the process of handing on the faith and the content of that faith. Tradition (uppercase) includes Scripture, the essential doctrines of the Church, and the Eucharist and the other sacraments. Changeable customs, institutions, teachings, and practices are included in tradition (lowercase).

Trent, Council of, the Catholic Church's principal response to the Protestant Reformation. It met in three different stages between 1545 and 1563. The council defined the canon of Sacred Scripture, the seven sacraments, and other major theological realities. It also shaped Catholicism from the sixteenth century to the Second Vatican Council in the mid-twentieth. The adjectival form is Tridentine, which often refers to a mentality that favors a more conservative, legalistic approach to Catholic doctrine and life.

Twelve, the, the twelve Apostles, symbolizing the twelve tribes of Israel, who were called and "sent" by Jesus to carry the gospel to the whole world.

two-swords theory, the medieval belief that the pope has power in both the temporal and the spiritual realms. It found its extreme expression in Pope Boniface VIII's bull *Unam Sanctam* (1302).

type, a person in whom the qualities of a greater or later reality are somehow "typified" or anticipated, for example, Mary as the type of the Church.

Ultramontanism (lit., "beyond the mountains" [the Alps]), an attitude of mind, developed initially in nineteenth-century France but later spreading throughout Europe, that was militantly loyal to the papacy, viewing it as the bulwark against political liberalism and philosophical and ethical relativism.

Uniate Churches, a pejorative term used by some in the Orthodox Churches to describe those Eastern Churches that remained in full communion with Rome. Such Churches are more accurately described as Eastern Catholic Churches.

Unitatis redintegratio. *See* Decree on Ecumenism.

Vatican, the city-state surrounded by Rome and under the jurisdiction of the pope. The more common ecclesiological application is to the headquarters of the Roman Catholic Church, including the papacy and the Roman Curia. It takes its name from Vatican Hill, which was located outside the city walls of classical Rome and is regarded as the site of the burial of St. Peter.

Vatican Council I, the ecumenical council (1869–70) that defined the dogma of papal infallibility and reaffirmed that of papal primacy.

Vatican Council II, the ecumenical council (1962–65) that inaugurated a new era of renewal and reform of the Church and brought the Tridentine and Baroque periods of Catholicism to an end. Vatican II emphasized the Church as the whole People of God, the active participation of the laity in the life and mission of the Church, the Church's need to enter into dialogue and cooperation with non-Catholic Christians and non-Christian religions alike, the Church's role as a servant of humankind, and the need to decentralize the structural operations of the Church.

Vicar of Christ, a traditional title for a bishop, but now exclusively applied to the pope.

Vicar of Peter, the more traditional title for the Bishop of Rome, designating his distinctive Petrine ministerial function in service to the universal Church and to his brother bishops.

World Council of Churches, the most visible international expression of the ecumenical movement in the twentieth century. First constituted in 1948, it consists of Churches and ecclesial communities that accept the WCC's self-description as "a fellowship of churches which confess the Lord Jesus Christ as God and Savior according to the Scriptures, and therefore seek to fulfill together their common calling to the glory of the one God, Father, Son and Holy Spirit." Although not a member Church, the Catholic Church participates in almost all of the programs of the WCC, including its Faith and Order Commission.

SELECT BIBLIOGRAPHY

This "Select" Bibliography makes no claim to completeness. There are many more references to individual books and articles on the Church in the Notes. The list below serves simply as a starting point for general readers, students, and teachers in the building of a longer bibliography, shaped to their own interests and needs.

General Works on the Church, Ecclesiology, and Basic Sources

Burghardt, Walter J., and William G. Thompson, eds. *Why the Church?* New York: Paulist Press, 1977.

Congar, Yves. "Church: Ecclesiology." Translated by Matthew J. O'Connell. In *The Encyclopedia of Religion,* edited by Mircea Eliade. New York: Macmillan, 1987. Vol. 3, pp. 480–86.

———. *Lay People in the Church: A Study for a Theology of the Laity*. Translated by Donald Attwater. Rev. ed. Westminster, MD: Newman, 1965.

———. *I Believe in the Holy Spirit*. Translated by David Smith. 3 vols. New York: Seabury, 1983.

Dulles, Avery. *Models of the Church.* Exp. ed. Garden City, NY: Doubleday, Image, 1987.

———. "A Half Century of Ecclesiology." *Theological Studies* 50/3 (September 1989): 419–42.

Gutiérrez, Gustavo. *A Theology of Liberation: History, Politics and Salvation.* Translated by Caridad Inda and John Eagleson. Maryknoll, NY: Orbis Books, 1973; new ed., 1988. See also Marc H. Ellis and Otto Maduro, eds. *The Future of Liberation Theology: Essays in Honor of Gustavo Gutiérrez.* Maryknoll, NY: Orbis Books, 1989.

Haight, Roger *Christian Community in History*. 3 vols. New York: Continuum, 2004, 2005, 2008.

Küng, Hans. *The Church.* Translated by Ray and Rosaleen Ockenden. New York: Sheed & Ward, 1967.

———. *The Catholic Church: A Short History*. Translated by John Bowden. New York: Modern Library, 2001.

McBrien, Richard P. *Catholicism.* Rev. ed. San Francisco: HarperSanFrancisco, 1994.

———. *101 Questions & Answers on the Church.* New York: Paulist Press, 1996.

———. ed. *The HarperCollins Encyclopedia of Catholicism.* San Francisco: HarperSanFrancisco, 1995.

O'Donnell, Christopher. *Ecclesia: A Theological Encyclopedia of the Church.* Collegeville, MN: Liturgical Press, 1996.

Ormerod, Neil. "The Structure of a Systematic Ecclesiology." *Theological Studies* 63/1 (March 2002): 3–30.

Paul VI, Pope. *Evangelii nuntiandi* ("On Evangelization in the Modern World"), apostolic exhortation, December 8, 1975. Washington, DC: United States Catholic Conference, 1976.

Phan, Peter, ed. *The Gift of the Church: A Textbook on Ecclesiology in Honor of Patrick Granfield, O.S.B.* Collegeville, MN: Liturgical Press, 2000.

Prusak, Bernard P. *The Church Unfinished: Ecclesiology Through the Centuries.* New York: Paulist Press, 2004.

Rahner, Karl. *The Church and the Sacraments*. Translated by W. J. O'Hara. New York: Herder and Herder, 1963.

Schillebeeckx, Edward. *Christ the Sacrament of Encounter with God*. Translated by Paul Barrett and N. D. Smith. New York and London: Sheed & Ward, 1963.

Schreiter, Robert J., ed., *Mission in the Third Millennium* (Maryknoll, NY: Orbis Books, 2001).

Sullivan, Francis A. *The Church We Believe In: One, Holy, Catholic and Apostolic.* New York: Paulist Press, 1988.

Tanner, Norman P., ed. *Decrees of the Ecumenical Councils.* 2 vols. Washington, DC: Georgetown University Press; London: Sheed & Ward, 1990.

Tillard, Jean-Marie R. *Flesh of the Church, Flesh of Christ: At the Sources of the Ecclesiology of Communion*. Translated by Madeleine Beaumont. Collegeville, MN: Liturgical Press, 2001.

Zizioulas, John D. *Being as Communion: Studies in Priesthood and the Church.* Crestwood, NY: St. Vladimir's Seminary Press, 1985.

Ecclesiology in and of the New Testament and the Early Church

Brown, Raymond E., and John P. Meier. *Antioch and Rome: New Testament Cradles of Catholic Christianity.* New York: Paulist Press, 1983.

Brown, Raymond E., et al., eds. *Peter in the New Testament.* New York: Paulist Press, 1974.

Collins, Raymond F. *The Many Faces of the Church: A Study in New Testament Ecclesiology.* New York: Crossroad, 2003.

Cwiekowski, Frederick J. *The Beginnings of the Church.* New York: Paulist Press, 1988.

Harrington, Daniel J. *The Church According to the New Testament: What the Wisdom and Witness of Early Christianity Teach Us Today.* Franklin, WI: Sheed & Ward, 2001.

Sullivan, Francis A. *From Apostles to Bishops: The Development of the Episcopacy in the Early Church.* New York: Paulist Press, 2001.

Vatican Council I

Butler, Cuthbert. *The Vatican Council 1869–1870.* Westminster, MD: Newman, 1962.

Pottmeyer, Hermann J. *Towards a Papacy in Communion: Perspectives from Vatican Councils I and II.* New York: Crossroad, 1998.

Vatican Council II

Alberigo, Giuseppe. *A Brief History of Vatican II.* Translated by Matthew Sherry. Maryknoll, NY: Orbis Books, 2006.

Alberigo, Giuseppe, Jean-Pierre Jossua, and Joseph A. Komonchak, eds. *The Reception of Vatican II.* Washington, DC: Catholic University of America Press, 1987.

Alberigo, Giuseppe, and Joseph A. Komonchak, eds. *History of Vatican II.* 5 vols. Maryknoll, NY: Orbis Books; Leuven: Peeters, 1995, 1997, 2000, 2003, 2006.

Bulman, Raymond F., and Frederick J. Parrella, eds. *From Trent to Vatican II: Historical and Theological Investigations.* New York: Oxford University Press, 2006.

Flannery, Austin, ed. *Vatican Council II: The Basic Sixteen Documents.* Northport, NY: Costello, 1996.

Hahnenberg, Edward P. *A Concise Guide to the Documents of Vatican II.* Cincinnati, OH: St. Anthony Messenger Press, 2007.

John XXIII, Pope. "Pope John's Opening Speech to the Council." In *The Documents of Vatican II,* edited by Walter M. Abbott, translated by Joseph Gallagher. New York: Guild Press, America Press, and Association Press, 1966. Pp. 710–19.

Miller, John H., ed. *Vatican II: An Interfaith Appraisal.* Notre Dame, IN: University of Notre Dame Press; New York: Association Press, 1966.

O'Malley, John W. *What Happened at Vatican II.* Cambridge, MA: Harvard University Press, 2008.

Rahner, Karl. "Towards a Fundamental Theological Interpretation of Vatican II." *Theological Studies* 40/4 (December 1979): 716–27. Also in his *Concern for the Church: Theological Investigations XX.* Translated by Edward Quinn. New York: Crossroad, 1981. Pp. 77–89.

Revord, Sherry, exec. prod. *Faithful Revolution: Vatican II.* 5-cassette video series. New York: Lyrick Productions, 1997.

Rynne, Xavier (Francis X. Murphy). *Vatican Council II.* Maryknoll, NY: Orbis Books, 1999.

Vorgrimler, Herbert, ed. *Commentary on the Documents of Vatican II*. 5 vols. New York: Herder and Herder, 1967–69.

The Papacy: Primacy and Infallibility

McBrien, Richard P. *Lives of the Popes: The Pontiffs from St. Peter to Benedict XVI*. Updated ed. San Francisco: HarperSanFrancisco, 2006.

Schatz, Klaus. *Papal Primacy: From Its Origins to the Present*. Translated by John A. Otto and Linda M. Maloney. Collegeville, MN: Liturgical Press, 1996.

Tierney, Brian. *Origins of Papal Infallibility 1150–1350: A Study on the Concepts of Infallibility*. Leiden: Brill, 1988; copyright, 1972.

Tillard, Jean-Marie R. *The Bishop of Rome*. Translated by John de Satgé. Wilmington, DE: Michael Glazier, 1983.

Magisterium

Curran, Charles E. *The Church and Morality: An Ecumenical and Catholic Approach*. Minneapolis: Fortress, 1993.

———. *Catholic Social Teaching, 1891-Present: A Historical, Theological, and Ethical Analysis*. Washington, DC: Georgetown University Press, 2002.

———. "Official Catholic Social and Sexual Teachings: A Methodological Comparison." In his *Tensions in Moral Theology*. Notre Dame, IN: University of Notre Dame Press, 1988. Pp. 87–109.

McBrien, Richard P. "An Ecclesiological Analysis of Catholic Social Teachings." In Oliver F. Williams and John W. Houck, eds., *Catholic Social Thought and the New World Order: Building on One Hundred Years*. Notre Dame, IN: University of Notre Dame Press, 1994. Pp. 147–77.

Sullivan, Francis A. *Magisterium: Teaching Authority in the Catholic Church*. New York: Paulist Press, 1983.

———. *Creative Fidelity: Weighing and Interpreting Documents of the Magisterium*. New York: Paulist Press, 1996.

Ministry

Cozzens, Donald B. *The Changing Face of the Priesthood: A Reflection on the Priest's Crisis of Soul*. Collegeville, MN: Liturgical Press, 2000.

Hahnenberg, Edward P. *Ministries: A Relational Approach*. New York: Crossroad, 2003.

Mahony, Cardinal Roger M. "As I Have Done for You." Pastoral letter on ministry. *Origins* 29/46 (May 4, 2000): 741, 743–53.

McBrien, Richard P., *Ministry: A Theological Pastoral Handbook*. San Francisco: Harper & Row, 1987.

O'Meara, Thomas F. *Theology of Ministry: Completely Revised Edition*. New York: Paulist Press, 1999.

Ecumenical Ecclesiology

For many diverse statements from the World Council of Churches and various dialogue groups, both national and international, see Part VI, n. 86, and VII.2.8.c of this book. Among the most important documents are: *The Nature and Mission of the Church* (WCC Faith and Order Paper 198, 2005); *Baptism, Eucharist and Ministry* (WCC Faith and Order Paper 111, 1982), and *Church and World: the Unity of the Church and the Renewal of the Human Community* (WCC Faith and Order Paper 151, 1990). For statements pertinent to the Anglican Communion, see Part VI, n. 97, and VII.2.8.b on ARCIC II's "The Gift of Authority." For the Windsor Statement, see www.anglicancommunion.org/windsor2004. Statements pertinent to specific major Protestant traditions are listed in the notes, cited above.

John Paul II. *Ut unum sint* ("On Commitment to Ecumenism"). Encyclical letter of May 25, 1995. Available on the Vatican Web site, www.vatican.va.

Lindbeck, George A. *The Future of Roman Catholic Theology: Vatican II—Catalyst for Change.* Philadelphia: Fortress, 1970.

The Church and Non-Christians: The Interfaith Dimension

For various statements on the Church's relations with Jews, see Part I, nn. 25–26; Part VI, nn. 76–78, 80; and in particular VI.3.2.

Dupuis, Jacques. *Christianity and the Religions: From Confrontation to Dialogue.* Maryknoll, NY: Orbis Books, 2002.

Sullivan, Francis A. *Salvation Outside the Church? Tracing the History of the Catholic Response.* New York: Paulist Press, 1992.

INDEX OF PERSONS

INDEX OF SUBJECTS

The reader should also consult the Glossary for clear definitions and descriptions of topics, most of which are included in this index, but some of which are not.